SECOND EDITION

SPORT LAW

A MANAGERIAL APPROACH

Linda A. Sharp
UNIVERSITY OF NORTHERN COLORADO

Anita M. Moorman
UNIVERSITY OF LOUISVILLE

Cathryn L. Claussen
WASHINGTON STATE UNIVERSITY

Holcomb Hathaway, Publishers
Scottsdale, Arizona 85250

Library of Congress Cataloging-in-Publication Data

Sharp, Linda A.
    Sport law : a managerial approach / Linda A. Sharp, Anita M. Moorman,
Cathryn L. Claussen. — 2nd ed.
        p. cm.
    ISBN 978-1-934432-00-6
    1. Sports—Law and legislation—United States.   I. Moorman, Anita M.   II.
Claussen, Cathryn L.   III. Title.

KF3989.S53 2010
344.73'099—dc22

                                                                2010011121

> *Dedicated to Dr. Betty van der Smissen—mentor, role model, and friend*

The information provided in this text is not intended as legal advice. It is intended solely for informational and educational purposes. Legal counsel should be consulted for advice in handling specific legal matters.

Please note: The authors and publisher have made every effort to provide current website addresses in this book. However, because web addresses change, it is inevitable that some of the URLs listed here will change following publication of this book.

Consulting Editor: Packianathan Chelladurai

Holcomb Hathaway, Publishers, Inc.
6207 North Cattletrack Road
Scottsdale, Arizona 85250
480-991-7881
www.hh-pub.com

ISBN 978-1-934432-00-6

10 9 8 7 6 5 4 3 2

Printed in the United States of America.

Brief Contents

Contents

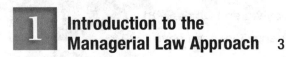

5 Employer Liability for Actions of Employees and Others 81

6 Hiring, Promotion, Termination, Compensation, and Leave 99

7 Harassment and Employee Expression Issues 135

8   Working Conditions   161

9   Labor Relations/ Collective Bargaining   191

10   The Law of Agency and Athlete Agents   231

Preface

In today's legal landscape, readers need to understand the issues of law that affect their current or prospective employment. Whether a reader works as a coach or a teacher; becomes a program administrator in a recreation program; manages a fitness or tennis/golf club; or works in a high school, college, Olympic, or professional sport organization, legal concerns will be inextricably woven into his or her managerial responsibilities. Thus, in *Sport Law: A Managerial Approach,* Second Edition, we use the term *manager* to refer to anyone, regardless of job title, who performs any of the managerial functions discussed throughout the text.

As the title suggests, this book is organized by managerial function and not by legal theory. We hope that this arrangement will make the legal theory useful and meaningful for readers. We discuss four broad business functions—(1) human resource management, (2) strategic management/governance, (3) operations management, and (4) marketing management—considering each managerial role in turn and the legal theories that apply to it. By integrating the legal information with managerial functions, we hope to help readers understand how legal concepts relate to specific management functions.

Part I deals with introductory legal concepts and introduces our approach to preventive law. An important theme in this book is the use of law to gain competitive advantage. Thus, for example, we discuss risk management not just as a method to minimize liability but as a strategy to make sport/recreation organizations more successful and more competitive. In this book, *competitive advantage* refers not just to increasing profits but also to achieving superior operations. A superior operation means a safer, better run organization, one that attracts more clients or participants. Thus, even in the nonprofit or public sector, achieving a competitive advantage is important because it results in a more efficient organization—one that better serves the needs of its constituents.

Part II, "Human Resource Management," addresses the tort, contract, and discrimination issues surrounding managerial decision making in hiring, firing, disciplining, and evaluating employees. Chapters in Part II also cover liability for the acts of employees and statutory law pertaining to working conditions. We include discussions of collective bargaining, labor relations, and the role of the sport agent.

Part III, "Strategic Management—Governance," deals with the intersection of legal and governance issues in collegiate, professional, and Olympic sport. We also describe the regulation of participants in high school sport, college sport, Olympic sport, and private clubs.

Part IV, "Operations Management," focuses on the legal issues pertinent to the operation of sports facilities and events, and sport/recreation programs. We also address spectator liability and participant violence, as well as the role of exculpatory agreements in operations management.

Part V, "Marketing Management," deals with intellectual property matters such as trademarks and copyrights, trade practices such as false advertising and ambush marketing, and contractual issues such as endorsement and sponsorship agreements. We also include constitutional and civil rights topics pertinent to sport marketing and sport media.

This book is intended for upper-level undergraduates and graduate students. It is our goal that this book be relevant to any law course preparing students to assume a broad range of responsibilities in education, recreation, or sport. It can also be used as a resource for sport managers in a variety of roles and contexts. To that end, we cover a wide range of "sport law" topics and include examples applicable to professional sport, recreation programs, physical education, fitness clubs, coaching, athletic training, Olympic sport, and sport marketing.

NEW TO THIS EDITION

his second edition of the book provides recent cases and updated information on the topics discussed. For example, we have added the following high-profile cases:

- *O'Brien v. Ohio State University*, a college coaching contract dispute (Chapter 4);
- *Williams v. Dallas Independent School District*, a First Amendment employee speech case (Chapter 7);
- *Parrish v. National Football League Players, Inc.*, concerning the duty to market the names and likenesses of retired NFL players (Chapter 9);
- *Pistorius v. International Association of Athletics Federations*, a case brought before the Court of Arbitration for Sport by an elite sprinter who runs with the aid of prostheses on both legs and who wanted to compete in international track events against able-bodied competitors (Chapter 12);
- *White v. NCAA*, an antitrust class action suit brought against the NCAA alleging that the NCAA limitation on athletics-based-aid was an unreasonable restraint of trade (Chapter 13);
- *Jennings v. University of North Carolina*, a sexual harassment case brought against a college soccer coach (Chapter 14);
- *Lanzilla v. Waterville Valley Ski Resort*, concerning whether a sport safety act could be construed to cover the activity of "snow tubing" even though the act did not refer to that activity (Chapter 15);
- *Sciarrotta v. Global Spectrum*, dealing with the application of the "limited duty" rule to an ice hockey spectator (Chapter 16);
- *Karas v. Strevell*, a participant violence case in ice hockey (Chapter 18);
- *Board of Supervisors of LSU v. Smack Apparel Company*, a trademark case exploring whether sport teams' color schemes can acquire secondary meaning (Chapter 19); and
- *C.B.C. Distribution and Marketing, Inc. v. Major League Baseball Advanced Media*, a right of publicity case dealing with fantasy baseball (Chapter 20).

Numerous websites pertaining to legal issues are featured throughout the text to prompt in-class discussions and further research. Relevant websites, with annotations, have also been added to the resource lists at the ends of chapters.

At the suggestion of adopters, we made changes to the book's organization. We moved the chapters on human resource management to precede those dealing with governance issues; this moves the discussion of contracts forward since they impact many of the legal issues discussed in subsequent chapters. In this edition, Chapter 16 combines two previous chapters (15, "Sport Facility and Event Issues," and 17, "Premises and Spectator Liability") to make it easy for readers to access all material related to facility and premises issues in one location.

SPECIAL FEATURES

 n an effort to make this book as useful as possible and to facilitate understanding and application of the material, we include the following text features:

Managerial Context Tables. One of our prime objectives is to help readers understand how legal theories affect the performance of managerial functions. To that end, each of Chapters 4–20 opens with an exhibit identifying the managerial contexts, the major legal issues, the relevant law, and illustrative cases for that chapter. These exhibits provide overviews of chapter content and reinforce the connections between management responsibilities and the legal material we present. Since the book chapters are organized by managerial function, these exhibits also make it easier for instructors to identify the major legal theories addressed in each chapter.

Case Opinions. Most chapters offer case opinions illustrating particular legal points. We selected cases that represent seminal treatments of important legal issues, stating the facts of the case in our own language but providing the actual language of the courts, somewhat abridged, so that readers can follow the courts' reasoning. By using these case excerpts, we hope readers will better understand how courts address legal theory and, as a result, develop a basis for making informed managerial decisions. Discussion questions follow each excerpted case.

Focus Cases. Each chapter presents several "mini" case opinions—highly condensed case opinions that emphasize a key discussion point. Readers will get the "flavor" of a court opinion in just a few paragraphs.

Hypothetical ("Considering . . . ") Cases. In each chapter, we offer one or more hypothetical but realistic situations to help readers understand the dynamic interplay between fact and legal theory. Some of the hypothetical cases are based on actual cases, but most are composites of fact patterns developed to highlight specific aspects of legal theory or core legal principles. Each hypothetical situation is followed by questions. The discussion and analysis of the scenarios are provided at the end of chapters. To encourage students to use the cases as a learning tool, have them make a few notes about how they would respond to the questions before they turn to the end of the chapter to check their understanding of the material.

Competitive Advantage Strategies. The boxed feature "Competitive Advantage Strategies" appears throughout the book to provide practical methods for eliminating or minimizing liability based on the legal concepts discussed in each chapter. These strategies can help readers understand how to use the law to make sound operational decisions and can assist them in working effectively with legal counsel.

Discussion Questions, Learning Activities, and Case Studies. The Discussion Questions and Learning Activities found at the end of each chapter emphasize important concepts and will aid readers in reviewing chapter material. Often, the activities ask readers to apply their experience as sport or recreation managers to develop policies or procedures. Case studies invite in-depth analysis of selected topics.

Website Resources, annotated. Each chapter includes a collection of web resources to help readers further explore legal issues and to bookmark for future professional use. Each URL is accompanied by a brief description that points out key links and benefits of the site.

Glossary of Legal Terms. Legal terms are defined when they first appear in the text as well as in a Glossary at the end of the book. Since the book is organized on the basis of managerial function and not legal concepts, this feature will be particularly helpful when readers need to refresh their understanding of a concept.

Ancillaries. An instructor's manual and PowerPoint presentation are available to instructors upon adoption of this text. Adopters will also have access to a Sport Law website that provides updates and discussion ideas to keep classes current and stimulating.

We have taken a unique approach in preparing this textbook. We hope that you and your students find our managerial law approach beneficial. Please write to us in care of our publisher to let us know about your experiences with this text.

Holcomb Hathaway, Publishers
6207 N. Cattletrack Rd., Suite 5
Scottsdale, AZ 85250
email: feedback@hh-pub.com

Linda A. Sharp
Anita M. Moorman
Cathryn L. Claussen

Acknowledgments

W e would first like to express our gratitude to Lisa Pike Masteralexis, who added greatly to the quality of this book by authoring Chapter 9, "Labor Relations/Collective Bargaining." Her expertise in this area is well-recognized and we appreciate her willingness to be a part of this endeavor.

We would like to thank the following individuals, who reviewed this book at various stages and offered suggestions for its improvement: Richard Bell, Mesa State College; Brian Crow, Slippery Rock University; Janet S. Fink, University of Connecticut; Chad. D. McEvoy, Illinois State University; Steve McKelvey, University of Massachusetts; Lori K. Miller, Wichita State University; Barbara Osborne, University of North Carolina; James Padilla, Grand Valley State University; Andrew T. Pittman, Baylor University; Glenn Steimling, University of Colorado at Colorado Springs; and Rey Treviño, University of Houston. The book has been improved substantially as a result of their well-informed input.

We are also grateful to the following individuals, who took time to respond to a survey and provide feedback and suggestions concerning this edition as we began work: James Allen, The University of Southern Mississippi; Susan K. Allen, University of Wisconsin-Parkside; Gregory Austin, Colby-Sawyer College; Robert S. Brown, Daniel Webster College; William Carroll, University of Mobile; Leigh Ann Danzey-Bussell, Ball State University; Mark Dodds, SUNY Cortland; Gil Fried, University of New Haven; Matt Garrett, Loras College; Glenn Gerstner, St. John's University; Curt Hamakawa, Western New England College; Christian E. Hardigree, University of Nevada, Las Vegas; Timothy Hatten, Rock Valley College; Richard Hsiao, Indiana University of Pennsylvania; J.V. Ippolito, Brevard College; Anastasios Kaburakis, Southern Illinois University Edwardsville; Roz Kelsey, University of Regina; John Knorr, St. Edward's University; Jordan Kobritz, Eastern New Mexico University; Robert Malekoff, Guilford College; William Manning, St. Mary's College of California; Lori Miller, Wichita State University; William Miller, University of Wisconsin-Parkside; Dennis Phillips, The University of Southern Mississippi; Ellen Roberts, Columbus State University; Chad Seifried, The Ohio State University; Alicia Stewart, Virginia Intermont College; James P. Strode, Ohio Dominican University; Robert Taylor, California University of Pennsylvania; James Velasquez, D'Youville College.

* * *

I would like to thank my co-authors, Anita Moorman and Cathy Claussen. They are not only stellar sport law scholars but wonderful colleagues and friends. Thank you for joining me in this project.

I am also thankful to all the staff at Holcomb Hathaway, Publishers, who have made this endeavor a joy with their professionalism, competence and support. In particular, I wish to thank Colette Kelly, who joined me in the vision for this project and supported me as a colleague and friend throughout.

I wish to thank Dianna Gray for her friendship and continuing support throughout my career in academe. She is always willing to lend her assistance in any way possible and I am grateful for her kindness.

I wish to thank all my sport management and sport law colleagues who, over the years, have encouraged me to write a sport law text. I wish to extend my gratitude to Packianathan Chelladurai, who has been a great supporter and who facilitated my involvement with Holcomb Hathaway. And thanks to all my students, who have asked insightful questions and allowed me the latitude to combine my quirky sense of humor with legal theory.

Finally, we have dedicated this edition of the book to Dr. Betty van der Smissen. I am truly grateful for the opportunity to have worked with her and known her as a friend. She was a wonderful mentor and role model. She has set the standard of excellence in sport law and I hope that this book exemplifies the standard of rigorous scholarship that she set for us all.

L.S.

Special thanks to my co-authors: to Linda Sharp for sharing her vision for this text and her dedicated mentorship throughout my career, and to Cathy Claussen for her constant friendship and motivation throughout this project and our careers. Thanks to all my sport law and recreation law colleagues for continually challenging and inspiring my scholarship and passion for the law.

I want to thank Alison Miner for her continued friendship, support, and encouragement. I also must thank my mother and father, Donald and Patricia Moorman, for putting me through law school and always supporting my professional career choices.

I would like to thank my colleagues at the University of Louisville for making me better every day. And thanks to my graduate assistants, Marion Hambrick and Jason Simmons, who helped research, review, and provide a student perspective on many chapters in the text.

I am also deeply grateful to the staff at Holcomb Hathaway, Publishers, who have been amazing and patient partners in the project.

A.M.

To my co-authors, Anita Moorman and Linda Sharp—co-authoring a book with outstanding colleagues who are also good friends is indeed a blessing. Thank you both for the privilege of playing on this team.

I am grateful to Colette Kelly and Gay Pauley and the other staff at Holcomb Hathaway, Publishers, for their patience, good humor, and commitment to excellence.

I wish to thank Brenda Butler Moore, Alma Robinson, and Professor Wendy W. Williams, of Georgetown University Law Center, whose support and encouragement during my law school days meant everything.

Thank you to all my students, who challenge me to think creatively and who manage to laugh on demand at my attempts to bring humor to sport law.

A most special thanks to Kathy Browder for your unflagging belief in me. Your friendship is my treasure always.

My deepest thanks to Carol Gordon and Bogey, in whose unsurpassed patience, confidence, and love I have been sustained throughout the process of preparing the second edition, and to Mary Lou Enberg, whose "you can do it" will always sound in my heart.

Finally, I dedicate my work on this book to my grandmother, whose love still holds my world together.

C.C.

About the Authors

Linda A. Sharp, J.D., received her juris doctorate from Cleveland Marshall College of Law and practiced corporate law in Ohio for seven years before continuing her studies at Kent State University in the areas of sport management, higher education administration, and sociology. After teaching in Indiana University's sport management program where she also held a joint appointment with the law school, she is now at the University of Northern Colorado as a professor in the UNC Sport Administration graduate program, teaching sport law and ethics.

Throughout her career, Sharp has lectured on more than 100 occasions on legal topics related to sport, recreation, and physical activity for audiences ranging from academics in sport law, sport management, and business law to university counsel, student affairs professionals, athletic directors, coaches, and managers of health and fitness clubs. Her lecture and workshop topics focus primarily on contract and tort law issues related to educational sport. Some representative presentations include liability issues related to coaching, risk management issues for college sport programs, employment law issues including negligent referral, negligent misrepresentation issues in education, contract issues in athletics including coaching contracts, liability concerns relating to the recruiting of student-athletes, medical concerns of college athletes, and liability issues related to on- and off-campus sports and recreational activities. She has presented workshops that deal with comprehensive risk management strategies in athletic and recreational sport programs. Sharp is also a consultant on legal issues in educational sport (www.sharplawprof.com).

She has written several book chapters and a monograph on the subject of sport law, a monograph addressing liability issues related to summer camps, as well as a number of articles in *Sport Marketing Quarterly, Athletic Business, Journal of Legal Aspects of Sport,* and *JOPERD.* She is a former president of the Sport and Recreation Law Association and a recipient of the Betty van der Smissen Leadership Award.

Anita M. Moorman, J.D., is a professor in Sport Administration at the University of Louisville where she teaches sport law and legal aspects of sport. She has a law degree from Southern Methodist University and, prior to her academic pursuits, practiced law in Oklahoma City in the areas of commercial and corporate litigation for 10 years. She also holds an M.S. degree in sport management from the University of Oklahoma and a B.S. in political science from Oklahoma State University.

Moorman was admitted to practice before the United States Supreme Court in 2000 when she served as co-counsel for nine disability sport organizations and prepared an amicus curiae brief in the landmark Americans with Disabilities Act case involving the disabled professional golfer, Casey Martin and the PGA Tour (*Martin v. PGA Tour, Inc.*).

Moorman has served on the editorial board of *Journal of Sport Management, Journal of Legal Aspects of Sport,* and *Sport Marketing Quarterly,* and she is the editor of a feature column in *Sport Marketing Quarterly* entitled "Sport Marketing and the Law." Moorman also actively participates in the North American Society for Sport Management, Sport & Recreation Law Association, and the Academy of Legal Studies in Business, and is a member of the National Sport Law Institute. Her research interests include commercial law issues in the sport industry and legal and ethical issues related to sport marketing practices, brand protection, and intellectual property issues in sport. She has published more than 20 articles in academic journals/proceedings, including the *Journal of Sport Management, Sport Management Review, Sport Marketing Quarterly, Journal of Legal Aspects of Sport, JOPERD, Leisure Science, International Sport Journal, Journal of Sport and Social Issues, Journal of the Academy of Marketing Science,* and ACSM's *Health and Fitness Journal,* and has given more than 40 presentations at national and international conferences. Moorman has also contributed 10 book chapters on legal topics in other sport management texts.

Cathryn L. Claussen, J.D., earned her law degree from Georgetown University Law Center. She has taught at Bowling Green State University, and Clemson University, and is now the Director of the Sport Management Program at Washington State University.

She brings a wealth of practical experience to her teaching and scholarship, including collegiate coaching experience and service as a race director and as co-director of a golf tournament, as well as having played tennis professionally. Additionally, she chaired Bowling Green State University's Equal Opportunity Compliance Committee, as well as the Gender Equity subcommittee of BGSU's Intercollegiate Athletics Committee.

Nationally known for her work in civil and constitutional rights in the context of sport, Claussen's many scholarly publications include book chapters on constitutional law issues, as well as product liability. She has published research in such journals as the *Journal of Legal Aspects of Sport, Journal of Sport Management, University of Miami Entertainment & Sports Law Review,* and *Marquette Sports Law Review,* among others. Specific research topics include gender equity in intercollegiate athletics, gambling on sport, ethnicity discrimination relative to the use of Native American team names and logos, disclosure of information regarding the HIV-positive status of student-athletes, and the constitutionality of mass searches of sports spectators.

Claussen has spoken at symposia on best teaching practices for sport law courses, as well as on sport governance issues for the NCAA. She is frequently consulted on issues of gender equity in athletics, and she is a trained external reviewer for the NCAA Certification program. She has also served on the editorial boards of *International Sports Journal* and *Journal of Legal Aspects of Sport* and as president of the Sport and Recreation Law Association. Claussen's many accomplishments were recognized by SRLA in awarding her the 2010 Betty van der Smissen Leadership Award.

PART I | **Introductory Legal Concepts**

T he first three chapters of this text are intended to give you an overview of some fundamental principles that you will need to understand the legal theory in this text and to attain maximum benefit from the approach we have chosen to use for this textbook. In Chapter 1 you will be introduced to the "managerial law" approach and how this book has been organized around managerial functions and not legal theories. You will learn how we have structured the book, what the unique features of this book are, and how you can use legal theory to attain a competitive advantage for your sport/recreation organization.

Chapter 2 is entitled "Managerial Strategies to Minimize Liability" and its focus is on developing a preventive law mentality for your organization. You will learn how the preventive law process works and how you may develop and implement a preventive law plan for your sport/recreation enterprise. This preventive law process is presented, once again, because it can help to attain a competitive advantage in the marketplace.

Chapter 3, entitled "The U.S. Legal System and Legal Research," provides information regarding our legal system, the anatomy of a lawsuit, and the way courts decide a variety of legal disputes. You will also learn about primary and secondary legal resources and about the process of conducting legal research. All of this information is necessary for you to be able to appreciate fully the legal theory and cases presented throughout the book.

Introduction to the Managerial Law Approach

LAW AND SPORT

Y ou have just been hired as the administrator of a local youth baseball league. As you begin your first week on the job you are overwhelmed by how many of your responsibilities have legal implications. How do you ensure that your coaches are competent and fit to work with young athletes? What emergency medical care is available for participants? Do you need to have automated external defibrillators (AEDs) on-site? What policies and procedures do you implement to make sure that the crowd does not pose a danger to game officials or to other fans or players? How do you maintain equipment and the playing fields? What provisions should you have in your contract with the vendors who will provide food and beverages at the games? What levels of insurance are necessary? All of these questions have both managerial and legal implications.

Whether you become a coach, an athletic director at a high school or college, the administrator of a sports league, a supervisor in a park district, a manager of a fitness club, a marketer for a sport organization, or the Commissioner of the National Football League (NFL), you will find the content of this course, known conventionally as sport/recreation law, to be quite useful to you.

Some commentators argue that there is no such legal theory as "sport law" (Shropshire, 1998). These commentators assert that the legal theory, e.g., of tort, contracts, labor relations, administrative law, or constitutional law, is the same regardless of whether the application is in the realm of sport and physical activity or whether the application pertains to other businesses or aspects of daily life. Other commentators argue that certain applications make sport unique enough that it may be appropriate to characterize a resultant body of knowledge as sport law (Gardiner, 1997). Regardless of which theoretical position you believe is correct, the reality is that the law is inextricably woven into the fabric of sport and recreation organizations.

As you read the sports pages in your local and national newspapers, note how much of the sports section is devoted to issues other than scores and game stories. As you watch ESPN or listen to other sports programs, you will realize that much of the commentary does not deal with events that happen during a contest. Many of the stories deal with legal issues pertaining to sport figures, sport organizations, and sport/recreational facilities. A few examples are presented in Exhibit 1.1.

These examples are only a small sample of the issues that recur frequently and are reported in the general media. There are, of course, many more examples of sport/recreation law issues that occur on a daily basis and do not receive the same level of media attention as some of those in Exhibit 1.1.

It is imperative not only that we recognize the pervasiveness of law as it affects sport and recreation but also that we understand that the legal system in our country sometimes leads to an abuse of the system because of our "open door" philosophy of hearing disputes. Our legal system operates under the belief that we should allow citizens as much access to the formal legal adjudication of disputes as possible. This philosophy is fine when people use the system only to bring claims that are indeed meritorious. However, "Americans will sue each other at the slightest provocation" (Taylor & Thomas, 2003, p. 44). In other words, our country's judicial system allows lawsuits to be filed that may seem nonsensical at first glance, and we, as a very litigious nation, look for responsible parties to blame. So long as these claims have an underlying basis in law, the claim can be filed.

SITUATION	LEGAL THEORY
Sample of legal issues pertaining to sport and recreation.	**EXHIBIT 1.1**
A university football coach leaves to coach at another university.	Contract law
A professional sports team has an issue with the "salary cap" in signing a player.	Collective bargaining and contract law
A prosecutor charges an athlete with sexual assault.	Criminal law
A female basketball coach at a college asserts that she should be paid the same as the men's basketball coach.	Equal Pay Act and Title VII (federal statutes)
A youth sport organization is held liable for a coach who molested a team member.	Tort law—negligent hiring
A health club and equipment manufacturer are liable for injury when weight equipment malfunctions.	Tort law—negligence Products liability
Congress investigates the fairness of the Bowl Championship Series.	Antitrust law
A sport business names its sports apparel with a name very similar to another product name.	Trademark law
A company terminates an endorsement contract with an athlete who was accused of criminal conduct.	Contract law
A whitewater rafting company uses a waiver to avoid liability for its own negligence.	Tort and contract law
A university eliminates the women's gymnastics team and the men's baseball team.	Title IX (a federal statute)
NCAA student-athletes sue videogame manufacturers based on the use of athletes' likenesses in games.	Right of publicity

For example, a cheerleading coach in California was sued when a student alleged that his failure to make the squad resulted from the coach changing his high score. The student's family sued, alleging that the coach sabotaged the student, demanding damages and the coach's dismissal (Taylor & Thomas, 2003). Another suspect lawsuit involved a volunteer youth league baseball coach sued by the father of a player after the team had a winless season. The suit alleged that the coach's incompetence cost the team a trip to an out-of-state tournament. Other frivolous suits have been filed after a coach benched a player during a critical hockey game, after two baton twirlers were cut from the majorettes program at a high school, and after an athlete was placed on the junior varsity team instead of the varsity team (Asquith, 2002).

What does this mean for us as prospective managers, supervisors, educators, or coaches in sport and recreation organizations? It means that we need to know as much about the law as possible to try to avoid lawsuits, meritorious or not. As you will learn in greater detail in Chapter 3, lawsuits are time consuming and expensive, regardless of whether a judgment is ever rendered against you or your organization. Therefore, we need to understand the law and use it as a tool to help prevent or lessen the consequences of these lawsuits.

We also need to look more closely at the law as a guide to creating better policies and procedures in our organizations, not just for the purpose of preventing litigation, but also in an effort to make our organizations safer and more hospitable environments for our internal (employees) and external (clients, customers, athletes) constituencies.

The law is, of course, only the starting point for having an ethical organization, as John C. Maxwell points out in his book entitled *There's No Such Thing as "Business" Ethics* (2003): "Some companies have given up entirely on trying to figure out what's ethical and are instead using what's legal as their standard for decision making. The result is moral bankruptcy" (p. 12). Although the study of ethical behavior is beyond the scope of this text, it is important to understand that compliance with the law is only the first step in developing an ethical culture in your organization.

This book is structured to help you understand the legal theory that is necessary to function effectively in your employment roles in sport and recreation organizations. The next section will explore the rationale for such an approach.

RATIONALE FOR A TEXT ON MANAGERIAL LAW FOR THE SPORT ENTERPRISE

This text is driven by management functions, not legal topics. The main benefit of presenting sport/recreation law information in this way is that you can use the information as a prospective sport/recreation manager, not as an aspiring attorney. It allows you, the reader, to understand how the legal concepts relate to each management function, an integration that is not usually accomplished when the content is organized according to legal topics.

In implementing the managerial approach, we have adopted the framework used by Antoni Brack in his article entitled "The Paradigm of Managerial Law" (1997). Brack, a professor of business law at a Dutch university, wrote this article to suggest how to structure the primary legal course in a business school curriculum. Brack's suggestion was to structure courses as "managerial law," which links law to business functions, in an attempt to train prospective business managers to be legally informed and better professionals. Structuring courses in this way emphasizes that law courses in business schools should have a business orientation because business professionals need to be able to recognize and deal with legal difficulties, problems, risks, and costs in a pragmatic way. Thus, the traditional legal structure of a course should give way, according to Brack, to the structures of business functions, which have more practical and operational meaning to prospective managers.

This managerial law approach is meritorious for the legal course in our curricula as well. As our sport and recreation programs become more sophisticated and as we strive to place students in sought-after positions in the sport and recreation fields, we need to approach legal material from the viewpoint of how you as a prospective sport or recreation manager might best learn and utilize the material.

Whether you are a prospective coach, physical educator, athletic director, recreation program supervisor, youth sport administrator, fitness club employee, or any of many roles, you will benefit from the managerial approach because managerial activities—such as hiring and overseeing personnel, supervising sport and recreation participants, providing sport and activity programming/instruction, administering sport and recreation facility operations, and overseeing games/events—are functions performed by a variety of persons working in sport, educational, and recreation organizations. Thus, the term "manager" as used in this book includes anyone, regardless of job title, who performs any of the managerial functions discussed throughout this text.

ORGANIZATION OF THIS TEXT

We have organized this text based on four commonly acknowledged business functions, with an orientation toward managerial law as mentioned above. These functions are: (1) human resource management; (2) strategic management—governance; (3) operations management; and (4) marketing management. The managerial law approach means that legal topics are subsumed under the managerial components of each function. The legal topics have to fit the function to provide "optimal operational and strategic use" (Brack, 1997, p. 240).

Part I, "Introductory Legal Concepts," introduces readers to material that is necessary for an understanding of the legal system, legal resources, and managerial strategies to minimize liability. The remainder of the book is organized according to the previously mentioned four business functions common to all sport organizations.

Part II, "Human Resource Management," first looks at the legal issues surrounding managerial decisions in hiring, firing, disciplining, and evaluating employees. This is done using the legal perspectives of contract law, tort law, and discrimination law. These chapters also cover liability for the acts of employees as well as statutory law pertaining to working conditions for employees. We include labor relations and collective bargaining matters within professional sport, and we address the role of the sport agent.

Part III, "Strategic Management—Governance," deals with governance issues in a variety of settings. We discuss regulatory issues concerning athletes in professional sport, high school and college sport, Olympic sport, and private clubs.

Part IV, "Operations Management," focuses on the legal issues pertinent to sport facilities and the development of events, including the safety of spectators. We discuss liability related to programmatic responsibilities. In these chapters, we also address participant violence. Finally, we present the role of exculpatory agreements as a component of this managerial function.

Part V, "Marketing Management," concerns the legal issues surrounding intellectual property matters such as trademarks and copyrights. In these chapters, we consider trade practices such as false advertising and ambush marketing. We present contractual issues such as endorsement and sponsorship contracts. We include constitutional and civil rights issues pertinent to marketing and address sports information, media, and public relations concerns, such as broadcasting agreements, privacy rights, and defamation.

As you see, we have integrated the legal theories and concepts pertinent to each business function in such a way as to enable you, in your roles in sport and recreation organizations, to better use the law as you engage in decision making relative to each business function. In this way, we are asking you to use the legal theories in a pragmatic manner, to solve real-life problems found in sport enterprise.

OBJECTIVES OF THIS TEXT

In conjunction with the managerial law approach discussed above, we have some specific objectives for the book, including:

- recognizing the role of legal knowledge in providing a competitive advantage.
- recognizing the role of law and regulation in strategic management.

- recognizing the role of preventive law.
- recognizing the role of negotiation in sport/recreation business.

Knowledge of the Law as a Competitive Advantage

Although the legal environment surrounding sport and recreation business is just one facet of the managerial landscape, it is an important one to consider. In fact, according to one author, "legal issues in general have emerged as the most important factor in the external environment in which business operates" (Siedel, 2002, p. 3). Instead of approaching legal issues from a negative or reactive perspective, i.e., as obstacles to organizational profitability and efficiency, we strive to present the issues in a manner that allows you to use your knowledge of the law to gain a competitive advantage over other organizations. In this way, legal "problems" may be transformed into opportunities for competitive advantage (Siedel, 2002). This is Siedel's premise in his book *Using the Law for Competitive Advantage* (2002). Bagley's book entitled *Winning Legally* (2005) also emphasizes that knowledge of legal issues should enable managers to create value, marshal resources, and manage risk in their organizations. Bagley writes, "Managers must ensure that their legal strategy aligns with their business strategy" (p. 5). The legal strategy cannot simply be an afterthought but must be integrated with business strategy. Bagley reframes the relationship of law to business and encourages managers to look at the law as not constraining them but rather to use the law to generate more value for the business.

In keeping with Siedel's and Bagley's approach to the law, this text will emphasize the competitive benefits of understanding and implementing the law properly within your sport organization. Competitive advantage, for our purposes, means not just your ability to make your business more profitable, but means that it is an opportunity to make your sport/recreation organization a superior one operationally. A superior operation translates into a safer, better run organization, which in turn will be one that attracts more clients/participants. Thus, even if you are in the nonprofit sector, a competitive advantage translates into your organization becoming more efficient, one that better serves the needs of your constituents.

A secondary benefit to recognizing the role of law in maximizing your ability to act assertively and competitively will occur when you make better use of your attorneys, whether they are in-house counsel or simply on retainer by your organization. We, as attorneys, recognize the degree to which managers often treat attorneys as "necessary evils." As you acknowledge the importance of using law as a competitive tool, you will be better able to use the legal counsel that is available to your organization. Instead of using your attorneys as "firefighters" to end the conflagration of ongoing legal problems, you will know how to use their talents proactively to help you draft policies, procedures, and contracts that will help you avoid or minimize liability from the outset. You will be able to integrate your legal decisions with your financial and operational strategies to better "manage" the law and your lawyers.

The Role of Law and Regulation in Strategic Management

As will be discussed in Part III of this text, you will need to understand how government and governing organizations affect an organization's operations. In the case of sport and recreation, legislative intervention such as federal or state statutes may dictate, at least in part, the operations of the organization. There are also judicial decisions that shape the parameters of organizational decision making.

A number of governing bodies affect how sport and recreation are organized and managed. In the case of collegiate sport, for example, innumerable rules and regulations must be followed to retain membership in the governing association, e.g., the National Collegiate Athletic Association (NCAA). For Olympic sport, various levels of governance affect the operation of a national governing body (NGB). In professional team sports, affiliation with the league must be considered, e.g., National Football League (NFL), Major League Baseball (MLB), National Hockey League (NHL), as well as relationships with players' associations. High school sport is governed by state high school athletic associations. Trade associations and professional organizations, e.g., the National Intramural and Recreational Sport Association (NIRSA) and the American College of Sports Medicine (ACSM), also provide standards and operational guidelines.

Working with all of these governing bodies provides legal challenges that you must understand. These challenges could be viewed solely as constraints in the operation and management of the sport or recreation enterprise. However, they can also provide opportunities for competitive advantage if you understand the law and use it to create value and reduce costs in your organization.

Although a managerial objective permeates the text, we have placed particular emphasis on the role of law and regulation in drafting Part II, "Human Resource Management" and Part III, "Strategic Management—Governance." For example, in these parts of the book, we address:

- **Employment discrimination.** Chapters 6 and 7 discuss many of the federal statutes affecting managerial decision making in the hiring, firing, and evaluation of employees, as well as harassment and employee expression issues. The prohibitions on firing a coach whom you perceive to be "too old" for the demands of the job is an example of Chapter 6's content.

- **Working conditions.** Chapter 8 discusses federal and state statutes regulating safety and health concerns in employment. The application of the Occupational Safety and Health Act (OSHA) to an athletic trainer's concerns about preventing disease transmission is a matter found in this chapter.

- **Labor relations/collective bargaining.** Chapter 9 deals with federal labor law, antitrust, and contract law affecting employees. The controversial case of Maurice Clarett, a football player from The Ohio State University, who challenged the NFL's rule on eligibility, is illustrative of a Chapter 9 dispute.

- **Governance issues in professional sport.** Chapter 11 addresses the power of the commissioner, the legal structure of a league, and antitrust issues related to ownership and relocation of sport franchises. The degree to which commissioners of professional sport leagues may discipline individual players is an issue for this chapter.

- **Governance of Olympic sport.** Chapter 12 focuses on the legal structure of governing bodies, disciplinary authority, and the Ted Stevens Olympic and Amateur Sports Act. The degree to which individual NGBs can have their own standards for drug testing or eligibility is covered in this chapter.

- **NCAA governance issues.** Chapter 13 discusses the relationship of university members to each other and to the governing body and how the courts have addressed issues such as antitrust. For example, an athlete's claim that the NCAA eligibility rules violate antitrust law is an example of a dispute discussed in this chapter.
- **Regulatory issues in amateur sport.** Chapter 14 deals with some of the regulations affecting the eligibility of high school and collegiate athletes and the legal principles affecting our interactions with athletes. Whether drug testing high school athletes violates their Fourth Amendment rights under the federal Constitution is an inquiry pertinent to this chapter.

The Role of Preventive Law

Although Chapter 2 deals specifically with this issue, the role of preventive law is emphasized throughout the text. Every chapter features sections entitled "Competitive Advantage Strategies" to help you use the legal material presented in ways that minimize liability and use the law to better manage your organization and achieve a competitive advantage in the world of sport and recreation.

Part IV, "Operations Management," includes numerous topics that lend themselves well to the application of preventive law concepts. Specifically, you may find the following chapters helpful:

- Liability for participant injury (Chapter 15)
- Safety of spectators (Chapter 16)
- Use of exculpatory agreements (Chapter 17)
- Participant violence in sport (Chapter 18)

The Role of Negotiation in Sport Business

Being an effective negotiator is an important managerial competency. Although this book will not focus on the interpersonal skills that will improve your negotiating abilities, preparation plays a very important role in attaining successful negotiating outcomes. In regard to that aspect, we present many types of issues and contracts for your use in understanding the legal parameters of the negotiations that are a part of sport and recreation business. For example, we include the following contract issues:

- Employment contracts (Chapter 4)
- Independent contractor agreements (Chapter 5)
- Professional athlete contracts (Chapter 9)
- Facility leases (Chapter 16)
- Game contracts (Chapter 16)
- Exculpatory agreements (Chapter 17)
- Endorsement, sponsorship, and broadcast contracts (Chapter 20)
- Licensing programs (Chapter 20)

In addition, a section in Chapter 3 deals with the role of alternative dispute resolution methods, including arbitration, mediation, and negotiation.

SPECIAL FEATURES OF THE TEXT

n an effort to accomplish the foregoing objectives, the following text features are designed to facilitate understanding and application of the material.

Managerial Context Tables

Since one of our prime objectives is to have you understand the connections between legal theory and how you may use the law in terms of your managerial functions, we have developed tables (in Chapters 4–20) to help with this. The introduction to each of these chapters includes a table that identifies the managerial contexts, the major legal issues, the relevant law, and illustrative cases for that chapter. This table will serve as an overview of chapter content and reinforce the connections between your management responsibilities and the legal material presented.

Glossary of Legal Terms

Although legal terms will be defined when they are first presented, there is also a glossary at the end of the book. Since the book is organized on the basis of managerial function and not legal concepts, this feature will be particularly helpful to refresh your understanding of legal concepts as you encounter them throughout the text.

Case Opinions

Most chapters contain one or more "Case Opinions" that have been chosen to illustrate particular legal points. We have stated the facts of the case in our own language but have used the actual language of the courts, in condensed versions, to give guidance on legal theory. Discussion questions follow each excerpted case. These cases will be helpful to you in understanding how courts address legal theory and how you can use court decisions to guide your business decisions. These cases are used because they represent landmark illustrations of important legal issues you need to understand as a sport or recreation manager.

Focus Cases

Within each chapter we present a number of "mini" case opinions, which we call "Focus Cases." These cases are very condensed (summarized) case opinions that are chosen to emphasize a key discussion point. You will get the "flavor" of a court opinion without reading a lengthy discussion of the case and rationale.

Hypothetical Cases

Within each chapter we also present the feature "Considering . . ."; these are hypothetical "factual situations" to be considered. Although sometimes these fact patterns are taken from actual cases, often we create examples that are composites of fact patterns or legal theory. These hypothetical examples are offered to help you understand the dynamic interplay between fact and legal theory. They also illustrate certain core legal principles in ways that emphasize how you may apply these principles to managerial decision making. Every hypothetical situation is followed by questions. To use this feature as a learning tool, make a few notes about how you would respond to the questions. Then see the "Analysis & Discussion" of the scenario at the end of the chapter to check and hone your understanding of the material.

Competitive Advantage Strategies

To place particular emphasis upon the managerial law concept, we provide "Competitive Advantage Strategies" throughout each chapter. These strategies provide you with several practical methods to eliminate or minimize liability based on the legal concepts discussed in that chapter. These strategies are also presented with the goal of helping you understand how to use the law to make better operational decisions and to assist you in working more effectively and knowledgeably with your legal counsel.

Discussion Questions, Learning Activities, Case Studies, and Website Resources

The discussion questions and learning activities found at the end of each chapter emphasize important concepts and will assist you in the review of chapter material. Both the questions and the activities require you to understand the legal principles; the activities may also ask you to *apply* your knowledge, often by developing policies or procedures as a sport or recreation manager in a particular factual circumstance. We also include one or more case studies to allow you to do a more in-depth analysis of a topic. Finally, because some of these activities require Internet research, we have provided an annotated list of websites related to the topics discussed in each chapter.

CONCLUSION

I n summary, we take a unique approach in this sport law textbook. We hope that you will find this managerial law approach beneficial as you learn how to make legally sound decisions. Your new knowledge of the law should help you make your organization more competitive and a better environment for participants and employees when you begin your career in sport and recreation business.

REFERENCES

Asquith, C. (2002, November 11). Sue the coach! *Sports Illustrated*, 21.

Bagley, C. E. (2005). *Winning legally*. Boston: Harvard Business School Press.

Brack, A. (1997). The paradigm of managerial law. *The Journal of Legal Studies Education, 15*(2), 237–244.

Gardiner, S. (1997). Birth of a legal area: Sport and the law or sports law? *Sport and Law Journal, 5,* 10.

Maxwell, J. C. (2003). *There's no such thing as "business" ethics*. New York: Warner Business Books.

Shropshire, K. (1998). Introduction: Sports law? *American Business Law Journal, 35*(2), 181–184.

Siedel, G. J. (2002). *Using the law for competitive advantage*. San Francisco: Jossey-Bass.

Taylor, S., Jr. & Thomas, E. (2003, December 15). Civil wars. *Newsweek, 142*, 42–53.

2

Managerial Strategies to Minimize Liability

INTRODUCTION

As we discussed in Chapter 1, one of this book's objectives is to emphasize the managerial use of legal principles so that you gain a competitive advantage for your organization. This chapter extends that theme into the realm of risk management or preventive law. Instead of looking at risk management as a necessary evil to ward off plaintiffs' lawyers, we will suggest ways in which the use of preventive legal strategies can add value to your organization. Even if there were no such phenomena as lawsuits or legal liability, the manager in your sport or recreation organization would be well advised to adopt the strategies mentioned in this chapter, not simply to avoid or minimize liability, but to make the organization a better one for employees, participants, and spectators alike.

USING RISK MANAGEMENT TO GAIN COMPETITIVE ADVANTAGE

In much of the literature relating to risk management, authors argue that risk management is necessary to avoid or minimize liability. Thus, risk management is often characterized as an obstacle, as the proverbial albatross around one's neck. This view seems rather narrowly focused. It makes better business sense to reframe risk management as an opportunity to make your sport or recreation organization more successful and, therefore, more competitive.

The vision of this book is to tie legal theory to managerial roles and functions to enable you to use the law to make better decisions for your organization. The essence of this vision as it pertains to risk management is to allow you to use these principles to fashion a better organization for all your constituents: employees, participants, and spectators. A better organization is a safer and more efficient one.

Therefore, your risk management strategies should be congruent with your organizational culture. If you are committed to building a climate of value and responsiveness to the needs of your constituents, risk management is simply one more business tool to aid in accomplishing that (Bagley, 2005; Hanssen, 2005). The underlying culture of an organization and its core values drive the way the organization views risk management and safety concerns. For example, Recer, in an article entitled "NASA Culture Blamed in Shuttle Report" (2003), discusses the way in which the NASA culture, "driven by schedule, starved for funds, and burdened with an eroded, insufficient safety program" (p. 1), led to the destruction of space shuttle *Columbia* in 2003 and the death of seven astronauts. Recer reports that the *Columbia* Accident Investigation Board found that the culture of NASA had changed little since the 1986 *Challenger* disaster, and the "flawed practices embedded in NASA's organizational system continued for 20 years" and led to both disasters. According to Recer, the disasters reflect an organizational culture that put a premium on scheduling and funding at the expense of human life. This example serves as a reminder that the cultural priorities of an organization drive all of its policies and practices—in this case, with horrendous consequences.

Risk management cannot be an afterthought. It cannot be viewed as a necessary evil. Risk management is at the core of what you stand for as an organization and must be interwoven with every aspect of your business. The safety and well-being of all your constituents should be one of your core values, and risk management is an important tool to carry out that imperative.

RISK MANAGEMENT OR PREVENTIVE LAW?

A ccording to Prairie and Garfield (2004), there is a distinct difference between risk management and preventive law. These authors define **risk management** as "the function or process by which [an organization] identifies and manages the risks of liability that rise from its activities" (p. 13). They note that the traditional view of risk management is often confined to risks related to a personal injury lawsuit or a property damage claim. These authors believe that the organization should focus more broadly and adopt a **preventive law** posture, one that looks at all risks that could affect the institution's financial health. They explain, "The scope of preventive law provides the broader focus, to include environmental, political, economic, regulatory, institutional and cultural risks" (p. 13). This broader view corresponds well to our view that the risk management process is holistic (Gurevitz, 2009) and is relevant to every aspect of your organization. Hereafter, the process will be discussed as one of preventive law, adopting the broader view of Prairie and Garfield.

THE PREVENTIVE LAW PROCESS

A s identified by Prairie and Garfield (2004), five steps make up the preventive law process. First, risk identification is undertaken, in which a legal audit is performed to identify all possible risks. Second, an assessment of the risks is undertaken. Third, the risks are evaluated. Fourth, a preventive law plan is designed. Fifth, the preventive law plan is implemented. Each of these steps will now be elaborated upon.

Risk Identification—The Legal Audit

Before any sport or recreation organization can develop a plan to prevent injury or loss, the legal landscape of possible liability must be explored. The approach to this task should be holistic. Of course, personal injury is a prime issue in sport/recreation organizations because of the nature of sport and physical activity; however, a review of the topics covered in this text and presented in Exhibit 2.1 will remind the reader that many of your prospective liabilities stem from issues other than personal injury. Exhibit 2.1 is based on the following hypothetical situation to illustrate the far-ranging nature of these liabilities:

> You are the newly hired general manager of Daily Fit, a health and fitness club. Your club has a gymnasium, a pool, and several exercise and weight rooms. You also have a sauna and offer child care. You operate a juice bar and a café for members, and you serve alcohol in the café. You have contracted with a number of personal trainers to give assistance to your members.
>
> You are a firm believer in preventive law, and you hire a consultant to perform a legal audit so you will have a better sense of what the landscape of liability may be. The consultant has prepared the list of possible liability concerns shown in Exhibit 2.1.

The list in Exhibit 2.1 reflects a holistic approach to preventive law and, although not exhaustive, can serve as a checklist for you to consider where you might have exposure to loss or liability. You will note that the list of concerns covers a wide range of legal issues: tort law, contract law, employment law, administrative law, and intellectual property law concepts are all embedded in the legal audit.

EXHIBIT   2.1   Possible liability concerns for a health and fitness club.

EMPLOYMENT ISSUES

Breach of employment contract

Wrongful termination suit

Defamation based on employment references

Discrimination based on race, gender, disability, age, religion, nationality

Sexual harassment

Vicarious liability for actions of employees

Negligent hiring/retention/supervision claims

Contracts with independent contractors such as personal trainers

Working conditions—Occupational Safety & Health Act and Fair Labor Standards Act

Workers' compensation

Labor relations issues if any employees are unionized

Employee theft

FACILITY ISSUES

Zoning issues

Lease issues

Disability access—Americans with Disabilities Act

Contracts with service providers

PREMISES LIABILITY

Slip and fall

Pool safety

Security in club and parking lot

Provision of emergency medical care including use of automated external defibrillators

Other types of emergencies such as severe weather or a bomb threat

Maintenance concerns

CLIENT/PARTICIPANT CONCERNS

Supervision

Instruction

Warnings

Equipment safety

Child care

Food/drink preparation at juice bar

Liability related to the service of alcohol

Use of waivers/agreements to participate

Invasion of privacy issues in locker room

INTELLECTUAL PROPERTY/ADVERTISING

Use of trademarks/copyrights

False advertising

Deceptive trade practices

Risk Assessment

The next step in the preventive law process is to assess risk. According to Prairie and Garfield (2004), risk assessment is the process of "determining the probability that particular risks will result in claims during a specified period and the magnitude of the potential liability arising from such claims" (p. 20). This assessment can be done by looking not only at the history of prior claims at your sport/recreation organization but also at the types of litigation that have been brought against similar organizations and what their degree of exposure has been. A trade association may compile statistics related to claims in your type of sport/recreation business. Current industry literature that discusses "hot topics" in litigation is one source of information about the kinds of risks that often turn into costly litigation. Chapter 3 references a number of legal resources for keeping abreast of current litigation in sport and recreation. Trade journals such as *Athletic Business, Athletic Management,* and *Fitness Management* have articles dealing with current cases and trends in litigation. You should also consult with your legal counsel and attend workshops to stay abreast of the trends in litigation related to your business. Newsletters or periodicals from trade associations or other membership associations frequently list upcoming seminars or workshops.

Exhibit 2.2 provides an excerpt from a risk assessment. This exhibit shows the assessment process relative to some of the premises liability risks listed in Exhibit 2.1.

Using information developed from the risk audit, you are able to assess the risks in view of their frequency of occurrence and the magnitude of the risk. In this way, you can set priorities as to which risks need to be addressed immediately and which risks can be handled in the normal course of maintenance and repair.

Risk Evaluation

The **risk evaluation** component of the preventive law process is closely aligned with the risk assessment component. Once you have assessed the probability and the magnitude of particular risks, you can evaluate these risks in conjunction with the mission of your organization and the importance of certain activities to your organization.

To illustrate, let's return to the health and fitness club example discussed in regard to the risk identification process. Let's assume that you have ascertained that the sale of alcohol poses a severe problem. Claims based on the improper sale of alcohol are highly probable, and when such a claim prevails, potential liability is very costly. For a health and fitness club, the sale of alcohol is really peripheral to your business. It is an amenity that you could eliminate without causing your clients great inconvenience. In evaluating this risk, you may choose to eliminate the sale of alcohol.

However, you also know that swimming pools often engender much litigation, and if a drowning occurs, the lawsuit would be quite costly. But, in contrast to the sale of alcohol, a swimming pool is at the core of your business activities. It would be inappropriate to shut down the pool operation because of the risk assessment. Rather, you will develop strategies to minimize the risk of liability in your pool operation.

Assessment of premises liability risks.			EXHIBIT **2.2**
TYPE OF RISK	**FREQUENCY OF RISK**	**MAGNITUDE OF RISK**	**HANDLING THE RISK**
Pool does not meet statutory standards regarding drain covers	Occasional	Severe—fatality could result	Install drain covers in the next 24 hours
Bleachers missing some slats	Occasional	Moderate—slip or fall	Repair bleachers before the next event
Slight irregularity in locker room tile—patron could trip	Frequent	Slight—bruised toe	Repair tile during usual maintenance period
No emergency training for employees in getting outside assistance	Frequent	Fatality could result if delay	Begin training employees by the end of the week

Development of the Preventive Law Plan

There are four possible strategies to cope with risks: (1) risk elimination; (2) risk retention; (3) risk transfer; and (4) risk control (Prairie & Garfield, 2004).

Risk elimination

Risk elimination should be used only if the exposure to risk greatly outweighs the benefits of retaining that activity or operation. The sale of alcohol is peripheral to a fitness club operation and may be eliminated based on the prospect of huge losses. Most likely, however, if you were the owner of a pro sport franchise, you would not eliminate the sale of alcoholic beverages at games. In this context, the service of alcohol is a part of the fan experience, and it is quite lucrative. You would most likely adopt transfer and control strategies as discussed below. Risk elimination is not the preferred strategy to deal with most loss exposures. If you have incorporated activities within your business because they are congruent with your mission and core values, you will opt to keep those activities and find ways to control the risk, not eliminate the activities.

Risk retention

Risk retention means that your organization chooses to bear the financial consequences of an activity. If your business is self-insured, you are retaining all the risk. Or, if you could not obtain insurance for a particular risk yet you have chosen to keep that activity, you are retaining the risk. For example, if you choose to run an event without terrorism insurance (because it is too costly) and the event must be cancelled because of a terrorist act, your organization will bear the brunt of that financial loss; you are retaining the risk.

Risk transfer

Risk transfer shifts the possible financial loss to another party. Organizations attempt risk transfer in a number of ways, including procuring insurance, hiring independent contractors, and using contractual provisions. We will discuss these methods in more detail in other chapters. The most common risk transfer method is the procurement of insurance. Insurance is a risk transfer method because any claim for a covered incident is paid by the insurance company.

Using an independent contractor, as we will discuss in Chapter 5, means that you shift the possible liability to that contractor. You will require the contractor to procure insurance for its own operations. For example, the vendor you hire for a pro sport facility to serve alcoholic beverages will be an independent contractor that must procure its own insurance. As you will learn in Chapter 5, a major benefit of using an independent contractor is that you avoid vicarious liability based on the actions of the independent contractor. Thus, you are using this method to shift risk to the independent contractor.

Contractual provisions can transfer risk. Using waivers with activity participants, as we will discuss in Chapter 17, essentially transfers the risk of financial loss to those participants, since they agree not to sue you if you have been negligent (see Chapter 15 for a discussion of negligence). You will also learn in Chapter 16 about the use of the indemnification clause, which essentially provides that Party A agrees to bear the liability of Party B's actions should a lawsuit result in a judgment against Party B. This type of risk transfer is common in commercial undertakings such as leases.

Risk control

Risk control is the key aspect of the preventive law plan, since it involves the actual reduction of risk, not just methods to deal with the financial consequences of the risk. This component addresses the risks that you identify in your legal audit and involves developing strategies to minimize the risks attendant to your operations. Since a sport or recreation organization, by its very nature, will always have inherent risks related to the activities that it provides, the focus here relative to possible physical injury is on reducing those risks that go beyond the inherent risks and arise from poor management, instruction, supervision, and so forth.

Implementation of the Preventive Law Plan

A critical factor in the implementation of your preventive law plan is making sure that the plan is congruent with your core values. As we have discussed, preventive law is simply one more management tool for attaining a competitive advantage in the sport/recreation marketplace. Therefore, all members of your organization must understand the importance of preventive law and embrace this concept as a daily part of their work. Making the organization better for all constituencies is at the heart of preventive law, so the preventive law plan should become a cornerstone of the operation.

Although a committee is typically responsible for the actual development and implementation of the preventive law plan, *all* members of the organization must understand the importance of preventive law and implement these strategies in their area of expertise. As a simple example, if the maintenance personnel in your business are not committed to preventive law, they will not view their role as vital to this agenda—and if they are not committed, you will likely fail to see the results you want in terms of keeping your facility clean and in good repair. This lack of cleanliness and good repair may lead to property damage or physical injury.

Implementing a preventive law plan includes the following key elements:

- Developing effective policies and procedures
- Drafting contracts that protect your interests
- Designing effective training programs
- Developing evaluation procedures

Develop effective policies and procedures

The preventive law plan begins with the promulgation of effective policies and procedures, such as the protocol to follow in a medical emergency or the protocol for hiring coaches to ensure that they are competent and suitable for your organization. Throughout this text we include Competitive Advantage Strategies in every chapter; these will be helpful as you develop policies and procedures for all the legal issues discussed throughout the book. Good policies and procedures not only provide evidence that you are acting reasonably, but they also communicate to all your constituents your commitment and concern. The policies are communication mechanisms for ensuring that all of your organization's personnel are in alignment regarding their obligations and performance standards.

Policies and procedures also ensure fairness and consistency in the workplace. They provide guidance for managers and employees alike in dealing with a variety of possible legal issues. Keep in mind that people may be less likely to bring a claim against your organization if they perceive that you are trying to "do the right thing" in terms of safety and fairness.

Draft contracts that protect your interests

One of the advantages in contract law is that, generally, you have adequate opportunity to conduct negotiations and work through several drafts of a contract in an effort to produce a document that protects your organization's interests. See Chapter 4 for a discussion of this process in terms of drafting a contract with the "worst case" scenario in mind. The point here is that you have adequate time to assess a contract: you do not have to rush into a contractual undertaking, and you can truly use a preventive law mentality in this area.

Be careful to draft contracts that are congruent with your business practice and values. For example, if you are concerned about possible injuries related to alcohol consumption by spectators, your contract with the alcohol concessionaire should ensure that the concessionaire trains employees properly, follows proper protocol in the service of patrons, and offers incentives for drivers to remain sober. Although standard contracts for many transactions are readily available in books and on the Web, they often do not reflect the nuances of your business or particular aspects of your state's laws and may do more harm than good. For example, if you copy a waiver form from a book, but it does not use the language relating to negligence required by your state, the document will not protect you. You should always consult an attorney to develop an effective waiver form for your organization. (See Chapter 17 for an in-depth discussion of waivers.)

Design effective training programs

The best policies and procedures are useless if they are not reflected in organizational practice. Therefore, effective training programs in such areas as employment practices, inspection and maintenance of facilities, proper supervision and instruction in your programs, and protection of your intellectual property are essential to the implementation of a preventive law program.

All employees, regardless of position, should become aware of the necessity of using preventive law strategies in all their work efforts. Everyone has a responsibility to

---

Competitive Advantage

STRATEGIES

Implementing Preventive Law

- Use the preventive law process as another opportunity to become more competitive in the marketplace.

- Develop the preventive law plan as an extension of your organization's core values, to enhance the experiences of all your constituents.

- Do not use the strategy of eliminating activities to reduce risks, unless the risks greatly outweigh the benefits of an activity.

- Use all available risk transfer strategies, including insurance, the use of independent contractors, and contractual means such as waivers and indemnification clauses.

- Make sure all employees understand and are involved in the development of the preventive law program.

- Allocate sufficient time and resources to the development of the preventive law plan so that employees understand how important it is to your organization.

foster a safe environment and to be cognizant of areas that could pose personal or financial risk (Eason, 2007). Since your preventive law plan is inextricably tied to your organizational core values, it is important to explain to employees just how the preventive law process enhances those values. For example, the manager of a health club might explain to employees that the preventive law plan will ensure that customers have a safe environment in which to exercise (Carman, 2008). Employees are more likely to follow policies and procedures if they understand the value of those policies and procedures for the organization.

Develop evaluation procedures

The preventive law process is ongoing. It does no good to deal with it in a piecemeal or haphazard manner. In fact, it may be detrimental to your organization to begin this process and then fail to follow through. For example, if you identify a risk, develop a policy to address it, but then fail to provide adequate resources or training to actually implement a risk control strategy, you may have evidenced more than mere negligence when someone is injured because of this risk. You will learn more about this in the discussion of gross negligence or willful and wanton behavior in Chapter 18.

You must have an organizational commitment to the preventive law process. It is not something that can be done once and then be forgotten. The cycle of risk identification, assessment, evaluation, plan design, and plan implementation is continual.

CONCLUSION

One of the underlying themes of this book is to tie managerial functions to legal theory in an effort to help managers in sport and recreation organizations to make their businesses more competitive in the marketplace. Competitive advantage stems, in part, from making your organization a better one for all your constituents. A better organization is one that enhances safety and minimizes loss to the organization.

A preventive law program should be an extension of your core values. It should be proactive and holistic in identifying all possible exposures for your type of organization. After you identify, assess, and evaluate your possible exposures to loss, you will design a prevention plan. This plan will focus on the nature of risk control as you implement strategies to help minimize the risks identified.

discussion questions

1. What is the difference between the traditional concept of risk management and preventive law?
2. What are the five steps of the preventive law process? Discuss each.
3. Why is the concept of risk control at the heart of the preventive law process?
4. Discuss the aspects of designing a prevention plan.
5. Explain the necessity for an ongoing plan to address risk in an organization.

learning activities

Using the key words "risk management" or "preventive law," conduct an Internet search to find policies and procedures of various sport organizations. Have the organizations adopted a holistic approach to identifying risk? Are there gaps in the risks identified? Does it appear that each organization's philosophy is to incorporate risk management/preventive law into the core values of the organization?

CASE STUDY

Assume that you have just been hired as the general manager of a minor league baseball team. Numerous lawsuits have been brought against the team in the past, ranging from personal injury claims to contract disputes, even a trademark infringement suit. You are convinced of the value of preventive law in any organization and feel that you need to begin the process with your franchise as soon as possible.

In view of what you have learned in this chapter, discuss the measures you would take to institute the preventive law process in your franchise.

REFERENCES

Bagley, C. E. (2005). *Winning legally.* Boston: Harvard Business School Press.

Carman, D. (2008, August). Safety first. *Recreation Management,* 6–11.

Eason, J. A. (2007, March). Due diligence. *Fitness Management,* 40–41.

Gurevitz, S. (2009, May). Manageable risk. Retrieved on July 1, 2009, at http://www.universitybusiness.com/viewarticlepf.aspx?articleid=1288

Hanssen, J. (2005, February–March). Corporate culture and operational risk management. *Bank Accounting & Finance, 18,* 35–38.

Prairie, M., & Garfield, T. (2004). *Preventive law for schools and colleges.* San Diego, CA: School & College Law Press.

Recer, P. (2003, August 26). NASA culture blamed in shuttle report. Online source found at http://news.findlaw.com/ap/o/1501/8-26-2003/20030826073007_059.html.

Siedel, G. J. (2002). *Using the law for competitive advantage.* San Francisco: Jossey-Bass.

WEBSITE RESOURCES

www.sadlersports.com ▪ This site sponsored by an insurance brokerage company has a great deal of free information on risk management for sports organizations. Risk management allows sports organizations to reduce their exposure to liability and make their organizations better places for employees, athletes, and spectators.

www.sportsmanagementresources.com ▪ The library link on this website allows you to find an Athletics Program Risk Checklist, which can help you add to your preventive law plan.

www.nata.org ▪ The website for the National Athletic Trainers' Association has a "Health and Safety" link that provides a series of organizational position statements on a variety of risk management concerns. These can help in the development of a preventive law plan.

www.nspf.com ▪ This is the website of the National Swimming Pool Foundation with links to education programs and courses, including materials on aquatic risk management.

The U.S. Legal System and Legal Research

INTRODUCTION

This chapter is intended to provide the reader with a basic understanding of the American legal system, as well as a rudimentary foundation for conducting legal research. If you have a solid grasp of these fundamentals, you will be in a position to converse intelligently with legal counsel should it become necessary, and you will be capable of exploring the legal ramifications of an issue that presents itself. Nevertheless, when you are faced with a legal problem, it is prudent to rely on an attorney's advice and use your own more limited research abilities only to develop an informative base upon which to interact with your lawyer.

THE U.S. LEGAL SYSTEM

The legal system of the United States is based on the balance of power created by having three branches of government—the executive, the legislature, and the judiciary. Each of these three branches is a source of law, and each fulfills a designated role in maintaining our system of government by rule of law, as may be seen in Exhibit 3.1.

A **constitution** is a foundational document that sets forth the basic operating principles of a government, including limits on governmental power. Each of the 50 states has its own constitution, which usually mirrors the federal Constitution in many of the protections provided to its citizens. **Statutes** are written laws created by legislatures, which are law-making bodies comprised of elected representatives. **Regulations** are rules that are created to operationalize statutes by providing more specific guidance. As you can see in Exhibit 3.1, the legislative branch is not alone in creating new law. The executive branch also creates new law when administrative agencies promulgate regulations intended to operationalize statutes. As enacted by a legislature, statutes are often "bare bones" and require regulations to flesh them out so that people know how the laws are meant to apply to real-world situations. For example, Title IX is one paragraph long, but the U.S. Department of Education is responsible for implementing regulations based on Title IX that fill several pages.

The courts may also create law when they render decisions that interpret existing laws as they apply to a particular case. This type of law is known collectively as

EXHIBIT 3.1	Relationship of law to branches of government.		
Branch of Government	Legislative Branch	Executive Branch	Judicial Branch
Source of Law	Congress and state legislatures	President or governor, administrative agencies	Federal and state courts
Type of Law	Statutes	Executive orders, agency regulations	Case law/common law
Role of Branch	Enact new laws, amend existing laws	Enforce existing laws	Interpret Constitution and other existing laws

the **common law,** or **case law.** Nevertheless, creation of new law is not the primary function of the courts, since they must operate within the frameworks of the laws that already exist. In contrast, the legislatures are elected to represent the will of the people in creating new laws.

The laws created by these three governmental branches, along with state and federal constitutions, are considered primary legal sources. That is, they *are* law and carry authority as such, in contrast to secondary sources (to be discussed later in this chapter), which are merely commentary on the law and hold only explanatory or persuasive value.

Structure and Functioning of the Judicial System

The courts are the ultimate arbiters of the various types of laws because in the end the courts are where disputes about the appropriate application of these laws to real problems are resolved. So let's focus now on understanding the structure of the judicial system and how it works.

Exhibit 3.2, which depicts the hierarchical nature of the judicial system, also shows how our judicial structure is split into two systems—the federal courts and the state courts. The court system of the state of Idaho is used in this exhibit.

Because the United States is a federal union of many states, we have both a federal court system and a state court system. Courts have differing **jurisdiction**—authority to hear a case—depending on their location and the subject matter of the case. As a general rule, the federal courts assert jurisdiction only over federal law claims, such as claims based on the U.S. Constitution or federal statutes or regulations. The primary exception is when the parties to a lawsuit involving $75,000 or more are residents of different states. In this instance, a case based on a state law claim may be brought in federal court under **diversity of citizenship jurisdiction** so that an objective decision can be made about which state's law should be applied. In the main, though, federal courts will hear only federal claims.

State courts, on the other hand, have **concurrent jurisdiction,** which means that they may hear both state law and federal law claims. Sometimes it becomes a strategic decision for the attorneys involved as to whether to bring a federal claim in federal court or in state court. For example, when the federal judiciary is predominantly composed of judges appointed by conservative presidents, a civil rights plaintiff may choose to bring a federal discrimination claim in state court, where the case may be heard by a more liberal, and thus more supportive, judge.

Court hierarchies—federal and Idaho.		EXHIBIT 3.2
	FEDERAL COURTS	**STATE COURTS**
Highest court	U.S. Supreme Court	Idaho Supreme Court
Appellate court	U.S. Circuit Court of Appeals	Idaho Court of Appeals
Trial court	U.S. District Court	Idaho District Court

In both federal and state court systems, the trial court is the lowest-level court in the hierarchy, the appellate court is the next level up, and the highest court is usually (but not always—the highest court in New York is called the New York Court of Appeals) called the supreme court and is the court of last resort. An adverse decision by a lower court may be appealed to the next highest court, but the highest court in each jurisdiction may select which cases it does and does not wish to review.

The U.S. Supreme Court is very selective about the cases it chooses to hear. Those who wish to take an appeal to the Supreme Court must petition the Court by requesting **certiorari**. A **denial of certiorari** simply means that the Supreme Court is declining to hear the case, and having done so, is allowing the decision of the lower court to stand. The same is true when state supreme courts refuse to hear an appeal. This does not mean that the higher court agrees with or is giving any endorsement to the lower court's decision; it means only that the court is choosing to hear cases that seem more important at that point in time, or ones that resulted in a split of opinion in several lower appellate courts and thus require immediate ultimate resolution.

A case may be appealed only on grounds of a **legal error**—that is, an erroneous interpretation of the law or application of legal procedure by the lower court. The trial court is entrusted with finding the facts—determining the credibility of the witnesses and the evidence. For example, when professional football player O.J. Simpson was put on trial for murdering his wife, the issue of whether or not a glove fit O.J.'s hand was a factual question for the jury to consider at the trial court level. The jury's conclusion on that issue would not be an appealable issue. However, whether or not the trial court properly admitted the glove into evidence would be an evidentiary legal issue that could serve as grounds for appeal, if that evidence should have been excluded as a matter of law. In deciding such issues, appellate courts review the trial court's record and the appellate briefs filed by the parties' attorneys, and hear the attorneys' oral arguments. They do not hear witness testimony or look at gloves or similar evidence; instead, they simply accept the outcomes of the fact-finding performed by trial courts.

An appellate court may choose to *affirm* the decision of the lower court, to *reverse* the decision (thus transforming the loser into the winner), or to *remand* the case back to the lower court with instructions for it to re-examine the facts in light of the appellate court's interpretation of the legal principles to be applied.

Anatomy of a Lawsuit

The judiciary is composed of civil courts and criminal courts. Criminal courts are where persons charged with a crime against the state are prosecuted. Civil courts hear cases that involve controversies of a noncriminal nature. Examples of **civil causes of action** (i.e., legal grounds upon which to sue) include contract disputes, employment discrimination, and **torts**—a civil wrong other than a breach of contract usually referring to the causing of damage to person or property or a person's reputation (e.g., slander or negligence) or harm to a person's commercial interests.

In a criminal case, the defendant has the right to a trial before a jury of his or her peers. Civil suits differ in that some are tried before a jury and some are heard by a judge with no jury. Criminal and civil courts also differ in the burden of proof required. In a criminal case, the prosecution must prove *guilt beyond a reasonable doubt* or the jury is supposed to vote to acquit the defendant. In contrast, in a civil trial the burden of proof is much lower. The plaintiff has only to prove his or her case by a *preponderance of the evidence;* that is, that his or her case is more likely than not to be true. Here the scales of justice merely move off-center, whereas in a criminal trial one side of the scales must drop all the way down with the weighty assurance of guilt.

Most sport law cases are brought in civil court, although occasionally a criminal case will arise that involves sports gambling, bribery, or excessive violence. For an excellent description of the civil (and criminal) trial processes, as well as more details on the anatomy of a lawsuit, see the website of the Idaho court system at www.isc.idaho.gov/overview.pdf. Exhibit 3.3 illustrates the process followed in a civil trial.

The following hypothetical example illustrates the civil trial process. Susan Spectator was injured in a 15-foot fall when the bridge she was crossing collapsed as she and several other spectators followed their favorite professional golfer to the next hole. Susan hired a tort lawyer with experience in negligence actions, who prepared a written **complaint** summarizing the allegations in Susan's case. This complaint included a statement of the cause of action (negligence in this case), the remedy requested, and a brief summary of the facts supporting Susan's claim that the defendant is responsible for her injury.

Susan's complaint was filed with the court. The country club then filed an answer to the complaint, admitting or denying each allegation. Alternatively, the country club's attorney could have filed a motion to dismiss the case, if it had been clear that the plaintiff did not have a legitimate case. The judge assigned to the case then ordered a period of discovery, during which the lawyers for both parties gathered their evidence by such means as **depositions** (oral testimony obtained under oath from witnesses or the parties in the case) and **interrogatories** (answers written under oath to a list of written questions). For example, Susan's lawyer deposed the club's maintenance staff about the condition of the bridge and requested maintenance records to ascertain whether the club had acted reasonably to keep the bridge in a safe state of repair.

Often, the results of discovery lead to an out-of-court settlement or to successful motions for summary judgment (explained below), allowing all parties to avoid the time and expense of a full trial. If, however, a sufficient controversy remains after discovery is completed, then plaintiff Susan will pursue the matter through a full **trial on the merits,** which means that the issues will be fully argued and a final decision reached. If the country club is found to have been negligent in maintaining the

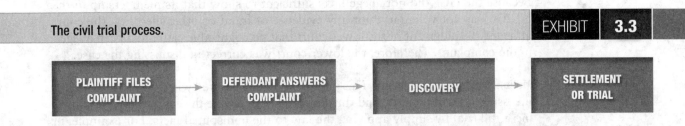

The civil trial process.   EXHIBIT   **3.3**

PLAINTIFF FILES COMPLAINT → DEFENDANT ANSWERS COMPLAINT → DISCOVERY → SETTLEMENT OR TRIAL bridge or in regulating the traffic flow based on the bridge's weight-bearing capacity, Susan will win her case and collect compensatory damages to compensate her for her injury. **Compensatory damages** are monetary payment for actual injury or economic loss, and may include compensation for such things as medical expenses or property damage. If the country club was found grossly negligent, the court could award punitive damages. **Punitive damages** are payment of an amount beyond that required to compensate for a victim's injuries; the additional damages award is intended to punish the defendant for grossly negligent or intentional misconduct.

Means of concluding a trial

You will encounter three common ways of concluding a trial, other than a decision on the full merits of the case:

1. Rule 12(b)(6) motion to dismiss for failure to state a claim upon which relief can be granted
2. Motion for summary judgment
3. Petition for a preliminary injunction

When a court grants any of these, the case to that point cannot carry any precedential value because it has not received a full trial on the merits. For researchers, the only value of such cases is their ability to shed light on how the courts might reason about the issue involved if the issue ever did make it to a full trial. The three ways of concluding a trial will be discussed in more detail below.

Motion to dismiss for failure to state a claim. This motion will be granted only when, even though all the plaintiff's factual allegations are accepted as true, the plaintiff fails to allege sufficiently a set of facts that would support a claim for relief based on the law invoked. For example, in *Pryor v. NCAA* (2002), the Third Circuit denied the NCAA's motion to dismiss the plaintiff's Title VI claim because the plaintiff had alleged sufficient facts indicating that the NCAA might have engaged in intentional race discrimination in raising the initial eligibility standards when it adopted Proposition 16.

In contrast, in *Hispanic College Fund, Inc. v. NCAA* (2005), the Indiana Court of Appeals affirmed a trial court's granting of defendant NCAA's motion to dismiss. Plaintiff Hispanic College Fund (HCF) had filed a claim alleging that the NCAA acted arbitrarily and capriciously in creating a special rule that prohibited HCF from sponsoring an extra preseason college football game while allowing the Black Coaches Association to do so. Indiana law does not permit judicial review of the decisions of voluntary membership organizations absent fraud or other illegality. Because the HCF did not allege facts sufficient to show that its membership in the NCAA was not voluntary, nor any evidence of fraud or other illegality, the court affirmed the judgment of the lower court that no cognizable claim had been alleged in the complaint. Therefore, the lower court was correct in dismissing the case.

Motion for summary judgment. This judgment will be granted when there are no genuine issues of material fact, and thus the judge can decide the case without conducting a full trial by simply applying the law to the undisputed facts. For example, in *Mid-South Grizzlies v. National Football League* (1983), the facts were undisputed that the Grizzlies were a potentially successful football team in a rival league to the NFL, and that when they later sought to become a franchise in the NFL, their request was denied. The court applied the law to those facts, finding that the NFL had not violated antitrust law in denying the Grizzlies' franchise request. Because the facts were not in dispute, the case did not have to go to a full trial for a determination as to which party's story was more credible. Instead, the court could grant the NFL's motion for summary judgment because all it had to do was apply existing law to agreed-upon facts. (For more information, see the Focus Case in Chapter 11.)

Preliminary injunction. This injunction will be granted when

1. The plaintiff has a substantial likelihood of prevailing on the merits of the case.
2. The plaintiff will suffer irreparable injury if the preliminary injunction is not issued.
3. Issuing the injunction will not inflict a greater injury on the defendant than the one threatening the plaintiff.
4. The injunction will not have an adverse effect on the public interest.

For example, in *Johnson v. Florida High School Activities Association* (1995), the U.S. District Court granted a preliminary injunction to order the Florida High School Activities Association (FHSAA) to allow a learning-disabled high school swimmer to compete during his senior year, even though he was 19 years old and in violation of the age limit rule, for the following reasons:

1. He was likely to prevail on his claim that denying him a waiver of the rule violated the Rehabilitation Act.
2. He would suffer irreparable injury if not allowed to compete during his final year of school.
3. Granting the waiver would not have significantly burdened the FHSAA and would have advanced the public interest in eliminating discrimination against individuals with disabilities.

Decision-Making Processes of the Courts

Courts must interpret statutes, regulations, constitutions, and common law (the law created by prior court decisions). In doing so, judges are supposed to act impartially. They attempt to follow certain guiding principles that restrain them from acting solely on personal philosophy, sympathy, or whim. It is important that you understand these principles so that you will be able to predict the outcome of cases related to your legal issues and so that you will be able to identify the pertinent facts that your lawyer will need.

Interpretation of statutes

When construing a statute, a court will use certain time-honored maxims as tools of argument to guide and justify its interpretation. These are known as **canons of statutory construction**. Often, though, these canons contradict each other. In fact, two opposing canons are available for use in arguing most points of statutory interpretation. In an article now treated as a classic, one noted legal scholar compiled a selection of these competing canons and labeled them as "thrusts" and "parries" (Llewellyn, 1950).

An example is "If the language is plain, it must be given effect." That is, it should be given a literal interpretation. A problem arises, though, when the statute is very old and a strict interpretation of the plain language would render an unjust result in light of contemporary circumstances. In this situation, another canon would be "Do not give effect to the plain language if a literal interpretation would lead to an absurd result or thwart the obvious purpose of the statute."

For example, assume a federal statute passed in 1940 prohibits gambling activities conducted over the telephone wires. In more modern times, gambling activities might be conducted via wireless computer access to a satellite. A literal interpretation of the statute might limit the legal prohibition to older technology, when in fact the probable intent of those who created that law was to prohibit easy access to gambling opportunities around the country—but they weren't aware at that time that future communications technology might not utilize telephone lines. So a literal interpretation of the statute would lead to an absurd result (gambling using a wireless connection is legal whereas it is prohibited if a telephone line is used) and would thwart the statute's obvious purpose.

Another type of problem arises when the statutory language is ambiguous and thus susceptible to differing reasonable interpretations. In such a case, a canon would indicate that the court must look to the original intent of the legislature to see what it had in mind when it enacted the statute. If the legislature thinks a court has misconstrued the legislative intent, it can pass a new statute amending the original law to assert its "true" intent. For example, Congress passed the Civil Rights Restoration Act of 1987 (CRRA) to correct the Supreme Court's misconstruction of the types of educational programs that Congress intended to count as recipients of federal funds under Title IX. The statutory language prohibited any educational "program or activity" that received federal funds from discriminating on the basis of sex. In *Grove City College v. Bell* (1984), the Supreme Court interpreted that language narrowly, holding that if a specific educational program did not receive federal funds, it need not comply with Title IX. In the CRRA, Congress said that the "program or activity" language was meant to be interpreted broadly, so that if any part of a university received federal funds, Title IX would apply to the entire educational program offered by that university.

Interpretation of regulations

With regard to interpreting regulations issued by administrative agencies, the general rule is that courts will afford great deference to the interpretation made by the agency responsible for promulgating and enforcing those regulations. For example, courts have uniformly deferred to the U. S. Department of Education's Office for Civil Rights' policy interpretations when construing the athletics regulations that flesh out how Title IX should be applied to interscholastic and intercollegiate athletics.

Interpretation of constitutions

The interpretation of a constitution, whether federal or state, is the particular responsibility of the courts—neither legislatures nor administrative agencies have any say about what a constitution might mean. Thus, court decisions interpreting

The U.S. Legal System and Legal Research **CHAPTER 3** **31**

constitutions are the final word on the subject. For example, the Establishment Clause in the First Amendment to the U.S. Constitution says that Congress shall pass no law respecting an establishment of religion. Based on the writings of the framers of the Constitution found in the Federalist Papers, we understand that they meant this clause to prohibit the establishment of a government-endorsed religion. However, the only interpretations of the Establishment Clause that have the authority of law—that is, that the courts will enforce—are the interpretations courts have handed down through the years as they decided cases in which that clause was implicated. Over time, the Supreme Court has interpreted that part of the First Amendment so that it now means something close to the idea that the government should remain almost completely neutral with regard to religion.

Interpretation of common law

Common law is the body of case law that has developed over time as court decisions have been rendered and then relied upon in subsequent cases. Our common law legal system involves both a cumulative and an interpretive process.

Cumulative process of the common law. The common law is cumulative in that it builds upon itself, adding layer after layer of case law to the edifice. Two guiding principles aid the cumulative process—stare decisis and binding precedent. **Stare decisis** means "let the decision stand." Under this principle, a court will usually refuse to change a ruling on an issue that has already been decided. Occasions when a court overrules a past decision are quite rare. For example, in 1972 the Supreme Court adhered to stare decisis in deciding not to overrule a 1922 Supreme Court decision, *Federal Baseball Club of Baltimore, Inc. v. National League of Professional Baseball Clubs.* The 1922 Court had ruled that professional baseball was not interstate commerce and hence not subject to antitrust laws. Although by 1972 pro baseball was obviously "big business" that crossed state lines, in *Flood v. Kuhn* (1972) the Court refused to violate stare decisis by overruling *Federal Baseball,* insisting that only Congress could eliminate the exemption from antitrust law for pro baseball that the earlier case had established.

The second guiding principle in the cumulative process of common law is the system of following binding precedent. There are actually two types of precedent— **binding precedent** and **persuasive precedent.** Within a given jurisdiction, the lower courts are bound by the precedent (or prior decisions) established by the courts above them. Decisions of the U.S. Supreme Court are binding precedent for all other courts in the land.

To illustrate how this works, let's assume the supreme court of Washington has decided that for Washington State University dropping men's swimming is an appropriate way to correct gender imbalance in its athletics program under Title IX and does not constitute reverse discrimination against male athletes. All the lower courts in the state of Washington must now adhere to that ruling and cannot decide otherwise. If that same issue has not yet reached the Idaho Supreme Court, the Idaho Court of Appeals may choose to rely on the rationale of the Washington Supreme Court and adopt the same holding because it finds the Washington precedent *persuasive.* The Washington decision is not *binding* on the Idaho court, however, because it was rendered in a different jurisdiction.

If the athletics director at the University of Idaho also then decides to drop men's swimming and is sued for reverse discrimination, she should be aware that although the Idaho court may adopt the position and rationale of the Washington Supreme Court, this might not occur. Not being bound by law decided in another jurisdiction, the Idaho court might decide to find in favor of the male swimmers. The Idaho athletics director could have more confidence in persuasive precedent from other jurisdictions if a majority of those jurisdictions have decided the issue the same way.

The combined effects of cumulative binding precedent and stare decisis lend uniformity, stability, and predictability to the law. The result is a society governed by the rule of law instead of the whimsy of whoever happens to be in power at a given moment in time. This system also enables individuals and businesses to make rational decisions about their actions with relative certainty about the legality of those actions, and it ensures that individuals residing in the same jurisdiction will receive similar and thus fair treatment in the courts. However, the downside of a cumulative common law system is that the law changes slowly, and the changes that do occur depend on the happenstance of real-world problems occurring and finding their way into court. Legislatures can speed the process of change by enacting statutes purposively to address new issues. However, achieving legislative consensus on a complex or controversial issue can be quite difficult.

Interpretive process of the common law. The saving grace of the common law system is that it is also an interpretive process. The law is made of words, and words are by nature subject to differing interpretations. The interpretive nature of judicial decision making thus builds flexibility into case law. In fact, it is this interpretive space that lawyers manipulate when arguing a case on behalf of a client.

The lawyer uses two primary methods to persuade the court that her client's position should prevail. If past precedent is relevant and supportive of her case, the lawyer will *analogize*. That is, she will argue that the facts in her case are so similar to the facts in the prior cases that those earlier, supportive decisions should apply to her case too. If, however, past cases are not supportive of her position, the lawyer will attempt to *distinguish* her case from those earlier cases by persuading the court of the significant factual and legal differences between them, thus justifying a different outcome in her case.

The result of this interpretive aspect of deciding case law is that a court can adapt existing law to situations that present a new twist on an issue. This flexibility is nevertheless constrained because the court must justify its decision based on the reasoned application of past cases. Thus, courts can adapt the law to social change, but they usually can only do so slowly. Again, this restrained flexibility contributes to legal and social stability.

ALTERNATIVE DISPUTE RESOLUTION

A lawsuit can be quite costly and time consuming. It is not unusual for court costs and attorneys fees to add up to a significant amount of money, sometimes several hundred thousand dollars, especially if several preliminary motions are filed. The average civil lawsuit takes two years to conclude and may take as many as six to eight years to wind its way through the system if, for example, there are a full trial on the merits and one or two appeals or remands. The discovery phase alone can take several months to complete. In contrast, arbitrations generally are concluded in less than a year.

Alternative dispute resolution (ADR) methods for resolving legal conflicts may allow parties to avoid a trial. In choosing ADR, the parties opt for a private dispute resolution procedure instead of going to court. The most commonly used forms of ADR are arbitration and mediation. Other forms of ADR involve privately hiring ex-judges or ombudspersons (the latter are individuals appointed within organizations to settle disputes internally).

The American Arbitration Association (AAA) is a national not-for-profit educational organization dedicated to the resolution of disputes of all sorts through arbitration, mediation, and other forms of ADR. The AAA was formed in 1926, is headquartered in New York City, and has offices in cities throughout the United States. More information on arbitration and mediation can be found at the AAA website at www.adr.org. After registering as an online user, you can access the link to the site's Reference Center. This site offers links to downloadable documents such as "Alternative Dispute Resolution Basics—FAQs" (see the website listing at the end of the chapter for more information and sample documents). Other related websites are included in the reference list at the end of this chapter.

Arbitration vs. Mediation

It is important to distinguish between arbitration and mediation since, although both are forms of alternative dispute resolution, they work in very different ways. **Arbitration** involves submission of a dispute to a neutral decision maker for *final and binding resolution*. Arbitrators affiliated with the AAA are trained to ensure that appropriate due process protections are observed throughout the arbitration process. Additionally, the arbitrator is granted the authority to award any relief that would have been available had the matter gone to court. **Mediation,** on the other hand, is submission of a dispute to an impartial mediator, who assists the parties in *negotiating a settlement of the dispute*. The mediator facilitates joint discussions between disputing parties and may also hold separate meetings with each side and suggest possible grounds for settlement. However, the mediator does not have authority to force the parties to settle or to reach an agreement regarding the dispute. The mediator helps the parties to compromise and reach a mutually satisfactory settlement of the dispute. Therefore, parties that will have an ongoing relationship might prefer mediation over arbitration because they will be more likely to continue a positive working relationship after the dispute is resolved. If the mediation process is not working, the parties are free to abandon mediation at any time after the first meeting and pursue remedies in court. If a settlement is reached through mediation, it will be written up as an enforceable settlement contract.

Alternative Dispute Resolution in Sports

The past decade has seen an increased emphasis on using ADR to resolve sport disputes. For example, CDM Fantasy Sports and Major League Baseball Advanced Media (MLBAM) entered into a nonbinding mediation process to try to reach agreement on a dispute over whether CDM can use player names and statistics for its baseball fantasy leagues without violating MLBAM's intellectual property rights. MLBAM asserted that CDM's use of that information without a license from MLBAM violated its ownership rights over that information. CDM, on the other hand, claimed that player statistics are, and properly belong, in the public domain (Fisher, 2005). The parties aired the dispute before a mediator, but were unable to reach an agreement. CDM then continued to seek a declaratory judgment on the issue pursuant to a claim it had filed in federal court. Ultimately, the 8th Circuit Court affirmed the decision of the federal district court that player names and statistics are already in the public domain, and thus their use by CDM Fantasy Sports is protected free speech under the First Amendment (*C.B.C. Distribution and Marketing, Inc. v. Major League Baseball Advanced Media,* 2007; see Chapter 20).

An agreement to arbitrate can appear in an individual contract with an athlete, in a collective-bargaining agreement between a players association and an owners group, or in a particular sport organization's constitution and bylaws. Most professional players association rules now require that disputes between agents must be resolved through arbitration. In addition, challenges to league rules and salary disputes between professional athletes and their teams are also subject to arbitration under the league's collective-bargaining agreement. (Salary arbitration is discussed in detail in Chapter 9.) The U. S. Olympic Committee (USOC) constitution and bylaws and the Ted Stevens Olympic and Amateur Sports Act require that arbitrations arising out of USOC athletics grievances be administered in accordance with the Commercial Arbitration Rules of the AAA (American Arbitration Association, "Commencing an arbitration"). See also the AAA document "Athletes' Frequently Asked Questions for Olympic Movement Disputes Administered by the AAA" at www.adr.org.

Other disputes involving professional sports, including disputes over partnership proceeds, termination of sports executives, the sale or relocation of a franchise, and payments under executive or partnership agreements, are also frequently resolved through ADR, primarily arbitration. Nevertheless, many issues are tried in the courts. A basic understanding of the fundamentals of legal research can help sport and recreation management professionals work effectively with their legal counsel if litigation occurs.

LEGAL RESOURCES

his section describes the many resources available to the public for conducting research on legal issues. Legal resources can be either primary or secondary resources.

Primary Legal Resources

As discussed earlier, primary resources in law consist of what actually is the law—that is, what may be relied upon in a lawsuit. These include constitutions, statutes, regulations, and case (common) law.

Constitutions, statutes, regulations

The U.S. Constitution provides the framework for the federal government and protects the fundamental rights of all citizens. Its protections of fundamental rights are applicable to the conduct of state governments by virtue of the 14th Amendment (cited as *U.S. CONST.* amend. XIV). Each of the 50 states has its own constitution, which provides citizens with protections similar to those in the U.S. Constitution. (Constitutions are cited in the following format: *N.Y. CONST.* art. X, § x.)

Federal statutes are codified in a series of volumes known as the U.S. Code (cited U.S.C. § x (year)). The U.S. Code Annotated (U.S.C.A.) is another series of volumes reporting federal statutes, but adding annotations regarding courts' interpretations of certain provisions, legislative history, and so forth.

The statutes of each state are similarly codified and published. An example is the Revised Code of Washington (cited as *Wash. Rev. Code* § x (year)). Many of the bound publications of these statutes contain annotations that identify court decisions construing the various sections or provisions of each statute. Recent amendments to the statutes are printed as pamphlets and placed in pockets at the back of the hardbound volumes until the volumes undergo a completely new printing. These pamphlets are known as "pocket parts."

Federal regulations are first proposed in the *Federal Register* and when finalized are codified in the *Code of Federal Regulations* (cited as volume XX C.F.R. § x (year)). For example, the gender equity in athletics regulations that implement Title IX are found in 34 C.F.R. § 106.41 (2009). Each state has regulations promulgated by various state agencies as well.

Court decisions

You may wish to read court decisions on a legal issue facing your sport or recreation organization so that you can determine whether the facts are analogous to your situation and gain an understanding of the courts' rationale for deciding the cases as they did. Court decisions are printed in case reporters, which exist for both federal and state court decisions. Public law libraries and libraries at law schools carry hard copies of collections of case reporters. Additionally, cases are reported online in several of the legal databases described in the sections of this chapter on electronic databases and websites. Exhibit 3.4 summarizes the citation abbreviations for case reporters for the federal courts.

Case reporters for federal courts.		EXHIBIT 3.4
COURT	**REPORTERS**	**ABBREVIATIONS**
U.S. District Courts	*Federal Supplement* (1st and 2nd Series)	F. Supp. and F. Supp. 2d
U.S. Courts of Appeals	*Federal Reporter* (1st, 2nd, & 3rd Series)	F., F.2d, and F.3d
U.S. Supreme Court	*U.S. Supreme Court Reports*	U.S.
	Supreme Court Reporter	S.Ct.
	Lawyer's Edition (1st and 2nd Series)	L.Ed. and L.Ed.2d

As Exhibit 3.4 shows, U.S. Supreme Court decisions are reported in three different case reporters, of which the official reporter is *United States Supreme Court Reports*. The most readily available and easiest to use version is the *Supreme Court Reporter,* and the third option is the *Lawyer's Edition*. In addition, full text versions of the Supreme Court's decisions are available at www.supremecourtus.gov.

State court decisions are reported in state case reporters, such as the *California Reporter*. Most law libraries do not carry state case reporters, preferring to save space by carrying only regional reporters, which report court decisions for all the states in a region. Exhibit 3.5 summarizes the regional reporters and the states they include.

All case reporters are referenced in the same manner: first the volume number, then name of the reporter, then the page number on which the first page of a particular case begins, and then the abbreviated name of the court and the year of the decision in parentheses. For example, *DeFrantz v. United States Olympic Committee* is reported at 492 F. Supp. 118 (D.D.C. 1980), which means that you can find the case in volume number 492 of the *Federal Supplement* on page 118, and that the case was decided in 1980 by the U.S. District Court of the District of Columbia. For Supreme Court cases, the name of the Court is not included in the parenthetical because the name of the reporter indicates that a Supreme Court case is being cited—only Supreme Court decisions are reported in the Supreme Court case reporters.

Secondary Legal Resources

Secondary resources are sources that are not in themselves law but that offer insight into or interpretation of the law. Secondary resources should never be relied upon as legal authority. They include the following:

Law dictionaries. *Black's Law Dictionary* provides definitions of legal terms, including Latin terms and phrases commonly used in the law.

Legal encyclopedias. *Corpus Juris Secundum* (C.J.S.) and *American Jurisprudence* (Am. Jur.) are legal encyclopedias that work like standard encyclopedias by providing a topical summary of a legal issue and referring the reader to other resources. These are a good place to begin your research if you know very little about your topic.

EXHIBIT 3.5	Regional case reporters of state court decisions.	
REGIONAL CASE REPORTER	**ABBREVIATIONS**	**STATES INCLUDED**
Atlantic Reporter	A. and A.2d	CT, DE, ME, MD, NH, NJ, PA, RI, VT
North Eastern Reporter	N.E. and N.E.2d	IL, IN, MA, NY, OH
North Western Reporter	N.W. and N.W.2d	IA, MI, MN, ND, NE, SD, WI
Pacific Reporter	P., P.2d, and P.3d	AK, AZ, CA, CO, HI, ID, KS, MT, NM, NV, OK, OR, UT, WA, WY
South Eastern Reporter	S.E. and S.E.2d	GA, NC, SC, VA, WV
Southern Reporter	So. and So.2d	AL, FL, LA, MS
South Western Reporter	S.W., S.W.2d, and S.W.3d	AR, KY, MO, TN, TX

Case summaries. *American Law Reports* (A.L.R.) covers both state and federal court decisions, providing case summaries as well as annotations with case commentaries and references to related cases. It is useful when you want to use a specific case as a starting point for your research.

Restatements. The restatements of the law (e.g., the *Restatement [Third] of Torts*) are written by legal experts who provide comprehensive summaries of the law on a broad topic such as torts. They contain exhaustive explanations and examples of application. These are most useful to someone who already has a working familiarity with the relevant area of the law. Often courts will rely on the restatements as a highly persuasive authority—although still not law—because they are written by the foremost legal analysts in their areas of expertise.

Treatises and hornbooks. Treatises and hornbooks are scholarly books written by expert legal scholars that provide an in-depth treatment of a legal topic. For example, *Prosser and Keeton on the Law of Torts* is considered one of the most definitive treatments of tort law ever written (Keeton, Dobbs, Keeton, & Owen, 1984). You might use a treatise such as this one if you seek comprehensive background knowledge on your topic. A treatise will contain extensive legal analysis and substantial references to other resources on the topic.

Law reviews. Law reviews are scholarly journals published by law schools that contain articles written by law professors, practicing attorneys, and advanced law students. These articles offer extensive analyses of narrow legal topics (e.g., the constitutionality of mass searches of sports spectators). They are a good place to start your research if your topic is a newly developing area of the law or if you already have a working familiarity with the general context of your specific topic. Some other academic journals focus on sport law (e.g., the *Journal of Legal Aspects of Sport*), and some business and academic journals, such as the *Sport Marketing Quarterly,* publish a law column as a regular feature.

Case digests. Case digests are subject indexes that correspond to the case law reporters described earlier. There are state, regional, and federal case digests, as well as an assortment of topical digests. These are useful when you want to locate cases relevant to your topic that were decided in a particular jurisdiction. To find cases in these digests, you must identify keywords relevant to your topic; they provide an index of keywords that can help. As a note of caution, the people who compile these digests often categorize topics according to somewhat archaic keywords used in legal classification. For example, sport-related topics can be located using the keywords "theatres and shows," and employment relationship topics might be listed under "master and servant." Law librarians at law libraries can help with identifying appropriate keywords.

Indexes. *Index to Legal Periodicals,* available in both book and electronic form, allows you to locate law review articles by topic or author.

Electronic databases. Electronic databases are available that contain primary legal resources and secondary sources, including full-text law review articles. Most law schools subscribe to the two predominant computerized legal databases, WEST-

LAW and LEXIS; however, their license agreements require them to restrict access to their own faculty and students. Most university libraries, though, subscribe to LEXIS-NEXIS Academic Universe, which any library user can access. The LEXIS-NEXIS Academic Universe legal database is not as comprehensive as the full LEXIS service, but it will suffice for most research needs. The NEXIS portion is a comprehensive compilation of news publications.

LEXIS and WESTLAW provide a variety of search methods, including searches by citation or keywords and natural language queries.

Websites. Websites give you access to many legal resources and are especially valuable in the event that you do not have access to any of the electronic databases. The following is a sampling of law-related websites:

- Cornell Law School's Legal Information Institute site is searchable for federal statutes (U.S. Code), state statutes, and Federal Rules of Civil Procedure, as well as federal and state court decisions. www.law.cornell.edu
- Two sites, www.findlaw.com and www.law.com, allow registered users to receive daily or weekly email updates on recent developments in topical areas such as sport law. The FindLaw database is searchable for federal and state law.
- Emory Law School's site is searchable for federal court decisions, which can be accessed at www.law.emory.edu by performing a site search using the search term *caselaw*.
- The Gender Equity in Sports Project (University of Iowa) site is searchable for information on gender equity in sports, including cases and recent developments in the news. http://bailiwick.lib.uiowa.edu/ge/
- Law Crawler—Legal Search is a comprehensive site for legal research. www.lawcrawler.findlaw.com
- The 'Lectric Law Library's Lexicon Lyceum site provides an online law dictionary. www.lectlaw.com/def.html
- The Library of Congress "Thomas" website is a comprehensive site for U.S. legislative materials and treaties. http://thomas.loc.gov
- The Marquette Law School site provides links to various sport law journals, which can be accessed at www.law.marquette.edu by highlighting the National Sports Law Institute link and clicking on *Publications*.
- The National Archives site is a useful online source for historical materials. www.archives.gov
- The National Center for State Courts provides a listing of court websites. www.ncsc.org
- KnowX offers a service for locating nationwide public records on people, businesses, and assets, for a fee. www.knowx.com
- The Sport & Recreation Law Association (SRLA) website provides a link to the Findlaw search database. www.srlaweb.org
- The United States Patent & Trademark Office (USPTO) website is searchable for registered trademarks and service marks. www.uspto.gov

Shepard's Citators. *Shepard's* is a citation system for updating your cases to ensure that you are not relying on out-of-date or overruled law—an essential component of doing legal research. However, it is complex and bewildering until you master it, so you should seek the help of a law librarian for your first attempt. *Shepard's* lists cases that have cited previous cases, as well as cases that have interpreted specific provisions of statutes. It codes cases according to whether they have been questioned, criticized, followed, reversed, or overruled.

CONDUCTING LEGAL RESEARCH

A s you realize by now, a myriad of resources are available for use in conducting legal research. Law libraries and legal research can be a never-ending maze in which you can waste much time, unless you start with a good research plan.

Stages of Legal Research

Good legal research generally progresses through five stages:

1. Identify the specific issue to be researched.
2. Find the relevant law.
3. Read and summarize the relevant law.
4. Update the relevant law.
5. Organize the information you have collected.

The plan outlined below should help keep you focused as you progress through these five stages.

Stage 1: Identify your issue

When you identify your issue, the more specific you can be, the better able you will be to narrow the parameters of your search for the relevant law. One strategy is to assess the facts of your problem by placing them in the following categories:

- Parties
- Objects
- Places
- Basic issue of the case
- Defenses
- Relief desired

This process of categorizing the facts will often suggest the specific legal issues that need to be researched. For example, let's categorize the following set of facts:

> "Big Mucky Muck the Giant Duck," the team mascot for the Seattle Ducks, was up in the stands entertaining the spectators with his antics, when one of the spectators seated on the third base line was hit in the face by a batted foul ball that he did not see coming because he was watching the Duck's antics. His eye socket was shattered, resulting in $25,000 in medical expenses.

What are the legal issues involved here?

Parties: injured spectator; stadium management

Objects: mascot entertainer; batted foul ball

Place: spectator at baseball game seated on third base line; jurisdiction in the state of Washington

Basic issue: Is management potentially liable to spectators for negligence?

Possible defenses: contributory negligence; assumption of risk

Relief sought: damages for injury

After categorizing the facts in this way, we can identify some of the specific legal issues involved:

- Does stadium management owe a duty of care to baseball game spectators to protect them from batted foul balls?
- If so, can management defend itself by arguing that spectators assume the risks inherent in being a baseball game spectator?
- If so, does employment of a mascot who entertains in the stands create an enhanced risk to spectators that they do not assume as an inherent risk?
- If so, can the injured spectator recover damages for injury? If so, in what amount?
- How does this jurisdiction determine the amount of blame, and thus the amount of damages, for which the defendant is responsible?

Once you have identified some specific legal issues, a law librarian or other legal expert can help you identify any relevant legal issues you may be unaware of and help you determine keywords, phrases, and legal terms of art that will increase the efficiency of your search for relevant law.

Stage 2: Find the relevant law

Approaches to finding the law that is relevant to your issue will vary depending upon your level of familiarity with that area of the law and your proficiency in legal research. If you are fairly familiar with negligence law in the context of sport, you might go directly to a case digest or electronic database such as LEXIS and immediately begin searching for relevant cases.

If you are unfamiliar with the topic, however, you might wish to gain some background knowledge to develop a context for understanding the specific legal issues involved. A legal encyclopedia can be a good place to start, or, if the issue is relatively new, reading a few recent law review articles will provide you with different analyses of your topic. Treatises or hornbooks may also be useful at this stage. Once you have acquired some comfort with the overall context, you can use A.L.R. to find relevant cases or the annotations (if you have a statutory issue) in the U.S. Code Annotated to find cases interpreting relevant statutory provisions.

You can also use the plain language search function of a computerized database such as LEXIS to begin to find cases. For example, you might click on the link for "Federal and State Cases" and then the link for a specific state, say California. Then, using a natural language search, type a first-level keyword, e.g., "inherent risk," into the *Search Terms* box. Then, search within results using a narrowing keyword, e.g., "baseball." You will get a list of approximately 116 cases, and you will find that around number 6 on the list is a case that deals with your precise issue: *Lowe v. California League of Professional Baseball*, 1997 Cal. App. LEXIS 532 (Cal. Ct. App. 1997).

Stage 3: Read and summarize the relevant law

Once you have collected the cases and other primary resources in Stage 2, you must read them carefully and evaluate them for their relevance to your issue. Evaluation of the relevance of cases is made much easier by briefing each case. A **case brief** is a succinct one- or two-page summary of a case that enables you to assess and compare it quickly with other cases. (A sample case brief is provided later in this chapter.) As you read, take notes on cases cited in the case you are reading, and read those cases too. Repeat this process until you find that you are turning up no new information and the sources are becoming repetitious, referring to the same legal principles and sources for support. At this point, you can feel reasonably sure that you have "closed the loop" and will not turn up any more relevant information.

Don't forget to search the law of jurisdictions other than your own to find persuasive precedent that may bolster your position. At this point, it would be a good idea, now that you have a grasp of the relevant law, to review all the primary sources you have found, refine the issue(s) of interest, and read or reread some law review articles or other secondary sources for their analytical perspectives.

Stage 4: Update the relevant law

It is extremely important to be sure that you are not relying on out-of-date or overruled law. *Shepard's* is the most commonly available search tool for updating the law in your collection. Electronic databases such as LEXIS also contain updating services. As discussed earlier, using *Shepard's* may be confusing, so it is advisable that you seek assistance from a law librarian when updating the law.

Stage 5: Organize your information

You are now ready to put your information into a format that will enable you to resolve your legal problem or formulate your position on your legal issue. Use the framework provided in Exhibit 3.6 to organize and write out your position. The acronym FIRAC may help you remember the steps.

Reading and Briefing a Case

As stated earlier, a case brief is a one- or two-page summary that outlines the key features of a case. The important components of a case brief are as follows:

- The citation information
- The facts
- The issue(s) presented

Competitive Advantage
STRATEGIES

Putting Basic Legal Strategies to Work

- If you are in doubt as to whether you need to seek legal advice, conducting some preliminary legal research on your issue should aid you in making that determination.

- Be careful not to apply the fruits of your legal research to a situation not germane to that body of law. Sometimes nonlawyers will attempt to extend a legal principle to a problem governed by a completely different area of the law because doing so appears logical from an untrained perspective. When in doubt, consult a lawyer instead of relying on your own conclusions.

- Use a preventive law approach and consider retaining a lawyer to assist in drafting contracts and policies, as well as risk management planning, for your sport or recreation organization. Such an approach can contribute to management success and increased profitability by helping to create and foster a safe and thus appealing business environment, and by helping you avoid costly litigation.

- A preventive approach depends on effective communication between a knowledgeable client and a lawyer. Be sure you have a working understanding of the basic legal issues facing your organization or event. To facilitate clear communication with your attorney, know what information is relevant to enable him to provide the best legal advice.

EXHIBIT	3.6	Framework for organizing legal information (FIRAC).

Facts: a statement of the facts that relate to your problem or your issue.

Pro baseball spectator on third base line was injured by batted foul ball when distracted by team mascot's antics in the aisle.

Issue: a statement of the specific legal issue(s) you wish to resolve.

Is management liable to spectator for negligence?

Relevant law: a collection of the relevant case briefs, statutory language, regulations, etc., that are most significant to your issue, placed in order of how relevant or significant they are.

Sample topics:

Case brief of *Lowe v. California League of Professional Baseball*

Briefs of other cases involving other types of spectator distractions

Briefs of cases on negligence liability of management for batted foul balls

Law review articles on these issues

Application of the law: a detailed analysis of how the law you found applies to the facts in order to resolve your issue. Try to be objective in your analysis by including a discussion (and then a refutation) of any existing support for your opponent's position. For example:

Spectator risks are increased by mascot antics, a risk that is not assumed because such distractions are not an inherent risk of baseball spectating. While being hit by a foul ball is an inherent risk, here the risk was unreasonably increased. But see cases and law review articles suggesting that similar distractions are either inherent risks or obvious risks, negating management liability. But these are distinguishable from the heightened distraction presented by a live mascot cavorting in the aisle, who intends to garner attention and is thus intentionally distracting.

Conclusion: a statement of the anticipated resolution of the issue and its practical implications for your organization:

Therefore, management should be held liable. Practical implications: keep mascot out of likely foul ball areas or out of stands altogether. Also, issue adequate warnings.

- The **holding** (or final ruling on the specific issue being decided)
- The **rationale** (or reasoning) used by the court to justify its decision

The rationale is the most difficult information to ascertain when you are reading a case, but it is also the most important information, next to the actual holding. Remember, a case goes to a full trial only for an issue that has not yet been squarely resolved in prior cases, and the *reasoning* in prior cases that have precedential value is what the courts will use as they apply the existing law to your new issue. Understanding the rationale of the courts in the cases you have collected allows you to guess how a court is likely to view your attempt either to analogize or to distinguish your case from past precedent.

As you read the rationale of an opinion, look for language that identifies what the court considers to be the major issues raised in the case. Then focus on how the court applies the relevant law to the facts surrounding those issues. Also note how it makes the arguments justifying its conclusions on those issues. For a good example of identifying the supporting arguments for specific issues in a case, examine the rationale provided for *Cohen v. Brown University* in Chapter 14. If you were to write a case brief on that case, your goal would be to achieve a similar understanding of the court's rationale and make a concise summary of the key points.

See Exhibit 3.7 for an example of a concise case brief.

Sample case brief.	EXHIBIT	3.7

CITE: *Knapp v. Northwestern University,* 101 F.3d 473 (7th Cir. 1996), *cert. denied,* 520 U.S. 1274 (1997).

FACTS: Knapp was offered a scholarship to play basketball at NU. During his senior year of high school, he suffered cardiac arrest, and an internal defibrillator was implanted. NU subsequently refused to allow him to play or practice, based on their team doctors' recommendations, but continued to honor his athletic scholarship. Knapp and his parents were willing to sign a liability waiver, but NU would not allow it. Knapp sued, claiming a violation of § 504 of the Rehabilitation Act, and ultimately sought a permanent injunction requiring NU to let him play. The District Court denied NU's motion for summary judgment and entered a permanent injunction prohibiting NU from excluding Knapp from playing on its basketball team for any reason related to his cardiac condition. NU appealed.

ISSUE: Does NU's refusal to allow Knapp to play violate the Rehabilitation Act?

HOLDING: No. The 7th Circuit reversed the decision of the district court and remanded it to the district court with instructions to enter summary judgment in favor of NU.

RATIONALE: Playing basketball is not a major life activity. Major life activities are not the job of one's choice; according to the ADA regulations, they are basic everyday functions that the average person can perform with little difficulty, such as walking and breathing. Learning is a major life activity, but Knapp still has his scholarship and can still get a college education, so NU's refusal to let him play does not place a substantial limitation on the major life activity of learning. Since there is no substantial limitation on a major life activity, Knapp is not disabled within the meaning of the law.

Even if he was found to be disabled, Knapp is not otherwise qualified to play basketball because there is a reasonable probability of substantial harm to him that cannot be eliminated—and this judgment was based on expert medical opinion. The EEOC regulations and the Supreme Court have recognized that direct threat to self is a valid defense.

According to the court in *Knapp,* medical decisions are best left to doctors, not to the courts. Here, NU doctors examined Knapp and his medical records, evaluated the severity of the risk and the possibility of future occurrences, and rationally reviewed and relied on consensus medical opinions in the pertinent field. So even if there were conflicting medical opinions (e.g., Knapp's doctor), the university acted reasonably and without discrimination.

CONCLUSION

You now have an understanding of the U.S. legal system and are acquainted with the basics of the legal research process. If your organization is confronted with a decision to make or policy to formulate that has legal ramifications, doing some research on specific relevant legal topics will give you a good sense of what your options are. Again, it is critically important that you remember that, if you are not a trained lawyer, you should rely on your research only for informational purposes. Once you are familiar with the legal issues relevant to your topic, you should seek out competent legal advice to make important policy decisions. A working knowledge of the legal issues you face will help you to work successfully with your lawyer in organizational planning, policy making, and risk management. It should also make your sport or recreation organization more attractive to your clientele and help you avoid financial loss due to litigation that might have been avoided.

discussion questions

1. When the higher court in a given jurisdiction declines to hear an appeal, how does that affect the decision rendered at the level below?

2. In your own words, explain the difference between a motion for summary judgment and a motion to dismiss for failure to state a claim. What precedential value do decisions on these motions have?

3. In your own words, explain the difference between binding precedent and persuasive precedent.

4. What are the pros and cons of a common law legal system founded on the principles of stare decisis and binding precedent?

5. What is the difference between mediation and binding arbitration? Why might parties in dispute choose alternative dispute resolution instead of litigating in court?

6. What is the difference between primary and secondary legal resources?

7. How would a manager faced with a potential legal problem benefit from conducting some legal research and reading some relevant cases?

learning activities

1. Using LEXIS-NEXIS or a similar online database, find a case on a sport law topic assigned by your professor and write a case brief summarizing it.

2. Consider the following sample statute:

   NO VEHICLES ALLOWED IN CITY PARKS. (Pullburg City Ordinance 1234.5(6)(a))

- What is the plain meaning of this statute?
- Does it apply to Tonka dump trucks? Bicycles? Baby strollers? Skateboards? Motorized scooters? Motorized wheelchairs? Emergency vehicles? Medi-vac helicopters?
- Is the statute more ambiguous than you initially thought?
- What might have been the legislative intent behind the law?

This exercise illustrates the interpretive nature of the law. It also makes clear why we need administrative agencies to issue regulations and courts to render rulings interpreting how statutes should be applied.

3. On the website of the National Center for State Courts (www.ncsc.org), find information on the state court structure and hierarchy for the state in which you reside.

CASE STUDY

1. Consider the following list of imaginary binding case precedents in your jurisdiction. Use it to analogize or distinguish the "cases" listed below.

1999—Discrimination against reds is not allowed.
2001—It is acceptable to exclude squares.
2003—Discrimination against greens is not allowed.

Case A: You feel you have been discriminated against because you are purple. How would your lawyer argue your case? What would the opposing lawyer argue?

Case B: You feel you have been discriminated against because you are a purple square. How would your lawyer argue your case? What would the opposing lawyer argue?

Case C: You feel you have been discriminated against because you are a triangle. How would your lawyer argue your case? What would the opposing lawyer argue?

Case D: You feel you have been discriminated against because you are a translucent sphere. How would your lawyer argue your case? What would the opposing lawyer argue?

2. Repeat the steps above, but make the following substitutions:

Native Americans for reds
Men for triangles
Black people for purples
Women for squares
Hispanics for greens
Israeli Jews for translucents
Transsexuals for spheres

R E F E R E N C E S

Cases

C.B.C. Distrib. & Mktg., Inc. v. Major League Baseball Advanced Media, 505 F.3d 818 (8th Cir. 2007), *cert. denied,* 128 S.Ct. 2872 (2008).

DeFrantz v. USOC, 492 F. Supp. 118 (D.D.C. 1980).

Federal Baseball Club of Baltimore, Inc. v. National League of Prof'l Baseball Clubs, 259 U.S. 200 (1922).

Flood v. Kuhn, 407 U.S. 258 (1972).

Grove City College v. Bell, 465 U.S. 555 (1984).

Hispanic College Fund, Inc. v. NCAA, 826 N.E.2d 652 (Ind. App. 2005).

Johnson v. Florida High Sch. Activities Ass'n, 899 F. Supp. 579 (M.D. Fla. 1995).

Knapp v. Northwestern Univ., 101 F.3d 473 (7th Cir. 1996), *cert. denied,* 520 U.S. 1274 (1997).

Lowe v. California League of Prof'l Baseball, 1997 Cal. App. LEXIS 532 (Cal. Ct. App. 1997).

Mid-South Grizzlies v. NFL, 720 F.2d 772 (3rd Cir. 1983).

Pryor v. NCAA, 288 F.3d 548 (3rd Cir. 2002).

Statutes

Civil Rights Restoration Act of 1987, 102 Stat. 28 (1988).

Other Sources

American Arbitration Association. (n.d.b.). *Commencing an arbitration for Olympic Movement disputes.* Retrieved June 14, 2009, from www.adr.org/sp.asp?id=22292.

American Arbitration Association (n.d.). *Commercial rules: Olympic and professional sports.* Retrieved June 14, 2009, from www.adr.org/sp.asp?id=28822.

Fisher, E. (2005, September 19–25). Mediator to hear evidence in MLBAM fantasy sports dispute. *Sports-Business Journal,* p. 6.

Keeton, W. P., Dobbs, D. B., Keeton, R. E., & Owen, D. G. (1984). *Prosser and Keeton on torts,* 5th ed. St. Paul, MN: West Group.

Llewellyn, K. N. (1950). Remarks on the theory of appellate decision and the rules or canons about how statutes are to be construed. *Vanderbilt Law Review, 3,* 395–406.

W E B S I T E   R E S O U R C E S

www.adr.org ▪ This website for the American Arbitration Association (AAA) provides links to downloadable documents relevant to sport managers. These include "A Guide to Mediation and Arbitration for Business People," "Alternate Dispute Resolution Basics—FAQs," "Athletes' Frequently Asked Questions for Olympic Movement Disputes Administered by the AAA," and "Sports Arbitration, Including Olympic Athlete Disputes."

www.isc.idaho.gov/overview.pdf ▪ The Idaho Supreme Court website has posted this description of the civil and criminal trial processes in its state, as well as details on the anatomy of a lawsuit.

www.ncsc.org ▪ The website of the National Center for State Courts provides information on state court structures and hierarchies.

www.supremecourtus.gov ▪ The official site of the Supreme Court contains the full text of the Court's case opinions.

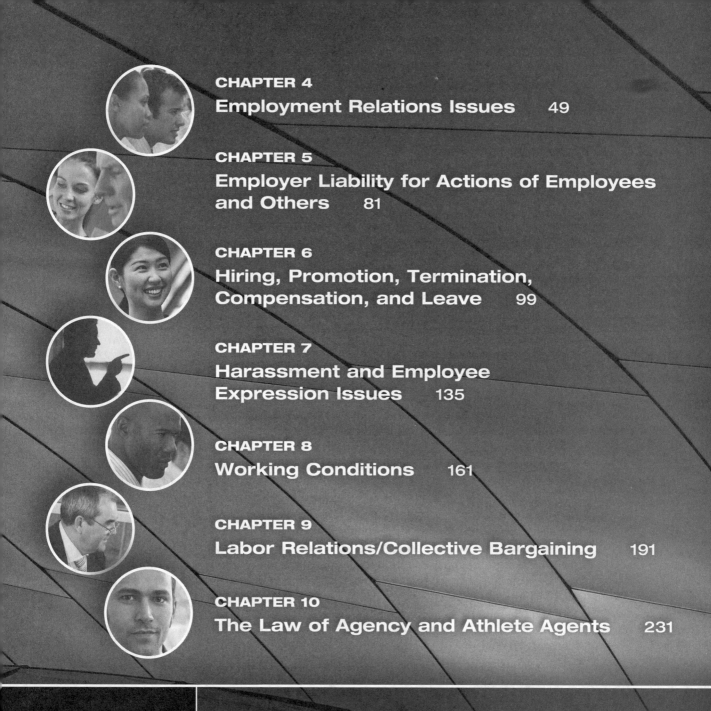

PART II | **Human Resource Management**

INTRODUCTION TO THE LAW IN HUMAN RESOURCES

M anaging human resources effectively is an essential component of gaining a competitive advantage in the world of sport and recreation. Highly motivated employees who are treated with respect and concern are at the core of any successful enterprise. Therefore, it is critical that you understand the legal concerns pertinent to hiring, supervising, disciplining, evaluating, and terminating employees. You also need to understand the legal issues relevant to working conditions and the legal landscape surrounding your interactions with a very important "human resource"—the athletes who participate in your setting.

If you perform any of the diverse responsibilities related to the management of human resources, you will encounter a number of legal issues. You and your organization can be much more successful if you possess a fundamental understanding of some of the legal areas implicated in the human resources management function of a sport organization.

LEGAL PRINCIPLES AND THE HUMAN RESOURCES FUNCTION

M any legal areas are implicated in human resource management. In Chapter 4 you will learn about employment relations issues, after an overview of contract law principles is given. Chapter 4 focuses primarily on contract law issues in employment, including the drafting of an employment contract and employment at-will principles, but it also addresses some tort theories as they pertain to employment. Chapter 5 focuses on the liability a sport/recreation organization may have for the acts of its employees, volunteers, or independent contractors. Chapter 6 has an extensive review of employment discrimination law, including aspects of race, gender, age, and disability discrimination. Chapter 7 continues to focus on employment discrimination, addressing sexual harassment and issues related to employee expression. Chapter 8 addresses legal aspects of working conditions, including the Fair Labor Standards Act, workplace safety, and workers' compensation law. Chapter 9 provides the fundamentals of labor relations law and collective bargaining. Chapter 10 focuses on the law related to athlete agents.

All of the human resource issues described in these chapters will require you to be knowledgeable in a variety of legal theories so that you can make effective decisions in the workplace. The following chapters explore each of these areas and their application in sport and recreation organizations.

Employment Relations Issues

INTRODUCTION

anaging human resources effectively is an essential component of gaining a competitive advantage in the sport marketplace. "Enduring advantages will come from making better use of people," according to one human resource text (Jackson & Schuler, 2000, p. 6). Highly motivated employees who are treated with respect and concern are integral to the success of any enterprise. Therefore, we discuss the legal issues pertaining to contract and tort concerns with employees in sport organizations to enhance your ability to make wise managerial decisions that are well-founded on legal principles. Concern for doing the right thing legally can translate into a more effective and efficient sport business.

This chapter discusses important contract principles related to employment relations. To help you understand those principles, it gives an overview of contract law as a foundation. Next, the chapter discusses the principle of employment at will and explores the issue of wrongful termination in that context. Finally, this chapter addresses a number of tort causes of action that are particularly applicable to employment matters. Exhibit 4.1 provides an overview of this chapter's managerial contexts, major legal issues, relevant law, and illustrative cases.

OVERVIEW OF CONTRACT LAW

As we discussed in Chapter 2 with regard to risk management, contract law is an excellent vehicle for using the law to gain a competitive advantage. Most contracts of any complexity are negotiated over a lengthy period of

EXHIBIT	4.1	Management contexts in which employee relations issues may arise, with relevant laws and cases.

MANAGEMENT CONTEXT	MAJOR LEGAL ISSUES	RELEVANT LAW	ILLUSTRATIVE CASES
Contract law principles	What are elements of a contract?	Contract law	
Authority to sign contract	When is organization bound by employee?	Actual vs. apparent authority	*Huyett*
Hiring employees	Employment contract	Reassignment clause	*Monson*
	Rights of competitors	Covenant not to compete	*Northeastern Univ. v. Brown*
Termination of contracts	Breach of contract	Perquisites	*Rodgers*
		Just cause termination	*O'Brien*
		Liquidated damages	*DiNardo*
Termination of employment	Term of employment	At-will employment	*Frazier*
Employment references	Liability for accuracy of information	Negligent misrepresentation/ fraud	*Randi W.*
Recruiting employees	Liability for interfering with existing contract	Tortious interference with contractual relations	*Bauer*

time, and there are usually multiple drafts before the final contract is signed. This means that you have more than adequate opportunity to reflect upon the agreement and to consult with your attorney in order to arrive at a document that will best serve your interests.

Contract law is, essentially, concerned with clarifying and enforcing the will of the parties in determining agreements. Courts are concerned with trying to give effect to the parties' intent; courts do not try to rewrite contracts to make a better document for the parties or to make sure that each party has the best deal possible.

Canons of Interpretation

Because of this underlying philosophy of contract law, you should understand a few basic principles about how courts interpret contracts, called the **canons of interpretation** (see Exhibit 4.2). First, the courts try to interpret a contract as an integrated whole. This means that the courts always try to interpret a contract in a way that makes sense for the entire contract. The court reads sections of the contract together in an attempt to discover if there is cohesion throughout the document. Clauses of the document are tied together, sometimes in very complex ways, and the document should reflect agreement in all its parts.

Another canon of interpretation is that, in the event of ambiguity, a document will be interpreted most strictly against the party that drafted the document. What does this mean for you? It means that if you are the party that has the advantage of actually drafting the document, you need to make sure that the contract is very clear in its meaning. If there is ambiguity in the document you (or your attorney) have drafted, that ambiguity may lead to the court's favoring the other party when it tries to resolve the ambiguity.

Whenever you begin a negotiation or start to draft a document, you should always take the perspective of the **worst case scenario.** Contracts are simply reflections of human understandings, and as with all relationships, sometimes the relationship may deteriorate. Consider the hiring of a college coach, for example. When a coach is hired, generally everyone is excited about the prospect of new leadership in a program. The last thing that most people would think about is the dissolution of this partnership. However, the reality is that coaching contracts are breached frequently, either by a college that wants to move a program in a new direction or by a coach who seeks greener pastures. Therefore, the coaching contract must be written with the worst case scenario in mind. The contract should be drafted to protect your organization's interests in the event the contract is terminated, either by you or by the other party.

Canons of interpretation of contract law.	EXHIBIT	4.2

1. The courts interpret a contract as an integrated whole.
2. The courts interpret a contract most strictly against the party that drafted the document, in the event of ambiguity.

Formation of a Contract

A **contract** is "a promise, or set of promises, for breach of which the law gives a remedy, or the performance of which the law in some way recognizes a duty" (Restatement [Second] of Contracts, 1981, § 1). The formation of a contract has four fundamental aspects: (1) agreement—offer and acceptance; (2) consideration; (3) capacity; and (4) legality.

Agreement—offer and acceptance

The formation of a contract begins with an offer, which is a conditional promise made to do or to refrain from doing something. For example, I may offer to sell you a certain piece of fitness equipment for $400. I have identified the terms of the offer; you know what piece of equipment we are discussing, and you know the price. I have communicated the offer to you.

If you agree to the terms as stated, you have given an **acceptance**. You have promised to pay me $400 when I deliver the equipment to you. If you do not mirror the offer with your acceptance, you may become the offeror of a **counteroffer**. For example, if your response is that you want the equipment but will pay only $300, you are effectively rejecting my initial offer and making a counteroffer to me based on a price of $300. If I agree to the reduced price, I have accepted the counteroffer.

Consideration

Consideration involves the exchange of value. Even if there has been an exchange of promises, there can be no contract until there is an exchange of value. One party gives up something of value in exchange for the other party's value. Often the bargained-for exchange is in terms of money for a promise to do X or to provide X.

If I promise to pay you $100 and ask for nothing in exchange, there is no contract. All we have is an unenforceable promise to make a gift to you of $100. However, if I agree to pay you $100 for a tennis racquet of yours that is barely serviceable, there is consideration. Further, courts do not generally inquire as to whether the consideration was too little or too much. Since, as discussed above, a basic premise of contract law is to allow private parties to engage in transactions of their own making, courts will not generally intervene to stop a bad deal from taking place. I made a bad choice to pay $100 for your much-abused racquet; however, I do so of my own volition and without any misrepresentations on your part about the condition of the racquet. Sometimes we may make good deals and other times we may make bad deals; it is not the prerogative of the courts to be intermediaries in the deals we make, only to ascertain that the law is followed.

Capacity

Capacity means the legal competence of the parties to the contract to enter into a contractual relationship. For example, minors are usually not bound by contracts since the law makes a presumption that a minor lacks the legal competence (capacity) to enter into contracts. Thus, if a minor signs a contract, it is generally voidable at the option of the minor. That is, a minor can set aside a contract and the legal obligations stemming from that contract. We will elaborate upon this concept in conjunction with the discussions of waivers in Chapter 17.

Other circumstances may affect competence. For example, mental incompetence or intoxication may also result in a lack of capacity.

Legality

Legality means that, to be enforceable, the subject matter of the contract must not violate state or federal law. A contract whose terms require the violation of law would be unenforceable. For example, since gambling is illegal in most places in the United States, a gambling contract in Ohio, where gambling is illegal, would not be enforceable.

Oral Contracts

If a contract has the elements of offer, acceptance, and consideration; the parties have capacity to enter into the agreement; and the subject matter is legal, must the contract be in writing to be enforceable? Generally speaking, oral contracts are enforceable, but the parties may have some difficulty establishing the terms of the contract since there is nothing in writing. As good managerial practice, regardless of what the law permits, you should put every contract in writing.

Under certain circumstances, the courts will not enforce oral contracts. States have statutes known as the **Statutes of Frauds,** which require certain types of contracts to be in writing. For our purposes in sport or recreation settings, the following types of transactions must be in writing:

- Agreements for the sale of land or an interest in land
- Contracts for the sale of goods priced at $500 or more
- Contracts that cannot be performed within one year of the formation of the contract (Cross & Miller, 2009)

A sport facility purchase or lease would fall under the first category of transaction. Purchasing any type of sporting equipment costing $500 or more exemplifies the second type. Finally, a game contract signed in 2010 for a game to be played in the year 2013 would be a contract that could not be performed within one year and thus must be in writing to be enforceable.

Contract Remedies

When one party fails to perform essential aspects of a contract, this is termed a **breach of contract.** Sometimes the breach may be remediable, but often the contract is terminated and the nonbreaching party is awarded the damages sustained as a result of the breach. In a contract case, the court is not attempting to punish the party that breached the contract; it is simply trying to compensate the innocent party for the loss of the bargain. Essentially, **contract damages** are designed to put nonbreaching parties in the position they would have held if the contract had been performed as promised (Restatement [Second] of Contracts, 1981, § 347).

Compensatory damages

In most contract cases, the nonbreaching party can be compensated for the loss of the bargain through monetary or **compensatory damages.** These damages arise directly from the loss of the bargain.

For example, let's assume a sporting goods store agrees to sell X a football helmet for $125. X agrees to buy the helmet for that price, but the store now refuses to sell X the promised good. The store is in breach of the contract, and X still needs to obtain the helmet. X goes to the two other stores in the area that sell that model of helmet and finds that Store A is selling the helmet for $135 and Store B is selling the helmet for $150. What damages can X recover?

First, the general rule in a breach of a sales contract is that the buyer can recover the amount equal to the difference between the contract price and the market price. In this case, however, there are two market prices, $135 and $150, for the same item. So can X recover $25 ($150 market price from Store B minus $125 contract price) or can X recover only $10 ($135 market price from Store A minus $125 contract price)? Assuming that the item is identical, X's damages are limited to $10. According to the principle of **mitigation of damages,** a nonbreaching party must act reasonably to lessen the consequences of the breach. In this case, that would mean that X must choose to buy the item for the lesser price of $135 ($10 damages). This obligation to reduce the damages, if possible, is not absolute. X only has to act reasonably; it is not necessary to get bids on this helmet from every vendor in the United States, just to deal with the vendors X usually has dealt with for this type of equipment.

The principle of mitigation of damages applies to all types of contracts, but it may be more difficult to implement than in the example just given. Suppose a university breaches its employment contract with a coach. The coach is obligated to mitigate damages by accepting a comparable offer of employment with another university. The coach, however, would not have to accept employment that was inferior in compensation, level of competition, geographic location, and so forth, just to lessen the damages; that would not be expected as a part of the duty to mitigate.

Specific performance

In certain rare circumstances, monetary damages will not suffice because the object of the contract is unique. If an item is unique, no matter what a breaching party pays, money damages will not compensate for the loss of the bargain because the item cannot be purchased on the open market. For example, suppose you agree to sell me a Babe Ruth uniform that he wore in a particular game against the Cleveland Indians. There is no other jersey worn by Babe Ruth on that date; it is unique. I agree to buy the jersey for $30,000. If you then breach the contract, money damages will not help me because that item cannot be obtained elsewhere. **Specific performance,** that is, compelling a party to fulfill the terms of a contract, is the appropriate remedy because that will force you to sell me the jersey for $30,000.

This remedy cannot be used with personal services contracts, however. If you owned the Miami Heat and LeBron James wanted to breach his employment contract with your franchise, you could not force LeBron to play for you by arguing that specific performance (playing) was necessary. Courts will not force people to compete against their will. Moreover, how would you ascertain that

LeBron's performance was acceptable? He may be on the floor, but how could you enforce a quality performance?

Liquidated damages and penalty provisions

Sometimes the proper amount of damages cannot be determined exactly. Although contract damages cannot be mere speculation, sometimes parties have to approximate the amount of damages that will be sustained. Employment contracts often have a **liquidated damages** provision because the parties would not be able to determine the amount of a breach exactly. The parties, therefore, agree to a liquidated damages provision that sets up the reasonable approximation of damages. Later in this chapter you will study the case of *Vanderbilt University v. DiNardo*, which illustrates this principle.

Care must be taken in drafting the liquidated damages provision because courts do not uphold **penalty provisions,** provisions that do not bear a reasonable relationship to the damages to be sustained and are simply punishing a party for breaching a contract. Courts will not uphold these provisions, nor will they award **punitive damages,** unless there is some fraudulent behavior.

Rescission and restitution

Rescission involves undoing the contract and returning the parties to the positions they had prior to the contract. It is often utilized when fraud, duress, mistake, or misrepresentation has taken place. **Restitution** involves returning the goods or property that was transferred under the contract. For example, if I pay you $1,000 for a tennis racquet because you misrepresent that it was used by Serena Williams in a tournament, I can rescind the contract and have the $1,000 restored to me if I ascertain that Serena Williams did not use this racquet.

Promissory estoppel

Promissory estoppel is a quasicontractual remedy, meaning that a party may have some recourse despite the fact that some elements of the contract may have been left out. A court may substitute detrimental reliance (see item 3 in the list below) for the element of consideration (Restatement [Second] of Contracts § 90). Promissory estoppel is used when a party relies upon another party's promises and suffers an injustice. Promissory estoppel has three elements:

1. A promise is made that should reasonably be expected to induce reliance.
2. There is reliance upon that promise.
3. Some detriment occurs to the party that relied upon the promise.

For example, in the case of *Bowers v. Federation Internationale de L'Automobile* (2007) a court held that plaintiff fans who sued the organizers of a car race because there were fewer competitors in the race than advertised could not prevail on their promissory estoppel claim. No reasonable racing fan would have regarded the race's "advertising" regarding the number of cars in the race as a promise upon which someone could reasonably rely.

Next, we explore promissory estoppel through a hypothetical situation in college athletics.

considering . . .   **PROMISSORY ESTOPPEL**

Larry Lance, a former basketball player at Sports R Us University (SRU), received a grant-in-aid for three years, but his athletic scholarship was not renewed for his senior year. A notice of nonrenewal was given to Lance in a timely fashion. Further, according to NCAA regulations a grant-in-aid can be granted only for a period of one academic year.

Lance acknowledges the foregoing facts of the situation, but he is concerned about the promises made to him when he was recruited to play at SRU. He decided to come to SRU only because the SRU basketball coach promised him that he would receive a scholarship for all four years at SRU, assuming Lance remained academically eligible, which he did. However, after three years on scholarship, the coach chose not to renew Lance's aid for his senior year.

Question

- Does Lance have any recourse?

Note how you would answer the question and then check your response using the Analysis & Discussion at the end of this chapter.

In a situation closely aligned to the hypothetical one above, a football player recruited by the University of Hawaii sued the school and the school's former defensive line coach on the basis of promissory estoppel. Daniel Smith was recruited by Hawaii, and he orally committed to play for that school. At the time of his oral commitment, Smith agreed to stop considering offers from other schools. However, the university did not follow through and formally offer Smith a scholarship. Smith's suit claims that he relied upon the assistant coach's representations that he would be offered a scholarship and did not pursue other schools after making the oral commitment to Hawaii (Staples, 2008).

Disparity of Bargaining Power

In some situations courts will find that a contract may violate notions of public policy and refuse to enforce the contract. See Chapter 17 for a discussion of public policy concerns and waivers. Another reason why some contracts are unenforceable is that an unconscionable **disparity of bargaining power** exists between the parties. The difference in power forces the signer to agree to the terms of the contract as dictated by the other party. There is no bargaining about the terms of the contract; the contract is written exclusively by one party, and the other party is forced to accept those terms in order to go forward with the transaction.

We have focused on the quasicontractual remedy that may exist in certain situations in which a coach promises something to a prospective student-athlete that induces that athlete to attend the university. In most situations, however, student-athletes are confined to contract remedies based on the documents signed. One of these documents is the **National Letter of Intent** (NLI), which is an agreement between the institution and the prospect that the prospect will attend that institution for one year and will be provided with a financial aid award ("About the National Letter of Intent," 2009). See the website http://www.ncaa.org/wps/wcm/connect/nli/nli for more information about the program. Once the NLI is signed, the recruiting process stops, and no other schools are entitled to make contact with that recruit.

Some commentators have asserted, however, that the NLI exemplifies a disparity of bargaining power in collegiate athletics (Meyer, 2004). This is so, argues Meyer, because the prospective athlete cannot negotiate, in any way, to alter the content of the standardized NLI form, which does not incorporate any of the representations that a coach may have made during the recruiting process pertaining to playing time and other matters. Meyer believes that the most egregious issue pertains to the departure of a coach. The NLI is signed with an institution, not a coach. Therefore, if the coach leaves after a student has signed the NLI, that is not grounds for the student-athlete to void the agreement. In fact, if the athlete then chooses not to honor the NLI and to transfer to another school, she can be forced to sit out for two years and to lose two seasons of eligibility.

Meyer (2004) argues that this is blatantly unfair, since the reality is that most athletes choose to attend an institution based on the coach, not on the institution itself. She suggests that athletes be given a limited release from the NLI, without penalty, in cases where the head coach who recruited that athlete leaves before the athlete enrolls in school. This limited release would allow the athlete to find another institution within a 30-day period.

Authority to Contract

Organizations can act only through their representatives, who are often employees of the organization. For the purposes of agency law, the organization is characterized as the **principal** and the person acting on behalf of the principal is the **agent** (see Chapter 10).

Agents have a scope of authority (see Chapter 10) to bind the organization contractually. Agents have **actual authority** to engage in certain transactions. This means that the principal has conveyed to the agent what his limits of authority may be. The concept of **apparent authority** means that the principal has somehow conveyed to a third party that the agent has authority to act, even though the agent does not have actual authority. The hypothetical case below illustrates these principles.

considering . . .   **APPARENT AUTHORITY**

The manager (agent) at a sporting goods store (principal) has actual authority to make contracts up to a value of $15,000. This actual authority has been conveyed in writing to the manager. The manager, however, has entered into several transactions with vendors for amounts in excess of $15,000, and the store owners have taken no action against the manager for violating his actual authority.

The manager purchases equipment for $25,000 from a vendor with whom he has exceeded $15,000 before. The store owners now want to void the agreement.

Question

- How can the third-party vendor argue that the store owners should be bound by the agreement even though the manager violated his scope of actual authority?

Note how you would answer the question and then check your response using the Analysis & Discussion at the end of this chapter.

In the next case, an employee unsuccessfully argued that the state board of education should be bound by actions taken by the university president as agent of the state board. Here, the court found that no actual or apparent authority existed.

Huyett v. Idaho State Univ.

FOCUS CASE | 104 P.3d 946 (Idaho 2004)

FACTS

Shirley Huyett was hired as the head women's basketball coach at Idaho State University (ISU) by the ISU President, Howard Gauthier, on June 29, 2001. It was a one-year contract. Huyett wanted a multiyear contract, and after Huyett began work at ISU Gauthier made some vague references to the possibility of this.

During her one-year employment term, Huyett and ISU engaged in negotiations for a multiyear contract. ISU prepared a draft of a three-year employment contract but rescinded the draft before either party signed it. Huyett was placed on administrative leave, and she filed suit for breach of an express or implied contract for multiyear employment.

The trial court entered summary judgment for the university, and Huyett appealed.

HOLDING

The Idaho Supreme Court affirmed, as it held that the state university did not have actual or apparent authority to enter into a multiyear employment contract with Huyett.

RATIONALE

In this case, the Idaho Board of Education is the principal and carries the authority to approve all employment contracts. The university and its employees are agents of the board. According to the policy and procedures of the board, no multiyear employment contracts are valid unless they have been approved by the board.

ISU did not have actual or apparent authority to enter into a multiyear agreement with Huyett. University presidents are given authority only to negotiate contracts but not to bind the board. Apparent authority is based upon representations from a principal to a third party, and the board never indicated that the draft contract for multiple years was anything but a draft.

EMPLOYMENT CONTRACT PROVISIONS

Certain provisions are commonly found in employment contracts. For the sake of illustration, we discuss these employment contract provisions in the context of the employment contract between a university and a coach. Detailed summaries of provisions in contracts between coaches and universities are available at the following websites:

www.fcsl.edu/node/174

www.usatoday.com/sports/graphics/basketball_contracts/flash.htm

www.usatoday.com/sports/college/football/2009-coaches-contracts-database.htm

See Chapter 9 for a discussion of professional athlete contracts.

Duties and Responsibilities

The duties and responsibilities section of the employment contract sets out the duties and responsibilities that the *employee* is expected to perform. For example, a college coach has many responsibilities in addition to evaluating talent, preparing players for competition, and developing game day strategies. Coaches often have numerous programmatic responsibilities in the areas of budgeting, recruiting, scheduling contests, evaluating assistant coaches, public and media relations, and fund-raising. These must all be set forth in this section of the contract. This section should also provide that the coach will devote his/her primary efforts to fulfilling the responsibilities of the position.

The contract should clearly state that the athletics program is only one aspect of the university's primary purpose of education. This should lead to a discussion of the coach's responsibility to make every effort possible to ensure that student-athletes meet their academic obligations.

Finally, there must be language that states the coach's obligation to abide by all NCAA, conference, and university rules and regulations. In fact, the NCAA (by-law 11.2.1) mandates that a stipulation in the coach's contract provide that a coach found in violation of NCAA regulations shall be subject to disciplinary action as set forth in the NCAA enforcement procedures. There should also be language that reinforces the coach's responsibility to oversee the assistant coaches to make sure that all members of the coaching staff comply with all pertinent rules and regulations.

Reassignment clause

A **reassignment clause** gives an employer the right to transfer an employee into a different employment position in the organization. For example, the university, as

---

Competitive Advantage

STRATEGIES

Contract Law

- Use the worst case scenario in developing contracts for your organization. Contracts should serve your interests when the contractual relationship encounters difficulties, such as in cases of breach or termination.

- Even though oral contracts may be enforceable in many situations, it is good business practice to put all your contracts in writing to avoid disputes regarding their content.

- Avoid making promises that go beyond what a written agreement conveys. Under the theory of promissory estoppel, you may be liable for promises.

- Enforce the limits of actual authority that your organization has conveyed to employees. Remember that third parties may be able to use the concept of apparent authority to your organization's detriment.

employer, may try to insert a reassignment clause into a coaching contract. This means that the university retains the right to transfer the coach to a different employment position in the university. The university could invoke this right of reassignment, for example, if it wants to make a coaching change but the coach has not breached the agreement. If the university were to terminate the coach, it would be subject to damages for breach. However, if a reassignment clause exists, the university may rightfully remove the coach from his current position and reassign him to other duties. If the coach refuses to accept the reassignment, that is a breach by the coach, and the university may terminate the contract for just cause (see below for a further discussion of the concept of just cause). However, if the university attempts to reassign a coach and it does not have the right to do so under the contract, the coach may argue that the university has breached the agreement by doing so. The coach would argue that this is a **constructive discharge,** which means that although the coach has not been actually fired, the impact of the reassignment is essentially to take away the responsibilities for which he was hired.

The reassignment clause is usually highly detrimental to an employee's interest. If someone is hired to be a football coach, for example, that person, regardless of compensation, does not want to become the golf coach or the compliance coordinator. Compensation is not the issue; a coach wants to retain the status associated with the original position and to coach in his/her area of competence. In the following case, the validity of a reassignment clause was upheld against a coach.

Monson v. State of Oregon

FOCUS CASE   901 P.2d 904 (Or. Ct. App. 1995)

FACTS

Don Monson coached the men's basketball team at the University of Oregon from 1983 to 1992. After the 1991–92 season ended, the athletic director met with Monson and advised him that the basketball program was not "going in the direction he wanted" (p. 906) and that Monson was being reassigned to golf coach. Monson protested, saying that to accept this reassignment would be professional suicide. After Monson failed to accept the new assignment, the university considered him to have resigned and paid him no further compensation.

Monson sued the university for breach of contract, asserting that he had performed his obligations as basketball coach and that the term of his employment contract did not expire until June 30, 1994. Monson argued that the attempt to reassign him was a constructive discharge. The university responded that it had the right to reassign Monson under a clause in the contract that stated: "The position as offered is subject to all applicable provisions of State and Federal law, State administrative rules, and the regulations and policies of the State System of Higher Education and the University of Oregon" (p. 905). These regulations permitted the reassignment of any state employee.

A jury trial was held, and Monson was awarded $292,087.93. The university appealed.

HOLDING

The Oregon appellate court reversed the judgment of the trial court and held that reassignment was permitted.

RATIONALE

The primary issue upon appeal was whether the university had a right to reassign Monson. The court reviewed the contract provisions that incorporated by reference all of the administrative rules and regulations governing all state employees, regardless of position. These rules and regulations did permit the reassignment of personnel. Therefore, the court reasoned that the university retained the right to reassign Monson and that, when it did so, it did not breach the employment contract with the coach.

Compensation

Compensation of the employee is a critical facet of any employment agreement. High-profile coaches with very competitive teams, for example, are often compensated quite well, especially football coaches and the coaches of men's basketball teams. As of March 2008, there were four university football coaches who received yearly compensation in excess of $3 million. The average earnings of the 120 major college football coaches reached $1 million. At least a dozen coaches are making $2 million or more per year (Wieberg & Upton, 2008). In December 2009, Mack Brown, football coach at the University of Texas, became the first college football coach to be paid more than $5 million annually in salary. Beginning with the 2010 season, Brown will be paid at least $5.1 million a year (Berkowitz, 2009). In a very controversial hiring, the University of Kentucky contracted with basketball coach John Calipari for a $31.65 million deal over 8 years (McMurray, 2009). Some commentators have found this excess of commercialism in coaches' contracts to be detrimental to the interests of the student-athletes (Greene, 2008).

Even with employees who are less highly compensated, the language relating to compensation must be clearly stated. If an employee receives only a base salary and fringe benefits such as life insurance, health insurance, and a pension plan, this is a rather straightforward matter. Often, however, a coach may be compensated beyond these amounts with benefits that are known as **perquisites (perks)**. In the case of a college coach, these perquisites may include such additional compensation as profits from radio and television shows; profits from summer sports camps held at the university; the use of an automobile and expenses for gas, insurance, and maintenance; payment for housing; membership in a variety of tennis and country clubs; and payments from endorsement contracts with athletic equipment suppliers. Note that some of these perks may be paid directly by the employer, but others may accrue to the coach's benefit from outside sources. There may also be bonus money forthcoming for a coach who takes a team to postseason competition or finishes with a certain number of wins or at a certain level in the conference. A contract might also include a bonus provision for team graduation rates or academic performance.

The point of contention with perquisites becomes apparent when an employer terminates an employee's contract without cause. In such a case, the employer is liable for damages, but the issue is whether it is liable for simply the amount due under the base salary and fringe benefits aspects of compensation or whether the organization may be liable for the perquisites, even if it does not actually pay out those benefits. This issue came to the fore in the following seminal case.

Rodgers v. Georgia Tech Athletic Association

FOCUS CASE   303 S.E.2d 467 (Ga. Ct. App. 1983)

FACTS

Pepper Rodgers was the football coach at the Georgia Institute of Technology in Atlanta in December 1979, when the university terminated Rodgers' employment without cause with two years remaining on his contract. After the university terminated Rodgers, it continued to pay him his normal monthly salary, pension, and insurance benefits, since the university had breached its contract with him. However, Rodgers asserted that the university owed him compensation for other items he lost when he was terminated. Twenty-nine "perquisite" items were mentioned in the suit, 10 of which were not paid by the Georgia Tech Athletic Association, his employer. These 29 items included auto use and expenses, housing, season tickets to college and pro games, country club memberships, profits from radio and television shows, and profits from Rodgers' summer football camp. Rodgers sued, claiming that he should receive these lost revenues from the university in addition to the base salary and fringe benefits that the university was paying. The university claimed that it had met its legal responsibility to Rodgers by paying lost wages and fringe benefits. The trial court agreed with the university and dismissed the suit. Rodgers appealed.

HOLDING

The Georgia Court of Appeals reversed in part and affirmed in part as it held that Rodgers may recover perquisites over and above what the Georgia Tech Athletic Association paid directly.

RATIONALE

The appellate court first reviewed the pertinent provisions of Rodgers' contract. The contract stated that "In addition to [regular compensation], as an employee of the Association, you will be entitled to various insurance and pension benefits **and perquisites** [emphasis added] as you become eligible therefor." This nebulous language regarding perquisites was sufficient, stated the court, to allow a jury to award some of the perquisites even though the employer did not pay them. Under contract damage principles, an employer may be responsible for some damages caused by its breach of contract even if a third party directly controlled the perquisite amounts.

The *Rodgers* case was a seminal decision regarding the recovery of perquisites by a coach if the university breaches its employment contract with the coach. Today, universities are very careful to identify exactly what amounts it may be responsible for in the event it breaches a contract. Generally, the practice is to identify, at the time the contract is negotiated, the damages that will be paid if a breach occurs. This practice is discussed below under the principle of liquidated damages.

Term of the Contract

Generally, the term of employment is stated as a number of years. Some states have laws forbidding any state employee to have a term of employment that exceeds one year. These laws sometimes provide exclusions for very high-profile coaching contracts so that universities may hire coaches for multiyear agreements.

Another approach to stating the term of employment is to use a **rollover clause.** This clause provides that when an employee has a commitment for a specific number of years, at the end of each year, the contract's term is automatically renewed for another year unless one party notifies the other of the intention not to roll over.

Rollover clauses are often ambiguously drafted, with the result that the term of the contract is quite unclear. Also, to prevent the rollover, an employer often has to give notice years in advance of its intention to let the contract expire. In the college athletics setting, this results in a "lame duck" coach who is likely to give less than complete effort since he knows that he is unwanted by the university.

Clauses Related to Termination

In any contractual relationship, the parties must envision the time when the contract ends. Sometimes the contract ends with the employer alleging that the employee breached the terms of the contract. When the employer ends the relationship in such a circumstance, it is taking the position that the termination is based on just cause. In other circumstances, the employer or employee may seek to end the contractual relationship without any acceptable reason to do so. This is known as a termination without just cause.

Termination for just cause

If an employer terminates an employee's contract for **just cause,** this means that the employer has not breached the employment contract; instead the employee has breached the contract by engaging in behavior that violates the standards of job performance established by the employer. The expectations of job performance must be clearly stated in the employment contract and employee manuals. The standards pertaining to a hearing process should also be clearly set forth in the contract, or the process set forth in the employee manual must be incorporated by reference in the contract.

In the case of *Cole v. Valley Ice Garden* (2005), the Supreme Court of Montana interpreted whether "just cause" could include a poor win–loss record by a coach. In this case, the coach of a junior hockey league team was terminated because of poor performance by the team. The coach argued that this termination was without cause and, therefore, that he was entitled to damages including lost wages and fringe benefits. The coach drafted the agreement and did not define "just cause" in the contract. The state high court held that just because the term "for cause" was not defined in the contract does not mean that it has no meaning. In fact, coaches are routinely terminated for failing to maintain a certain level of performance. In this case, since the employer did not act arbitrarily in terminating the contract and the termination was related to the needs of the business, the termination should be considered to be "for cause." This case demonstrates the need to have the performance expectations clearly set out in a contract.

A variety of behaviors are often included as grounds for a just cause termination. For example, if an employee grossly fails to perform the responsibilities of the job as set forth in the contract, this may be a ground for just cause termination. In addition, contracts usually include a clause designated as a **morals clause** that provides for just cause termination based on immorality, criminal behavior, or behavior reflecting poorly upon the employer. An example of such behavior is found in the case of *Maddox v. University of Tennessee* (1995), in which the court upheld the termination of an assistant football coach after the coach was arrested for driving under the influence of alcohol.

The employer, of course, wants to broaden the language in this clause to retain the option of terminating the employee for conduct unfavorable to the employer but not necessarily criminal in nature. For example, a university will want language that states that any behavior by the coach that would tend to bring public ridicule upon the college or any failure to meet the ethical or moral standards of the community should be considered behavior that could result in termination.

Most endorsement contracts also contain morals clauses. These clauses are negotiated under the same competing considerations as discussed above. That is, the athlete endorser seeks to have the morals clause and thus termination of the endorsement contract limited to situations in which the athlete is convicted of a felony involving moral turpitude. The advertising company, however, wants to broaden the clause to cover behavior that has an adverse effect on either the athlete's reputation or the product brand's reputation, regardless of the illegality of the act. The Tiger Woods scenario, involving multiple allegations of marital infidelity, is indicative of the public image issue. Several companies who had hired Woods as an endorser terminated their contracts with him, including AT&T, Accenture, and Gatorade ("Gatorade cuts all ties," 2010). Using morals clauses as protection for the contracting companies is a necessity of business (Auerbach, 2005).

The contracts of university coaches will always include a provision that a violation of NCAA rules (or conference or university rules) may result in termination. Usually, the types of rules violations that may lead to a just cause termination are intentional violations of major rules or repeated, willful violations of minor rules.

The following focus case concerns Jim O'Brien, who was fired as the men's head basketball coach at The Ohio State University and sued the university, claiming that he was wrongfully terminated. The dispute centered on an interpretation of the language defining violation of NCAA or Big 10 rules as grounds for termination for cause.

O'Brien v. Ohio State University

2007 Ohio App. LEXIS 4316 (Sept. 20, 2007)

FOCUS CASE

FACTS

In 1997, plaintiff O'Brien was hired as the men's basketball coach at the defendant university. On May 14, 1998, Alex Radojevic, a talented basketball player from Yugoslavia, arrived on campus for an unofficial visit. At the time of the visit Radojevic was enrolled at a community college in Kansas and was playing basketball for that community college.

In the fall of 1998, O'Brien learned that Radojevic had played professional basketball for a Yugoslavian team. At trial O'Brien testified that he believed Radojevic was not eligible to play college basketball since he had played professionally. However, O'Brien's staff continued to recruit Radojevic, and on November 11, 1998, Radojevic signed a National Letter of Intent with Ohio State and came for his official visit to the university in December 1998.

Later in December 1998, O'Brien was asked to provide some financial assistance to the Radojevic family, and O'Brien gave the family $6,000 from a drawer in his office desk. Plaintiff testified that he was certain that this "loan" did not violate NCAA rules since Radojevic was not able to be a college player.

Thereafter, however, in February 1999, when the defendant's athletic director, Andy Geiger, asked the plaintiff about Radojevic's status, O'Brien stated that he believed that Radojevic could regain his amateur status. Geiger had no knowledge of the loan to Radojevic. Radojevic never enrolled at Ohio State. He entered the NBA draft and was drafted by the Toronto Raptors.

In March 1999, O'Brien completed a very successful season with the team, advancing to the Final Four in the NCAA Tournament. Based on this performance Ohio State rewarded plaintiff with a new employment contract, with a substantial increase in compensation, effective September 12, 1999. On September 15, 1999, O'Brien signed an NCAA Certificate of Compliance certifying that during the 1998–1999 academic year he had "reported through the appropriate individuals any knowledge of violations of NCAA legislation involving [the] institution."

In April 2004, the plaintiff informed Geiger of the loan because the plaintiff knew that a lawsuit had been filed in which the loan would be revealed. After an internal investigation of this matter, the plaintiff was terminated in June 2004. The termination was a "for cause" termination, and the defendant alleged that the plaintiff had violated Section 4.1(d) of his employment contract, which required him to "know, recognize, and comply" with all applicable rules and regulations of the NCAA and to "immediately report to the Director [of Athletics] and to the Department of Athletics Compliance Office" if he had "reasonable cause to believe that any person had violated such laws, policies or regulations." The defendant university took the position that O'Brien's failure to report the loan made to Radojevic violated the above section and was a material breach of contract for which the university could terminate the contract for cause under Section 5.1(a), which stated that the university can terminate a contract if a material breach occurs. Section 5.1(b) was not mentioned as a reason for termination, but the language of that section referred to a rules violation committed by a coach that leads to a "major" infraction investigation by the NCAA or the Big Ten Conference. Defendant university received a notice from the NCAA that it was investigating the men's basketball program in May 2005. Three of the violations cited by the NCAA pertained to the Radojevic loan.

The plaintiff alleged that the university breached his employment contract in terminating him for cause. A trial was held in the Ohio Court of Claims, and the Court of Claims rendered judgment for O'Brien as it held that the university had breached the employment contract with plaintiff.

HOLDING

The Ohio Court of Appeals affirmed.

RATIONALE

The Court of Claims' judge, who served as the fact finder, found that O'Brien made the loan for humanitarian reasons. He also found that Radojevic was ineligible to participate in athletics at the time that the loan was made even though O'Brien had continued to recruit Radojevic after learning that he had played professional basketball in Yugoslavia.

The Court of Claims held that O'Brien's "single, isolated recruiting infraction" and O'Brien's failure to disclose that violation was not a material breach under the contract entitling Ohio State to terminate O'Brien for cause. Although O'Brien did breach his contract by making a loan under the circumstances given, this single failure of performance was not "so egregious as to frustrate the essential purpose of the contract."

The appellate court agreed with the Court of Claims' finding that there was no material breach in this situation. First, the court noted that the extent to which Ohio State was deprived of the benefit it expected from the employment contract was not as significant as Ohio State asserted—the NCAA sanctions were minor and the damage to Ohio State's reputation was minor. Second, the breach of trust was reparable. Also, O'Brien forfeited substantial salary and benefits, and he had made a good faith effort to resolve the dispute.

The Court also held that the wording of the contract favored the employee and, therefore, must be enforced absent unconscionability. Specifically, §5.1(b) contemplates that the coach could retain employment during an investigation and remain employed unless serious sanctions were imposed. The court must honor the parties' agreement, which, in this case, greatly favored the coach.

The Ohio State Supreme Court declined to hear the *O'Brien* appeal, so O'Brien was owed almost $3 million from Ohio State University. This case points out the consequences of a termination clause that was extremely unfavorable to the university.

At least one university has added Academic Progress Rate requirements to its coaching contracts. Mississippi State University is adding clauses into the coaches' contracts that allow for termination for cause if a coach's team faces a ban from post-season play for failing to meet APR levels. The NCAA is also considering implementing a lifetime APR for coaches that will allow prospective employers to assess a coach's ability to meet APR requirements ("An APR for coaches," 2009).

The employment contract should always provide for some type of internal hearing to allow the employee to present evidence regarding why, in the employee's view, his behavior does not qualify as behavior allowing the organization to terminate the contract for just cause. This is a due process protection intended to ensure that the termination is done in a fair manner.

Termination without cause

Circumstances may arise in which an employer wishes to "fire" an employee who has not engaged in any behavior that would serve as "just cause" for termination. Also, an employee may wish to sever her relationship with an employer, usually to go on to another, better job. If there is no legitimate justification for terminating the contract before the term expires, this is known as termination without cause. That is, one party is breaching the contract by terminating it without legitimate justification for doing so under the contract provisions.

In the current climate of intercollegiate sports, the ability to win games is often valued above all other considerations. Therefore, a coach's performance may be judged primarily by the standard of a win–loss record. The win–loss record is not generally included in the performance measures allowing a university to terminate a coach for just cause. However, many coaches are "fired" simply because of a failure to win enough games. A coach's timeline to succeed has been shortened from five years, the previously accepted timetable for success. Steve Wieberg, in a *USA Today* article, stated that a coach must now establish a winning record within three years of being hired at a Division I-A school or be fired (2005). This type of termination, assuming the coach's contract term has not expired, is a breach of contract by the university because there is no just cause for terminating the coach. If the coach brings a cause of action against the university, the complaint alleges **wrongful termination:** the employee was terminated contrary to the terms of the contract. Similarly, if a coach fails to complete the term of his/her contract, the coach has breached the contract.

To anticipate an employee's or employer's breach of the employment contract, common practice is to include a liquidated damages clause, sometimes termed a **buy-out** provision. As mentioned previously, if the exact amount of damages that will be suffered if a party breaches the contract cannot be ascertained at the time the contract is signed, the parties may agree to an amount of damages that reasonably approximates the damages that would be sustained. The liquidated damages provision must be intended by the parties to be a reasonable estimation of the anticipated damages; the clause will not be upheld if it is a penalty clause drafted simply to coerce performance by punishing a breach. Employment contracts for coaches often include liquidated damages provisions for a breach by the employer and may also include liquidated damages provisions for a breach by the coach. Remember the concept of mitigation discussed earlier in this chapter. A university that breaches may argue that the damages should be reduced because the coach failed to accept a reasonable coaching opportunity, thus failing to lessen the consequences of the breach.

The following Focus Case provides an example of a liquidated damages provision that was upheld against the coach.

Vanderbilt University v. DiNardo

FOCUS CASE	174 F.3d 751 (6th Cir. 1999)

FACTS

In 1990, Gerry DiNardo signed a contract to coach football at Vanderbilt University for five years, ending in 1995. The contract included a liquidated damages clause providing that if DiNardo breached the contract, he would pay his net salary back to the university for the number of years still remaining on his contract. In addition, an Addendum to the contract signed in 1994 allegedly extended the term of the contract through the 1997 season. At the end of the 1994 season, DiNardo left Vanderbilt to become the head football coach at Louisiana State University. Vanderbilt University sued for breach of contract, seeking the liquidated damages owed. The federal district court held that the liquidated damages clause was enforceable, and judgment was entered against DiNardo for $281,886.43. DiNardo appealed.

HOLDING

The 6th Circuit Court of Appeals affirmed the decision in regard to the enforceability of the liquidated damages clause.

RATIONALE

The primary issue before the court was whether the liquidated damages clause was valid or should be stricken as a penalty clause. The court noted that, to be upheld, the provision must be reasonable in relation to the anticipated damages for breach, measured prospectively at the time the contract is signed. In this case, the use of a formula based on DiNardo's salary was reasonable since the damage to be sustained by Vanderbilt went well beyond the cost of hiring a replacement coach. When DiNardo was hired, both parties knew that a long-term commitment was important to the stability of the football program. In this circumstance it was very difficult to ascertain damages with exact certainty, and using the number of years left in the contract multiplied by net salary per year was a reasonable way to calculate damages. The court found that the clause was not a penalty clause meant to coerce performance.

Another dispute concerning a buyout provision involved Rich Rodriguez, a football coach, who chose to terminate his contract with West Virginia University to coach at the University of Michigan. Rodriguez breached his contract with WVU in December 2007, and the university sued him for $4 million, the buyout amount specified in his employment contract (Ruibal, 2008). Rodriguez asserted, however, that he signed the contract under false pretenses and that the university president agreed to reduce or eliminate the buyout clause (Smith, 2008). The matter was settled in July 2008, when the University of Michigan agreed to pay $2.5 million and Rodriguez paid $1.5 million to WVU ("Michigan to pay $2.5M," 2008).

Restrictive Covenant/Covenant Not to Compete

Employment contracts often include a **restrictive covenant** or a **covenant not to compete** to protect the interests of the employer. These clauses may take various forms, but they essentially restrict the ability of the employee either to terminate the contract early or to take a comparable job at another organization considered a competitor. For example, if a coach breaches his employment contract, the restrictive covenant may provide that he may not accept an employment opportunity that is in competition with the employer.

The enforceability of this type of clause is determined by state law. Generally, it is disfavored because it attempts to restrict an employee's ability to secure a new position. However, clauses that are drafted narrowly in terms of scope, geographic area, and time period usually are upheld. For example, if a university drafted a restrictive covenant attempting to prevent a football coach from ever coaching college football again anywhere in the United States, that clause would be overly restrictive and not enforced. However, if a football coach's contract with a Big 10 university had a clause preventing him from taking a head football coaching position at another Big 10 school in the next two years, that clause would most likely be upheld as a reasonable restrictive covenant.

The covenant not to compete clause is certainly relevant in other employment situations as well. For example, in the case of *Nike, Inc. v. McCarthy* (2004), a director of sales at Nike left his job to become vice president of footwear sales at Reebok, one of Nike's prime competitors. Nike sued to prevent McCarthy from working for Reebok for a year, arguing that the noncompete agreement McCarthy signed as an employee of Nike prevented him from working for a competitor for a year after his employment with Nike ended. The court upheld the clause, noting that Nike had a legitimate interest in enforcing the agreement because McCarthy could use confidential information he gained at Nike to help the competitor, Reebok.

A contract dispute relating to a college football coach illustrates the covenant not to compete issue.

Northeastern University v. Brown

17 Mass. L. Rep. 443 (Mass. Super. Ct. 2004)   **FOCUS CASE**

FACTS

Don Brown had been under contract with Northeastern University as its football coach since 2000. In July 2003, he signed a new contract with Northeastern, with a term through 2007–08. Article VII of his employment contract provided that he was not to negotiate or accept other employment during the term of his contract without first obtaining the written consent of the university president. A liquidated damages clause in the contract provided for a payment of $25,000 if Brown left Northeastern before the end of his contract.

In January 2004, Northeastern denied a request from the University of Massachusetts (UMass) to discuss employment with Brown. Nonetheless, Brown told his athletic director that UMass had offered him the position of football coach and he had declined. Brown submitted his resignation three days later in order to accept employment with UMass. Northeastern sued Brown, seeking a preliminary injunction to prevent Brown from coaching at UMass.

HOLDING

The Superior Court of Massachusetts granted the injunction against Brown.

RATIONALE

The issue before the court was whether Northeastern's only remedy was the liquidated damages provided for in the employment contract, or whether it could obtain an injunction preventing Brown from coaching at UMass. First, the court was very displeased with Brown's conduct, which it characterized as a "willful and intentional" breach of contract. In fact, the court said that Brown's "word was no good and his promises were lies." Further, Brown's breach was "obvious, brazen and defiant."

According to Massachusetts law, liquidated damages are not the exclusive remedy. An injunction may be granted to enforce a duty even if there is a provision for liquidated damages.

In this case, there is strong evidence of irreparable harm to be suffered by Northeastern and its football program. The court noted that Brown knows all of Northeastern's plays and procedures, and he could use that knowledge against Northeastern. He also will try to recruit the same student-athletes, and the schools are rivals in the same conference. Therefore, the court issued an injunction forbidding Brown from working as an employee of UMass until further order of the court.

Competitive Advantage
STRATEGIES

Employment Contracts

- Employment contracts should be developed with care and cover all the necessary aspects as indicated in this section.

- The termination clauses and liquidated damages provisions should be given particular attention.

- An employee cannot be terminated for just cause unless the prohibited behavior is carefully delineated and understood.

- An employee should not be reassigned to another position in the organization unless the employment contract explicitly permits this.

After the *Brown* ruling, Northeastern and UMass worked out a settlement. Brown was barred from coaching on the sidelines for three UMass games, and UMass paid Northeastern $150,000 ("Coach thieves beware," 2004). This lawsuit illustrates the type of remedy available against an employee who blatantly violates a covenant not to compete provision.

Miscellaneous Provisions

This section presents two additional provisions, one specific to collegiate athletics coaching and the other applicable to many other types of employment contracts.

Athletically related income

Pursuant to NCAA by-law 11.2.2, coaching contracts must stipulate that the coach annually provide to the institution's CEO a written, detailed account of athletically related income from sources outside the institution. In addition, the approval for the receipt of such income must be consistent with the institution's policy related to outside income for all employees. Sources of athletically related income include sport camps, country club memberships, payments for TV or radio shows, and endorsement contracts for athletic equipment.

Arbitration clause

Many disputes related to an employment contract may best be resolved by submission to an impartial third party. The arbitration clause sets forth what types of disputes may be submitted to an arbitrator. It also states whether arbitration is compulsory and whether the arbitrator's decision is final and binding upon the parties. An article by Moberg (2006) is instructive on this issue.

EMPLOYMENT AT WILL

In many circumstances, employees do not have a contract designating their term of employment. The employment has no specified duration—it is "indefinite." In these cases, the employment is termed **at will,** which means that the employer may fire the employee at any time, for any reason or for no reason. This rule also allows the employee to quit at any time for any reason. However, in practice the rule is usually more favorable to the employer's position than to the employee. The following Focus Case deals with employment at will and a football coach.

Frazier v. University of the District of Columbia

FOCUS CASE

742 F. Supp. 28 (D.D.C. 1990)

FACTS

Bobby Frazier was the head football coach at the University of the District of Columbia. After being employed at the university for approximately seven years, he was terminated from his position with no explanation. Frazier had no employment contract. Frazier sued for wrongful termination.

HOLDING

The federal district court granted the university's motion to dismiss.

RATIONALE

The coach was an at-will employee; he was never employed for a fixed period of time. Therefore, the rule applies that the coach may be terminated at any time, for any reason or for no reason at all. There is no wrongful discharge here, since the employer could discharge the coach at any time.

Contract Law Exceptions

The right to discharge employees at will is not absolute. The right to discharge is subject to exceptions based on contract law and exceptions based on public policy. These exceptions are discussed below.

Employment at Will

■ Personnel manuals should be developed with care and have language consistent with the underlying employment contracts or employment relationships (employment at will). The manual should include language disclaiming your intent to alter the employment contracts or relationships in any way.

■ The exceptions to employment at will vary greatly from state to state. Consult an attorney when developing your employment policies related to employment at will.

■ Be familiar with your state's whistleblower statutes.

■ Be familiar with your state's stance regarding the covenant of good faith and fair dealing.

Implied contracts

Some courts hold that there is an implied contract of employment even if there is no written contract. To ascertain the content of the implied contract, courts will look to other documents that have been provided to employees, such as a personnel manual. For example, the personnel manual may state that employees may be dismissed only for good cause. This statement is, of course, at odds with the concept of at-will employment. Therefore, employers should make sure that the information provided in personnel manuals is consistent with the relationship it has established with its employees.

Covenant of good faith and fair dealing

In addition to concerns related to language in personnel or policy manuals, some courts look at whether a discharge violated the contract **covenant of good faith and fair dealing.** This covenant is an expectation that both parties to a contract will act fairly in their contractual dealings. When applied to the concept of employment at will, it necessitates that an employer act in good faith when terminating an employee.

The covenant of good faith and fair dealing is applied differently to employment contracts in different jurisdictions. Currently, 21 states imply some form of the covenant in employment contracts. The states that currently recognize some form of claim for the covenant of good faith and fair dealing in the employment relationship are Alabama, Alaska, Arizona, Arkansas, California, Connecticut, Delaware, Idaho, Illinois, Indiana, Louisiana, Massachusetts, Nevada, New Hampshire, New Jersey, New York, Oklahoma, Pennsylvania, South Carolina, Vermont, and Wyoming. This number has remained constant for the last 10 years (Dau-Schmidt & Haley, 2007).

Public Policy Exceptions

The most prevalent exception to the employment at will doctrine relates to public policy concerns. The majority of states have some sort of public policy exception, meaning that a dismissal is wrongful if an employer fires an employee for engaging in conduct that affects the employee and also affects some interest of the public at large.

For example, both Congress and the states have passed antidiscrimination statutes prohibiting employment discrimination on the basis of race, ethnicity, gender, age, and so forth. Even if a person could not prevail on such a statutory claim—for example, if the employer does not have enough employees to be subject to statutory requirements (see Chapter 6 for a discussion of employment discrimination), it would still offend societal notions of fairness to allow an employer to fire an at-will employee because of one of these protected characteristics. Other unacceptable reasons for discharge under the public policy exception are presented in Exhibit 4.3.

Unacceptable reasons for discharge under the public policy exception.	EXHIBIT	4.3

Employment discrimination on the basis of race, ethnicity, gender, age, etc.

Blowing the whistle about illegal conduct by the employer

Cooperating in the investigation of a charge against the company

Filing unfair labor practice charges with the National Labor Relations Board

Complaining or testifying about safety hazards in the workplace

Reporting OSHA violations

Source: Jackson & Schuler, 2000.

The public policy exceptions are interpreted narrowly, however. The public policy must be well established and well defined in the jurisdiction in which the claim is filed.

In addition to the judicially created public policy exceptions, the federal government as well as many states have passed **whistleblower statutes** providing that employees who report illegal activities allegedly committed by their employer shall not be subject to discrimination or retaliation by the employer. Not all employee disclosure or whistleblowing is protected; however, most of the statutes protect employees who report violations or suspected violations of a state or federal statute (Earle & Madek, 2007). A whistleblowing case arose from the California Whistleblower Protection Act (CWPA) when a strength and conditioning coach at a university filed an administrative complaint alleging that the head football coach had retaliated against him. The retaliation arose after the strength and conditioning coach reported improprieties relating to the misappropriation of athletic department property and possible violations of NCAA rules regarding the conduct of football practices to the university auditor (*Ohton v. Board of Trustees California State Univ.*, 2007).

TORT THEORIES AND EMPLOYMENT

Chapter 3 introduced tort law, that very broad area of the law that encompasses a variety of legal causes of action not arising from contract. This chapter, so far, has dealt with employment issues related to contract law. Now we turn our attention to some tort theories as they are applied to employment concerns.

Defamation

Chapter 20 discusses the elements of the cause of action in defamation. In that chapter you will learn that defamation is a tort that protects one's reputation. In this chapter we discuss how this tort has been claimed against employers who provide references for employees.

Many employers refuse to give references at all because of the threat of defamation liability. In some cases, employers make no statements regarding an employee's performance; they simply acknowledge that Employee X has been with the company for a certain number of years in a particular capacity. Obviously, a prospective employer's effort to select a good employee is severely hampered when little or no information is available from a current or past employer.

Truth is a complete defense to a defamation claim. Therefore, the information disclosed should be in the employee's file, documented as fact. No comments relating to an employee's personality should be disclosed nor should any secondhand information be discussed.

Most states also provide that an employer has a **qualified privilege** to disclose pertinent information. This means that an employer who acts in good faith may disclose information concerning an employee's work performance to individuals inside the current employer's operation or to prospective employers. The privilege is lost if the reference is given with actual malice—if it is intentionally or recklessly injurious to the employee. This privilege thus serves as type of immunity against defamation claims, although the privilege does not prevent a lawsuit from being filed.

Negligent Misrepresentation/Fraud

The courts have not yet adopted a cause of action forcing an employer to say anything about a current or former employee when a prospective employer inquires. Although the practice of withholding information may be detrimental to the prospective employer's ability to select wisely, there is no affirmative duty to disclose.

However, if information is disclosed, then a duty arises to give accurate disclosure; an employment reference may not "distort" the information given. Giving inaccurate information may constitute negligent misrepresentation or fraud.

Under Restatement (Second) of Torts § 311, one who negligently gives false information to another, where the party reasonably relies upon that information resulting in harm to another, may be liable for **negligent misrepresentation. Fraud** is similar, but it involves intentional misrepresentations that are intended to induce or that the individual should realize are likely to induce action by another, thus resulting in harm (Restatement [Second] of Torts § 310). The following Focus Case addresses these concepts.

Randi W. v. Muroc Joint Unified School District

FOCUS CASE | 929 P.2d 582 (Cal. 1997)

FACTS

A school vice-principal, Robert Gadams, sexually molested a middle school student. The student sued Gadams and also sued the administrator's former employers who gave positive recommendations about Gadams to his current employer.

Gadams had worked in three school districts prior to this incident. In each situation, Gadams had engaged in various types of inappropriate sexual behavior with students. However, none of these problems were disclosed in employment references that were relied upon by the current employer. In fact, some of the references referred to Gadams' "genuine concern" for students and described him as an "upbeat, enthusiastic administrator who related well to the students."

The plaintiff sued the former employers for negligent misrepresentation and fraud, alleging that the failure to disclose material information relating to Gadams' fitness for the job induced the current employer to hire Gadams, leading to the sexual assault upon the plaintiff.

The trial court upheld the defendants' motions to dismiss. The California Court of Appeals affirmed in part and reversed in part. The plaintiff appealed to the California Supreme Court.

HOLDING

The California Supreme Court affirmed in part, holding that the "misleading half-truths" supplied by former employers were actionable.

RATIONALE

The court held that the writer of a recommendation letter owes a duty not to misrepresent the facts and the character of a former employee, if making those misrepresentations would cause a foreseeable risk of physical injury to the prospective employer or to third persons (students, in this situation). It was not appropriate for defendants to make positive comments about the candidate without disclosing the rest of the information they possessed concerning his misconduct. The representations that Gadams was fit to interact appropriately and safely with female students were false and misleading, in view of the defendants' knowledge of Gadams' repeated sexual improprieties.

The *Randi W.* case was an important step in holding employers accountable for giving a complete picture of a job candidate. It stopped short, however, of forcing an employer to disclose. So in this case, if one of the former school districts had said absolutely nothing about Gadams except that he worked for the district for X years in certain positions, there would have been no liability. Some commentators have argued that this is unacceptable, that employers should be forced to divulge information about an employee in a situation like this one where the health and well-being of a very vulnerable population is at stake (Swerdlow, 1991). The cause of action on this ground is known as **negligent referral**.

Tortious Interference with Contractual Relations

Tortious interference with contractual relations prohibits improper interference with existing contracts (Gleason, 2008). In considering whether a defendant's interference with a contract or a prospective contract is improper, a court will address a number of factors, including the motives and interests of the interfering party (Restatement [Second] of Torts § 767, 1977).

The following case deals with these principles.

Competitive Advantage
STRATEGIES

Tort Theories and Employment

- When giving employment references, do not discuss employees' personalities. Stick to the facts that you have documented in the employees' files.

- If you choose to disclose information about employees, give a balanced reference: provide information about the employee's strengths and weaknesses. Do not provide favorable information without also providing unfavorable—assuming that you have evidence to support anything you say about the employee.

- In recruiting an employee, do not attempt to induce that person to breach an existing employment contract.

Bauer v. Interpublic Group of Companies, Inc.

FOCUS CASE   255 F. Supp. 2d 1086 (N.D. Cal. 2003)

FACTS

The plaintiff, Francis Bauer, is a sports agent whose clients are professional football players. During the 2001 college football season, David Carr was quarterback for Fresno State University. Bauer met with Carr and his father in the summer of 2001 and was told that the father, Rodger, would handle all dealings with agents.

After Bauer held several conversations with Rodger and his wife, Sheryl, David Carr signed a representation agreement with Bauer on January 1, 2002. Soon thereafter, David Carr decided that he was uncomfortable being represented by Bauer, and he terminated the relationship within two weeks of the contract's execution.

Bauer believed that David Carr terminated the contract because he received information from the Interpublic Group of Companies, Inc., a competitor in the sport agent business and parent company of Octagon Football. In contrast, David Carr stated that he had initiated the contact with defendant company (Octagon) and that the decision to terminate the agreement with Bauer had no relationship to any communications with Octagon.

Bauer sued Interpublic for intentional interference with contract and unfair competition.

HOLDING

The court granted the defendant's motion for summary judgment.

RATIONALE

First the court noted the elements of a claim for intentional interference with contract. The elements are (1) a valid contract between a plaintiff and a third party; (2) defendant's knowledge of this contract; (3) defendant's intentional acts designed to induce a breach or disruption of the contractual relationship; (4) actual breach or disruption of the contractual relationship; and (5) resulting damage.

The court then reviewed the evidence presented by plaintiff Bauer. If Carr did receive any information containing negative information about Bauer, there is no evidence that the defendant sent the information. There is no evidence that the defendant made any disparaging remarks about Bauer to Carr. Further, there is no evidence that the defendant had any input into Carr's decision to terminate the contract with Bauer. Carr was the party who initiated contact with the defendant after he decided to terminate his contract with Bauer.

In light of this evidence, Bauer could not show that the defendant induced Carr to terminate his contract with Bauer.

The *Bauer* case illustrates the type of situation that is often indicative of this tort. In the case of *Northeastern University v. Brown,* discussed earlier in the context of a coach violating the covenant not to compete, a case could be made against UMass for tortious interference with contractual relations if evidence showed that UMass acted to induce a breach of Brown's coaching contract with Northeastern University.

In the case of *Harrick v. National Collegiate Athletic Ass'n* (2006), a former basketball coach sued the NCAA for tortious interference with his employment contract asserting that his termination was due to the NCAA's involvement. The federal district court held that the coach had no cause of action because there can be no tortious interference unless a party is a "stranger to the contract." In this case, the NCAA, although not a party to the employment contract, was not a stranger to the contract since universities have to comply with NCAA rules and terminate employees who commit NCAA violations.

CONCLUSION

Managing human resources effectively can help you gain a competitive advantage in the sport marketplace. To make good management decisions in this realm, you need a thorough understanding of contract law and employment law principles. This chapter provided an overview of contract law followed by a discussion of employment contracts. We also reviewed the legal principles pertaining to employment at will and wrongful termination. Finally, we addressed a number of tort causes of action that are applicable in employment matters. Understanding these legal principles should enable you to make sound decisions related to human resources and to assist in making your organization a better one for employees.

discussion questions

1. What are the benefits of using a worst case scenario approach in drafting contracts?
2. Explain the concepts of agreement, consideration, capacity, and legality in the formation of contracts.
3. Are oral contracts generally enforceable? When are oral contracts not enforceable? Give some examples from a sport setting to illustrate Statute of Frauds principles.
4. What are the remedies available in breach of contract actions? What is the usual remedy? What are the limitations upon using specific performance?
5. What is the principle of mitigation of damages?
6. Contrast actual authority with apparent authority. When can a third party use apparent authority to bind an organization to a contract?

learning activities

1. As the current athletic director at a Division I university, you are in the process of negotiating an employment contract with I. Will Wynn, your new football coach. Answer the following questions in your role as athletic director in order to protect the university's interests in the contract.

a. Discuss the purpose of the reassignment clause and whether it is in the university's best interest to have this in the contract with Wynn. If you attempt to reassign a coach and there is no reassignment clause permitting this, what may be the legal outcome?

b. Discuss the covenant not to compete (restrictive covenant) and how you may use it to your benefit in the contract with Wynn.

c. Would the university prefer to have a stated term of years or a rollover clause? Explain.

d. Discuss five other clauses that you would like to incorporate into the coaching contract to protect the university's interests.

2. Conduct an Internet search to find out how many college football coaches now have compensation "packages" that exceed $2 million per year. Try to ascertain how much of the compensation is base salary, how much is in the form of perquisites, and what those perquisites may be.

CASE STUDY

Review the *O'Brien* Focus Case on pages 65–66 and then answer the following questions related to that case.

1. The Court of Claims' judge in this case interpreted the facts in favor of O'Brien when the judge characterized the loan as given for humanitarian reasons and not given to gain an improper recruiting advantage. What facts might support a more sinister interpretation of the coach's conduct?

2. Discuss how Ohio State could have strengthened its grounds for termination for cause.

3. Discuss the implications of this decision relative to other colleges that may wish to terminate coaches "for cause."

4. Review Section V of the Greenberg article listed in "Other Sources" at the end of this chapter and consider the language of other termination provisions in coaches' contracts to determine how a termination clause may be written which favors the university. You may also consider the termination clauses in the coaches' contracts, which may be found by using the coaches' contract databases listed in the list of relevant websites below.

 *considering . . .*   **ANALYSIS & DISCUSSION**

Promissory Estoppel (p. 56)

Lance cannot win on contract principles. The grant-in-aid (the contract between the student and the university) clearly states that it can only be for a one-year period, and notice of nonrenewal was given timely. Under promissory estoppel principles, Lance does have a case. First, a promise was made by the coach that Lance would receive aid for all four years. This promise should reasonably be expected to induce reliance, since the coach is the person who makes decisions related to scholarships. Lance chose to attend SRU based upon the coach's promises, and Lance suffered a detriment since he received no aid in his senior year. The relationship between the coach and the prospect also contributes to the strength of Lance's case, since the disparity in bargaining power between coach and player makes reliance even more likely to occur.

Apparent Authority (p. 57)

The third-party vendor will argue that there was apparent authority to enter into the $25,000 contract. Since the store owners had taken no action before when the manager entered into contracts exceeding his actual authority, the third-party vendor reasonably believes that the agent has the authority to act. The principal will be bound to the agreement.

REFERENCES

Cases

Bauer v. Interpublic Group of Cos., 255 F. Supp. 2d 1086 (N.D. Cal. 2003).

Bowers v. Federation Internationale de L'Automobile, 489 F.3d 316 (7th Cir. 2007).

Cole v. Valley Ice Garden, 113 P.3d 275 (Mont. 2005).

Frazier v. University of the D.C., 742 F. Supp. 28 (D. D.C. 1990).

Harrick v. National Collegiate Athletic Ass'n, 454 F.2d 1255 (N.D. Ga. 2006).

Huyett v. Idaho State Univ., 104 P.3d 946 (Idaho 2004).

Maddox v. University of Tenn., 62 F.3d 843 (6th Cir. 1995).

Monson v. Oregon, 901 P.2d 904 (Or. Ct. App. 1995).

Nike, Inc. v. McCarthy, 379 F.3d 576 (9th Cir. 2004).

Northeastern Univ. v. Brown, 17 Mass. L. Rep. 443 (Mass. Super. Ct. 2004).

O'Brien v. Ohio State Univ., 2007 Ohio App. LEXIS 4316 (September 20, 2007).

Ohton v. Board of Trustees Cal. State Univ., 56 Cal. Rptr. 3d 111 (Ct. App. 2007).

Randi W. v. Muroc Joint Unified Sch. Dist., 929 P.2d 582 (Cal. 1997).

Rodgers v. Georgia Tech Athletic Ass'n, 303 S.E.2d 467 (Ga. Ct. App. 1983).

Vanderbilt Univ. v. DiNardo, 174 F.3d 751 (6th Cir. 1999).

Other Sources

About the National Letter of Intent (NLI). Retrieved December 1, 2009, from www.ncaa.org/wps/wcm/connect/nli/nli.

An APR for coaches. (2009, Feb/March). *Athletic Management, 8.*

Auerbach, D. (2005, Summer). Morals clauses as corporate protection in athlete endorsement contracts. *DePaul Journal of Sports Law & Contemporary Problems, 3,* 1–18.

Berkowitz, S. (2009, Dec. 10). Brown's new salary is Texas-sized: $5.1M. *USA Today,* p. 1C.

Coach thieves beware (2004, November 27). College Athletics Clips. Found at www.collegeathleticsclips.com/archives/000326.html.

Cross, F. B., & Miller, R. L. (2009). *West's legal environment of business: Text, cases, ethical, regulatory, international and e-commerce issues.* 7th ed. Cincinnati, OH: West.

Dau-Schmidt, K. G., & Haley, T. A. (2007, Winter). Governance of the workplace: The contemporary regime of individual contract. *Comparative Labor Law & Policy Journal, 28,* 313–349.

Earle, B. H., & Madek, G. A. (2007, Spring). Article: The mirage of whistleblower protection under Sarbanes-Oxley: A proposal for change. *American Business Law Journal, 44,* 1–54.

Gatorade cuts all ties to Tiger Woods. (2010, Feb. 26). *Chicago Tribune.* Retrieved March 30, 2010, from www.chicagotribune.com/topic/ktla-gatorade-drops-tiger,0,6106587.story.

Gleason, J. P. (2008, May). Comment: From Russia with love: The legal repercussions of the recruitment and contracting of foreign players in the National Hockey League. *Buffalo Law Review, 56,* 599–654.

Greenberg, M. J. (2006, Fall). Symposium: National Sports Law Institute Board of Advisors: Termination of college coaching contracts: When does adequate cause to terminate exist and who determines its existence? *Marquette Sports Law Review, 17,* 197–257.

Greene, L. S. (2008, Spring). UMKC sports law symposium: Emerging legal issues affecting amateur & professional sports: Football coach contracts: What does the student-athlete have to do with it? *UMKC Law Review, 76,* 665–696.

Jackson, S. E., & Schuler, R. S. (2000). *Managing human resources: A partnership perspective.* 7th ed. Cincinnati, OH: South-Western College Publishing.

McMurray, J. (2009, April 2). Big green: Calipari's contract loaded with perks. Retrieved on June 29, 2009 from http://www.universitybusiness.com/newssummary.aspx?news=yes&posted=18689.

Meyer, S. (2004, Fall). Comment: Unequal bargaining power: Making the National Letter of Intent more equitable. *Marquette Sports Law Review, 15,* 227–247.

Michigan to pay $2.5M, Rodriguez $1.5M to satisfy WVU buyout. (2008, July 9). Retrieved June 29, 2009, from http://sports.espn.go.com/ncf/news/story?id=3479493.

Moberg, B. C. (2006, Winter). Navigating the public relations minefield: Mutual protection through mandatory arbitration clauses in college coaching contracts. *Journal of Legal Aspects of Sport, 16*(1), 85–120.

NCAA, Division I Manual By-law 11.2.1 and 11.2.2 (2008–09).

Restatement (Second) of Contracts (1981).

Restatement (Second) of Torts (1977).

Ruibal, S. (2008, January 24). State of W. Va. still feeling spurned. *USA Today,* p. 5C.

Smith, V. (2008, January 29). Rodriguez files $1.5M letter of credit. Retrieved June 29, 2009, from http://news.findlaw.com/scripts/printer_friendly.pl?page=?ap_stories/s/2060/01-29-2008/20.

Staples, A. (2008, April 17). Hawaii lawsuit headed to court. Retrieved June 29, 2009, from http://sports illustrated.cnn.com/2008/writers/andy_staples/04/17/recruiting.notebook/index.html.

Swerdlow, J. (1991). Negligent referral: A potential theory for employer liability. *Southern California Law Review, 64*(2), 1645–1673.

Wieberg, S. (2005, January 5). Win now or pack your bags. *USA Today,* pp. 1C, 6C.

Wieberg, S., & Upton, J. (2008, March 28). College football coaches calling lucrative plays. Retrieved June 29, 2009, from http://www.usatoday.com/sports/college/football/2007-12-04-coaches-pay_N.htm?POE=click-refer.

WEBSITE RESOURCES

www.fcsl.edu/node/174 ▪ This database of college football and basketball coaches' contract provisions is made available by the Center for Law and Sports at Florida Coastal School of Law. The site includes detailed summaries of contract provisions for coaches in various conferences.

www.usatoday.com/sports/graphics/basketball_contracts/flash.htm ▪ This *USA Today* site sets forth contract provisions dealing with compensation for Division I men's basketball coaches whose teams competed in the 2006 NCAA basketball tournament. PDF files for many of the actual contracts are included.

www.usatoday.com/sports/college/football/2009-coaches-contracts-database.htm ▪ This *USA Today* site sets forth contract provisions dealing with compensation for Football Bowl Subdivision coaches. PDF files for many of the actual contracts are included.

www.ncaa.org/wps/wcm/connect/nli/nli ▪ This site provides information about the National Letter of Intent Program, which is administered through the NCAA Eligibility Center office.

5

CHAPTER

Employer Liability for Actions of Employees and Others

INTRODUCTION

This chapter discusses the circumstances in which employers will be held responsible for the actions of their employees. First, the concept of *respondeat superior* will be addressed: employers are generally responsible for the actions of employees so long as the actions are taken within the scope of employment. Next, we discuss the legal theories of negligent hiring, supervision, and retention, followed by the issue of whether an employer may be liable for the actions of an independent contractor or volunteer. Last, we address the matter of whether a university may be vicariously liable for actions of its athletes.

This chapter extends the notion addressed in Chapters 4, 6, and 7 that managing human resources effectively is an essential component of gaining a competitive advantage in the sport marketplace. In Chapters 4, 6, and 7 we discuss this notion in conjunction with effective legal strategies for handling the concerns of employees. In this chapter, we explore ways in which you as a manager can minimize your organization's exposure to liability based on the actions of personnel, whether the personnel are employees, independent contractors, volunteers, or college athletes. See Exhibit 5.1 for an overview of this chapter's managerial contexts, major legal issues, relevant law, and illustrative cases.

LIABILITY RELATED TO EMPLOYEES

This section provides an introduction to vicarious liability principles and discusses various forms of negligence that can occur in making employment-related decisions.

EXHIBIT 5.1	Management contexts in which liability for actions of employees and others may arise, with relevant laws and cases.

MANAGEMENT CONTEXT	MAJOR LEGAL ISSUES	RELEVANT LAW	ILLUSTRATIVE CASES
Oversight of employees	Liability for actions of employees	Vicarious liability/ *respondeat superior*	
	Employer liability for actions of employees	Scope of employment	*Smith*
Hiring employees	Liability for hiring improperly	Negligent hiring	
Supervision of employees	Liability for supervising improperly	Negligent supervision	
Retention of employees	Liability for retaining improperly	Negligent retention	
Hiring independent contractors	Who is an independent contractor?	Criteria defining independent contractor	*Lang*
	Liability for actions of independent contractor	Negligent selection	
Choosing volunteers	Liability for acts of volunteer	Vicarious liability	*Lasseigne*
Oversight of college athletes	Liability for acts of student-athlete	Vicarious liability	*Kavanagh*

Vicarious Liability Principles

The doctrine of **vicarious liability** or *respondeat superior* (let the master respond) holds an employing organization (employer) responsible for certain acts of its employees, not because of any wrongdoing by the employer, but because the law has deemed it appropriate for the employer to be held accountable for the actions of its employees. Thus, the employer's liability is secondary or derivative in the sense that the employer itself is not a wrongdoer. As a policy matter, this doctrine is based on the belief that the employer generally receives the benefits of its employees' actions; therefore, when the employee does something that is not beneficial, the employer should also bear that responsibility. The doctrine is also predicated on the employer's ability to control employees and to procure insurance that covers the actions of employees. In short, an employer should bear employee liability as a cost of doing business.

The general rule of *respondeat superior* is that an employer will be responsible for the acts of an employee so long as the acts are done within the scope of employment, to advance the business of the employer. Conduct is considered to be within the employee's **scope of employment** if "it is of the kind he is employed to perform; it occurs substantially within the authorized time and space limits; and it is actuated, at least in part, by a purpose to serve the master" (Restatement [Second] of Agency § 228). For example, if a driver of a delivery truck owned by a sporting goods store drives negligently and injures a third party, that negligence of the employee is imputed to the employer under the principle of *respondeat superior* so long as the accident occurred in the scope of employment, that is, while the employee was in the process of making deliveries for the employer.

Please note that an employee's job description as written in an employee handbook or an employee contract is usually not synonymous with the concept of scope of employment. Job descriptions do not generally encompass all of the duties actually performed by employees. Often the employment contract includes a rather nebulous phrase to the effect that the employee is expected to do X, Y, Z, and "other duties as may be assigned." For example, if a coach drives negligently while transporting players to an away match, that negligence will certainly be within the coach's scope of employment, even if the duty of transporting players was not specifically delineated within the coach's contract.

The case of *Smith v. Gardner* deals with a college assistant baseball coach and whether his actions were within the scope of employment.

Smith v. Gardner

| 998 F. Supp. 708 (S.D. Miss. 1998) | **FOCUS CASE** |

FACTS

Plaintiff was injured in a two-car automobile accident in the early morning hours of March 17, 1996. Plaintiff sued the driver of the other vehicle, Gardner, and Gardner's employer, San Jacinto College, based on Gardner's negligent driving. Gardner was employed as an assistant baseball coach with the college, and he was on a road trip with the team.

After the team was settled into a hotel on the night of March 16, Gardner left the hotel at midnight to buy some beer. He returned to the hotel and drank some of the beer. He then decided to go out again and purchase smokeless tobacco. He left again, driving the school van, and at 3:22 a.m. he was involved in the accident in question. He was driving while intoxicated.

The plaintiff asserted that the college should be vicariously liable for the actions of Gardner, arguing that Gardner's actions were within the scope of employment.

HOLDING

The federal district court granted the college's motion for summary judgment, as it held that Gardner's actions were not within the scope of employment.

RATIONALE

First, the court addressed the definition of "scope of employment," since an employer is not responsible vicariously for the actions of an employee unless the actions are taken within the scope of employment. If an action is within the scope of employment, the employee is taking action in the course of and as the means to accomplish the purposes of employment and therefore in furtherance of the master's business. In contrast, if an employee abandons his employment and is engaged in some purpose of his own, this is not considered to be within the scope of employment.

In this case, Gardner, in driving around town after drinking enough beer to become intoxicated, was not in any sense about any conceivable business of the college, nor was he performing any act that could be considered incidental to his employment. Gardner was obviously a "frolicking employee engaged in affairs of his own."

Therefore, concluded the court, the college is not liable for Gardner's alleged negligence relating to the auto accident in question.

To extend the above discussion, it becomes apparent, therefore, that most acts of an intentional nature done by an employee are outside the scope of employment. Intentional torts, which are deliberate actions taken—such as assault and battery, as discussed in Chapter 18—are usually undertaken to serve the employee's own interests, not to benefit the employer. Therefore, the general rule of *respondeat superior* does not usually apply to cover intentional torts.

While vicarious liability can be difficult to establish in cases dealing with intentional torts such as sexual assault, one case illustrates that, given certain facts, a youth organization may be held vicariously liable for its representative's sexual assault of a child. In the case of *Southport Little League v. Vaughan* (2000) an appellate court in Indiana upheld a finding of vicarious liability against a Little League baseball club. The abuser was an equipment manager who molested several children in an equipment shed where he took them supposedly to

---

Competitive Advantage

STRATEGIES

Liability Related to Employees

- Develop protocols for hiring employees and ensure that they are followed in all circumstances, even if a candidate is "known" by the organization.

- Make sure that all protocols provide for reasonable investigation into applicants' backgrounds. What is reasonable investigation will vary depending upon the type of position and the person's involvement with vulnerable populations. For

(continued)

distribute and check the fitting of baseball uniforms and equipment. One notable fact was that the abuser, through his roles as Little League official and equipment manager, had organizational authority to be alone with a participant in the equipment shed (Preston, 2006). Although this is only one situation, Gibbons and Campbell (2003) speculated that it could mark a trend in courts to reconsider holding employers liable for their employees' sexual assaults of children, particularly if the organizations place their employees in a position of trust and authority. Regarding the implications of *Southport Little League*, they remarked that "Courts may find that coaches and administrators that sexually assault players accompanying them on team trips are, at least in part, acting within the scope of their employment" (p. 215).

Also, in some circumstances an intentional tort may be considered to be within the scope of employment because the employer has engaged in some behavior that ratifies or condones the employee's propensity to engage in acts of that nature—this is the **ratification/condonation principle** (27 Am. Jur. 2d *Employment Relationship* § 381, 2005). In Chapter 18 the case of *Tomjanovich v. Los Angeles Lakers* (1979) is presented. In the case, Tomjanovich was severely injured by a punch thrown by Kermit Washington, a Lakers player, who was rewarded by the Lakers for his rough play. The Lakers, therefore, essentially condoned Washington's violent propensities, which led to this foreseeable attack upon Tomjanovich. This is an example of the ratification or condonation of behavior that would normally be outside the scope of employment. Ugolini (2007) provides an interesting law review discussing the NFL's responsibility for the behavior of its players.

The hypothetical case presented in the negligent retention discussion later in the chapter illustrates the ratification/condonation principle as well as negligent retention.

Negligence in Making Employment-Related Decisions

In contrast to the theory underlying *respondeat superior,* liability based on negligent hiring, supervision, or retention is predicated on the negligence of a managerial employee in making an employment-related decision. The basic tenets of negligence law apply (see Chapter 15's discussion of the elements of negligence). The standard of care imposed upon a manager who is making a hiring decision is to act as a reasonably prudent manager in the circumstance.

Competitive Advantage

STRATEGIES

Liability Related to Employees (cont.)

example, extra care should be taken when hiring employees who will work closely with children or with disabled individuals. Use criminal background checks to the extent permitted by state law.

- Require job applicants to sign a form authorizing you to obtain employment information from prior employers.

- Use a job application form that requires applicants to divulge whether they have been convicted of a felony and the details surrounding any conviction.

- Check the references provided and carefully document the responses.

- If you work in a youth sport organization, educate parents regarding issues of proper coaching relationships with young players and encourage parental involvement in observing coaching behaviors. Implement a reporting mechanism for parents to raise concerns with organization administrators.

- Train managers to supervise employees reasonably and to discipline employees in accordance with organizational policy.

- Develop a "no tolerance" policy regarding workplace violence. Violent or inappropriate behavior should never be overlooked or condoned by an organization, even if the person seems to be performing well in other aspects of the job.

- Train managers to deal with employees in stressful situations such as terminations and labor disputes.

- Train all employees to resolve workplace disputes through negotiation and respectful dialogue.

- Develop a Threat Assessment and Response Team to investigate any threats of violence and develop appropriate responses.

Negligent hiring

The basic question underlying **negligent hiring** is whether a manager acted reasonably in choosing a particular person to fill a position. The tort of negligent hiring is concerned with the risk created by exposing members of the public to a potentially dangerous or unfit person. As the Restatement (Second) of Agency § 213 (1958) provides: "a person conducting an activity through servants or agents is subject to liability for harm resulting from his conduct if he is negligent or reckless . . . in the employment of improper persons." Negligent hiring occurs when an employer breaches its duty to hire safe and competent employees (Minuti, 1988). The manager must first ask, Does that employee or candidate have the appropriate qualifications?

For example, there is considerable controversy regarding personal trainers and their qualifications (as discussed in Chapter 15). Since there is no overarching national standard, a manager must be diligent in choosing a personal trainer who has the necessary competence to deal safely and effectively with clients. A lawsuit against Crunch Fitness illustrates this issue. A client at a Crunch Gym in New York believed that the personal trainer provided by the gym was an expert. However, the client suffered a brain hemorrhage and died as a result of the trainer's recommendations. Even though the trainer knew that the client had high blood pressure, the trainer recommended diet supplements containing ephedra, which was clearly life-threatening advice. The trainer was hired despite his lack of any certification or knowledge regarding either weight training or nutrition (Cotten, 2009).

In addition to qualifications, the manager must also ask, Is the candidate suitable for the position in terms of personal characteristics and qualities? Is there something in the person's background that would affect the person's ability to do the job? If a factor was neglected that should have been discovered by a manager who had acted with reasonable diligence in the hiring process, the manager may be liable for negligent hiring.

The following hypothetical case illustrates a rather prevalent scenario, the hiring of a coach for youth sport.

considering . . .   **NEGLIGENT HIRING**

You are the chief administrator of a local youth softball league in charge of hiring coaches for the upcoming season. The coaches are not well paid, and it is difficult to get enough coaches for your eight teams. The participants in the program are young girls, ages 8 to 14.

The season is fast approaching and you need to fill the last coaching position very quickly. Finally, a man applies who has just moved to your area. He seems very personable, and he tells you that he has coached softball for the last 10 years in other youth organizations. You are very impressed with this person's knowledge of the sport and his outgoing personality, so you hire him, doing no reference checks whatsoever.

If you had done any investigation, you would have found out that his last coaching position ended with accusations against him of sexual abuse of his female players. Also, if you had done a criminal background check, you would have uncovered a conviction for a sexual offense with a minor.

One month after being hired, this coach sexually molests a girl on his team.

Question

■ What liability can exist?

Note how you would answer the question and then check your response using the Analysis & Discussion at the end of this chapter.

Unfortunately, this type of scenario is frequently repeated across the United States. The nature of youth sport with close ties between coaches and participants increases the opportunity for child abuse to occur. Abuse may include sexual, emotional, and physical abuse and neglect (Brackenridge, Bringer, & Bishopp, 2005). In terms of the heinous specter of child abuse, pedophiles often seek to serve as youth coaches because this role gives them easy access to a large number of potential victims. Organizations that work with children, such as youth leagues, YMCA/YWCA, and Boys' and Girls' Clubs, must be very vigilant in their hiring practices because of the predatory nature of pedophiles and, of course, the very vulnerable populations that they serve.

Several initiatives have been taken to address the prevalence of sexual predators in youth sport. In Florida, the Lunsford Act was passed in 2005 requiring sports officials and other independent contractors to clear a fingerprinting and background check before being allowed on public school grounds when students are present. The difficulty with the law is that it has led to a drastic drop in officials, not because the referees are criminals but because many would-be officials are reticent to go through the check because of its cost and because it is burdensome to do so (Ramirez, 2007). In addition, the National Recreation and Park Association has developed a comprehensive national volunteer management program that screens, identifies, and educates volunteers in parks and recreation programs across the country (Bynum, 2007).

Negligent supervision

In **negligent supervision,** the basic question is whether a manager acted reasonably in guiding and overseeing an employee's actions. The degree and type of supervision considered reasonable is always related to the particular circumstance. The following hypothetical case illustrates negligent supervision.

considering . . .   NEGLIGENT SUPERVISION

You are employed at a tennis club as the head teaching pro. According to your job description, you are responsible for making sure that the assistant pros run instructional drills properly. Since you are very busy with your own lessons, you have not watched any of the drill sessions run by Freddie Forehand. If you did observe any of the drill sessions, you would see that Forehand is not following good safety practices as he sets up the overhead drills. He is having students hit overheads while the people on the other side of the net are doing another drill. Someone is hit by an overhead and seriously injured.

Question

- What liability can exist?

Note how you would answer the question and then check your response using the Analysis & Discussion at the end of this chapter.

Negligent retention

The underlying question in regard to **negligent retention** is whether a manager acted reasonably in retaining an employee's services. This issue may arise when a manager receives negative feedback about an employee or has direct knowledge of an employee's misdeeds yet does nothing to discipline or discharge that employee. The following hypothetical case illustrates negligent retention.

considering . . . NEGLIGENT RETENTION

Bob Strong is the general manager of Fit and Well, a health and fitness club that is owned by Win Corporation. Strong is in charge of all employment-related matters, including hiring, firing, and disciplining employees.

Six months ago, Strong hired Adam Easton to be the club's director of fitness. Easton came highly recommended with superb credentials. After one week on the job, Strong received a complaint from another employee, Tammy Riley, that Easton had screamed at her for making a scheduling mistake and had essentially backed her into a corner as he screamed, using his size and strength to intimidate her. Strong listened to Riley's story but did not investigate further and did not talk to Easton about this incident.

After one month on the job, Strong received another complaint about Easton's violent behavior from Jessica Barker, another club employee. On this occasion, Easton screamed obscenities at Barker and grabbed her arm to emphasize a point. Strong again listened to Barker's report but chose to do nothing, since Easton was doing a great job outside of these outbursts.

Over the course of the next five months, Strong received similar complaints from five other employees and one club patron about Easton's increasingly violent behavior. Strong once had a "chat" with Easton about the issue, but he never took any disciplinary action.

In the sixth month, Easton exploded and punched one of the club's patrons, sending her to the hospital with a broken jaw and a concussion. This patron is now going to sue Strong and Win Corporation based on Easton's intentional tort (battery). (Note that a criminal case could also be made against Easton.)

Question

- On what bases could the patron win her lawsuit?

Note how you would answer the question and then check your response using the Analysis & Discussion at the end of this chapter.

The negligence of a manager in hiring, supervising, or retaining may lead to vicarious liability for the employer, since the actions of the manager in dealing with these employment-related decisions are, most likely, within the manager's scope of employment and, therefore, will be imputed to the employer under the usual rule of *respondeat superior.*

LIABILITY FOR ACTS OF INDEPENDENT CONTRACTORS

One of the major benefits of engaging an **independent contractor,** a party doing work without the control of the hiring party except as to the ultimate result of the work, is that an employer avoids the prospect of vicarious liability based on the actions of the independent contractor. The rule is that one who hires an independent contractor is generally not liable for the negligent or intentional acts or omissions of the contractor.

Factors Determining Independent Contractor Status

The independent contractor is hired to produce a certain result but is not controlled as to the method in which he obtains that result; this is the prime factor that courts look at when ascertaining whether a party should be considered to be an independent contractor. When the courts attempt to determine the degree of control asserted, they look at a number of factors, as shown in Exhibit 5.2.

In the following Focus Case, a horse owner was sued on the basis that he should be vicariously liable for the actions of a jockey he had hired to ride in a particular race.

Factors used to determine independent contractor status.   EXHIBIT   **5.2**

1. The right to control the manner in which the work is performed
2. The right to discharge
3. The method of payment
4. Whether taxes are deducted from the payment
5. The level of skill required to perform the work
6. The furnishing of necessary tools, material, or equipment

Source: Lang v. Silva, 1999.

Lang v. Silva

FOCUS CASE 715 N.E.2d 708 (Ill. App. Ct. 1999)

FACTS

Plaintiff Danny Lang, a jockey, was injured when his horse fell during a race at Sportsman's Park racetrack. Lang alleged that the accident occurred because of the careless riding of jockey Carlos Silva. Silva was cited for careless riding and disqualified from the race. Lang sued Silva for negligence and willful and wanton conduct. Lang also sued Crown's Way Farm and Ronald Dicicilia, owners of the horse ridden by Silva, alleging that they should be liable for Silva's actions under vicarious liability principles. The circuit court granted summary judgment on behalf of Crown's Way Farm and Dicicilia. Lang appealed.

HOLDING

The Illinois Appellate Court affirmed the dismissal of the claims against Crown's Way Farm and Dicicilia.

RATIONALE

The critical issue for determination was whether jockey Silva was an employee or an independent contractor. If he is considered to be an independent contractor, then Crown's Way Farm and Dicicilia cannot be liable for Silva's actions under vicarious liability principles.

First the court looked at how the relationship between Silva and Crown's Way Farm was structured. [See Exhibit 5.2 for a list of the factors addressed by the court.] The court emphasized that the right to control the manner in which the work is performed is the predominant factor in determining whether a person is an employee or an independent contractor.

In this circumstance, as the court addressed the listed factors, it concluded that Silva was an independent contractor. Silva had retained an agent to obtain and schedule races for him; he rode on a per-race basis for various owners; Crown's Way did not pay Silva directly, but rather the money came from the racetrack, which withdrew money from the horse's guarantee; Crown's Way did not provide insurance for Silva, and Silva provided his own saddle. Also, Silva's occupation requires considerable specialized skill. Finally, as to the critical issue of control, the prerace discussions held with Silva provided only a familiarization with the horse and were not intended to override Silva's professional judgment in how the race was to be ridden.

As a matter of law, the court concluded that Silva was an independent contractor. There was no vicarious liability, and summary judgment for Crown's Way Farm and Dicicilia was proper.

The factors listed in Exhibit 5.2 and used in the *Lang* case are the ones that courts generally address in ascertaining whether a party is an independent contractor. The question of degree of control is critical. Control over *results* is consistent with a finding that a party is an independent contractor, but control as to the day-to-day *details* of how a party is to work reflects an employer–employee relationship. In the case of youth sport game officials, the trend is for courts to hold that they should be considered as independent contractors. At least 13 states have passed laws classifying sports officials as independent contractors for the purposes of workers' compensation analysis, an analysis which primarily addresses the degree of control factor discussed above (Popke, 2008; Sushner, 2005).

When you determine that you want an independent contractor relationship to exist, you should have a contract that clearly states that this is the case. However, you must treat the contractor, in all circumstances, in ways that are consistent with that relationship. For example, you wish to hire a personal trainer for your fitness club, and you want to avoid vicarious liability by having that person serve as an independent contractor. But since the person will not make a great deal of money and you need to add to your insurance enrollment to get better rates, you offer the person the opportunity to join the group health policy. This seemingly innocuous gesture may completely destroy the independent contractor relationship you attempted to set up. It is likely that a court would conclude you were treating the personal trainer as an employee, and you would likely have difficulty in establishing that your club should not be vicariously liable for the actions of that personal trainer. It is important that you set up the relationship properly and treat the person in ways that are consistent with that relationship. See Exhibit 5.3 for an example of language used in an independent contractor agreement.

Competitive Advantage

STRATEGIES

Liability for Acts of Independent Contractors

- If you wish to set up an independent contractor relationship, remember that you cannot control the details of the day-to-day operation if you wish to avoid vicarious liability. Your practice with the independent contractor must be consistent with your documentation.

- To avoid liability for negligent selection, develop a list of necessary credentials for the independent contractor and hire only contractors that meet those criteria.

- Require prospective independent contractors to provide you with a list of references. Check those references carefully.

Terms and conditions of an independent contractor agreement.   EXHIBIT   **5.3**

1. **Independent Contractor; Relationship of the Parties.** The parties aver that:
   a. The Contractor is not subject to Company's control as to the means and methods of accomplishing the work to be performed hereunder, but the Company may specify and control the result to be accomplished including any specifications, standards, requirements, and deliverables;
   b. The Contractor selects its own customers or clients and is free to contract with others during the term of this Contract;
   c. The Contractor selects its own employees; and
   d. This Contract shall not be construed to create any partnership, joint venture, nor other agency relationship between the parties, who are independent of one another. It is expressly understood and agreed that the enforcement of the terms and conditions of this contract and all rights of action relating to such enforcement, shall be strictly reserved to the Company and the named Contractor. Nothing contained in this Contract shall give or allow any claim or right of action whatsoever by any other third person. It is the express intention of the parties that any such person or entity, other than the parties hereto, receiving services or benefits under this Agreement shall be deemed an incidental beneficiary only.

Negligent Selection

There is an exception to the general rule of nonliability for the actions of independent contractors. That exception is based on the theory of **negligent selection,** a concept closely analogous to negligent hiring. You have a duty to choose an independent contractor in a reasonable fashion, just as in negligent hiring the employer has a duty to hire reasonably. The elements of negligence (see Chapter 15) apply here as they do to negligent hiring. The following hypothetical case illustrates the theory of negligent selection.

considering . . .   NEGLIGENT SELECTION

C. Lou Less, the athletic director at Cleveland High School, is reviewing bids from bus companies. The high school needs to use an outside company to transport athletes to some of the away games. The contract with the chosen company will be set up as an independent contractor relationship.

The Ace Bus Company has, by far, the lowest bid for the services, and Ms. Less decides to take that bid without doing any investigation of the company. If an investigation had been undertaken, the record would have shown that several of Ace's drivers have been cited for reckless driving or driving while intoxicated.

En route to an away basketball game, one of the buses is involved in a serious vehicular accident. It was caused by an Ace driver who was driving while under the influence of alcohol. Several of the school's athletes are injured in the crash, and numerous lawsuits have been filed against the school district.

Ms. Less feels confident that there can be no liability for the school district in this case, because the contract with Ace Bus Company clearly designates it as an independent contractor, for which the school district has no vicarious liability.

Question

- Is Ms. Less correct in believing that there can be no school district liability here?

Note how you would answer the question and then check your response using the Analysis & Discussion at the end of this chapter.

The hypothetical case illustrates the legal principle that an organization can be held liable for the actions of an independent contractor if someone in the organization fails to use due care in the selection of the independent contractor. Although the organization will not be vicariously liable for the actions of the independent contractor, it can have liability based on negligent selection if it fails to use proper care in the choice of the independent contractor. The cost of a contract should not be the sole factor in hiring an independent contractor.

Although we used a hypothetical case to illustrate this point, there has been concern that some universities may be using charter bus companies that do not meet federal safety standards. ESPN disclosed that at least 85 Division I universities used charter bus companies during 2007 and 2008 that have had one or more deficient federal safety scores (Holtzman, 2009). This emphasizes the need to research bus companies and to choose those with proven safety records that meet federal safety standards; if proper research is not done and the incompetent bus company is at fault, the university may be liable for negligent selection.

LIABILITY FOR THE ACTS OF A VOLUNTEER

A *volunteer* is someone who agrees to assist your organization in some capacity for no compensation. The question of whether an organization is liable for the acts of a volunteer is very closely aligned to the question of control discussed earlier in regard to independent contractors. The following Focus Case explores this issue.

Competitive Advantage

STRATEGIES

Liability for the Acts of a Volunteer

- Screen and select volunteers with the same care that you use for employees in the same capacities.

- Take particular care to screen volunteers who will be in positions of authority and trust with minors.

Lasseigne v. American Legion Nicholson Post #38

543 So.2d 1111 (La. Ct. App. 1989)   **FOCUS CASE**

FACTS

The plaintiff was injured while participating in a Little League baseball practice. He was hit in the head by a ball thrown by a teammate. The plaintiff alleged that the coaches were negligent in the way that they oversaw practice and in failing to advise the injured player's parents of his injury. The local post of the American Legion was also sued for vicarious liability based on the actions of the coaches.

The coaches were volunteers, and they were not selected by the local post. Each team was responsible for hiring its own coaches. The post simply oversaw the location of game sites, organized schedules, and provided umpires and team scorers.

The trial court granted the defendant post's motion for summary judgment.

HOLDING

The Louisiana Court of Appeal affirmed summary judgment for the post, as it held that there was no vicarious liability for the coaches' actions.

RATIONALE

The core issue was whether the local American Legion post could be vicariously liable for the actions of the coaches. The court noted that the coaches were not employees of the post. They were volunteers who were chosen by the private sponsors of the teams. The post had absolutely no control over the manner in which the coaches conducted practices. Absent any control over the way in which the coaches conducted their business, the post cannot be vicariously liable for the actions of the coaches.

As shown by the Focus Case, the fact that a person is a volunteer and is not paid for her work is not the essential point for determining the vicarious liability of an organization. The question is whether the organization exerted sufficient control over the actions of the volunteer in terms of the day-to-day execution of the volunteer's responsibilities. If that level of control exists, then vicarious liability may exist. The following hypothetical case illustrates this notion of control.

considering . . .   CONTROL OVER VOLUNTEERS

Joe Goodheart agreed to assist the coaches of the men's basketball team at Small Community College (SCC) by performing various tasks as directed by Coach Light. Coach Light asked Goodheart, who had a valid driver's license, to pick up a recruit at the airport and drive him to the hotel near campus. While on his way to the hotel, Goodheart drove negligently and the recruit was injured in the accident.

Question

- Can SCC be liable under vicarious liability even though Goodheart was a volunteer?

Note how you would answer the question and then check your response using the Analysis & Discussion at the end of this chapter.

LIABILITY FOR THE ACTS OF A COLLEGIATE ATHLETE

Most courts have consistently held that the relationship between a university and its athletes is not one of employer–employee. See Chapter 8 for a discussion of the workers' compensation cases dealing with this issue.

In the following Focus Case, a plaintiff attempted to argue that an athlete should be considered an agent of the university in order to impose vicarious liability upon the university.

Kavanagh v. Trustees of Boston University

FOCUS CASE | 795 N.E.2d 1170 (Mass. 2003)

FACTS

The plaintiff, Kenneth Kavanagh, played basketball for the intercollegiate team at Manhattan College. The team was playing an away game at Boston University (BU) when Kavanagh was injured in a scuffle. Kavanagh attempted to break up a fight between the opponents and was punched in the nose by Levar Folk, a BU player. The blow broke Kavanagh's nose.

Kavanagh's claim against BU was based on vicarious liability, as he claimed that Folk was an agent of BU. This claim was dismissed by the trial court. Kavanagh appealed.

HOLDING

The Supreme Judicial Court of Massachusetts affirmed the dismissal of the action against Boston University.

RATIONALE

The court held that the relationship between a university and its athletes cannot be viewed as one of employment nor agency. A student is a buyer of education, not an agent of the school, and a student does not attend a university to do its bidding. The receipt of a scholarship by an athlete does not transform the relationship into an employment situation. Further, an athlete may be considered to be a "representative" of a school in some senses, but not in the legal sense.

The *Kavanagh* case reflects the current majority position: university athletes are not agents of their universities, nor are they employees. Therefore, imposing vicarious liability upon a university based on actions of its athletes is not warranted.

CONCLUSION

T he legal reality of *respondeat superior* means that sport organizations will have liability for the actions of employees while the employees are furthering the business of the employer (acting within the scope of employment). That is a cost of doing business.

However, it is entirely possible to avoid liability for negligent hiring, supervision, or retention if managers who are in charge of hiring, disciplining, and terminating employees are trained to act in a reasonably prudent manner. Organizations should adopt protocols to ensure that screening and selection of employees and volunteers are performed carefully.

If you desire to create an independent contractor relationship in order to avoid the prospect of vicarious liability, the document reflecting that relationship should clearly delineate that the organization retains control only as to the outcome of the work, not as to the details of how to accomplish it. The working relationship with the independent contractor should be consistent with that understanding.

discussion questions

1. What is the underlying rationale for *respondeat superior*? Explain why it is a derivative theory of liability as opposed to a direct theory of liability.

2. What is your understanding of the concept of scope of employment? Give examples from sport organizations of situations when an employee may be acting within the scope of employment, and give examples of situations when an employee may be acting on his or her own behalf.

3. When could a plaintiff use the argument that behavior was ratified or condoned by an employer? Give examples.

4. Explain the theory of negligent hiring. Explain how you can find vicarious liability for an organization based on the negligence of a manager or administrator in hiring.

5. Explain why an organization may wish to set up an independent contractor relationship. What are the factors that courts look at in ascertaining whether a situation is an employment relationship or an independent contractor relationship?

learning activities

Many Internet sites deal with issues related to youth sport and the hiring of coaches and other personnel. Do an Internet search and find three different hiring or selection protocols followed by youth sport leagues or associations to ensure that those hired are suitable to work with children.

CASE STUDY

The coach of Midwest University's men's basketball team, Bill Beam, has an excellent win–loss record, but he has a violent temper and often verbally abuses his players, both on and off the court. The athletic director has heard this abuse and has also seen the coach push and slap players on a number of occasions at practice. The athletic director, who is Beam's immediate superior, is intimidated by Beam and has never spoken to Beam about this behavior or in any way tried to discipline Beam.

One day, after a humiliating loss to a rival university, Beam, in a fit of rage, grabs a player and slams him against a locker. The player suffers a concussion and a severe neck injury.

If the player sues, what are the possible causes of action against Beam, the athletic director, and Midwest University?

considering . . .   **ANALYSIS & DISCUSSION**

Negligent Hiring (p. 86)

Given the facts in the case above, you acted negligently in hiring this coach, and the league will be liable under the usual *respondeat superior* principles for your negligent hiring, which occurred while you were in the scope of employment. The league cannot be responsible under *respondeat superior* principles directly for the actions of the coach, since the sexual abuse is not within the coach's scope of employment. Also, there was no ratification or condonation of behavior, since the coach did not engage in any bad behavior at *this* job before he molested the player.

In this case, you have a duty to act reasonably in choosing coaches for the youth teams. No reasonable person would hire someone to coach children without investigating the applicant's credentials. No references were checked. An investigation would have ascertained that this coach was certainly an unfit choice to coach youth players, since a person with this background is likely to repeat this heinous behavior. Therefore, you breached your duty of care by hiring this person, which resulted in injury to a player.

Negligent Supervision (p. 87)

First, Forehand will be liable. He is acting negligently considering the way in which he is setting up the drills. See Chapter 15 for a discussion of negligence in instruction.

Second, the tennis club, as Forehand's employer, will be liable under the principles of *respondeat superior*. Forehand acted negligently while he was performing duties within the scope of employment.

Third, you will be liable for your negligence in supervising Forehand. You had a responsibility to oversee his teaching practices, and you failed to do so.

Fourth, the tennis club (your employer) will be responsible for your negligent supervision under the principles of *respondeat superior*. You acted negligently in supervising Forehand, and your negligence was within the scope of your employment, since your duties included the supervision of the assistant teaching pros.

Negligent Retention (p. 88)

First, there is negligent retention. Strong was put on notice that Easton had violent propensities and never took adequate action to discipline Easton or, if necessary, terminate Easton's employment. Strong had a duty of care to other employees and to patrons to act reasonably to facilitate a safe environment at the club. Strong's failure to do so resulted in a foreseeable event, the serious attack upon a patron. Since Strong acted negligently within the scope of his employment with Win Corporation, the employer is also liable under the general rule of *respondeat superior*.

This fact pattern also lends itself to an analysis under the ratification/condonation concept discussed earlier. Although Easton's behavior would not normally fall under *respondeat superior* since the battery was not within the scope of employment, it is arguable that Strong's failure to intervene over the months in which he had knowledge of Easton's violent behavior was a ratification or condonation of that behavior, thus essentially making it within the scope of employment.

Negligent Selection (p. 92)

Unfortunately, Ms. Less has overlooked the principle of negligent selection. In this case, the school district, through the negligence of Ms. Less, may be liable for choosing unwisely. There is a duty to use reasonable care in the selection of an independent contractor. That duty was breached in this case because no investigation concerning the competency of the drivers was done. If it had been done, it would have shown that Ace was not a wise choice because several of the drivers had poor driving records. This unreasonable choice of bus company led directly to the injuries. Under these facts, it would be quite easy to establish the negligence of Ms. Less, an employee of the school district, in choosing Ace Bus Company, and liability is a given.

Control over Volunteers (p. 94)

In this case, the answer is yes since Goodheart was negligent while he was performing a task directed by the coach. Goodheart was under the control of the coach when the incident occurred.

REFERENCES

Cases

Kavanagh v. Trustees of Boston Univ., 795 N.E.2d 1170 (Mass. 2003).

Lang v. Silva, 715 N.E.2d 708 (Ill. App. Ct. 1999).

Lasseigne v. American Legion Nicholson Post #38, 543 So.2d 1111 (La. Ct. App. 1989).

Smith v. Gardner, 998 F. Supp. 708 (S.D. Miss. 1998).

Southport Little League v. Vaughan, 734 N.E.2d 261 (Ind. Ct. App. 2000).

Tomjanovich v. Los Angeles Lakers, 1979 U.S. Dist. LEXIS 9282 (S.D. Tex. 1979).

Other Sources

27 Am. Jur. 2d *Employment Relationship* (2005).

Brackenridge, C. H., Bringer, J. D., & Bishopp, D. (2005). Managing cases of abuse in sport. *Child Abuse Review, 14*(4), 259–274.

Bynum, M. (2007, March). Getting to know you. *Athletic Business,* 95–97.

Cotten, D. (2009, January). Do your certification homework. *Fitness Management,* 52.

Gibbons, M., & Campbell, D. (2003). Liability of recreation and competitive sport organizations for sexual assaults on children by administrators, coaches, and volunteers. *Journal of Legal Aspects of Sport, 13,* 185–229.

Holtzman, B. (2009, March 31). Bus safety an issue for colleges. Retrieved June 9, 2009, from http://sports.espn.go.com/espn/otl/news/story?id=3997988.

Minuti, M. (1988). Note: Employer liability under the doctrines of negligent hiring: Suggested methods for avoiding the hiring of dangerous employees. *Delaware Journal of Corporate Law, 13,* 501–534.

Popke, M. (2008, September). Who makes the call? *Athletic Business, 78*–84.

Preston, M. B. (2006, October). Note: Sheldon Kennedy and a Canadian tragedy revisited: A comparative look at U. S. and Canadian jurisprudence on youth sports organizations' civil liability for child sexual exploitation. *Vanderbilt Journal of Transnational Law, 39,* 1333–1372.

Ramirez, E. (2007, March 14). Referees cry foul in Citrus County over school screening requirements. *St. Petersburg Times,* p. 10.

Restatement (Second) of Agency (1958).

Sushner, M. (2005, Spring). Are amateur sports officials employees? *Sports Lawyers Journal, 12,* 123–154.

Ugolini, J. M. (2007). Even a violent game has its limits: A look at the NFL's responsibility for the behavior of its players. *University of Toledo Law Review, 39,* 41–58.

WEBSITE RESOURCES

www.naso.org ▪ This is the website of the National Association of Sports Officials. There is a special report on this site called "Officials & Independent Contractor Status" that deals with the history of determining whether officials should be classified as independent contractors.

www.nrpa.org/tlc2 ▪ This section of the National Recreation and Park Association website allows organizations to become part of the volunteer management program entitled Operation TLC²: Making Communities Safe. This program has a focus on screening, identifying, and educating volunteers—all actions that can help an organization avoid situations where it may be liable for the negative actions of a volunteer.

www.sadlersports.com/riskmanagement/index.html ▪ This website of a company specializing in insuring sports and recreation organizations provides a variety of reports on risk management issues including one on types of background checks for volunteers in youth sport. This is a useful resource for employers or future employers concerned about minimizing liability.

Hiring, Promotion, Termination, Compensation, and Leave

CHAPTER

6

INTRODUCTION

A critical aspect of human resource management is avoiding illegal employment discrimination. Employment discrimination may occur in many different forms and contexts. This chapter explores the legal issues involved in hiring, promotion, and termination decisions based illegally on race, sex, religion, age, or disability. Also covered here are compensation discrimination in salary arrangements and decisions regarding employee leave. Other forms of illegal employment discrimination, such as harassment and discriminatory treatment based on different forms of employee expression, are discussed in Chapter 7.

The U. S. Constitution and several federal statutes apply to these types of employment discrimination, and most states and many cities have also enacted civil or human rights statutes and ordinances to provide relief for victims of illegal employment practices. However, the focus of this chapter is on examining the applicable *federal* laws. For a summary of the issues, relevant laws, and primary cases discussed in this chapter, see Exhibit 6.1.

HIRING, PROMOTION, AND TERMINATION DECISIONS

T his section discusses decisions to hire, promote, or terminate employees that involve intentional discrimination or the use of seemingly neutral employment policies that can disadvantage an entire group of people.

Discrimination on the Basis of Race or Sex

Although intentional discrimination on the basis of race or gender appears to be on the decline, obvious inequities remain in the realm of sport. Continuing dispari-

EXHIBIT 6.1	Management contexts in which employment discrimination may arise, with relevant laws and cases.

MANAGEMENT CONTEXT	MAJOR LEGAL ISSUES	RELEVANT LAW	ILLUSTRATIVE CASES
Hiring/promotion/termination	Race/sex discrimination	Title VII	*Morris, Wynn*
		Title IX	
		Equal Protection Clause	*Ludtke*
	Age discrimination	ADEA	
		§ 504	
	Disability discrimination	ADA	*Lemire*
Compensation determinations	Sex discrimination	Title VII, Title IX, Equal Pay Act, EEOC regulations	*Stanley, Perdue*
Employee leave decisions	Pregnancy	PDA	
	Family leave	FMLA	

ties in employment patterns and compensation raise questions about the causes of these differences—are they the result of lifestyle choices, educational background, or lack of preparation? Or are they, in fact, due to prejudicial stereotypes and attitudes manifesting themselves in discriminatory employment practices that are prohibited by law? This is a particularly difficult question in the case of high-profile coaching and administrative positions because employment decisions are infused with a large amount of subjectivity on the part of the employer. Often few objective criteria exist on which to compare applicants, and "organizational fit" is a major (and quite subjective) part of the hiring decision. Also, standard institutional hiring procedures often are not followed when universities hire big-time coaches. In 2008 the NCAA's Minority Opportunities and Interests Committee began to seek NCAA legislation that would require athletic departments to document that they follow institutional hiring procedures when they fill vacancies (McKindra, 2008). When they do not, discrimination can be impossible to prove. However, when there *is* evidence of discriminatory conduct, federal laws are in place that can provide a remedy.

Title VII

One such law is Title VII of the Civil Rights Act of 1964, as amended by the Civil Rights Act of 1991. Title VII focuses on employment discrimination. (See Exhibit 6.2.)

The phrasing "terms, conditions, or privileges of employment" applies to employment decisions related to such things as hiring, firing, layoffs, job training, discipline, job classifications, and provision of benefits.

Scope of coverage. Title VII applies to employers that impact interstate commerce and that have 15 or more employees who work at least 20 calendar weeks in a given year. These employers may be governmental or in the private sector and may include educational institutions, labor unions, or players associations. Title VII does not apply to independent contractors. **Bona fide membership clubs** (such as exclusive country clubs that do not serve the general public) are exempt from Title VII, as are American Indian tribes and religious organizations hiring employees to

---

Section 703 of Title VII of the Civil Rights Act of 1964.   EXHIBIT   **6.2**

(a) It shall be an unlawful employment practice for an employer—

(1) to fail or refuse to hire or to discharge any individual, or otherwise to discriminate against any individual with respect to his compensation, terms, conditions, or privileges of employment, because of such individual's race, color, religion, sex, or national origin; or

(2) to limit, segregate, or classify his employees or applicants for employment in any way which would deprive or tend to deprive any individual of employment opportunities or otherwise adversely affect his status as an employee, because of such individual's race, color, religion, sex, or national origin.

perform religious functions. Covered employees include U. S. citizens employed by American employers outside the United States and non-U. S. citizens employed within the United States.

Protected classes. The protected classes listed in the statute (race, color, religion, sex, and national origin) are the only ones covered by Title VII. The term "race" refers to ethnicity, rather than being limited to the traditional anthropological definition of race, and thus protects identifiable ethnic groups such as Hispanics or Jews. Color-based discrimination refers to unlawful treatment on the basis of actual skin color, and national origin discrimination refers to an improper focus on place of ancestry. Place of ancestry is not the same as citizenship. The latter refers to where a person holds citizenship, not the nation in which a person or her ancestors were born. Because citizenship is not a protected class, an American ice hockey referee was unsuccessful in using Title VII to sue the National Hockey League for allegedly discriminating against U. S. citizens by hiring mostly Canadian citizens as referees (*Dowling v. United States,* 1979).

Title VII protects both women and men from sex discrimination. In *Medcalf v. University of Pennsylvania* (2001), a male was rejected for a job coaching a collegiate women's rowing team, and a female was hired instead. In denying the university's motion for summary judgment, the court found sufficient evidence of intentional sex discrimination in several statements made by the senior associate athletic director. In these statements, she indicated that the university preferred to hire a woman for the job in order to balance the mostly male coaching staff and to provide a female role model for the athletes.

Finally, in addition to the long-established religions, Title VII protects people professing unorthodox beliefs that are sincerely held and not simply adopted as an ulterior means to some desired end (such as creating a religion to justify using unlawful hallucinogenic drugs).

Individuals who belong to other groups that tend to suffer from discrimination do not have a remedy under Title VII. For example, because sexual orientation is not listed as a protected class, a man who was not hired because he is gay cannot use Title VII to seek justice. It should be noted, however, that 20 states plus the District of Columbia have added sexual orientation as a protected class to their state employment discrimination laws. These states are California, Colorado, Connecticut, Hawaii, Illinois, Iowa, Maine, Maryland, Massachusetts, Minnesota, Nevada, New Hampshire, New Jersey, New Mexico, New York, Oregon, Rhode Island, Vermont, Washington, and Wisconsin. Additionally, Title IX and the Equal Protection Clause have been used successfully to challenge adverse employment decisions made on the basis of sexual orientation or gender identity (Women's Sports Foundation, 2009).

Administration and procedure. The federal agency that administers and helps enforce Title VII is the Equal Employment Opportunity Commission (EEOC). The EEOC issues regulations for implementing Title VII that are generally enforced by the courts. Occasionally, the EEOC also issues guidelines for analyzing discrimination cases. Courts typically do not feel compelled to enforce mere guidelines but are free to use them if they find the reasoning behind them persuasive.

An example of these guidelines that applies specifically to sport is the *Enforcement Guidelines on Sex Discrimination in the Compensation of Sports Coaches in Educational Institutions* (EEOC, 1997), discussed later in this chapter.

Remedies. The remedies available under § 706(g) of Title VII include:

- **Back pay** for work missed due to the adverse employment action
- **Front pay** for future earnings that would have been received absent the discrimination
- Reinstatement of the employee to the position
- Retroactive seniority
- **Injunctive relief** ordering the employer to cease unlawful practices or to engage in affirmative action
- Attorneys fees
- Compensatory and punitive damages

Types of loss that may be compensated include financial loss (past and future) and pain and suffering. The most typical relief granted is back pay for wages and benefits lost due to the illegal discrimination.

Theories of liability and defenses. Courts use two primary theories of liability in deciding Title VII cases—disparate treatment and disparate impact. **Disparate treatment** applies when an employer has *intentionally* discriminated against a member of a protected class. The **disparate impact** theory is used when an employer's *neutral* employment practice has had a discriminatory *effect* on a protected class of which the plaintiff is a member. Defenses include some legitimate nondiscriminatory reason for the adverse action, business necessity, and bona fide occupational qualification. These two theories of liability and the defenses are explained below.

Disparate treatment: Direct evidence. A disparate treatment claim requires a finding of intentional discrimination, which may be proved in two ways: with direct evidence of intent or by means of an inference from circumstantial evidence relating to the way the employer has treated others. An example of direct evidence of intentional discrimination is found in *Biver v. Saginaw Township Community Schools* (1986). In this case, the court found evidence of intentional discrimination in a school superintendent's statement that "hell would freeze over before he would hire a woman for a boys' coaching position." Such statements serve as direct evidence of intentional discrimination when they are directly related to the allegedly discriminatory action. In *EEOC v. NBC* (1990), Roth, the female plaintiff, had evidence that she had been the target of several sexist remarks during her attempts to be hired into the position of television sports director. But she was unable to provide evidence connecting those remarks to the hiring decision process, so the court found that her "direct evidence" of discrimination was inadequate.

Disparate treatment: Inference. In most instances, direct evidence of intent to discriminate is hard to come by. Thus, the more commonly used method of proving discriminatory intent is through the inferential *McDonnell Douglas* test established

| EXHIBIT | 6.3 | *McDonnell Douglas* burden-shifting analysis. |

1. Plaintiff has burden of proof to establish a prima facie case of discrimination.
2. Defendant has burden of production to support its defense.
3. Plaintiff has burden of proof to establish that the defense is pretext.

in *McDonnell Douglas Corp. v. Green* (1973). This is a burden-shifting test in which the plaintiff and defendant take turns shouldering evidentiary burdens (see Exhibit 6.3). Evidentiary burdens include the burden of production and the burden of proof. The **burden of production** is the responsibility to produce evidence without any burden to prove that the defense (in this case) is true. The **burden of proof** is the responsibility to prove the truth of an issue.

Under the *McDonnell Douglas* test, a plaintiff must first prove a **prima facie case** that discrimination has occurred (that is, provide initial support that the allegation is true) (see Exhibit 6.4).

Once the plaintiff has established by a **preponderance of the evidence** (i.e., the weight of the evidence tips in his favor) that a prima facie case of discrimination exists, the burden of production, but not the full burden of proof, shifts to the defendant to provide evidence that the adverse action was taken for *some legitimate, nondiscriminatory reason* (the elements of this requirement are known by the acronym SLNDR). If the defendant is successful in producing such evidence, the full burden of proof now rests upon the plaintiff to prove that the defendant's SLNDR defense is pretext, that is, a sham disguising intentional discrimination. If the plaintiff is successful in proving pretext by a preponderance of the evidence, she wins the lawsuit. An example of a disparate treatment claim alleging both race and sex discrimination is found in the *Morris* case.

| EXHIBIT | 6.4 | *McDonnell Douglas* three-prong test to prove that discrimination has occurred in hiring or job performance situations. |

In a hiring situation, a prima facie case is shown by establishing that:

1. The applicant is a member of a protected class.
2. The applicant applied and was qualified but was rejected.
3. The employer hired a nonminority candidate or continued to search.

In a job performance situation, a prima facie case is shown by establishing that:

1. The employee is a member of a protected class.
2. The employee was performing the job satisfactorily but was fired or given adverse treatment in working conditions.
3. The employee's work was given to a nonminority employee.

Morris v. Wallace Community College–Selma

125 F. Supp. 2d 1315 (S.D. Ala. 2001)   **FOCUS CASE**

FACTS

Plaintiff Morris is a White female coach who had been employed full-time by a southern Black community college, Wallace Community College–Selma, since 1992. Although Morris expressed interest in being promoted to the position of athletics director in 1997, a Black male, Raji Gourdine, was chosen instead. The college said that it never accepted applications for the position of athletics director, but instead appointed someone in 1996 and also in 1997. The college also asserted that one of the criteria for the position was to hire an administrator, not a coach. However, the first person offered the position was a chemistry professor, not an administrator. The athletic director also claimed that Morris had been a trouble-maker who had often spoken unfavorably about the administration, had failed to follow proper travel procedures, and had scheduled games without obtaining approval. However, all of her annual performance evaluations had been positive, and she had never received a written reprimand for any objectionable behavior. In fact, the college president appointed her to the position of assistant athletics director when Gourdine was appointed head athletics director.

As a coach, Morris was paid less than comparable Black male and female coaches, but she also had had less work experience than they did when she was hired. She had had no prior coaching experience, and her only experience related to physical education had been teaching three classes at the YMCA and aerobics at church. Morris was also offered a summer camp coaching job with less than a full load (and thus less compensation) than her Black colleagues, who received more lucrative summer employment.

Morris sued under Title VII, alleging race and sex discrimination for failure to promote, inequity in coaching compensation, and inequity in the awarding of summer employment contracts. The defendant moved for summary judgment on all these claims.

HOLDING

Morris produced evidence sufficient to create genuine issues of material fact sufficient to defeat the summary judgment motions on all the above claims.

RATIONALE

In this case, a court would apply the *McDonnell Douglas* test to decide the failure to promote claim.

(*Plaintiff's Burden of Proof to Establish a Prima Facie Claim*) Morris obviously belongs to a protected class as a female (prong 1; see Exhibit 6.4), since Title VII protects against sex discrimination. Her claim of race discrimination is covered under Title VII even though she is White, because the statute prohibits race discrimination regardless of what race a person is. Here, we have a White person seeking a promotion in an historically Black institution, a place where she is definitely in the minority. Therefore, the first prong of the *McDonnell Douglas* test is met.

The "applied for the job" part of prong 2 (see Exhibit 6.4) of the test is satisfied because she expressed interest in being promoted to the position of athletics director when the job came open. An employer cannot avoid liability by appointing someone to an open position instead of accepting applications. If someone has learned of the job opening and expressed a desire to be considered for the position, the employer has a duty to consider that person along with the other potential appointees.

The "qualified for the job" part of prong 2 is harder to determine, given these facts. However, the college's nonadherence to its hiring criterion of prior administrative experience, as evidenced by its first offering the athletics director job to a chemistry professor, casts doubt on the required qualifications for the job. Such inconsistency suggests that Morris could satisfy prong 2 by proving that she was at least minimally qualified. Her appointment as assistant athletics director shows that the administration must have thought she could perform the functions of an athletics director role sufficiently to assist the head director of athletics. This makes her appear to be at least as qualified as the chemistry professor, so the second prong is satisfied.

Prong 3 (see Exhibit 6.4) is met if Morris shows that she was rejected in favor of someone not in the protected class. In this case, a Black male was hired as director of athletics. Once again, Title VII protects against discrimination on the basis of race even if a plaintiff is White. Also, Gourdine is in the majority ethnic group at the historically Black college, a fact that makes Morris' claim of race discrimination look a bit stronger. As a female, she is also a member of a protected class in this situation.

Therefore, Morris has successfully made a prima facie claim of both race and sex discrimination.

(*Defendant's Burden of Production*) It is now the college's turn to bring a SLNDR defense. It must produce evidence that it had some legitimate nondiscriminatory reason for denying Morris the promotion. The college argued that she was not promoted because she was a troublemaker, and also because she was not an administrator and therefore did not meet one of the qualification criteria.

(*Plaintiff's Burden of Proof of Pretext*) The burden now shifts back to Morris to prove that the two aspects of the SLNDR defense are pretext. She showed that the promotion was not denied on the basis that she was a troublemaker by the fact that she had consistently received positive performance reviews and never received any written reprimands. She also succeeded in proving that the college did not really deny her the promotion because she lacked the required qualification of being an administrator by the fact that the college first offered the job to a chemistry teacher. Thus, Morris proved that the college's SLNDR defense was bogus. Since the college could not articulate a legitimate reason for failing to promote her, the inference to be drawn is that the failure to promote must have been based on the fact that she is White and/or that she is female.

With regard to the claim that Morris suffered compensation discrimination, the college did not prove that she was paid equitably in comparison with similarly situated Black and/or male coaches. Finally, with regard to the alleged discrimination in summer employment contracts, there are no facts that indicate that the college had some legitimate nondiscriminatory reason for giving her less favorable summer contracts than the Black and/or male coaches. Thus, the college will be unable to satisfy its burden of producing evidence for a SLNDR defense on this issue.

Disparate impact. As mentioned earlier, the disparate impact theory is used when, instead of evidence of discriminatory intent, a plaintiff has appropriate statistical evidence that a "neutral" employment practice has had a disparate impact or effect on members of a protected class in the relevant workforce pool. A burden-shifting test is used here as well, with the parties taking turns establishing evidentiary burdens in the same fashion as the *McDonnell Douglas* test: first the plaintiff's prima facie case, then the defendant's defense, and finally the plaintiff's chance to prove the defense is pretext for discrimination.

In disparate impact cases, the defense is a little different from the SLNDR defense used in disparate treatment cases, in that it is specifically tied to the employer's action being job-related. In these cases, once the prima facie case of disparate impact is established, the burden shifts to the employer to provide evidence that the neutral practice is job-related and a business necessity; that is, it is necessary as a means to achieving a legitimate business objective. If the defendant employer is successful in establishing business necessity, the burden shifts back to the plaintiff to prove that the ostensibly neutral employment practice is in fact pretext for discrimination. A way to prove pretext is to provide evidence that other methods are available for accomplishing the stated business goal that do not adversely impact the protected class.

Successful disparate impact claims are rare because of the difficulty in establishing that an appropriate workforce pool has been negatively impacted. An example of this difficulty is found in the case of *Wynn v. Columbus Municipal Separate School District*.

Wynn v. Columbus Municipal Separate School District

692 F. Supp. 672 (N.D. Miss. 1988)   **CASE OPINION**

[FACTS

Plaintiff Wynn was hired at Lee High School in 1963 as a physical education instructor, and since then has also coached various girls' athletics teams. She also initiated several female sports teams that did not exist before she was employed. The person who served as both head football coach and athletics director resigned in 1969, and the superintendent of schools and later the principal performed the duties of athletics director after that resignation. In 1971, separate job descriptions for athletics director and for head football coach were created. Then, in 1977 the Board of Trustees decided to return to the earlier practice of having the position of athletics director combined with that of head football coach, but no combined job description was ever produced. The board's decision to combine the two positions was based on the trustees' perception that football was the "dominant" sport in the school district and that it was the major revenue producer as well as the major cost item in the overall athletics program.

The board concluded that it was logical to have the head football coach also be the athletics director.

Johnny Bruce served as both head football coach and athletics director until his resignation in 1984, during which time, plaintiff Wynn testified, Wynn was performing many of the athletics director's duties. She also testified that she had worked in all sports in some capacity, including football, and had been placed in charge of all money and ticket sales for varsity football; she also prepared financial statements for the school district superintendent. Based on her 20 years of coaching experience and her hands-on experience with the duties of the athletics director position, Wynn applied for the open athletics director position on February 15, 1984. The board had never advertised for applications for the single position of athletics director when the position opened, but Wynn and Bob Williford (the boys basketball coach) nevertheless applied for the position of athletics director, and Bill Wilkerson (the assistant football coach) applied for the dual position of head football coach and athletics director. Wilkerson was appointed head football coach in March 1984, but the high school principal served as athletics director until May 1984 because the superintendent was considering recommending that the positions be split again. In May, the principal recommended that Wilkerson be appointed athletics director in addition to his position as head football coach, and the board named him the athletics director. Wilkerson had only five years of experience in the school district, and his experience was limited to football, basketball, cross-country, and an off-season training program.

The board maintained that its decision was primarily influenced by the fact that Wilkerson was qualified to serve as head football coach, while Wynn and Williford were not. They did concede that the combined position effectively excluded women from the position of athletics director because it would be rare that a woman would be qualified to be the head football coach. Plaintiff Wynn contended that the requirement that the athletics director also serve as head football coach had a disparate impact on females and unlawfully excluded females from consideration for the position of athletics director under Title VII.]

HOLDING

The court dismissed plaintiff's disparate impact claim, although it upheld her claim for disparate treatment based on sex (the latter claim is not excerpted herein).

RATIONALE

The disparate impact model is one which is often used by plaintiffs in Title VII cases but one which is often misunderstood or misapplied. As the Fifth Circuit has cautioned: "The disparate impact model applies only when an employer has instituted a specific procedure, usually a selection criterion for employment, that can be shown to have a causal connection to a class imbalance in the workforce." . . .

[P]laintiff characterizes the requirement that Athletic Director also be qualified to act as Head Football Coach as a facially neutral, objective employment criterion which has a disparate impact on females seeking the position of Athletic Director. Although the court agrees that the requirement has a disparate impact on individuals seeking the Athletic Director position who are not qualified to serve as Head Football Coach—including male and female basketball, volleyball, track, and baseball coaches—the court is not convinced that the requirement has a disparate impact on females only.

As her statistical pool, plaintiff utilizes all Athletic Directors throughout the state of Mississippi. Plaintiff asserts that since only 62 of 192 individuals who are not head football coach have been selected to serve as athletic director, the requirement that Athletic Director serve as Head Football Coach has had a disparate impact on females. Plaintiff's proof also establishes that of 192 athletic directors statewide, only two are females. Plaintiff has also established that no head football coach in Mississippi is a female.

The court is of the opinion that plaintiff's disparate impact theory is flawed in two respects. First and foremost, the court concludes that plaintiff has chosen an improper pool of applicants from whom [sic] to draw her statistics. The fact that very few women across the State of Mississippi are selected to serve as Athletic Director bears only a tenuous relationship at best, if any relationship at all, to the issue of whether Columbus Schools discriminates in its selection of Athletic Directors. . . .

Secondly, plaintiff's statistical evidence is drawn from a universe of individuals including both members and non-members of the protected class of females among whom plaintiff is included. The numerous male coaches who are not qualified as head football coach who are thus denied consideration for an athletic director's job—including in this case Bob Williford, who was denied the Lee High Athletic Director job along with plaintiff—are not within an identifiably or arguably protected class under Title VII.

The court is of the opinion that the only proper group for consideration in the case at bar are those female coaches in the Columbus Schools who have applied for and been denied the position of Athletic Director because of their lack of qualifications for the job of Head Football Coach. Clearly, the court is only concerned here with the alleged discriminatory acts of the defendants in this action, not some larger group of all school districts throughout the state of Mississippi who have not appointed women as athletic directors. The alleged discriminatory practice of requiring the Athletic Director to serve also as Head Football Coach is applied *only* to prospective employees of Columbus Schools.

* * *

In view of the fact that Wynn is the only female coach who has ever applied for the position of Athletic Director within the Columbus Schools, the court concludes that she has failed to establish a prima facie case of disparate impact inasmuch as she has failed to establish a causal connection between the requirement that Athletic Director also serve as Head Football Coach and any *actual* effect of excluding a disproportionate number of members of a protected class from employment opportunities.

The court holds that although Wynn applied for an available position for which she was qualified and for which she was rejected, Wynn has failed to make out a prima facie case of sexually-motivated disparate impact. Plaintiff's disparate impact proof fails to show that Columbus Schools practiced any distinguishable pattern of rejecting female applicants for Athletic Director.

* * *

[The court acknowledged in a footnote that plaintiff had shown that of six female coaches in the school district, none was serving as head football coach and therefore all would have been excluded from consideration for the combined job at Lee High School. According to the court, "If plaintiff had offered proof that these individuals had prior knowledge that the Athletic Director was required to serve as Head Football Coach and females were therefore discouraged from applying for the position, Wynn's disparate impact theory might be more persuasive." The *Wynn* case thus illustrates the difficulties in providing appropriate statistical proof of disparate impact—the court may require evidence that many members of the protected class have in fact been turned down for the position, or that at least they considered applying but were discouraged from doing so because of the facially neutral hiring rule.]

Questions

1. How did the school district's "neutral" hiring rule affect the likelihood of a female being hired as athletics director? Cite evidence brought by plaintiff Wynn in her attempt to prove a prima facie case of disparate impact sex discrimination.

2. The court rejected Wynn's evidence of disparate impact. According to the court, what kind of evidence would have been acceptable instead? Could she have produced such evidence? Why or why not?

3. What policy judgment seems to underlie making it more difficult to establish a prima facie case under the disparate impact theory than under the disparate treatment theory?

BFOQ defense. In cases of alleged gender discrimination, an additional available defense is known as the **bona fide occupational qualification** (BFOQ) **defense.** Here, the employer must show that the alleged discrimination was justified because members of the excluded protected class could not effectively perform the essential job functions. This defense is construed narrowly and is rarely successful. For example, in *EEOC v. Sedita* (1991), the defendant health club, Women's Workout World, refused to hire men as fitness instructors or as management staff, asserting that its all-female clientele had a privacy interest in not being disturbed by the presence of males. Thus, they argued that being female was a BFOQ for filling those jobs. The court ruled that there was no evidence that the female clients would have left the club if males were employed, and that a female privacy interest did not appear to be disturbed at the nation's many other health clubs that hire employees of both sexes.

In a 2003 case dealing with a BFOQ, the Phoenix Suns settled a Title VII lawsuit brought by Kathryn Tomlinson, who had been employed by the Suns' "Zoo Crew" halftime entertainment troupe. After performing well in her job the first year, Tomlinson was not rehired because the next year the Suns restricted the hiring of Zoo Crew members to "males with athletic ability and talent." The Suns could not establish why sex was a BFOQ for working as a member of the Zoo Crew and agreed to a settlement payment of $82,500 in damages ("Suns settle," 2003).

Generally, customer preference does not count as grounds for a BFOQ defense. In *Morris v. Bianchini* (1987), a health club management's desire to maintain a macho image for its customers by hiring only male athletics directors was determined to be unlawful reliance on customer preference. Such a policy would only perpetuate the entrenched gender stereotype that females are less capable of performing such jobs.

In contrast, religion can often succeed as a BFOQ in hiring decisions. A religious institution is allowed to hire a person of a particular religious persuasion if the job requires the performance of religion-related tasks. For example, a Catholic institution cannot be forced to hire a Baptist to teach religion classes. However, for nonsectarian activities, such as coaching the Catholic university's basketball team, the institution may not be able to restrict hiring to Catholic coaches, because propagation of the Catholic faith is not necessarily an integral part of the activity of intercollegiate basketball competition.

Title IX

If an inappropriate employment action is taken by an employer that is an educational institution and a recipient of federal funds, the aggrieved employee may have, in addition to a Title VII claim, a cause of action under Title IX of the Education Amendments of 1972 (see Exhibit 6.5).

In *Cannon v. University of Chicago* (1979), the Supreme Court recognized that Title IX afforded a private right of action to plaintiffs, and in *North Haven Board of Education v. Bell* (1982), the Court established that Title IX applies to claims of sex discrimination on the part of employees of educational institutions. Subpart E of the Title IX regulations specifically addresses employment discrimination in education institutions. The courts are split, however, as to whether a Title IX employment discrimination claim is precluded by the availability of a Title VII claim in the same lawsuit. In the employment context, courts that *do* allow both

| EXHIBIT | 6.5 | Title IX of the Education Amendments of 1972, 20 U.S.C. § 1681. |

No person in the United States shall, on the basis of sex, be excluded from participation in, be denied the benefits of, or be subjected to discrimination under any education program or activity receiving federal financial assistance.

claims usually analyze the Title IX claim similarly to a Title VII claim anyway, using the same *McDonnell Douglas* burden-shifting framework (see *Blalock v. Dale County Board of Education*, 1999).

Equal Protection Clause

In instances where a branch of the state or federal government is the employer, an employee may also bring a discrimination claim under the **Equal Protection Clause** found in the Fourteenth Amendment to the U.S. Constitution (see Exhibit 6.6). It is important to remember here that a constitutional law action is triggered only when state action has occurred. That is, the government must have been the "bad actor"—the entity that has allegedly deprived the plaintiff of Constitutional rights—in order for that plaintiff to claim the protection of the Constitution. Public schools and universities are considered branches of state government and hence are state actors for purposes of constitutional law.

The essence of equal protection is that similarly situated people must be treated similarly under the law unless there is a constitutionally permissible reason to do otherwise. If the government *purposefully* deprives someone of a fundamental right guaranteed to all citizens (such as the right to vote or the right to travel freely among the states), or purposefully singles out someone for differential treatment based on his or her status as a member of a prescribed group, the Equal Protection Clause provides a way to challenge the constitutionality of the rule or law through which the government has done this. However, a law that has an *unintended* discriminatory effect is not actionable under the Equal Protection Clause.

Most sport-related litigation under the Equal Protection Clause involves differential treatment on the basis of race or sex. Over time, the courts have established a hierarchy of three tests that are used to determine whether the Equal Protection Clause has been violated (see Exhibit 6.7). These three tests are based on the type of group classification found in the allegedly discriminatory rule or law. Strict scrutiny is the hardest test for a government rule to pass, and rational basis review is the easiest.

Strict scrutiny. The strictest test, called **strict scrutiny,** is reserved for **suspect classifications** (including race, ethnicity, national origin, and alienage) and requires the court to scrutinize closely the law in question. It is based on the premise that there is almost never a good reason for a law to differentiate on the basis of an im-

---

Amendment XIV of the U.S. Constitution.   EXHIBIT   **6.6**

SECTION 1

All persons born or naturalized in the United States, and subject to the jurisdiction thereof, are citizens of the United States and of the state wherein they reside. No state shall make or enforce any law which shall abridge the privileges or immunities of citizens of the United States; nor shall any state deprive any person of life, liberty, or property, without due process of law; nor deny to any person within its jurisdiction the equal protection of the laws.

mutable characteristic such as race. This test states that a law that incorporates a racial classification must be *necessary* to achieve a *compelling* government interest. The words *necessary* and *compelling* are key—they should be read as "absolutely necessary" and "extremely compelling."

A government rule passed strict scrutiny when a Japanese American sued the government for placing him (and many others like him) in a detention camp because of his race after Japan bombed Pearl Harbor in World War II. He claimed that he had been denied the equal protection of the laws based on his race. The U.S. Supreme Court ruled, however, that the government had a compelling interest in protecting national security and that detaining Japanese Americans was necessary to achieve that goal by ensuring they were not spying for Japan (*Korematsu v. United States,* 1944). This is one of the few cases in which a race-based classification has passed the difficult test of strict scrutiny. In almost every other conceivable kind of case where a racial classification is used (most situations are not as compelling as protecting national security!), courts will rule that there is no compelling reason to use such a classification; to do so is almost always uncalled for.

Although not an employment discrimination case, *St. Augustine High School v. Louisiana High School Athletic Association* (1967) is a sport-related case that provides an example of a rule that did not pass strict scrutiny. In this case, the LHSAA added a new show-of-hands vote requirement to the existing criteria for attaining membership (and thus opportunity to participate in post-season tournaments, for example) at the very meeting in which all-Black St. Augustine's membership application to the then all-White-school LHSAA was being considered. Without using the actual "compelling government interest" code words, the court applied the first part of the strict scrutiny test in finding that the state could have no compelling reason (other than perpetuating racial segregation) to add the new membership vote requirement to existing criteria. The court thus did not need to determine whether the vote requirement was necessary to achieve a compelling government interest because there was no compelling reason for implementing such an arbitrary rule. So the court ordered the LHSAA to admit St. Augustine High School as a member, and enjoined it from refusing membership to any school that met the established written membership criteria solely on the basis of an arbitrary vote.

EXHIBIT 6.7	Equal Protection Clause tests.	
GROUP CLASSIFICATION	**NAME OF TEST**	**LANGUAGE OF TEST**
Suspect class: race, ethnicity, alienage, national origin	**Strict scrutiny:** court will give rule a very hard look and *almost always* strike it down	Rule must be *necessary* to achieving a *compelling* government interest
Quasi-suspect class: gender, legitimacy of birth	**Intermediate scrutiny:** court will give rule a fairly hard look and *usually* strike it down	Rule must be *substantially related* to achieving an *important* government interest
Nonsuspect class: all other groups singled out for differential treatment	**Rational basis review:** court will uphold rule if it seems reasonable	Rule must be *rationally/reasonably related* to achieving a *legitimate* government goal

Intermediate scrutiny. Down a notch in the hierarchy of Equal Protection Clause tests is the one used for gender-based classifications, the **intermediate scrutiny** test. This test assumes that rarely, but occasionally, there may be an important reason for the government to rely on a law that differentiates on the basis of sex. The courts are required to scrutinize such a law closely, but not quite as critically as they would a race-based law. The intermediate scrutiny test states that the law in question must be substantially related to achieving an important government interest. Although the words *substantially related* sound a lot like *necessary,* and *important* sounds a lot like *compelling,* the courts intend the intermediate scrutiny test to be a little easier for governments to pass. Therefore, these words are not to be construed as synonymous and should be viewed as code words for the level of critical review a law will receive from the courts.

An example of a case in which a governmental rule passed intermediate scrutiny is *Rostker v. Goldberg* (1981). In this case, the Court concluded that women were unsuited to combat roles, so excluding women from the draft registration was substantially related to achieving the government's important goal of maximizing military flexibility, since those serving in noncombat roles might need to be shifted to combat roles during a confrontation. Most of the time, however, gender-based classifications do not survive intermediate scrutiny because they often reflect archaic notions about women's capabilities, or function to treat women differently without a good reason. An example of a case in which a gender-based rule failed the intermediate scrutiny test is found in *Ludtke v. Kuhn* (1978).

Ludtke v. Kuhn

461 F. Supp. 86 (S.D.N.Y. 1978)   **CASE OPINION**

[FACTS

In 1975, Major League Baseball Commissioner Bowie Kuhn implemented a policy that called for all major league baseball teams to take a unified stand against the admission of women sportswriters into clubhouses. During the 1977 World Series, plaintiff Melissa Ludtke, a sportswriter for *Sports Illustrated* magazine, was denied admission to the locker room of the New York Yankees when she sought to join her male counterparts there immediately after a game to conduct postgame interviews. Ludtke sued, claiming an Equal Protection Clause violation because she was being intentionally treated differently from similarly situated sportswriters who were male.]

HOLDING

The court found that the rule in question did violate the Equal Protection Clause and enjoined the defendants from enforcing the policy of totally excluding female sports reporters from the locker rooms, requiring them to adopt an alternative means of preserving player privacy.

RATIONALE

Defendants say women reporters are excluded in order (1) to protect the privacy of those players who are undressed or who are in various stages of undressing and getting ready to shower; (2) to protect the image of baseball as a family sport; and (3) [to ensure] preservation of traditional notions of decency and propriety.

Another pivotal fact that is also not disputed is that fresh-off-the-field interviews are important to the work of sports reporters and will give a competitive advantage to those who have access to the ballplayers at that juncture, particularly during World Series games.

Another critical consideration is the admission that there are several other less sweeping alternatives to the present policy of blanket exclusion of women reporters. Counsel for the defendants admitted that those players who are desirous of undressing can retreat to their cubicles in the clubhouse. There the players can be shielded from the "roving eyes" of any female reporters by having each cubicle furnished with a curtain or swinging door. It is also conceded that the player who is undressed and wishes to move about in that state can use a towel to shield himself from view.

* * *

[The court went on to use an entwinement test to find that Yankee Stadium was so entwined with city government, because of its devotion to public use, its lease to the Yankees from the city, and the extensive involvement of public funds in the renovation and maintenance of the facility, that the defendants who use the facility could be considered state actors for purposes of the Equal Protection Clause analysis. It further found that the defendants had intentionally treated Ludtke differently from her colleagues solely on the basis of her sex.]

* * *

"To withstand constitutional challenge . . . classifications by gender must serve important governmental objectives and must be substantially related to achievement of those objectives." *Craig v. Boren*, 429 U.S. 190, 197 (1976). . . . Defendants have asserted, as justification for the complete exclusion of female reporters from the clubhouse at Yankee Stadium, their interest in protecting the privacy of the ballplayers while undressing in the locker room.

The right to privacy is of constitutional dimension, and its protection is thus undeniably an important objective. It cannot be said on these facts, however, that there is a sufficiently substantial relationship between that objective on one hand and the total exclusion of women from the Yankee locker room on the other to pass constitutional muster. . . .

At least during the World Series games, male members of the news media with television cameras have been allowed to enter the Yankee locker room immediately after the games and broadcast live from that location. In this connection, only a backdrop behind the player standing in front of the camera is provided to shield other players from the "roving eye" of the camera. These locker room encounters are viewed by mass audiences, which include many women and children. This practice, coupled with defendants' practice of refusing to allow accredited women sports reporters to enter the locker room, shows that the latter is "substantially related" only to maintaining the locker room as an all-male preserve.

* * *

The court holds that defendants' policy of total exclusion of women sports reporters from the locker room at Yankee Stadium is not substantially related to the privacy protection objective and thus deprives plaintiff Ludtke of that equal protection of the laws which is guaranteed her by the Fourteenth Amendment.

Questions

1. The New York Yankees and Major League Baseball are not government actors. How did the court justify allowing plaintiff Ludtke to use the Equal Protection Clause to sue Major League Baseball? Why do you think they justified it?

2. Why did the defendants' exclusionary policy flunk the intermediate scrutiny test?

3. Does this case provide any hints as to why sex discrimination claims are given intermediate, rather than strict, scrutiny?

Rational basis review. The easiest test to pass, and thus the lowest of the three in the hierarchy, is called **rational basis review**. This test is used for group classifications other than gender or suspect classifications. Under this test, the government must simply have a rational basis for adopting the questioned law to accomplish a legitimate goal. In other words, the law must reflect a reasonable means of achieving a legitimate government interest. Almost all laws to which this test is applied are upheld by the courts. All it takes is a reasonable rationale supporting the rule.

For example, assume that a public university has a policy of refusing to hire student-athletes for certain jobs on campus. If an affected student-athlete were to challenge the policy on the grounds that student-athletes were being unfairly singled out from the rest of the student body, this claim would receive rational basis review. The group "student-athletes" is not a suspect class like race or a quasi-suspect class like sex. As long as the university could articulate a legitimate goal for the hiring policy—for example, that it would promote the educational welfare of athletes by protecting their available study time—and could show that the policy is a rational means of accomplishing that goal, the policy would withstand an equal protection challenge.

Discrimination on the Basis of Age

Discrimination based on the age of the employee is becoming increasingly relevant in today's workplace as businesses seek to cut costs. Older employees making higher salaries may be targeted for termination because a younger staff is generally a less expensive staff. The federal statute that protects older workers was passed in 1967 and is called the Age Discrimination in Employment Act (ADEA; see Exhibit 6.8). The ADEA applies to employers with 20 or more employees and, unlike Title VII, it covers employees in American Indian tribes, religious organizations, and private membership clubs, such as country clubs. However, in *Kimel v. Florida Board of Regents* (2000), the Supreme Court ruled that, unlike Title VII, the ADEA does not allow a private right of action against state government employers.

Employees over the age of 40 are protected by the ADEA, and currently there is no upper age limit. That is, an employer must treat an 80-year-old employee the same as a 30-year-old. Although research has shown that older workers are more reliable and committed to their jobs, are absent less often, and are harder working than younger employees, often employers have the opposite perception (Bennett-Alexander & Pincus, 1998). The ADEA was intended to protect older workers who may be limited by such stereotypical views about their ability or willingness to perform. Consequently, it does not protect young workers from discrimination based on the notion that they

| The Age Discrimination in Employment Act of 1967, 20 U.S.C. § 623. | EXHIBIT | 6.8 |

Section 4(a) It shall be unlawful for an employer—

(1) to fail or refuse to hire or to discharge any individual or otherwise discriminate against any individual with respect to his compensation, terms, conditions, or privileges of employment, because of such individual's age;

(2) to limit, segregate, or classify his employees in any way which would deprive or tend to deprive any individual of employment opportunities or otherwise adversely affect his status as an employee, because of such individual's age; or

(3) to reduce the wage rate of any employee in order to comply with this chapter.

are too young (*General Dynamics Land Systems, Inc. v. Cline*, 2004). Examples of age discrimination that would be covered under the statute include:

- Forcing retirement due to age
- Including age preferences in job advertisements
- Assigning older workers to jobs that do not allow them to be competitive for higher-level jobs within the organization
- Promoting a younger worker over an older one because the older worker may be planning to retire soon
- Hiring a younger worker over an older worker who is better qualified

Because the language of the ADEA mirrors the language of Title VII, the courts usually analyze ADEA claims in the same manner as Title VII disparate treatment claims, using the *McDonnell Douglas* burden-shifting analysis (discussed earlier) for claims resting largely on circumstantial evidence (see *Reeves v. Sanderson Plumbing, Products, Inc.*, 2000). That is, the plaintiff must prove a prima facie case of age discrimination, then the defendant must offer a SLNDR defense, and then the plaintiff must disprove the proffered defense or show that it is pretext for discrimination. The disparate impact theory of liability is not allowed under the ADEA, nor are mixed-motives claims, in which a plaintiff alleges that the adverse action stems from both permissible and impermissible employer motives (*Gross v. FBL Financial Services, Inc.*, 2009). Instead, a viable age discrimination suit requires the plaintiff to sustain the burden of proving intentional discrimination.

The statute enumerates additional defenses that employers may use in responding to an ADEA claim, which include good cause, bona fide occupational qualification, reasonable factors other than age, and seniority. When employees' job performance is deemed unsatisfactory or they have violated workplace rules, an employer may discipline or discharge them, regardless of their age, under the **good cause** defense. If an age classification is a BFOQ that is reasonably necessary for satisfactory performance of the job, then the employer is justified in imposing an age restriction. In such a case, the employer would have to prove a factual basis for believing that older workers could not safely and effectively perform the essential job functions. This BFOQ defense is usually a difficult defense to prove, and in cases of jobs that impact public safety (e.g., firefighters and police officers) the ADEA already provides an exemption allowing the imposition of mandatory retirement.

The ADEA provides the **reasonable factors other than age** defense for use when, for example, an employer has taken adverse action against an employee because restructuring an organization required the elimination of a position or because the employee's work performance had deteriorated to the point of being unsatisfactory. In the latter case, the argument would be that the person was no longer doing acceptable work and was fired for that reason, not because of their age. The Supreme Court has interpreted this defense to mean that an adverse employment action motivated by an age-neutral factor that somehow correlates with age does not constitute disparate treatment of an older worker and thus does not violate the ADEA (*Hazen Paper Co. v. Biggins*, 1993—termination of employee to avoid paying pension benefits was not age discrimination).

The following hypothetical case illustrates how this defense might be applied in the context of a sport-related employment action.

considering . . .   REASONABLE FACTORS OTHER THAN AGE

Assume the Charlottesville Parks and Recreation Department has a hiring policy that ties salary to years of experience; thus, the more years of experience, the higher the salary that must be paid to a new hire. Two people apply for the job of Physical Activities Director. One is Juanita Oldpro, who is 56 years old and has 25 years of experience in similar positions. The other is Justin Newby, who is 30 years old and has five years of relevant experience. The organization cannot afford to hire Oldpro because her years of experience require a salary that exceeds its budget by $10,000, so Newby is hired instead.

Questions

- If you were the hiring official at the Parks and Recreation Department, what would you tell Oldpro when you informed her that she did not get the job?

- If Oldpro threatened to sue you based on the fact that you hired a less qualified younger person, how would you respond to her?

- If Oldpro did in fact sue the Parks and Recreation Department for age discrimination, would your reason for not hiring her, if proven to be true, be considered acceptable under the ADEA?

For a sport-related case, see _Austin v. Cornell University_ (1995).

Note how you would answer the questions and then check your responses using the Analysis & Discussion at the end of this chapter.

Discrimination on the Basis of Disability

As of May 2009, people with disabilities constitute approximately 22.9 percent of the potential workforce in America. The unemployment rate for people with disabilities is approximately 13.7 percent compared to 8.9 percent for persons with no disabilities (U. S. Dept. of Labor, 2009). Many employment decisions about disabled applicants are grounded in stereotypes, fear, or ignorance about the disability involved or the capabilities of individuals with disabilities. Two federal statutes operate to protect persons with disabilities from workplace discrimination: § 504 of the Rehabilitation Act of 1973 and the Americans with Disabilities Act of 1990 (see Exhibit 6.9).

Section 504 applies to recipients of federal funds, so it was not until the passage of the ADA in 1990 that protection of the employment rights of disabled persons was extended to the private sector (more specifically, to employers with 15 or more employees). This extension of protection to the private sector is the primary difference between the two laws. In fact, the courts have used virtually the same analysis in deciding ADA cases as was developed for § 504 cases.

These laws prohibit discrimination against a qualified individual with a physical or mental impairment that substantially limits one or more major life activities, if the individual, with or without reasonable accommodation, can perform the essential duties of the job. There is no all-inclusive list of covered disabilities; instead, the courts are supposed to make their decisions on a case-by-case basis, paying attention to the particular facts in each case. If an accommodation is necessary to enable an

EXHIBIT	6.9	Federal statutes that protect persons with disabilities from employment discrimination.

Section 504 of the Rehabilitation Act of 1973

No otherwise qualified individual with handicaps in the United States shall, solely by reason of his handicap, be excluded from the participation in, be denied the benefits of, or be subjected to discrimination under any program or activity receiving federal financial assistance or under any program or activity conducted by any executive agency.

Title I of the Americans with Disabilities Act (ADA)

No covered entity shall discriminate against a qualified individual with a disability because of the disability of such individual in regard to job application procedures, the hiring, advancement, or discharge of employees, employee compensation, job training, and other terms, conditions, and privileges of employment.

employee to perform the essential job functions, it must be reasonable in scope and cost and not impose an undue hardship on the employer or constitute a fundamental alteration of the nature of the employer's program.

The Supreme Court has ruled that the ADA may not be used to sue a state government employer because Congress did not intend this statute to abrogate the Eleventh Amendment **sovereign immunity** (i.e., governmental immunity) from lawsuits enjoyed by the states (*University of Alabama v. Garrett,* 2001). With this ruling, legal recourse against public school and university employers was narrowed. Aggrieved employees have to bring their disability claims under either § 504 or the Equal Protection Clause. Equal protection claims will be analyzed using rational basis review because disability is not considered a suspect classification (*City of Cleburne v. Cleburne Living Center, Inc.,* 1985).

The ADA was amended by the Americans with Disabilities Act Amendments Act of 2008 (ADAAA), which became effective in January 2009 and made some significant changes with regard to the interpretation and application of the ADA. The stated purpose of the ADAAA is to reinstate the availability of a broad scope of protection by rejecting certain requirements established in Supreme Court decisions and in EEOC regulations that are more restrictive than Congress intended (ADAAA, 2008). In particular, the ADAAA states that the terms "substantially limits" and "major life activity" must not be interpreted as significantly restrictive, and instructs the EEOC to revise its regulations accordingly. As a result of the new law, a significant amount of case law may now be of questionable reliability as precedent for deciding future cases brought under the ADA. A helpful resource for understanding the ADAAA is an official "Notice" on the EEOC's website (www.eeoc.gov/ada/amendments_notice.html) that provides a concise explanation of the changes made by the new law (EEOC, 2009).

Elements of a § 504/ADA claim

The elements necessary for a successful § 504/ADA claim include:

- Plaintiff has a covered disability.

- The disability substantially limits a major life activity.
- Plaintiff was discriminated against on the basis of that disability.
- No reasonable accommodation was made.

Covered disabilities. Examples of covered disabilities include:

- *Physical impairments* such as blindness, deafness, and cerebral palsy
- *Mental/psychological disorders* such as learning disabilities, schizophrenia, epilepsy, and dyslexia
- *Infectious/contagious diseases* such as tuberculosis and the human immuno-deficiency virus (HIV)

The Court in *Toyota Motor Mfg. v. Williams* (2002) held that a **disabling impairment** is one that is permanent or long-term and that is not likely to be overcome with rest or treatment. This decision attempts to clarify the distinction between true disabilities that are covered by the laws and temporary injuries or conditions that are not. Earlier, the Supreme Court had also ruled that impairment corrections such as eyeglasses and high blood pressure medicine should be mitigating factors in determining whether the treated condition substantially limited a major life activity (*Sutton v. United Airlines, Inc.,* 1999). Some of the standards enunciated in these two cases have been renounced by the ADAAA of 2008. For example, the only treatment measures allowed to be considered as mitigating factors on substantial limitation of a major life activity are ordinary eyeglasses or contact lenses. And the statute specifies that a non-covered transitory impairment is one with a duration of six months or less (ADAAA, 2008).

In addition to people with current disabilities, the ADA covers people with past disabilities when the individual's record of having had an impairment might lead to discrimination. Examples include past drug addiction or alcoholism, where the individual is no longer engaged in substance abuse.

The ADA also covers situations where individuals are discriminated against because they are perceived as having a disability, when in fact they do not. Examples might be someone with severe facial scarring or someone who is a cancer survivor. Some employers believe that facial disfiguration might negatively impact the employee's ability to deal successfully with customers, or that cancer will recur, and thus they are unwilling to hire people with these characteristics even though they are not truly disabled.

The ADAAA makes clear that a plaintiff using the "regarded as having" provision is not required to prove that the perceived disability substantially limits a major life activity. While at first glance this provision would seem to open the door to nearly any perceived disability being covered by the ADA with no need to prove substantial limitation, there is another provision meant to limit abuse of this provision by excluding users of the "regarded as having" prong from being entitled to receive a reasonable accommodation. A "regarded as having" plaintiff could thus try to sue to get her job back, for example, but would not be able to get it back if she could not perform the essential job duties without reasonable accommodation. However, if a "regarded as having" plaintiff who did not have a truly disabling condition succeeded in winning a lawsuit, then he could seek reinstatement to his job. According to one commentator, this last scenario illustrates the essence of an ADA claim—to prevent employment discrimination based on fears, myths, and stereotypes about disability (Long, 2008).

Substantial limit on a major life activity. After determining that an applicant has a covered disability, the next step in the analysis is to assess whether or not that impairment substantially limits a **major life activity.** Major life activities include but are not limited to fundamental aspects of human living, such as "caring for oneself, performing manual tasks, seeing, hearing, eating, sleeping, walking, standing, lifting, bending, speaking, breathing, learning, reading, concentrating, and working" (ADAAA, 2008, Sec. 3(2)(A)). A disability substantially limits working, for example, when the individual's ability to perform a broad range of jobs, not just one particular job or skill, is substantially limited (*Otis v. Canadian Valley-Reeves Meat Co., 1995*). A disability substantially limits learning when it affects learning in a broad sense, instead of limiting learning only in one type of skill. The new law has added a nonexhaustive list of major bodily functions that also count as major life activities, such as immunal, digestive, neurological, respiratory, circulatory, and reproductive functions (ADAAA, 2008, Sec. 3(2)(B)).

The *Lemire v. Silva* (2000) case illustrates how courts determine what counts as a covered disability and how they analyze whether that disability substantially limits a major life activity. The court's opinion also demonstrates the burden-shifting analysis used to determine liability in disability discrimination cases.

Lemire v. Silva

104 F. Supp. 2d 80 (D. Mass. 2000)   **CASE OPINION**

[FACTS

Plaintiff Cassie Lemire was a field hockey coach at Sandwich High School from 1992 to 1996. She suffered from a panic disorder with agoraphobia, and her symptoms included anxiety attacks, fear of going to public places, and fear of being alone, among others. She was taking antidepressant medication during her coaching employment, but even with medication she would suffer occasionally from her symptoms. Lemire's psychiatrist reported that her disorder had inhibited her ability to travel far from home, her ability to interact with others outside her family, and her ability to work outside of her home.

In 1995, fliers were distributed at one of the field hockey games that contained a copy of one of Lemire's appointment cards for her psychological treatment, and that further read: "Do you think this person should be coaching your child? This is not a stable person." Some parents later complained to the principal and the athletic

director about the suitability of Lemire as a coach based on the idea that her panic disorder made her unstable. In 1997, the principal decided to institute a formal application process for the position of field hockey coach and told Lemire she would have to apply and be considered for rehire by a search committee. Plaintiff claims she was the only incumbent coach ever to have to be screened by a search committee. The search committee recommended that Lemire be rehired, and she was. Then a petition was circulated protesting her appointment, and the principal appointed an independent counselor to meet with the players and report back to him. The counselor's report indicated that the athletes respected Lemire's technical expertise but distrusted her because her behavior was unprofessional and demoralizing to them. Plaintiff then was discharged, and she brought suit under the Americans with Disabilities Act. Defendants moved for summary judgment.]

HOLDING

The court denied defendants' motion for summary judgment on her ADA claim.

RATIONALE

The defendant has admitted, for purposes of summary judgment, that the plaintiff suffers from a mental impairment within the meaning of the ADA. The defendant argues, however, that plaintiff's impairment fails to limit substantially any of her major life activities. The plaintiff claims in response that her mental impairment has substantially limited major life activities: working and interacting with others. . . .

Working is undoubtedly a major life activity under the ADA. The EEOC has defined it as such in its implementing regulations. See 29 C.F.R. section 1630.2(i) (1999).

* * *

The ability to interact with others, if defined broadly to include the most basic types of human interactions, is a major life activity. Human beings are fundamentally social beings. The ability to interact with others is an inherent part of what it means to be human. . . . The ability to interact is . . . also essential to contemporary life. . . .

The ability to travel is also a major life activity. . . . The ability to leave one's home and travel short distances is necessary in most cases to form and maintain social ties, earn a living, and purchase food and clothing. It is thus also at least as significant and as basic as learning and working.

The ability to concentrate is not a major life activity. . . . [L]imitations on the ability to concentrate can be more appropriately framed as limitations on the major life activities of working, learning, or speaking.

* * *

The evidence proffered by plaintiff demonstrates a genuine issue of material fact as to whether Mrs. Lemire was substantially limited in her ability to work [and] interact with others. . . .

* * *

In determining whether the plaintiff is substantially limited in a major life activity, a court must consider three factors: (1) the nature and severity of the impairment; (2) the duration or expected duration of the impairment; and (3) the permanent or long term impact, or the expected permanent or long term impact of or resulting from the impairment. The court must take into account, also, the mitigating measures the plaintiff employs, such as medication.

In order to demonstrate that her ability to work is substantially limited, plaintiff must show that she is "significantly restricted in the ability to perform either a class of jobs or a broad range of jobs in various classes as compared to the average individual having comparable training, skills, and abilities. The inability to perform a single, particular job does not constitute a substantial limitation in the major life activity of working."

The plaintiff . . . had to quit a security job in 1996 after four months of employment because she experienced several panic attacks while at work. . . . Her treating psychiatrist, Dr. Julius Treibergs, has stated that her psychiatric disorder impairs her ability to work outside the home, to interact with people outside her family, and travel far away from home. A jury could infer from this evidence, if credited, that the plaintiff's mental impairment forecloses her from a sufficiently broad range of jobs to limit substantially her ability to work.

* * *

According to Ms. Lemire's treating psychiatrist . . . her ability to interact with others in crowded places . . . has and will continue to be impaired. A genuine dispute of material fact exists as to whether plaintiff's inability to interact with others in crowded places is a substantial limitation on her ability to interact with others.

* * *

An examination of an employee's "qualified" status requires consideration of whether the employee could perform the essential functions of the job and, if not, whether any reasonable accommodation by the employer would enable her to perform those functions. . . . The plaintiff has provided a sufficient explanation for a jury to find that . . . she was able to perform the essential functions of her job at the time her employment was terminated.

* * *

The plaintiff has presented a prima facie case of discrimination. . . . The burden thus shifts to the defendants to demonstrate a legitimate, non-discriminatory reason for firing plaintiff.

The defendants claim that they dismissed plaintiff because of Mrs. Warren's independent [counselor's] report. In those circumstances, the plaintiff needs to show that a reasonable jury could infer from the proffered evidence of record that defendants' stated reason is a mere pretext.

I conclude that the plaintiff has proffered sufficient evidence to warrant a reasonable jury in finding pretext. The testimony of Amy Orrico and Lee Reis is indirect evidence that the real reason for plaintiff's dismissal was her mental impairment. [Their testimony included evidence that a teammate's parent, Joseph Silva, told them plaintiff was an unsuitable coach because of her panic disorder; that he convinced the team to circulate the petition protesting Lemire's being rehired; that he met with the principal to urge him to fire Lemire; and that he had told them Lemire had been fired because she was seeing a psychiatrist.] The defendants' failure to inform plaintiff of the reason for her dismissal at the time is further indirect evidence that the real reason was discrimination. Finally, inconsistencies among defendants' contentions about when and on what basis Principal Norton decided to fire plaintiff are further indirect evidence of pretext.

Questions

1. How did the court reason that Lemire's panic disorder substantially limited her major life activities?

2. Could the defendants have done anything differently that might have given the court less reason to find that their SLNDR defense might be pretext for discrimination?

Competitive Advantage

STRATEGIES

Hiring, Promotion, and Termination

- Review all job application materials and interview questions to ensure that there are no inappropriate questions about information such as marital status and childcare, since these could be construed as evidence of sex discrimination.

- Advertise open positions and recruit applicants in such a way as to encourage a diverse pool of applicants.

- If you choose to implement an affirmative action plan, be sure to use a temporary method to move toward hiring goals. Do not state hiring goals (which are legitimate targets) in the form of strictly specified numerical requirements (which are unlawful quotas).

- Review workplace policies to ensure that hiring, training, scheduling, benefits, promotion, leave taking, and termination processes are provided or applied fairly to *all* employees.

(continued)

Discrimination based on the disability. The alleged discriminatory treatment must be based on the plaintiff's disability rather than on other factors. For example, in the *Lemire* case, the plaintiff had to establish that she was fired not because the independent counselor determined that she had engaged in a pattern of unprofessional conduct but because she had a panic disorder.

No effort at reasonable accommodation. If the disabled applicant or employee can, with reasonable accommodation, perform the essential functions of the job, he must not be subjected to employment discrimination. According to § 101 of the ADA, **reasonable accommodations** may include:

- Rendering facilities and equipment readily accessible to and usable by those with disabilities

- Restructuring jobs by such means as modifying work schedules

- Reassigning an employee to a vacant position (only required when there is an existing reassignment policy available to all employees)

- Modifying qualifying examinations or training materials, and providing interpreters or readers

The courts have approved accommodations costing up to $15,000 as reasonable, but what is considered reasonable rather than an **undue hardship** (excessive monetary cost or administrative burden) will depend in part upon the financial resources of the organization. The U. S. Department of Labor calculated average costs of accommodations held reasonable by the courts between 1992 and 1999, and found that 20 percent cost nothing, 51 percent cost under $500, 11 percent cost between $501 and $1,000, 6 percent cost between $1,001 and $2,000, 8 percent cost between $2,001 and $5,000, and 4 percent exceeded $5,000 (Job Accommodation Network, 1999). Thus, two-thirds of accommodations deemed reasonable by the courts cost less than $2,000, with half costing less than $500. Of employers surveyed between 2004 and 2006, 46 percent reported that accommodations they had made cost nothing, 45 percent reported a one-time cost, typically of approximately $500 ("Workplace accommodations," 2009).

Aside from the issue of expense, types of accommodations held to be unreasonable include:

- Tolerating employee misconduct stemming from a disability (*Maddox v. University of Tennessee,* 1995)
- Tolerating frequent absences from work (*Jackson v. Veterans' Administration,* 1994)
- Redesigning a job by eliminating many of the essential job functions that the employee could no longer perform (*Russell v. Southeastern Pennsylvania Transportation Authority,* 1993)

Significant risk exception

The significant risk exception to an ADA claim is exemplified in *School Board of Nassau County v. Arline* (1987), where the court assessed whether a teacher with tuberculosis posed a significant risk to her students. The analysis involves examining the severity of the risk and the likelihood of transmission occurring, as well as potential means of reducing the risk. If the risk is or can be made insignificant, the employee is protected by the law and must be allowed to continue performing the job. If, however, the risk does pose a direct threat to the safety and well-being of others, the employer is under no legal obligation to hire or maintain the employment of the affected individual.

In many sports-related disability cases, an issue arises as to whether an individual's disability poses a significant risk to others. The risk might be collision with an assistive device such as a metal brace or wheelchair, or contracting an infectious disease. For example, Magic Johnson, while an employee of the Los Angeles Lakers basketball team, was diagnosed as HIV-positive. If he had been terminated due to his disease and had sued, the central issue would have been whether his HIV-positive status posed a direct threat (significant risk) of harm to the other participants.

Competitive Advantage

STRATEGIES

Hiring, Promotion, and Termination (cont.)

- In case it becomes necessary to justify dismissal of an employee, keep records of performance appraisals that evaluate employees' performance as objectively as possible.

- Carefully define the essential functions of the jobs for which employees are hired. Review all job announcements and position descriptions to ensure that only the duties essential to the job are presented.

- Make reasonable accommodations for employees with disabilities by ensuring that facilities are accessible and assistive equipment is available.

- Be aware that employers may not require a medical examination except *after* an offer of employment has been made. They then may withdraw the job offer based on the exam results *only* if the exam results show that the applicant cannot perform the job requirements after reasonable accommodation has been made.

- Seek external perspectives when trying to determine whether a proposed accommodation for a disability is reasonable or constitutes an undue hardship. The EEOC provides helpful information on its website at www.eeoc.gov/policy/docs/accommodation.html.

- Avoid asking interview questions with potentially discriminatory implications (see Exhibit 6.10). Interview questions for applicants with disabilities should center on what kinds of things applicants *can* do and what qualifications they *do* possess relative to the job instead of what they cannot do or whether they have disabilities (see Exhibit 6.11).

EXHIBIT	6.10	Guide to appropriate pre-employment inquiries.

TOPIC	ACCEPTABLE	UNACCEPTABLE (POTENTIALLY DISCRIMINATORY)
Citizenship	Statement by employer that, if hired, applicant may be required to submit proof of authorization to work in the United States	"Are you a U.S. citizen?" Requirement that applicant produce naturalization papers or first papers
Age	"Are you over 18 years of age?" "If hired, can you furnish proof of age?"	"How old are you?" "What is your birthdate?"
Marital/Family Status	"Do you have any responsibilities that would conflict with your ability to perform your job duties?"	"Are you married?" "Do you have any children?" "What are your childcare arrangements?"
Religion	None	"What is your religious denomination?" "What religious holidays do you observe?"
Race/Ethnicity	None	Complexion, color of skin, or other questions directly or indirectly indicating race or ethnicity
Arrests/Convictions	"Have you ever been convicted of a crime?" (Clarify that conviction will be considered only as it relates to ability to perform the indicated job.)	"Have you ever been arrested?"
Education	Applicant's academic, vocational or professional education; schools attended	"What year did you graduate from high school (college)?"
Physical Condition	"Can you perform all of the duties outlined in the job description?"	"Do you have any physical disabilities?"

In *Anderson v. Little League Baseball* (1992), a man confined to a wheelchair had served as first-base coach for three years without incident when the national Little League imposed a policy forbidding people in wheelchairs from coaching the bases. The policy was based on the idea that the wheelchair posed a significant risk to players who might be attempting to catch a foul ball. The court ruled that there was no evidence of significant risk, since he had served as first-base coach safely for three years, and that the policy was based on stereotypes about the capabilities of people in wheelchairs.

Defenses

To defend against a disability claim, an employer must show that the adverse employment action was not *solely* due to the plaintiff's disability but was job-related. For example, in *Maddox v. University of Tennessee* (1995), an assistant football coach alleged that he was fired because of his disability, which was alcoholism. The court found that the university terminated him not solely because of his alcoholism but because he embarrassed his employer by being arrested for drunk driving and being uncooperative with the arresting officer. Therefore, the court upheld his dismissal.

An employer could also show that the disabled person was fired or not hired because she could not perform the essential functions of the job. To succeed on this type of job-relatedness defense, the essential job functions must have been *objectively* defined by the employer such that they conform to business necessity and must not have been formulated with the purpose of excluding employees with disabilities.

Examples of questions related to disabilities that an employer should not ask on an application or during an interview.	EXHIBIT	6.11

Do you have a heart condition? Do you have asthma or any other difficulties breathing?

Do you have a disability that would interfere with your ability to perform the job?

How many days were you sick last year?

Have you ever filed for workers' compensation? Have you ever been injured on the job?

Have you ever been treated for mental health problems?

What prescription drugs are you currently taking?

Source: EEOC, www.eeoc.gov/facts/jobapplicant.html.

An employer may not require a medical examination of a prospective employee until after an employment offer has been made. If that exam shows that the applicant, with reasonable accommodation, would remain unable to perform the essential job duties, then the employer may retract the offer. The Rhode Island Commission for Human Rights awarded $20,000 in back wages to a man who was passed over for a high school softball coaching job partly because he refused to take a physical examination unlawfully requested by school district officials before an employment offer after they found out about his prior medical history (Davis, 2006).

Moreover, even if all the elements for a successful disability claim are met, an employer may escape liability if the accommodation necessary to allow a disabled person to do the job would impose an undue burden on the employer or require a fundamental alteration in the nature of the employer's business. In *PGA Tour, Inc. v. Martin* (2001), the Supreme Court held that granting a waiver of the rule mandating that professional golfers walk the course to a golfer with a severe circulatory disorder in his legs would not constitute a fundamental alteration in the game of golf. Thus, the Tour was required to grant the waiver as a reasonable accommodation of Casey Martin's disability. This case, however, was decided under Title III of the ADA (discrimination in places of public accommodation) rather than as an employment discrimination case because individual sport professional athletes are not considered employees. Therefore, we discuss this case in Chapters 14 and 16 when we cover private clubs, places of public accommodation, and sport facility/event issues.

COMPENSATION DISCRIMINATION

During the 1990s the issue of gender equity in coaching salaries surfaced in the sport industry. Coaches of women's college teams, primarily in the sport of basketball, have filed lawsuits seeking salaries comparable to their counterparts coaching the men's basketball team at the same university. These lawsuits claim that sex-based compensation discrimination occurred because the coaches of the women's teams were being paid less for doing the same job as the coaches of the men's teams. These suits are typically brought under three laws: Title VII, Title IX, and the Equal Pay Act of 1963.

The elements of sex discrimination claims under Title VII and Title IX were discussed earlier. The Equal Pay Act (29 U.S.C. § 206(d)(1)), which is part of the Fair Labor Standards Act, requires that women be paid a similar wage to what men receive for doing similar work. That is, gender cannot be the basis for giving lower pay to an employee who does substantially equal work, which is defined as work requiring "equal skill, effort, and responsibility, and which [is] performed under similar working conditions." In the context of sport, coaching skills and effort required are not generally disputed. Instead, as we will see in the *Stanley* and *Perdue* cases, the central issue is usually differences in coaching responsibilities, such as revenue generation by filling stadiums or arenas with fans, public speaking, and fund-raising activities.

Under the Equal Pay Act, pay differentials are permitted when they are based on seniority or merit, or for any reason other than gender. It is a comparison of the content of jobs, not a comparison of job titles, that determines whether the jobs will be considered similar. The jobs must be substantially equal in order for the court to find for the plaintiff.

The landmark case on this issue to date is *Stanley v. University of Southern California* (*Stanley II,* 1999), in which Marianne Stanley, then coach of the University of Southern California (USC) women's basketball team, refused during contract renegotiation to accept a salary less than that of George Raveling, then coach of the USC men's basketball team. USC refused to match his salary, and Stanley sued the university under the Equal Pay Act.

In reviewing Stanley's request for a preliminary injunction to keep her job (*Stanley I,* 1994), the 9th Circuit Court initially held that coaching women's basketball was not substantially the same job as coaching men's basketball at the Division I level for three reasons: men's basketball coaches had greater responsibilities relative to public speaking and fund-raising than did coaches of women's basketball; the pressure on the men's coach to generate 90 times the revenue of the women's team was greater; and Coach Raveling had substantially better skills, qualifications, and experience than Stanley. Raveling had an educational background in marketing and nine years of experience in that field. He had 31 years of coaching experience whereas Stanley had 17. Additionally, Raveling had experience as an author, actor, and television commentator. In comparison, Stanley had had several speaking engagements, had won four national championships (Raveling had won none), and she had taken her team to three NCAA tournament playoffs while she was at USC.

In the eyes of the court, however, Stanley's qualifications did not match up to Raveling's. The court ultimately concluded that the question of substantial equality of the two coaching jobs need not be decided because the case could be decided on other grounds. The court based its final decision on the grounds that Stanley's lower pay was justified by a reason other than gender—that is, USC paid her less because she was less qualified as a coach than her counterpart (*Stanley II,* 1999).

In contrast to *Stanley* is *Perdue v. City University of New York* (1998). Molly Perdue, former women's basketball coach and women's sports administrator at Brooklyn College, successfully sued the college under the Equal Pay Act for salary discrepancies between her coaching salary and that of the men's basketball coach, and her administrator's salary and that of the men's athletics administrator. Regarding her coaching responsibilities, Perdue established that she and the men's coach "coached 'basically' the same season, the same number of games, the same number of players, and the same number of practices. . . . Moreover, they both managed their team's budgets, scholarships, assistant coaches, scouting of opponents, game preparation, and ordering of equipment. . . . [T]hey both were responsible for the supervision, guidance, and counseling of athletes, and for team conduct . . . [and] were accountable to the same person" (*Perdue,* 1998, p. 334).

With respect to her duties as an athletics administrator, Perdue provided evidence that she and the men's program administrator "had the same eleven duties . . . [including responsibility] for the daily operations of sports, game scheduling, organizing team budgets, organizing student orientation, and administering the athletic program . . . [and] both reported to the same individual" (*Perdue,* 1998, p. 334). Thus, the court concluded that the jury had appropriately found that Perdue performed substantially equal work on jobs requiring equal skill, effort, and responsibility, under similar working conditions, as her male counterparts, but for less pay. Therefore, it awarded her $134,829 in back wages, $5,262 in unpaid retirement benefits, and $134,829 in liquidated damages, in addition to $85,000 in compensatory damages, for a total of $359,920, plus prejudgment interest on the back pay and compensatory damages in the sum of $83,264.94 through May 31, 1998, and $43.25 *per diem* to the date that judgment was entered. It also awarded Perdue attorneys fees in the amount of $339,399.60 and expenses in the amount of $16,982.19.

The major limitation of the application of Title VII and the Equal Pay Act to the coaching salary equity issue is that the sex of the team and not the sex of the coach is the primary determinant of lower salaries for coaches of women's sports. These two laws, however, provide a remedy based on the sex of the employee. In *Jackson v. Armstrong School District* (1977), the women's basketball coaches in the school district were all earning the same salary regardless of their gender, whereas coaches of men's basketball were more highly paid. The court ruled that Title VII protects claimants on the basis of *their* sex and not the sex of the team they coach.

Over half of collegiate women's basketball teams are coached by men, and thus salary discrimination based on the sex of the team coached would negatively affect male coaches as well as females. So if Geno Auriemma, coach of the University of Connecticut women's basketball team, were receiving a lower salary than the UConn men's basketball coach, he would have no remedy under Title VII or the Equal Pay Act. The only recourse for him would be a Title IX claim. However, the 6th Circuit Court has suggested in dictum that a male coach of a women's team is not a member of a class protected by Title IX, even though he is affiliated with a protected class (the members of his team; *Arceneaux v. Vanderbilt University,* 2001). The courts have determined that Title IX employment discrimination claims should be analyzed in the same manner as Title VII claims, so most of the time Title IX has been as ineffective as Title VII in resolving the coaching salary issue (but see *Tyler v. Howard University* (1993), where the plaintiff women's basketball coach prevailed under Title IX and the Equal Pay Act, and *Pitts v. Oklahoma* (1994), where the women's golf coach successfully sued under Title VII and Title IX).

In 1997, the EEOC issued its *Enforcement Guidelines on Sex Discrimination in the Compensation of Sports Coaches in Educational Institutions.* These guidelines, while not law, may be used by the courts as a persuasive indication of the intent behind the law when they decide future coaching salary cases. The existence of these guidelines, the success of some plaintiffs in the courts, and the desire to avoid the costs and negative publicity of litigation appear to have encouraged many university athletic departments with high-profile women's basketball teams to adjust the salaries of their women's team coaches to amounts comparable to their male counterparts (Claussen, 1995).

The EEOC guidelines run counter to some of the case law in several ways (see in particular *Stanley v. University of Southern California,* 1994 and 1999, discussed earlier). First, the courts have often, though not always, required that coaches of the same sport be used as the appropriate comparator for purposes of the Equal Pay Act. The *Guidelines,* however, assert that coaching tasks and skills are common across many sports, so a female basketball coach is encouraged to use male coaches from sports besides basketball as comparators.

Second, the *Guidelines* state that "pay discrimination cannot be justified if the differences relied on for the proposition that the two jobs are not substantially equal are themselves based on discrimination in the terms and conditions of employment" (EEOC, 1997, p. 2). Thus, if a university has distributed marketing and promotional resources in a discriminatory fashion among men's and women's teams, revenue generation could not be used as a "factor other than sex" to justify salary disparity.

Third, the *Guidelines* say that sex of the athlete coached is not acceptable as a "factor other than sex" that can justify salary disparity where the institution has limited females to coaching only female athletes and they earn less than male coaches of male athletes. Such a situation would mean that the sex of the athletes coached was not a gender-neutral factor in the creation of the salary disparity.

It remains to be seen whether courts that face this issue in the future will adopt these guidelines. If they do, the *Stanley* decision may become an aberration.

EMPLOYEE LEAVE

Employment discrimination can encompass adverse employment actions other than improper hiring, firing, and promotion decisions or compensation discrimination. Sometimes employees are subjected to employment discrimination because of their desire to take an extended leave of absence because they are pregnant or because they must contribute to the childcare needs of the family.

Pregnancy

In 1978, Title VII was amended by the addition of the Pregnancy Discrimination Act (PDA). This law was added in response to the growing numbers of women in the workforce who were being fired from their jobs because they became pregnant. This is an ongoing concern. According to the EEOC, pregnancy discrimination claims increased by 31 percent from 1992 to 2005 (Thompson, 2006). Often, employers believe that they should not have to accommodate the lengthy leaves that maternity may require (maternity leave provisions are not always a feature of employee leave policies). Another common attitude is that new mothers will become unreliable employees because of the demands of caring for a newborn child, given society's expectation that the mother be the primary caregiver. The PDA essentially requires employers to treat pregnancy like any other temporary inability to work and allow pregnant women to take leave time, and it forbids employers from using pregnancy as a factor in a decision to engage in an adverse employment action.

Although many female managers have confronted pregnancy discrimination, it has not been a high-visibility issue in sport so far. This could change now that women play professional basketball in the Women's National Basketball Association. The 1999 collective bargaining agreement between the WNBA and the Women's National Basketball Players Association (WNBPA) included a section titled "Pregnancy Disability Benefit." This section provided that a player who could not perform her services as a result of her pregnancy would receive 50 percent of her base salary in accordance with the payment schedule in her standard player contract for the duration of the time she was unable to play due to pregnancy, or for the remaining term of her contract, whichever was shorter. It also provided that a player whose contract was terminated while she was pregnant would continue to receive medical benefits until the end of that playing season, or until the birth of her child, whichever was later in time (WNBPA, 1999). These provisions of the Pregnancy Disability Benefit were continued in the 2008 collective bargaining agreement with one change: a player terminated while pregnant is now eligible to receive medical benefits until the end of that playing season or three months after the birth of her child, whichever comes later (WNBA, 2008).

The collective bargaining agreement thus provided for a partially paid leave and implied that a player would not have her contract terminated due to her pregnancy. However, it did not include any provision prohibiting the use of pregnancy as a factor in the decision whether to renew a player's contract. This omission might allow management to terminate pregnant players by simply not renewing their contracts.

Family Leave

For employees who have worked at least one year, the Family and Medical Leave Act of 1993 guarantees up to 12 weeks of unpaid leave per year that may be used for childbirth or adoption or to care for sick primary family members. It also requires employers to provide the same job or its equivalent upon the employee's return.

CONCLUSION

Employment discrimination can occur in the sport industry in several forms, including adverse employment actions based on a person's membership in a protected class, inequitable compensation on the basis of sex, and discriminatory application of employee leave policies. This chapter presented various grounds for pursuing employment discrimination claims that arise in the context of sport, as well as strategies to help managers avoid courses of action that could result in employment discrimination litigation. Familiarity with the application of various laws pertaining to illegal discrimination on the basis of race, sex, age, disability, and religion is an important aspect of human resource management. But it is even more important to put knowledge into practice by taking proactive steps to manage human resources in ways that accommodate differences that do not make a difference in job performance.

discussion questions

1. How does disparate impact analysis differ from disparate treatment analysis? Explain the different types of factual situations that would give rise to each theory of liability. Also, explain the different kinds of prima facie cases the plaintiff must prove for each. What are the implications for sport managers who are developing hiring criteria?

2. Would a professional baseball pitcher's shoulder injury that prevents him from pitching for one season be considered a covered disability under the Americans with Disabilities Act? Why or why not?

3. What are the primary arguments that support the position that employers are justified in paying coaches of male college athletics teams more than coaches of female teams? What are the primary counterarguments?

learning activities

1. Assume you are the director of athletics at Studyhard University. R. A. Winner, your longtime head football coach, who was stricken with a degenerative disease two years ago and now can no longer walk, must be carried on and off the field by his assistant coaches, but he continues to perform nearly all of the duties expected of the head coach. Some in the community are calling for you to replace Coach Winner because he presents such an appearance of weakness. Write a memo to the university president explaining why you have decided not to succumb to pressure to terminate Coach Winner's employment contract on the basis of his disability.

2. Assume you are the director of athletics at Awesome University, an NCAA Division I powerhouse in both men's and women's basketball. You must hire a new women's basketball coach, and a press conference is scheduled for this evening at which sports reporters from the national media will be asking whether you plan to hire a woman or a man and whether you intend to pay the new coach a salary comparable to the whopping salary the men's team coach is being paid. How will you respond to those questions?

3. Assume you are the athletics director at Planet Mars Junior College, and you are about to hire a new head football coach. One of the hiring criteria the search committee wants to establish is that successful applicants must have at least two years of football playing experience at the college level. Do you have any reservations about including this criterion to be put in the written position announcement? If so, write an email memo to the search committee members describing your concerns. (You may wish to remind them that Bela Karolyi, former coach of the United States Women's Olympic Gymnastics team, has never competed on the uneven parallel bars or the balance beam!)

4. Go to the U. S. Department of Labor's website at www.dol.gov and read more about the Family and Medical Leave Act.

5. Go to the Equal Employment Opportunity Commission's website at www.eeoc.gov and locate and read the entire document titled *Enforcement Guidelines on Sex Discrimination in the Compensation of Sports Coaches in Educational Institutions.*

CASE STUDY

Based on *Jackson v. National Football League,* 1994 U.S. Dist. LEXIS 8303 (S.D.N.Y. 1994).

The World League of American Football (WLAF) operated in 1991 and 1992 as a professional football league with teams in 10 cities in the United States, Canada, and Europe. In May 1990, Jerome Vainisi, vice president in charge of football operations, contacted various people in order to compile a list of potential applicants for coaching positions. The final list contained the names of 547 potential applicants. The WLAF had a goal of hiring two Black head coaches and two Black general managers for its 10 teams.

Plaintiff James Jackson III, an African American, applied for a coaching position. He had been the head coach of a minor league football team in Connecticut from 1979 to 1988, where he compiled a win–loss record of 74–24–4 and won three minor league "Super Bowl" championships. Before that, Jackson had been head coach for a semipro football team in New York and an assistant head coach for a high school football team. He did not receive an interview, nor was he hired by any of the WLAF teams, and Vainisi testified that he believed Jackson was not qualified for those positions. Although Vainisi testified that he tried to recruit Black coaches and that offers were made to several Black coaches, all of the head coaches he hired were White. There was also some evidence that WLAF may have made offers to Black coaches who were not likely to accept them because they already had jobs in the NFL, which provided them with better job security and compensation, or because they had geographic location preferences.

During the lawsuit, Vainisi testified that "primarily at least being a head coach in college and maybe a coordinator at a professional level would be the minimum" required experience. Vainisi also admitted that the hiring criteria were not written anywhere. Moreover, he indicated that he might credit some minor league coaching experience as professional coaching experience, "depending upon the coach himself and what his prior experience was."

Furthermore, although some of the successful candidates had experience coaching in the NFL or major college programs, at least one, Roman Gabriel, had no such experience. Although Gabriel had been an offensive coordinator for a United States Football League team, Vainisi testified in his deposition that he approved Gabriel to coach the Raleigh–Durham franchise despite reservations about Gabriel's qualifications. Vainisi's approval was based largely on Gabriel's experience as a player in the NFL and the "special business consideration" that "Gabriel is a legend" in the Raleigh–Durham area and "there was almost no other person you could name as the head coach down there, because of Gabriel's reputation in the community."

Finally, the plaintiff's personal notes of a telephone conversation with Vainisi indicate that Vainisi told the plaintiff that "we couldn't name you to Germany because they don't want a black man as head coach there. . . . They're not ready for a black head coach." There is no evidence that Vainisi informed the plaintiff during that conversation that the plaintiff was not hired because he was not qualified.

1. On what grounds can the plaintiff successfully establish a prima facie case of race discrimination in hiring?
2. How would the defendant argue in favor of some legitimate nondiscriminatory reason for not hiring Jackson?
3. How would the plaintiff make the argument that the WLAF's defense is pretext for discrimination?
4. In your estimation, who should win this case?

considering . . .　　　ANALYSIS & DISCUSSION

Reasonable Factors Other Than Age (p. 117)

You should tell Oldpro that although she was well qualified for the position, the organization could not afford to hire her based on the established pay scale. Her threat to sue should be met either with a polite refusal to comment or with a repeated statement of the reason she was not hired, coupled with a statement that this decision was completely unrelated to her age.

If Oldpro does in fact sue, your reason for not hiring her should be considered acceptable under the ADEA. If Oldpro makes out a prima facie case of age discrimination, your defense would be that linking salary to years of relevant work experience is an acceptable business practice and that she was not hired because of a reasonable factor other than age. That is, based on the organization's salary policy, Oldpro was not hired for budgetary reasons. (See *EEOC v. Francis W. Parker School,* 1994).

REFERENCES

Cases

Anderson v. Little League Baseball, 794 F. Supp. 342 (D. Ariz. 1992).

Arceneaux v. Vanderbilt Univ., 2001 U.S. App. LEXIS 27598 (6th Cir. 2001).

Austin v. Cornell Univ., 891 F. Supp. 740 (N.D.N.Y. 1995).

Biver v. Saginaw Township Cmty. Sch., 805 F.2d 1033 (6th Cir. 1986).

Blalock v. Dale County Bd. of Educ., 84 F. Supp. 2d 1291 (M.D. Ala. 1999).

Cannon v. University of Chicago, 441 U.S. 677 (1979).

City of Cleburne v. Cleburne Living Ctr., Inc., 473 U.S. 432 (1985).

Dowling v. United States, 476 F. Supp. 1018 (D. Mass. 1979).

EEOC v. Francis W. Parker Sch., 1994 U.S. App. LEXIS 29366 (7th Cir. 1994), *cert. denied,* 115 S.Ct. 2577 (1995).

EEOC v. National Broadcasting Co., 753 F. Supp. 452 (S.D.N.Y. 1990).

EEOC v. Sedita, 755 F. Supp. 808 (N.D. Ill. 1991).

General Dynamics Land Systems, Inc. v. Cline, 124 S.Ct. 1236 (2004).

Gross v. FBL Financial Services, Inc., 2009 U.S. LEXIS 4535 (2009), Stevens, *dissenting*.

Hazen Paper Co. v. Biggins, 507 U.S. 604 (1993).

Jackson v. Armstrong Sch. Dist., 430 F. Supp. 1050 (W.D. Pa. 1977).

Jackson v. NFL, 1994 U.S. Dist. LEXIS 8303 (S.D.N.Y. 1994).

Jackson v. Veterans' Admin., 22 F.3d 277 (11th Cir. 1994).

Kimel v. Florida Bd. of Regents, 120 S.Ct. 631 (2000).

Korematsu v. United States, 323 U.S. 214 (1944).

Lemire v. Silva, 104 F. Supp. 2d 80 (D. Mass. 2000).

Ludtke v. Kuhn, 461 F. Supp. 86 (S.D.N.Y. 1978).

Maddox v. University of Tenn., 62 F.3d 843 (6th Cir. 1995).

McDonnell Douglas Corp. v. Green, 411 U.S. 792 (1973).

Medcalf v. University of Pa., 2001 U.S. Dist. LEXIS 10155 (E.D. Pa. 2001).

Morris v. Bianchini, 1987 U.S. Dist. LEXIS 13888 (E.D. Va. 1987).

Morris v. Wallace Cmty. Coll.–Selma, 125 F. Supp. 2d 1315 (S.D. Ala. 2001).

North Haven Bd. of Educ. v. Bell, 456 U.S. 512 (1982).

Otis v. Canadian Valley-Reeves Meat Co., 52 F.3d 338 (10th Cir. 1995).

Perdue v. City Univ. of N. Y., 13 F. Supp. 2d 326 (E.D.N.Y. 1998).

PGA Tour, Inc. v. Martin, 532 U.S. 661 (2001).

Pitts v. Oklahoma, No. CIV-93-1341-A (W.D. Okla. 1994).

Reeves v. Sanderson Plumbing Products, Inc., 120 S.Ct. 2097 (2000).

Rostker v. Goldberg, 453 U.S. 57 (1981).

Russell v. Southeastern Pa. Transp. Auth., 1993 U.S. Dist. LEXIS 12358 (E.D. Pa. 1993).

School Board of Nassau County v. Arline, 480 U.S. 273 (1987).

Stanley v. University of S. Cal., 13 F.3d 1313 (9th Cir. 1994) [*Stanley I*]; 178 F.3d 1069 (9th Cir. 1999) [*Stanley II*].

St. Augustine High School v. Louisiana High School Athletic Ass'n, 270 F. Supp. 767 (E.D. La. 1967), *aff'd*, 396 F.2d 224 (5th Cir. 1968).

Sutton v. United Airlines, Inc., 527 U.S. 471 (1999).

Toyota Motor Mfg. v. Williams, 122 S.Ct. 681 (2002).

Tyler v. Howard Univ., No. 91-CA11239 (D.C. Super. Ct. 1993).

University of Ala. v. Garrett, 531 U.S. 356 (2001).

Wynn v. Columbus Municipal Separate Sch. Dist., 692 F. Supp. 672 (N.D. Miss. 1988).

Constitution

U.S. CONST. amend. XI.

U.S. CONST. amend. XIV.

Statutes and Regulations

Age Discrimination in Employment Act, 20 U.S.C. § 621 *et seq.*

Americans with Disabilities Act Amendments Act of 2008, Pub. L. No. 110–325, 122 Stat. 3553. Retrieved June 15, 2009, from http://frwebgate.access.gpo.gov.

Americans with Disabilities Act of 1990, 42 U.S.C. § 12101 *et seq.*

Equal Pay Act of 1963, 29 U.S.C. § 206(d)(1).

Family and Medical Leave Act of 1993, 29 U.S.C. § 2611 *et seq.*

Pregnancy Discrimination Act, 42 U.S.C. § 2000e(k).

Rehabilitation Act of 1973, 29 U.S.C. § 701 *et seq.*

Title VII of the Civil Rights Act of 1964, as amended by the Civil Rights Act of 1991, 42 U.S.C. § 2000e *et seq.*

Title IX of the Education Amendments of 1972, 20 U.S.C. § 1681 *et seq.*

Title IX regulations, 34 C.F.R. § 106.51(a)(1) (1994).

Other Sources

Bennett-Alexander, D. D., & Pincus, L. B. (1998). *Employment Law for Business*. 2nd ed. Boston: Irwin/McGraw-Hill.

Claussen, C. L. (1995). Title IX and employment discrimination in coaching intercollegiate athletics. *University of Miami Entertainment & Sports Law Review, 12*(2), 149–168.

Davis, P. (2006, October 5). Man denied coaching job could net $20,000 in back pay. *The Providence Journal*. Retrieved October 10, 2006, from www.projo.com.

Equal Employment Opportunity Commission. (October 1997). *Enforcement guidelines on sex discrimination in the compensation of sports coaches in educational institutions.* www.eeoc.gov/policy/guidance.html.

Equal Employment Opportunity Commission. (March 2009). Notice concerning the Americans with Disabilities Act (ADA) Amendments Act of 2008. Retrieved June 14, 2009, from www.eeoc.gov/ada/amendments_notice.html.

Job Accommodation Network. (1999). Accommodation benefit/cost data. www.jan.wvu.edu/media/Stats/BenCosts0799.html.

Long, A. B. (2008). Introducing the new and improved Americans with Disabilities Act: Assessing the ADA Amendments Act of 2008. *Northwestern University Law Review Colloquy, 103*, 217–229.

McKindra, L. (2008, February 1). Minority panel asks for accountability in hiring. *The NCAA News.* Retrieved February 7, 2008, from www.ncaa.org.

Suns settle sexual discrimination suit. *Associated Press State & Local Wire,* October 10, 2003. Retrieved January 14, 2006, from LEXIS-NEXIS.

Thompson, A. (2006, March 31). When becoming a mom means losing your job. Retrieved March 31, 2006, from www.msnbc.msn.com/id/12100070/print/1/displaymode/1098/.

U.S. Department of Labor. (May 2009). May 2009 disability statistics released. Retrieved June 14, 2009, from www.dol.gov/odep.

Women's National Basketball Association (2008). Women's National Basketball Association Collective Bargaining Agreement. Retrieved June 14, 2009 from http://en.wikipedia.org/wiki/Women_National_Basketball_Association, References #9.

Women's National Basketball Players Association. (1999). WNBA Collective Bargaining Agreement. Retrieved from www.wnbpa.org.

Women's Sports Foundation. Laws and legal resources for addressing discrimination or harassment based on sexual orientation and gender identity. Retrieved June 14, 2009, from www.womenssportsfoundation.org.

Workplace Accommodations: Low Cost, High Impact. *Job Accommodation Network-Fact Sheet Series.* Retrieved June 14, 2009, from www.jan.wvu.edu/research/index.htm.

WEBSITE RESOURCES

www.diversityinsport.com/ ▪ The Laboratory for Diversity in Sport at Texas A&M University focuses on how diversity affects organizational and team performance. Their assessment of exemplars and best practices looks at issues ranging from diversity in marketing to diversity training and is available under the "Publications and Projects" link.

www.dol.gov ▪ This is the U. S. Department of Labor's website. Among other things, it contains information about the Family and Medical Leave Act.

www.dol.gov/odep/categories/research/ ▪ This U. S. Department of Labor site contains research and resources on disabilities and the workplace, including disability employment statistics.

www.eeoc.gov ▪ This is the website of the Equal Employment Opportunity Commission. It contains much useful information on application of the federal employment discrimination laws. Among the many linked documents is the EEOC's *Enforcement Guidelines on Sex Discrimination in the Compensation of Sports Coaches in Educational Institutions.*

www.eeoc.gov/ada/amendments_notice.html ▪ This section of the EEOC site contains a helpful resource for understanding the Americans with Disabilities Act Amendments Act of 2008 (ADAAA). It provides a concise explanation of the changes made by the new law.

www.eeoc.gov/policy/docs/preemp.html ▪ The Equal Employment Opportunity Commission site has resources for both employers and potential employees about the workplace and job application process. At this site, you will find the document *ADA Enforcement Guidance: Preemployment Disability-Related Questions and Medical Examinations,* an explanation of the EEOC guidelines on hiring practices. It includes examples of questions related to disabilities that an employer should not ask on an application or during an interview.

www.jan.wvu.edu/ ▪ The website for the Job Accommodation Network (from the Office of Disability and Employment Policy) provides information and resources on how employers can accommodate workers with disabilities. Those seeking to avoid discrimination in their hiring, promotion, or termination practices can visit the A to Z guide, grouped by conditions, at www.jan.wvu.edu/media/atoz.htm.

www.tidesport.org ▪ The Institute for Diversity and Ethics in Sport at the University of Central Florida "serves as a comprehensive resource for issues related to gender and race in amateur, collegiate and professional sports." It posts annual Racial and Gender Report Cards for organizations like the NBA, WNBA, MLB, and college sports, under the "Racial & Gender Report Card" link.

www.womensbasketballonline.com/wnba/wnbacbawnbacba 08.pdf ▪ You can view the WNBA's 2008 Collective Bargaining Agreement at this site, which governs the employment relationship between the organization and its players.

www.womenssportfoundation.org ▪ The Women's Sports Foundation website provides news and information about resources for addressing discrimination or harassment in sport based on gender, sexual orientation, and gender identity.

Harassment and Employee Expression Issues

INTRODUCTION

A s we saw in the previous chapter, avoiding illegal employment discrimination is a critical aspect of human resource management. That chapter
discussed the legal issues involved in hiring, promotion, and termination
decisions and in determinations regarding compensation and employee leave. Here
in Chapter 7, we explore several other forms of illegal employment discrimination,
such as harassment and discriminatory responses to different forms of employee
expression. In particular, this chapter discusses sexual and racial harassment in
the employment context and discriminatory treatment of employees for engaging
in different forms of expressive activity. These may include seeking justice under
antidiscrimination laws, whistleblowing, dress or grooming choices, speech while
on the job, observance of religious practices, and unionizing activity.

Harassment is included in this chapter rather than Chapter 6 because most
harassing behaviors are expressive activity—verbal, physical, or pictorial/symbolic
statements are the substance of harassment. Because of this, people often believe
that the First Amendment should protect their right to harass others. From the
point of view of people in the workplace, harassment may appear to be a form
of employee expressive activity, so we have chosen to address it in that context.
It should be kept firmly in mind, however, that in the eyes of the law, this type
of behavior is harassing *conduct* rather than speech. Hence, the laws prohibiting
harassment do not run afoul of the First Amendment.

As was true for the types of employment discrimination discussed in Chapter
6, the Constitution and several federal statutes apply to the types of employment
discrimination we discuss in this chapter, as do civil or human rights statutes and
ordinances enacted by most states and many cities. However, once again, the focus
of this chapter is on examining the applicable *federal* laws. For a summary of the
issues, relevant laws, and primary cases discussed in this chapter, see Exhibit 7.1.

EXHIBIT 7.1	Management contexts in which employment discrimination may arise, with relevant laws and cases.		
MANAGEMENT CONTEXT	**MAJOR LEGAL ISSUES**	**RELEVANT LAW**	**ILLUSTRATIVE CASES**
Workplace harassment	Sexual/racial/religious	Title VII (and Title IX with regard to sex)	*Bowman, Cameli, Faragher*
	Age and disability	ADEA and ADA	
	Sexual orientation	State & municipal laws	
Employer responses to employee expression	Employer retaliation	Title VII Title IX	*Cox* *Lowrey, Jackson*
	Dress/grooming codes	First Amendment and Title VII	
	Injudicious speech/whistleblowing	First Amendment	*Dambrot, Williams*
	Religious speech & team prayer	First Amendment and Title VII	*Lumpkin, Borden, Johnson*
	Religious practices	Title VII	*Simmons*
	Union activity speech	NLRA	

SEXUAL AND RACIAL HARASSMENT

Sometimes employment decisions are made contingent upon the performance of sexual favors. For example, a supervisor may threaten to deny an employee's promotion if the employee refuses to accede to a demand for sex. At other times, sexual or racial harassment can create an abusive work environment that makes it very difficult for an employee to perform his or her job. Situations like these are considered forms of sex or race discrimination prohibited under Title VII. Exhibit 7.2 presents the Equal Employment Opportunity Commission's regulations defining sexual harassment. In 2008, 13,867 sexual harassment charges were filed, and 16 percent of those charges were filed by men ("Dillard's to pay," 2009).

Sexual Harassment

Based on the EEOC definition, courts have further defined two types of sexual harassment: quid pro quo and hostile environment.

Quid pro quo harassment

Quid pro quo harassment occurs when an employer conditions a job-related benefit, such as a promotion or pay raise, upon an employee's willingness to engage in sexual behavior. An example of this might be a fitness club manager promising a promotion to the aerobics instructor if she will engage in a sexual relationship with him. This effectively constitutes sexual bribery, and an actionable claim of quid pro quo sexual harassment requires only one instance of such conduct.

Hostile environment harassment

A second type of sexual harassment, known as **hostile environment harassment,** is much more difficult to define and consequently more difficult for courts to address. Hostile environment sexual harassment occurs when an employee is subjected to repeated unwelcome behaviors that do not constitute sexual bribery but are sufficiently severe and pervasive that they create a work environment so hostile that it substantially interferes with the harassed employee's ability to perform his or her job. The Supreme

---

EEOC Sexual Harassment Regulations, 29 C.F.R. § 1604.11(a) (2009).   EXHIBIT **7.2**

Sexual harassment is defined as unwelcome sexual advances, requests for sexual favors, and other verbal or physical conduct of a sexual nature where:

1. Submission to the conduct is made a term or condition of employment;

2. Submission to or rejection of such conduct is used as a basis for employment decisions;

3. The conduct has the purpose or effect of unreasonably interfering with an individual's work performance; or

4. The conduct has the purpose or effect of creating an intimidating, hostile, or offensive working environment.

Court, in *Harris v. Forklift Systems* (1993), listed several factors that courts may consider in determining whether a sexually hostile environment exists, including:

- The frequency of the offensive conduct
- The severity of the offensive conduct
- Whether the conduct is physically threatening or humiliating or merely an offensive utterance
- Whether the conduct unreasonably interferes with an employee's work performance

It is necessary, therefore, to examine all the factual circumstances of a case to determine whether a hostile environment exists. Many types of behaviors fall into the gray area where courts must make a judgment call based on the specific facts of each case. See Exhibit 7.3 for examples.

In *Harris*, the Supreme Court established that plaintiffs in hostile environment cases do not need to wait until they have proof of psychological injury before they can invoke the protection of the law. The Court also established that hostile environment claims are to be subjected to a two-pronged test, one prong being objective and the other subjective:

1. From an objective perspective, would a **reasonable person** in the same situation have perceived the resulting climate as hostile?
2. Did the plaintiff subjectively experience the conduct as sufficiently severe and pervasive that it created a hostile work environment for him or her, thereby making it difficult to perform his or her job?

(Courts use the concept of an abstract "reasonable person" as an "objective" standard to judge behavior in several areas of the law. A reasonable person would be a person exercising judgment that meets societal expectations for prudence in decision making.)

Hostile environment sexual harassment claims may be brought in two types of cases:

1. Where the offensive speech or conduct is sexual in nature
2. Where the offensive speech or conduct is harassment based on the victim's gender and is thus "based on sex" but not necessarily sexual in content

Bowman v. Shawnee State University (2000) provides an example of a hostile environment sexual harassment case in which both types of offensive conduct are discussed.

EXHIBIT	7.3	Examples of conduct that may contribute to a sexually hostile work environment.

- Unwelcome sexual touching, pinching, patting, hugging
- Whistling or cat-calling
- Sexually suggestive or obscene notes, letters, or email
- Leering or sexually oriented gestures
- Obscene jokes or other vulgar language
- Display of sexually suggestive materials, including posters, calendars, or cartoons

Bowman v. Shawnee State University

220 F.3d 456 (6th Cir. 2000)

CASE OPINION

[FACTS

Plaintiff Thomas Bowman became a full-time instructor of physical education courses at Shawnee State University in 1988. Jessica Jahnke was hired in 1990 and soon became the Dean of Education. In 1991, Bowman was selected to serve as Sports Studies Coordinator. Bowman claims that beginning in 1991 Jahnke sexually harassed him on multiple occasions, including one instance where she rubbed his shoulder for two seconds until he jerked away and said "no." Another incident occurred at a 1992 Christmas party where Jahnke grabbed Bowman's buttocks when he was leaning against the stove in her house. Bowman told her that if someone did the same thing to her, she would have them fired. Jahnke responded that she "controlled [Bowman's] ass and she would do whatever she wanted with it" (p. 459). On two occasions, Jahnke suggested that Bowman share her whirlpool or swimming pool with her, without his girlfriend present. Bowman alleged numerous other instances of harassing behavior, but they were unrelated to sexual activity. In 1995, Jahnke wrote a memo to Bowman stating that she was angry at him for lying to her about teaching a class at Ohio University and was stripping him of his responsibilities as Sports Studies Coordinator. This removal was short-lived, as the Provost rescinded the removal within a few days, and Bowman's salary was never reduced. Nevertheless, Bowman brought a sexual harassment suit against the university and Jahnke. The district court dismissed the claim against Jahnke because individual liability does not attach under Title VII unless the individual defendant is the actual employer.]

HOLDING

The circuit court affirmed the district court's decision that Bowman's sexual harassment claim failed because the harassment did not rise to the level necessary to have created a hostile work environment.

RATIONALE

To prevail [against an employer on a quid pro quo claim] under a sexual harassment claim without showing that the harassment was severe or pervasive, the employee must prove the following: (1) that the employee was a member of a protected class; (2) that the employee was subjected to unwelcomed sexual harassment in the form of sexual advances or requests for sexual favors; (3) that the harassment complained of was on the basis of sex; (4) that the employee's submission to the unwelcomed advances was an express or implied condition for receiving job benefits or that the employee's refusal to submit to the supervisor's sexual demands resulted in a tangible job detriment; and (5) the existence of respondeat superior liability.

* * *

Even if we assume that the loss of the Coordinator position constitutes a significant change in employment status, there is no tangible employment action in this case because the very temporary nature of the employment action in question makes it a non-materially adverse employment action. [Thus, the court concluded there was no quid pro quo sexual harassment.]

* * *

A plaintiff may [however] establish a violation of Title VII by proving that the sex discrimination created a hostile or abusive work environment without having to prove a tangible employment action. In order to establish a hostile work environment claim, an employee must show the following: (1) the employee is a member of a protected class, (2) the employee was subject to unwelcomed sexual harassment, (3) the harassment was based on the employee's sex, (4) the harassment created a hostile work environment, and (5) the employer failed to take reasonable care to prevent and correct any sexually harassing behavior.

* * *

Non-sexual conduct may be illegally sex-based and properly considered in a hostile environment analysis where it can be shown that but for the employee's sex, he would not have been the object of harassment. . . .

* * *

We agree with the district court that while Bowman recites a litany of perceived slights and abuses, many of the alleged harassing acts cannot be considered in the hostile environment analysis because Bowman has not shown that the alleged harassment was based upon his status as a male. . . . Bowman has not alleged that Jahnke made a single comment evincing an anti-male bias. . . .

* * *

The only incidents that may arguably be considered in the hostile work environment analysis are the 1991 shoulder rubbing incident, the 1992 Christmas party incident, the 1994 whirlpool incident, the 1994 swimming pool incident, and the 1995 meeting in Jahnke's office [in which she pushed him on the chest]. . . . [T]he incidents that may properly be considered are not severe or pervasive and, thus, do not meet the fourth element of the hostile environment analysis.

Questions

1. Why was this case treated as a hostile environment case rather than as a case of quid pro quo sexual harassment?

2. On what grounds did the court reject the idea that plaintiff Bowman had been subjected to a hostile working environment by his supervisor?

3. Do you think the decision in this case might have been different if it had been a male supervisor and a female victim instead of the other way around?

Bowman illustrates how a court deals with a hostile environment sexual harassment claim. Hostile environment harassment claims may also be brought for harassment on the basis of one's race or religion under Title VII, one's age under the ADEA, or one's disability under the ADA. The courts deal with these additional types of hostile environment harassment claims by using the same *Harris v. Forklift Systems* factors for analysis that are used with hostile environment sexual harassment claims. Additionally, sexual harassment that occurs in educational institutions that receive federal funds may be actionable under Title IX as well as Title VII.

Racial Harassment

The *Cameli* case illustrates how a court dealt with a hostile environment racial harassment claim.

Cameli v. O'Neal

FOCUS CASE   1997 U.S. Dist. LEXIS 9034 (N.D. Ill. 1997)

FACTS

Plaintiff Cameli, who is White, served as varsity basketball coach at predominantly Black Thornton High School from 1982 through 1994. In 1990, Richard Taylor, the superintendent of schools, forced Cameli to hire a Black assistant coach, Rocky Hill, to sit on the bench during varsity games. Cameli did not get along with Hill and thought he was a negative influence on the players. William O'Neal became principal of Thornton in 1993. O'Neal engaged in a series of decisions in which he forced Cameli not to cut players that Cameli wished to cut and reinstated players Cameli had cut from the team. Cameli alleged that he was also subjected to an atmosphere of repeated racial insults that rose to the level of a "hostile environment" for Title VII purposes. Particularly, he claims that Principal O'Neal told him on two separate occasions that Thornton would have a Black coach, that he had trouble relating to Black students, that it would look good to the Black community if he had another Black assistant on his bench, and that "no White coach was going to treat Black ball players that way." He also claims that O'Neal told the plaintiff's assistants that the plaintiff could not relate to Black students and that the athletic director and assistant principal also told the plaintiff that he would be Thornton's last White head coach.

Cameli sued under Title VII claiming he had been subjected to a racially hostile work environment. The defendant moved for summary judgment.

HOLDING

The court found that the conduct complained of by Cameli was not sufficiently severe or pervasive to create a hostile environment and granted defendant's summary judgment motion.

RATIONALE

Even though Cameli may have *subjectively* perceived his environment to be permeated with racial hostility, the *objective* test was not met here. Although several of the comments may have been racially insensitive and indeed unwarranted, Cameli was not subjected to vicious racial insults or ridicule, nor to physically threatening or humiliating actions that a reasonable person would conclude were severe enough or frequent enough over an extended period of time to create an abusive work environment. Moreover, Principal O'Neal's interference with Cameli's coaching decisions, although inappropriate and bothersome to the point of creating hostility, did not contribute substantially to a *racially* hostile atmosphere in Cameli's place of work.

Same-Sex/Same-Race Harassment

Increasingly, plaintiffs are bringing hostile environment claims when they have been harassed by someone of the same sex or same race. Although Title VII does not explicitly protect against discrimination on the basis of sexual orientation, in *Oncale v. Sundowner Offshore Services, Inc.* (1998), the Supreme Court ruled that same-sex sexual harassment may be a violation of Title VII where the harassment is not simply based on the harassee's sexual orientation but is harassment of a sexual nature perpetrated by a person of the same sex. For example, repeated derisive comments such as "everyone knows you're a faggot" and "everyone knows you take it up the ass" are based on an employee's sexual orientation, and by themselves they would not trigger the protection of Title VII (*Bibby v. Philadelphia Coca-Cola Bottling Co.*, 2000). However, where sexually related taunts, forcible sexual acts and gestures, and physical assaults of a sexual nature are perpetrated by a same-sex harasser, Title VII is violated because the Supreme Court has interpreted such actions as being "based on sex" (*Oncale*, 1998). The Court further ruled that such conduct need not be motivated by sexual desire in order to be actionable. In June 2009, Dillard's department store company, under an EEOC consent decree, agreed to pay $110,000 to two male employees who had been sexually harassed by their male supervisor. The supervisor had exposed himself, propositioned them, and made sexually explicit and derogatory remarks to them ("Dillard's to pay," 2009).

Competitive Advantage
STRATEGIES

Sexual and Racial Harassment

- Adopt a harassment policy separate from a general antidiscrimination policy, and ensure that it is disseminated, explained, and enforced. Be sure that it covers racial and religious harassment in addition to sexual harassment. Ensure that the policy specifies alternatives to the immediate supervisor for receiving complaints.

- When creating policies that include definitions of prohibited behaviors (e.g., sexual harassment), make the definitions broader than what is actually defined by the law as illegal conduct so that enforcement of the policy cannot be construed as an admission of liability. An example would be:

  Unwelcome conduct of a sexual nature is prohibited, regardless of whether it rises to the level of creating a hostile environment (Neil, 2003).

- Do not assume that everyone understands what harassment is. It is a good idea to conduct employee training workshops that define harassment and describe procedures for handling harassment incidents.

- A clear and strong harassment policy should have, at a minimum, the components shown in Exhibit 7.4. For an example of an actual sexual harassment policy, see the policy appended to the court's opinion in *Robinson v. Jacksonville Shipyards, Inc.* (1991).

Relying on the recognition of same-sex sexual harassment by the Court in *Oncale*, the Eighth Circuit held that an African American employee could bring a claim of same-race racial harassment against a supervisor who repeatedly called him "nigger" and "black boy" and referred to his Caucasian wife as "whitey" (*Ross v. Douglas County*, 2000).

Employer Liability for Harassment

When a supervisor is guilty of harassing an employee, the supervisor's employer may be held strictly liable (under the principle of vicarious liability; see Chapter 5) if the employer knew or should have known the harassment was occurring and an adverse employment action (such as discharge, demotion, or undesirable reassignment) was the tangible result (the typical quid pro quo case). The employer's only available defense is to disprove the claims of the plaintiff. Additionally, when the harassment is perpetrated by a nonsupervisory employee or a nonemployee such as a client or customer, the employer may be held strictly liable if the employer knew or should have known it was occurring and failed to take reasonable steps to prevent it.

A different situation is presented by hostile environment cases where adverse, tangible job consequences may have been threatened by a supervisor but did not occur. In *Burlington Industries, Inc. v. Ellerth* (1998), the Supreme Court ruled that in such cases the employer can still be held vicariously liable for the harassing actions of a supervisory employee. However, the employer may assert an **affirmative defense** (i.e., a defense that excuses rather than denies blame) by showing both of the following:

1. The employer exercised reasonable care to prevent and promptly correct any sexually harassing behavior
2. The plaintiff employee unreasonably failed to take advantage of any preventive or corrective opportunities provided by the employer

The *Ellerth* decision further noted that while having an antiharassment policy with an explicit procedure for dealing with complaints is not always required to establish a successful affirmative defense, the existence of such a policy is a relevant factor for courts to consider under the first prong of the affirmative defense. Additionally, if an employer can demonstrate that the aggrieved employee unreasonably failed to use the established complaint procedure, this will normally suffice to meet the second prong of the affirmative defense.

To understand the rationale underlying employer liability for hostile environment sexual harassment, let's look at *Faragher v. City of Boca Raton* (1998).

| Essential elements of a harassment policy. | EXHIBIT | 7.4 |

- A philosophy of zero tolerance for harassing behavior
- A description of the legal definition of sexual, racial, and religious harassment, along with examples specific to your business
- Reporting procedures for harassment complaints that make clear the following:
  - Steps to take if you are a target of harassment
  - How to register a complaint and with whom (competence to handle such a complaint is an issue; also, employees should have an option to bypass their immediate supervisor in cases where the supervisor is the harassing party)
  - Retaliation against a complainant will not be tolerated
- An investigation process that makes clear the following:
  - The confidentiality of the process
  - Who will investigate the validity of the complaint
  - Procedures for investigating the complaint
- A description of applicable sanctions or disciplinary actions
- An appeals process

Faragher v. City of Boca Raton

| 118 S.Ct. 2275 (1998) | FOCUS CASE | |

FACTS

Beth Ann Faragher brought an action against the City of Boca Raton and her supervisors after resigning from her employment as an ocean lifeguard, alleging that the supervisors had created a "sexually hostile atmosphere" at work by repeatedly subjecting her to "uninvited and offensive touching," by making lewd remarks, and by speaking of women in offensive terms. Faragher never complained to management about these incidents, although another female lifeguard had complained about harassment that she and other lifeguards, including Faragher, had endured. Although the city had a sexual harassment policy, it had not disseminated this policy to beach employees.

HOLDING

The Supreme Court held that an employer is vicariously liable for harassment caused by a supervisor, but that this liability is subject to an affirmative defense that addresses the reasonableness of the employer's conduct and the conduct of the plaintiff.

RATIONALE

The Supreme Court found that sexual harassment by a supervisor is not an act contemplated within the scope of his or her employment. However, the Court noted that an employer may be vicariously liable for such actions by employees under the Restatement (Second) of Torts § 219(2)(d), which provides that an employer "is not subject to liability for the torts of his servants acting outside the scope of their employment unless . . . the servant purported to act or speak on behalf of the principal and there was reliance on apparent authority, or he was aided in accomplishing the tort by the existence of the agency relation." The Court agreed with Faragher's argument that the sexual harassment engaged in by her supervisors was made possible by the abuse of their supervisory authority, and it found that the aided-by-agency-relation principle was sufficient to hold an employer vicariously liable. The Court noted that the employment (agency) relationship allows the unwelcome contact between a supervisor and an employee and that the victim may be reluctant to complain about the actions of a supervisor. Also, when a supervisor discriminates against a subordinate, those acts depend on the supervisor's position of power over the employees who report to him or her.

The Court then noted that the city would have the opportunity to raise an affirmative defense but that this defense would likely be unsuccessful in this case because of the city's failure to disseminate its sexual harassment policy to the beach employees. Additionally, the city officials had made no attempt to keep a record of complaints or to monitor supervisors' conduct. Furthermore, the harassment policy did not contain a procedure for bypassing one's supervisor to register a complaint in situations where the harassing party was the supervisor.

EMPLOYEE EXPRESSION

Sometimes employees provoke adverse employment actions by the way in which they choose to express themselves in the work environment. In this section we discuss legal issues of this nature that may arise in the sport or recreation context.

Retaliation for Seeking Justice/ Whistleblowing Under Title VII or Title IX

Title VII protects employees from employer **retaliation** for the employee's efforts to obtain justice under the statute. In *Cox v. National Football League* (1998), a plaintiff sued his employer under Title VII on the grounds that the employer had retaliated against him. Bryan Cox alleged he was fined one game day's pay ($87,500) in retaliation for his filing of a race discrimination lawsuit against the NFL for its failure to take measures to prevent racial harassment of players by fans. The court found that Cox had not demonstrated a causal link between the fine and the protected expression because over two years had passed between the two events and because there was ample evidence that the real basis for Cox's fine was his multiple instances of abusing fans and officials with profanity and obscene gestures.

The courts have ruled that Title IX also prohibits retaliation, including retaliation for whistleblowing—that is, for criticizing the employing institution for gender inequities in athletics. In *Lowrey v. Texas A & M University System* (1998), Jan Lowrey was demoted from her position as Women's Athletics Coordinator after she spoke out on Title IX issues with regard to Tarleton State University's athletic department. The court ruled that Title IX retaliation claims should be analyzed in the same way as Title VII retaliation claims, in that both should utilize the *McDonnell Douglas v. Green* (1973) burden-shifting framework. In the context of a retaliation claim, the plaintiff must prove a prima facie case by showing:

1. She engaged in activity protected by the statute
2. The employer took adverse action against her
3. A causal connection existed between the protected activity and the adverse employment action

In *Lowrey,* the court decided that because she had been demoted, even though she received no less pay, Lowrey made out a prima facie case of retaliation under Title VII. With regard to the Title IX cause of action, the court ruled that she had enough evidence in a memo from the athletic director to the president of the university to support a prima facie case of retaliation for whistleblowing under that statute as well. In the memo, the athletic director recommended demoting Lowrey and complained that she "has taken her concerns, complaints, and issues directly to others on campus outside the Athletics Department since the beginning, effectively undermining any viable working relationship we might have had" (p. 914). The president acted on the athletic director's recommendation in demoting Lowrey, and thus there was some causal evidence linking the demotion to the administrators' displeasure with Lowrey's Title IX activity.

In *Jackson v. Birmingham Board of Education* (2005), Roderick Jackson, a male coach of a high school girls' basketball team, sued under Title IX claiming that he was fired in retaliation for complaining that his team was being treated inequitably. The Board of Education argued that Title IX does not provide a private right of action for a retaliation claim, but the Supreme Court disagreed, finding it important to protect those who report discrimination in order to enable the Title IX enforcement scheme to work as Congress envisioned. The Court held that there is indeed an implied private right of action for retaliation claims under Title IX. Subsequently, in 2007, Fresno State University agreed to pay $9 million to its former women's basketball coach and $5.2 million to its former volleyball coach after they each sued for sex discrimination and retaliation (Daysog, 2009; "Lesbian basketball coaches," 2008).

Dress/Grooming Codes

The federal courts are split on the issue of whether dress and grooming codes imposed by government actors violate the First Amendment right to freedom of expression. Most of these cases involve dress and grooming codes in schools, so they are discussed in greater detail in Chapter 14.

In the private sector, courts have generally ruled that employers may impose reasonable rules governing the appearance of their employees without running afoul of the sex discrimination provision of Title VII. For example, courts have upheld company policies stipulating appropriate hair length and appropriate clothing for the different sexes (see e.g., *Lockhart v. Louisiana-Pacific Corp.,* 1990; *Albertson's v. Washington Human Rights Comm'n,* 1976; *Fagan v. National Cash Register,* 1973; *Willingham v. Macon Telegraph Pub. Co.,* 1975). However, grooming or dress codes that differentiate on the basis of race or sex *and* that subject members of those groups to different conditions of employment as a result (for example, requiring females, but not males, to wear skimpy, sexually suggestive clothing that results in the women being subjected to leers and lewd comments) would probably not be tolerated by the courts.

A related issue is the use of training or employee manuals that direct employees to adjust their behavior on the basis of racist or sexist stereotypes. For example, Shawn Brooks, who was hired as an account executive by the Philadelphia Eagles Radio Network, was urged by his supervisor to use a best-selling book titled *Dress for Success* as a training manual for his job. One chapter, "When Blacks and Hispanics Sell to Whites (and Vice Versa)," included some advice that Brooks, who is Black, found offensive. One passage reads:

> Blacks selling to whites should not wear Afro hair styles or any clothing that is African in association. If you're selling to corporate America it is very important that you dress, not as well as the white salesmen, but better than them.

Another passage reads:

> If you are a Hispanic (Mexican, Puerto Rican, Cuban or other Latin American), you should avoid pencil-line mustaches, any articles of clothing that have Hispanic associations, and anything that is very sharp or precise. Also avoid any hair tonic that tends to give a greasy or shiny look to the hair; this also triggers a strong negative reaction.

When Brooks complained to an administrator, he was referred back to the offending supervisor. He resigned and filed a race discrimination and racial harassment claim with the Pennsylvania Human Rights Commission, which found in his favor ("Eagles' exec files," 2003).

Injudicious Speech and Whistleblowing Under the First Amendment

The First Amendment to the U. S. Constitution protects the right of federal or state government workers to enjoy some freedom of speech when speaking as citizens on matters of public concern (*Connick v. Myers,* 1983; *Pickering v. Board of Education,* 1968). See Exhibit 7.5. According to the Supreme Court in *Pickering,* the interests of the employee as a citizen in commenting upon matters of public concern are to be balanced against the interests of the government employer in promoting efficiency of its services (the *Pickering* balancing test; see Exhibit 7.6). In *Connick,* the Court established that determining whether a specimen of speech refers to a matter of public concern (i.e., a matter that concerns important social or political ideas) depends

EXHIBIT	7.5	Amendment I of the United States Constitution.

Congress shall pass no laws respecting an establishment of religion, or prohibiting the free exercise thereof; or abridging the freedom of speech, or of the press; or the right of the people peaceably to assemble, and to petition the government for a redress of grievances.

The *Pickering* balancing test.   EXHIBIT 7.6

Interests of a citizen employee commenting on matters of public concern

Interests of the government employer in promoting efficiency of its services

on examining its content, form, and context. This issue of whether speech counted as speech about a public concern was central to the *Dambrot v. Central Michigan University* (1995) case.

In *Dambrot,* on multiple occasions the men's basketball coach at Central Michigan University (CMU) had referred to several of his players as "niggers." As a result, he was fired, and he sued claiming his freedom of speech had been violated. The court applied the *Connick* analysis of examining the content, form, and context of the speech to determine whether it touched on a matter of public concern. Finding that the coach's use of the word "nigger" communicated no socially or politically important message to his players and that the form and context of the speech was intended to be motivational rather than to communicate important social and political ideas, the court ruled that Coach Dambrot's use of the word "nigger" was not a matter of public concern. Instead, it was merely a racial slur that was of such low value as not to be the type of meaningful expression the First Amendment was designed to protect. Thus, the court did not have to proceed further to apply the *Pickering* balancing test in upholding the university's right to terminate the coach.

In 2006 the Supreme Court decided the case of *Garcetti v. Ceballos,* which altered somewhat the application of the *Pickering* balancing test regarding the right to free speech of government employees. In this case, a deputy district attorney was denied a promotion for writing a memo recommending that the district attorney's office dismiss a case due to improper police behavior.

The *Pickering* analysis goes as follows:

1. Does the speech focus on a matter of public concern?
2. If not, there is no First Amendment protection.
3. If yes, then the *Pickering* balancing test will be applied.

In *Garcetti,* the Supreme Court held that the First Amendment does not prohibit managerial discipline of public employees for speech made pursuant to their official job duties. This ruling thus seems to add to the *Pickering* analysis a threshold inquiry into whether the speech was part of the employee's job. According to the dissent, however, a supervisor should be able to take disciplinary action when an employee's speech is inflammatory or misguided but not when it is legitimate yet unwelcome (e.g., whistleblowing).

The dissent also argued that it can be difficult to draw a clear line between a government employee speaking as a citizen and speaking as an employee. This difficulty is exemplified in the *Lumpkin* case discussed in the next section on "Religious Speech." As you read about that case, consider whether, when Reverend Lumpkin made his views known to the media, he was speaking as a citizen (albeit a minister) or as an employee of the San Francisco Human Rights Commission.

The Focus Case that follows illustrates how one court has applied the *Garcetti* decision to a controversy arising in the sport context.

Williams v. Dallas Indep. Sch. District

FOCUS CASE   480 F.3d 689 (5th Cir. 2007)

FACTS

Williams was a high school athletic director and head football coach. During the 2003 school year, he had to ask the principal's office repeatedly for budget account balance information, and his requests were repeatedly ignored by the office manager. Two months later, he wrote a memorandum to the principal expressing his concerns about the handling of the school's athletics funds compared to standard operating procedures at other high schools in the school district. In the memo, Williams also implied that some corrupt practices were occurring in the management of athletics accounts.

Four days later, the principal removed Williams from his position as athletic director, and subsequently the school district declined to renew Williams' employment contract. Later that same month, the school district placed the principal and his office manager on administrative leave pending an investigation of their financial practices.

Williams sued, alleging that the retaliatory employment action violated his free speech rights. The district court granted summary judgment for the school district, holding that Williams' memo did not address a matter of public concern and thus did not warrant First Amendment protection.

HOLDING

The Fifth Circuit affirmed.

RATIONALE

The court stated that the *Garcetti* decision had added a threshold requirement to the *Pickering* analysis that requires shifting the focus from the content of the speech to the role the speaker occupied when the statements were made. The court acknowledged that the *Garcetti* opinion did not explicate the definition of speaking "pursuant to" one's "official duties," except to say that a formal job description is not dispositive on the issue. The court noted that the district court found Ceballos was acting pursuant to his official duties because he was performing a required task when he wrote his offending memo alleging police impropriety. And the court acknowledged that here, the athletic director was not required to write critical memos regarding athletics accounts to the high school principal. So the question the court engaged was the extent to which, under *Garcetti*, a public employee's speech is protected by the First Amendment if it is not made as part of a required job duty but is nevertheless related to expected duties.

The court distinguished Williams' memo from other cases: schoolteacher Pickering's protected speech in writing to a newspaper about the funding policies of his school board, and another school teacher's protected speech when she complained to her principal about the school's discriminatory hiring practices. In the eyes of the court, these were speech activities that could be engaged in by citizens who were not working for the government. In contrast, the statements Williams made in his memo were made in the course of performing his job as athletic director because he needed financial information to do his job effectively. It was part of his job to communicate with the principal's office about the athletics budget. Therefore, his statements were made pursuant to his official duties and, under *Garcetti,* were not protected by the First Amendment.

It is important to note that in *Garcetti* the Supreme Court expressly stated that it was not deciding whether the new threshold inquiry as to employee versus citizen status applied to the context of teaching or scholarship. Therefore, we may expect to see divergent applications of *Garcetti* by the circuit courts to issues arising in an educational context. (For a law review article addressing this issue, see Hutchens (2008).) Additionally, even though First Amendment protection may be limited in scope, various state and federal whistleblower laws may provide statutory protection to government employees who experience retaliation for whistleblowing activity.

Religious Speech: First Amendment

In addition to freedom of speech, the First Amendment also protects our freedom of religion. There are two religion clauses in the First Amendment—the Free Exercise Clause and the Establishment Clause (see Exhibit 7.5). The **Free Exercise Clause** protects our fundamental right to the free exercise of our religious beliefs, unless these beliefs illegally cause harm to society (e.g., human sacrifice can be prohibited). The **Establishment Clause** was intended to prevent the establishment of a government-endorsed religion, but it has been broadly interpreted over the years to the point where now it is interpreted to mean that the government must be neutral with respect to religious matters.

Occasionally, an employee will express a religious viewpoint or take a political stance that is informed by a religious perspective. In such a case, the First Amendment may be implicated. For example, in *Lumpkin v. Jordan* (1997), a Baptist minister who was a member of the San Francisco Human Rights Commission was fired after he made statements to the media denouncing homosexuality as a sinful abomination. One of the goals of the Human Rights Commission was to lead the community toward respect for homosexual citizens. When the plaintiff minister sued the city for religious discrimination, the court applied the *Pickering* balancing test (Exhibit 7.6) in ruling in favor of the city. Finding that the plaintiff was fired because he made public statements at odds with his position of employment on the commission, the court held that he was not fired solely because of his religious beliefs. The court stated that because Reverend Lumpkin was a policymaker in the mayor's administration, his remarks would undermine the very policies the administration was striving to implement—a situation that the First Amendment principle of free speech would not protect.

Further, the court found that Lumpkin's removal did not violate the Free Exercise Clause because the mayor's interest in preventing disruption of his administration's goals outweighed Lumpkin's right to religious expression. Finally, Lumpkin's termination did not violate the Establishment Clause because the adverse employment action could not reasonably be construed as an endorsement of a particular religious view. The following hypothetical case involves a similar situation in a sport context.

considering . . .   RELIGIOUS SPEECH

The fact pattern in *Lumpkin* is somewhat similar to a scenario involving Bill McCartney, former football coach at the University of Colorado and founder of the conservative Christian men's organization known as the Promise Keepers. While he was still employed as head football coach, McCartney used his position as a platform for expressing his religious views that abortion and homosexuality are sinful, and he even utilized the university setting to disseminate his message. The university responded by forbidding McCartney from continuing to use the university setting to promote his personal views, and McCartney acquiesced (Monaghan, 1992).

However, suppose that McCartney instead had been terminated for those activities and then sued for religious discrimination.

Questions

- What are the differences between the employment positions held by McCartney and Reverend Lumpkin?
- What is the difference between the mission of the University of Colorado and the mission of the San Francisco Human Rights Commission?
- Would these factual differences make a difference to the court as it decided the freedom of speech issue? The Free Exercise Clause issue? The Establishment Clause issue?

Note how you would answer the questions and then check your responses using the Analysis & Discussion at the end of this chapter.

Team Prayer: First Amendment

Sometimes religious speech takes the form of prayer. Let's examine the issue of team prayer in the Focus Case below.

Borden v. Sch. Dist. of Township of East Brunswick

FOCUS CASE   523 F.3d 153 (3rd Cir. 2008)

FACTS

Borden was a high school football coach who had, for 23 years, participated in praying with his football team at pre-game meals and in the locker room. He often organized and led these prayer activities. After a few parents complained, the athletic director/principal of the school told Borden to stop leading prayer. A few days later, the school district's lawyer told Borden that all team prayer had to be student-initiated and that he should not encourage, lead, or coerce student prayer. Nor should he even participate in student-initiated prayer because that would be considered an unconstitutional endorsement of religion.

Borden agreed to abide by the new policy but continued to participate by bowing his head silently during subsequent pre-game meal prayers and by remaining in a kneeling position throughout subsequent pre-game prayers that followed pre-game locker room strategy talks. Borden claimed that these postures were intended as secular demonstrations of his respect for the players, the prayers, and East Brunswick's football tradition. Because Borden also then directed the team captains to poll each of the players as to whether they wished to continue to "follow the same [prayer] practices as last year," and the captains did so by personally phoning each player, there is some question as to whether an element of coercion was present in the minds of the athletes. Borden also filed suit, claiming that applying the new policy violated his Constitutional rights.

HOLDING

The District Court granted summary judgment in favor of Borden, and the Third Circuit reversed, concluding that his silent participation in team prayer activity was not protected speech and did violate the Establishment Clause.

RATIONALE

(Free Speech Issue) Because Coach Borden was a state employee, the Third Circuit used the *Connick/Pickering* analysis to determine whether the prayer policy had been applied to him in a way that violated his freedom of speech. First, the court declined to use the *Garcetti* threshold requirement of identifying the role of the speaker as citizen or employee—citing the Supreme Court's expressed refusal to decide the issue of whether the *Garcetti* requirement applies to teaching and scholarship in the educational context.

Next, in order to determine whether the prayer activity was a matter of public concern, the court used the *Connick* test to examine the content, flow, and context of the speech. Because the content of Borden's silent acts of expression was focused on promoting team morale and solidarity, and not, for example, on making a social statement about the value of public prayer, the court found that the message did not involve a matter of public concern. In the court's view, the form and context of the prayer activities reinforced its non-public nature. The praying occurred at invitation-only meals and in closed locker rooms, and was not meant for public airing. Therefore, the Third Circuit concluded that the team prayers were not matters of public concern and so were not entitled to First Amendment protection. Therefore, it was unnecessary for the court to engage in the *Pickering* balancing test because Borden did not have a free speech right that would call for it.

(Establishment Clause Issue) There are three tests for violations of the Establishment Clause: (1) endorsement test; (2) coercion test; (3) *Lemon* test. Use of the endorsement test is appropriate when the government is participating in religious activity, as was the case here. The endorsement test asks this question: Would a reason-

able observer who is familiar with the history and context of "the display" (here, praying) perceive it to be an endorsement of religion? If so, then it violates the Establishment Clause and can be restricted.

The court found that Borden's 23 years of past team prayer activity (including leading, selecting, orchestrating, and participating) were an unconstitutional endorsement of religion that impacted the interpretation of his current silent acts of expression. Considering the history and context of his prayer behavior, the court concluded that an objective observer could draw a reasonable inference that Borden's behavior went beyond a secular show of respect and was actually intended to preserve participation in team prayer at his school. Therefore, the school district's policy was upheld as it applied to Coach Borden.

Writing in concurrence, one judge expressed the view that Borden's silent bowing and kneeling could constitute an impermissible endorsement of religion, even without his 23-year history of endorsement factored in. This judge also believed that Borden's actions might not pass the coercion test because of his role in getting the team captains to poll the players without ensuring that their responses were anonymous. In contrast, another judge wrote in a separate opinion that a reasonable observer would have no reason to believe Coach Borden was lying about the changes he had made in his behavior and could instead believe that the respectful acts to which Borden now limited himself did not cross the line into impermissible endorsement of religion.

Religious Speech: Title VII

Title VII may present an avenue for recourse in cases where employers take adverse action on the basis of religious speech, as demonstrated in the *Johnson* case.

Johnson v. National Football League

FOCUS CASE   1999 U.S. Dist. LEXIS 15983 (S.D.N.Y. 1999)

FACTS

Plaintiff J. Edwards Johnson V, also known as Yacub Abdul-Matin, who is African American, converted to Islam while he was a football player at the University of Miami. Because of his religious involvement, he wrote two articles about race and religion that were published in the university newspaper, and that he claims did not meet with the approval of his football coaches. He was also involved in a public controversy over his religion. Several professional football teams had expressed interest in Johnson, but all eventually changed their minds, allegedly due to the controversy he had been involved in while in college. Johnson filed suit, claiming that the NFL discriminated against him on the basis of his race and his religion by refusing to hire him as a professional football player. The NFL defendants moved to have the suit dismissed for failure to state a claim upon which relief may be granted, claiming the complaint failed to allege any circumstances that could allow an inference that the NFL had engaged in discrimination.

HOLDING

The court denied the defendants' motion to dismiss.

RATIONALE

The court found that Johnson's claim alleged that he was profiled as a troublemaker because of the positions he took in college on religious issues and racial pride and the incidents that arose because of this. His complaint further alleged that this profiling resulted in his name being withdrawn by the Atlanta Falcons after they drafted him and that he was blackballed, causing other NFL teams to abandon interest in him. The court ruled that the complaint did in fact allege that Johnson was denied employment because of a combination of his race and his religion, and therefore it did state a claim upon which, if substantiated, relief could be granted under Title VII.

Religious Practices

Religious expression may arise in the employment context in situations where an employee refuses for religious reasons, to adhere to an assigned work schedule that conflicts with the worker's observance of a Sabbath day or religious holiday or to an employer's policy regarding appropriate conduct, dress, or grooming. An employee who is terminated for this may have a cause of action under Title VII, which, in addition to race, color, national origin, and sex, prohibits discrimination on the basis of religion. The worker's religion need not be an organized, widely recognized religion, as long as it involves sincerely held beliefs and takes the place of religion in the worker's life. Thus, even atheism has been construed as a "religion" under Title VII.

Religion is treated differently from the other classes protected under Title VII, in that the employer is required to make a reasonable accommodation for the employee's religious practice unless doing so would cause undue hardship. The courts consider several factors in determining whether a religious accommodation is reasonable or constitutes an undue hardship. These are listed in Exhibit 7.7.

The *Simmons* case shows how a court decides whether an organization has made a reasonable religious accommodation.

Factors to consider in determining the reasonableness of religious accommodations.	EXHIBIT 7.7

- Size of the staff
- Type of job employee does
- Whether other employees were asked for their assistance in making the accommodation
- The willingness of other employees to assist in making the accommodation
- Cost of the accommodation
- Administrative burdens of the accommodation
- What has been done by similarly situated employers

Simmons v. Sports Training Institute

FOCUS CASE   1990 U.S. Dist. LEXIS 4877 (S.D.N.Y. 1990)

FACTS

Plaintiff Bertrand Simmons was hired as a maintenance worker for the Sports Training Institute in July 1981. In August 1983, Simmons converted to the Seventh Day Adventist faith, which prohibits working on the Sabbath, which is considered to be from sundown Friday until sundown on Saturday. The plaintiff told his supervisor of his religious reason for no longer being able to work on Saturdays, and his work schedule was adjusted to accommodate his religious requirement. Simmons failed to tell his supervisor, however, that Friday afternoons were off-limits too.

Later, the plaintiff agreed to his supervisor's request to change his work schedule so that the plaintiff's brother, who was also employed there, could work during the day because he had been having difficulty staying awake at work. This change, however, meant that the plaintiff was once again scheduled to work on the Sabbath because his brother had been scheduled to work on Friday evening. Therefore, on the next Friday, the brothers traded shifts so that the plaintiff could observe his Sabbath. This upset the supervisor because it reinstated the plaintiff's brother to a double-shift situation in which he would again have "sleeping on the job" problems. When the plaintiff now made the supervisor aware of the Friday portion of the Sabbath, the supervisor accommodated Simmons' religious observance request again, which resulted in his being scheduled for the graveyard shift.

In September 1984, the plaintiff took a three-week vacation when his supervisor had granted him only two weeks. When he returned, plaintiff refused to give a satisfactory explanation for his delayed return, demanded to be returned to the morning shift, and refused to work graveyard. He was fired and subsequently sued the Sports Training Institute, alleging religious discrimination under Title VII.

HOLDING

The court dismissed the complaint.

RATIONALE

The court found that the plaintiff was terminated for insubordination based on his threat not to work the graveyard shift and the fact that he had taken an unauthorized week of vacation. Insubordination was a legitimate, nondiscriminatory reason for plaintiff's dismissal, and the court found that this reason was not pretext for religious discrimination. Indeed, the supervisor had tried twice to accommodate Simmons' religious practice.

In the following hypothetical situation, an athlete violated a league rule because of his religious beliefs and was punished for it.

considering . . .   **RELIGIOUS PRACTICES**

During the 1996 NBA basketball season, Denver Nuggets guard Mahmoud Abdul-Rauf (formerly known as Chris Jackson), who had converted to Islam in 1991, refused to stand for the playing of the national anthem at his games. According to Abdul-Rauf, standing for what he termed "a nationalistic ideology" would impermissibly come between him and Allah. His refusal violated a league rule that required all players, coaches, and athletic trainers to stand in line in a dignified manner during the playing of the national anthem. The NBA responded by suspending him without pay (Mossman, 1996).

Questions

- If Abdul-Rauf sued the NBA for religious discrimination under Title VII, how should the court decide the case?
- What action should the NBA take to provide a reasonable accommodation?

Note how you would answer the questions and then check your response using the Analysis & Discussion at the end of this chapter.

Some religious faiths prohibit the shaving of facial hair, and this might conflict with an organization's grooming code that is designed to ensure an appropriate public image for the organization. In such a case, a reasonable accommodation might be to reassign the employee to a position that does not involve dealing with the public, such as stocking shelves or handling paperwork.

Speech in the Context of Unionizing Activity

Section 8(a)(3) of the National Labor Relations Act (NLRA) makes it an **unfair labor practice** for an employer "by discrimination in regard to hire or tenure of employment to encourage or discourage membership in any labor organization" (29 U.S.C. § 158(a)(3)). This rule applies to employees who staff sports facilities and events who might be members of labor unions, as well as to professional athletes' involvement with players associations. An athlete who suffered an adverse employment action because of any expressive activity in support of a players association would be protected by the NLRA.

Competitive Advantage

STRATEGIES

Employee Expression

- Be sensitive to cultural differences that may relate to ethnicity, gender, age, or religion and that may affect the work environment. For example, such differences might impact celebrations of special events or clothing and grooming requirements.

CONCLUSION

Employment discrimination can occur in the sport industry in several forms, including harassment perpetrated by employers or by fellow employees and unequal treatment of employees because of their expressive activity.

This chapter presented various grounds for pursuing these types of employment discrimination claims, as well as strategies to help managers avoid employment discrimination litigation.

discussion questions

1. How do hostile environment harassment claims (whether based on race or sex) differ from quid pro quo harassment claims?
2. What is the advantage to the employer of having the affirmative defense available in claims where there is no tangible adverse employment action?
3. For what two types of potentially discriminatory situations is an employer required to provide reasonable accommodation to an employee, unless doing so would cause undue hardship or cause a fundamental alteration of the business?
4. What kind of reasonable accommodation for religious practices could management offer to an employee in a situation where reassignment to a less visible work setting is impossible—for example, when the employee is an NBA player?

learning activities

1. Assume you are an upper-level manager at ESPN and have been given the responsibility of developing a sexual harassment policy for the entire company. Draft such a policy and then write a memo to your supervisor suggesting sound guidance for its dissemination, implementation, and enforcement.
2. Assume you are the Commissioner of the NBA. Write a memo to the team owners providing guidelines for how they should handle future cases similar to the scenario in which Mahmoud Abdul-Rauf refused to stand for the playing of the National Anthem before his basketball games. Be sure to include a statement explaining why these guidelines are important, as well as practical suggestions for reasonable accommodations.
3. On the Web, find a sport or recreation organization's harassment policy and critique it to see if it contains the critical components suggested in this chapter.

CASE STUDY

The National Basketball League (NBL) is suffering from image problems. Several of the top players in the league have had repeated brushes with the law, and as a result the widespread popular perception is that the league is full of thugs. Approximately 75 percent of the players in the NBL are Black. Most of these players contribute to the league's negative public image by embracing "hip-hop" culture and wearing clothing that reinforces the "gangster" image.

With the popularity of the NBL's entertainment product in decline in corporate America (source of sponsorship and advertising dollars) and among the White middle-class viewing audience, NBL Commissioner David Firm has decided the league needs an image facelift. He has proposed implementation of a dress code to become effective at the beginning of the next season of play. This dress code is to be enforced by the individual teams and is mandatory for all players. Punishment in the form of monetary fines and suspensions may be imposed for violations.

The proposed dress code requires that players dress in "business casual" style at all times while on team or league business, except for specified types of occasions where other attire is appropriate (e.g., special events, basketball clinics, etc.). Additionally, it prohibits headgear of any kind while a player is on the bench or in the stands during a game, during media interviews, and during other team or league events. Also forbidden are chains, pendants, or medallions worn on the outside of a player's clothing, sunglasses worn indoors, and headphones (except in the team locker room, team bus, or team plane). According to one player, "Almost one hundred percent of the guys in the league who are young and Black players wear big chains."

Several players have publicly voiced their objection to the proposed dress code. In fact, many have said it will affect mostly the Black players, is in fact targeted at Blacks, and is a racist attempt to suppress Black "hip-hop" style and culture. Not surprisingly, sport sociology professors have entered the dialogue, with about two-thirds of them suggesting that the dress code is indeed evidence of lingering racist attitudes. On the other hand, some players, coaches, and noted sport scholars have expressed support for the proposal. Their position is that the dress code is not targeted at suppressing Black cultural expression but is instead a long overdue "good business" response to the need to repair the league's image in the eyes of the paying customers and corporate sponsors.

Because the dress code affects employment conditions and the employer–employee relationship, it is a mandatory topic for collective bargaining (see Chapter 9 for further discussion of this topic). That is, management cannot unilaterally impose it on the players. Instead, the players association will have to agree to accept the dress code as part of its overarching collective bargaining agreement with management, due to be renegotiated next month.

Immediately after Commissioner Firm first announced the proposed dress code one month ago, 45 players began to engage in expressive activities designed to encourage a greater level of player involvement in the players association, in an effort to forge a strong union position against agreeing to accept the dress code. Additionally, three of the "activist" players (I. M. Pacer, M. E. Sixer, and I. Warrior) filed a lawsuit against the NBL two weeks ago, claiming that the proposed dress code constitutes racial harassment. The 45 "activist" players have noticed that they are being more closely scrutinized and are receiving more disciplinary sanctions by management for violations of team and league rules than are "nonactivist" players. Among the 45 "activists," Pacer, Sixer, and Warrior seem to be receiving the most scrutiny and sanctions.

1. If Pacer, Sixer, and Warrior came to you seeking advice on whether they should withdraw their lawsuit claiming that the proposed dress code constitutes racial harassment, how would you respond and why?

2. Those same players also want your advice about whether they should file a new lawsuit claiming that the proposed dress code violates their free speech right to express themselves and their cultural values through their clothing style choices.

3. They also ask your advice about bringing an unfair labor practice claim under the National Labor Relations Act.

4. They also want to know what you would advise about bringing a claim alleging employer retaliation under Title VII.

5. Commissioner Firm has decided to hold a press conference to address the accusations of racism, which have been receiving a huge amount of play in the media. He has formed a committee of NBL staff members to assist him in preparing his remarks. You are a member of that committee. What advice would you give the commissioner?

considering . . . **ANALYSIS & DISCUSSION**

Religious Speech (p. 150)

As we saw in the *Dambrot* case, public employees are entitled to First Amendment protection for expressing their views on matters of public concern, a category that definitely includes perspectives on homosexuality and abortion. Let's assume that *Garcetti* does not apply to McCartney's speech as a coach (educator). And let's assume further that if a court did decide *Garcetti* is applicable, that his speech was not speech made in the scope of his employment (adopting here the type of analysis on this issue that the Fifth Circuit used in the *Williams* case). Applying the *Pickering* balancing test (Exhibit 7.6) to the McCartney hypothetical requires us to balance McCartney's interest in being able to comment freely on matters of public concern with the university's interest in maintaining an efficient, regularly functioning school environment. The four factors to be considered in applying the *Pickering* balancing test include:

1. Whether the statements were directed to persons McCartney would normally be in contact with in his daily work

2. Whether the statements had an adverse effect on discipline by superiors or harmony among co-workers

3. Whether the employment relationship is the kind that necessitates personal loyalty and confidence for its proper functioning

4. Whether the statements in any way impeded the employee's proper performance of his duties or interfered with the regular operation of the employer's organization

In this hypothetical, the second and fourth factors are the ones potentially seriously affected by McCartney's speech. His speech activity may have adversely affected harmony among his colleagues at the university. Additionally, misappropriating public resources for the purpose of publicly expressing ideas unrelated to his employment could be considered an interference with the regular operation of the university.

With regard to the freedom of religion issues, the court might follow the reasoning in *Lumpkin* and hold that the university's interest in furthering its educational mission of inquiry outweighed McCartney's right to free exercise of his religion. Or it might find that the educational mission of the university should embrace the exercise of diverse viewpoints, including religious viewpoints. Or it might distinguish this case from *Lumpkin* and say that McCartney does not hold a policymaking position in which he must conform his behavior to the goals of the administration, and therefore his freedom to express his religious views is not outweighed by any interest of the university. Finally, with regard to the Establishment Clause, the court could rule that firing Coach McCartney could not reasonably be construed as an establishment of a preferred religious view by the university and that therefore it did not violate the Constitution. There is no clear answer to the question of how a court is likely to resolve such a case. If the case were decided purely on freedom of speech grounds, the university would likely win. But if the religion clauses of the First Amendment are also invoked, the waters are muddied considerably.

Religious Practices (p. 155)

In this case, the court is likely to find that the Muslim faith is a sincerely held belief and that, if Abdul-Rauf's practice is in accord with Muslim practice, the NBA should provide a reasonable accommodation for him. Eventually, the NBA did accommodate Abdul-Rauf by allowing him to remain in the locker room during the national anthem.

REFERENCES

Cases

Albertson's v. Washington Human Rights Comm'n, 544 P.2d 98 (Wash. Ct. App. Wa. 1976).

Bibby v. The Philadelphia Coca-Cola Bottling Co., 85 F. Supp. 2d 509 (E.D. Pa. 2000).

Borden v. Sch. Dist. of Township of East Brunswick, 523 F.3d 153 (3rd Cir. 2008), *cert. denied,* 2009 U.S. LEXIS 1640.

Bowman v. Shawnee State Univ., 220 F.3d 456 (6th Cir. 2000).

Burlington Indus., Inc. v. Ellerth, 118 S.Ct. 2257 (1998).

Cameli v. O'Neal, 1997 U.S. Dist. LEXIS 9034 (N.D. Ill. 1997).

Connick v. Myers, 103 S.Ct. 1684 (1983).

Cox v. NFL, 29 F. Supp. 2d 463 (N.D. Ill. 1998).

Dambrot v. Central Mich. Univ., 55 F.3d 1177 (6th Cir. 1995).

Fagan v. National Cash Register, 481 F.2d 1115 (D.C. Cir. 1973).

Faragher v. City of Boca Raton, 118 S.Ct. 2275 (1998).

Garcetti v. Ceballos, 126 S.Ct. 1951 (2006).

Harris v. Forklift Systems, Inc., 510 U.S. 17 (1993).

Jackson v. Birmingham Bd. of Educ., 125 S.Ct. 1497 (2005).

Johnson v. NFL, 1999 U.S. Dist. LEXIS 15983 (S.D.N.Y. 1999).

Lockhart v. Louisiana-Pacific Corp., 795 P.2d 602 (Or. Ct. App. 1990).

Lowrey v. Texas A & M Univ. Sys., 11 F. Supp. 2d 895 (S.D. Tex. 1998).

Lumpkin v. Jordan, 1994 U.S. Dist. LEXIS 17280 (N.D. Cal. 1994), aff'd, 109 F.3d 1498 (9th Cir. 1997).

McDonnell Douglas Corp. v. Green, 411 U.S. 792 (1973).

Oncale v. Sundowner Offshore Services, Inc., 523 U.S. 75 (1998).

Pickering v. Board of Educ., 88 S.Ct. 1731 (1968).

Robinson v. Jacksonville Shipyards, Inc. 760 F. Supp. 1486 (M.D. Fla. 1991).

Ross v. Douglas County, 234 F.3d 391 (8th Cir. 2000).

Simmons v. Sports Training Inst., 1990 U.S. Dist. LEXIS 4877 (S.D.N.Y. 1990).

Williams v. Dallas Indep. Sch. Dist., 480 F.3d 689 (5th Cir. 2007).

Willingham v. Macon Telegraph Pub. Co., 597 F.2d 1084 (5th Cir. 1975).

Constitution

U.S. CONST. amend. I.

Statutes and Regulations

National Labor Relations Act, 29 U.S.C. § 158(a)(3).

Sexual Harassment Regulations, 29 C.F.R. § 1604.11(a) (2009).

Title VII of the Civil Rights Act of 1964, as amended by the Civil Rights Act of 1991, 42 U.S.C. § 2000e *et seq.*

Title IX of the Education Amendments of 1972, 20 U.S.C. § 1681 *et seq.*

Other Sources

Anon. (2008, July 28). Lesbian basketball coaches call foul. *Inside Higher Ed.* Retrieved August 6, 2008, from www.insidehighered.com.

Anon. (2009, June 11). Dillard's to pay $110,000 for same-sex harassment. Retrieved June 14, 2009, from www.eeoc.gov/press/6-11-09.html.

Daysog, R. (2009, April 14). Former Hawaii basketball coach sues UH over his dismissal. Retrieved April 24, 2009, from www.honoluluadvertiser.com.

Eagles' exec files (2003, December 1) discrimination suit based on "insensitive" book. *Sports Lawyer's Update,* www.sportslaw.org/members/news/novnl2003.htm.

Hutchens, N. H. (2008). Silence at the schoolhouse gate: The diminishing First Amendment rights of public school employees. *Kentucky Law Journal, 97,* 37–77.

Monaghan, P. (1992, November 11). U. of Colorado football coach accused of using his position to promote his religious views. *The Chronicle of Higher Education,* p. A35, A37.

Mossman, J. (1996, March 13). Anthem boycott costs NBA's Abdul-Rauf. *The BG News* (Bowling Green State University student newspaper), p. 8.

Neil, M. (2003). When sexual harassment hits home. *ABA Journal Report,* September 26, 2003. Retrieved September 26, 2003, from www.abanet.org/journal.

WEBSITE RESOURCES

www.eeoc.gov/laws/types/sexual_harassment.cfm ▪ This U.S. Equal Employment Opportunity Commission website provides a definition of harassment, a statement of when an employer is liable for harassment, and statistics on the number of harassement charges the EEOC has received and resolved. It also provides links to a number of enforcement and guidances and policy documents as well as links to Title VII of the Civil Rights Act of 1964, the Age Discrimination in Employment Act of 1967 (ADEA), and the Americans with Disabilities Act of 1990 (ADA)—which, if violated, can constitute harassment.

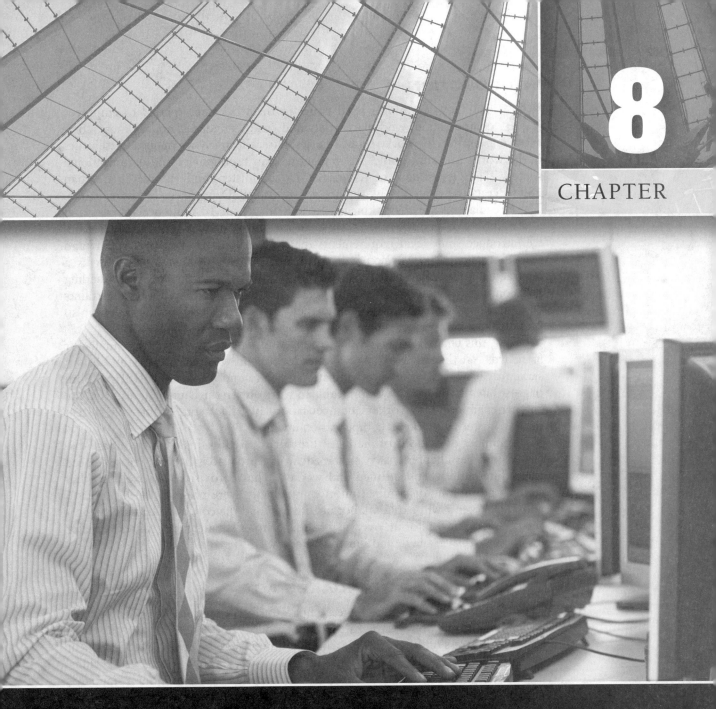

8

Working Conditions

INTRODUCTION

This chapter explores legal issues in the workplace related to employee compensation, workplace safety and health standards, and workers' compensation for work-related injuries. How effectively we manage these issues in the workplace can significantly impact worker productivity and organizational success. The Department of Labor (DOL) administers and enforces more than 180 federal laws related to workplace activities (U.S. Department of Labor, n.d.e). These regulations cover workplace activities for about 10 million employers and 125 million workers. Obviously, we cannot examine each of these laws. Instead, we introduce some legal requirements that regularly affect workers in sport and recreation organizations. You will recall that the employment relationship is a contractual relationship between an employer and an employee. Issues surrounding that contractual relationship were presented in Chapter 4. In addition to restraints or limitations arising from the employment contract, federal and state laws also provide for a number of regulations affecting employers and employees.

First, this chapter covers laws affecting wages provided for in the Fair Labor Standards Act (FLSA). Next, the chapter focuses on workplace safety and health standards provided for in the Occupational Safety and Health Act (OSHA). Both of these laws are federal laws applicable to worksites in the United States. Last, the chapter examines state workers' compensation laws. Each state has its own system for administering workers' compensation laws.

A number of sections of the FLSA are not covered in this chapter but are discussed in other chapters, such as the equal pay provisions prohibiting sex-based wage differentials between men and women. These provisions, as well as other statutes prohibiting discrimination in employment, were presented in Chapters 6 and 7. Chapter 9 will explain labor negotiation and the collective-bargaining process. See Exhibit 8.1 for an overview of this chapter's managerial contexts, major legal issues, relevant law, and illustrative cases.

THE FAIR LABOR STANDARDS ACT

The law that has the greatest impact on working conditions in terms of wages and hours is the Fair Labor Standards Act. The FLSA was passed by Congress on June 25, 1938, and it is administered by the U. S. Department of Labor's Wage and Hour Division. The main objective of the FLSA was to eliminate "labor conditions detrimental to the maintenance of the minimum standards of living necessary for health, efficiency, and general well-being of workers" (FLSA, 2009, § 202). The FLSA establishes standards for minimum wages, overtime pay, recordkeeping, and child labor. These standards affect more than 80 million workers, both full-time and part-time, in the private and public sectors. However, FLSA does not regulate or require (1) vacation, holiday, severance, or sick pay; (2) meal or rest periods, holidays off, or vacations; (3) premium pay for weekend or holiday work; (4) pay raises or fringe benefits; or (5) a discharge notice, reason for discharge, or immediate payment of final wages to terminated employees.

The FLSA can apply to workers in one of two ways. First, the FLSA provides what is known as **enterprise coverage,** which applies to employees who work for certain businesses or organizations that have at least two employees and do at least

| | | | EXHIBIT | 8.1 |

Management contexts and legal issues pertaining to working conditions, with relevant laws and cases.

MANAGEMENT CONTEXT	MAJOR LEGAL ISSUES	RELEVANT LAW	ILLUSTRATIVE CASES
Determining employee compensation and job duties	Overtime pay Minimum wages Exemptions for administrative employees and amusement businesses	FLSA	*Adams* *Bridewell* *Jeffery* *Liger*
Use of interns and trainees	Exemptions for interns and non-payment of interns	FLSA	
Creating a safe workplace	On-the-job injuries Employees handling dangerous substances or being exposed to blood or dangerous pathogens	OSHA	
Employer liability for injuries to employees	Workers compensation for on-the-job injuries Professional and college athletes as employees	State Workers' Compensation Regulations and Programs	*Jones, Dozler, Savage Elmhurst, Park, Hallal* *Pro Football, Inc., Van Horn, Waldrep, Rensing,*

$500,000 a year in business (U. S. Department of Labor, n.d.b). Enterprise coverage also includes hospitals, businesses providing medical or nursing care for residents, schools and preschools, and government agencies. Second, the FLSA provides for **individual coverage** in cases where an organization does not qualify as an enterprise but an employee regularly engages in activities involving interstate commerce or the production of goods for interstate commerce. Regularly sending and receiving postal mail, making and receiving long-distance telephone calls, shipping goods to another state or receiving goods from other states, and keeping records of those goods all qualify as engaging in interstate commerce. Thus, it is highly unlikely that a business would not be subject to the FLSA in today's global economy.

Minimum Wage and Overtime Requirements

The FLSA originally established maximum working hours of 44 hours per week for the first year after its passage, 42 for the second, and 40 thereafter. Minimum wages of 25 cents per hour were established for the first year and 30 cents for the second, rising to 40 cents over the next six years. Of course, that was in the late 1930s and early 1940s. Since that time, the maximum working hours per work week remains at 40. The minimum wage increase that took place in 2007 established an incremental increase in the minimum wage to $5.85 in 2007 and to $7.25 beginning July 2009. Hourly employees who work in excess of 40 hours per week are entitled to the established overtime rate of at least one and one-half times the employee's regular hourly wage for all hours worked in excess of 40 hours.

Nonexempt (or covered) **employees** include any employee who does not meet a specific exemption provided for in the FLSA. Nonexempt employees cannot waive their right to overtime pay, nor can an employee agree to work more than 40 hours at regular pay. The overtime requirements apply to a work week. Hence, overtime pay is not required just because an employee works more than eight hours in a day; rather, the critical time period is the work week. A **work week** is a period of 168 hours in seven consecutive days (7 x 24 = 168). A work week may begin on any given day and hour as determined by the employer. Each work week stands alone, so that the time an employee works cannot be averaged over, for example, a month. In addition, to qualify for overtime pay, an employee must have actually worked 40 hours. Thus, if an employee works 40 hours during one work week and also is paid for an eight-hour holiday day, bringing the total hours paid to 48, the employee is not entitled to overtime pay for the eight hours above 40, since she did not actually work more than 40 hours in a given work week. Employers are not required to pay extra to an employee who works on a holiday, although this is a fairly common practice.

Calculating overtime pay is straightforward. For example, David is a customer service representative (salesperson) for Dick's Sporting Goods with a regular hourly wage of $12 per hour. David works 45 hours in a week. For the five hours over the 40 hours, David must be paid time-and-a-half. In this case, it would be 1.5 x $12 = $18 x 5 overtime hours = $90. The employee's total wage for that week would be $12 x 40 hours = $480 + $90 (overtime pay) = $570.

Exemptions Under FLSA

The FLSA contains a number of exemptions for certain employee groups from the mandatory overtime provisions (U. S. Department of Labor, n.d.a). Three exemptions are frequently encountered in the sport industry: (1) executive or administrative exemption, (2) amusement or recreation exemption, and (3) trainee/intern exemption.

Executive or administrative exemption

Section 13(a)(1) of the FLSA, codified at 29 U.S.C. § 213(a)(1), exempts from both minimum wage and overtime pay any employee employed in a bona fide executive, administrative, or professional capacity or in the capacity of outside salesperson (these are often referred to as the **white-collar exemptions**). Generally, these employees are salaried and receive higher rates of pay. The rationale behind the exemption is that these employees enjoy a professional position at a set salary and, therefore, should not receive an additional benefit for working more than 40 hours per week.

The exemptions were premised on the belief that the exempted workers typically earn salaries well above the minimum wage. These workers were presumed to enjoy other compensatory privileges, such as above-average fringe benefits, greater job security, and better opportunities for advancement, compared to the workers entitled to overtime pay (29 C.F.R. Part 541, 2005). Further, the type of work that exempt workers performed was difficult to standardize to any time frame and could not be easily extended to other workers, making enforcement of the overtime provisions difficult.

The applicability of the white-collar exceptions or any other exemption under the FLSA must be affirmatively established by the employer. To qualify for one of the white-collar exemptions, the employer cannot simply classify an employee as an outside salesperson or an administrative employee. The employee's title or job description does not determine whether his position qualifies for an exemption. Under the FLSA, the employer must evaluate both the *salary level* and the employee's *job duties* to determine whether overtime pay is due.

As of August 23, 2004, the DOL revised its rules for employee coverage. Now, employees considered exempt from overtime pay are subject to new overtime rules and base salary tests (U.S. Department of Labor, n.d.c). The employer must be able to satisfy these tests in order to be exempt from the minimum wage and overtime requirements.

For example, a minor league baseball team may hire Corey as an assistant promotions manager and want to pay him a small starting salary of $18,000 (approximately $346 per week or $8.65 per hour—clearly above the minimum wage), expecting Corey to work his normal 40-hour week in the office as well as conduct promotions at dozens of events during evenings and on weekends. It is entirely likely that Corey could work in excess of 70 hours per week, which would reduce Corey's hourly wage to $4.94 per hour (clearly below the minimum wage). Thus, the reasoning behind the new exemption rules is that simply giving an employee such as Corey a manager's title and a small salary and then demanding well over a 40-hour work week is unacceptable and not permitted under the FLSA. Under the FLSA's new exemption requirements, Corey's employer would be in violation of the minimum wage and overtime laws unless it pays Corey at least $23,660 annually.

The new DOL regulations provide for a three-part test for the white-collar exemptions from overtime pay:

1. **Salary basis test:** The employee must be paid a set and fixed salary that is not subject to variations because of quantity or quality of work.
2. **Salary test:** The amount of the salary must meet a minimum level.
3. **Duties test:** The employee's duties must be primarily involved in the executive, administrative, or professional functions of the business.

An organization that believes it qualifies for one of the white-collar exemptions but is unable to satisfy one of the exemption tests faces considerable risk. For example, a business could be liable for thousands of dollars in penalties, back wages, and legal costs if it incorrectly categorizes an employee as an exempt employee and fails to pay overtime or minimum wages.

Salary basis test. To meet the salary basis test for exemption from overtime, the employee must be paid a set sum of money for each work week regardless of the number of hours actually worked. An employee must be paid for this time period regardless of quantity or quality of work and must be paid if the employee works any period of time within a particular work week. The employer also cannot deduct pay from the employee's salary for work stoppages controlled by the employer. Thus, salaried employees of the NHL were still required to be paid by their individual team employers even though a work stoppage occurred when the owners and players reached an impasse in their labor negotiations in 2004. The employers would have had to terminate the employees in order to avoid paying their salaries. They could not unilaterally require the salaried employees to accept less pay for working fewer hours. If an employee is ready, willing, and able to work during a specific pay period, she must be paid for that period to meet the salary basis test and to qualify for the exemption from minimum wage and overtime pay.

Salary test. The 2004 exemption amendments also established new and clearer salary requirements and duty lists. Under the new salary test, an employee's weekly salary must be at least $455 (which equates to a minimum annual salary of $23,660). This is a $300 increase from the prior weekly salary test of $155. Simply stated, any employee paid less than $23,660 will always be covered by FLSA protections and will be entitled to overtime pay regardless of the job duties.

Job duties test. Under the new duties test, the employee's job duties must fit into one of the following categories in order to qualify for an exemption: executive, administrative, learned professional, creative professional, computer employee, or outside sales employee. See Exhibit 8.2.

To qualify for the "white-collar exemption," the employer must satisfy all three of these tests. Recall Corey's employment as an assistant promotions manager. Corey's job duties must fall within one of the exempt categories, such as the administrative category, but the minor league baseball team must meet the other two tests as well. Under the salary basis test, Corey must be paid his salary when the team is traveling, even though Corey may work fewer than 40 hours during such a week. Under the salary test, Corey must be paid a minimum of $23,660 annually or $455 weekly. If the team fails to meet any of these tests, Corey is not an exempt employee, and the team must pay overtime wages.

Assistant coaching and athletic training positions are significantly affected by the exemption amendments. Head coaches and head athletic trainers may be exempt as learned professionals, but assistant coaches and assistant athletic trainers are probably not exempt. Coaches and trainers who work significantly more than 40 hours per week, are paid a relatively low salary, and do not supervise other employees and exercise direct and independent judgment will have to be paid at least $23,660 per year to comply with the FLSA, assuming the other exemption tests are also satisfied (see Baechli, 2004).

Amusement or recreational exemption

A second exemption commonly present in the sport or recreation industries is the Amusement or Recreational Employee exemption. Section 213 of the Fair Labor Standards Act (hereinafter "FLSA") provides as follows:

Exemptions

(a) Minimum wage and maximum hour requirements. The provisions . . . shall not apply with respect to—

(3) any employee employed by an establishment which is an amusement or recreational establishment, [or] organized camp, . . . , if

(A) it does not operate for more than seven months in any calendar year, or

(B) during the preceding calendar year, its average receipts for any six months of such year were not more than 33 1/3 per centum of its average receipts for the other six months of such year . . .

	EXHIBIT	8.2
Exempt employee categories under Fair Labor Standards Act.		

JOB DUTY EXEMPTION CATEGORY	JOB DUTIES	EXAMPLE REPRESENTATIVE POSITIONS
Executive	Primarily manages an enterprise, subdivision, or customarily recognized department Regularly directs the work of at least two other full-time employees; is authorized to hire or fire, or influences decisions to hire/fire/promote other employees Minimum salary = $455 per week paid on a salary basis	Associate athletic director for marketing in a college athletic department
Administrative	Primarily performs office or nonmanual work directly related to general business operations Must exercise discretion and independent judgment with respect to matters of significance (discretion and independent judgment means making independent choices free from immediate direction and supervision) Minimum salary = $455 per week paid on a salary basis	Ticket sales manager with a professional sports team
Learned professional	Primarily performs work requiring advanced knowledge in a field of science or learning, defined as work predominantly intellectual in character and requiring consistent exercise of discretion and judgment Employee acquired advanced knowledge through a prolonged course of specialized intellectual instruction Minimum salary = $455 per week paid on a salary basis	College faculty
Creative professional	Primarily performs work requiring invention, imagination, originality, or talent in a recognized field of artistic or creative endeavor Minimum salary = $455 per week paid on a salary basis	Professional photographer
Computer employee	Computer systems analyst, computer programmer, software engineer, or other similarly skilled worker in the computer field Primarily applies systems analysis techniques and procedures Is compensated either on a salary basis at not less than $455 per week ($23,660 per year) OR $27.63 per hour if on an hourly basis	Webmaster for a high school athletic program
Outside sales employee	Primarily makes sales or obtains orders or contracts for services or use of facilities Is regularly engaged away from the employer's place of business No minimum salary	Sales representative for a sport medicine supply company

In order to qualify for the exemption the employer must demonstrate that it satisfied one of the two tests set forth in the exemption. These two tests are either (1) the seven months operations test or (2) the average receipts test. An excellent example of a seasonal or recreational enterprise is an amusement park or swimming pool or summer camp that operates for only a few months each year and then closes down completely. However, both major league and minor league sports teams have often asserted this exemption with mixed results. For example, in *Adams v. Detroit Tigers, Inc.* (1997), the Detroit Tigers were sued by a number of batboys who claimed that they were not paid overtime compensation and minimum wages for their work in violation of state and federal law. The baseball team argued that it was exempt. Specifically, the baseball team contended that it was an amusement or recreational establishment that either operated for not more than seven months in a calendar year or had average receipts for any six months of a calendar year that are less than 33 1/3 percent of average receipts for the remaining months of that year. Both parties agreed that the baseball team as a whole was a recreation or amusement establishment. The court further found that the batboys were an intricate part of this establishment and were not independent of the baseball team. However, the court granted the Tigers' motion for summary judgment because the Tigers had shown that the baseball team met the wage-hour exemptions since the batboys were only employed for seven months of the year and the off-season receipts were less than 33 1/3 percent of the average of in-season receipts for the remainder of the year. The court dismissed the batboys' wage-hour cause of action.

In *Bridewell v. The Cincinnati Reds* (1995), maintenance employees for the Cincinnati Reds sued for overtime wages. The United States District Court for the Southern District of Ohio had granted summary judgment in favor of the Reds and found that it was not liable for plaintiffs' overtime wage claims because it was entitled to the exemption for recreational and amusement establishments that operate less than eight months per year under the FLSA. But the court of appeals reversed, concluding that the Reds held regular season home games at Cincinnati's Riverfront Stadium and that the Reds had the exclusive right to sell advertising on signs at the stadium throughout the year, to operate the scoreboard during baseball and football games, and to contract with a concessionaire to operate at baseball and football games. The court of appeals also noted that the Reds employed 120 employees year-round and as many as 700 employees at peak periods. The court of appeals held the team was not entitled to the exemption under the FLSA for recreational and amusement establishments because the facts established that the defendant, in fact, operated year-round in various capacities.

Finally in *Jeffery v. Sarasota White Sox, Inc.* (1995), the plaintiff was a groundskeeper employed by the Sarasota White Sox to maintain a baseball complex. The city owned the complex, which was open year-round, but used by the defendant only on a seasonal basis. The plaintiff sued the defendant seeking damages for unpaid overtime wages pursuant to the FLSA, 29 U.S.C.S. § 201 et seq. On appeal, the court affirmed the trial court's grant of summary judgment for defendant since defendant was an amusement or recreational establishment exempt from the mandatory overtime provisions of the FLSA. An establishment was seasonal if it satisfied the six-month receipts test, even if the establishment was open for more than seven months a year.

The following Case Opinion is useful to examine how a court has recently compared the holdings in *Bridewell* and *Jeffery* and explore whether a major league sports team could successfully assert the Amusement and Recreational exemption as compared to a minor league sports team.

Liger v. New Orleans Hornets NBA Ltd. Partnership

565 F. Supp. 2d 680 (E.D. La. 2008) and
2006 U.S. Dist. LEXIS, 72670, 11 Wage & Hour Cas. 2d (BNA) 1857 (E.D. La. 2006).

CASE OPINION

[FACTS

The Plaintiffs filed this action on May 27, 2005. Plaintiffs are former employees of the Hornets and are seeking compensation for allegedly unpaid overtime wages. The plaintiffs worked in the "business enterprise" of the organization, specifically in sales and fan relations. Under the Fair Labor Standards Act, "FLSA," the maximum work week for an employee of an enterprise engaged in commerce is forty hours. 29 U.S.C. § 207(a)(1) (2006). If an employee works longer, he must receive overtime compensation at a rate of at least one and one-half times his regular rate of pay. The Hornets argued that they were an amusement or recreational establishment which is exempt from the overtime and minimum wage compensation requirement.]

HOLDING

The court held that the Hornets were a year-round operation, and thus could not qualify for the amusement and recreation exemption.

RATIONALE

The Hornets are an organization that is involved in the amusement or recreation of professional basketball games. The Hornets argued that it was not liable to the sales employees because it was exempt under the Seasonal Amusement and Recreation Exemption of the FLSA. The statute provides two elements under which an amusement or recreational establishment may be found exempt from minimum wage and maximum hour requirements: "if (A) it does not operate for more than seven months in any calendar year, or (B) during the preceding calendar year, its average receipts for any six months of such year were not more than 33 1/3 per centum of its average receipts for the other six months of such year."

The sales employees relied on the decision in *Bridewell v. The Cincinnati Reds* which held that the Cincinnati Reds were a year-round operation. The Hornets relied on *Jeffery v. Sarasota White Sox, Inc.*, to argue that it only operated for seven months of the year. The court held that reliance upon *Jeffery*, however, was insufficient to find in favor of the Hornets. In *Jeffery*, the Eleventh Circuit found that a minor league baseball team did not operate for seven months out of the year, although some employees were employed year-round. In that case there was no dispute regarding the length of the operating season. The court was not convinced that the operative scale of a minor league baseball team was analogous to that of an NBA franchise.

The sales employees' reliance on *Bridewell* was more appropriate. In *Bridewell*, the Sixth Circuit found that a major league baseball team was a year-round operation, despite the fact that they did not provide "amusement and recreation" year-round. Additionally, the court observed that "the fact that the Reds employ 120 year-round workers compels the conclusion that they 'operate' year-round." (stating, "[w]hile a truly seasonal business that employs an insignificant number of workers year-round could conceivably qualify for the exemption, the fact that the Reds employ 120 year-round workers compels the conclusion that they 'operate' year-round."). The Hornets admit that it employs over 100 personnel in year-round positions. In addition, the NBA regular season typically begins in October and ends in April; in combination with pre-season and post-season games, the Hornets have the opportunity to participate in games for nine months each year. Finally, the NBA draft occurs each June; thus, the Hornets operate in the summer even when they do not make the playoffs. Therefore, the court found the reasoning and holding of *Bridewell* to be more analogous to Liger's situation than *Jeffery*. Consequently, the court found that the Hornets were a year-round operation, and thus, could not qualify for the exemption under FLSA, 29 U.S.C. § 213 (a)(3)(A).

Questions

1. Why did the court determine that the operations of a National Basketball Association team were more analogous to the operations of a Major League Baseball team rather than a minor league baseball team?

2. What were the key characteristics of the Hornets operations that led the court to conclude it was a year-round operation?

Trainee or intern exemption

One area in which the sport industry is often criticized relating to wages and hours involves the use of interns. The value of experiential learning has been well documented in business and academic journals (Briggs, 2000; Cates-McIver, 1998; Crumbley & Sumners, 1998; Haghighi, 1998; Kelsey, 2002; Singer, 2000; Whalen & Barnes, 2001). Sport management students are encouraged to volunteer and seek internships to improve their employment opportunities. It could easily be argued that no single step in a sport management career path is as important and valuable as the internship. However, how the sport industry compensates interns has been criticized (Stier, 2001; Genzale, 2005; Shellenbarger, 2009).

Under the Fair Labor Standards Act, it may not be necessary to pay interns who qualify as trainees (29 U.S.C. §§ 203(e)(2)(A); Kaplan, 1994). The Supreme Court has held that the words "to suffer or permit to work," as used in the FLSA to define the term "employ," do not make all persons employees who work for their own advantage on the premises of another without any agreement for compensation. Whether trainees or students are employees under the FLSA will depend upon all of the circumstances surrounding their activities on the premises of the employer.

Trainee status is determined by using six criteria set forth by the Department of Labor. If all of the following six criteria are met, the trainee or student is not an employee for purposes of the FLSA:

1. The intern is not displacing a regular employee position and works under close supervision.

2. The intern is not entitled to a job at the end of the internship.

3. Both the sponsor organization and the intern understand that the intern is not entitled to any wages during the internship.

4. The intern receives training from the sponsor organization, even if it takes time away from work and is of no immediate advantage to the employer.

5. The training includes actual hands-on experience with equipment or processes used in the industry.

6. The training primarily benefits the student, not the sponsor organization. (U.S. Department of Labor, n.d.g)

Most state labor agencies do an excellent job of providing current information and resources about wage and labor issues, including the use of trainees. For example, the following information is provided by the Texas Workforce Commission to help educate employers in Texas about the correct use of trainees.

> In an administrative letter ruling dated February 22, 1974, the DOL stated that if a person is considered a "trainee," that person is not considered an "employee" and does not have to be paid minimum wage and overtime. The letter gave . . . six criteria for the designation of a person as a trainee; commentary on each criterion follows in italics.

See Exhibit 8.3 for the criteria and commentary.

The burden is on the employer to demonstrate that the exemption applies and that all the criteria are satisfied. Essentially, if a company is using interns as a low-cost or no-cost replacement for regular employees, it may have difficulty meeting the trainee criteria. Organizations in other industries, such as entertainment, financial services, and architectural services, have been investigated and fined by the Department of Labor for rampant misuse of the trainee exemption (Gregory, 1998; Lisser, 1995).

The following hypothetical case explores the trainee exemption in the context of the sports industry.

considering . . .   INTERNS UNDER THE FLSA

Assume you have recently been hired as the marketing and promotions director for a minor league professional sports team. You have two full-time salespeople who also help with game day promotions and operations, but you want to partner with the local university's sport management program to provide opportunities for the students to learn about the professional sports industry and also to get some help for your game day promotions and operations. You have a limited budget and will not be able to pay the students for their help.

Questions

- What options do you have to use these students without paying for their services?
- How would you structure your internship program to make sure it is compliant with the FLSA?

Note how you would answer the questions and then check your responses using the Analysis & Discussion at the end of this chapter.

Volunteers under the FLSA

Volunteerism is a significant element of the sport and recreation industry. Not only is volunteerism an important way for students to gain meaningful experience, but many sport organizations rely heavily on volunteers to aid in event manage-

| EXHIBIT | 8.3 | DOL criteria for the designation of a person as a trainee and the Texas Workforce Commission's *commentary (in italics)* (Texas Workforce Commission, 2008). |

1. The training, even though it includes actual operation of the facilities of the employer, is similar to that which would be given in a vocational school.

   The closer it is to a classroom or educational setting, the easier it will be to consider the individuals to be trainees. The arrangement might also result in a training certificate that could be listed as a job qualification on subsequent job applications. It would also help if the individual and the entity providing the training could first develop an individualized training plan that would be tailored to help the individual qualify for a specific job or range of jobs with a variety of companies via the training course.

2. The training is for the benefit of the trainees.

   This would be an easy argument to make in the case of individuals participating in welfare-to-work programs but also in any training or internship programs that tend to increase their "hireability" in the open job market.

3. The trainees do not displace regular employees, but work under close observation.

   This would also be an easy argument to make, especially in the case of a training "academy" run by a company, but also for a work experience program sponsored by a governmental entity. In the latter case, the government agency would be able to show that were it not for the work experience program, the activities in question would not be taking place. In a true training environment, the trainees are not going to be trusted to do much actual work for the company; the actual production would presumably be done by regular employees, who of course are already trained.

4. The employer that provides the training derives no immediate advantage from the activities of the trainees, and on occasion his operations may actually be impeded.

   This goes hand-in-hand with item 3 above. It would be important here to document the training process and the before and after figures for comparison. Again, the actual productive work will be done by regular employees; any productive work done by trainees would have to be insubstantial in nature and amount and also be secondary to the training process.

5. The trainees are not necessarily entitled to a job at the completion of the training period.

   Again, this is related to item 3 above. The work would not be done at all, or at least certainly not on the schedule that exists, were it not for the existence of the training school or program under which the individuals receive training. The courts find it important to have a written agreement to the effect that trainees have no expectation or guarantee of employment upon completion of the training.

6. The employer and the trainees understand that the trainees are not entitled to wages for the time spent in training.

   The courts find it important that there be a written agreement to the effect that payment for the services is neither intended nor expected.

ment. The Olympic Organizing Committees for Barcelona, Atlanta, and Sydney used more than 141,000 volunteers combined, and Beijing reportedly used 2 million volunteers during the 2008 summer Olympic games. Even a small local event may have operational difficulties without the aid of volunteers.

The Fair Labor Standards Act defines employment very broadly, i.e., "to suffer or permit to work." However, the Supreme Court has made it clear that the FLSA was not intended "to stamp all persons as employees who without any express or implied compensation agreement might work for their own advantage on the premises of another." Individuals who volunteer or donate their services, usually on a part-time basis, for *public service, religious, or humanitarian objectives,* not as employees and without contemplation of pay, are not considered employees of the religious, charitable, or similar **nonprofit** organizations that receive their service (DOL, 2009).

For example, members of civic organizations may volunteer to drive a school bus to carry a football team or school band on a trip. Similarly, an individual may volunteer to help in a youth program as a camp counselor, scoutmaster, to solicit contributions or participate in a benefit program for a university athletic team, or to volunteer other services required by charitable, educational, or religious programs. These volunteers are not employees for purposes of minimum wage and overtime pay requirements under FLSA.

However, under the FLSA, employees may not volunteer services to **for-profit** private sector employers. When Congress amended the FLSA in 1985, it made clear that people are allowed to volunteer their services to public agencies and their community but with one exception— public sector employers may not allow their employees to volunteer without compensation. Public sector employees may not volunteer additional time to do the same work for which they are employed. There is no prohibition on anyone employed in the private sector from volunteering in any capacity or line of work in the public sector. Note that an employee can not volunteer to do the work for which they should be paid. However, if UPS were sponsoring a local sporting event and agreed to recruit volunteers from among its employees, those employees may volunteer their time to the local organizing committee. Many large employers actually offer additional benefits to employees who choose to volunteer in the community as a "representative" of their employer.

Competitive Advantage
STRATEGIES

Complying with the Fair Labor Standards Act

- Regularly review and prepare employee position descriptions and duties lists for existing employees based upon operational needs.
- Create complete employee position descriptions and duties lists for all new hires based upon operational needs.
- After reviewing the FLSA exemption requirements, determine which employees are nonexempt and pay overtime when appropriate.
- Evaluate status of seasonal employees to determine whether amusement and recreation exemption applies.
- Evaluate employee work habits to determine whether employees are "suffered or permitted" to work extra hours in the day, such as working during lunch or prior to or after regular work hours.
- Maintain employee work records for at least three years.
- Evaluate part-time employees to determine whether minimum wage and overtime practices are compliant.
- Review agreements with independent contractors. If a person has more characteristics of an employee than an independent contractor (see Chapter 5), wage and hour requirements may apply.
- Review how interns are used and determine whether such use meets the "trainee" exemption from paying minimum wage and overtime.
- Use a written internship agreement addressing the trainee criteria.

Penalties for Violations of FLSA

The Department of Labor has a clear policy of investigating alleged violations of the FLSA. In 2007, the DOL initiated more than 30,000 compliance actions resulting in $10.3 million in civil penalties and $220 million in payment of back wages. Employers that willfully or repeatedly violate the minimum wage or overtime pay requirements are subject to a civil monetary penalty of up to $1,100 for each such violation. A second conviction may result in imprisonment. The Department of Labor may also bring suit for back pay and an equal amount in liquidated damages, and it may obtain injunctions to restrain persons from violating the act. It is also a violation to fire or in any other manner discriminate against an employee for filing a complaint or for participating in a legal proceeding under FLSA.

WORKPLACE SAFETY AND HEALTH

The Occupational Safety and Health Act of 1970 is administered by the Occupational Safety and Health Administration and covers all employers and their employees in the 50 states, the District of Columbia, Puerto Rico, and other U. S. territories. Employers have a general duty to provide their employees with a safe and healthful work environment free from serious hazards. Safety and health conditions in most private industries are regulated by OSHA or OSHA-approved state programs.

Employers covered by the act must comply with the regulations and the safety and health standards promulgated by OSHA. OSHA enforces the act through workplace inspections and investigations. The act defines an employer as any "person engaged in a business affecting commerce who has employees, but does not include the United States or any state or political subdivision of a State" (OSHA, 2007). Therefore, the act applies to employers and employees in such varied fields as manufacturing, construction, retail, agriculture, law, and medicine and includes nonprofits, organized labor, and private educational institutions. The act establishes a separate program for federal government employees and extends coverage to state and local government employees only through the states' OSHA-approved plans. Sport organizations can be affected in a number of ways, ranging from safety standards applicable to a new sports stadium construction project to the ergonomic design of a computer station in a ticket office.

OSHA has two primary regulatory functions:

1. Setting standards
2. Conducting inspections to ensure that employers are providing safe and healthful workplaces

OSHA may set a **specific hazard standard** that must be met by an employer and may require that employers adopt specific practices, means, methods, or processes reasonably necessary and appropriate to protect workers on the job. Regardless whether OSHA has set forth a standard addressing a specific hazard, employers also must comply with the **general duty** clause in the act. The general duty clause (Section 5(a)(1)) states that each employer "shall furnish . . . a place of employment which is free from recognized hazards that are causing or are likely to cause death or serious physical harm to his employees" (OSHA, 2007).

Employers must become familiar with the specific standards applicable to their establishments and eliminate those specific hazards as well as general hazards that are likely to cause death or serious injury to employees. Compliance with standards may include ensuring that employees have been provided with, have been effectively trained on, and use personal protective equipment when required for safety or health. Employees must comply with all rules and regulations that apply to their own actions and conduct.

Many specific OSHA standards relate to manufacturing, construction, and transportation industries. For example, OSHA opened an investigation during the Dallas Cowboys new stadium construction project following a crane accident. Between April 2006 and May 2008, the construction manager of the Cowboys stadium project reported 175 incidents to OSHA ("OSHA is investigating recent accidents," 2008). During Louisville's construction of its new downtown arena, the construction company entered into a site-based construction partnership agreement with the Kentucky Department of Labor OSHA as part of a Construction Partnership Program run by OSHA's Division of Education and Training. A Construction Partnership Program agreement is a voluntary agreement that allows OSHA to make quarterly consultations and site visits to conduct safety and health surveys and requires construction company employees to complete extensive safety training programs (Louisville Arena Authority, 2008). The training programs include a variety of topics including rigging safety, fall protection, forklift safety, accident analysis, hazard communication, bloodborne pathogens, first aid/CPR defibrillator, top driver safety, fire protection safety, respirator training, and scaffolding safety.

Such a program is a proactive approach to OSHA compliance and avoiding OSHA claims. Entering into a program such as this can also serve to improve financing and bonding opportunities for new facility financing. Organizations should also retain all documents pertaining to construction in the event of an accident and resulting OSHA investigation. For example, following the collapse of the Dallas Cowboys' practice facility in May, 2009, OSHA investigators were looking for building and construction documents that under Texas law must be retained for the lifetime of the structure. However, documents for the collapsed practice facility were lacking, with only a few documents indicating where the facility was to be located. Documentation regarding construction materials and inspections were not properly maintained. Sport managers who are involved in the construction of a new sports facility must be proactive in meeting their obligations under OSHA as well as other building code requirements.

A typical sport organization, by contrast, may only be indirectly affected by OSHA. Most sport organizations will be covered primarily by the general duty clause; that is, they need to ensure that their place of employment is free from hazards. For example, an employee of a minor league hockey team is responsible for placing signage around the ice rink prior to each game. One day, as the employee is hanging the signage behind the hockey goal, a player who is also on the ice practicing hits the employee in the back of the head with the puck and knocks him unconscious. The employee does not have any permanent injury, but an injury requiring more than minor first aid must be reported to OSHA. This is the type of injury that OSHA would expect the employer to have provided standards and training to avoid. It is quite likely that permitting the hockey players to practice on the ice at the same time that employees are setting up the event creates an unsafe

Competitive Advantage
STRATEGIES

Workplace Safety and Health

- Be sure all required OSHA information and posters are displayed for employees.

- Determine which OSHA standards and regulations apply to your organization.

- Conduct safety compliance audits of your company to identify and correct any violations.

- Establish a team to deal with catastrophic occurrences, fatalities, and OSHA-related public relations issues.

- Determine who will be responsible for overseeing safety and health concerns in your organization, and designate that person as your OSHA contact.

- Regularly review your safety records to ensure that your organization is in compliance with recordkeeping and reporting requirements.

- Make sure all training manuals, safety manuals, and other written employee training programs are up to date and easily accessible.

working condition. This condition could easily be remedied by implementing safety procedures to monitor access and usage of the ice rink when employees are present and by properly training employees as to these safety procedures.

Another notable segment of the sport industry affected by OSHA involves athletic trainers and medical personnel. Knowledge of OSHA guidelines for preventing disease transmission is essential for these individuals. OSHA's regulations regarding the prevention of transmission of bloodborne pathogens detail a number of requirements that affect athletic training or medical staff members. Of particular importance is the requirement that employers establish an exposure control plan to eliminate or minimize employee exposures. Employers must also provide personal protective equipment such as gloves, gowns, and masks, and provide information and training to employees covering the dangers of bloodborne pathogens, preventive practices, and postexposure procedures.

For a simple example of how these requirements should be implemented, consider an athletic trainer who is working at a men's basketball game when a member of the team is struck in the head resulting in a bloody nose. As we watch on television or at the game, we may see the trainer grab a bandage or gauze pad and place it on the injury to stop the bleeding. In fact, it was not at all uncommon a few years ago for the trainer not to wear protective gloves when treating this type of injury. However, under the OSHA guidelines on bloodborne pathogens, an exposure control plan should require all employees to have protective gloves immediately available and mandate that all employees must use these gloves when treating any injury where bleeding is present.

OSHA encourages states to develop and operate their own job safety and health programs. OSHA approves and monitors these "state plans," which operate under the authority of state law. Currently 26 states and jurisdictions operate complete state plans (covering both the private sector and state and local government employees), and four (Connecticut, New Jersey, New York, and the Virgin Islands) have plans that cover state and local government employees only (DOL, 2009). States with OSHA-approved job safety and health plans must set standards that are at least as effective as the federal standards. Most but not all of the state-plan states have adopted standards identical to the federal standards.

The act also provides protection for employees who report safety or health concerns. Employers may not discriminate or retaliate against an employee who raises or reports safety or health concerns. Provisions in most public safety laws and many environmental laws protect employees who complain about violations of the law by their employers. These provisions are known as whistleblower protections (see Chapter 4). If an employer discriminates or retaliates, the employee can file a complaint with OSHA. OSHA enforces the whistleblower protections in most laws. Remedies can include job reinstatement and payment of back wages.

WORKERS' COMPENSATION LAW

Workers' compensation statutes have been passed by each state to provide compensation for individuals who are injured while on the job. These statutes, many of which were enacted in the early part of the twentieth century, were put into effect because workers were not able to recover against their employers, under common law principles, for injuries on the job. Thus, many workers were left without a remedy for injuries that occurred at their place of employment.

To remedy this injustice, state legislatures passed workers' compensation statutes requiring the employer to pay compensation for work injuries and illnesses. Workers' compensation laws are designed to ensure that employees who are injured or disabled on the job are provided with fixed monetary awards, eliminating the need for litigation. These laws also provide benefits for dependents of workers whose work-related accidents or illnesses resulted in their death. These laws also protect employers and fellow workers by limiting the amount an injured employee can recover from an employer and by eliminating the liability of co-workers in most accidents.

Coverage of Workers' Compensation Laws

An employee is entitled to workers' compensation benefits for any work-related injury or illness regardless of who was at fault. An injury may be the result of a single incident, such as tripping over a box of promotional items in your office and breaking your wrist, having your foot run over by a Gator utility vehicle while unloading merchandise at a stadium, or even just bending over. An injury may also be the result of work activities extending over a period of time. For example, an employee who has lifted heavy objects at work and eventually develops pain in the back or other parts of the body may have suffered a work-related injury. Another example is that of a college football facility that ignites fireworks and sounds a very loud horn after each home team touchdown. An employee who is required to stand close to the fireworks and the horn may suffer hearing loss over time that would be covered by workers' compensation. An injury may also be the result of a disease or illness that is produced, contributed to, or aggravated by the employment. For example, a worker's exposure to stress may accelerate the development of heart disease.

Elements for a workers' compensation claim

Although the specific language of the statutes varies from state to state, three essential elements must be met for an injured employee to be entitled to workers' compensation (see Exhibit 8.4).

Essential elements entitling an injured worker to workers' compensation.   EXHIBIT   **8.4**

1. A compensable injury must have occurred.
2. The injury must be accidental.
3. The injury must arise out of employment.

When a claim falls within the coverage of the workers' compensation statute, that claim is exclusive, meaning that the worker's *only* remedy is under workers' compensation. The employee's compensation is determined by a schedule of compensation under the statute. For example, under the Massachusetts workers' compensation schedule, an employee who suffers the total loss of use of one eye would receive a sum equal to the average weekly wage in the commonwealth at the date of the injury multiplied by 39 (A.L.M., 2009). The use of the multiplier 39 is simply the formula adopted by the Commonwealth of Massachusetts to set a value for the injury. Clearly, it is difficult to place a dollar value on the loss of an eye, but one purpose of the workers' compensation formula is to provide specific recovery amounts for a broad range of injury types. A different state may use a different multiplier. An employee is limited to recovering the predetermined amount based on the worker's level of impairment, payments for medical expenses, and degree of disability as determined by the state's workers' compensation scheme and formulas. As we will discuss later, employees may seek to show that workers' compensation is not applicable to their injury because the benefits are limited.

Compensable injuries. Generally, to have a **compensable injury,** a worker must suffer a physical injury or illness. Psychological or emotional injuries are often excluded from the coverage of the act. In addition, laws may exclude compensation for injuries that are intentional or self-inflicted; result from the employee's horseplay or voluntary intoxication (either alcohol or drug-induced); arise from voluntary participation in off-duty recreational, social, or sporting events; result from "acts of God" (unless a person's job exposes him to a greater risk of injury from such acts); or are inflicted by someone else for personal reasons unrelated to employment.

Accidental injuries. Injuries that result from intentional acts are not considered accidental injuries for purposes of workers' compensation. For example, if a worker punches a co-worker on the job, this is not an accidental injury and is not compensable. Sexual harassment at the workplace may be considered intentional conduct and may be excluded under the statute. However, even in cases where the employee's own negligence may have contributed to his injury, he is still entitled to workers' compensation. For example, LaShonda, a special events coordinator for a local nonprofit organization, has transported several boxes of promotional items to be given away at the annual celebrity golf scramble. When LaShonda arrives at the golf course pro shop to unload her car, she mistakenly puts the car in reverse instead of park, causing the car to roll over her as she attempts to unload the boxes. While certainly LaShonda's own negligence has contributed to her injury, she is still entitled to recover workers' compensation for her injuries, since the injury was the result of an accident.

Injuries arising out of employment. The third element for entitlement to workers' compensation is whether the injury "arose out of employment." This is often a difficult issue to resolve. Often courts look at whether the injury is tied to some condition, activity, or requirement of employment. Although each state may use different language to decide whether the injury "arose out of employment," courts often consider the following factors, although no single factor is determinative (van der Smissen, 1990):

1. Whether the injury occurred during working hours
2. Whether the injury occurred on the employer's premises
3. Whether the injury occurred during an activity initiated by the employer
4. Whether the employer exercised any degree of control or direction over the employee's activity
5. Whether the employer benefited or stood to benefit from the employee's activity

An injury does not have to occur at the employer's worksite or while the employee is actually working. Injuries to employees who are making deliveries or walking through parking lots may fall within the reach of workers' compensation. If an employer urges employees to participate in employer-sponsored activities, such as a fitness event or a company softball game, there may be liability under workers' compensation. In a case from Ohio, a company was held responsible for death benefits under the workers' compensation statute after an employee suffered a heart attack while participating in a foot race held during a company-sponsored fitness day (*Jones v. Multi-Color Corp.,* 1995). The activities were held to be work-related, and thus the heart attack arose out of employment.

In a case that involved a school district, a teacher/coach tore his Achilles tendon while playing basketball in an evening fund-raising game, which was held to benefit the school's basketball program (*Dozier v. Mid-Del Sch. System,* 1998). A team of teachers, coaches, and former school athletes had been playing against employees of a radio station. The teacher/coach's claim for workers' compensation benefits was initially denied on the basis that the injury occurred during a voluntary recreational activity, but an appellate court reversed, holding that the injury "arose out of employment." The court noted that the teacher/coach was encouraged to participate in the fund-raiser to help the athletic programs survive. Under the language of the statute, the employer "derived a substantial direct benefit from the activity," and the injury was compensable under the workers' compensation law.

In another case, a teacher who was injured during a basketball game between students and teachers was able to recover workers' compensation (*Highlands County Sch. Bd. v. Savage,* 1992). This case was easier to resolve because the game was held during regular school hours and teachers were required to participate or at least attend the game as spectators.

Even an employee who is engaging in voluntary physical activity during business hours may be acting within the scope of his employment for purposes of workers' compensation. A fitness instructor, Murphy, injured his leg while playing wallyball during his work shift at the Elmhurst Park fitness facility. Murphy was found to be entitled to workers' compensation even though the park district had argued the game was a voluntary recreational activity. The Illinois court of appeals agreed with the findings of the workers' compensation commission that the instructor's participation clearly benefited the park's business, that recreation was inherent in Murphy's job, and that his reason for participating was not for his own diversion but for his employer's benefit (*Elmhurst Park District v. Illinois Workers' Compensation Commission,* 2009).

The following Focus Case and subsequent hypothetical case further examine how the *scope of employment* factors may be applied to a sport organization.

Hallal v. RDV Sports, Inc.

FOCUS CASE　682 So. 2d 1235 (Fla. App. 1996)

FACTS

Keith Hallal was attending the University of Massachusetts as a full-time student, pursuing a bachelor's degree in sports management. In the spring of 1994, he was selected for an internship with the marketing office of the Orlando Magic. Shortly after beginning work with the Magic, Mr. Hallal sustained an injury to his ear when his head struck an antenna that was protruding from a radio mounted on the wall of the supply and copy room. Mr. Hallal later filed suit against the Magic for negligent maintenance of its premises. The Magic moved for summary judgment, asserting that it was immune from tort liability under the Florida Workers' Compensation Law. The trial court agreed and entered final summary judgment in favor of the Magic.

HOLDING

The trial court properly concluded that Mr. Hallal was an "employee" under the Florida Workers' Compensation Act when he was injured.

RATIONALE

Section 440.03, Florida Statutes (1995), provides that every employer and every employee is bound by the provisions of the Workers' Compensation Law. Section 440.02(13)(a) defines "employee" as "any person engaged in any employment under any appointment for contract of hire or apprenticeship, express or implied, oral or written, whether lawfully or unlawfully employed, and includes but is not limited to aliens and minors." Specifically excluded from the definition of "employee" is the term "volunteer." Section 440.02(13)(d)6 provides that "[a] person who does not receive monetary remuneration for his services is presumed to be a volunteer unless there is substantial evidence that valuable consideration was intended by both employer and employee." Mr. Hallal contends that he falls within the statutory definition of a volunteer because he did not receive monetary remuneration for his services as an intern and because the record does not contain substantial evidence that he and the Magic intended to exchange valuable consideration. We disagree.

The record establishes that interns with the Magic are required, among other things, to attend all Magic home basketball games and that in exchange they are paid $25 a game. Mr. Hallal attended ten home games and received a total of $250. Such payment constitutes monetary remuneration. Therefore, Mr. Hallal was not a "volunteer." Moreover, even if no monetary remuneration had been received by Mr. Hallal, summary judgment would have been appropriate in this case because Mr. Hallal's participation in the internship program constituted valuable consideration in that such participation was necessary in order for him to satisfy the requirements of his degree.

Bob Jackson owns a sports marketing firm with about a dozen employees. To build goodwill and teamwork, he sponsors a company softball team and strongly encourages all of the employees to play. In fact, Jackson gives special benefits to those who play on the team. During a league game after work hours at a public softball field, the team's shortstop, Mary, sprains her ankle while running the bases.

Questions

- Can Jackson's company be held responsible for paying Mary's workers' compensation claim?

- What factors would a court look at when deciding whether this injury arose out of employment?

Note how you would answer the questions and then check your responses using the Analysis & Discussion at the end of this chapter.

Workers' Compensation and the Professional Athlete

In professional sports, the accidental nature of the injury is a critical issue, since many injuries are possible in sport due to the physical and possibly violent nature of the game. Many workers' compensation cases arising on the professional sport level involve professional athletes who argue that workers' compensation law is not applicable. They make this argument because the workers' compensation benefits are very limited and are often considered insufficient compensation for professional athletes, who may be receiving very large salaries. However, most states have specifically included professional athletes in their workers' compensation programs. The following Focus Case examines a professional athlete's claim for worker compensation benefits.

Pro-Football, Inc. v. Uhlenhake

558 S.E.2d 571 (Va. App. 2002)	**FOCUS CASE**

FACTS

The Workers' Compensation Commission (WCC) entered an award of permanent partial disability benefits in favor of Jeffrey A. Uhlenhake, a professional football player, for injury to his left foot. Pro-Football, Inc. (Washington Redskins) contends that injuries to a professional football player are not covered by the Workers' Compensation Act. Beginning in 1996, Uhlenhake was employed by Pro-Football as an offensive lineman for the Washington Redskins football team. During his career, Uhlenhake experienced a number of physical injuries in training, practices, and games. Specifically, Uhlenhake injured his left foot, left ankle, and left knee. An orthopaedic surgeon examined Uhlenhake in 1999 and determined that he had a permanent impairment of his left ankle due to arthritis and of his left knee due to the ACL injury. Uhlenhake filed a claim for permanent partial disability worker compensation benefits based upon injuries to his left ankle and foot and to his left knee. Following an evidentiary hearing, the WCC ruled that injuries sustained in employment by professional athletes are covered by the Workers' Compensation Act and that Uhlenhake was entitled to permanent partial disability benefits for 5 percent loss of the use of his left foot and 14 percent loss of use of his left leg and for medical benefits. Pro-Football appealed.

HOLDING

The Virginia appellate court held that the WCC correctly ruled that professional football players are covered under the Workers' Compensation Act when they suffer injuries in the game they are employed to perform.

RATIONALE

Pro-Football contended that injuries resulting from voluntary participation in activities where injuries are customary, foreseeable, and expected are not accidental within the meaning of the workers' compensation laws. The Workers' Compensation Act provides that "'injury' means only injury by accident arising out of and in the course of employment." The Act does not . . . specifically define the term "injury by accident." To establish an "injury by accident," a claimant must prove (1) that the injury appeared suddenly at a particular time and place and upon a particular occasion, (2) that it was caused by an identifiable incident or sudden precipitating event, and (3) that it resulted in an obvious mechanical or structural change in the human body.

The principle is well established that "to constitute injury by accident it is not necessary for the Plaintiff to prove that there must be a . . . 'fortuitous circumstance' . . . [or] that there should be an extraordinary occurrence in or about the work engaged in." The evidence proved that Uhlenhake was engaged in an activity required by his employment. He was employed by Pro-Football to train, practice, and play in football games, which is the business of Pro-Football. This is not a case of an injury "resulting from an employee's voluntary participation in employer-sponsored off-duty recreational activities which are not part of the employee's duties." Likewise, this is not a case in which the "injury was the direct result of [an employee] taking a risk of his own choosing, independent of any employment requirements, and one that was not an accepted and normal activity at the place of employment." Uhlenhake was at all relevant times engaged in an activity within the scope of his employment contract.

In addition to explaining when an injury is a result of an accident that would permit workers' compensation benefits to be paid, the *Uhlenhake* case also addresses the nature of football as a dangerous sport and the matter of whether players should expect to be injured. Pro-Football had argued that by engaging in conduct that is physically dangerous and that has a high likelihood of injury, players must "automatically" expect to be injured. In support of its contentions, Pro-Football cited two appellate court decisions in other jurisdictions, *Rowe v. Baltimore Colts* (1983), and *Palmer v. Kansas City Chiefs Football Club* (1981).

However, the appellate court stated that "the *Rowe* and *Palmer* decisions are contrary to the decisions in the great majority of jurisdictions. Injuries in [professional] sports are so routinely treated as compensable in the great majority of jurisdictions that they seldom appear in reported appellate decisions" (Arthur Larson, Workers' Compensation Law § 22.04[1][b], 2001). Larson further notes that *Palmer* "is the only surviving appellate decision denying compensation for injury in a professional team sport. To say that football injuries are not accidental because of the probability of injury is . . . no more than to say that any activity with a high risk factor should be ruled noncompensable." The *Uhlenhake* court emphasized that the business of Pro-Football is to engage in the activity of professional football. It employs individuals to constantly perform in a strenuous activity that has risks and hazards. As with coal miners, steel workers, firefighters, and police officers, who are covered by workers' compensation, other classes of employees are regularly exposed to known, actual risks of hazards because "the employment subjects the employee to the particular danger." Therefore, despite a few decisions to the contrary, the court decided that "it is clear that professional football players are covered workers when they suffer injuries in the game they are employed to perform."

Workers' Compensation and the Collegiate Athlete

In the course of playing a sport for an institution, a player may suffer an injury. Some players have argued that they should receive workers' compensation for such injures. Although a few players were able to convince courts in early cases (*Van Horn v. Industrial Accident Comm'n,* 1963; *University of Denver v. Nemeth,* 1953) that they should be considered "employees" of the university, most courts today are in agreement that student-athletes at universities should not be considered employees. The student-athlete's claim for workers' compensation is based on the argument that the receipt of an athletic scholarship constitutes an employment contract in which the athlete exchanges the work of athletic performance for the pay of scholarship monies.

An interesting case from Texas (*Waldrep v. Texas Employers Ins. Ass'n,* 2000) concerns Kent Waldrep, a former football player at Texas Christian University (TCU), who became a quadriplegic when he broke his neck during a game in 1974. TCU had no insurance coverage and informed Waldrep that it was not liable for his medical bills. Waldrep filed a claim for workers' compensation. On March 23, 1993, the Texas Workers' Compensation Board ruled in Waldrep's favor and awarded benefits. Later, a jury decided that Waldrep was not an employee of TCU and was not entitled to workers' compensation benefits. The Texas Court of Appeals also found that Waldrep was not an employee, explaining that both Waldrep and TCU evidenced an intention that Waldrep be considered an amateur. This position is consistent with the NCAA's policies and rules that consider the "athlete as an integral part of the educational program and the athlete as an integral part of the student body, and by doing so, retain a clear line of demarcation between college athletics and professional sports." The holding in *Waldrep* is consistent with most courts' determinations that student-athletes are not university employees.

In the following Focus Case, the court also found that a student-athlete is not an employee for the purposes of workers' compensation.

Rensing v. Indiana State University Board of Trustees

FOCUS CASE 444 N.E. 1170 (Ind. 1983)

FACTS

Rensing suffered an injury on April 24, 1976, during the team's spring football practice that left him a quadriplegic. Rensing filed a claim with the Industrial Board of Indiana (Industrial Board) seeking recovery under workers' compensation for permanent total disability as well as medical and hospital expenses incurred due to the injury. The Industrial Board found that an employer–employee relationship did not exist between Rensing and the Indiana State University Board of Trustees (Trustees) and denied Rensing's claim for benefits. Rensing appealed, and the Indiana court of appeals reversed the decision of the Industrial Board on the basis that Rensing was an "employee" for pay within the meaning of the statute and his employment by the Trustees was also within the coverage of the statute. ISU then appealed to the Indiana Supreme Court.

HOLDING

The court of appeals incorrectly concluded that Rensing was an employee under the Workmen's Compensation Act. The decision of the Industrial Board is reinstated.

RATIONALE

The contested issue is whether the requisite employer–employee relationship existed between Rensing and the Trustees so as to bring him under the coverage of the Workmen's Compensation Act. It is clear that while a determination of the existence of an employee–employer relationship is a complex matter involving many factors, the primary consideration is that there was an intent that a contract of employment, either express or implied, did exist. In other words, there must be a mutual belief that an employer-employee relationship did exist. It is evident from the documents that formed the agreement in this case that there was no intent to enter into an employee–employer relationship at the time the parties entered into the agreement.

In this case, the National Collegiate Athletic Association's (NCAA) constitution and by-laws were incorporated by reference into the financial aid agreements. A fundamental policy of the NCAA, which is stated in its constitution, is that intercollegiate sports are viewed as part of the educational system and are clearly distinguished from the professional sports business. The NCAA has strict rules against "taking pay" for sports or sporting activities. Any student who does accept pay is ineligible for further play at an NCAA member school in the sport for which he takes pay. An athlete receiving financial aid is still first and foremost a student. All of these NCAA requirements designed to prohibit student–athletes from receiving pay for participation in their sport were incorporated into the financial aid agreements that Rensing and his parents signed.

Courts in other jurisdictions have generally found that such individuals as student athletes, student leaders in student government associations, and student resident hall assistants are not "employees" for purposes of workmen's compensation laws unless they are also employed in a university job in addition to receiving scholarship benefits.

The *Rensing* case is indicative of the modern rule finding that the student-athlete is not an employee of the university. The discussion about whether student-athletes should be considered employees, however, has many ramifications beyond the workers' compensation issue. Some commentators view the designation of the student-athlete as an "amateur" who is not an employee of the educational institution to be inaccurate and not reflective of the reality of college sport, especially at the Division I level (Sack & Staurowsky, 1998; Gurdus, 2001). In 2001, a group of college athletes organized the Collegiate Athletes Coalition (CAC), a collegiate players association, to voice student-athlete concerns. Even though the CAC enlisted the help of a major labor union, the CAC believes that student-athletes are not "employees" within the meaning of the federal labor laws. Others argue that the student's athletic performance is given as consideration for the athletic grant-in-aid, and this athletic scholarship should be considered as creating an employer-employee relationship. Although a viable policy argument may be made that student-athletes should be employees within the meaning of the workers' compensation law or federal labor laws, most courts addressing the issues have held that student-athletes are not employees of the universities for which they play.

Competitive Advantage
STRATEGIES

Workers' Compensation

- When sponsoring teams or other activities, do not mandate participation or reward employees who participate in these activities.

- Communicate with employees regarding the events and make sure that they understand that participation is *truly* voluntary.

- Do not hold sport or fitness events on company premises.

- Do not attempt to control these events; confine your support to providing only economic support.

- Workers' compensation insurance is expensive. Do your homework and get lower-risk classifications for your business and employees, where possible.

Premiums for Workers' Compensation Insurance

Since employers have no choice but to provide workers' compensation to employees, employers must secure insurance to cover these claims. There are two important points to consider regarding the cost of this insurance. First, the cost of premiums declines as the number of workplace injuries declines. Therefore, it is in an employer's interest to have safety and risk management programs in place. Second, employers must understand the classification systems for types of workers and ensure that workers are not placed in a "high risk" category, for which the premiums are higher. For example, all employees in a fitness club do not have the same physical demands, yet some employers allow their clerical employees to be classified with their fitness instructors, which results in a higher premium than necessary for those employees who are in a "harmless" desk job. Also, care must be taken that the entire operation is not lumped together with high-risk endeavors, which also have high premiums. For example, some states classify as an "amusement" business anything ranging from the health, fitness, or tennis club to the traveling carnival. Obviously, the carnival operation can be expected to have a much higher rate of injury than the health club. The health club owner will be greatly disadvantaged if she does not see that the club receives the proper classification.

CONCLUSION

This chapter explored legal issues in the workplace related to employee compensation, workplace safety and health standards, and workers' compensation for work-related injuries. We identified and discussed laws affecting wages as provided in the Fair Labor Standards Act and issues arising in the sport industry such as the use of interns and administrative employee exemptions. We explained workplace safety and health standards required under the Occupational Safety and Health Act, and we examined state workers' compensation laws and the treatment of student-athletes and professional athletes as workers for purposes of workers' compensation. How well a manager knows and understands these legal issues can provide her with a competitive advantage in the workplace and lead to increased employee productivity and effectiveness.

discussion questions

1. Identify and explain the rights that employees are given under the Fair Labor Standards Act.
2. Explain the three tests used to determine whether an employee is exempt from overtime requirements under the FLSA.
3. Identify the five factors used in determining whether a person is working within the scope of employment under workers' compensation principles.

learning activities

1. A football player at Star University suffered a serious neck injury during last week's game. He has retained an attorney for the purpose of filing a workers' compensation claim against the university. What are the player's chances of prevailing under such a claim? You should read *Rensing v. Indiana State Univ.* (1983) and *Coleman v. Western Michigan Univ.* (1983). You may also want to consider the following comment offered by the court in *Waldrep v. Texas Employers Ins. Ass'n* (2000):

   In conclusion, we note that we are aware college athletics has changed dramatically over the years since Waldrep's injury. Our decision today is based on facts and circumstances as they existed almost twenty-six years ago. We express no opinion as to whether our decision would be the same in an analogous situation arising today; therefore, our opinion should not be read too broadly.

2. As you know, many organizations including sport organizations experienced financial difficulty during the economic recession that began in late 2008 and early 2009. As a result many companies had to make difficult choices about whether or not they should furlough employees in order to reduce costs. Visit the Department of Labor website located at the following link: www.dol.gov/whd/flsa/index.htm. From this page, locate information or

guidance on the legal issues that arise from an organization's decision to furlough any or all of its employees. Specifically, see if you can find an answer to whether a salaried exempt employee can voluntarily take time off work due to lack of work.

CASE STUDY

You have obtained an internship with a professional baseball team, and you were injured when several boxes of dashboard promotional toys fell on you in the supply and copy room at the team offices. You receive a meal voucher and free parking for each game for helping with promotions at the 50 home games required under your internship agreement. Are you entitled to workers' compensation?

Review *Hallal v. RDV Sports* (1996), where an appellate court held that workers' compensation was the exclusive remedy in a similar situation. The court noted that the student was not a volunteer under the statute.

considering . . .   ANALYSIS & DISCUSSION

Interns Under the FLSA (p. 171)

In order to use these students as interns without paying for their services, you have to demonstrate that the trainee exemption is applicable to your organization. It would be a good idea to develop a formal intern/student trainee handbook outlining the relationship. This handbook could specifically address the six criteria the DOL would consider in exempting the students from the overtime and minimum wage laws, as discussed earlier on pages 170–172. When using students as interns, consider these guidelines:

1. Make sure the students are not displacing regular employees. Since you will retain your two salespersons, this element should be satisfied.

2. Complete a written agreement with the trainees stating there is no expectation or guarantee of employment upon completion of the internship and no expectation of wages during the internship.

3. You must provide close supervision and a hands-on experience. This may mean that you have to limit the number of student interns you have, in order to provide the level of supervision and experience needed. Thus, two or three student interns may satisfy these elements, whereas six or eight may be more difficult, since you are the only supervisor.

4. The internship must be more beneficial to the students than to your organization, so it may be a good idea to limit internships to only those students who are receiving academic credit for the experience and to structure several professional development activities into the internship, such as mock interviews and sitting in on planning or strategy sessions. Typically, in these higher-level meetings the organization is being benefited very little by the involvement of the intern, but the experience is very helpful for the student.

Injuries Arising Out of Employment (p. 181)

Jackson can be held liable for Mary's injuries if it is determined that the injury arose out of Mary's employment. Thus, we must apply the five factors identified on page 179 and consider results from similar cases to reach a conclusion. Of the five factors, the first two do not help Mary's case, since the event was not during normal working hours and was not held on company premises. However, the remaining three factors must be considered. Jackson sponsors the event, strongly encourages employees to participate, and even provides employees special benefits if they participate. It is likely that these facts alone would demonstrate that the employer initiated and controlled the activity sufficient to find that Mary's injury arose from her employment. We saw a similar result in the *Jones* case, where the employee was urged to participate in a company-sponsored fitness day event. With regard to whether the employer stood to benefit, while it is not as clear a case as *Dozier* or *Savage,* where the employer's fund-raising event benefited from the employee's participation, one could still certainly argue that the company's desire to build goodwill and teamwork were sufficient benefits to conclude that the injuries arose from Mary's employment, similar to the *Elmhurst Park* case.

REFERENCES

Cases

Adams v. Detroit Tigers, Inc., 961 F. Supp. 176 (E.D. Mich. 1997).

Bridewell v. The Cincinnati Reds, 68 F.3d 136 (6th Cir. 1995).

Coleman v. Western Mich. Univ., 336 N.W.2d 224 (Mich. Ct. App. 1983).

Dozier v. Mid-Del Sch. Sys., 959 P.2d 604 (Okla. Ct. App. 1998).

Elmhurst Park District v. Illinois Workers' Compensation Commission, 917 N.E.2d 1052 (Ill. App. 2009).

Hallal v. RDV Sports, 682 So.2d 1235 (Fla. Dist. Ct. App. 1996).

Highlands County Sch. Bd. v. Savage, 609 So.2d 133 (Fla. Dist Ct. App. 1992).

Jeffery v. Sarasota White Sox, Inc., 64 F.3d 590 (11th Cir. 1995).

Jones v. Multi-Color Corp., 108 Ohio App. 3d 388 (Ohio Ct. App. 1995).

Liger v. New Orleans Hornets NBA Ltd. Partnership, 565 F. Supp. 2d 680 (E.D. La. 2008).

Liger v. New Orleans Hornets NBA Ltd. Partnership, 2006 U.S. Dist. LEXIS, 72670, 11 Wage & Hour Cas. 2d (BNA) 1857 (E.D. La. 2006).

Pro Football, Inc. v. Uhlenhake, 558 S.E.2d 571 (Va. Ct. App. 2002)

Rensing v. Indiana State Univ., 444 N.E.2d 1173 (Ind. 1983).

Rowe v. Baltimore Colts, 53 Md.App. 526, 454 A.2d 872 (Md. App. 1983).

University of Denver v. Nemeth, 257 P.2d 423 (Colo. 1953).

Van Horn v. Industrial Accident Comm'n, 33 Cal. Rptr. 169 (Cal. Ct. App. 1963).

Waldrep v. Texas Employers Ins. Ass'n, 21 S.W.3d 692 (Tex. Ct. App. 2000).

Statutes

Annotated Law of Massachusetts, GL, ch. 152, § 36 Payment for Certain Specific Injuries (2009).

Fair Labor Standards Act of 1938, 29 U.S.C. §§ 201 *et. seq.* (2005).

Mass. Gen. Laws Ann. ch. 152, § 36 (2005).

Occupational Safety and Health Act of 1970, 29 U.S.C. §§ 651 *et seq.* (2005).

Other References

Baechli, M. P. (2004, August 7). White collar exemptions in the academic workplace. Client publication of Littler Mendelson. Washington, DC: Author.

Boegle, J., & Kleinendorst, S. (2000). The law comes down on unpaid internships. *Reno News & Review.* Retrieved April 5, 2000, from www.studentadvantage.com/ article_story/1,1075,c2-i21-t0-a11445,00.html.

Breed, A. G. (2004, November 28). Jockey's plight affects sport; Athlete paralyzed at W.Va. track puts spotlight on problems with insurance. *Charleston Gazette-Mail*, p. 1A.

Briggs, T. W. (2000, February 21). Stint on copy desk helps an intern correct his course. *USA Today*, p. 6D.

California State University (2004). *The Fair Labor Standards Act (FLSA): White Collar Exemption Guidelines*. Long Beach, CA: Author.

Cates-McIver, L. (1998, October). The value of internships and co-op opportunities for college students. *Black Collegian, 29*(1), 72–74.

Crumbley, D. L., & Sumners, G. E. (1998, October). How businesses profit from internships. *The Internal Auditor, 55*(5), 54–58.

Department of Labor. (2009, January 1). State occupational safety and health plans. Retrieved May 23, 2009, from http://www.osha.gov/dcsp/osp/index.html.

Drobka, M. E., Denecke, A. E., & Fuhr, C. (2004, July 22). Significant changes to FLSA "White Collar" exemptions effective August 23, 2004. *Findlaw.com*. Retrieved October 10, 2005, from http://library.findlaw.com/2004/Jul/22/133522.html.

Dunn, L. E. (1992). "Protection" of volunteers under federal employment law: Discouraging voluntarism? *Fordham Law Review, 6*, 451–472.

Ex-Steeler fails to score with workers' comp. suit. (2002, August 31). *The Entertainment Litigation Reporter*. Retrieved October 9, 2005, from the LEXIS-NEXIS Academic database.

FLSA restrictions on volunteerism: The institutional and individual costs in a changing economy. (1993). *Cornell Law Review, 78*, 302–335.

Genzale, J. (2005, July 11). Use interns, get more than you pay for. *Street & Smith's SportsBusiness Journal, 8*(11), 26.

Gregory, D. L. (1998). The problematic employment dynamics of student internships. *Notre Dame Journal of Law, Ethics & Public Policy, 12*, 227–264.

Gurdus, J. (2001, Spring). Note: Protection off of the playing field: Student athletes should be considered university employees for purposes of workers' compensation. *Hofstra Law Review, 29*, 907–930.

Haghighi, H. (1998, December 20). The right tools. *New York Times*, p. 30.

Hays, D. (2003, August 18). Numbers games: Workers' comp & baseball. *National Underwriter, 107*(33), 14.

InfoDirect (n.d.). FLSA: *What was changed in the "White Collar" exemptions?* Retrieved October 10, 2005, from http://infodirect.adp.com/julAug2004/main1.asp?id=111111.

Injured National Hockey League players fail to prevent their employers from being reimbursed, under New York workers' compensation law, for salaries they were paid while not playing. (2005, July). *Entertainment Law Reporter*. Retrieved October 9, 2005, from the LEXIS-NEXIS Academic database.

Jaros, R. L. (1999, November). Workers' compensation: Implications for clinicians. *Athletic Therapy Today, 4*(6), 39–40.

Johnston, J. T. (2003). Show them the money: The threat of NCAA athlete unionization in response to the commercialization of college sports. *Seton Hall Journal of Sport Law, 13*, 203–237.

Kaplan, R. K. (1994, May). Hiring student interns. *Small Business Reports, 19*(5), 9–13.

Kelsey, J. M. (2002). Fighting fires with interns: Building a program that keeps YOU on track. *Public Relations Quarterly, 47*(3), 43–45.

Lisser, E. (1995, March 1). Firm in Atlanta settles dispute over interns. *Wall Street Journal*, p. S1.

Louisville Arena Authority. (2008, November 20). Press Release: Arena construction company to sign unprecedented agreement with OSHA regarding oversight. Retrieved March 31, 2010, from www.arenaauthority.com/news.aspx.

Lyncheski, J. E. (2000, September/October). When are volunteers "employees" who must be paid for their time? *Balance, 4*(5), 25.

Minor leaguer pitchers win against Marlins in workers' comp battle. (1999, August 31). *The Entertainment Litigation Reporter*. Retrieved October 9, 2005, from the LEXIS-NEXIS Academic database.

Ortner, C. J. (1998). Adapting Title VII to modern employment realities: The case for the unpaid intern. *Fordham Law Review, 66*, 2613–2647.

OSHA is investigating recent accidents at new Cowboys stadium. (2008, June 17). Street & Smith's SportsBusiness Daily. Retreived March 31, 2010, from www.sportsbusinessdaily.com/article/121657.

Paralyzed football player not entitled to workers' compensation benefits. (2000, July 27). *HR on Campus, 3*(7). Retrieved October 9, 2005, from the LEXIS-NEXIS Academic database.

Preis, Jr., E. F., & Johnson, R. C. (2004, Autumn). Coverage under the FLSA and the new regulations. *Employee Relations Law Journal, 30*(2), 30–50.

Professional boxer held not entitled to benefits. (1998, January 6). *New York Law Journal, 21*. Retrieved October 9, 2005, from the LEXIS-NEXIS Academic database.

Sack, A. L., & Staurowsky, E. J. (1998). *College athletes for hire: The evolution and legacy of the NCAA's amateur myth*. Westport, CT: Praeger.

Selingo, J. (2000, April 4). Florida Supreme Court says university is liable for intern's injury. *The Chronicle of Higher Education.* Retrieved April 4, 2000, from http://chronicle.com/daily/2000/04/2000040404n.htm.

Shellenbarger, S. (2009, January 28). Do you want an internship? It'll cost you. *The Wall Street Journal,* p. D1.

Singer, J. M. (2000, February 21). Students leap into internships and land jobs after college. *USA Today,* p. 6D.

Stier, B., Jr. (2001). Sport management internships—A double edged sword. *The ClipBoard (NASPE),* 2(3), 5.

Texas Workforce Commission. (2008). Especially for Texas Employees: Student interns—trainees. Retrieved May 23, 2009, from http://www.twc.state.tx.us/news/efte/advanced_flsa_issues.html#interns_trainees.

The applicability of the Fair Labor Standards Act to volunteer workers at nonprofit organizations. (1986). *Washington and Lee Law Review, 43,* 223–243.

U.S. Department of Labor (n.d.a). *Exemptions.* Retrieved October 10, 2005, from www.dol.gov/elaws/esa/flsa/screen75.asp.

U.S. Department of Labor (n.d.b). *Fact sheet #14: Coverage under the Fair Labor Standards Act (FLSA).* Retrieved October 11, 2005, from www.dol.gov/esa/regs/compliance/whd/whdfs14.htm.

U.S. Department of Labor (n.d.c). *Fact sheet #17C: Exemption for administrative employees under the Fair Labor Standards Act (FLSA).* Retrieved October 11, 2005, from www.dol.gov/esa/regs/compliance/whd/fairpay/fs17c_administrative.htm.

U.S. Department of Labor (n.d.d). *Fact sheet #18: Section 13(a)(3) exemption for seasonal amusement or recreational establishments under the Fair Labor Standards Act (FLSA).* Retrieved October 11, 2005, from www.dol.gov/esa/regs/compliance/whd/whdfs 18.htm.

U.S. Department of Labor (n.d.e). *General information on the Fair Labor Standards Act (FLSA).* Retrieved October 11, 2005, from www.dol.gov/esa/regs/compliance/whd/mwposter.htm.

U.S. Department of Labor (n.d.f). *School-to-work.* Retrieved October 10, 2005, from www.dol.gov/elaws/esa/flsa/scope/ee15astw.asp.

U.S. Department of Labor (n.d.g). *Trainees.* Retrieved October 10, 2005, from www.dol.gov/elaws/esa/flsa/docs/trainees.asp.

U.S. Department of Labor (n.d.h). *Volunteers.* Retrieved October 10, 2005, from www.dol.gov/elaws/esa/flsa/docs/volunteers.asp.

van der Smissen, B. (1990). Legal liability and risk management for public and private entities, § 25.342. Cincinnati, OH: Anderson.

Wage and Hour Division letter dated September 5, 2002. http://www.dol.gov/esa/WHD/opinion/FLSA/2002/2002_09_05_8_FLSA.htm.

Whalen, E., & Barnes, A. (2001, July–August). Internship payoffs . . . and trade-offs. *The Quill, 89*(6), 18–19.

Workers' comp and the company softball game. (2005, May 30). *Texas Lawyer.* Retrieved October 9, 2005, from the LEXIS-NEXIS Academic database.

WEBSITE RESOURCES

www.dol.gov/elaws/esa/flsa/screen75.asp ▪ The U.S. Department of Labor (DOL) developed this Elaw Advisor to help employees and employers understand the exemptions to the overtime pay provisions of the Fair Labor Standards Act (FLSA).

www.dol.gov/esa/whd/regs/compliance/fairpay/fs17c_administrative.pdf ▪ This fact sheet provides general information on the exemption from minimum wage and overtime pay provided by Section 13(a)(1) of the FLSA.

www.dol.gov/esa/whd/regs/compliance/whdfs18.pdf ▪ This fact sheet provides information about the Section 13(a)(3) exemption from minimum wage and overtime pay to seasonal and recreational employee under the FLSA.

www.dol.gov/esa/whd/regs/compliance/posters/minwagebwp.pdf ▪ The Wage and Hour Division of the DOL has created this poster, which summarizes the Fair Labor Standards Act's minimum wage provisions.

www.dol.gov/elaws/esa/flsa/docs/volunteers.asp ▪ This fact sheet explains the FLSA definition of volunteers.

www.dol.gov/elaws/esa/flsa/docs/trainees.asp ▪ This fact sheet explains the criteria for determining whether trainees or students are employees of an employer under the FLSA.

9

Labor Relations/Collective Bargaining

Chapter contributed by Lisa Pike Masteralexis.

INTRODUCTION

M anagers who understand and properly manage their labor force in a union-ized setting are at a competitive advantage over those who do not invest the proper time with labor relations. Labor peace keeps businesses moving forward in a position of strength, and if workers are satisfied, presumably they are more productive. In fact, creating a setting in which businesses could achieve industrial peace was a goal of Congress in enacting the National Labor Relations Act. Congress created the labor laws to develop an environment that balanced the rights and interests of workers and employers.

Not only are labor problems a distraction from running one's business, but they have consequences for others not directly involved in the dispute. For instance, when there is a strike or lockout in professional sports, the labor stoppage affects employees within and outside of the bargaining unit. The longer the labor stoppage lasts, the more likely it is that employees will lose jobs as their employer loses revenue. The lack of games shortens the schedule for the facility, causing facility employees to go without work as long as the labor dispute continues. Other related businesses, such as hotels, restaurants, and transportation in the area surrounding the venues, also suffer lost revenue from the economic impact of the events.

EXHIBIT 9.1	Management contexts in which labor problems may arise, with relevant laws and cases.		
MANAGEMENT CONTEXT	**MAJOR LEGAL ISSUES**	**RELEVANT LAW**	**ILLUSTRATIVE CASES**
Union organizing and operating activities	Unfair labor practices: interference/discrimination by employer against union members	National Labor Relations Act	*Morio v. NASL*
Collective bargaining Unilateral implementation of change in working conditions	Unfair labor practices by union or management: refusing to bargain in good faith violating collective bargaining agreement	National Labor Relations Act	*NFLPA v. NLRB & NFL Management Council*
Workplace discrimination	Unfair labor practices: employer discrimination or retaliation against union member union discrimination or retaliation against non-member	National Labor Relations Act	*Nordstrom, d/b/a Seattle Seahawks & NFLPA*
Duty of fair representation	Union unfair labor practice: unfairly treating employee who is a union member or non-member	National Labor Relations Act	*Peterson v. Kennedy*
Unilateral implementation of change in working conditions	Unfair labor practices by union or management: refusing to bargain in good faith violating collective bargaining agreement	National Labor Relations Act	*NFLPA v. NLRB & NFL Management Council*
Arbitration/dispute resolution	Arbitrator's authority Scope of review by court	Labor	*Major League Baseball Players Association v. Garvey*
Rights of retired employees	Contractual and fiduciary duties re marketing of retired players	Contract, agency	*Parrish v. National Football League Players, Inc.*

To understand and manage your labor force, it is crucial to have a working knowledge of labor laws and to make management decisions with the labor laws in mind. Protecting your management decisions and knowing when to work with a union are important. Further, making sure that all supervisors who report to you are knowledgeable in labor laws is key to a successful relationship with your employees in a unionized setting.

Sport managers will most likely encounter unionized workforces in facility management, interscholastic and intercollegiate athletics, and professional team sports. Facility executives may manage employees from a variety of unions, such as laborers, carpenters, and clerical unions, all with different collective bargaining agreements. In some cases, interscholastic coaches may be members of a teachers union. In collegiate athletics, staff members are often unionized but coaches are not. One exception is the Pennsylvania state college system, which has a coaches union.[1]

Exhibit 9.1 provides an overview of this chapter's managerial contexts, major legal issues, relevant law, and illustrative cases.

LABOR LAWS

L abor laws exist on both the state and federal level. In most cases, state labor laws apply to public entities, such as a state university's athletic department, and federal labor laws apply to private employers engaged in a business involving interstate commerce. Interstate commerce occurs when a business crosses state lines, so virtually all businesses are engaged in interstate commerce. The following examples illustrate the types of entities governed by state versus federal labor laws:

- Staff members in the athletic department at the University of Massachusetts are members of Service Employees International Union, the professional staff union at the university, which is a (public) state agency. The professional staff on the campus is organized into a local unit whose activities are governed by Massachusetts state labor laws.

- The athletes of the Boston Celtics, Boston Bruins, Boston Red Sox, and New England Patriots are also union members working in Massachusetts, but they are members of national bargaining units (players associations) that negotiate with private multiemployer bargaining units (leagues). Therefore, the professional athletes' employment relationship is governed by the federal National Labor Relations Act and the Labor Management Relations Act (LMRA).

- Employees at the University of Massachusetts' arena, the Mullins Center, are members of the public employees union and are governed by state labor laws, while their counterparts at the TD BankNorth Center (where the Celtics and Bruins play) are members of private local units of a large national union governed by federal law.

[1]See www.apscuf.org/contracts/index.html#coaches. The Pennsylvania State System of Higher Education (PASSHE) and Association of Pennsylvania State College and University Faculties (APSCUF) have recently negotiated their third collective bargaining agreement. APSCUF represents approximately 350 athletic coaches at the 14 state-owned universities represented by PASSHE.

Labor Law History

Labor law is a body of law that has evolved from federal labor statutes. Prior to the enactment of federal labor legislation, there were some common law decisions involving the labor movement in the state courts. By and large, these decisions were not favorable to the labor movements involved. Although judges had discretion under common law, the ability of unions to act varied by state and by political climate, and, in most circumstances, pro-business doctrines dictated the legality of union conduct (Feldacker, 2000).

In the nineteenth century, state courts often considered concerted activities by workers (strikes, work slowdowns, and picketing) to be criminal conspiracies. In the first recorded American labor law case, *Commonwealth v. Pullis* (1806), a group of Philadelphia cordwainers were convicted under the criminal conspiracy doctrine for attempting to impose a policy to force shoemakers within the city to hire only those cordwainers who were union members charging uniform prices the group had set for their wage (Commons, et. al, 1958). Today that action would be classified as a closed shop.[2] One exception was *Commonwealth v. Hunt* (1842), in which the Supreme Judicial Court of Massachusetts refused to find that the actions of the Boston Journeymen Bootmakers Society rose to the level of a criminal conspiracy (*Hunt*, p. 128). The association, whose constitution stated that its purpose was to engage in concerted activity to better wages and working conditions, had simply joined together to express their intent to do so, to encourage their members to require certain wages from their employers, and to pressure employers to hire members of the Boston Journeymen Bootmakers Society. The court found that those actions did not constitute criminal conspiracy but could have constituted it if their goals were achieved through criminal means rather than through economic pressure (*Hunt*, pp. 129–136).

Commonwealth v. Hunt marked the beginning of the judicial recognition of employees' right to engage in concerted actions to better their employment conditions. Any benefit gained, however, was short-lived. Employers soon began using the Sherman Act of 1890 as their legal maneuver to fight employee challenges. Section 1 of the Sherman Act of 1890 prohibits contracts, combinations, and conspiracies that restrain trade or commerce. The theory of antitrust law is to prevent groups of competitors from reducing competition in the market. Employing the Sherman Act, employers argued that the actions of the employees engaged in concerted activity had the effect of reducing competition and injuring consumers.

The U. S. Supreme Court agreed that the Sherman Act applied to combinations of employees as well as to businesses, upholding a treble damage suit against a labor movement (*Loewe v. Lawlor*, 1908). This resulted in federal courts regularly issuing injunctions against union activity, even if the Sherman Act was not ultimately applied to the labor activity. By issuing the injunctions, the courts assisted employers in thwarting concerted activities of employees. After *Loewe v. Lawlor,* the use of the injunction to stop concerted activity coupled with the threat of the Sherman Act's treble damage award produced a chilling effect on union activities.

The Clayton Act of 1914, by limiting the use of antitrust laws against labor unions, created a statutory labor exemption from antitrust laws. It stated that the

---

[2]A closed shop is a rule requiring that an employee be a union member in order to be hired.

labor of a human being was not commerce, and, thus, the Clayton Act's intent was to protect unions acting lawfully in their own self-interest from being deemed illegal combinations or conspiracies. Courts interpreted this to mean that antitrust laws were unenforceable against unions engaged in legitimate objectives. However, courts continued to issue injunctions against labor when they determined that a union's activities, such as a boycott of its employer's customers or a sympathy strike, were not legitimate objectives (*Duplex Printing Press, Co. v. Deering,* 1921). As a result, the U. S. Supreme Court continued to allow federal courts to grant injunctions against union activity that they deemed interfered with the free flow of goods in commerce (*Duplex Printing Press, Co. v. Deering,* 1921).

In response, the Norris LaGuardia Act of 1932 defined and limited the powers of federal courts to grant injunctions in labor disputes unless there was a threat of violence or there were provisions in the collective bargaining agreement to allow for it. In doing so it reinforced the Clayton Act's intent to exempt the normal activities of a union from antitrust laws (see *United States v. Hutcheson,* 1940, and *Boys Markets, Inc. v. Retail Clerks' Union, Local 770,* 1970).

National Labor Relations Act

Enacted in 1935, the National Labor Relations Act (NLRA) applies to private employers. Its preamble set forth the policy of the United States to

> eliminate . . . or mitigate the causes of certain substantial obstructions to the free flow of commerce . . . by encouraging collective bargaining and by protecting the exercise by workers of full freedom of association, self-organization, and designation of representatives of their own choosing, for the purpose of negotiating the terms and conditions of their employment or other mutual aid or protection. (NLRA, § 151, 2005)

With this language, the NLRA set forth employee rights, among them the right to negotiate with an employer over hours, wages, and terms and conditions of employment, to encourage workplace harmony between private employers and employees through collective bargaining. The NLRA applies to employees and employers in the private sector, drawing distinctions between employees for assignment to bargaining units such that employees who are in the same bargaining unit need not do the exact same job but must have common bargaining interests. It also established procedures for union certification and the obligations of management once a union is in place.

The law also created a new federal agency, the National Labor Relations Board (NLRB), to administer labor laws in the United States. Congress established the NLRB because it mistrusted the manner in which courts made labor decisions, which were historically aligned with employer interests, and because it believed that a specialized agency charged with administering, developing, and applying labor relations expertise was necessary. The two primary activities of the NLRB are as follows:

1. To conduct secret ballot union elections for certification and decertification
2. To prevent and remedy unfair labor practices committed by management or union

Taft-Hartley Act of 1947

From its focus on employee rights and unfair labor practices of employers, there is no doubt that the NLRA was pro-labor. A dozen years later, the Taft-Hartley Act amended the NLRA to balance the employee–employer relationship by stipulating

> the legitimate rights of both employees and employers in their relations affecting commerce, to provide orderly and peaceful procedures for preventing the inter-ference by either with the legitimate rights of the other, to protect the rights of individual employees in their relations with labor organizations whose activities affect commerce, to define and proscribe practices on the part of labor and man-agement which affect commerce. . . . (LMRA, § 141, 2005)

For example, NLRA § 7 gives employees the right to join or assist unions; the Taft-Hartley Act added to that the right of employees to choose *not* to join or assist unions. Further, NLRA § 8 prohibits management from discriminating against an employee on the basis of union membership; Taft-Hartley added a provision that prohibits the union from similar behavior against nonunion members. NLRA § 9 was amended to include decertification to the NLRB's responsibilities. Once the Taft-Hartley Act amended the NLRA, the latter was renamed the Labor Management Relations Act of 1947 (LMRA). Often the names NLRA and LMRA are used interchangeably.

Fair Labor Standards Act of 1938

The Fair Labor Standards Act sets forth minimum hourly wage, overtime wages, and child labor protections for workers. It also requires recordkeeping on those aspects of the law by employers. The FLSA contains a number of exemptions from the overtime pay and minimum wage provisions and some exemptions from the child labor provisions. Exemptions are narrowly construed against the employer asserting them. Consequently, employers and employees should always closely check the exact terms and conditions of an exemption in light of the employee's actual duties before assuming that the exemption might apply to an employee. The burden of proving that the exemption applies rests with the employer.

Exemptions that are likely to apply in the sport and recreation industries include those for individuals working in executive or administrative positions and those for individuals engaged in commissioned sales for the retail or service industry, of which sports and recreation are a part. (See Chapter 8 for more information on the FLSA.)

LABOR RELATIONS APPLIED TO PROFESSIONAL SPORT

Although the National Labor Relations Act was enacted in 1935, it was not until the late 1960s and early 1970s that the labor movement took hold in the sport industry. This was not for a lack of attempts; baseball players first organized in 1885, when John Montgomery Ward formed the Brotherhood of Professional Base Ball Players to challenge the National League's salary cap, reserve clause, and sale of players (Jennings, 1990). The years between that first labor movement and the National Basketball Players Association's signing of the first sports labor contract in 1967 saw numerous attempts at creating players' associations. The players' attempts at collective action in earlier eras are probably best described as attempts to engage owners in negotiations and to solicit pension benefits, rather than attempts at full-blown unionization. In some cases, shrewd moves by owners fractured the solidarity in the players' group, such as when the NHL Board of Governors crushed the 1958 formation of the National Hockey League Players' Association (Cruise & Griffiths, 1991). In other situations, the labor movements were turned into company unions (Weiler, 2000).

The decision that opened the door to union certification in professional sports involved baseball umpires. In *The American League of Professional Baseball Clubs and the Association of National Baseball League Umpires* (1969), Major League Baseball challenged the NLRB's jurisdiction. MLB argued that because it was exempt from antitrust laws under the 1922 Supreme Court decision in *Federal Baseball,* it should likewise be exempt from labor laws. As a result of other professional sports being subject to antitrust laws, the NLRB found that it could not be seriously accepted that baseball was not engaged in interstate commerce. Next, MLB argued that it had an internal system of self-regulation, so there was no need for NLRB involvement. The NLRB disagreed, arguing that the system that MLB was relying on would put the umpire before the commissioner for a final resolution of disputes involving the Uniform Umpire's Contract, the Major League Agreement, and the Major League Rules. The NLRB recognized that the system was designed by the employers, and these employers were the same individuals who hire and manage the commissioner. Thus, there was no evidence of a neutral third party as the final arbiter. The NLRB noted that although this case involved just umpires, professional baseball clubs employ a host of other employees, including professional athletes, clubhouse attendants, front office staff, scouts, groundskeepers, and maintenance staff, who would potentially seek assistance from the NLRB in the future.

Professional Sport Labor Unions

Today, virtually all major league teams are unionized workplaces for professional athletes, but not for their coaches or front office staff.[3] The reasons for this are varied, and among them might be the following:

- There are far fewer white-collar workers in unions.
- There is high turnover in front office and coaching positions.
- With intense competition for jobs, people might not be open to working together in a democratic union organizing movement.
- Organizing front office staff or coaches on a national, multiemployer level as the professional athletes have done is a challenging task.

Unionized workplaces for professional athlete-employees have been years in the making and are unique. The dynamics of the professional sports labor relationship

[3]Unions exist in Major League Baseball (MLBPA), the National Basketball Association (NBAPA), the National Football League (NFLPA), the National Hockey League (NHLPA), Major League Soccer (MLSPU), the Women's National Basketball Association (WNBAPA), the Arena Football League (AFLPA), the Women's United Soccer Association (WUSAPA), and the Major Indoor Lacrosse League (MILLPA). Minor league hockey players in the AHL and ECHL are members of one union, the Professional Hockey Players Association (PHPA).

make every collective bargaining negotiation a battle. Athlete-employees are union members with short-term careers and short-term union membership. The turnover rate for sport union members is much higher than for other union members because athletes' careers are far shorter than those of employees in other industries. Most professional athletes have little job security. As a result, most players want to achieve the best deal possible in the collective bargaining negotiations. With an average career length in professional sports hovering around three years and most collective bargaining agreements having three- to six-year terms, players are motivated to negotiate for the best wages and working conditions possible. Comparing their bargaining goals with the average unionized hotel worker or teacher, who might be looking ahead to a 30-year career and five to ten collective bargaining negotiations in their careers, one can see that there is less pressure in the short term on the hotel worker or teacher.

Further, there is a great disparity between players' talent and, thus, their need for the union. A player such as Alex Rodriguez of the New York Yankees does not need the services of the union as much as a late-round draft pick or a recently released free agent trying to make his way back onto an MLB roster. In fact, it could be argued that well-paid superstars like Rodriguez, LeBron James, or Peyton Manning do not need a union. Their concerns in collective bargaining may be very different from the rank-and-file player or league journeyman. Players associations must represent star athletes making millions of dollars as well as those earning league minimums.[4] When negotiating for the collective interests of the players, unions must struggle to keep the superstars and the players on the bench equally satisfied. Without the solidarity of all players, a players association loses its strength.

Players associations are national (versus local) employee bargaining units that negotiate with a transnational multiemployer bargaining unit. The turnover rate for sport union members is much higher than it is for members of other types of unions. This forces players associations to constantly communicate their message to new members. In spreading the message, the players associations face logistical challenges of representing employees on different teams throughout the United States and Canada. Similarly, the multiemployer bargaining unit comes with its own challenges. It may also have vastly disparate bargaining priorities. For instance, compare the collective bargaining goals of George Steinbrenner, owner of the large-market New York Yankees, to those of Robert Nutting, owner of the small-market Pittsburgh Pirates. Despite their differences in revenue and team payroll, in collective bargaining sessions the two must agree on their negotiating positions and strategies. The negotiations are pressure-packed league-level meetings that are highly publicized events followed as intently by the media as a pennant race.

Despite the owners' propensity to "go to war" with their league's players association, ironically professional leagues favor unionized workforces. Professional sport is probably one of the only places where management "needs" the union almost as much as the employees do in order to counter the many restrictive policies, such as the draft and free agency limitations. These provisions on their own would be subject to antitrust scrutiny, but if they are the product of collective bargaining, these restrictive policies are immune from antitrust suit under the labor

---

[4]For established leagues, the minimum salaries are six-figure salaries with excellent benefits, but in some of the newer leagues, the salaries of rank-and-file players are still inadequate to earn a living. In the WNBA, for example, salaries generally range between $30,000 and $80,000 annually.

exemption (*Brown v. Pro Football, Inc.,* 1996). This doctrine will be discussed in greater detail later in the chapter.

LABOR LAW IN PRACTICE

A t the core of labor law are the rights granted to workers in § 7 of the National Labor Relations Act. From this core flows the employees' right to negotiate as a group with their employer, thereby "leveling the field" in their attempt to bargain for better benefits and working conditions. This "balancing" of power is accomplished through the protections guaranteed in § 7, the enforcement mechanisms of § 8, and the right to become an appropriate bargaining unit set forth in § 9.

Employee Rights

Section 7 of the NLRA sets forth three seminal employee rights:

1. The right to join or assist unions
2. The right to engage in collective bargaining through a representative of one's own choosing
3. The right to engage in concerted activity for one's own mutual aid and protection (29 U.S.C. § 157, 2005)

These rights guarantee that workers can choose to join unions, and they make the union the exclusive bargaining representative for all workers. Workers seeking to enforce these rights and collectively bargain with management can do so through two approaches. Employers may voluntarily recognize the employees in a union, or they may force the employees to force them to recognize the union. This is done when 30 percent of the employees file authorization cards with the NLRB authorizing an election. The authorization cards are not to authorize a union but rather to authorize an election.

Certification of appropriate bargaining unit

Once the NLRB receives authorization cards, it evaluates whether the employees seeking an election are an appropriate unit for bargaining.

Certifying workers in appropriate bargaining units brings stability to the collective bargaining process and facilitates agreement between the parties. If members of the unit were from disparate jobs, the needs and goals involved in the bargaining process would also be disparate. This would create division within the union negotiating group and quite likely lead to a breakdown in the process.

To certify a bargaining unit as appropriate, the NLRB examines the community of interests of proposed unit members to determine if they have enough in common to make bargaining successful. **Community of interests** includes such factors as:

- Commonality of supervision
- Commonality of personnel policies and work rules
- Shared work areas and similarity of job duties and working conditions
- Similarity of methods for evaluation
- Similarity in pay and benefits

- Integration and interdependence of operations
- History, if any, of collective bargaining between the parties (Feldacker, 2000; Gold, 1998)

In a case involving the North American Soccer League, the league challenged the NLRB's certification of all players into a national bargaining unit for purposes of collective bargaining (*North American Soccer League v. NLRB,* 1980). The NASL argued that local team units were the appropriate form of the bargaining unit. The NLRB disagreed, finding that where an employer has assumed sufficient control over the working conditions of the employees of its franchisees or member-employers, the NLRB may require employers to bargain jointly. Thus, the issues in the case were whether there was a joint employer relationship among the league and its member clubs and, if so, whether the designated bargaining unit of players was appropriate. The court agreed that labor relations were conducted on a league level, not delegated to individual teams, and, thus, the NLRB's designation was appropriate.

From the union's perspective, if the NASL had been successful in limiting bargaining to the local level, solidarity could easily have been threatened, since employers could conceivably trade away union supporters and undermine the union's strength. Such a system could also undermine the union's strike threat. For instance, if a team in New York went on strike, the league could continue to play and just give any team playing New York a bye for that game. If the league could continue without that franchise, the power of the strike would be severely limited; games could continue, broadcasting would still occur, and only New York would lose revenue. With the shared revenue structures in place in most leagues, under such a circumstance the New York franchise would still receive a cut of revenues from the other games. Such a situation would severely disable the negotiating power of the players union.

When a union is designated as an appropriate bargaining unit, then elections are held and the union is certified as the exclusive bargaining representative for employees. At this point two important changes occur for employees. First, management is put on notice that it has a duty to bargain in good faith with the union. Second, the union has a duty of fair representation for its employee members.

The following hypothetical case explores the process of forming a union and its likely impact on the employer as well as the employees in a sport facility.

considering . . .   **LABOR LAW IN PRACTICE**

Big City Arena (BCA) is owned and operated by Big City Sports and Entertainment (BCSE). BCSE operates its headquarters out of BCA. BCA is the only facility BCSE owns, but its facility management subsidiary operates numerous arenas throughout North America. BCSE also owns an NBA franchise, a WNBA franchise, and an NHL franchise, all of which play their home games at the BCA. A Major Indoor Lacrosse League franchise is also a tenant, and the BCA attracts many major tours, from concerts to family events, as well as an occasional amateur sports championship. Needless to say, the arena is busy most nights of the year.

Carrie Stevens is the general manager of the BCA. When she was promoted to the general manager position, the workers rejoiced. She had started at BCA as an usher while putting herself through college. Upon graduation, Carrie was hired as an event coordinator, and over 10 years she worked her way to the top. She tries her best to accommodate employees' needs and create a positive work environment, but the reality is that BCSE is always under pressure to generate revenue through its arena operations to spend on its major league teams.

When BCSE acquired the teams, all budgets at the arena were cut. The BCA works on a skeletal staff compared to those at the other arenas that BCSE manages. Carrie feels tremendous pressure running the facility that is the home headquarters for the company. Having events virtually every night of the year is leading to morale problems for BCA staff. It is clear to the employees at the bottom of the organization that they do not and never will get the same perks as their BCSE colleagues on the professional teams.

In this environment, Carrie overhears BCA head usher Jim Stone leading a group of employees in a conversation about their working conditions. Carrie hears them complaining about their low salaries; the long hours setting up before and cleaning up after games, concerts, and sporting events; and their lack of benefits (pension, healthcare coverage, and the like). The complaints become very frank and personal. At one point Jim says, "Carrie has forgotten her roots. She no longer cares about the people who work for her. She is up with the big dogs now and only cares about moving up in the company." Carrie knows the employees are fed up and something must be done.

At the end of the discussion, Jim Stone vows to do something about it, saying, "I'm going to call my friends at the Staples Center and find out the name of their union."

Questions

- If Jim chooses to organize his workplace, what steps must he take?
- If Jim starts an organizing campaign, what should Carrie do? Should she voluntarily recognize the union and then sit down with Jim to negotiate for better working conditions? Should she try to stop Jim's union organizing? Can she fire Jim or others helping him to unionize BCA?

Note how you would answer the questions and then check your responses using the Analysis & Discussion at the end of this chapter.

Duty to engage in collective bargaining

Once a union is in existence, management *must* engage in collective bargaining over mandatory subjects of bargaining or risk being charged with an unfair labor practice under § 8 (a)(5) of the NLRA for failing to bargain in good faith (*NLRB v. Katz,* 1962). **Mandatory subjects** are hours, wages, and terms and conditions of employment. They are those things "plainly germane to the 'working environment' and not those 'managerial decisions which lie at the core of entrepreneurial control'" (*Ford Motor Co. v. NLRB* at 498, 1979). Good faith bargaining over mandatory subjects is required to achieve a contract called a collective bargaining agreement (CBA). Provisions in the CBA for wages include salaries; bonuses; severance and termination pay; and fringe benefits, such as life or disability insurance, health coverage, and practically anything else that has monetary value. The concept of hours includes any time spent at work; in professional sport this may include such provisions as training camp, practices, season, schedule, number of games, and so forth. Terms and conditions of employment cover the majority of the remaining provisions in an employee's work life, including seniority, medical issues, grievance arbitration provisions, drug-testing provisions, safety concerns, and the like. In professional sports there are additional provisions that may affect more than one of these subjects. For instance, the draft provision affects wages. The position or slot into which someone is drafted affects the amount of money the athlete will earn in salary and bonuses. The draft also affects terms and conditions of employment, as it determines the team and geographic location where a player will work, as well as other factors, such as playing time (depending on the other players on that team or in the club's farm system), rosters, and coaches (*Mackey v. National Football League,* 1976).

In addition to mandatory subjects, there are also permissive subjects for bargaining. **Permissive subjects** are those that management is not obligated to negotiate over and that the union cannot bargain to impasse over. An **impasse** is a stalemate in negotiations that often leads to an economic weapon being used by the union, in the form of a strike, or by management, in the form of a lockout. An example of a permissive subject might be the National Hockey League Players Association (NHLPA) asking for its logo to appear on the NHL team uniforms or in NHL advertisements. There is no legal obligation for the NHL to negotiate with the NHLPA for such a provision, but the NHL can do so if it chooses.

Duty of fair representation

After certification by the NLRB, a union becomes the exclusive bargaining representative for *all* employees. The **duty of fair representation** requires that a union represent all employees in the bargaining unit fairly, even if the employees are not union members (*Steele v. Louisville & Nashville Railroad Co.,* 1944). If the union does not represent its employees fairly, the NLRB has ruled that it qualifies as an unfair labor practice under § 8(b)(1)(A), the section that prohibits interference with § 7 rights (*Miranda Fuel Co.,* 1962). Unions must represent employees without acting in an arbitrary, bad faith, or discriminatory manner (*Vaca v. Sipes,* 1967). For example, in *Vaca v. Sipes,* the plaintiff alleged that the union's decision to drop the pursuit of his grievance through the arbitration process was arbitrary and discriminatory. The U. S. Supreme Court held that a union's duty of fair representation "includes a statutory obligation to serve the interest of all members without hostility or discrimination toward any, to exercise its discretion with complete good faith and honesty, and to avoid arbitrary conduct" (*Vaca* at 177). Most breach of the duty of fair representation cases challenge a union's decision to pursue grievances on behalf of employees. In *Peterson v. Kennedy and NFLPA* (1985), the plaintiff NFL player sued his union for failing to represent him fairly when it made an error in filing his grievance, thus causing the issue to be time-barred under the process set forth in collective bargaining. The court held that since the union's conduct amounted to no more than negligence, it did not meet the standard required for a duty of fair representation case. The court emphasized that unions are not liable for good faith, nondiscriminatory errors of judgment made in processing grievances. Thus, unions are not held liable for errors in judgment about whether to pursue a grievance, interpretations of collective bargaining agreements, and representing an employee in the grievance arbitration process (*Vaca*).

Concerted activity

The last § 7 right, the right to engage in concerted activity, gives employees the right to strike or undertake similar activities (picketing, work slowdowns, etc.) to better their economic conditions (mutual aid) or address poor working conditions (protection). The right to engage in concerted activity provides protection for employees to work together to improve their working conditions. However, there is a limit as to the behavior that is protected. Any activity that interferes with the employer's ability to conduct business with customers (such as threatening customers or blocking entrances) or that leads to violence is not protected.

Unfair Labor Practices

Section 8 of the NLRA and the LMRA establishes employer and union unfair labor practices and provides enforcement mechanisms. See Exhibit 9.2.

Employer retaliation for union activity

As noted in Exhibit 9.2, it is an unfair labor practice for an employer to interfere with, restrain, or coerce employees who are engaged in union activity (NLRA, § 8(a)(1)). It is also an unfair labor practice to discriminate against employees for such activity or for showing support of the union (NLRA, § 8(a)(3)). In theory, this is straightforward, but in practice, it becomes difficult to apply. Often decisions about discipline, retention, and termination come from mixed motives, so for managers it is very important to keep a well-documented paper trail on union employees in the event that you have to let a worker go.

Mixed-motive cases often arise for professional athletes who are released from their jobs for a lack of skill, poor performance, or misconduct but who are heavily

---

Unfair labor practices of employers and unions as established by the National Labor Relations and Labor Management Relations Acts, 29 U.S.C. § 158 (2005).   EXHIBIT **9.2**

EMPLOYER UNFAIR LABOR PRACTICE	UNION UNFAIR LABOR PRACTICE
8(a)(1)—To interfere with, restrain, or coerce employees in the exercise of § 7 rights	8(b)(1)—To restrain or coerce employees in their exercise of § 7 rights
8(a)(2)—To dominate or interfere with a union or contribute financial or other support to it	8(b)(2)—To cause employer to discriminate against employee
8(a)(3)—By discrimination in regard to employment or any term or condition of employment to encourage or discourage membership in any labor organization	8(b)(3)—To refuse to bargain collectively with an employer
8(a)(4)—To discharge or discriminate against an employee because he has filed an unfair labor practices complaint or given testimony under NLRA	8(b)(5)—To require employees to pay excessive dues or discriminatory fees for membership under union security clause
8(a)(5)—To refuse to bargain collectively with employee's representative	8(b)(6)—To cause an employer to pay for services not performed

involved in union activity. As club management compares two similarly talented players, if one is heavily engaged in union activities, it is easy to imagine how that factor might influence the decision as to which of the two to sign, release, or demote. By their contracts, athletes agree to be released at any time for lack of skill or ability. The challenge of determining whether a termination was related to a lack of skill or due to union involvement can be difficult. The analysis is compounded by the fact that union leaders tend to be league veterans whose performance may be in decline.

In *Nordstrom, d/b/a Seattle Seahawks and NFLPA* (1989), wide receiver Sam McCullum successfully challenged his release by the Seattle Seahawks as retaliation for his union activities. McCullum was a starting wide receiver for the Seattle Seahawks from 1976 to 1981. In 1981 he became his team's union player representative, which brought him a prominent role in union activities. McCullum orchestrated a "solidarity" handshake with the opposing team at the start of a preseason game, which led to tension with his head coach, Jack Patera. Despite that, McCullum started all preseason games. At the end of training camp, McCullum was released when the Seahawks made a trade for another wide receiver.

The test for determining whether an employer has violated § 8(a)(3) requires that an employee show that union activities were a motivating factor in the firing (*Wright Line, a Division of Wright Line, Inc.,* 1980). Then, the burden shifts to the employer to prove the employee would have been fired even if he had not engaged in union activities. McCullum was successful in showing that the acquisition of another wide receiver would not have occurred in the absence of management's animus against McCullum for being an outspoken supporter of the union. He also showed evidence of this animus by proving that the fines imposed on him for the solidarity handshake greatly exceeded those imposed on other NFL players. McCullum not only proved the unfair labor practice but was awarded back pay and damages (*Nordstrom,* 1991). Due to the speculative nature of professional sport playing careers and compensation, this was an exceptional feat.

Another case illustrating employer retaliation against players who exercised their § 7 right to strike is *NFL Management Council and NFLPA* (1992).

NFL Management Council and NFLPA

FOCUS CASE   309 N.L.R.B. 78 (1992)

FACTS

In the 1987 season, the NFL players went on strike as a result of reaching an impasse in collective bargaining negotiations. The NFL Management Council decided that if the NFLPA went on strike it would use replacement players, many of whom were available since a competitor league, the USFL, had recently disbanded. These replacement players generally were those cut from prior training camps. After a one-week game cancellation, the NFL was able to schedule two weeks of games using replacement players, which caused a number of striking players to cross the picket lines and return to the playing field.

The NFLPA then called off the strike and sent the players back to their clubs effective Thursday, October 15. The league, however, imposed a rule (followed by all clubs) that striking veterans were not allowed to play the following weekend unless they had reported back to their clubs by 1:00 p.m. Wednesday. Yet, the clubs used replacement players that weekend who had signed in as late as 4:00 p.m. on Saturday for Sunday's game and 4:00 p.m. Monday for the Monday night game. The NFLPA filed an unfair labor practice charge against the league, stating that the rule violated § 8 of the National Labor Relations Act. The NFLPA claimed that the rule discriminated against striking players and deprived them of 1/16 of their annual salaries.

HOLDING

The NLRB upheld the complaint of an unfair labor practice against the NFL.

RATIONALE

The NLRB set forth the following standard for judging the NFL Management Council's conduct. The NLRB first noted that the U. S. Supreme Court has recognized that some practices are inherently so prejudicial to union interests and so devoid of economic justification . . . that the employer's conduct carries an inference of unlawful intent so compelling that no one could believe the employer's protest of innocence. If the employer acts in this manner, the Court has given the NLRB free rein to find an unfair labor practice, even if management introduces evidence that the conduct was motivated by business considerations. On the other hand, if the employer shows evidence of legitimate and substantial business justifications for its conduct, and the NLRB determines that the impact on employee rights is comparatively slight, an antiunion motivation must be proved to sustain the unfair labor practice charge.

Applying the above principle, the NLRB found that the Wednesday deadline clearly constituted discriminatory conduct toward union members because it applied a different standard to the strikers and also adversely affected worker rights, namely the right to strike. The NLRB and courts have recognized that the right to strike includes the right to an unconditional application to return to work. The teams argued that the Wednesday deadline was required for them to have sufficient time to prepare returning players and to take care of administrative changes. The NLRB found the NFL Management Council's justifications were weak, since the NFL had never before imposed such a deadline, not even when players held out and tried to renegotiate their contracts. Players in such a situation either returned to the club or were placed on an exempt list that still provided the players with compensation and service time. Further noting the late deadlines used for replacement players, the NLRB rejected the NFL justifications.

Duty to bargain in good faith

Once a union is certified by the NLRB, management has a duty to bargain in good faith over hours, wages, and terms and conditions of employment. In fact, both sides have such a duty. Either party can negotiate to impasse and decide whether to use an economic weapon of imposing a strike or a lockout. In practice, management may unilaterally implement its last best offer and still fulfill the duty to bargain in good faith (*Brown v. Pro Football*, 1996). There is no duty to bargain over permissive subjects, and there is no right to negotiate to impasse over them. Thus, employers can unilaterally impose permissive subjects and those that deal primarily with "management rights." Management rights generally encompass managerial decisions that "lie at the core of entrepreneurial control" (Rabuano, 2002). Management need not negotiate these decisions with a union, but they may have to negotiate their effect if they affect hours, wages, or terms and conditions of employment.

Commissioners of professional sport leagues are granted power by their owner-employers to maintain the integrity of the game. They do this by approving player contracts to ensure that the contracts do not circumvent rules; making rules for conduct on and off the field; resolving disputes between players and owners, teams, or the league; resolving disputes between owners and between owners and the league; and disciplining players, clubs, owners, game officials, and other league and club employees. As a result, commissioners' decisions within their owner-granted powers may clash with the duty to bargain over mandatory subjects. It may be difficult for management to accept a requirement to bargain over rules and policies that historically have been unilaterally mandated by the league or commissioner. For instance, in *NFLPA v. NLRB* (1974), the NFLPA argued that the action of the commissioner of the NFL in imposing a rule and corresponding fines without negotiating with the union was a refusal to bargain in good faith.

NFLPA v. NLRB

503 F.2d 12 (8th Cir. 1974)   **CASE OPINION**

[FACTS

The National Football League Players Association petitioned the Eighth Circuit Court of Appeals to review an NLRB order dismissing a complaint against the NFL's Management Council (owners' collective bargaining representative). The complaint alleged that the NFL violated § 8(a)(5) and § 8(a)(1) of the NLRA by unilaterally establishing a rule that "any player leaving the bench area while a fight is in progress on the field will be fined $200." The court was not asked to judge the wisdom of the rule, but rather whether the NLRB erred in dismissing the complaint on the ground that the rule was adopted and promulgated by the NFL commissioner rather than by the owners.

On January 22, 1971, the NLRB certified the NFLPA as the exclusive bargaining representative for NFL players, and negotiations for a collective bargaining agreement began. The NFLPA, NFL, and each of the clubs signed the CBA on June 17, 1971. In early 1971, NFL Commissioner Pete Rozelle discussed with his staff the problem of injuries to players through violence on the field. He directed a member of the NFL staff to discuss this problem with the owners' competition committee to deal with proposed changes in policy on the competitive aspects of football. The committee recommended a rule be established to fine players who left the bench during a fight on the field. At the March 25 meeting of the owners, the commissioner explained the proposal to the clubs and they adopted the rule. Rozelle subsequently fined 106 players under the rule.

The NFLPA appealed the imposition of the fines on the grounds that the players had not been notified of the new rule and that the rule violated the CBA, which provided for good faith negotiations on any changes in employment conditions. Commissioner Rozelle responded that the rule was passed by the clubs and that he had jurisdiction to impose the fines under the powers vested in him as commissioner. On December 29, 1971, the NFLPA withdrew the matter from the commissioner and requested the council to begin negotiations on the rule. The council refused on the grounds that the commissioner was acting within his powers and that the players only had the right to an appeal to him. The NFLPA filed an unfair labor practice charge with the NLRB on December 10, 1971, alleging the NFL's unilateral adoption of the rule was a refusal to bargain.

The NLRB found: (1) the union conceded the commissioner had a right to adopt the bench-fine rule; (2)

the bench-fine rule had in fact been promulgated by the commissioner, and the owners engaged in no meaningful or substantial conduct with respect to its adoption or promulgation; and (3) as a matter of law there is no substantive difference between the commissioner's imposing individual fines for conduct detrimental to the game after notice and hearing and promulgating the bench-fine rule. Thus, promulgation of the rule was within the commissioner's authority.

The NFLPA appealed.]

HOLDING

The Eighth Circuit Court of Appeals reversed and remanded the case to the NLRB.

RATIONALE

The record does not support the NLRB's finding that the NFLPA conceded that the Commissioner had the right under the CBA to adopt and promulgate the bench-fine rule; to the contrary, the NFLPA denied he had such a right. The NFLPA agreed only that the Commissioner had a right pursuant to the CBA to fine a player for conduct detrimental to the NFL *after notice and hearing*. The distinction was a meaningful one. If the Commissioner's power is limited in the manner the NFLPA suggests, each player who has been notified he is being charged with conduct detrimental to the game can at the hearing attempt to prove that the conduct in question is not, in fact, detrimental and to prove he did not engage in the proscribed conduct. If the Commissioner, *after notice and hearing*, decides that a player has been guilty of conduct detrimental to professional football, then the Commissioner shall have complete authority to fine or suspend.

The record also does not support the NLRB's finding that the bench rule was adopted by the Commissioner without meaningful or substantial conduct on the part of the Owners. The Commissioner discussed with his staff "his feeling that from now on if a player left the bench area during a fight, he felt he would have to fine him." But, he was obviously concerned about the reaction of the Owners to such a course of action and instead of announcing his policy or simply imposing a fine, he asked a staff member to discuss the matter with the competition committee—a committee in which only management is represented. When that committee indicated its approval, he had the committee bring a recommended resolution to the Owners for their approval. It was only after Owners voted 24–2 in favor of the rule that the Commissioner sent out a press release that the bench-fine rule was in effect. At no time prior to the press release did the Commissioner discuss the problem of players leaving the bench during fights with the NFLPA. If, as the Employers contend, the Commissioner is the agent of both the NFL and the NFLPA, and promulgated the rule as their agent, one must assume a serious breach of ethics by the Commissioner if he talked to only one of his principals. And, no one suggests the Commissioner is an unethical man.

To summarize, every fact and inference supports the administrative law judge's conclusion that the rule was adopted and promulgated by the Owners. We hold the NFL, by unilaterally promulgating and implementing a rule providing for an automatic fine to be levied against any player leaving the bench area while an on-field fight or an altercation is in progress, have engaged in unfair labor practices within the meaning of § 8(a)(5) and § 8(a)(1) of the Act.

Questions

1. Do you agree with the decision that the NFL bench-clearing rule was not promulgated by Commissioner Rozelle? Why or why not?

2. If such a rule is, in fact, within the Commissioner's power, how might he have unilaterally imposed it without facing an unfair labor practice charge?

§ 10(j) injunctions

When an unfair labor practice is alleged, the NLRB, through its attorneys, may seek a court order, called a § 10(j) **injunction,** to stop the employer from committing the unfair labor practice. In *Morio v. NASL* (1980), a § 10(j) injunction was sought by Winifred Morio, regional director for the NLRB, against the North American Soccer League.

Morio v. NASL

501 F. Supp. 633 (S.D.N.Y. 1980)

CASE OPINION

[FACTS

Morio seeks a temporary injunction pursuant to § 10(j) of the NLRA, pending the final disposition of matters before the NLRB. Respondents are the North American Soccer League and its 21 U.S.-based clubs. The NASL is a 24 team, nonprofit association, of which 21 are U.S.-based and three are based in Canada. Each of the constituent members is engaged primarily in the business of promoting and exhibiting professional soccer contests for the public. Collectively, these clubs annually gross revenue in excess of $500,000 and purchase and import interstate commerce goods and materials in excess of $50,000. The NLRB has found, and the 5th Circuit affirmed, that the NASL and its constituent member clubs are joint employers and that a collective bargaining unit comprised of all NASL players on clubs based in the United States is appropriate.

All professional soccer players employed by NASL constitute a unit appropriate for collective bargaining within the meaning of § 9(b) of the act. This unit includes players on active, temporarily inactive, disabled, suspended, ineligible, and military eligibility lists. The unit does not include NASL officials, managerial/executive personnel of NASL or clubs, or players employed by the Canadian clubs. Since September 1, 1978, the union, by virtue of § 9(a) of the act, has been the exclusive representative of all employees for collective bargaining.

Morio alleges that she has reasonable cause to believe that NASL interfered with, restrained, and coerced employees in the exercise of rights guaranteed them under § 7 of the act by unilaterally changing the employment conditions when:

1. On October 19, 1978, and thereafter, NASL required players to get permission from their clubs whenever a particular brand of footwear, other than selected by each NASL club, is desired by an employee.
2. On April 10, 1979, NASL initiated plans for a new winter indoor soccer season from November 1979 to March 1980.
3. On November 24, 1979, and continuing thereafter, NASL required players to participate in the winter indoor soccer season.

4. On October 16, 1979, NASL initiated and implemented plans to increase the 1980 regular summer outdoor soccer season schedule by two games and two weeks and also reduced the maximum roster of all NASL clubs during the regular summer outdoor season from 30 to 26 players.
5. Commencing on October 19, 1978, through March 1979, and continuing thereafter, NASL bypassed the union and dealt directly with players in the unit. It solicited players to enter into individual employment contracts, then negotiated and actually entered into individual employment contracts with them.

NASL conceded that it has done all of these actions and unilaterally changed the conditions of employment. The evidence introduced at the court hearing established that Morio had reasonable cause to believe that the individual contracts NASL entered into with employees since September 1, 1978, constitute 96.8 percent of the existing individual contracts. The other 3.2 percent of the current individual player contracts were entered into prior to the union's certification.]

HOLDING

The district court for the Southern District of New York found reasonable cause to believe that NASL engaged in unfair labor practices and that Morio was, therefore, entitled to injunctive relief, pending the final determination of the charges before the NLRB.

RATIONALE

It is undisputed that NASL refused to bargain with the Union. However, NASL claims it had a right to refuse to bargain with the Union while pursuing their appeal of the NLRB's determination of an appropriate collective bargaining unit. NASL's duty to bargain with the Union arose at the time that the Union was certified as the exclusive bargaining representative. The fact that NASL was pursuing its right to appeal did not, absent a stay of the NLRB's order, obviate their duty to bargain with the Union and does not constitute a defense to an application for relief under § 10(j) of the Act where, as here, NASL has apparently repeatedly refused to bargain with the Union and continuously bypassed the Union and dealt directly with employees.

NASL's most vigorous opposition comes in response to Morio's application for an order requiring NASL to render voidable, at Union's option, all individual player contracts, whether entered into before or after the Union's certification. NASL claims that such power in the hands of the Union would result in chaos in the industry and subject NASL to severe economic loss and hardship since these individual contracts are the only real property of NASL. The relief requested by Morio is not a request to have all individual contracts declared null and void, nor that the "exclusive rights" provision of the individual contracts, which bind the players to teams for a certain time, be rendered voidable. Moreover, Morio seeks an order requiring NASL to maintain the present terms and conditions in effect simply until NASL negotiates with the Union unless and until an agreement or a good faith impasse is reached through collective bargaining. Morio does not, however, seek to rescind that unilateral provision which provided for the present summer schedule. The NLRB has consciously limited its request for relief to prevent any unnecessary disruption of NASL business. The NLRB is seeking to render voidable only those unilateral acts taken by the NASL which it admits have occurred. These unilateral changes modify all existing individual contracts entered into before September 1, 1978, in derogation of the Union's right to act as the exclusive bargaining agent of all employees. The individual contracts entered into since September 1, 1978, are apparently in violation of the duty of the NASL to, in accordance with the Act, bargain collectively with the Union. The obligation is exclusive. This duty to bargain with the exclusive representative carries with it the negative duty not to bargain with individual employees.

Morio is entitled to an injunction enjoining NASL from giving effect to individual contracts entered into prior to September 1, 1978, or any modification, continuation, extension or renewal thereof "to forestall collective bargaining." *J. I. Case Co. v. NLRB,* 321 U.S. 332, 341 (1944). NASL has refused to recognize that only the Union has the right to waive its right to be the exclusive bargaining representative. In *National Licorice Co. v. NLRB,* 309 U.S. 350 (1940), the Supreme Court held that the NLRB has the authority to order an employer not to enforce individual contracts with its employees which were found to have been in violation of the NLRA. The evidence discloses that Morio has reasonable cause to believe that NASL has used, and will continue to use, the individual contracts entered into prior to September 1, 1978, to forestall collective bargaining, and to continue to enforce them is to bypass and undermine support for the Union. With such contracts in place, NASL's determination not to bargain with the Union is well fortified so there simply is no incentive for NASL to bargain with the Union.

The NLRB is, therefore, entitled to the relief which it seeks requiring NASL to render voidable certain provisions in the existing individual contracts which the Union requests, as set forth above. The Union has been permitted by the court to intervene in this action as a party petitioner. The court finds it is not the intent of Morio, as the NASL claims, to visit punitive actions on the NASL and the requested relief with respect to the individual contracts has been carefully tailored to avoid chaos and economic hardship.

Questions

1. Why was it determined that local bargaining units were inappropriate for collective bargaining purposes?

2. Do you agree with the NASL's position that Morio's request to declare all contracts voidable (at the union's option) would result in chaos and subject NASL to severe economic loss and hardship, since these individual contracts are the only real property of NASL?

3. Clarify in lay terms what Morio is actually requesting of the court. Is it to "undo" all player contracts in the NASL? Do you believe this is a proper remedy under the circumstances?

4. Should a union have a right to determine whether a player's contract is voidable in this situation? What if the player decides that he does not want to void the contract? Should the union be able to overrule the players' wishes for the good of the other members of the union? How should collective versus individual bargaining be balanced in unionized workplaces?

COLLECTIVE BARGAINING

When employees form a union and begin collective bargaining, their goal is to negotiate a contract *with management* that contains the mandatory subjects of their workplace. The process is one that favors compromise between the two sides to further a peaceful and productive work environment. Collective bargaining in professional sports addresses negotiations over policies that are restrictive to employees, such as drafts, limits on free agency, salary caps, and the like. These restrictive practices have been challenged by players on antitrust grounds. As a result, federal courts have been presented with unique questions as to whether these restrictive provisions are in fact protected from antitrust scrutiny when they are negotiated with the players union. The following discussion elaborates on the law as it stands in this area.

Convergence of Labor and Antitrust Law

Antitrust law has long influenced professional sports since many of the restrictive policies and structures of professional sport leagues lend themselves to antitrust challenges. Restrictive practices are those that limit a player's ability to earn money or to move through a free market and include such practices as the draft, the salary cap or luxury tax, and restrictions on free agency (*Mackey v. NFL,* 1976; *Smith v. Pro Football, Inc.,* 1978). Under labor laws, these practices that might otherwise violate players' antitrust rights may be shielded from antitrust liability if negotiated for through the collective bargaining process (*McCourt v. California Sports, Inc.,* 1979; *Brown v. Pro Football,* 1996; *Wood v. NBA,* 1987; *Clarett v. NFL,* 2004). Thus, it is a competitive advantage for leagues to negotiate their restrictive practices through the collective bargaining process with a players union—so much so that in 2000, the NLRB filed a complaint against the Arena Football League and its member clubs seeking to decertify the AFL Players Organizing Committee (AFLPOC), claiming that owners coerced players into joining the union (IBL, 2000). Two players had complained to the NLRB that the AFL illegally recognized and supported the AFLPOC in order to form a union that would be sympathetic to management and to try to shield the owners from player antitrust suits. The complaint describes numerous instances in which the AFL and its teams, among other things, engaged in the following activities:

- "Rendered unlawful assistance" to the AFLPOC
- "Solicited employee players" to sign union cards
- "Promised benefits to employee players if they formed or joined a union and engaged in collective bargaining"
- "Threatened employee players" with reprisals and "threatened to discharge and release employee players" who refused to engage in collective bargaining
- Released players "to discourage employees" from refusing to form a union

All of these activities are unfair labor practices. The NLRB investigated as a result of complaints brought by two players and found that the AFLPOC has never been supported by a majority of AFL players and was illegally recognized by the AFL owners and that the AFL owners threatened AFL players and illegally promised benefits to AFL players to coerce them to form a union (IBL, 2000). Another example occurred in 1996 when many star NBA players sought to decertify the NBPA, and NBA Commissioner David Stern publicly supported players who favored keeping the players association.

All professional sport organizations except MLB are subject to antitrust laws. MLB is exempt because over 80 years ago, the U. S. Supreme Court found that baseball was not engaged in interstate commerce and, thus, was not a business Congress intended to be subject to the Sherman Act (*Federal Baseball Club of Baltimore v. National League of Professional Baseball Clubs*, 1922). MLB's antitrust exemption survived two further Supreme Court challenges, and much of it remained intact despite the adoption of the Curt Flood Act of 1998 (*Toolson v. New York Yankees*, 1953; *Flood v. Kuhn*, 1972).

The Curt Flood Act allows major league level players to sue their employers under the Sherman Act, but it does not remove baseball's immunity, since the exemption still applies to business areas and the league's employment relationship with minor league players. While at first blush it appears the Curt Flood Act opens MLB to increased antitrust litigation, it does not. Baseball, like all other unionized professional sports leagues, is shielded from antitrust liability by the labor exemption. It is well established that during the term of a collective bargaining agreement, terms negotiated in that agreement are exempt from antitrust scrutiny (*Allen Bradley Co. v. Local No. 3, I.B.E.W.*, 1945; *United Mine Workers v. Pennington*, 1965; *Local No. 189, Amalgamated Meat Cutters & Butcher Workmen v. Jewel Tea Co.*, 1965). Provided that the defendant proves the plaintiff is, was, or will be a party to the collective bargaining agreement, that the subject being challenged on antitrust grounds is a mandatory subject for bargaining (hours, wages, and other terms and conditions of employment), and that the collective bargaining agreement was achieved through bona fide arms' length bargaining (bargaining that occurs freely, without one party having excessive power or control over the other), the defendant's actions will be exempt from antitrust (*Reynolds v. NFL*, 1978; *McCourt v. California Sports, Inc.*, 1979; *Wood v. NBA*, 1987; *Brown v. Pro Football*, 1996; *Clarett v. NFL*, 2004). In *Wood v. NBA* (1987) and *Clarett v. NFL* (2004), the Second Circuit held that players outside of the process at the time a collective bargaining agreement is negotiated are still precluded from a successful antitrust challenge to a provision agreed to in collective bargaining. Further, *Clarett* extended this to anything that is a product of the collective bargaining process and the collective bargaining relationship, in Clarett's case specifically draft eligibility rules contained in the NFL constitution and by-laws.

A number of cases have raised the issue of whether the labor exemption continues to protect parties from antitrust scrutiny after a collective bargaining agreement has expired (*Bridgeman v. NBA*, 1987; *Powell v. NFL*, 1989; *NBA v. Williams*, 1995; *Brown v. Pro-Football*, 1996). In *Brown v. Pro-Football, Inc.*, which is discussed below, the U. S. Supreme Court noted that when a bargaining relationship exists between a league and a players association, labor policy favors limiting antitrust liability. Thus, provided that the league is engaged in lawful collective bargaining activities, the labor exemption will continue to insulate the employer from antitrust liability. The Court clarified, however, that it did not intend its holding to "insulate from antitrust liability every joint imposition of terms by employers, for an agreement amongst employers could be sufficiently distant in time and circumstances from the collective bargaining process that a rule permitting antitrust intervention would not significantly interfere with that process" (*Brown* at 250). Yet the Court did not give an example of such time and circumstance, as is shown in this Case Opinion.

Brown v. Pro Football, Inc.

| 518 U.S. 231 (1996) | CASE OPINION |

[FACTS

In 1987 the NFL–NFLPA CBA expired. The NFL and NFLPA began to negotiate a new contract, and in March 1989, during the negotiations, the NFL adopted Resolution G-2, a plan that would permit each club to establish a "developmental squad" of up to six rookies who, as free agents, had failed to secure a position on a roster. Squad members would practice and play in regular games as substitutes for injured players. Resolution G-2 provided that the club owners would pay all squad members the same weekly salary.

In April, the NFL presented the developmental squad plan to the NFLPA. The NFL proposed a fixed squad player salary of $1,000 per week. The NFLPA disagreed, insisting that the club owners give developmental squad players benefits and protections similar to those provided regular players and that they allow players to negotiate their salaries individually. Two months later negotiations on the issue of developmental squad salaries reached an impasse. The NFL then unilaterally implemented the developmental squad program by distributing to the clubs a uniform contract that embodied the terms of Resolution G-2 and the $1,000 proposed weekly salary. The NFL advised club owners that paying developmental squad players more or less than $1,000 per week would result in disciplinary action, including the loss of draft choices.

In May 1990, 235 developmental squad players brought this suit against the NFL, claiming that their employers' agreement to pay them a fixed $1,000 weekly salary violated the Sherman Antitrust Act. The federal district court denied the employers' claim of exemption from the antitrust laws; it permitted the case to reach the jury, and it subsequently entered judgment on a jury treble-damages award that exceeded $30 million. The NFL and its member clubs appealed.

The Court of Appeals (by a split 2-to-1 vote) reversed. The majority interpreted the labor laws as waiving antitrust liability through the collective bargaining process, so long as such restraints operate primarily in a labor market characterized by collective bargaining. The court held, consequently, that the club owners were immune from antitrust liability. Brown appealed to the U. S. Supreme Court.]

HOLDING

The U. S. Supreme Court upheld the Appeals Court decision that the development squad fixed wage was immune from antitrust liability due to the labor exemption.

RATIONALE

The immunity is what the Supreme Court has called the "nonstatutory" labor exemption from the antitrust laws. The petitioners and their supporters concede, as they must, the legal existence of the exemption. They also concede that, where its application is necessary to make the statutorily authorized collective bargaining process work as Congress intended, the exemption must apply both to employers and employees. Consequently, the question in this case is one of determining the exemption's scope: Does it apply to an agreement among several employers bargaining together to implement after impasse the terms of their last best good-faith wage offer? Assuming that such conduct is unobjectionable as a matter of labor law and policy, we conclude that the exemption applies.

Labor law itself regulates directly, and considerably, the kind of behavior here at issue—the post-impasse imposition of a proposed employment term concerning a mandatory subject of bargaining. Both the NLRB and the courts have held that, after impasse, labor law permits employers unilaterally to implement changes in pre-existing conditions, but only insofar as the new terms meet carefully circumscribed conditions. For example, the new terms must be "reasonably comprehended" within the employer's pre-impasse proposals (typically the last rejected proposals), lest by imposing more or less favorable terms, the employer unfairly undermined the union's status. The collective bargaining proceeding itself must be free of any unfair labor practice, such as an employer's failure to have bargained in good faith. These regulations reflect the fact that impasse and an accompanying implementation of proposals constitute an integral part of the bargaining process. . . .

Although the prior case law focuses upon bargaining by a single employer, no one here has argued that labor law does, or should, treat multiemployer bargaining differently in this respect. Indeed, NLRB and court decisions suggest that the joint implementation of proposed terms after impasse is a familiar practice in multiemployer bargaining.

* * *

In these circumstances, to subject the practice to antitrust law is to require antitrust courts to answer a host of important practical questions about how collective bargaining over wages, hours, and working conditions is to proceed—the very result that the implicit labor exemption seeks to avoid. And it is to place in jeopardy some of the potentially beneficial labor-related effects that multiemployer bargaining can achieve. That is because unlike labor law, which sometimes welcomes anticompetitive agreements conducive to industrial harmony, antitrust law forbids all agreements among competitors (such as competing employers) that unreasonably lessen competition among or between them in virtually any respect whatsoever. If the antitrust laws apply, what are employers to do once impasse is reached? If all impose terms similar to their last joint offer, they invite an antitrust action premised upon identical behavior (along with prior or accompanying conversations) as tending to show a common understanding or agreement. If any, or all, of them individually impose terms that differ significantly from that offer, they invite an unfair labor practice charge. Indeed, how can employers safely discuss their offers together even before a bargaining impasse occurs? A pre-impasse discussion about, say, the practical advantages or disadvantages of a particular proposal invites a later antitrust claim that they agreed to limit the kinds of action each would later take should an impasse occur. The same is true of post impasse discussions aimed at renewed negotiations with the union. Nor would adherence to the terms of an expired collective bargaining agreement eliminate a potentially plausible antitrust claim charging that they had "conspired" or tacitly "agreed" to do so, particularly if maintaining the status quo were not in the immediate economic self-interest of some. All this is to say that to permit antitrust liability here threatens to introduce instability and uncertainty into the collective bargaining process, for antitrust law often forbids or discourages the kinds of joint discussions and behavior that the collective bargaining process invites or requires.

We do not see any obvious answer to this problem. We recognize, that, in principle, antitrust courts might themselves try to evaluate particular kinds of employer understandings, finding them "reasonable" (hence lawful) where justified by collective bargaining necessity. But any such evaluation means a web of detailed rules spun by many different non-expert antitrust judges and juries, not a set of labor rules enforced by a single expert administrative body, namely the NLRB. The labor laws give the NLRB, not antitrust courts, primary responsibility for policing the collective bargaining process. And one of their objectives was to take from antitrust courts the authority to determine, through application of the antitrust laws, what is socially or economically desirable collective bargaining policy.

Petitioners also say that irrespective of how the labor exemption applies elsewhere to multiemployer collective bargaining, professional sports is "special." We can understand how professional sports may be special in terms of, say, interest, excitement, or concern. But we do not understand how they are special in respect to labor law's antitrust exemption. We concede that the clubs that make up a professional sports league are not completely independent economic competitors, as they depend upon a degree of cooperation for economic survival. In the present context, however, that circumstance makes the league more like a single bargaining employer, which analogy seems irrelevant to the legal issue before us.

We also concede that football players often have special individual talents, and, unlike many unionized workers, they often negotiate their pay individually with their employers. But this characteristic seems simply a feature, like so many others, that might give employees (or employers) more (or less) bargaining power, that might lead some (or all) of them to favor a particular kind of bargaining, or that might lead to certain demands at the bargaining table. We do not see how it could make a critical legal difference in determining the underlying framework in which bargaining is to take place. Indeed, it would be odd to fashion an antitrust exemption that gave additional advantages to professional football players (by virtue of their superior bargaining power) that transport workers, coal miners, or meat packers would not enjoy. Ultimately, we cannot find a satisfactory basis for distinguishing football players from other organized workers. We therefore conclude that all must abide by the same legal rules.

For these reasons, we hold that the labor exemption applies to the employer conduct at issue here. That conduct took place during and immediately after a collective bargaining negotiation. It grew out of, and was directly related to, the lawful operation of the bargaining process. It involved a matter that the parties were required to negotiate collectively. And it concerned only the parties to the collective bargaining relationship.

Our holding is not intended to insulate from antitrust review every joint imposition of terms by employers, for an agreement among employers could be sufficiently distant in time and in circumstances from the collective bargaining process that a rule permitting antitrust intervention would not significantly interfere with that process. We need not decide in this case whether, or where, within these extreme outer boundaries to draw that line. Nor would it be appropriate for us to do so without the detailed views of the NLRB, to whose specialized judgment Congress intended to leave many of the inevitable questions concerning multiemployer bargaining bound to arise in the future.

Questions

1. According to *Brown v. NFL*, when are actions involving labor relations in professional sport leagues no longer exempt from antitrust liability?
2. Is it fair to the union that the Court did not settle on a particular point in time at which the exemption from antitrust laws would end (i.e., expiration of the CBA, a strike or lockout, or impasse)?

Collective Bargaining Agreements

In collective bargaining negotiations, employees working with their union and employers through a management team negotiate over mandatory subjects of bargaining, resulting in a contract called the **collective bargaining agreement.** Exhibit 9.3 presents excerpts from three CBAs. (The documents as a whole can be hundreds of pages long.)

EXHIBIT	9.3	Excerpt from collective bargaining agreements.

NFL - ARTICLE XI COMMISSIONER DISCIPLINE (available at nflpa.org)

Section 1. **League Discipline:** Notwithstanding anything stated in Article IX (Non-Injury Grievance):

(a) All disputes involving a fine or suspension imposed upon a player for conduct on the playing field other than as described in subsection (b) below, or involving action taken against a player by the Commissioner for conduct detrimental to the integrity of, or public confidence in, the game of professional football, will be processed exclusively as follows: the Commissioner will promptly send written notice of his action to the player, with a copy to the NFLPA. Within twenty (20) days following such written notification, the player affected thereby, or the NFLPA with the player's approval, may appeal in writing to the Commissioner.

(b) Fines or suspensions imposed upon players for unnecessary roughness or unsportsmanlike conduct on the playing field with respect to an opposing player or players shall be determined initially by a person appointed by the Commissioner after consultation concerning the person being appointed with the Executive Director of the NFLPA, as promptly as possible after the event(s) in question. Such person will send written notice of his action to the player, with a copy to the NFLPA. Within ten (10) days following such notification, the player, or the NFLPA with his approval, may appeal in writing to the Commissioner.

(c) On receipt of a notice of appeal under subsection (a) or (b) above, the Commissioner will designate a time and place for a hearing to be commenced within ten (10) days thereafter, at which he or his designee (other than the person appointed in (b) above) will preside. The hearing may be by telephone conference call, if the player so requests. As soon as practicable following the conclusion of such hearing, the Commissioner will render a written decision which will constitute full, final and complete disposition of the dispute and will be binding upon the player(s) and Club(s) involved and the parties to this Agreement with respect to that dispute. Any discipline imposed pursuant to subparagraph (b) above may only be affirmed, reduced, or vacated by the Commissioner in such decision, and may not be increased.

Section 2. **Time Limits:** Each of the time limits set forth in this Article may be extended by mutual agreement of the Commissioner and the player(s) and the Club(s) involved.

Section 3. **Representation:** In any hearing provided for in this Article, a player may be accompanied by counsel of his choice. A representative of the NFLPA may also participate in such hearing and represent the player. In any such hearing, a Club representative may be accompanied by counsel of his choice. A representative of the Management Council may also participate in such hearing and represent the Club. The NFLPA and Management Council have the right to attend all hearings provided for in this Article. At the hearing, the player, the NFLPA and the Management Council will have the right to be present, by testimony or otherwise, any evidence relevant to the hearing. All hearings shall be transcribed.

Section 4. **Costs:** Unless the Commissioner determines otherwise, each party will bear the cost of its own witnesses, counsel and the like.

Section 5. **One Penalty:** The Commissioner and a Club will not discipline a player for the same act or conduct. The Commissioner's disciplinary action will preclude or supersede disciplinary action by any Club for the same act or conduct.

Section 6. **Fine Money:** Any fine money collected pursuant to this Article will be contributed to the Brian Piccolo Cancer Fund, the Vincent T. Lombardi Cancer Research Center, ALS Neuromuscular Research Foundation, and the NFLPA Players Assistance Trust ("P.A.T."). Any such fine money shall be allocated equally among the four (4) organizations mentioned in the preceding sentence.

NBA - ARTICLE VI PLAYER CONDUCT (available at nbpa.org)

Section 2. Practices.

(a) When a player, without proper and reasonable excuse, fails to attend a practice session scheduled by his Team, he shall be subject to the following discipline: (i) for the first missed practice during a Season—$2,500; (ii) for the second missed practice during such Season—$5,000; (iii) for the third missed practice during such Season—$7,500; and (iv) for the fourth (or any additional) missed practice during such Season—such discipline as is reasonable under the circumstances.

(b) Notwithstanding Section 2(a) above, when a player, without proper and reasonable excuse, refuses or intentionally fails to attend any practice session scheduled by his Team, he shall be subject to such discipline as is reasonable under the circumstances.

MLB - ARTICLE XII DISCIPLINE (available at mlbplayers.com)

D. Compliance

(1) Nothing contained in this Grievance Procedure shall excuse a Player from prompt compliance with any discipline imposed upon him.

(2) Club Fines. A fine imposed by a Club pursuant to Regulation 5 of the Uniform Player's Contract in excess of $2,000 may not be deducted from the Player's salary until such fine is finally upheld in the Grievance Procedure or the time in which to file a Grievance has expired.

(3) Fines Imposed by the Vice President, On-Field Operations or Commissioner.

    (a) A fine imposed by the Vice President, On-Field Operations or the Commissioner in excess of $3,000 may not be deducted from the Player's salary until such fine is finally upheld in the Grievance Procedure or the time in which to file a Grievance has expired.

    (b) The Player's employing Club is authorized, at the request of the Vice President, On-Field Operations, or the Commissioner, to deduct the amount of the fine from the Player's salary and transmit such sum to the Commissioner once the fine may be deducted from the Player's salary.

The CBA is a document that represents the culmination of collective bargaining negotiations. The collective bargaining relationship, however, is an ongoing one. After the document is drafted and ratified, during the term of the contract, there may be a need for changes. To adopt changes, the moving party (union or management) must initiate discussions and negotiations on issues that involve mandatory subjects. Either side has the right to convince the other side to come back to the bargaining table to discuss or negotiate over a new or current term of employment. Managers who understand that unilateral changes in the workplace must be negotiated with the union before implementation will have a better relationship with employees and be less likely to face unfair labor practice charges. An exception to this rule occurs when the change qualifies as a management right, so-called "managerial decisions which lie at the core of entrepreneurial control" (*Ford Motor Co. v. NLRB* at 498, 1979).

Professional sports league CBAs have some key provisions that make up mandatory subjects for bargaining. These include the provisions shown in Exhibit 9.4.

As you can see, some of the provisions do not fit neatly in the categories chosen for them, and some actually fit in more than one category. For instance, no strike–no lockout provisions do affect hours, because they give an expectation that players will work and will be allowed to work. They also, obviously, affect wages. The same can be said for the draft, free agency, and other player mobility provisions. In the next section, we explore in greater detail some of the critical aspects of collective bargaining.

Arbitration

A critical component in the collective bargaining relationship is the reliance on arbitration to resolve disputes. Arbitration is a process whereby the parties to a dispute choose to resolve it by jointly hiring a neutral third-party arbitrator to render a decision that is final and binding (see Chapter 3). It is a less costly, more efficient

| EXHIBIT | 9.4 | Provisions in professional sports CBAs. |

WAGE PROVISIONS	HOUR PROVISIONS	TERMS AND CONDITIONS OF EMPLOYMENT
Salary caps/taxes (teamwide or based on players' service)	Training camp/spring training	Grievance arbitration, including injury, medical, and labor grievance
Minimum salaries	Season schedule	Free agency
Fines	Postseason play	Draft
Salary arbitration	Travel	Discipline
Termination/severance pay	All-star game	Drug testing
Licensing revenues	Exhibition games	Travel, locker room, parking policies
Per diem pay	Charitable requirements	Player conduct
Fringe benefits (pensions, life and health insurance, etc.)	Winter or summer leagues	Health issues (medical care, access to records, right to second opinion)
Tickets	No strike–no lockout	Rosters
Charitable contributions	Public relations commitments	Anticollusion

alternative to the court system or to a strike or a lockout as a means of resolving a disagreement. Arbitration clauses are common in labor agreements and create a mechanism for employees and employers to resolve disputes over interpretations of the CBA or to challenge disciplinary action. **Rights arbitration** is for disputes over the interpretation or application of the contract. **Interest arbitration** deals with disputes over the terms of contracts, such as salary arbitration (*Silverman v. MLBPRC*, 1995). Salary arbitration is discussed in the next section.

Regardless of the quality of the negotiating or the clarity of the language in the CBA, it would be unrealistic to think that disputes would not arise during the course of the agreement. These disputes can be lodged through a grievance process that should be negotiated into the CBA. The first step in the process takes place when one party files a grievance against the other. Unions generally file these on behalf of their employees. Grievance processes typically include the five steps shown in Exhibit 9.5.

For arbitration to work, both sides must agree in collective bargaining that the decision of the arbitrator(s) is final and binding. Three cases decided by the U. S. Supreme Court in 1960, known collectively as the *Steelworkers* Trilogy, established federal policy that:

- Courts should enforce arbitration clauses.
- They should do so without inquiring into the merits of a grievance.
- They should not intervene in an arbitrator's decision, provided that the arbitrator's award is based on the essence of the collective bargaining agreement.

(See *U.S. Steelworkers v. American Mfg. Co.*, 1960; *U.S. Steelworkers v. Warrior Gulf Co.*, 1960; *U.S. Steelworkers v. Enterprise Corp.*, 1960.) In other words, a court should presume that parties with a contract containing an arbitration clause should use it, and a court should not substitute its decision for the arbitrator's. A court can overturn a decision only where the plaintiff can prove that the arbitrator exceeded the scope of her authority, for example by conflicting with express terms of the CBA, imposing disciplinary action, or crafting a resolution that is not expressly allowed in the contract.

Steps for resolving disputes, leading to arbitration.	EXHIBIT	9.5

1. An employee discusses a grievance with the union rep or steward or reports it directly to a supervisor.

2. If the union representative and the employee agree the grievance has merit, they submit a formal written grievance.

3. The union representative and a management representative attempt to resolve the grievance.

4. The grievance may be heard before a committee to assist the two sides in resolving the dispute.

5. An arbitration hearing is held and a decision is rendered by an independent arbitrator or panel of arbitrators.

The following Case Opinion illustrates how the Supreme Court strictly upholds the decision of an arbitrator in line with the *Steelworkers* Trilogy discussed above.

Major League Baseball Players Association v. Garvey

532 U.S. 504 (2001)	CASE OPINION

[FACTS

In the late 1980s the Major League Baseball Players Association (MLBPA) filed grievances against Major League Baseball Clubs claiming the clubs had colluded in the market for free-agent services after the 1985, 1986, and 1987 seasons in violation of the industry's collective bargaining agreement. A free agent is a player who may contract with any Club, rather than one whose right to contract is restricted to a particular Club. In a series of decisions, arbitrators found collusion by the Clubs and damage to the players. The MLBPA and Clubs entered into a Global Settlement Agreement pursuant to which the Clubs established a $280 million fund to be distributed to injured players. The MLBPA also designed a "Framework" to resolve individual player's claims, and applying that Framework, recommended distribution plans for claims relating to a particular season or seasons. The Framework provided that players could seek an arbitrator's review of the distribution plan. The arbitrator would determine "only whether the approved Framework and the criteria set forth therein have been properly applied in the proposed Distribution Plan." The Framework set forth factors to be considered in evaluating players' claims, as well as specific requirements for lost contract-extension claims where a player had a specific offer that was made and withdrawn due to collusion.

Steve Garvey, a retired, highly regarded first baseman, submitted a claim for damages of approximately $3 million. He alleged that his contract with the San Diego Padres was not extended to the 1988 and 1989 seasons due to collusion. The Association rejected Garvey's claim in February 1996, because he presented no evidence that the Padres actually offered to extend his contract. Garvey objected, and an arbitration hearing was held. He testified that the Padres offered to extend his contract for the 1988 and 1989 seasons and then withdrew the offer after they began colluding with other teams. He presented a June 1996 letter from Ballard Smith, Padres' President and CEO from 1979 to 1987, stating that, before the end of the 1985 season, Smith offered to extend Garvey's contract through the

1989 season, but that the Padres refused to negotiate with Garvey thereafter due to collusion. The arbitrator denied Garvey's claim, after seeking additional documentation from the parties because he doubted Smith's credibility due to the "stark contradictions" between the 1996 letter and Smith's testimony in the earlier arbitration proceedings.

Garvey moved in Federal District Court to vacate the arbitrator's award, alleging that the arbitrator violated the Framework by denying his claim. The District Court denied the motion. The Court of Appeals for the Ninth Circuit reversed by a divided vote. The court acknowledged that judicial review of an arbitrator's decision in a labor dispute is extremely limited. But it held that review of the merits of the arbitrator's award was warranted in this case, because the arbitrator "dispensed his own brand of industrial justice." The court recognized that Smith's prior testimony with respect to collusion conflicted with the statements in his 1996 letter. But in the court's view, the arbitrator's refusal to credit Smith's letter was "inexplicable" and "border[ed] on the irrational," because a panel of arbitrators, chaired by the arbitrator involved here, had previously concluded that the owners' prior testimony was false. The court rejected the arbitrator's reliance on the absence of other corroborating evidence, attributing that fact to Smith and Garvey's direct negotiations. The court also found that the record provided "strong support" for the truthfulness of Smith's 1996 letter. The Court of Appeals reversed and remanded with directions to vacate the award.

The District Court then remanded the case to the arbitration panel for further hearings, and Garvey appealed. The Court of Appeals reversed the District Court and directed that it remand the case to the arbitration panel with instructions to enter an award for Garvey in the amount he claimed.]

HOLDING

The Ninth Circuit Court of Appeals erred in reversing the order of the District Court denying the motion to vacate the arbitrator's award, and it erred further in directing that judgment be entered in Garvey's favor.

RATIONALE

Judicial review of a labor-arbitration decision pursuant to such an agreement is very limited. Courts are not authorized to review the arbitrator's decision on the merits despite allegations that the decision rests on factual errors or misinterprets the parties' agreement. It is only when the arbitrator strays from interpretation and application of the agreement and effectively "dispense[s] his own brand of industrial justice" that his decision may be unenforceable. When an arbitrator resolves disputes regarding the application of a contract, and no dishonesty is alleged, the arbitrator's "improvident, even silly, factfinding" does not provide a basis for a reviewing court to refuse to enforce the award.

To be sure, the Court of Appeals here recited these principles, but its application of them is nothing short of baffling. The substance of the court's discussion reveals that it overturned the arbitrator's decision because it disagreed with the arbitrator's factual findings, particularly those with respect to credibility. The Court of Appeals, it appears, would have credited Smith's 1996 letter, and found the arbitrator's refusal to do so at worst "irrational" and at best "bizarre." But even "serious error" on the arbitrator's part does not justify overturning his decision, where, as here, he is construing a contract and acting within the scope of his authority.

In *Garvey II*, the court clarified that *Garvey I* both rejected the arbitrator's findings and went further, resolving the merits of the parties' dispute based on the court's assessment of the record before the arbitrator. For that reason, the court found further arbitration proceedings inappropriate. But again, established law

ordinarily precludes a court from resolving the merits of the parties' dispute on the basis of its own factual determinations, no matter how erroneous the arbitrator's decision. Even when the arbitrator's award may properly be vacated, the appropriate remedy is to remand the case for further arbitration proceedings. The Court of Appeals usurped the arbitrator's role by resolving the dispute and barring further proceedings, a result at odds with this governing law.

For the foregoing reasons, the Court of Appeals erred in reversing the order of the District Court denying the motion to vacate the arbitrator's award, and it erred further in directing that judgment be entered in Garvey's favor. The petition for a writ of certiorari is granted, the judgment of the Court of Appeals is reversed, and the case is remanded for further proceedings consistent with this opinion.

Questions

1. According to *MLBPA v. Garvey,* what is the standard for a court to use to vacate an arbitrator's award?

2. Supreme Court Justice Stevens strongly dissented with the majority decision in the *MLBPA v. Garvey* decision above. Stevens argued that even in cases where the court sees clearly that the arbitrator's decision is irrational and the correct disposition of the matter is perfectly clear to the court that the only solution under *Garvey* would be to remand the decision for a new arbitration case, and thus, he found such a solution flawed. Do you agree or disagree with Stevens that courts should have some limited power to overturn arbitration decisions when it is obvious that the arbitrator erred?

Salary arbitration

As stated previously, arbitration clauses in CBAs specify that disputes over certain players' salaries be settled through arbitration. For example, both Major League Baseball and the National Hockey League provide for disputes between an owner and an eligible player over the player's salary to proceed through arbitration. The processes that are used resulted from collective bargaining negotiations. The two systems share the same end goal of determining a player's worth for the upcoming season, but the systems are notably different. For instance, baseball's system is "final offer," meaning that the arbitrators must choose one side or the other's final offer. The arbitrators do this by choosing the midpoint between the two offers and determining whether the player is worth more or less than that midpoint. If more, the player's salary demand is met. If less, the club's salary offer becomes the salary for the upcoming season. In hockey, arbitrators have the ability to choose either an offer or an amount between the two offers. It is not a process for the faint of heart, as a player is forced to listen to the team argue as to why the player is not worth the value he seeks.

Player eligibility, the specific process, and the criteria for judging a player's worth also differ between baseball and hockey. Baseball players with at least three years and less than six years of major league service are eligible to file for salary arbitration. Those players considered "super twos" (the top 17 percent of major league service time for second-year players) and those free agents whose clubs have elected salary arbitration are also eligible. As a general rule, NHL players are eligible for salary arbitration after four years in the league. NHL clubs also have the right to elect salary arbitration in lieu of making a qualifying offer[5] for two classes of players: those who earned more than $1.5 million in their previous season, and Group II[6] players eligible for salary arbitration who themselves choose not to go to salary arbitration. Exhibit 9.6 compares the baseball and hockey processes.

Discipline

Most CBAs have at least one provision devoted to employee discipline. The discipline provisions are intertwined with grievance arbitration, which serves as the mechanism to challenge disciplinary action. The phrase "just cause" often appears in discipline provisions. This refers to a level of scrutiny used in evaluating whether an employee deserves the discipline rendered and, thus, sets limits on employers' authority.

In professional sports the players association's negotiation of discipline provisions has served as a means to limit or at the very least define commissioner powers. Grievance arbitration has also cut into the commissioner's powers, since historically the commissioner has been positioned as the arbitrator in disputes between players and the league or teams. In many cases, the grievance process specifies that the player must first take his grievance to the commissioner and then, based upon the outcome of that decision, may accept it or proceed to a neutral arbitration process. An example of a commissioner discipline clause was given in Exhibit 9.3.

Drug testing

The NLRB has held that drug and alcohol testing of employees is a mandatory subject for bargaining (*Johnson-Bateman Co. v. International Association of Machinists,* 1989). Although recently Congress has begun to press all sports for uniform drug testing, policies achieved through collective bargaining are more likely to be effective in protecting the rights and obligations of employees and employers, especially employee rights. Through a bargaining process, manage-

---

[5]A qualifying offer is an offer that must be extended to a restricted free agent to retain negotiating rights to that player. Players making less than $600,000 must be offered 110 percent of the previous year's salary. Those earning from $600,000 up to $1 million must be offered 105 percent, and those earning over $1 million must be offered 100 percent.

[6]Group II is a category of players determined by a formula that uses the player's age and years of service in the league.

ment and players will negotiate to develop fair provisions in regard to issues such as players' privacy rights, confidentiality surrounding the testing process and the results of tests, medical concerns that arise from the testing, the determination of which drugs to test for and what amounts of those drugs in one's system will subject a player to suspension, concerns over "what else" the organization might test for or might discover in testing, and the role of drug-testing results in international competition.

Salary arbitration in MLB and the NHL.		**EXHIBIT** **9.6**

SALARY ARBITRATION	MAJOR LEAGUE BASEBALL	NATIONAL HOCKEY LEAGUE
Eligibility	All players with 3, but less than 6 years major league service time Super 2s—top 17 percent of players with at least 2 but less than 3 years of service time and at least 86 days of service in the immediately preceding season Free agents whose clubs opt for salary arbitration	Group 2 free agents may opt for it provided the following conditions of first signing age and service time: ■ 18–20 with 4 years service ■ 21 with 3 years service ■ 22–23 with 2 years service ■ 24+ with 1 year service Club may opt for it if: ■ Player is eligible for qualifying offer and is Group 2 free agent with prior salary plus bonuses in excess of $1.5 million ■ Player is Group 2 free agent that has not accepted qualifying offer
Criteria	Contribution to club during past season Length & consistency of career contribution Past compensation Comparable baseball salaries (most weight to players within 1 year of player's service time) Physical or mental defects Recent club performance	Overall performance of player & comparables Number of games Length of service Overall contribution to club success Special leadership, public appeal Compensation of comparables
Inadmissible Evidence	Info on noncomparable players Financial condition of player and club (inability to pay) Testimonials, newspaper clips, etc. Prior offers or negotiation history Cost to the parties of the arbitration process Salaries in other sports or professions	Info on noncomparable players Testimonials, newspaper clips, etc. Reference to actual or potential walk-away rights Financial condition of club Prior offers or negotiation history Any prior award made to player
Arbitrator's Decision	No written decision or opinion, just chooses club offer or player demand Decision made within 24 hours of hearing	Written decision includes contract term, base salary, bonuses, inclusion of minor league salary, statement of reasons for decision Decision made within 48 hours of close of hearing

Further, at the bargaining table the two sides may consider whether to include educational and rehabilitative components in the policies. The two sides can also negotiate the testing policies and procedures in the context of other aspects of their employment relationship, such as disciplinary actions and arbitration provisions. Finally, the collective bargaining process is just that—a process. It is the negotiation of an agreement that will be interpreted and administered on a daily basis—an agreement that can be renewed, reviewed, and renegotiated when the parties find that conditions have evolved in such a way as to require the two sides to come back to the bargaining table to reopen the agreement. See Exhibit 9.7 for penalties and discipline provisions of the performance-enhancing drug policies in the CBAs for the NBA, MLB, NHL, and NFL.

Drug-testing provisions cover two categories of drugs: substances of abuse and performance enhancers. Substances of abuse are recreational drugs such as marijuana, cocaine, LSD, and the like. Performance enhancers are drugs such as anabolic steroids, amphetamines, and so forth. Drug-testing provisions may include penalties, opportunities for rehabilitation, and education on substances.

EXHIBIT	9.7	Disciplinary provisions of performance-enhancing drug policies in the CBAs for the NBA, MLB, NHL, and NFL.

NBA - ARTICLE XXXIII ANTI-DRUG PROGRAM

Section 9. Steroids, Performance-Enhancing Drugs and Masking Agents Program

(c) Penalties.

Any player who (i) tests positive for a SPED pursuant to Section 5 (Reasonable Cause Testing), Section 6 (Random Testing), or Section 14 (Additional Bases for Testing), or (ii) is adjudged by the Grievance Arbitrator pursuant to Section 5(e) above to have used or possessed a SPED, shall suffer the following penalties:

(A) For the first such violation, the player shall be suspended for ten (10) games and required to enter the SPED Program;

(B) For the second such violation, the player shall be suspended for twenty-five (25) games and, if the player is not then subject to in-patient or aftercare treatment in the SPED Program, be required to enter the SPED Program;

(C) for the third such violation, the player shall be suspended for one (1) year from the date of such violation and, if the player is not then subject to in-patient or aftercare treatment in the SPED Program, be required to enter the SPED Program; and

(D) for the fourth such violation, the player shall be immediately dismissed and disqualified from any association with the NBA or any of its Teams in accordance with the provisions of Section 11(a) below.

MLB's JOINT DRUG PREVENTION AND TREATMENT PROGRAM

8. DISCIPLINE

B. Player Tests Positive for a Performance Enhancing Substance

1. First positive test result: a 50-game suspension;

2. Second positive test result: a 100-game suspension; and

3. Third positive test result: permanent suspension from Major League and Minor League Baseball; provided, however, that a Player so suspended may apply, no earlier than one year following the imposition of the suspension, to the Commissioner for discretionary reinstatement after a minimum period of two years.

C. Player Tests Positive for a Stimulant

1. First positive test result: follow-up testing pursuant to Section 5 above;

2. Second positive test result: a 25-game suspension;

3. Third positive test result: an 80-game suspension; and

4. Fourth and subsequent positive test result: a suspension for just cause by the Commissioner, up to permanent suspension from Major League and Minor League Baseball, which penalty shall be subject to challenge before the Arbitration Panel.

NHL - ARTICLE 47 PERFORMANCE ENHANCING SUBSTANCES PROGRAM

47.7 Disciplinary Penalties. Positive tests for performance enhancing substances will result in mandatory discipline as follows:

(a) for the first positive lest, a suspension of twenty (20) NHL Games without pay, and mandatory referral to the SABH program for evaluation and possible treatment;

(b) for the second positive test, a suspension of sixty (60) NHL Games without pay, and mandatory referral to the SABH program for evaluation and possible treatment;

(c) for the third positive lest, a "permanent" suspension without pay, although a Player so suspended can reapply for discretionary reinstatement after a minimum period of two (2) years by making an application to the Committee.

NFL POLICY ON ANABOLIC STEROIDS AND RELATED SUBSTANCES (2008)

6. Suspension and Related Discipline

Players with a confirmed positive test result will be subject to discipline by the Commissioner as outlined in the Policy below.

Step One: The first time a player violates this Policy by testing positive; attempting to substitute, dilute or adulterate a specimen; manipulating a test result; or by violation of law (see Section 5), he will be suspended without pay for a minimum of four regular and/or postseason games.

Step Two: The second time a player violates this Policy by testing positive; attempting to substitute, dilute or adulterate a specimen; manipulating a test result; or by violation of law (see Section 5), he will be suspended without pay for a minimum of eight regular and/or postseason games.

Step Three: The third time a player violates the Policy by testing positive; attempting to substitute, dilute or adulterate a specimen; manipulating a test result; or by violation of law (see Section 5), he will be suspended without pay for a period of at least 12 months, subject to any appeal (see Section 10). Such a player may petition the Commissioner for reinstatement after 12 months. Reinstatement, and any terms and conditions thereof, shall be matters solely within the Commissioner's sound discretion.

Labor Relations and Collective Bargaining

- If you serve as a sport manager in a unionized workplace (or one that could become unionized), have a working knowledge of labor laws.

- As a manager employing unionized workers, strive to understand and abide by the processes, procedures, and rules set forth in the collective bargaining agreement. It is useful to ask legal counsel to guide you through collective bargaining and related employment decisions. For instance, if disciplining a union member, managers must follow the protocol and procedures set forth in the CBA to avoid the possibility of facing a grievance or arbitration.

- Before implementing management decisions, consult the CBA or your human resources or legal counsel to ensure that your decisions are in line with your organization's labor agreement.

Salary caps

Collective bargaining over compensation encompasses all of the wage and benefit provisions delineated in Exhibit 9.4, and then some. With the exception of salary caps, luxury taxes, fines, tickets, and licensing revenues, the list tends to be the same regardless of the field that the labor agreement covers.

The past three decades in professional sports have seen salaries rise at increasing rates as players have engaged in collective bargaining. As a result, negotiations in professional sports have increasingly centered on salary caps and other wage restrictions, as well as on luxury tax systems designed to limit the percentage of revenue devoted to player salaries. Creative negotiators on each side have created hard caps, with no or a minimum of exceptions for exceeding the team cap limits, as well as soft caps, which allow for exceptions such as room to sign veteran players or to replace injured or retired players. As a result of effective bargaining by the MLBPA, MLB is the only major league without some form of a salary cap. MLB does, however, have a luxury tax—clubs are taxed on the portion of team salary that exceeds a set, agreed-upon figure for team salaries.

The salary cap was used in professional sports prior to its adoption in the NBA in 1984, but in most recent memory, it has come to prominence through its use in the NBA and the NFL. Since it is a mandatory subject for bargaining, a salary cap cannot be unilaterally imposed but must be negotiated with the players. The salary caps are very complex collective bargaining provisions, which take up numerous pages in the CBA. A cottage industry has developed for experts with the labor and financial know-how to maneuver through these provisions; they are known as **capologists.** In addition to the team salary cap, there are also caps that single out a particular group of players, such as rookies.

Exhibit 9.8 attempts to break down some of the major components of the three league salary caps (NBA, NFL, and NHL). Due to the complexity of the caps, the exhibit is greatly simplified.

Salary caps operate by calculating in the aggregate certain league revenues that are defined in the CBA. The players receive a percentage of those defined revenues, and that number is divided by the number of clubs in the league. The resulting figure is the team salary cap. Lock (1998, pp. 322–323) explains that

> from an accounting standpoint, the operation of the [NFL] salary cap is straightforward and inflexible: the cumulative cap dollars contained in a team's player contracts simply cannot exceed the salary cap. The calculation of cap dollars expended by a team in its player contracts for any particular year, however, does not necessarily equal the actual dollars in its player contracts or dollars actually paid to its players. Instead, the salary cap creates a theoretical ceiling on the amount of money teams can spend on players in any particular year, subject to the league's rules for calculating cap dollars. Under league rules, the ceiling can be exceeded from a cash flow standpoint, depending on a team's attitude toward risk and its willingness to push cap dollars into future contract years.

Salary caps in MLB and the NHL.		EXHIBIT	9.8

SALARY CAP PROVISION	NBA	NFL (owners have currently opted out of NFL salary cap after 2010)	NHL
Defined revenues	Gate receipts National broadcast rights NBA properties Novelty, program, concession sales Team sponsorship Team promotions Arena club seating Summer camp proceeds Non-NBA tournaments Mascot/dance team performance Premium seat license proceeds 40% luxury suite proceeds 40% arena signage 50% arena naming rights	Gate receipts National broadcast rights NFL ventures Luxury box suite revenues Premium seating revenues Personal seat licenses Concessions Parking Signage Local advertising, promotion, & sponsorships Stadium lease or use agreements Equity instruments received from third parties	Gate receipts National, international, local, & digital broadcast rights NHL networks Concessions Merchandise Luxury boxes & premium seats Signage Sponsorships Parking
Players' percentage	Approximately 57% depending on league revenues	Approximately 64–65% depending on league revenues, but players are only guaranteed 50%	54–57% depending on league revenues
Team payroll cap	(51% of BRI – Projected Benefits) / (# of Teams) . . . Subject to numerous adjustments	(57.5% of TR – Projected Benefits) / (# of Teams) . . . Subject to numerous adjustments (2009)	[1.05 x [(% dependent on HRR x HRR) – Projected Benefits] / (# of Teams)] + $8 million
Team payroll floor	75% of salary cap	87.6% of salary cap (2009)	[1.05 x [(% dependent on HRR x HRR) – Projected Benefits] / (# of Teams)] – $8 million

Individual versus collective bargaining

Unique to professional athletes' unions is the individual bargaining power of the employees. Employee-athletes can and do have separate individual contracts that bind them to their employer-clubs, but they are also parties, through their players associations, to CBAs. The hierarchy of the agreements is such that the CBA takes precedence over the individual contract, but the two must work in concert. If not, the individual contract may violate provisions in the CBA. For example, assume the minimum salary in a league is $300,000. If a player is willing to play for $200,000, and his agent negotiated such a salary, it would undermine the union's work in negotiating for a higher minimum. As a result, the union has the right to "control" agents through the collective bargaining relationship. This is allowed under labor and antitrust laws so the union can protect its collective bargaining terms, because agents might otherwise "undercut" the terms that the union has negotiated on behalf of players. Unions cannot act to restrict agents' activities in other aspects of the players' professional career and decision making, such as marketing or financial advising.

Unions and rights of retired players

The National Football League Players Association and its marketing arm, Players, Inc. recently settled a lawsuit over their contractual and fiduciary duties to market retired players. The retired players, in *Parrish v. National Football League Players, Inc.* (2009), won a jury award of $28.1 million due to the NFLPA and Players, Inc.'s breach of its duty to market their names and likenesses. At issue was whether the defendants undertook a fiduciary duty to promote and to market all retired players who had signed Retired Player Group License Agreements (RPGLAs), but yet made no effort to do so and, further, whether the defendants' true commercial motive was to create an illusion of representation so that no one else would seek to sign up the retired players and to market them. The case raises questions as to what is the duty of players unions to retired players. And particular to the NFL retired players, a question has arisen as to what responsibilities the unions and leagues have to retired players who find in later years that they are subject to debilitating health as a result of injuries in their playing careers. Complicating the NFLPA case is the fact that retired players have not felt the union has represented their interest. The challenge here, as in many unions, is that current players pay the dues and vote on the union's leadership, thus leaving the union leaders to focus on current players at the risk of selling out the rights of past or future union members.

CONCLUSION

L abor relations are a critical piece of the work environment in sports. Labor law has been a critical component to the U. S. workforce as it has created structures for employees to bargain for safe and productive work environments. Labor laws, along with employment laws, delineate the conduct that is acceptable in the work environment. The NLRA in particular sets forth the parameters of conduct by employers and employees in private-sector unionized workplaces. It sets forth a process of collective bargaining that allows employees and employers to determine what issues must be resolved in their particular workplace and address them through the negotiation process to develop a contract for their workplace. We find the most unionized workforces in the sport industry among professional athletes and in the facility management world. As a manager in the sport industry, it is critical that you make management decisions with an eye toward the collective bargaining agreement and its rules, policies, and procedures, lest you find yourself facing a grievance and arbitration process.

discussion questions

1. What factors make labor relations in professional sports unique, as opposed to labor relations in other industries?
2. What employee rights were gained through the National Labor Relations Act?
3. What do the National Labor Relations Act and Labor Management Relations Act set forth as unfair labor practices?

4. Name five collective bargaining provisions for each mandatory subject of bargaining (hours, wages, and terms and condition of employment).
5. What is the role of arbitration in labor relations?
6. What is the labor exemption to antitrust? What is its relevance to professional sports labor relations?

learning activities

1. Conduct an Internet search to find professional sport organization collective bargaining agreements. They are often available on the union or league website. Examine the provisions in the collective bargaining agreements and assess whether the provisions relate to mandatory or permissive subjects for bargaining. Also, note how many niche or minor league sports are unionized. Good places to start are with the WNBA and the Pro Hockey Players Association.
2. Examine professional sport league collective bargaining agreements to compare and contrast the various provisions across leagues, such as those relating to drug testing, salary arbitration, grievance arbitration, salary caps, drafts, pensions, and other benefits. Also, discover whether there are provisions that are unique to each league.
3. Assume you are negotiating a new collective bargaining agreement in a league that has an expiring agreement. Research the key items for the negotiation and develop a strategy for CBA negotiations on the union or management side.

CASE STUDY

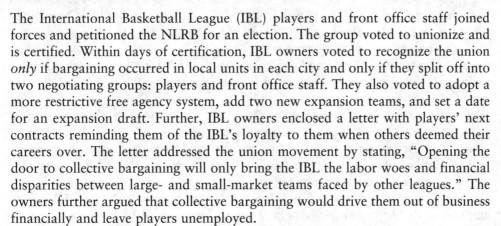

The International Basketball League (IBL) players and front office staff joined forces and petitioned the NLRB for an election. The group voted to unionize and is certified. Within days of certification, IBL owners voted to recognize the union *only* if bargaining occurred in local units in each city and only if they split off into two negotiating groups: players and front office staff. They also voted to adopt a more restrictive free agency system, add two new expansion teams, and set a date for an expansion draft. Further, IBL owners enclosed a letter with players' next contracts reminding them of the IBL's loyalty to them when others deemed their careers over. The letter addressed the union movement by stating, "Opening the door to collective bargaining will only bring the IBL the labor woes and financial disparities between large- and small-market teams faced by other leagues." The owners further argued that collective bargaining would drive them out of business financially and leave players unemployed.

The letter mobilized the player negotiating team. The lead negotiator is Tim Davis, a former NBA player who was banned two years ago for testing positive for marijuana and cocaine. Since then Davis underwent successful rehabilitation treatment and has been drug-free for two years. In fact, he recently spoke at the NBA–NBPA rookie training session on why players should avoid drugs. Davis is currently playing in the IBL to showcase his talents and get back on an NBA team.

Davis left for a six-city tour to meet with IBL players and held meetings in hotels far away from team facilities. During his meeting in Queens (NY), Davis found himself face-to-face with the IBL commissioner, who had been tipped off by one of the league's coaches. Their encounter ended in a shouting and shoving match. When Davis reported to training camp the next month, he was the only player forced to submit to an IBL-ordered drug test. The drug testing continued on a daily basis, leading many players to assume Davis was back using drugs. Every test was negative. Davis was also subjected to name-calling and criticism in the press by the coaching staff. This went on for three weeks, until Davis cracked under the pressure and punched his coach. Later that evening, Davis was notified that he was banned from the IBL.

1. Discuss whether Davis has any rights under labor laws.
2. What other information would you need to gather to discover whether Davis could challenge the commissioner's decision?

considering . . .   ANALYSIS & DISCUSSION

Labor Law in Practice (p. 200)

The first step for Jim to take is to gather and bring to his nearest NLRB regional office signed authorization cards from at least 30 percent of the employees in an appropriate bargaining unit in his workplace. An appropriate bargaining unit is one in which the employees have common interests and will be seeking common goals in negotiation. The authorization cards are simply to authorize the NLRB to come in and run an election at the workplace, not to authorize a union. Once the cards are turned over the NLRB and the unit is determined to be appropriate, the NLRB will come on-site to conduct an election. Often, workers in a union-organizing campaign will seek authorization cards from a majority of employees and then request that management voluntarily recognize the bargaining unit as the exclusive bargaining representative for the employees.

In terms of Jim's organizing his co-workers, the NLRB has developed organizing rights for oral solicitation and literature distribution. In both cases, the solicitations must be made on the employee's free time. This could be free time within the constraints of the workday, such as during a break or during any time when employees are allowed to converse over nonwork matters. The NLRB and courts have established the organizing rights and obligations of outside organizers and off-duty employees, but these issues are beyond the scope of this discussion.

In response to the question about what Carrie should do, she should not voluntarily recognize the union in accordance with § 9 of the NLRA. Like most employers, BCSE probably does not want to lose control of business decisions regarding its employees. Under § 7 of the NLRA, once a union is in place, the employer must collectively bargain with employees over hours, wages, and terms and conditions of employment.

Further, what if the union led by Jim Stone is not the only emerging union effort in the facility? If BCSE chooses Jim's union over others, then further problems in the workplace may occur. Moreover, what if Jim's complaints and actions are not representative of the rest of the employees at BCA? Then, by unilaterally and voluntarily recognizing Jim's union, Carrie may have given a segment of her employees what they want, but she has not determined whether the whole workplace is interested in unionization. By going through the election and certification processes, BCSE will be assured that workers are properly placed in appropriate units for collective bargaining purposes. For instance, BCA's clerical staff might be best served in a different union group than its laborers or ushers and ticket takers.

If BCA does not want a unionized workplace, once management at BCSE is aware of a growing labor movement, it may decide to take active steps to stop the union from organizing. BCSE managers would have to move carefully in this effort so as not to violate the labor laws that protect employees organizing, joining, or assisting unions. It is important for Carrie to have a working knowledge of labor relations in her repertoire of skills.

Carrie could present an antiunion speech to try to dissuade the employees from organizing. Carrie's speech can express her own or BCSE's opinions about the union, but it cannot include any threats to employees supporting the union, it cannot state that voting for the union is futile, it cannot appeal to racial prejudices, and it cannot promise benefits if the union is defeated. Under the *Peerless Plywood* rule, Carrie may speak against the union-organizing campaign on company time and may require her employees to attend a meeting and listen as a "captive audience." Carrie may not give an antiunion speech to a mass audience within 24 hours of the scheduled election, and she may not call employees into management areas that might intimidate them when she speaks to them about the union.

Carrie must proceed carefully in dealing with Jim Stone so as not to discriminate or retaliate. Doing so could make her vulnerable to an unfair labor practice charge for violating his NLRA § 7 rights to join or assist a union. Carrie should also seek out legal advice from BCSE attorneys before proceeding.

REFERENCES

Cases

Allen Bradley Co. v. Local No. 3, I.B.E.W., 325 U.S. 797 (1945).

Boys Markets, Inc. v. Retail Clerks' Union, Local 770, 398 U.S. 235 (1970).

Bridgeman v. NBA, 838 F. Supp. 172 (D.N.J. 1987).

Brown v. Pro Football, Inc., 518 U.S. 231 (1996).

Clarett v. NFL, 369 F.3d 124 (2nd Cir. 2004).

Commonwealth v. Hunt, 45 Mass. 111 (Mass S.J.C., 1842).

Commonwealth v. Pullis, Philadelphia Mayor's Court (1806).

Duplex Printing Press, Co. v. Deering, 254 U.S. 443 (1921).

Federal Baseball Club of Baltimore v. National League of Professional Baseball Clubs, 259 U.S. 200 (1922).

Flood v. Kuhn, 407 U.S. 258 (1972).

Ford Motor Co. v. NLRB, 441 U.S. 488, 498 (1979) *quoting* Fibreboard Corp. v. NLRB, 379 U.S. 203, 222–23 (1964) (Stewart, J. concurring).

Johnson-Bateman Co. v. International Ass'n of Machinists, 295 N.L.R.B. 180 (1989).

Local No. 189, Amalgamated Meat Cutters & Butcher Workmen v. Jewel Tea Co., 381 U.S. 676 (1965).

Loewe v. Lawlor, 208 U.S. 274 (1908).

Mackey v. NFL, 543 F.2d 606 (8th Cir. 1976).

Major League Baseball Players Assn. v. Garvey, 532 U.S. 504 (2001).

McCourt v. California Sports, Inc., 600 F.2d 1193 (6th Cir. 1979).

Miranda Fuel Co., 140 N.L.R.B. 181 (1962).

Morio v. NASL, 501 F. Supp. 633 (S.D.N.Y. 1980) *aff'd*, 632 F.2d 217 (2d Cir. 1980).

NASL v. NLRB, 613 F.2d 1379 (5th Cir. 1980).

NBA v. Williams, 45 F.3d 684 (2d Cir. 1995).

NFL Management Council and NFLPA, 309 N.L.R.B. 78 (1992).

NFLPA v. NLRB, 503 F.2d 12 (8th Cir. 1974).

NFL Management Council, 503 F.2d 12 (8th Cir. 1974).

NLRB v. Katz, 369 U.S. 736 (1962).

Nordstrom, d/b/a Seattle Seahawks and NFLPA, 292 N.L.R.B. 899 (1989).

Nordstrom, d/b/a Seattle Seahawks and NFLPA, 304 N.L.R.B. 78 (1991).

Parrish v. National Football League Players, Inc., No. C07-00943 WHA (n.d. Calif. 2009).

Peerless Plywood Co., 107 N.L.R.B. 427 (1953).

Peterson v. Kennedy, 771 F.2d 1244 (9th Cir. 1985).

Powell v. NFL, 930 F.2d 1293 (8th Cir. 1989).

Reynolds v. NFL, 584 F.2d 280 (8th Cir. 1978).

Silverman v. MLB Player Relations Comm., 880 F. Supp. 246 (S.D.N.Y. 1995).

Smith v. Pro Football, Inc., 593 F.2d 1173 (D.C. Cir. 1978).

Steele v. Louisville & Nashville R.R. Co., 323 U.S. 192 (1944).

The American League of Professional Baseball Clubs and the Association of National Baseball League Umpires, 180 N.L.R.B. 190 (1969).

Toolson v. New York Yankees, 346 U.S. 917 (1953).

United Mine Workers v. Pennington, 381 U.S. 657 (1965).

United States v. Hutcheson, 32 F. Supp. 600 (E.D. Mo. 1940).

U.S. Steelworkers v. American Mfg. Co., 363 US 564 (1960).

U.S. Steelworkers v. Enterprise Corp., 363 U.S. 593 (1960).

U.S. Steelworkers v. Warrior Gulf Co., 363 U.S. 574 (1960).

Vaca v. Sipes, 386 U.S. 171 (1967).

Wood v. NBA, 809 F.2d 954 (2d Cir. 1987).

Wright Line, a Division of Wright Line, Inc., 251 N.L.R.B. 1083 (1980), *enforced,* 662 F.2d 899 (1st Cir. 1981), *cert. denied,* 455 U.S. 989 (1982).

Statutes

Clayton Act of 1914, 15 USCS § 17 (2006).

Labor Management Relations Act (Taft-Hartley Act of 1947), 29 USCS § 141, *et seq.* (2005).

National Labor Relations Act, 29 USCS § 151, *et seq.* (2005).

Norris-LaGuardia Act of 1932, 29 USCS §§ 101–115 (2006).

Sherman Antitrust Act of 1890, 15 USCS § 1, *et. seq.* (2006).

Other Sources

Commons, J. R., Phillips, U. B., Gilmore, E. A., Sumner, H. L., & Andrews, J. B. (1958). *A documentary history of American industrial society, vol III.*, 59–248.

Cruise, D., & Griffiths, A. (1991). *Networth: Exploding the myth of pro hockey.* Toronto: Penguin.

Feldacker, B. (2000). *Labor guide to labor law*, 4th ed. Upper Saddle River, NJ: Prentice Hall.

Gold, M. E. (1998). *An introduction to labor law*, 2d ed. Ithaca, NY: ILR Press/Cornell University Press.

IBL, Class Action Reporter, September 19, 2000. Retrieved January 10, 2006, from http://bankrupt.com/CAR_Public/000919.MBX.

Jennings, K. M. (1990). *Balls and strikes: The money game in professional baseball.* New York: Praeger Publishers.

Lock, E. (1998). The regulatory scheme for player representatives in the National Football League: The real power of Jerry Maguire, *35 American Business Law Journal 319,* 322–323.

Rabuano, M. M. (2002). Comment: An examination of drug testing as a mandatory subject of collective bargaining in Major League Baseball. *University of Pennsylvania Journal of Labor and Employment Law, 4,* 439.

Weiler, P. C. (2000). *Leveling the playing field.* Cambridge, MA: Harvard University Press.

WEBSITE RESOURCES

www.apscuf.org/contracts/index.html#coaches ■ The website for the Association of Pennsylvania State Colleges and Universities (APSCU) contains the collective bargaining agreement regarding athletic coaches between the association and the Pennsylvania State System of Higher Education (PASSHE). The Pennsylvania state college system is the only system that has a coaches union. While collegiate athletic staff members are often unionized, most coaches are not.

The Law of Agency and Athlete Agents

INTRODUCTION

A thlete representation, also known as the athlete agent or sport agent business, is a visible and highly publicized element of the sport industry. This segment of the sport industry presents many unique challenges for sport managers. This chapter introduces basic notions of agency law and how those principles apply in a sport management context, exploring in detail the specific laws applicable to athlete agents and the unique legal issues related to athlete representation. The first section discusses the creation of an agency relationship, the scope of authority of agents, and the duties between principals and agents. The second section focuses on specific issues and disputes that may arise between athletes and agents. The last section focuses on the regulation of athlete agents regarding their dealings with student-athletes who still possess amateur eligibility and discusses the role of professional players associations in promoting the interests of professional athletes. Exhibit 10.1 presents the management contexts and applicable laws discussed in the chapter.

THE LAW OF AGENCY

A gency is the fiduciary relationship that arises when one person (a "principal") manifests a desire to have another person (an "agent") act on the principal's behalf and remain subject to the principal's control, which the agent consents to do (Restatement [Third] of Agency § 1.01 Agency Defined, 2006). Simply put, the term "agency" describes a relationship between two parties in which one party (the agent) agrees to act as a representative of the other party (the principal). The principal is the person hiring or engaging the agent to act on behalf of the principal or to perform certain duties for the principal. The typical athlete representation relationship involves the athlete (principal) hiring the athlete agent (agent) to negotiate a contract with a professional sport team where the sport team agrees to pay for the athletic services of the athlete. The principal (athlete) has an objective to

EXHIBIT 10.1	Management contexts pertaining to agency, with relevant laws and cases.		
MANAGEMENT CONTEXT	**MAJOR LEGAL ISSUES**	**RELEVANT LAW**	**ILLUSTRATIVE CASES**
Negotiation of business transactions	Creation of agency relationships	Agency Law Contract Law	
Employer liability for employee acts	Authority of agents to act Duties and responsibilities of agents/principals	Agency law, contract law, tort law	*Detroit Lions* *Jones, Clark Advertising Agency*
Player representation	Regulation of athlete agents	UAAA SPARTA Professional Player Association rules	*Alabama v. Goggins* *Hilliard v. Black*
Student-athletes' amateur status	NCAA eligibility *Dealings with agents*	Agency law UAAA SPARTA	*U.S. v. Piggie*

obtain a favorable contract with the professional team, and the athlete agent (agent) is the one employed to act on the athlete's behalf to achieve that objective.

In addition to the athlete representation relationship, agency relationships exist in a multitude of situations, many of which we experience on a daily basis. Almost everyone has dealt with an agent. Even the simplest transaction at a retail store involves an agent (sales clerk) and a principal (store employer). As another example, if you worked in a college stadium ticket office, such as Papa John's Cardinal Stadium at the University of Louisville, you would be an agent for the University of Louisville Athletic Association (ULAA), and the ULAA would be your principal. Virtually anyone who has had a job has served in a representative capacity for her employer and has been affected by agency law.

Almost every business enterprise requires the efforts of more than one person—engaging those persons to assist the enterprise is the essence of the agency relationship. Agency law governs relationships when one person hires or employs another to do his work, sell his goods, and/or acquire property on his behalf. The resulting transaction is as valid as if the employer were present and acting in person. A person can be hired to do work for another in a variety of ways. Three basic types of agency relationships exist:

1. Employee and employer relationship (this relationship results when an employer hires an employee to perform some form of service).
2. Principal and agent relationship (this relationship results when a principal hires an agent and gives that agent authority to act and enter into contracts on the principal's behalf).
3. Principal and independent contractor relationship (this relationship results when a person or business that is not an employee is employed by a principal to perform a certain task on the principal's behalf). Critical factors in determining independent contractor status were presented in Chapter 5.

Most agency relationships occur as part of an employment relationship, and the nature of that relationship was discussed in Chapter 4. However, the other two types of employment or contractual relationships are also quite visible in the sport industry. An example of the second type of agency relationship, the classic principal and agent relationship, is the athlete agent and professional athlete. The third agency relationship is illustrated by a university and a general contractor for a new stadium construction project, a common independent contractor relationship.

All contractual relationships involve the realization of a benefit to one party through the performance of another party. However, the principal–agent relationship is distinct from the traditional employee–employer and principal–independent contractor relationship due to the *fiduciary nature* of the principal–agent relationship. A **fiduciary** is defined as a person who acts primarily for the benefit of another. The nature of the fiduciary relationship is that one person entrusts his or her interests to another and that the agent must act loyally for the principal's benefit in all matters connected with the agency relationship. The traditional employee–employer relationship does not normally create a fiduciary relationship. Thus, an assistant athletic director for development at a university would likely not be in a fiduciary relationship with her employer. She would of course be required to perform tasks that benefit her employer and comply with various company policies, but the heightened duties associated with a fiduciary relationship would not exist in this relationship. On the other hand, the relationship between a professional athlete and his agent is a fiduciary relationship. The easiest way to distinguish fiduciary relationships from other types of contractual agency relationships is to ask whether a high degree of trust or confidence is vested by the principal in the agent. Fiduciary duties and other unique issues involving agency relationships are covered in this chapter.

Creation of the Agency Relationship

Agency relationships can only be created by the mutual consent of the parties. Thus, the creation of the agency relationship essentially involves two steps—(1) manifestation by the principal and (2) consent by the agent (Kleinberger, 2008). An agency relationship can be established by informal oral agreements or by more formal written agreements. Consider the following examples of when an agency relationship has been created (Kleinberger, 2008). Naomi is disappointed to learn that her favorite hiking guide, Max, will be unavailable during her upcoming trip to the Grand Canyon, and she sends the following email to Max: "So sorry you are not available, could you locate and hire me another guide of your quality and price range for the dates I sent you." Max hits the "reply" button and types, "Sure, no problem." He promptly receives an automated "out of the office" reply from Naomi indicating that she is gone for two weeks. A principal–agent relationship has been created. Naomi has manifested her intent to engage Max as her agent, and Max has consented to serve in that capacity. It is irrelevant that the principal, Naomi, may yet be unaware of the agent's consent.

Now consider the following: Max contacts Eric, explains the situation with Naomi, and determines that Eric is willing and available to guide Naomi during her trip. Max then emails Naomi a description of Eric's qualifications and rate. Naomi checks her email during her layover in Dallas and replies, "Great, go ahead." Max tells Eric, "The job is yours." And Eric replies, "Thanks. I have it on my schedule." Now, Naomi and Eric are principal and agent. The principal's (Naomi's) consent was communicated indirectly through her agent Max, but it is still effective and Eric has consented.

An agency agreement is a contract; thus, as discussed in Chapter 4, basic contract principles will apply. For example, the underlying objective of the agency relationship must relate to a lawful purpose, and both parties (agent and principal) must have the legal capacity to enter into the agency agreement. (See Chapter 4 regarding the essential elements of a contract and legal capacity.) Assuming the objective of the principal is lawful and both parties have the legal capacity to enter into the agree-

EXHIBIT	10.2	Creation of agency relationships.
	Express agency	Formal written or oral agreement is made between the parties.
	Implied agency	Agency relationship is implied from the conduct of the parties.
	Apparent agency	Third party relies on conduct of the principal suggesting that agent has authority, so principal is estopped from denying agency relationship.
	Ratification of agency	No actual agency exists, but the principal accepts or ratifies the unauthorized acts of the agent.

ment, an agency relationship can be created in four ways: (1) express agency, (2) implied agency, (3) apparent agency, and (4) ratification. See Exhibit 10.2.

Express agency

Express agency is created when the parties make a written or oral agreement. An example of an express agency would be the Standard Representation Agreement for a professional sports league that must be used between sports agents and their professional athlete clients (principals). Although an express agency can be an oral agreement, written agreements are more common. Such an agreement might begin with declarations as follows:

> WHEREAS, Johnny Newby (hereinafter referred to as "Player") and Samuel Smart (hereinafter referred to as "Agent") have agreed upon the terms of Agent's representation of Player pursuant to the National Roundball League Players Association Standard Representation Agreement (the "Agreement");
>
> WHEREAS, Player desires to engage Agent's services for the enhancement of Player's athletic, professional, and community profile; and
>
> WHEREAS, Player and Agent desire to memorialize their agreement related to Player's full range of compensable activities, the parties agree as follows . . .

You may want to review a sample Standard Representation Agreement for one of the professional players associations, such as NFLPA (www.nflpa.org).

Implied agency

An **implied agency** is not created by any written or oral agreement, but rather is implied by the conduct of the parties. The implied authority extends to those areas that are necessary for the agent to complete the objectives of the principal. For example, Chad is employed as the manager of a retail sporting goods store, Dick's Sporting Goods. Chad probably does not have a written or oral employment agreement detailing every task or decision he must accomplish or make, but he will have the implied authority to make agreements and engage in transactions that customarily go with a manager's operation of the store. Thus, when Chad directs an employee to ship inventory using UPS overnight delivery to another store, UPS will naturally invoice Dick's for the shipping costs. Dick's would not be able to avoid paying the charges simply because Chad's employment agreement did not expressly authorize him to ship inventory. Chad's authority is implied because shipping inventory is a customary act of a store manager.

Apparent agency

Apparent agency is created by the conduct of the principal that leads a third party to believe another individual serves as her agent. If the third party relies on the principal's conduct, the principal will not be permitted to deny the existence of an agency relationship simply because there is no formal agreement.

Ratification of agency

An agency relationship can also be created through ratification. **Ratification** occurs when the agent did not in fact have authority to act on behalf of the principal, but the principal accepts or ratifies the agent's act after the fact. For example, Bob's co-worker Sarah is offering to sell two tickets to a Cincinnati Reds baseball game. Bob is not an agent for his friend, Paul, but is certain Paul would want the tickets. Bob tells Sarah that his friend wants to purchase the tickets, so Sarah sets the tickets aside for Paul. Paul is not bound to buy the tickets because Bob has misrepresented his relationship as an agent for Paul. However, if upon learning that Bob has agreed on his behalf to purchase the tickets, Paul decides to purchase the tickets, Paul has accepted Bob as his agent and is bound to purchase the tickets from Sarah because he has ratified Bob's authority to act on his behalf.

Duties Involved in the Agency Relationship

As mentioned previously, the principal–agent relationship is considered a fiduciary relationship that carries with it a number of duties between the agent and the principal. The nature of the **fiduciary relationship** is that one person entrusts his interests to another and that the agent must act loyally for the principal's benefit in all matters connected with the agency relationship. These interests could include money, property, or other legal rights and responsibilities. Thus, the essence of an agency relationship requires that the agent owes his or her principal the utmost loyalty and good faith to act in the best interest of the principal, to follow the instructions of the principal, and to exercise reasonable care, competence, and diligence. In serving the interests of the principal the agent may not engage in self-dealing and must avoid conflicts of interest and competing interests. The agency must also account to the principal for any funds or property coming into the agent's possession (Restatement [Third] of Agency § 8.02–8.12, 2006).

Similarly, the principal owes duties to her agent. The principal must compensate the agent for his services as well as reimburse the agent for customary expenditures incurred in acting on behalf of the principal, such as travel expenses or telephone charges. The principal also has a duty to provide safe working conditions for the agent (see Chapter 8). The principal must also cooperate with the agent so that the agent is able to perform his duties (Restatement [Third] of Agency § 8.14–15, 2006). Thus, if Mary hired Steve to sell her baseball card collection on eBay, Mary must allow Steve reasonable access to the collection to photograph and inventory it so that Steve will be able to fulfill his obligations as Mary's agent. See Exhibit 10.3 for a summary of the duties involved in an agency relationship.

EXHIBIT 10.3	Summary of duties in an agency relationship.
DUTIES OF THE PRINCIPAL TO THE AGENT	**DUTIES OF THE AGENT TO THE PRINCIPAL**
Duty of compensation and reimbursement	Duty of loyalty (good faith)
Duty of cooperation	Duty of performance (reasonable care and skill)
Duty to provide safe working conditions	Duty of accounting (for funds and property)
	Duty of obedience (to follow instructions)

Another example of the duties involved in an agency relationship is offered in the case of *Detroit Lions, Inc. and Billy Simms v. Jerry Argovitz* (1985). In that case, an agent breached his duty, and, as a result, the court rescinded (canceled) the contract that had been executed between Billy Simms and the Houston Gamblers. The district court found that the Houston contract resulted from an unconscionable breach of a fiduciary duty. This case illustrates how an agent, in this case Argovitz, breached the duty of loyalty and good faith that lies at the heart of a fiduciary relationship.

The Detroit Lions and Billy Simms v. Jerry Argovitz

767 F.2d 919 (6th Cir. 1985)   **CASE OPINION**

[FACTS

In 1980 the Detroit Lions, a National Football League franchise, drafted Simms and signed him to a four-year contract that expired on February 1, 1984. Argovitz entered into an agency agreement with Simms early in 1980 and counseled him on numerous matters. Simms and Argovitz developed a confidential relationship in which, Argovitz testified, Simms looked up to him like a father. Simms sought Argovitz's advice on significant professional, financial, and personal matters.

From April 1982 through June 1983, Argovitz negotiated with the Lions for a renewed contract with Simms. On May 5, 1983, Argovitz announced at a press conference that his application for what became the Gamblers franchise had been approved. Simms was present at the press conference. The district court found that Argovitz manipulated Simms' contract negotiations with the Lions during the spring of 1983 in light of Argovitz's own interest in the Gamblers. The court also found that Argovitz misrepresented the negotiations with the Lions as not progressing when in fact they were progressing well. Simms received information on the Lions' negotiations only from Argovitz, the court found.

During May or June 1983, Argovitz decided to seek a contract for Simms with the Gamblers. On June 29, 1983, Simms arrived in Houston, believing that the Lions were not negotiating in good faith and were not really interested in his services. On June 30, 1983, the Gamblers offered Simms a $3.5 million, five-year contract that included nonmonetary fringe benefits Simms valued greatly. Argovitz told Simms that he thought the Lions would match the Gamblers' financial package and offered to telephone them. Although Simms told Argovitz not to call the Lions, the district court found

that to have two teams bidding for a single athlete is "the dream of every agent," and that Argovitz breached his fiduciary duty to Simms by not following the common practice described by both expert witnesses of informing the Lions of the Gamblers' offer.

On the afternoon of June 30, while negotiations were proceeding, the Lions' attorney called Argovitz. Argovitz was present at his office but declined to accept the call. Argovitz attempted to return the call only after 5:00 p.m., when the Lions' attorney had left for the July 4th weekend. The district court found these actions to further breach Argovitz's fiduciary duty toward Simms. Argovitz then left for the holiday weekend. The next day, July 1, 1983, Simms signed an exclusive contract with the Gamblers.

In July 1983, uninformed by any one of these events, the Lions sent Simms a further offer through Argovitz. On November 12, 1983, at Argovitz's instigation, Simms met with him and reexecuted the Gamblers' contract. Simms also signed a waiver of any claim he might have against Argovitz. Although at this time Argovitz had sold his agency business and no longer represented Simms, Argovitz did not inform Simms' new agent of his intention to have Simms sign a waiver. Nor did Argovitz, despite his fiduciary relationship with Simms, advise Simms to seek independent advice before signing the waiver. On December 16, 1983, Simms executed a second exclusive contract with the Lions for $1 million more than his Gamblers contract.

On December 18, 1983, the Lions and Simms brought this suit in Michigan state court against Argovitz and the Gamblers seeking rescission of the Gamblers' contract with Simms.]

HOLDING

The district court's rescission of the contract between Billy Simms and the Houston Gamblers is AFFIRMED.

RATIONALE

The district court granted rescission of the contract between the Gamblers and Simms because it found that Argovitz had breached his fiduciary duty as Simms' agent and confidant. It is uncontested that Argovitz had a personal interest in Simms' contracting with the Gamblers, who as a new team in a new football league would greatly benefit from the star attraction of a player of Simms' caliber. Argovitz's self-dealing arose from this conflict with his fiduciary duty to advance Simms' best interests.

As the district court found, under Texas law, where an agent has an interest adverse to that of his principal in a transaction in which he purports to act on behalf of his principal, the transaction is voidable by the principal unless the agent disclosed all material facts within his knowledge that might affect the principal's judgment. . . . This remains true even if the contract is fair.

The district court found as a matter of fact that "[a]t no time prior to December 1, 1983, was Simms aware" of all material facts regarding Argovitz's involvement with the Gamblers and Argovitz's failure to pursue Simms' interests in negotiations with the Lions. Argovitz accepts the legal standard as defined by the district court. He maintains that he satisfied his duty of disclosure simply by telling Simms that he was partial owner of the Gamblers and by telling Simms that the Lions would match the financial elements of the Gamblers' offer. A review of the facts as found by the district court reveals that these are but a few of the material disclosures that Argovitz should have made.

Questions

1. According to the court of appeals, if an agent has a conflict of interest with the interests of his principal, what must the agent disclose to the principal before entering into a transaction?

2. What information do you think Argovitz should have provided to Simms to avoid breaching his fiduciary duty?

Contractual Liability of the Principal and the Agent

Our discussion of how agency relationships are created, the scope of the agent's authority, and the duties owed between the principal and the agent is particularly important to understanding how agency law affects business transactions. An agent has the ability to bind both herself and her principal in contract (see Chapter 4) and in tort. With regard to contractual obligations, agency law defines the rights of third parties who enter into agreements with agents and the corresponding liability of the agent or the principal for those agreements.

Classifications of principals

Contractual liability will depend on how the principal is classified and the scope of authority of the agent. A principal can be *disclosed, unidentified,* or *undisclosed* (Restatement [Third] of Agency § 1.04, 2006). If the principal is **disclosed,** this simply means the third party is aware of the identity of the principal and that the agent is acting on behalf of the principal, such as in a registered athlete agent's contract negotiations on behalf of a professional athlete. A principal is **unidentified** if the third party is aware that the agent is acting on behalf of another but does not know the identity of the principal. For example, a sport marketing consulting company may be attempting to match a number of its clients with sponsorship opportunities with a sport organization. The sport organization may be unaware which clients the consulting company wants to secure a sponsorship for, but it is aware that the consulting company is acting on behalf of another. An **undisclosed** principal exists

EXHIBIT	10.4

Classifications of the principal and the liability of the principal and agent.

CLASSIFICATION	PRINCIPAL	AGENT
Disclosed	Liable	Not liable
Unidentified	Liable	Possibly liable
Undisclosed	Liable	Liable

if the third party is not aware that the agent is acting on behalf of another, such as when a buyer on eBay bids on an item during a sport memorabilia auction. The seller of the item has no way of knowing whether the buyer is purchasing the item for his own use, for resale to a third party, or on behalf of a specific third party; thus, if the purchase is on behalf of another, the principal is undisclosed.

The classification of the principal is important for determining the liability of the principal as well as the agent. If an agency relationship is disclosed, the principal is bound by the contracts entered into by the agent and is liable to the third party to those contracts. However, the agent is not liable to the third party because the third party knew he was dealing with an agent in a representative capacity for the principal. Thus, if a professional athlete, a disclosed principal, breaches his agreement with a professional sport franchise, the professional sport franchise cannot sue the agent for the breach of contract; its only recourse is against the athlete (principal). As Exhibit 10.4 indicates, the principal is always liable for the authorized acts of an agent; however, the agent's liability varies depending upon whether the existence of the principal is disclosed to the third party with whom the agent is dealing.

The following Focus Case illustrates the notion that if an agency relationship is disclosed to a third party who enters into a contract negotiated by an agent, only the principal is liable for a breach of that agreement.

Jones v. Archibald

360 N.Y.S.2d 119 (App. Div. 1974)	**FOCUS CASE**

FACTS

All-Pro represented Nate Archibald, a professional athlete, in contract negotiations and financial management. The plaintiff, Jones, contacted Nate Archibald to make a one-day appearance at Jones' boys' camp and was told by Archibald to contact his agent, All-Pro. All-Pro informed plaintiff that Archibald would appear at the camp on August 15. Jones paid the agreed amount for Archibald's appearance. On August 9, All-Pro was notified by Archibald that circumstances would prevent him from making the appearance. All-Pro sent this information by mail to Jones on August 10 (five days before the scheduled appearance), along with a refund of the money previously paid by Jones. Jones received this letter on August 14. Jones sued Archibald, as principal, and All-Pro, as agent, alleging that All-Pro was Archibald's authorized agent in the transaction, that Archibald willfully breached the contract, that All-Pro knew or should have known that Archibald would not appear, that All-Pro knew or should have known that its method of communicating to plaintiff that Archibald would not appear would not allow sufficient time to secure a replacement, and that as a result Jones was damaged in the amount of $200,000.

HOLDING

The court held that the agent, All-Pro, could not be held liable for any breach of the appearance agreement.

RATIONALE

The court first observed that where there is a disclosed principal–agency relationship, as in this case, the agent is not personally bound unless there is clear and explicit evidence of the agent's intention to substitute or add his personal liability for, or to, that of his principal. A disclosed agent who acts for another in negotiating a contract in the business interests of his principal will not be deemed to have intended to bind himself personally unless the intent to do so is manifested with reasonable clarity. All of the contracts between plaintiff and All-Pro were by correspondence. Nothing contained in the record indicates any intention on All-Pro's part to assume or undertake any individual, independent responsibility or obligation. As such, All-Pro could not be held liable for any breach of the appearance agreement. However, the court did state that Jones still had his cause of action against the principal, Nate Archibald.

If the principal is unidentified, both the agent and the principal are considered parties to the contract, and each may be liable for the contract.

Consider the following example of an unidentified principal at the famous auction house Christie's with which you may be familiar. Christie's conducts dozens of auctions and private sales each year of fine art, antiques, jewelry, and other expensive collectibles. For example, in 2008, Christie's conducted an auction of maritime art that included fine paintings and nautical antiques. Many of the bidders at these auctions are agents attempting to secure the item for their principal. However, the identity of the principal is not disclosed. Christie's as well as the other bidders certainly know a bidder may be acting in a representative capacity but have no idea who the agent represents or who is the ultimate purchaser of the item. In this case, both the agent and the principal may be liable for the contract. If the agent fails to pay the sale price as agreed, the agent will likely be liable to Christie's directly. However, assuming the agent is less able to pay than his wealthy principal, Christie's may also be able to seek payment from the principal if Christie's can prove the identity of the principal and can prove the agent acted with actual authority (Kleinberger, 2008, p. 29).

If the principal is undisclosed, both the agent and the principal may be liable on the contract, but the third party may have to sue them alternatively. (Suing alternatively means that if either the agent or principal denies liability, the third party must choose which one it will seek to hold accountable on the contract, and once the third party makes this choice, she is precluded from suing the one not chosen.)

Scope of agent authority

Another important consideration for determining liability is the scope of authority of the agent. Recall that agents have a duty of obedience, which means they must follow the instructions of the principal and may not exceed the authority granted by the principal (scope of authority). Furthermore, the principal is not liable if the agent does not have the authority to act on his behalf. If an agent has no authority to act on behalf of the principal or exceeds her authority, then the agent cannot bind the principal to a contract. If an agent enters into an unauthorized agreement with a third party, the agent will be liable to the third party. Also, if an agent knowingly misrepresents her alleged authority, she may be liable to the third party both on the contract and in tort (see Chapter 5 regarding tort liability of agents and employees).

Authority may be expressly stipulated in the agency agreement, which is known as **actual authority.** For example, assume an agent and a professional athlete have entered into a Standard Player Representation Agreement. This agreement empowers the agent to negotiate the player's compensation with the team. In the agreement, compensation is specifically defined as salaries, signing bonuses, reporting bonuses, roster bonuses, and any performance incentives earned by the player during the term of the contract. This agency agreement, however, would not authorize the agent to negotiate for endorsements on behalf of the athlete or perform financial or investment services for the athlete. Thus, if the agent represented himself to Nike as possessing the authority to act on behalf of the athlete and executed an endorsement agreement on behalf of the athlete with Nike, that contract would not be enforceable against the athlete. Nike, however, would have a claim for breach of contract against the agent.

In contrast, as discussed earlier, apparent authority is the power held by an agent to affect a principal's legal relations with third parties when a third party reasonably believes the actor has authority to act on behalf of the principal and that belief is traceable to the principal's manifestations (Restatement [Third] of Agency § 2.03 Apparent Authority, 2006). Apparent authority is created by a person's (principal's) manifestation that another person (agent) has authority to act with legal consequences for the person and that a third party reasonably believes the actor (agent) to be authorized, a belief traceable to the principal's manifestation. (Restatement [Third] of Agency § 3.03 Creation of Apparent Authority, 2006).

The following Focus Case demonstrates the concept and scope of apparent agency.

Clark Advertising Agency, Inc. v. Tice

| 490 F.2d 834 (N.D. Tex. 1974) | **FOCUS CASE** |

FACTS

Clark Advertising Agency (Clark) sued the American Hot Rod Association (AHRA) and its president, James Tice, for payment under a contract for advertising and promotional services. The parties had a previous written contract for advertising services for the 1971 Winter Nationals Race in Phoenix, Arizona, but proceeded under an oral contract for the race in question in West Palm Beach, Florida. Clark and Tice held initial talks regarding expenditures and fees, and such fees were to approximate those under the prior agreement for Phoenix. However, further discussions regarding an increase in fees and costs were held between Clark and two other AHRA officers, the vice president (Ballah) and the comptroller (Harkins). When Clark presented a total bill under the oral contract seeking the increased fees and costs discussed with Ballah and Harkins, AHRA refused payment, and Clark sued. AHRA contended that Ballah and Harkins did not have authority to bind AHRA during negotiations with Clark.

HOLDING

The court decided in favor of Clark.

RATIONALE

Whether or not either of these officers actually had express or implied authority to bind AHRA, the court held that there is ample evidence to find that they had apparent authority. The court stated that apparent authority exists whenever a principal manifests to a third person that an officer or agent may act in its behalf, and the third person believes in good faith that the authority exists. When that third person reasonably relies upon that apparent authority to his detriment, the principal is estopped to deny the authority (Restatement [Second] of Agency § 8, 1958; Henn, *Law of Corporations,* § 226, 2d ed., 1970). Tice testified that he did not know all the terms of the "loose verbal agreement," since he ceased to be personally involved and left the negotiations to Ballah and Harkins. Similarly, after the race Tice left it to Harkins to negotiate with Clark for a settlement of his services in Florida. By leaving the detailed negotiation work to Ballah and Harkins, Tice created the appearance that they had authority to conduct those negotiations.

ATHLETES AND ATHLETE AGENTS

In addition to breach of fiduciary duty as discussed in the *Detroit Lions and Simms v. Argovitz* case in the previous section, the relationship between athlete agents and both student-athletes and professional athletes can raise a number of complex legal issues. Legal issues affecting athletes and agents primarily arise in two areas: (1) the relationship between the athlete agent and the athlete once an agency relationship is created and (2) the interactions of athlete agents with student-athletes in an attempt to secure an agency relationship.

The first area involves the conduct of the agency relationship itself, as discussed in the first section of this chapter, such as whether an agent has acted in the best interests of the principal or whether the principal has interfered with the agent's ability to perform. These legal issues usually involve an athlete agent and either a professional athlete or a student-athlete who is actively pursuing a career as a professional athlete. The primary focus is on the adequacy of the performance of the agency agreement either by the athlete (principal) or the athlete agent (agent).

The second area involves the interaction of athlete agents with student-athletes who may have amateur eligibility remaining. In this latter area, the legal issues that arise relate to whether the athlete agent has complied with existing athlete agent laws and acted properly and truthfully with the student-athlete so that, if the student-athlete chooses to engage the agent's services, she does so with full knowledge of the effect it may have on her amateur status and eligibility. In this second area involving student-athletes, additional legal issues arise related to protecting the interests of colleges and universities that may be subject to NCAA penalties and incur significant financial losses if an ineligible student-athlete participates in the institution's intercollegiate athletic program after engaging an agent. For example, the University of Massachusetts and the University of Connecticut were both stripped of their victories in the 1996 NCAA men's basketball tournament and suffered financial penalties for the illegal acceptance of gifts from an agent by players Marcus Camby of UMass and Kirk King and Ricky Moore of UConn (Cavanaugh, 1997). Camby ultimately repaid UMass $151,000 for revenues forfeited by UMass due to the NCAA penalties ("Camby repays tourney money," 1997). The next sections of this chapter will examine a number of the legal issues that arise in the dealings of student-athletes and professional athletes with athlete agents.

STUDENT-ATHLETES AND AGENTS

E specially relevant for sport managers today is the ever-increasing amount of state and federal regulation of athlete agents. Legal issues relating to athlete agents' dealings with student-athletes are currently subject to a patchwork of both state and federal regulations. The regulatory law for sport agents may indeed be one of the most confusing and complex areas in the sport industry. Athlete agents, university compliance officers, student-athletes, professional athletes, employees of the NCAA enforcement staff, and contract negotiators for a professional sports team—all should understand the legal issues and laws affecting athlete agents.

Athlete Agent Regulation

Fierce competition among athlete agents and fears of unscrupulous athlete agent practices have led to significant developments in the intercollegiate/interscholastic industry segments. Consider the following statement from the National Conference of Commissioners of Uniform State Laws (University of Pennsylvania Law School, n.d.):

> With the proliferation of professional sport franchises in the United States, and the immense sums now paid to athletes for commercial endorsement contracts, it is no surprise that the commercial marketplace in which athlete agents operate has become very competitive. And while maximizing the income of one's clients is certainly the "American way" (as well as good business practice), the recruitment of a student-athlete while he or she is still enrolled in an educational institution may cause substantial eligibility or other problems for both the student and the school, especially where the athlete is not aware of the implications of signing the agency agreement or where agency is established without notice to the athletic director of the school. The problem becomes even more acute where an unscrupulous agent misleads a student. While several states have enacted legislation to address these issues, agent registration and disclosure requirements vary greatly from state to state, causing confusion among student athletes, athletic departments, educational institutions, and the agents themselves.

As of February 2010, 41 states and U.S. territories had adopted the Uniform Athlete Agents Act (NCCUSL, 2010). Three states have enacted their own versions of athlete agent legislation, such as California's enactment of the Miller-Ayala Sports Agent Act. However, seven states and one U. S. territory have no existing laws regulating athlete agents. Exhibit 10.5 summarizes U. S. state and territory regulation of athlete agent activities.

Due to this gap in state regulation, in September 2004, the U. S. Congress passed the Sport Agent Responsibility and Trust Act (SPARTA) to supplement the requirements of the UAAA and to provide some protection for student-athletes located in those states with no current form of athlete agent regulation. Add to this the penalties potentially imposed by the NCAA on its members (universities) if a student-athlete has had dealings with an agent and continues to compete as an amateur, and the landscape of athlete agency has become complex and challenging for sport managers. Thus, a basic understanding of the state and federal regulation of athlete agents is needed. This section will introduce the common elements in both the state and federal laws, and some unique features and limitations of the current legislative acts.

The Uniform Athlete Agents Act

Prior to the availability of the Uniform Athlete Agents Act, at least 28 states had adopted some form of athlete agent regulation. However, those state statutes varied considerably from state to state, and compliance with an athlete agent act in one state was effective only in that state. Thus, an athlete agent seeking to do business in each

---

EXHIBIT 10.5 U. S. state and territory regulation of athlete agent activities (NCCUSL, 2010).

States and others that have adopted the Uniform Athlete Agents Act:

Alabama, Arizona, Arkansas, Colorado, Connecticut, Delaware, District of Columbia, Florida, Georgia, Hawaii, Idaho, Indiana, Iowa, Kansas, Kentucky, Louisiana, Maryland, Minnesota, Mississippi, Missouri, Nebraska, Nevada, New Hampshire, New Mexico, New York, North Carolina, North Dakota, Oklahoma, Oregon, Pennsylvania, Rhode Island, South Carolina, South Dakota, Tennessee, Texas, Utah, U. S. Virgin Islands, Washington, West Virginia, Wisconsin, and Wyoming

States where adoption of the Uniform Athlete Agents Act is currently under consideration:

California and Illinois (2010)

States with their own versions of athlete agent legislation:

California, Michigan, Ohio

States and territories with no existing laws regulating athlete agents:

Alaska, Illinois, Maine, Massachusetts, New Jersey, Puerto Rico, Vermont, and Virginia

Current and updated information regarding enactment of the UAAA is available via the following link: http://www.nccusl.org/Update/uniformact_factsheets/uniformacts-fs-aaa.asp

state was required to comply with 28 different sets of requirements and 28 different regulatory schemes. Thus, the National Conference of Commissioners of Uniform State Laws (NCCUSL) began to investigate whether a uniform act was needed to eliminate some of the inconsistency among the various state statutes. The NCCUSL (n.d.c) identified six principal purposes that would be served by a uniform act:

1. Provide for reciprocity of registration
2. Authorize denial, suspension, or revocation of registrations based upon similar actions in another state
3. Regulate the conduct of individuals who contact athletes for the purpose of obtaining agency contracts
4. Require notice to educational institutions when an agency contract is signed by a student athlete
5. Provide a civil remedy for an educational institution damaged by the conduct of an athlete agent or a student athlete
6. Establish civil and criminal penalties for violation of the act

The NCCUSL approved a final proposed uniform act on November 30, 2000. Since that time, as mentioned above, 41 states and U. S. territories have adopted the Uniform Athlete Agent Act.

UAAA definitions. Section 2 of the UAAA contains the relevant definitions of persons and contracts covered by and subject to the act. The key definitions are for an **athlete agent,** a **student-athlete,** and an **agency contract.** These are set out in Exhibit 10.6.

The definition of an athlete agent is very broad and includes those individuals who recruit and solicit potential student-athletes as well as those who actually

---

Section 2(1) (2) and (12) of the UAAA definitions of athlete agent, student-athlete, and agency contract.   EXHIBIT **10.6**

(1) "Agency contract" means an agreement in which a student-athlete authorizes a person to negotiate or solicit on behalf of the student-athlete a professional-sports-services contract or an endorsement contract.

(2) "Athlete agent" means an individual who enters into an agency contract with a student-athlete or, directly or indirectly, recruits or solicits a student-athlete to enter into an agency contract. The term includes an individual who represents to the public that the individual is an athlete agent. The term does not include a spouse, parent, sibling, [or] grandparent, [or guardian] of the student-athlete or an individual acting solely on behalf of a professional sports team or professional sports organization.

(12) "Student-athlete" means an individual who engages in, is eligible to engage in, or may be eligible in the future to engage in, any intercollegiate sport. If an individual is permanently ineligible to participate in a particular intercollegiate sport, the individual is not a student-athlete for purposes of that sport.

enter into an agency agreement with a student-athlete. Thus, the definition includes "runners" working for an agent to recruit or solicit student-athletes to enter into an agency contract. However, only individuals are within the definition of athlete agent and therefore subject to the act. Corporations and other business entities do not come within the definition of athlete agent and therefore are not covered by the act. Individuals employed as athlete agents by a corporation or other business entity, such as IMG or Athletes First, are required to register in their individual capacity. Representatives of "professional sports teams or professional sports organizations," such as football or hockey teams, are excluded from the definition of athlete agent as long as they are acting for their teams or organizations. For example, a professional athlete who gives a student-athlete information about the qualifications of an athlete agent is not required to register under the UAAA unless the professional athlete also attempts to recruit or solicit the student-athlete to sign an agency contract.

The definition of student-athlete is also particularly important, since the UAAA expressly excludes, for purposes of a particular intercollegiate sport, any individual who is permanently ineligible to participate in that sport. Thus, the UAAA does not in any way apply to or affect the activities of athlete agents who work with athletes who are already professional athletes or who do not have any amateur eligibility remaining. However, the definition of student-athlete does apply to a two-sport athlete who has eligibility remaining in one sport. For example, an individual who has signed a contract to play professional baseball is not a student-athlete in baseball but is a student-athlete in football. Thus, any individual dealing with that student-athlete regarding professional services or endorsement contracts in professional football would be covered by the UAAA. The definition of student-athlete also includes individuals who are not yet in college. It includes high school students, high school dropouts, and high school graduates who may have future eligibility for intercollegiate sports.

UAAA requirements. The basic requirements of the Uniform Athlete Agents Act mandate *registration, disclosure, notification,* and *penalties/remedies.* In particular, the UAAA provides for the uniform *registration,* certification, and background checking of athlete agents who seek to represent student-athletes. The UAAA requires that specific warnings and *disclosures* be provided to student-athletes in the agency agreement and further requires *notification* be provided to educational institutions when an agent and a student-athlete enter into an agency agreement. The UAAA also permits an educational institution to bring a civil cause of action for damages resulting from a breach of the UAAA duties.

Agent registration. Sections 4 and 5 of the UAAA require agents to register and disclose their training, experience, and education. Registration requirements are stated in Section 4 (see Exhibit 10.7).

Agents must register in each state in which they have established sufficient minimum contact that would normally make them subject to the jurisdiction of the state courts. For example, if an individual whose principal place of business is in State A contacts a student-athlete in State B, the agent is acting as an athlete agent in both states and is therefore required to register in both states. However, subsection (b) of § 4 provides a safe harbor for an unregistered individual with

Agent registration requirements as specified in Section 4 of the UAAA.	EXHIBIT	10.7

(a) Except as otherwise provided in subsection (b), an *individual may not act as an athlete agent in this State without holding a certificate of registration* under Section 6 or 8.

(b) Before being issued a certificate of registration, an individual may act as an athlete agent in this State for all purposes except signing an agency contract, if:

> (1) a student-athlete or another person acting on behalf of the student-athlete *initiates* communication with the individual; and

> (2) *within seven days after an initial act* as an athlete agent, the individual submits an application for registration as an athlete agent in this State.

(c) An agency contract resulting from conduct in violation of this section is void and the athlete agent shall return any consideration received under the contract. [italics added for emphasis]

whom a student-athlete *initiates* communications. If a student-athlete in the state of Oklahoma (where the UAAA was adopted) contacts an athlete agent with an athlete representation firm in New Jersey (with no UAAA yet), the New Jersey athlete agent has not violated the Oklahoma UAAA if she attempts to enter into an agency agreement, so long as she registers in Oklahoma within seven days of the initial contact by the student-athlete. The individual must apply for registration within seven days from the *beginning* of any effort to recruit or solicit the student-athlete to enter into an agency contract. If the agent does not attempt to recruit or solicit the student-athlete to sign an agency contract, she does not have to register. Agents who are issued a valid certification of registration in one state may cross-file that application in all other states that have adopted the UAAA. This aspect of the act simplifies regulatory compliance for athlete agents and enables all jurisdictions to obtain dependable, uniform information on an agent's professional conduct in other states.

Disclosure. The loss of intercollegiate eligibility can have serious consequences for both the student-athlete and the university for which he plays. Because student-athletes may be unaware that their eligibility may be at risk when they enter into an agency agreement, the UAAA requires all agency contracts to be in a recorded form and signed by the student-athletes. The agency contract must also contain the warning shown in Exhibit 10.8 in close proximity to the signature of the student-athlete.

This warning is intended to make sure the student-athlete is aware that her amateur eligibility may be lost if she enters into an agency agreement. Student-athletes also have a statutory right to cancel an agency contract within 14 days after the contract is signed, without penalty. A student-athlete who opts to void an agency contract under this section is required to return any consideration received as an inducement to the signing of the agency contract, because such inducement is prohibited.

It is important to note that even if a student-athlete exercises his right to cancel the contract and the contract is canceled, this may not restore his eligibility. For

EXHIBIT	10.8	UAAA warning requirement for student-athlete agency contracts.

WARNING TO STUDENT-ATHLETE

IF YOU SIGN THIS CONTRACT:

(1) YOU MAY LOSE YOUR ELIGIBILITY TO COMPETE AS A STUDENT-ATHLETE IN YOUR SPORT;

(2) IF YOU HAVE AN ATHLETIC DIRECTOR, WITHIN 72 HOURS AFTER ENTERING INTO THIS CONTRACT, BOTH YOU AND YOUR ATHLETE AGENT MUST NOTIFY YOUR ATHLETIC DIRECTOR; AND

(3) YOU MAY CANCEL THIS CONTRACT WITHIN 14 DAYS AFTER SIGNING IT. CANCELLATION OF THIS CONTRACT MAY NOT REINSTATE YOUR ELIGIBILITY.

example, under the NCAA rules, a student-athlete loses his eligibility if he does any of the following:

- Enters into an agreement with an agent (NCAA Division I Manual, by-law 12.1.1(g))
- Retains an agent (by-law 12.2.4.3)
- Accepts transportation or other benefits from an agent (by-law 12.3.1.2)
- Ever has agreed (orally or in writing) to be represented by an agent for the purpose of marketing his or her athletics ability or reputation in that sport (by-law 12.3.1)

The NCAA is not required to reinstate a student-athlete's eligibility just because the student-athlete legally cancels the agency agreement (NCAA, n.d.a, n.d.b).

Notification. The potential loss of a student-athlete's eligibility is a serious concern for athletic programs at educational institutions; thus, Section 11 of the UAAA requires *both* the agent and the student-athlete to notify the athletic director that an agency agreement has been entered into within 72 hours of signing the agreement or before the athlete's next scheduled athletic event, whichever occurs first. The purpose of notification is to protect an educational institution from sanctions or other penalties that could result from allowing an ineligible player to participate. The penalties imposed by the NCAA can be quite severe, such as loss of scholarships, prohibition from championship events, probation, negative publicity, and forfeiture of tournament winnings or other revenue. The monetary penalties can be very substantial when revenues are lost from participation in a football bowl game or a postseason basketball tournament. Courts have recognized the adverse impact, both financial and operational, that NCAA penalties can have on educational institutions. For example, in *United States v. Piggie* (2002), Myron Piggie had created a secret scheme to pay talented high school athletes to play for his "amateur" summer team. The scheme produced multiple violations of NCAA rules since many of these athletes later signed letters of intent to play collegiate basketball. The ultimate ineligibility of these athletes resulted in NCAA violations and lost scholarships for several universities including UCLA, Duke,

Section 14 of the UAAA describing prohibited conduct for athlete agents.   EXHIBIT   **10.9**

(a) An athlete agent, with the intent to induce a student-athlete to enter into an agency contract, may not:

   (1) give any materially false or misleading information or make a materially false promise or representation;

   (2) furnish anything of value to a student-athlete before the student-athlete enters into the agency contract; or

   (3) furnish anything of value to any individual other than the student-athlete or another registered athlete agent.

(b) An athlete agent may not intentionally:

   (1) initiate contact with a student-athlete unless registered under this [Act];

   (2) refuse or fail to retain or permit inspection of the records required to be retained by Section 13;

   (3) fail to register when required by Section 4;

   (4) provide materially false or misleading information in an application for registration or renewal of registration;

   (5) predate or postdate an agency contract; or

   (6) fail to notify a student-athlete before the student-athlete signs or otherwise authenticates an agency contract for a particular sport that the signing or authentication may make the student-athlete ineligible to participate as a student-athlete in that sport.

---

the University of Missouri, and Oklahoma State University. Total costs for those universities neared $250,000.

Remedies and penalties. Section 14 of the UAAA describes the athlete agent conduct prohibited under the act that will give rise to both civil and criminal penalties (see Exhibit 10.9). The following hypothetical case illustrates how the UAAA provisions are applied.

considering . . .   **ATHLETE AGENT BEHAVIOR**

Josh is a "runner" for Steve Shady, a prominent sports agent. While on campus at Bigtime University in the State of Missolina, Josh meets (without informing the administration of his presence on campus) with Marcus Goode, Bigtime's star runningback. Goode is a sophomore and has two years of eligibility remaining in the NCAA. Bigtime University competes in NCAA FBS Division I. The State of Missolina adopted the UAAA in 2002. Josh represents that Shady is prepared to provide the following to Goode should he agree to be represented by Shady:

(1) the keys to a Mercedes-Benz S-500 parked right outside Goode's apartment

(2) $5,000 cash

(3) training at Shady's posh Fort Lauderdale, FL, workout facility in preparation for the NFL draft camp

Questions

- Is the meeting between Goode and Josh subject to the provisions of the UAAA?
- Assume Goode agrees to be represented by Shady at this meeting. Has the UAAA been violated, and what are the potential penalties?
- Assume further that Goode later signs a representation agreement. Would either the meeting or the signing of the representation agreement adversely affect his amateur eligibility with the NCAA?
- Assume that 13 days after signing the representation agreement, Goode has a change of heart and notifies Shady that he wants to cancel the contract. May he do so? What, if any, impact will the cancellation have on Goode's amateur eligibility?

Note how you would answer the questions and then check your responses using the Analysis & Discussion at the end of this chapter.

Sections 15 and 16 of the UAAA establish the civil and criminal penalties available for violations of the act. For example, the UAAA prohibits athlete agents from providing materially false or misleading information or making a materially false promise or representation with the intent of inducing a student-athlete to enter into an agency contract, and from furnishing anything of value to a student athlete or another person before that athlete enters into an agency contract. The act imposes criminal penalties for a violation, and each state adopting the UAAA must determine whether the criminal penalty will be a misdemeanor or a felony. The type of criminal penalties to be imposed was left to the states because of a wide variation in the criminal penalties provided for by existing acts. Remember, prior to the availability of the UAAA, 28 states had already adopted some form of athlete agent regulation, so Section 15 gives each state the flexibility to adopt penalties it believes best serve the interests of its citizens. It was debated whether athlete agents should be subjected to criminal sanctions, and the sheer size of the financial motivation in professional sport athlete representation led to the conclusion that some potential criminal penalty was necessary to discourage those individuals who are willing to engage in improper or illegal conduct.

Alabama is one of those states that has taken a firm stance toward athlete agent misconduct by including criminal penalties for violations. For example, in August of 2008, Raymond Lee Savage Jr., CEO and president of Savage Sports Management, was indicted for allegedly having a part in the illegal contact of former University of Alabama wide receiver, Tyrone Prothro. The action was brought by the Alabama Attorney General's office to enforce its UAAA. The state previously brought charges against another employee of Savage Sports Management named Jason Goggins. The State of Alabama presented two charges against Savage and Goggins: (1) not registering as an athlete agent in Alabama, which is a felony, and (2) initiating contact with a student-athlete, which is a misdemeanor. Eventually the misdemeanor charge against Savage was dropped.

But Savage and Goggins still must defend themselves against the felony charge, which carries a potential penalty of up to ten years in prison and a $5,000 fine. (Mullen, 2008; Heitner, 2009).

Section 16 creates a civil remedy specifically for educational institutions. It permits a college or university to sue either the athlete agent or former student-athlete for damages, including losses and expenses incurred as a result of the educational institution's being penalized, disqualified, or suspended from participation. Section 16 also allows the educational institution to recover its costs and reasonable attorneys fees.

As many states have included both civil and criminal penalties in athlete agent regulations, it behooves someone interested in this sector of the sport industry to become familiar with the relevant body of law.

Educational institutions are typically reluctant to bring an action against a former student-athlete, since suing a former student-athlete could easily create negative publicity for the university and hinder future recruiting of athletes. However, there are instances, such as that described earlier involving the University of Massachusetts and Marcus Camby, of highly improper conduct by student-athletes who ultimately received lucrative professional contracts even though their conduct caused serious financial losses to their educational institutions. Section 16 keeps open the possibility of a civil action against those individuals, but educational institutions must carefully consider whether to exercise the right to sue the individual student-athlete. Section 16 does not specifically authorize an action by a student-athlete against an athlete agent because the student-athlete can bring an action against an athlete agent under existing agency law, as was discussed in the first section of this chapter, for breach of contract or breach of fiduciary duty.

Sport Agent Responsibility and Trust Act

As mentioned earlier, even though 41 states and U.S. territories have adopted the UAAA as of February 2010, several states still have no laws regulating athlete agents. Thus, in those states student-athletes and educational institutions have had little if any protection from unscrupulous athlete agents. To address this gap in state regulation, Congress passed the Sport Agent Responsibility and Trust Act in September 2004 to supplement the requirements of the UAAA and to provide some protection for student-athletes located in those states with no form of athlete agent regulation (*Sports Agent*, 2003).

SPARTA provides some of the protections of the UAAA but is not as comprehensive. Like the UAAA, SPARTA seeks to prevent agents from luring student-athletes into signing agency contracts by offering valuable gifts and providing false or misleading information. SPARTA designates certain conduct by athlete agents regarding their contractual dealings with student-athletes as an unfair and deceptive trade practice subject to the regulatory authority of the Federal Trade Commission. SPARTA specifically prohibits an athlete agent from providing false or misleading information; making false or misleading promises; and providing anything of value, such as gifts, cash, or loans, to student-athletes.

SPARTA also requires that the agent provide the student-athlete with disclosures and warnings similar to those required in the UAAA regarding the effect on their eligibility of entering into an agency contract. Failure to make the required disclosures is a violation of the act. Violating any portion of the act exposes the athlete agent to civil fines of up to $11,000 per day, per offense. In addition, SPARTA extends enforcement authority to the individual states' Attorney General offices so that each state can impose fines on athlete agents who violate the act. SPARTA lacks the UAAA's extensive registration requirement, and in § 8 of SPARTA Congress specifically urges the states to "enact the Uniform Athlete Agents Act of 2000 . . . to protect student-athletes and the integrity of amateur sports from unscrupulous sports agents" (see NCAA, n.d.c).

PROFESSIONAL ATHLETES AND AGENTS

When you think of a sports agent or athlete agent, you might envision a bargaining table with Scott Boras on one side and George Steinbrenner on the other negotiating Alex Rodriguez' mammoth 10-year, $275 million contract with the New York Yankees (Freedman, 2008). However, most professional athlete contract negotiations do not involve hundreds of millions of dollars, nor the dynamic personalities of George Steinbrenner and superstar agent Scott Boras. Even in its most basic form, though, the main job of a sport agent is still contract negotiation. Thus, it is important that athlete agents possess the necessary training and expertise to be effective negotiators. The agency relationship is an express agency at the major league level, since major league professional sports require the athlete representatives to be certified by the players association and to use a Standard Player Representation agreement for agents and athletes.

However, athlete representation where the agent serves as financial consultant or endorsement representative, which is becoming more prevalent, could involve any of the various types of agency relationships described earlier and thereby raise additional issues involving the agent's mishandling of an athlete's funds. These types of disputes involve tort law principles, discussed in Chapter 4, such as fraud and misrepresentation, in addition to contract issues. Many of these issues were present in the highly publicized case involving sport agent Tank Black, chairman and CEO of the athlete representation firm Professional Management, Inc. (PMI). Black involved several NFL players in a pyramid and money laundering scheme in coordination with two different companies Black operated. While Black was president of Black Americans of Achievement, Inc. (BAOA), this organization produced a board game celebrating the accomplishments of African Americans. Black arranged for his PMI clients to promote BAOA's board game in exchange for free, restricted BAOA stock. However, the clients (athletes) were never informed of these arrangements and never agreed to endorse the BAOA board game. BAOA issued two million shares of free stock in the names of 15 PMI clients, and BAOA sent stock certificates to PMI. Black in turn sold the BAOA stock to his clients at PMI for prices that were above current market prices at the time. Black sold the BAOA stock to Ike Hilliard and other PMI clients for $1,240,000. Black then directed PMI clients to pay for BAOA stock with checks made payable to PE Communications, Inc. (PE), a shell company also created by Black. Black also directed that over $1 million in funds be transferred from the PE account to his personal bank accounts. Ultimately Black was decertified as an NFLPA player agent, and on May 7, 2002, he was sentenced to serve 60 months in prison and ordered to pay $12 million in restitution stemming from charges that he defrauded his athlete clients in multiple investment schemes over a three-year period (*Hilliard v. Black*, 2000).

As described in the previous section, a number of states have enacted protection for student athletes who are victimized by unscrupulous athlete agents. The UAAA and SPARTA both focus on protecting student-athletes and educational institutions. However, for those athletes who are no longer student-athletes but instead are active professional athletes, only traditional contract, tort, and agency law is available to protect them from a breach of an agency agreement, breach of fiduciary duty, or fraud. As a result, most professional players associations (labor unions for professional athletes, see Chapter 9) have developed registration and certification procedures for agents and impose limitations on fees as a means of minimizing the potential for athlete agents to exploit athletes.

For example, consider the following scenario of an NFL player agent who signs a player to a Standard Representation Agreement for a fee of 3 percent. The agent then negotiates and the player signs a two-year NFL Player Contract with salaries of $5 million per year. The agent's compensation would be $150,000 for 2010 and $150,000 for 2011 (3 percent of $5 million). It becomes a bit more complicated when the negotiated compensation includes signing bonuses, reporting bonuses, and performance incentives, and even more complicated when a player hires a new agent to renegotiate his player contract. But the players association regulations specifically address these eventualities. Ultimately, the restrictions imposed by the players association help to ensure that individuals serving as athlete agents possess the competency and skills necessary to assist the athlete.

The rigor of the certification process varies significantly among the professional leagues. For example, in 2005, the National Basketball Players Association agent certification process involved virtually no rigor, and of the 350 certified agents, fewer than 100 currently had an active client in the league (Masteralexis & Tryce, 2005). The Major League Baseball Players Association (MLBPA) and the National Football League Players Association (NFLPA) have more unique and rigorous features. For example, MLBPA's certification statement requires prospective agents to demonstrate knowledge of the MLB collective bargaining agreement, and the NFLPA requires that contract agents hold an advanced degree beyond the bachelor's degree and pass a qualifying examination (see http://www.

Competitive Advantage
STRATEGIES

The Law of Agency and Athlete Agents

- When establishing an agency relationship, follow basic contract principles, such as clearly identifying the parties, desired outcomes or objectives of the agency agreement, the duration of the agency, and the scope of authority of the agent.

- Even though oral agency agreements are enforceable, a better practice is to put agency agreements in writing.

- Athlete agents must educate themselves regarding the requirements of state laws such as UAAA and federal laws such as SPARTA before contacting prospective clients or embarking on a sport agency enterprise.

- Athlete agents should seriously evaluate the economic potential in the highly competitive field of athlete representation, since approximately half of all athlete agents do not have a single active player.

- Those working in college athletics at any level should be familiar with the legal restrictions on athlete agents as well as those imposed by the NCAA or other amateur athletic association to protect the interests of the university in the event a student-athlete's eligibility becomes an issue.

- A university compliance officer may want to create informational brochures and conduct informational and educational seminars for student-athletes to aid them in understanding what contact is permissible with agents.

nflplayers.com/user/template.aspx?fmid=181&lmid=233&pid=0&type=l for more information). Ultimately, the limitation on fees that can be charged by an agent for contract negotiation services is one of the best and most consistent restrictions imposed by the professional players associations.

CONCLUSION

Typically, legal issues affecting athletes and agents arise in two main areas—agency for professional athletes and agency for student-athletes. This chapter introduced basic notions of agency law, including how agency relationships are created, the scope of an agent's authority, and the duties existing between agents and principals. This chapter also identified the numerous ways in which athlete agents are regulated in their dealings with student-athletes, including state regulations, the Uniform Athlete Agents Act, and the federal statute SPARTA. Last, this chapter summarized other, private restrictions imposed on athlete agents by professional players associations and sport governing bodies. A solid understanding of basic agency law is important to enable any sport manager to function effectively as a representative (employee) of a sport organization. In addition, a thorough understanding of how agency laws have been applied to athlete agents and the regulations in this area will be very useful for sport managers who negotiate player contracts, evaluate athletic eligibility for a university or the NCAA, or pursue a career as an athlete agent.

discussion questions

1. What are the different ways in which an agency relationship may be created?
2. Identify and explain each of the duties owed by the principal to the agent and by the agent to the principal.
3. How is apparent agency different from express agency?
4. Explain the different classifications of principals and how the classification affects the liability of the principal for the actions of an agent.
5. What are the four primary requirements of the Uniform Athlete Agents Act? Explain and demonstrate your understanding of each of the requirements.
6. What is the primary purpose of SPARTA? What are its limitations?

learning activities

Using the Internet, find out what information is available for student athletes from the NCAA regarding athlete agents. From that information, can you determine the difference between an advisor and an agent? What is the significance of that difference? Go to www.ncaa.org and search for "agent information." (See also Grant, 1999.)

CASE STUDY

Len Bias played basketball at the University of Maryland in the mid-1980s. He was an outstanding player and was projected to be a top NBA draft selection. On June 17, 1986, the Boston Celtics drafted him into the NBA. Two days later, he was found dead in his dorm room from a cocaine overdose. Prior to his death, he had instructed his agent, Advantage International, Inc., to take out a $1 million life insurance policy. The policy was not issued prior to his death. Bias' estate sued Advantage for failing to take out the policy.

1. What duties has Advantage allegedly breached, if any?
2. What do you think the court's decision was? See *Bias v. Advantage International, Inc.* 905 F.2d 1558 (D.C. Cir. 1990).

considering . . .   **ANALYSIS & DISCUSSION**

Athlete Agent Behavior (p. 249)

Shady would clearly fall within the definition of an athlete agent under the UAAA because he represents himself to the public as an athlete agent. Josh would also come under the athlete agent definition because it applies to anyone who directly or indirectly recruits or solicits a student-athlete to enter into an agency agreement. Goode meets the definition of a student-athlete since he still has amateur eligibility remaining. As such, all the parties involved are subject to the acts. Josh and Shady must be registered under the act; thus, if Josh is not registered, his meeting would constitute a violation since he initiated the contact. Had Goode initiated the contact, Shady or Josh could have met with Goode and registered later. Assuming that Josh is registered, the meeting itself does not violate any of the restrictions imposed in UAAA.

Neither Shady nor Josh may offer Goode anything of value unless and until Goode executes an agency agreement. Thus, the verbal promises made by Josh violate the act, even though the promises were only offers to give Goode money or items of value if he signed with Shady. The inducement to sign is prohibited. If, during the course of the meeting, the proper disclosures are made and Goode executes the agency agreement, Shady or Josh may offer money or items of value to Goode. Remember, the primary purpose of the UAAA is to provide the student-athlete with adequate notice of the type of relationship he is entering into and the ramifications of that decision.

Once Goode agrees to be represented by Shady, whether in a formal agency agreement or just verbally, his amateur eligibility will likely be lost based upon the NCAA restrictions on student-athletes and agents. If Goode decides he would like to cancel the contract, the UAAA gives him 14 days to so. He could cancel it, return anything of value provided to him by Shady, and no longer be bound to the agency agreement. However, even if he legally cancels the agreement and returns any items of value or money received, the NCAA is not obligated to reinstate his amateur eligibility.

REFERENCES

Cases

Bias v. Advantage Int'l, Inc., 905 F.2d 1558 (D.C. Cir. 1990).

Clark Adver. Agency v. Tice, 490 F.2d 834 (5th Cir. 1974).

Detroit Lions, Inc. v. Argovitz, 767 F.2d 919 (6th Cir. 1985).

Hilliard v. Black, 125 F. Supp. 2d 1071 (N.D. Fla. 2000).

Jones v. Archibald, 360 N.Y.S.2d 119 (App. Div. 1974).

United States v. Piggie, 303 F.3d 923 (8th Cir. 2002).

Statutes

Restatement (Third) of Agency § 1.04 Terminology (2006).

Restatement (Third) of Agency § 8.01 General fiduciary principle (2006).

Restatement (Third) of Agency § 8.02 No self-dealing (2006).

Restatement (Third) of Agency § 8.03 No conflict of interest (2006).

Restatement (Third) of Agency § 8.04 Avoid competition or competing interests (2006).

Restatement (Third) of Agency § 8.05 No misuse property of funds of principal; avoid disclosure of confidential information (2006).

Restatement (Third) of Agency § 8.08 Duty of care, competence, and diligence (2006).

Restatement (Third) of Agency § 8.09 Duty to act within scope of authority and comply with lawful instructions (2006).

Restatement (Third) of Agency § 8.10 Duty of good conduct—refrain from actions that may damage principals enterprise (2006).

Restatement (Third) of Agency § 8.11 Duty to provide information to principal (2006).

Restatement (Third) of Agency § 8.12 Duty of accounting (2006).

Restatement (Third) of Agency § 8.14 Duty to indemnify (2006).

Restatement (Third) of Agency § 8.15 Deal fairly and in good faith, such as information about risks of physical harm or pecuniary loss (2006).

Sports Agent Responsibility and Trust Act, 15 U.S.C. § 7801 et seq. (2009).

Other Sources

Camby repays tourney money. (1997, June 21). *The New York Times*, p. 1(28) (Late Edition).

Cavanaugh, J. (1997, May 9). UMass and UConn lose '96 honors. *The New York Times*, p. B21 (Late Edition).

Golka's Athlete Agent Regulation Blog. Retrieved from www.athleteagent.blogspot.com/.

Grant, C. G. (1999, May 20). Memorandum to directors of athletics of NCAA Division I institutions. NCAA Division I Subcommittee on Amateurism and Agents. Retrieved October 6, 2005, from www1.ncaa.org/membership/enforcement/agents/sa_info/agent_packet/baseball_memo?ObjectID= 32829&ViewMode=0&PreviewState=0.

Heitner, D. (2009, March 31). Raymond Lee Savage Jr. has misdemeanor charge dropped. *Sports Agent Blog.com*. Retrieved June 6, 2009, from www.sportsagent-blog.com/2009/03/31/raymond-lee-savage-jr-has-misdemeanor-charge-dropped/.

Kleinberger, D. S. (2008). *Agency, partnerships, and LLCs* (3rd ed.). New York: Aspen Publishers, Inc.

Masteralexis, L. P., & Tryce, S. A. (2005, March). *Sport agent regulations: Making sense of the maze of conduct-governing rules, regulations and statutes*. Paper presented at the meeting of the Sport Recreation and Law Association, Virginia Beach, Va.

Mullen, L. (2008, November 10). State of Alabama says agent ran afoul of tough recruiting laws. *Street and Smith's SportsBusiness Journal*, p. 13.

National Collegiate Athletic Association. (n.d.a). *Applicable agent legislation*. Retrieved June 5, 2009, from www1.ncaa.org/membership/enforcement/agents/sa_info/legislation.html.

National Collegiate Athletic Association. (n.d.b). *Institutional guidelines sports agents-runners-financial advisors NCAA professional sports liaison committee*. Retrieved June 5, 2009, from www1.ncaa.org/membership/enforcement/agents/sa_info/agent_packet/inst_guidelines?ObjectID= 32823&ViewMode=0&PreviewState=0.

National Collegiate Athletic Association. (n.d.c). *Uniform athlete agents act (UAAA) history and status*. Retrieved June 5, 2009, from www1.ncaa.org/membership/enforcement/agents/uaaa/history.html.

National Conference of Commissioners on Uniform State Laws. (2010). *A few facts about the . . . Uniform athlete agents act*. Retrieved April 1, 2010, from www.nccusl.org/Update/uniformact_factsheets/uniformacts-fs-aaa.asp.

National Conference of Commissioners on Uniform State Laws. (n.d.b). *Uniform Athlete Agents Act, Legislative Fact Sheet*. Retrieved June 5, 2009, from www.nccusl.org/Update/uniformact_factsheets/uniformacts-fs-aaa.asp.

National Conference of Commissioners on Uniform State Laws. (2002). *Uniform Law Commission: Athlete Agents*

Act. Retrieved June 5, 2009, from www.nccusl.org/Update/ActSearchResults.aspx.

National Conference of Commissioners on Uniform State Laws. (n.d.c). *Summary: Uniform athlete agents act*. Retrieved June 5, 2009, from www.nccusl.org/Update/uniformact_summaries/uniformacts-s-aaa.asp.

National Conference of Commissioners on Uniform State Laws. (2000, November 30). *Uniform athlete agents act (2000)*. Retrieved June 5, 2009, from www.law.upenn.edu/bll/ulc/uaaa/aaa1130.htm.

Sports agent responsibility and trust act: Hearing before the Subcommittee on Commercial and Administrative Law of the Committee on the Judiciary, House of Representatives, 108th Cong., 1 (2003).

University of Pennsylvania Law School. (n.d.). Uniform athlete agents act: Policy statement. Retrieved June 5, 2009, from www.law.upenn.edu/bll/ulc/uaaa/aaps0615.htm.

WEBSITE RESOURCES

www.nccusl.org/Update/uniformact_factsheets/uniformacts-fs-aaa.asp ▪ This site presents current and updated information regarding enactment of the UAAA.

www.nflplayers.com/user/template.aspx?fmid=181&lmid=233&pid=0&type=l ▪ This site provides information about NFL agent regulations and certification requirements.

www.ncaa.org/wps/portal/ncaahome?WCM_GLOBAL_CONTEXT=/ncaa/NCAA/Legislation+and+Governance/Eligibility+and+Recruiting/Agents+and+Amateurism/Agent+Info+for+Student-Athletes/ ▪ This site provides information about the NCAA's regulations regarding student-athletes and agents.

http://athleteagent.blogspot.com, www.sportsagentblog.com ▪ These two blogs focus on athlete agents, are useful tools for students conducting research about athlete agents and related issues in professional sport.

PART III | **Strategic Management—Governance**

LEGAL ISSUES ARISING IN GOVERNANCE CONTEXTS

I n both amateur and professional sport, governing bodies generate, implement, and enforce rules and policies that define the manner in which their particular sports operate. Examples of such governing bodies include the United States Olympic Committee (USOC), the National Collegiate Athletic Association (NCAA), and the National Basketball Association (NBA). Specifically, a sport organization such as the NCAA must define and regulate its own structure and functioning, the relationship between it and the entities it governs, and the conduct of those entities. Governed entities may include other organizations. For example, Major League Baseball governs the various professional baseball teams within the National League, the NCAA governs (in some respects) the athletics programs of its various member universities, and the USOC governs national governing bodies such as USA Track & Field. Governed entities may also include coaches, officials, and administrators, as well as athletes, who are subject to the rules and regulations of the governing bodies of their particular sport.

In regulating its sport, a sport governing body may find its strategic management actions subject to legal challenge. Examples might include decisions regarding:

- exercising a commissioner's authority to act in the best interests of the sport;
- how to structure a new league;
- how to regulate league expansion, contraction, and franchise location;
- what limitations will be placed on types of acceptable equipment;
- how events will be selected and controlled;
- the nature of security, disciplinary, and dispute resolution procedures;
- the scope of control exerted in processes for determining participant eligibility;
- regulating coaching compensation and the integrity of officiating;
- controlling athletic conference membership and revenue agreements;
- and how to conduct business to best advantage with respect to the tax laws.

Strategic decision making in these areas involves issues of fairness to individuals and organizations, as well as fair competition in the marketplace.

LEGAL PRINCIPLES AND THE STRATEGIC MANAGEMENT FUNCTION

S everal legal principles are relevant to strategic decision making by sport governing bodies, including procedural fairness under the law of private associations and the Constitutional right to due process, and freedom from unfair discrimination in the provision of services. Additionally, due to the entertainment business aspects of professional, collegiate, and Olympic sport, one of the most frequently invoked legal principles is fair competition under antitrust law. Chapter 11 discusses the legal principles relevant to the governance of professional sport and is primarily focused on antitrust issues. Chapter 12 covers governance issues in Olympic sport and deals with a variety of legal principles, including application of the Ted Stevens Olympic and Amateur Sports Act (OASA), antidiscrimination laws, and procedural fairness. In addition, Chapter 12 is not limited to governance issues like Chapters 11 and 13, but also contains information on regulating participation in Olympic sport. We combine discussion of governance and regulation of participants in Olympic sport in one chapter because Olympic sport differs significantly in these areas from sport in other amateur settings.

Chapter 13 discusses the legal principles involved in the governance of high school and college athletics. These include antitrust law as well as procedural fairness, freedom from discrimination, and compliance with contract and tax law. Finally, Chapter 14 addresses issues pertinent to participants in private clubs and high school and college athletics.

The purpose of Part III is to provide information about the legal issues and principles pertaining to sport governance because when management makes a poor governance decision, it may have costly consequences. You can enhance your success in strategic management by possessing a fundamental understanding of the legal implications of various types of decisions often faced in the context of sport governance.

Governance Issues in Professional Sport

INTRODUCTION

Governance of professional sport may be roughly divided into governance of team sports by professional sports leagues and governance of individual sports by players associations operating professional tours. To help you understand the governance issues, this chapter first provides an overview of antitrust law as a foundation. Next, the chapter examines governance issues pertinent to the authority of professional sports leagues, including the power of the commissioner, the legal structure of leagues, applications for sport franchises, team ownership, franchise relocation, rival leagues, and equipment regulation. The chapter then examines governance issues related to individual professional sports, including organizational structure of tour players associations, control of events, equipment regulation, and disciplinary authority. Legal issues with respect to the governance of professional sport include contract law, labor law, the law of private associations, and limits on owners imposed by federal antitrust law. Exhibit 11.1 depicts the management contexts and applicable law discussed in this chapter.

OVERVIEW OF ANTITRUST LAW

Section 1 of the Sherman Act prohibits **concerted action** (i.e., joint action between two or more parties) that unreasonably restrains trade in a **relevant market**. "Relevant market" refers to the economic market in which the defendant business operates. Section 2 prohibits predatory or exclusionary conduct that is designed to enable an organization to acquire or maintain monopoly power in a relevant market. The purpose of these antitrust laws is to promote and protect the operation of free market capitalism, with the resulting benefits to consumers of better products at lower prices.

EXHIBIT 11.1	Management contexts in which governance issues may arise, with relevant laws and cases.

MANAGEMENT CONTEXT	MAJOR LEGAL ISSUES	RELEVANT LAW	ILLUSTRATIVE CASES
Sport league governance	Commissioner power	Private associations; labor law	*Finley, Chicago National League*
	League structures	Sherman Act	*Fraser, Brown*
	Franchise applications	Sherman Act	*Mid-South Grizzlies*
	Cross-ownership	Sherman Act	*NASL v. NFL*
	Ownership transfer	Sherman Act	*Piazza*
	Franchise relocation	Sherman Act	*Raiders I*
	Rival leagues	Sherman Act	*NASL v. NFL, Philadelphia World Hockey, USFL v. NFL, AFL v. NFL, Hecht*
	Equipment regulation	Sherman Act	*Schutt*
Individual sport tour governance	Event control	Sherman Act	*Volvo, JamSports, PGA Tour v. Martin*
	Equipment regulation	Sherman Act	*Gunter Harz, Weight-Rite, Gilder*
	Disciplinary authority	Sherman Act	*Blalock, Hipperdinger*

Professional sports (particularly those with teams in a league structure) present a unique challenge to the traditional application of antitrust law to businesses. Conventional businesses such as Reebok, adidas, and Nike compete for consumers and have an economic interest in putting rival companies out of business. Pro sports teams, on the other hand, have an interest in not competing too strongly economically with rival teams. To attract and retain consumers, leagues must maintain a competitive balance across teams so that the outcomes of games are truly contested and uncertain, in order to maximize entertainment value. To provide such an entertainment product successfully requires collective action between competitor teams in the form of league decisions to maintain economic competitiveness among its various teams. It is important to distinguish between playing competitiveness and economic competitiveness as you explore the application of antitrust law to sport governance. It is maintaining *economic* competitiveness that is the focus of antitrust law.

Per se violations of antitrust law are wrongdoings that are so obviously improper restraints on free trade that little other analysis is needed. Examples include agreements to fix prices so that one company doesn't undersell another, or dividing the geographic market into exclusive business territories. The interdependence of teams within a pro sports league necessitates agreements, such as market divisions, that would normally be per se or automatic violations of § 1 of the Sherman Act if engaged in by conventional businesses. Therefore, the courts have established that instead of strictly applying a per se antitrust analysis to sport organizations, they will apply a rule of reason analysis that can accommodate the economic competitive balance needed to provide a successful professional sport entertainment product (see Exhibit 11.2). The **rule of reason analysis** requires a court to balance the procompetitive (economically) effects of a rule against its anticompetitive effects. If the net effect dampens economic competition in the relevant market rather than promoting it, the rule will be found to violate § 1 of the Sherman Act.

Section 2 of the Sherman Act does not prohibit monopolies that have occurred naturally as the result of one competitor having a superior product or exercising better business sense, or by historic accident. Rather, it forbids *predatory behav-*

Rule of reason analysis applied to sport organizations. EXHIBIT **11.2**

In *Law v. National Collegiate Athletic Association* (1998, p. 1019), the Tenth Circuit summarized the application of the rule of reason analysis to sports league restraints as follows:

> [T]he plaintiff bears the initial burden of showing that an agreement had a substantially adverse effect on competition. . . . If the plaintiff meets this burden, the burden shifts to the defendant to come forward with evidence of the pro-competitive virtues of the alleged wrongful conduct. . . . If the defendant is able to demonstrate pro-competitive effects, the plaintiff then must prove that the challenged conduct is not reasonably necessary to achieve the legitimate objectives or that those objectives can be achieved in a substantially less restrictive manner. . . . Ultimately . . . the harms and benefits must be weighed against each other in order to judge whether the challenged behavior is, on balance, reasonable.

ior by which a competitor attempts to establish or maintain a monopoly. As an example, if Fly-rite Frisbee Company invents Frisbees and turns out to be the only manufacturer that produces Frisbees that fly well, it will quickly establish a natural monopoly—and that is fine. However, if Fly-rite seeks to protect its monopoly by buying up all potential competitors, it would be guilty of willful monopolization in violation of § 2 of the Sherman Act.

Defining the relevant geographic and product markets is an important part of the analysis for determining whether a violation of § 1 or § 2 has occurred. The more broadly a geographic market is defined, the smaller the market share of the alleged monopolist will be, and thus the less likely it is to be found guilty of a Sherman Act violation. Similarly, the more interchangeable the alleged monopolist's product is with the products of competitors, the less the market dominance of the alleged monopolist. A 70 percent share of the relevant market is generally considered the threshold for a finding of monopoly power.

Although teams within a given league do compete with each other for fan dollars, this intrabrand competition must be limited by agreements or rules designed to maintain the economic health of all the teams in the league. In the labor relations context, such agreements include efforts to spread athletic talent across teams, such as the draft system and limits on free agency. These efforts are discussed in Chapter 9. In the organizational governance context, such agreements include rules establishing restrictions on league structure and restrictions on franchise or event ownership and location.

GOVERNANCE AND STRUCTURE OF PROFESSIONAL SPORTS LEAGUES

Most professional team sports are structured as a league that is governed by three bureaucratic layers: the commissioner, the league's board of governors or owners committee, and the centralized league office. The athletes are usually (but not always) members of a players association that is the functional equivalent of a labor union. Relations between management and the players association are governed by the collective-bargaining agreement reached after a negotiation involving both sides.

Power of the Commissioner

Typically, the scope of the commissioner's power is defined in the league's constitution and by-laws. The commissioner's role is complex, because the owners have authority to hire and fire him, yet the commissioner typically has authority to impose disciplinary measures on the owners. According to Lentze (1995), the fact that a league commissioner usually has disciplinary authority, dispute resolution, and other decision-making powers makes the governance model of pro sports leagues different from the traditional corporate governance model of a board of directors and a chief executive officer (CEO). In the latter model, the CEO is under the direct control of the board and does not possess powers over the board similar to the powers of the league commissioner. Some have questioned whether these powers make a commissioner a neutral party, or whether he remains primarily an agent of the owners who employ him (see *National Football League Players Association v. National Labor Relations Board*, 1974). The players believe that the commissioner is "on the side" of the employers or owners as a group; however, in certain situations owners also find themselves desiring to limit the power of the commissioner.

The constitution and by-laws of pro leagues typically authorize the commissioner to engage in discretionary decision making in the following areas:

- Approval of player contracts
- Rule making
- Dispute resolution between player and club, between clubs, or between player or club and the league
- Disciplinary matters involving players, clubs, front office personnel, owners, and others

Additionally, the commissioner's role often includes restraining excessive exercise of owners' power that would be detrimental to fans, serving as lead negotiator for league-wide contracts such as television deals, and serving as a negotiator for the owners in labor disputes with players associations. (For analyses of the role of commissioners, see Lentze, 1995; Arcella, 1997.) Finally, league by-laws generally grant commissioners discretion to act "in the best interests of the game." This was the authority wielded by David Stern, the commissioner of the NBA, when he imposed a season-long suspension on Indiana Pacers basketball player Ron Artest for his role in a violent brawl during a Pacers–Pistons game in 2004. In 2009, NFL Commissioner Roger Goodell fined Bud Adams, the 86-year-old owner of the Tennessee Titans, $250,000 for making obscene hand gestures at Buffalo Bills fans while celebrating his team's victory (Walker, 2009).

The discretionary power of the commissioner is not all-encompassing, however, but is constrained by various provisions of the league's constitution and by-laws. For example, the commissioner may not fine a player in an amount greater than the rules allow. Additionally, the commissioner's power is limited by the terms agreed to by players and owners in the league's collective-bargaining agreement. For example, some players associations have successfully negotiated for commissioner decisions regarding disciplinary action against athletes to be subject to review through arbitration procedures. For example, following Commissioner Stern's decision to suspend Ron Artest, Jermaine O'Neal, and two other Indiana Pacers who participated in the 2004 brawl with fans in the stands, the National Basketball Players Association (NBPA) filed an appeal to an arbitrator under the league's collective-bargaining agreement. The arbitrator upheld the commissioner's decision to suspend the players but reduced the length of O'Neal's suspension from 25 to 15 games. The NBA challenged the authority of the arbitrator to review Stern's decision. The district court ruled that the provisions of the collective-bargaining agreement made clear that while the commissioner's authority to impose discipline for on-the-court misbehavior was unarbitrable, the arbitrator had the authority to review the commissioner's disciplinary actions for off-the-court misconduct (*NBA v. Artest*, 2004).

Direct judicial review of a commissioner's actions is also available. However, courts will typically accord substantial deference to the commissioner's judgment on issues within the scope of his authority. Courts are willing, though, to invoke the law of private associations to assert judicial review of a sport organization's actions. The law of private associations (also known as the law of voluntary associations or contractual due process) refers to a common law principle enabling a court to review the actions of a private association. Based on the idea that members of such associations are in a contractual relationship with the association, that organization must provide them with reasonable due process. Thus, a court may review the actions of such an association when it has allegedly violated its own rules or implemented arbitrary and capricious decisions that violate procedural fairness. In so doing, a court will require that a commissioner's actions

- be within the scope of his defined authority.
- be made in good faith.
- comport with basic tenets of procedural fairness.
- not be made in violation of state or federal law.

The application of the law of private associations as it relates to judicial review of decisions made by a commissioner is discussed more fully in the *Finley* case.

Charles O. Finley & Co. v. Kuhn

569 F.2d 527 (7th Cir. 1978), *cert. denied,* 439 U.S. 876 (1978)

CASE OPINION

[FACTS

Plaintiff Finley & Co., then owner of the Oakland Athletics baseball club, sold their contract rights to three star players just before the trading deadline. They sold the rights to Joe Rudi and Rollie Fingers to the Boston Red Sox for $2 million and the rights to Vida Blue to the New York Yankees for $1.5 million. Three days later, baseball Commissioner Bowie Kuhn disapproved these contract assignments on the basis that they were contrary to the best interests of baseball. He was particularly concerned that the arrangements would debilitate the Oakland A's, disrupt the competitive balance among teams in the American League by allowing the more affluent clubs to buy up the best talent, and exacerbate the then unsettled status of the reserve system. The owner of the A's then brought this suit, alleging that the Commissioner had exceeded the scope of his authority, and that he had breached his contract with the baseball clubs because his disapproval of the sales was arbitrary and capricious. Also at issue in a subsequent request for declaratory judgment was whether the covenant not to sue (waiver of recourse to the courts) found in the Major League Baseball Agreement was valid and enforceable. The lower court ruled in favor of the Commissioner on

all of the above claims, and the owner of the Oakland A's brought this appeal.]

HOLDING

The 7th Circuit affirmed the rulings of the district court.

RATIONALE

Basic to the underlying suit brought by Oakland and to this appeal is whether the Commissioner of baseball is vested by contract with the authority to disapprove player assignments which he finds to be "not in the best interests of baseball."

* * *

In November, 1920, the major league club owners ... all signed what they called the Major League Agreement, and Judge Landis assumed the position of Commissioner. . . . The agreement, a contract between the constituent clubs of the National and American Leagues, is the basic charter under which major league baseball operates.

The Major League Agreement provides that "the functions of the Commissioner shall be ... to investigate . . . any act, transaction or practice . . . not in the best interests of the national game of Baseball" and "to determine . . . what preventive, remedial or punitive action is appropriate in the premises, and to take such action. . . ." Art. I, Sec. 2(a) and (b).

* * *

He has also been given the express power to approve or disapprove the assignments of players. In regard to nonparties to the agreement, he may take such other steps as he deems necessary and proper in the interests of the morale of the players and the honor of the game.

The Major League Agreement also provides that "in the case of conduct by Major Leagues, Major League Clubs, officers, employees or players which is deemed by the Commissioner not to be in the best interests of Baseball, action by the Commissioner for each offense *may include*" a reprimand, deprivation of a club of representation at joint meetings, suspension or removal of non-players, temporary or permanent ineligibility of players, and a fine not to exceed $5,000 in the case of a league or club and not to exceed $500 in the case of an individual. Art. I, Sec. 3.

* * *

The district court considered the plaintiff's argument that the enumeration in Article I, Section 3 of the sanctions which the Commissioner may impose places a limit on his authority inasmuch as the power to disapprove assignments of players is not included. The court concluded that the enumeration does not purport to be exclusive and provides that the Commissioner *may* act in one of the listed ways without expressly limiting him to those ways.

* * *

Oakland was contending that the Commissioner could set aside assignments only if the assignments involved a Rules violation or moral turpitude. In its briefs on appeal, Oakland summarized this branch of its argument by stating that the Commissioner's "disapproval of the assignments . . . exceeded [his] authority under the Major League Agreement and Rules; was irrational and unreasonable; and was procedurally unfair."

* * *

The plaintiff has argued that it is a fundamental rule of law that the decisions of the head of a private association must be procedurally fair. Plaintiff then argued that it was "procedurally unfair" for the Commissioner to fail to warn the plaintiff that he would "disapprove

large cash assignments of star players even if they complied with the Major League Rules."

* * *

We conclude that the evidence fully supports, and we agree with, the district court's finding that "the history of the adoption of the Major League Agreement in 1921 and the operation of baseball for more than 50 years under it, including: the circumstances preceding and precipitating the adoption of the Agreement; the numerous exercises of broad authority under the best interests clause by Judge Landis and . . . Commissioner Kuhn; the amendments to the Agreement in 1964 restoring and broadening the authority of the Commissioner; . . . and most important the express language of the Agreement itself—are all to the effect that the Commissioner has the authority to determine whether *any* act, transaction or practice is 'not in the best interests of baseball,' and upon such determination, to take whatever preventive or remedial action he deems appropriate, whether or not the act, transaction or practice complies with the Major League Rules or involves moral turpitude." Any other conclusion would involve the courts in not only interpreting often complex rules of baseball to determine if they were violated but also, as noted in the *Landis* case, the "intent of the [baseball] code," an even more complicated and subjective task.

* * *

The Rudi–Fingers–Blue transactions had been negotiated on June 14 and 15, 1976. On June 16, the Commissioner sent a teletype to the Oakland, Boston and New York clubs and to the Players' Association expressing his "concern for possible consequences to the integrity of baseball and public confidence in the game" and setting a hearing for June 17. Present at the hearing were 17 persons representing those notified. At the outset of the hearing the Commissioner stated that he was concerned that the assignments would be harmful to the competitive capacity of Oakland; that they reflected an effort by Boston and New York to purchase star players and "bypass the usual methods of player development and acquisition which have been traditionally used in professional baseball"; and that the question to be resolved was whether the transactions "are consistent with the best interests of baseball's integrity and maintenance of public confidence in the game." He warned that it was possible that he might determine that the assignments not be approved. Mr. Finley and representatives of the Red Sox and Yankees made statements on the record. No one at the hearing, including Mr. Finley, claimed that the Commissioner lacked the authority to disapprove the assignments, or objected to the holding of the hearing, or to any of the procedures followed at the hearing.

On June 18, the Commissioner concluded that the attempted assignments should be disapproved as not in the best interests of baseball. In his written decision, the Commissioner stated his reasons which we have summarized . . . . The decision was sent to all parties by teletype. The Commissioner recognized "that there have been cash sales of player contracts in the past," but concluded that "these transactions were unparalleled in the history of the game" because there was "never anything on this scale or falling at this time of the year, or which threatened so seriously to unbalance the competitive balance of baseball." The district court concluded that the attempted assignments of Rudi, Fingers and Blue "were at a time and under circumstances making them unique in the history of baseball." We conclude that the evidence fully supports, and we agree with, the district court's finding and conclusion that the Commissioner "acted in good faith, after investigation, consultation and deliberation, in a manner which he determined to be in the best interests of baseball" and that "whether he was right or wrong is beyond the competence and the jurisdiction of this court to decide."

* * *

We must then conclude that anyone becoming a signatory to the Major League Agreement was put on ample notice that the action ultimately taken by the Commissioner was not only possible but probable. The action was neither an "abrupt departure" nor a "change of policy" in view of the contemporaneous developments taking place in the reserve system, over which the Commissioner had little or no control, and in any event the broad authority given to the Commissioner by the Major League Agreement placed any party to it on notice that such authority could be used.

Questions

1. How broad is the scope of the commissioner's power, according to the *Finley* court?

2. Is the commissioner's discretionary power to act unilaterally in the best interests of the game limited to certain topics, such as player misconduct? If not, to what areas of "baseball life" does the commissioner's "best interests" power extend?

3. How did the court apply the law of private associations in deciding this case? What are the implications for limits on the decision-making power of the commissioner?

The *Finley* case stands for the proposition that courts will not interfere with the authority of the commissioner to act in the best interests of the game, as long as the action falls within the constraints found in the league's constitution and by-laws and in the collective-bargaining agreements, as well as within traditional notions of due process.

Compare this decision with the ruling in *Chicago National League Ball Club v. Vincent* (1992). In this case, the court asserted its right to review baseball Commissioner Vincent's decision to restructure the divisions of the National League. The court ruled that the commissioner exceeded his authority when he ordered the transfer of the Chicago Cubs to the Western Division of the National League over the team's objection. A team's right to veto a transfer decision is provided in the league's constitution, and the court found that the best interests of baseball clause did not supersede enumerated rights in the constitution and by-laws.

Legal Structures of Pro Sports Leagues

Recently, professional sports leagues have experimented with different types of organizational structures, in part to attempt to reduce their exposure to antitrust liability. This section explores the legal ramifications of differing league structures.

Traditional structure

Professional sports leagues have traditionally been structured as nonprofit incorporated or unincorporated associations of clubs, where each member club has separate and independent ownership. Different sports have differing rules regarding club ownership, as we shall see later in the chapter. Exhibit 11.3 suggests how responsibilities are divided in a traditionally structured pro sport league.

The primary advantage of the traditional structure is its promise of profit-making potential for individuals who want to make an ownership investment, and thus the incentive it provides for those owners to maximize the value of each team. Sharing league-wide revenues also links the individual owners' interests to the general welfare of the league.

The primary disadvantage of the traditional model is that the necessary agreements among owners "for the good of the league as a whole" subject the league to potential liability under the antitrust laws for entering into agreements that unreasonably restrain free trade under § 1 of the Sherman Act.

Single entity structure

In several lawsuits, traditional sports leagues attempted to argue that they were in fact a single entity offering a league-generated entertainment product rather than a collection of individual entities in economic competition with one another. Thus, the argument goes, owner agreements that restrain trade are "agreements" between

---

Traditional pro sports league structure and division of responsibilities.   EXHIBIT 11.3

League office conducts centralized league operations such as:

- Scheduling games
- Hiring and training officials
- Disciplining players
- Marketing and licensing logoed merchandise
- Negotiating broadcasting contracts

League board of directors or owners committee oversees policy making on issues such as:

- Franchise relocation
- League expansion or contraction
- Playing facility issues
- Collective bargaining
- Rules of play
- Revenue sharing of non–locally generated revenue

Individual teams have responsibility for matters such as:

- Facility acquisition or leasing
- Team marketing
- Ticket sales and luxury seating
- Arrangements for local broadcasting contracts

internal parts of one entity and so do not restrain trade between competing entities; hence, they do not violate antitrust law. Most of the time, the courts have rejected the "single entity defense," finding that leagues are in fact associations of individually owned teams that do compete with each other economically as well as on the field or court (see, e.g., *North American Soccer League v. National Football League*, 1982; *Los Angeles Memorial Coliseum v. National Football League (Raiders I)*, 1984; *Sullivan v. National Football League*, 1994; but contrast *San Francisco Seals, Ltd. v. National Hockey League*, 1974; *American Needle, Inc. v. NFL*, 2008). Otherwise, why would leagues need agreements limiting franchise proximity to each other, for example? Therefore, league rules that restrain trade are subject to antitrust challenge, and courts will apply the rule of reason analysis to determine potential violations of the Sherman Act.

In recent years, several new leagues have attempted to structure themselves explicitly as single entities to avoid antitrust exposure. Thus, all of the investors would own undivided interests in the whole league and share all expenses and revenues based on the percentage of their respective ownership interests in the league. The leagues that have attempted to achieve deliberate single entity status include Major League Soccer (MLS), the Women's United Soccer Association (WUSA), the Women's National Basketball Association (WNBA), and the Arena Football League (AFL). The WUSA abandoned the single entity structure in its last-gasp effort to attract new investors before it folded in 2003. The WNBA has likewise returned to the traditional model of individual ownership in an apparent effort to create stability independent of the NBA's support structure.

In *Fraser v. Major League Soccer* (2002), several soccer players sued the league under the Sherman Act, claiming that the single entity structure was an attempt to unreasonably restrain trade by limiting economic competition among teams and depressing player salaries. The court upheld the validity of the single entity structure and ruled against the players, although it also found that the structure of the MLS was in actuality a hybrid that combined some elements of a single entity structure with elements of a traditional league.

The Supreme Court touched on this issue in *Brown v. Pro-Football, Inc.* (1996), stating that professional sports clubs must cooperate for their economic survival and so are not completely independent competitors. However, the Court did not rule on the issue of whether a league is a group of cooperating separate entities subject to the Sherman Act or an integrated single entity that does not compete with itself and thus is not subject to the Sherman Act. For now, the decisions of the lower courts provide the primary legal guidance for leagues. It appears that the courts will require deliberate and genuine structuring and functioning as a single entity for a league to avoid being subjected to antitrust challenges for unreasonable restraint of trade in the context of league governance issues. For a thorough discussion of single entity structure, see McKeown (2009).

Applications for Sport Franchises

Professional sports leagues have rules governing a team's application for a franchise within the league. Prospective owners have argued that such rules constitute concerted action that unreasonably restrains trade in violation of § 1 of the Sherman Act. Let's look at the *Mid-South Grizzlies* case, in which the court had to decide this issue.

Mid-South Grizzlies v. *National Football League*

| 720 F.2d 772 (3rd Cir. 1983) | **FOCUS CASE** |

FACTS

In 1974 and 1975, the Grizzlies, with their hometown in Memphis, Tennessee, were part of the World Football League. After the league disbanded in midseason in 1975, the Grizzlies applied to the NFL for a franchise in that league. The NFL had no franchise in Memphis, and placing a team there would not have infringed on the home territory of any existing NFL franchise. The Grizzlies provided evidence that they were an established enterprise with a reasonable chance of business success in a desirable market location. Nevertheless, the NFL rejected the Grizzlies' application for a franchise, and the Grizzlies sued under antitrust law, alleging that the rejection was made in bad faith out of ill will because the team had played in a rival league to the NFL. Essentially, the Grizzlies claimed that the NFL's negative vote on their franchise application constituted an antitrust violation because it unreasonably restrained trade by preventing them from competing within the NFL. The lower court granted summary judgment for the NFL, and the Grizzlies appealed.

HOLDING

The Third Circuit affirmed the decision of the District Court, holding that the NFL's rejection of the Grizzlies' franchise application did not violate the Sherman Act.

RATIONALE

The court applied the rule of reason analysis typically used to analyze the competitive effects of concerted action by league members under § 1 of the Sherman Act. (Refer back to Exhibit 11.2.) Here, the court found that the Grizzlies failed to satisfy their initial burden of showing any actual or potential injury to economic competition resulting from the denial of their franchise application. The nearest NFL franchise to Memphis was over 280 miles away in St. Louis, and thus there was no evidence that a Memphis team and a St. Louis team would compete for the same spectators, local broadcasters, merchandise customers, and so forth. Therefore, in the eyes of the court, there was no potential intraleague competition in the relevant product market that the NFL could be harming with its denial of a franchise to the Grizzlies. Moreover, the court believed that the NFL could show procompetitive interleague effects because the rejection left Memphis available as a future site for a franchise in a competing league, as well as leaving the Grizzlies club as a potential competitor in a future rival league. Therefore, the court concluded that the Grizzlies failed to make the necessary showing of injury to competition necessary to succeed on their antitrust claim.

Team Ownership

Leagues typically have ownership rules that set eligibility criteria for acceptable types of owners. Major League Baseball has no formal criteria, but it does consider such things as commitment to the local franchise area, amount of financial capital, and an ownership structure that poses no conflicts with the interests of the league (Friedman & Much, 1997). The NFL, on the other hand, has fairly restrictive ownership requirements. It prohibits public ownership of a franchise (with the exception of the Green Bay Packers, who were publicly owned before the NFL created this rule and were grandfathered in). It also prohibits corporate ownership of a franchise (again with one exception: in the mid-1980s former owner Eddie DeBartolo transferred ownership of the San Francisco 49ers to a property development corporation he owned, and the NFL fined him but let the new ownership arrangement stand (Lite, 1999)). The NFL also completely prohibited cross-ownership until it watered down its rule in 1997. None of the other Big 4 men's professional sports leagues (MLB, NBA, and NHL) forbids cross-ownership.

Cross-ownership

Cross-ownership is ownership of more than one sports franchise. In 1982, the former North American Soccer League (NASL) sued the NFL, alleging that the football league's rule banning cross-ownership of teams in competing leagues violated § 1 of the Sherman Act (*North American Soccer League v. National Football League,* 1982). The court found that the market supply of investors with sufficient capital and skill to purchase expensive sports franchises was quite limited, and that the NFL's ban on cross-ownership served to restrict significantly that supply, thereby creating a substantial restraint on free trade that harmed the capital-poor NASL. Therefore, the Second Circuit struck down the NFL's cross-ownership ban (as applied in that court's jurisdiction).

In 1997, the NFL weakened its strict ban on cross-ownership to allow an NFL team owner to own another sports franchise in the same geographic market (which allowed, for example, Wayne Huizenga to purchase the Miami Dolphins even though he already owned the Florida Marlins and the Florida Panthers hockey team). The rule change also allows an NFL team owner to own another sports franchise in another market as long as that market has no NFL team (which allowed, for example, Paul Allen to purchase the Seattle Seahawks even though he already owned the Portland Trailblazers).

Transfer of ownership

League restrictions on transferring team ownership can run afoul of antitrust law. In *Piazza v. Major League Baseball* (1993), the plaintiffs sought to buy the San Francisco Giants and relocate them to Florida. They were not allowed to purchase the franchise and sued, alleging a conspiracy among MLB owners to interfere with their efforts to buy. Eventually, the team sold for $15 million less than the plaintiffs had offered, which was evidence that the action of the owners had had the effect of reducing competition among bidders for the team. The court allowed the plaintiffs' antitrust claim to proceed, and the case was eventually settled out of court, with Major League Baseball agreeing to apologize and pay the plaintiffs $6 million (Sanchez, 1994). Other courts have rejected the *Piazza* analysis, reasoning that the point of antitrust law is not to protect sports entertainment producers (e.g., team owners or potential owners) from each other, but to protect against consumer harm by preventing anticompetitive conduct by those producers (*Baseball at Trotwood, L.L.C. v. Dayton Professional Baseball Club, L.L.C.,* 1999).

Courts tend to allow leagues to reject ownership transfers to prospective owners when the rejection is based on sufficient evidence of a lack of adequate financial capital, a lack of character, or insufficient business skills. According to the courts, these kinds of rejections serve to enhance interbrand competition (e.g., the ability of Major League Baseball to compete with other types of sports entertainment offerings) by preserving the quality of the league's product. (See *National Basketball Association v. Minnesota Professional Basketball, L.P.,* 1995.)

Franchise Relocation

The franchise rights of team owners include **territorial rights,** which prevent a franchise from relocating into a competitor team's market territory without league permission and adequate compensation for the potential loss of market share caused by the incursion. Franchise relocation restrictions can include a requirement that the move be approved by a three-fourths vote of the owners or a majority vote of the board of governors, for example. Typical justifications for restrictions on franchise relocation include ensuring that:

- Relocation sites have sufficient demographic and other characteristics to maintain league stability.
- Relocation does not negatively affect team travel and scheduling of games.
- The new territory does not encroach on existing team territorial rights.
- Relocation does not reduce the geographic diversity required for successful league-wide marketing.
- Relocation honors contractual and ethical duties (including loyalty) to cities.

Let's look at the *"Raiders I"* case to see how a court analyzed a franchise relocation in the NFL.

Los Angeles Memorial Coliseum v. National Football League (Raiders I)

| 726 F.2d 1381 (9th Cir. 1984), *cert. denied,* 469 U.S. 990 (1984) | **FOCUS CASE** |

FACTS

In 1978, the Los Angeles Rams moved their operation from the Los Angeles Coliseum to Anaheim Stadium, leaving the Coliseum without a major tenant. After their lease with the Oakland Coliseum expired that same year, the Oakland Raiders participated in negotiations for a move to the L.A. Coliseum and, in 1980, entered into an agreement to do so. Subsequently, the NFL owners voted 22-0, with five abstentions, against the move, under Rule 4.3 of the NFL Constitution. Rule 4.3 required the approval of three-fourths of the owners for a franchise relocation to a different city, regardless of whether the move was within or outside the team's original home territory. The Raiders then sued the NFL, claiming that Rule 4.3 violated § 1 of the Sherman Act, which prohibits concerted actions resulting in unreasonable restraints on trade. The District Court ruled in favor of the Raiders, and the NFL appealed.

HOLDING

The Ninth Circuit affirmed the decision of the district court and enjoined the NFL from preventing the Raiders' relocation to Los Angeles.

RATIONALE

The court found that Rule 4.3 divides up the market among the 28 teams of the NFL, which, in a nonsport situation, would violate § 1 of the Sherman Act. However, it also found that in order to produce the sports entertainment product, a professional league needs to be able to divide the market with territorial restrictions. Therefore, the court did not find a per se violation of antitrust law. Instead, it applied the rule of reason analysis, comparing the procompetitive effects of the rule to its anticompetitive effects.

Among the procompetitive effects identified by the court were:

- Exclusive territories aid new teams in achieving financial stability.
- Stability helps to maintain competitive performance balance among teams.
- Territories foster fan loyalty and team rivalries, which contribute to greater spectatorship, both live and televised.
- Preventing relocations that would take place before local governments can recover their investment maintains public confidence and interest in the NFL.
- Geographic diversity aids in collective negotiation of television rights with the networks.

The court balanced these against the anticompetitive effect of insulating teams from intraleague economic competition with each other, which allows them to set monopoly prices that harm consumers.

According to the court, there were less restrictive means to accomplish the same procompetitive goals. For example, the NFL could adopt a set of objective guidelines to follow in making franchise relocation decisions, thus eliminating the subjectivity (and hence possible bias) of a vote by the owners. Objective factors might include such things as population base, fan loyalty, economic impact projections, location continuity, facilities, and regional balance of teams. Here, the NFL made no evidentiary showing that the Los Angeles market could not sustain two pro football teams or that the relocation would harm the league's regional balance or have a negative effect on the league itself. Finally, the NFL failed to prove that the rule's effect of promoting interbrand competition (providing a strong league-wide product that could compete successfully against other professional sports and entertainment options) was greater than the negative effect on intrabrand (intraleague) competition.

Three years after it decided *Raiders I*, in *National Basketball Association v. SDC Basketball Club, Inc.* (1987) the Ninth Circuit stated that although leagues could use the objective factors identified in *Raiders I* to justify a relocation restriction rule, reliance on such objective factors was not a *necessary* condition for establishing the rule's legality. Therefore, at least for franchise relocations in the states located in the Ninth Circuit's jurisdiction, a professional sports league may not have to justify a restrictive relocation rule with an objective analysis, as long as it can identify sufficient procompetitive effects to counterbalance the negative effects of the rule.

In addition to league efforts to restrict relocation, the soon-to-be-abandoned host city will often try to retain its team. The City of Oakland attempted to use its power of **eminent domain**—the power of the government to appropriate private property for public use without the owner's consent—to take ownership of the Raiders and thus prevent them from moving to Los Angeles. However, a California appellate court ruled that such a taking would be unconstitutional because of the inhibitory negative effect it could have on interstate commerce by enabling the city to prevent the team's relocation out of Oakland indefinitely (*City of Oakland v. Oakland Raiders*, 1985).

Perhaps the most effective way for a city to protect its investment in a professional sports franchise and encourage a team to stay put is to include a liquidated damages clause in the facility lease contract that would require a team to pay several million dollars to the city if it breaches the lease agreement by relocating elsewhere. Cities that have brought breach of contract lawsuits based on a facility lease have also succeeded in persuading courts to enjoin a team from playing home games elsewhere until the expiration of the lease (see, e.g., *City of New York v. New York Jets Football Club, Inc.*, 1977; *City of New York v. New York Yankees*, 1983; *Metropolitan Sports Facilities Commission v. Minnesota Twins Partnership*, 2002).

Competitive Advantage STRATEGIES

Working Within Antitrust Law

If you are considering adopting league-wide rules regarding team ownership or franchise location, be sure to ask an attorney familiar with antitrust law to help you determine how to define the relevant market. Also seek help with weighing the projected anticompetitive effects of your new rule versus the projected procompetitive effects on economic competition within that market. Share with your attorney any sport-related case law of which you are aware that seems analogous to your proposed issue. Ask her to share with you the most recent case precedent in your jurisdiction. With all this information, you and your lawyer can attempt to predict how a court would decide your case if your rule were challenged under the antitrust laws. This will give you guidance as to whether to adopt your proposed rule, to alter it, or to abandon the idea.

Rival Leagues

American professional team sports tend not to sustain more than one professional league per sport for very long. When new leagues threaten existing leagues, the existing leagues have occasionally taken steps to preserve their market position that risk violating antitrust law. In the past, leagues have attempted to thwart rivals in several ways, including: (1) using cross-ownership rules to limit initial investment capital; (2) restricting the supply of players through the use of a reserve clause; (3) tying up television contracts to limit media exposure; and (4) limiting the availability of sites for rival teams by adding expansion teams or controlling playing facilities.

Using cross-ownership rules to limit initial investment capital

In *North American Soccer League v. National Football League* (1982), the fledgling professional soccer league NASL claimed that the NFL's ban on cross-ownerships violated § 1 of the Sherman Act because it prevented NASL clubs' access to a substantial segment of the market supply of investors with sufficient sport management skill and capital to become owners of a pro team. The court agreed that the cross-ownership ban was anticompetitive because it would have kept at least some NASL teams from competing effectively with the NFL for spectators and television revenue. Therefore, the Second Circuit remanded the case with instructions for the lower court to enter a permanent injunction prohibiting the NFL's ban.

Restricting the supply of players

One way the supply of players has been limited is through the use of a **reserve clause** in player contracts that functions to give teams a perpetual right to keep their players unless traded or released. The NHL's use of a reserve clause in the standard contract was challenged by the rival upstart World Hockey League as an illegal monopolization effort because it restricted the available pool of capable professional hockey players (*Philadelphia World Hockey Club, Inc. v. Philadelphia Hockey Club, Inc.,* 1972). The court agreed that the NHL's intent was to maintain its monopoly over the supply of major league hockey players and thus its position as the only major professional hockey league. The court therefore issued a preliminary injunction against the enforcement of the NHL's reserve clause.

Restricting television exposure

Another suit by an upstart league against the NFL was brought by the United States Football League (USFL), alleging that the NFL exercised illegal monopoly power by entering into television contracts with all three major networks (thus tying them up) and pressuring them to refuse to broadcast USFL games (*United States Football League v. National Football League,* 1988). According to the USFL, acquiring a network contract was essential to its survival as a league, and the NFL's actions prevented them from doing so. The court found that the NFL's television contracts were not exclusive and that there was plenty of prime-time space left in which the networks could have broadcast USFL games. It further found that the USFL had moved several teams out of desirable television markets into smaller cities and had changed from a spring to a fall playing season, putting it into direct competition with the NFL, and that these changes had reduced the USFL's attractiveness to investors and the television networks. The court concluded that these management decisions were the real reason that the USFL lacked a network television contract and affirmed the jury's verdict in favor of the NFL.

Restricting playing sites

In another suit against the NFL, the upstart American Football League claimed that the NFL's expansion by adding new teams in Dallas and Minneapolis was an unlawful effort to monopolize pro football. Section 2 of the Sherman Act prohibits predatory or anticompetitive conduct designed to enable the willful acquisition or maintenance of monopoly power in a relevant market. In this case, the NFL already had 12 teams in 11 other cities at the time of the expansion, and the AFL had eight teams in eight cities. The court found that 31 American cities had a sufficient population base to make them desirable sites for franchises and that the NFL occupied 11 of those, so the AFL could compete for the other 20.

Moreover, in the court's view, the relevant geographic market in which franchises could be established was not limited to those 31 cities but was actually nationwide. It further found that when in direct competition for the same site, each league had won once. Also, the fact that the NFL already occupied the most desirable cities could not be held against it simply because it happened to have been first on the scene. Under the law, an entity that has natural monopoly power because of the success of its business is allowed to enjoy and build on that power unless it misuses that power to further its monopoly. In the court's words, "[w]hen one has acquired a natural monopoly by means which are neither exclusionary, unfair, nor predatory, he is not disempowered to defend his position fairly" (*American Football League v. National Football League,* 1963, p. 131). The court concluded that the NFL had not monopolized the market for professional football.

Exclusive facility leases are another means of restricting playing sites. In *Hecht v. Pro-Football, Inc.* (1977), the D. C. Circuit Court found that the Washington Redskins' 30-year exclusive-use lease of Robert F. Kennedy (RFK) Stadium was a restrictive covenant that could violate the **essential facility doctrine.** This doctrine holds that refusing to share an essential facility that would be economically unfeasible for a would-be competitor to duplicate, when that refusal would constitute a severe impediment to prospective market entrants, is an unreasonable restraint of trade. The court found that the plaintiff presented sufficient evidence that in 1965 RFK Stadium was indeed the only stadium in the area suitable for professional football and that for the Redskins to share the stadium with an AFL franchise was practical as long as proper agreements were made regarding scheduling, use of locker rooms, and so forth. The case was remanded for a new trial in light of these findings.

Regulation of Equipment

Often pro sports teams sign exclusive contracts with equipment suppliers. Whether exclusive contracts constitute illegal use of monopoly power has also been addressed in the courts. In *Schutt Athletic Sales Co. v. Riddell, Inc.* (1989), the NFL had granted an exclusive right to Riddell to place its logo on its football helmets used during NFL games. Under the terms of the contract, players who wore helmets manufactured by other companies were not allowed to display those companies' logos on their helmets. The plaintiff alleged that high school and college consumers would make helmet purchase decisions based on what they saw the pro football players were using. The court ruled that the plaintiff had not provided sufficient evidence that this exclusive contract would adversely affect competition in such a broad market and upheld the contract.

GOVERNANCE OF PROFESSIONAL INDIVIDUAL SPORTS

Professional individual sports have very different organizational structures than professional team sports. Differences in organizational structure mean that governance of individual sports will also differ from governance of professional team sports. For example, because individual sport athletes are not employees, employment discrimination and labor laws are not applicable to them, nor is the labor exemption from antitrust law (see Chapter 9). However, following the Supreme Court's decision in *PGA Tour, Inc. v. Martin* (2001; see Chapter 16) touring pros are likely to be considered contestants with the right to be protected from discrimination in access to tournament play under the place of public accommodations provisions in several civil rights statutes.

Organizational Structure

Professional individual sports are generally organized around events or combinations of events into tours, and they are often governed by players associations comprised of active players and other stakeholders, such as tournament directors. These athletes are not "owned" by a team and are not salaried employees, but must earn their keep by winning prize money and garnering appearance fees. For example, the WTA (Women's Tennis Association) Tour, governed by an eight-person board of directors, is the major professional tennis tour for women. In 2008, more than 2,200 players from 96 nations competed for $86 million in prize money at 51 tour events and 4 grand slams held in 31 countries (WTA, 2009). The Ladies Professional Golf Association (LPGA), the major professional golf tour for women, has been operational since 1950. In 2009, the LPGA Tour included 31 events with prize money totaling over $49 million (LPGA, 2009). The LPGA is a nonprofit organization governed by a commissioner and the LPGA board of directors. The men's Professional Golfers' Association Tour (PGA Tour) is also a nonprofit organization. In 2005, the PGA Tour offered 48 official tournaments with over $250 million in prize money. It also operates with a commissioner (PGA Tour, 2005).

Control of Events

The person or entity in charge of an individual sports event is typically known as the owner, producer, or promoter of the event and is entitled to all the revenue unless it has agreed to share with other entities. For example, a contractual arrangement may be made so that concessions revenues are shared with the facility owner or parking revenues are shared with the host city.

When a players association or organized tour is involved, the producer of an individual event will generally have to agree to players association or tour rules about how the event is operated. Players associations often "sanction" or officially recognize certain events and not others as counting toward player rankings, and they may require event producers to pay a fee for the privilege of being a sanctioned event. The event producer usually also has to yield some control over an event to the players association or tour. For example, the producer may give up the authority to select officials, schedule the event independent of the tour schedule, or control who is eligible to participate. Finally, the event producer may have to agree to surrender certain revenue-generating processes to the tour, such as the sale of exclusive sponsorship signage and advertising rights or the negotiation of television contracts. Nevertheless, the event producer often retains significant responsibilities for staging the event, such as procuring equipment, arranging for parking and transportation to the venue(s), providing security systems and personnel, arranging for concessions services, and handling operations during the event. The complexity of the relationships among the event producer, players association, and tour organization often makes it difficult to say who is actually "producing" the event.

The *Volvo* case is one in which the complex relationships discussed here caused the district court judge to believe that antitrust law did not apply to the dispute. The circuit court reinstated the claims dismissed by the district court, finding sufficient evidence to support the pleadings. After the case was remanded to the district court, the parties settled out of court, so a trial on the merits did not take place. Nevertheless, the case serves to illustrate the challenges of applying antitrust law to sports tours where it may be difficult to identify who really controls events—and thus also difficult to identify the procompetitive and anticompetitive effects of the parties' actions.

Volvo North America Corp. v. Men's International Professional Tennis Council

857 F.2d 55 (2nd Cir. 1988)   **FOCUS CASE**

FACTS

The plaintiffs, Volvo, IMG, and ProServ, were owners and producers of certain men's professional tennis events. The Men's International Professional Tennis Council (MIPTC), the precursor to the Association of Tennis Professionals (ATP), along with the International Tennis Federation (ITF), sanctions and schedules professional tennis events, including Davis Cup events and Grand Prix events including the four grand slam tournaments. At the time this lawsuit was filed, Volvo had owned, produced, and sponsored only sanctioned tournaments, but IMG and ProServ had owned and produced both sanctioned events and non-sanctioned special events. A rival tour, World Championship Tennis (WCT), had owned eight Grand Prix events before being integrated into the Grand Prix as the result of an earlier antitrust lawsuit. Volvo had been the overall sponsor of the Grand Prix tournament series for several years but was passed over by the MIPTC in 1984 in favor of another sponsor. In 1985, Volvo assigned its contract rights with Madison Square Garden and NBC to the MIPTC. In exchange, the MIPTC agreed to sanction one of Volvo's tennis events on the condition that Volvo agree not to sponsor any special events in the United States during other Grand Prix tournaments or in any Grand Prix host city. After that agreement was reached, a senior administrator of the MIPTC allegedly attempted to intimidate tournament owners and producers into avoiding any association with Volvo in future Grand Prix events.

Volvo, IMG, and ProServ sued the MIPTC under antitrust laws, claiming that several MIPTC rules limited their ability to compete with events sanctioned by the MIPTC and owned and produced by the WCT. One such rule required tennis players who wanted to compete in any Grand Prix event to sign a Commitment Agreement that required them to participate in an expanded minimum number of Grand Prix tournaments and to limit their participation in nonsanctioned events. Another required owners and producers of sanctioned events to agree to contribute to a bonus pool of money used to reward players who performed well at sanctioned events. The district court found no claim upon which relief could be granted, seeing no evidence of an antitrust violation, and dismissed the case after the pleadings stage.

HOLDING

On appeal, the Second Circuit reversed and remanded the case back to the district court, finding that sufficient evidence existed to support a complaint for violations of antitrust law.

RATIONALE

The court found that the complaint adequately alleged that the MIPTC engaged in price fixing, horizontal market division, and group boycott behavior under § 1 of the Sherman Act, as well as monopolization, attempted monopolization, and conspiracy to monopolize under § 2. The plaintiffs had alleged that event producers had to agree to ceilings on player compensation in order to get their event sanctioned, and the court said that, if true, this was price fixing. The court also found that the MIPTC's agreement with the WCT when it was integrated into the Grand Prix divided the market between the two formerly competing tennis circuits through their arrangement to schedule their respective events in different cities and during different weeks, thus giving the WCT preferential treatment over other event producers such as Volvo. The court further found evidence of a group boycott in the players' Commitment Agreements, which prevented participation by any player who did not accept the conditions imposed in that agreement. Moreover, the extraction of Commitment Agreements from players, the earlier merger with the WCT, and the required contributions to the bonus pool all served to support the plaintiff's § 2 monopolization claims. Thus, the circuit court reinstated Volvo's case and remanded it back to the district court to allow it to go forward. It was later settled out of court.

The *Volvo* case serves to illustrate the fact that antitrust law may present limits on a professional tour's ability to control the events in its sport.

As we saw in the *Volvo* case, antitrust law has implications for how managers handle competition from rival tours. In *JamSports v. Paradama Productions, Inc.* (2005), the event control issue was whether Clear Channel Communications, Inc. violated the law in taking actions to prevent JamSports from competing as a new entrant in the professional motocross tour market. JamSports brought claims under antitrust law as well as claims of tortious interference with contract.

In this case, JamSports had entered into a 90-day exclusive negotiating period with the American Motorcyclist Association (AMA) regarding a contract to be the exclusive promoter for AMA Pro Racing's "supercross" dirt bike events. Clear Channel, the previous promoter, attempted to derail the deal during that 90-day period by such means as: approaching AMA Pro to attempt to get the contract for itself even though aware of the agreement for an exclusive negotiating period; attempting to lock up several supercross stadiums so JamSports would be unable to promote its tour at those venues by "arm-twisting" the facility managers, using leverage from the other motorsports events and concert business arms of Clear Channel; and attempting to close a deal with the international federation for motorcycle sports to start a rival supercross tour, which would subject AMA Pro to risk of expulsion from the international federation if it contracted with JamSports.

The court granted summary judgment in favor of Clear Channel on JamSports' claim that Clear Channel had violated the essential facilities doctrine, finding instead that there were several adequate stadiums from which JamSports had not been blocked. However, it found that a reasonable jury could conclude that had Clear Channel not prevented JamSports from promoting AMA Pro's tour, both companies would have promoted competing series, resulting in increased fan consumption opportunities and potentially lower ticket prices—procompetitive effects. The court therefore denied Clear Channel's motion for summary judgment that was based on the idea that JamSports could not show antitrust-type injury. Moreover, based on the strong-arm tactics Clear Channel used to try to lock up key stadiums, the court found sufficient evidence of conduct intended to hinder competition to allow JamSports' § 2 monopolization claim to survive a motion for summary judgment (*JamSports*, 2004).

When the case was finally tried, the jury found that Clear Channel had knowingly interfered with JamSports' prospective contract for its own competitive advantage, but it then inexplicably rejected JamSports' antitrust claims. The jury assessed compensatory damages of over $17 million and punitive damages of $73 million against Clear Channel for tortiously interfering with the contract and for doing the same to gain prospective competitive advantage. It also assessed compensatory damages of $169,000 against AMA Pro for breaching its prospective contract with JamSports. In a later appeal, the district court expressed its view that the jury had rejected the antitrust claims because it was confused by the complexity of the issues. To address the confusion and render a coherent ruling, the court reversed the judgment on the interference with prospective competitive advantage claim and ordered a new trial on the issue of damages with respect to the regular tortious interference with contract claim (*JamSports*, 2005).

As was evident in the *JamSports* case, courts are willing to review the authority of professional sports tours to control their events in legal contexts other than antitrust challenges. In another example, the U. S. Supreme Court intervened in the governance of professional golf by overturning the PGA Tour's decision to deny a waiver of one of its rules in the context of a disability discrimination lawsuit. In *PGA Tour, Inc. v. Martin* (2001), the tour had denied Casey Martin a waiver of its rule that players must walk the course. He had requested to be permitted to ride in a golf cart due to a debilitating circulatory disorder that made it extremely painful and dangerous for him to walk far. Martin sued the tour under the Americans with Disabilities Act, and the Court held in his favor. According to the Court, the PGA Tour's walking rule was a peripheral rule that had nothing to do with the essence of golf, which is shot-making. Therefore, waiving the walking rule would not work a fundamental alteration in the rules of golf that would constitute an unreasonable accommodation of Martin's disability. The Court thus held that in Casey Martin's case, a waiver of the walking rule was a reasonable accommodation and affirmed the decision of the Ninth Circuit ruling that the PGA Tour must allow him to ride in a cart.

Regulation of Equipment

Most professional sports have rules specifying what counts as acceptable equipment and what is considered illegal equipment. Equipment that would confer an unfair advantage, present safety concerns, or fundamentally alter the nature of the sport is likely to be prohibited. Occasionally, the justification for an equipment restriction is less clear, and the equipment manufacturer will bring suit alleging that the rule prohibiting its equipment is an unreasonable restraint of trade. The *Gunter Harz* case provides an example of the arguments that may be made by both sides in a dispute about the appropriateness of a new development. Here, the development pertains to tennis racquet stringing.

Gunter Harz Sports, Inc. v. United States Tennis Association, Inc.

FOCUS CASE   511 F. Supp. 1103 (D. Neb. 1981)

FACTS

The United States Tennis Association (USTA) is the recognized sanctioning organization for amateur and professional tournament tennis in America. It is a member of the International Tennis Federation (ITF), which is the organization recognized by the International Olympic Committee as the international governing body for the sport of tennis. The ITF is responsible for upholding the uniform international Rules of Tennis that it promulgates. Changes to the Rules of Tennis can be made only upon a two-thirds majority vote of the ITF's Committee of Management. The USTA is bound to adhere to ITF rules in order to ensure its athletes' eligibility for international competition.

During the early 1970s, a new method of stringing a tennis racquet, called "double stringing," was developed that imparted significantly greater spin on the ball and hence greater control. After conducting an inquiry into the effects of double stringing, as well as taking notice of player threats to boycott the French Open Championship to protest its use, the ITF's Committee voted to issue a temporary ban on the use of racquets with that string pattern to give the ITF more time to conduct research on its effects on match play. Two weeks later, the USTA announced that it would honor the ITF's temporary ban.

Approximately seven months later, the ITF announced that it would be introducing a new rule on acceptable tennis racquet specifications. This rule would include a provision requiring stringing patterns to conform to specifications that would outlaw double stringing. According to the ITF, the purpose of this rule was to prevent undue spin on the ball that could result in a fundamental change in the character of the game of tennis. The vote passed by the two-thirds majority needed, and therefore all national associations belonging to the ITF, including the USTA, were expected to adopt the new rule.

Meanwhile, the manufacturer of a double-strung racquet had begun marketing its racquet and stringing kits. After the new rule was adopted, the manufacturer sued under § 1 of the Sherman Act, claiming that the rule was the result of a group boycott by the tennis governing bodies intended to restrain trade in the manufacture and distribution of this new racquet and stringing kit.

HOLDING

The court held that the USTA's endorsement of the temporary ban and ultimate adoption of the new rule were rationally related to legitimate goals and did not constitute an unreasonable restraint of trade under § 1.

RATIONALE

As a preliminary matter, the court dismissed the idea that the USTA was "forced" to adopt the ITF's rule as a condition of membership, saying that acquiescence in an illegal scheme is just as illegal as creating it. It then went on to apply the rule of reason analysis, which entailed deciding on four issues:

1. Whether the concerted action by the governing bodies was intended to accomplish an end consistent with the policy
2. Whether the action was reasonably related to that goal
3. Whether the action was narrowly tailored to achieving that goal
4. Whether procedural safeguards were in place to prevent arbitrariness and allow for judicial review

First, it found that the collective action in adopting the ban and ultimately the new rule was intended to accomplish the legitimate goals of preserving the essential character and integrity of the game of tennis and of preserving competition by attempting to govern the game in an orderly manner with uniform rules. Second, the court found that the actions of the ITF and USTA were reasonably related and indeed necessary to preserving the character of the game by preventing exaggerated spin on the ball. Third, it determined that the temporary ban was narrowly tailored to ensuring that the game was conducted in an orderly manner, and that an appeals procedure was built into the rule so that a case-by-case determination could be made as to whether an individual racquet met the acceptable standard. Finally, the court found that the actions of the USTA were procedurally adequate with regard to the plaintiff because they did provide a reasonable response to him in a letter when he finally requested an appearance to promote his product. Thus, the court held that the USTA had not violated the Sherman Act.

Competitive Advantage

STRATEGIES

Governance of Professional Individual Sports

- In the *Martin* case, we see the Supreme Court overriding the PGA Tour's authority, as the governing body of professional golf in the United States, to define the rules of its sport. Taken together, the *Volvo, JamSports,* and *Martin* cases show that if you are an event producer or tour operator, you must be careful to consider a variety of potential legal challenges when making decisions about rules to control your event(s). Familiarize yourself with the implications of antitrust, contract, tort, and other laws for decisions about event control so that you will be able to exercise foresight in decision making and avoid costly litigation and negative publicity.

- If you are a manager in an individual sport that has not yet regulated equipment but is moving that direction, be sure to identify strong, legitimate policy reasons to support your regulation, and ensure that your regulation is not overbroad but goes no further than necessary to accomplish your policy goals.

- If you are working at the management level in an individual professional sport, invite your lawyer to meet with your executive board to share his perspective on how antitrust law might apply to your activities, and use this information when creating or changing rules and policies.

- When designing, modifying, and implementing disciplinary procedures, find a way to avoid the *"Blalock"* problem of active athletes subjectively imposing sanctions on fellow competitors.

Most of the time, as in *Gunter Harz,* courts grant substantial deference to sport organizations' decisions that regulate equipment. For example, in *Weight-Rite Golf Corp. v. United States Golf Association* (1991), a ban on a wedged shoe designed to improve weight distribution during the golf swing was upheld. However, occasionally a court interferes with such decisions. In *Gilder v. PGA Tour* (1991), the court affirmed a preliminary injunction striking down a ban on clubs with U-shaped grooves on the face instead of the usual V-shaped grooves. In *Gilder,* there was conflicting evidence as to the degree to which the new design improved players' scores by enabling them to impart more spin on the ball. Several players testified that the clubs with the U-shaped grooves imparted more control, thus decreasing the level of skill required to keep golf shots in the fairways and taking away the advantage previously possessed by those with more skill. In fact, 60 percent of the tour players polled supported the ban on these clubs. However, conflicting testimony came from other players who felt the shape of the grooves was irrelevant. The appellate court held that the lower court had not abused its discretion in issuing a preliminary injunction until a full trial on the merits could be completed.

It is difficult to distinguish the *Gilder* court's reasons for overturning the PGA Tour's ban from the courts' affirmations of similar bans in the *Gunter Harz* and *Weight-Rite* cases. *Gilder* may stand for the proposition that sports governing bodies may be subject to challenge if they attempt to ban equipment that does not have significant game-altering potential. The lesson for managers is probably that it is important to marshal evidence justifying equipment regulations in case you are sued and the court decides to question your decision.

Gilder notwithstanding, rules specifying acceptable equipment standards are rarely challenged in court. For example, MLB regulates materials in bats and sizes of gloves, and the United States Golf Association continues to regulate golf club design. The question we are left with is this: what is acceptable technological development and what changes the game enough in an undesirable direction that a ban would be justified? New composite frames have certainly changed the game of tennis from the way it was when all the racquets were made of wood, but those changes were seemingly considered acceptable because, unlike the double stringing in *Gunter Harz,* the new frames were not prohibited.

Now, let's examine a hypothetical case in which a technological development does not alter the game of golf significantly.

considering . . .

Shalloway, Inc. designs, manufactures, and sells a golf club called the Longshot. The shaft of the Longshot is made with new technology that enables a golfer consistently to drive the ball 10 yards farther than with a traditional driver. The United States Golf Association (USGA) governs the game of golf in the United States, Canada, and Mexico, and it is the source of the Official Rules of Golf adhered to in those countries. The Royal & Ancient Golf Club of St. Andrews (R & A) plays the same role in Europe.

The USGA bans the Longshot as a nonconforming club—that is, the club does not conform to the USGA's rules regulating acceptable equipment. The R & A, however, finds the club acceptable. As a result of the USGA's ban, pro shops at golf courses throughout the United States are unwilling to stock many of the Longshot clubs, which will harm Shalloway's business prospects.

Questions

- If Shalloway sues the USGA claiming that the ban constitutes an unreasonable restraint of trade under § 1 of the Sherman Act, how is the court likely to rule?

- How would it affect your analysis if the USGA and the R & A entered into an agreement, in the interest of international parity, to jointly ban the Longshot?

Note how you would answer the questions and then check your responses using the Analysis & Discussion at the end of this chapter.

Disciplinary Authority

Disciplinary authority in individual sports presents an interesting dilemma: active players may be in a position to make disciplinary decisions affecting their fellow competitors. This was the case in *Blalock v. Ladies Professional Golf Association* (1973). Professional golfer Jane Blalock was observed by monitors to have illegally moved her ball during tournament play. Blalock's penalty for cheating was decided by the LPGA's Executive Board, which was comprised of five active fellow golfers. Initially, the board recommended that Blalock be fined $500 and put on probation for the remainder of the season. A few days later, the members of the board changed their minds and imposed a one-year suspension instead of the shorter probation period. Blalock sued the LPGA, claiming that her suspension was a group boycott that was a per se restraint of trade. Under the LPGA rules, a member could not compete for prize money in non–LPGA sanctioned tournaments, so Blalock's suspension completely restrained her ability to earn a living as a player for one year.

The court held that the suspension was indeed a per se, or obvious, restraint of trade that did not require application of the rule of reason analysis. Central to the court's holding was the fact that Blalock's penalty was determined by her competitors in a completely subjective manner, which could have been motivated by self-interest in eliminating her as a competitor for a while. The defendants argued that two prior cases established precedent for the idea that disciplinary action in a self-regulated sport did not violate antitrust law (*Molinas v. National Basketball Association,* 1961; *Deesen v. Professional Golfers' Association of America,* 1966). However, the court distinguished those two cases on the basis that in neither was a majority of the decision makers comprised of active competitors.

Because professional individual sport athletes serve on the executive boards of their players associations, they have an influential voice in shaping governance policies, including provisions establishing disciplinary procedures. Although professional tennis is not known for having a large drug abuse problem, the men's players association—the Association of Tennis Professionals (ATP)—voluntarily implemented a drug-testing program in the late 1980s that focused on recreational drugs. In 1990, testing was extended to performance-enhancing drugs (International Tennis Federation, 2005).

The sport of tennis seems to be serious about its drug policy. In 2004, the ATP issued the maximum-length two-year suspension to #491 ranked player Diego Hipperdinger for testing positive for cocaine, in addition to requiring him to forfeit all ranking points and prize money earned since the date of his positive test (Association of Tennis Professionals, 2004). Hipperdinger appealed his case to the international Court of Arbitration for Sport (CAS; see Chapter 12). The panel upheld the two-year suspension as reasonable in length and stated that Hipperdinger should have known better than to chew unknown leaves for several days in Chile without inquiring as to what they were. Because he had an otherwise clean drug history and there was some question as to the accidental nature of his cocaine consumption, the CAS allowed his two-year suspension to start from the date of the urine sample collection instead of from the date of the decision by the original antidoping tribunal. Thus, his suspension was cut short by approximately five months (*Hipperdinger v. ATP Tour, Inc.,* 2005).

The International Tennis Federation manages, administers, and enforces the tennis antidoping program at all ATP-sanctioned events since 2006 and at WTA events since 2007. This is done in full compliance with the World Anti-Doping Agency (WADA) Code. (See Chapter 12 on governance of Olympic sport for more details on WADA.) Appeals are to be brought to the CAS rather than in an American court of law (International Tennis Federation, "The tennis anti-doping programme," n.d.). In 2008, both the LPGA and the PGA Tours implemented their own drug testing programs (Sirak, 2008). Both organizations also joined with other golf governing bodies worldwide to adopt a model antidoping policy effective in 2008 (LPGA, "Leading golf organizations come together," n.d.).

CONCLUSION

Many aspects of professional sport governance can raise legal issues, particularly in the area of antitrust law. Although many of the governance issues facing professional team sport managers differ from those that a manager of professional individual sport tours will confront, the underlying legal principles are similar. Governance activity relative to professional sports organizations is fraught with risks of running afoul of the Sherman Act because governing body decision making often has economic consequences—often intentionally so since the purpose of professional sport is to make a profit by providing an entertainment product. The more managers of professional sport organizations know about the potential legal ramifications of their policies and rule making, the better able they will be to compete successfully in the sport industry.

discussion questions

1. It is arguable that the court in *Mid-South Grizzlies v. NFL* (1983) ignored the anticompetitive effect of the NFL's franchise rejection on football fans. Refusing to expand the league to accommodate fan demand for additional franchises would have a negative effect on competition by denying those fans consumption opportunities. Adding a franchise ought to increase intrabrand (within-league) economic competition among NFL clubs; at the very least, it wouldn't reduce such competition. Was this case decided correctly?

2. Would reducing intrabrand competition by limiting the number of franchises in a league actually have a procompetitive effect by increasing the potential for interbrand competition of the league with leagues in other sports that may have, for example, an overlapping season?

3. Would a league's unilateral decision to eliminate one or more economically inviable teams violate the antitrust laws by reducing intrabrand competition?

4. How would you distinguish between new composite materials for tennis racquet frames that have changed the game by adding more power and "double stringing" that would have changed the game by adding more control? Is there a real difference? According to tennis champion Martina Navratilova, the new frames have significantly changed the game because the much-improved groundstrokes make it very difficult for serve-and-volley players to succeed (*Tennis,* 2006). If not, can you speculate as to why technology changes in frames have not been challenged but double-strung racquets were banned?

5. In the *Blalock* case, the court found a per se violation of § 1 of the Sherman Act. If the court had applied the rule of reason balancing of the procompetitive and anticompetitive effects of the suspension, would Blalock still have come out the winner? If not, why not? Was *Blalock* wrongly decided?

learning activities

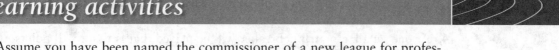

1. Assume you have been named the commissioner of a new league for professional women's football, the National Women's Football League (NWFL). You are considering trying to structure the NWFL as a single entity rather than as a traditional league. Examine the *Fraser v. Major League Soccer* (2002) and *Brown v. Pro-Football, Inc.* (1996) cases for clues as to what factors courts deem important in finding the existence of a legitimate single entity structure. Then write a two-column outline comparing the pros and

cons of the two league structures. Finally, write a two- to three-page memo to your prospective investors/team owners "selling them" on the virtues of your preferred structure. Be sure to read the McKeown (2009) law review article for additional information.

2. Legendary baseball player Pete Rose was banned for life from involvement with professional baseball for allegedly gambling on his sport. Using the Internet, find information about this. Was his punishment reviewed by an arbitrator? Did it get judicial review? Find information about the suspensions of John Rocker (Atlanta Braves) and Ron Artest and Jermaine O'Neal (Indiana Pacers), and compare their situations with that of Pete Rose. What justifies the huge disparity in their penalties?

3. If the NHL were to adopt a rule that each player must wear a safety helmet at all times while on the ice, could the league be liable under the antitrust laws for imposing an unreasonable restraint on trade if it handed down significant suspensions for players who broke the rule? If, on the other hand, the NHL does not adopt such a rule, is it potentially liable under other laws for failing to insist on proper safety equipment? The Commissioner of the NHL has asked you to develop a policy that he can seek to implement to address these issues. Draft that policy.

CASE STUDY

This case study is based on the trial proceedings for *Bryan v. ATP Tour, Inc.*, 2005 WL 2576512 (S.D. Tex. 2005).

The Executive Board of the Men's Professional Tennis Tour (MPTT) has announced changes to its rules pertaining to doubles play for the upcoming tour season. The Executive Board consists of three player representatives and three tournament directors. The MPTT "Doubles Enhancement" rules changes, listed below, apply to all MPTT Tour events except the four grand slam tournaments, which are not controlled by the MPTT. (However, grand slam seeding is determined by points accumulated during the previous 12 months of MPTT Tour competition.)

1. Sets will be first to five games instead of six.

2. Tie-breakers will be played at 4–4 instead of 6–6.

3. Instead of regular scoring, games will use no-ad scoring, meaning that at deuce, the receiving team will choose whether the serve will go to the deuce or ad court, and whoever wins the next point will win the game.

4. At one set all, a match tiebreaker will be played that is first to 10 points, win by two.

5. Players are prohibited from entering a doubles draw unless they also enter the singles draw, instead of being able to enter one or the other or both.

6. Doubles draws shall be seeded according to the players' combined singles and doubles rankings, instead of based on the players' best ranking in either singles or doubles.

The MPTT's stated goal in implementing these rule changes is to make doubles a more attractive and vital part of the men's pro tennis circuit, by making doubles matches shorter and of a more predictable length for ease in scheduling and more showcasing on feature courts; offering entertainment that will be more marketable to fans, sponsors, and television broadcasters; and making doubles matches less demanding in an attempt to attract more recognized players from the singles draw. The MPTT has included in press releases about the rules changes the following quote from the 2005 Master's Cup doubles champion: "It's better to play shorter doubles matches to encourage singles players to play more doubles. If the rules changes result in more singles players playing doubles, it will be better for the game, better for doubles, better for the tournament and the fans."

Not everyone feels the same way. As professional tennis has evolved, specialization has occurred, and high-level doubles play requires a very different set of skills from high-level singles play. Several of the world's top doubles players are doubles specialists who do not have very high singles rankings. In fact, very few highly ranked singles players play doubles, and many doubles specialists do not play singles at all. Many top-ranked singles players have stated that they would not be induced by the new rules to participate in doubles, because they prefer to concentrate their energy on their singles play.

Forty-five doubles specialists, led by Joe Dublin, have joined as plaintiffs to sue the MPTT. The plaintiffs have defined men's professional tennis as the relevant product market, with submarkets of singles and doubles. They contend that the new rules "will upset tradition and unfairly change the system to exclude doubles specialists in favor of singles players." The plaintiffs assert that not only will the new seeding system exclude doubles players in regular Tour events, it will also exclude most doubles players from the doubles draw at the grand slam events because those draws are seeded according to Tour rankings based on play during the preceding year.

Rules that have the effect of replacing doubles specialists with singles players in the doubles draw will increase the profits of tournament directors by reducing the costs of providing housing for a separate group of doubles players, reducing the costs of marketing and promoting doubles, and reducing the costs of offering lucrative prize money to compete with other tournaments for the best doubles entrants. The plaintiffs contend, therefore, that the tournament directors, who are business competitors, have joined in an agreement that unreasonably restrains trade under § 1 of the Sherman Act. They also claim that the new rules constitute a group boycott in violation of § 1 because they force out doubles specialists.

For their § 2 claim, the plaintiffs will have to prove that the MPTT is engaging in a willful attempt to assert or maintain monopoly power in the product market of men's professional tennis. Plaintiffs argue that the MPTT Tour enjoys monopoly power over men's professional tennis, including its submarkets of singles and doubles. They further argue that the new rules were enacted with a specific intent to ensure that the singles submarket enjoys monopoly power by destroying competition in the doubles submarket (tournaments will no longer have to compete for the best doubles players). This will harm consumers by turning doubles into a sideshow of singles players, providing a less skilled and therefore less attractive entertainment product. Effectively, doubles will be reduced from being its own legitimate sport to being a marketing tool—an opening act—for the singles tournaments.

The plaintiffs seek a permanent injunction against implementation of the new rules, as well as court costs, attorneys fees, and any further relief the court deems proper.

1. Are the plaintiffs likely to succeed on their § 1 claim?
2. Are the plaintiffs likely to succeed on their § 2 claim?
3. Should the MPTT's Executive Board reconsider the rule changes in light of the lawsuit?
4. If so, what new changes to the "Doubles Enhancements" would enable the MPTT to turn this situation into a public and player relations success story?

considering . . .   ANALYSIS & DISCUSSION

Equipment Standards (p. 285)

A § 1 violation requires concerted (joint) action in restraint of trade. Here, the USGA is acting alone, so the court would probably reject this claim. If, however, the USGA and the R & A agree to ban the Longshot, there is concerted action. The next question is whether that agreement unreasonably restrains trade. Following the rule of reason analysis used by the majority of courts and exemplified in the *Gunter Harz* case, the court would probably find the ban reasonable. First, the ban is intended to achieve international parity in equipment standards, thus ensuring a level playing field for golfers. Second, the ban seems reasonably related to that goal. Third, the ban seems narrowly tailored to accomplishing the stated goal, since there is no other way to protect against the advantage the club confers on those who use it. Fourth, there is no evidence of procedural unfairness to Shalloway, which successfully sells several other models of golf clubs. Thus, competition in the market for golf drivers is not unreasonably restrained by the ban on this one club. Therefore, the court would probably uphold the ban. However, if the court felt that the advantage conferred by the Longshot (a mere 10 yards) was not likely to alter the nature of the game significantly, following *Gilder* there is a possibility that it might find the ban unreasonable in relation to the golf organizations' stated goal and thus a violation of § 1.

REFERENCES

Cases

AFL v. NFL, 323 F.2d 124 (4th Cir. 1963).

American Needle, Inc. v. NFL, 538 F.3d 736 (7th Cir. 2008).

Baseball at Trotwood, L.L.C. v. Dayton Prof'l Baseball Club, L.L.C., Case No. C-3-98-260 (S.D. Ohio 1999) (unpublished opinion).

Blalock v. LPGA, 359 F. Supp. 1260 (N.D. Ga. 1973).

Brown v. Pro-Football, Inc., 518 U.S. 231 (1996).

Bryan v. ATP Tour, Inc., 2005 WL 2576512 (S.D. Tex. 2005)(trial pleadings).

Charles O. Finley & Co. v. Kuhn, 569 F.2d 527 (7th Cir. 1978), *cert. denied*, 439 U.S. 876 (1978).

Chicago National League Ball Club, Inc. v. Vincent, 1992 U.S. Dist. LEXIS 14948 (N.D. Ill. 1992).

City of NY v. New York Jets Football Club, Inc., 394 N.Y.S.2d 799 (N.Y. Sup. Ct. 1977).

City of NY v. New York Yankees, 458 N.Y.S.2d 486 (N.Y. Sup. Ct. 1983).

City of Oakland v. Oakland Raiders, 1985 Cal. App. LEXIS 2751 (Cal. Ct. App. 1985).

Deesen v. PGA, 358 F.2d 165 (9th Cir. 1966).

Fraser v. MLS, L.L.C., 284 F.3d 47 (1st Cir. 2002).

Gilder v. PGA Tour, Inc., 936 F.2d 417 (9th Cir. 1991).

Gunter Harz Sports, Inc. v. USTA, 511 F. Supp. 1103 (D. Neb. 1981), aff'd, 665 F.2d 222 (8th Cir. 1981).

Hecht v. Pro-Football, Inc., 570 F.2d 982 (D.C. Cir. 1977), cert. denied, 436 U.S. 956 (1978).

Hipperdinger v. ATP Tour, Inc., Arbitration CAS 2004/A/690 (2005).

JamSports v. Paradama Prods, Inc., 336 F. Supp. 2d 824 (N.D. Ill. 2004) (Motions for Summary Judgment); 382 F. Supp. 2d 1056 (N.D. Ill. 2005).

Law v. NCAA, 134 F.3d 1010 (10th Cir. 1998).

Los Angeles Mem'l Coliseum v. NFL (Raiders I), 726 F.2d 1381 (9th Cir. 1984), cert. denied, 469 U.S. 990 (1984).

Metropolitan Sports Facilities Comm'n v. Minnesota Twins P'ship, 638 N.W.2d 214 (Minn. Ct. App. 2002).

Mid-South Grizzlies v. NFL, 720 F.2d 772 (3rd Cir. 1983).

Molinas v. NBA, 190 F. Supp. 241 (S.D.N.Y. 1961).

NASL v. NFL, 670 F.2d 1249 (2nd Cir. 1982), cert. denied, 459 U.S. 1074 (1982).

National Football League Players Ass'n v. National Labor Relations Bd, 503 F.2d 12 (8th Cir. 1974).

NBA v. Artest, 2004 U.S. Dist. LEXIS 26249 (S.D.N.Y. 2004).

NBA v. Minnesota Prof'l Basketball, L.P., 56 F.3d 866 (8th Cir. 1995).

NBA v. SDC Basketball Club, Inc., 815 F.2d 562 (9th Cir. 1987).

PGA Tour, Inc. v. Martin, 532 U.S. 661 (2001).

Philadelphia World Hockey Club, Inc. v. Philadelphia Hockey Club, Inc., 351 F. Supp. 462 (E.D. Pa. 1972).

Piazza v. MLB, 831 F. Supp. 420 (E.D. Pa. 1993).

San Francisco Seals, Ltd. v. NHL, 379 F. Supp. 966 (C.D. Cal. 1974).

Schutt Athletic Sales Co. v. Riddell, Inc., 727 F. Supp. 1220 (N.D. Ill. 1989).

Sullivan v. NFL, 34 F.3d 1091 (1st Cir. 1994).

USFL v. NFL, 842 F.2d 1335 (2nd Cir. 1988).

Volvo N. Am. Corp. v. Men's Int'l Prof'l Tennis Council, 857 F.2d 55 (2nd Cir. 1988).

Weight-Rite Golf Corp. v. USGA, 766 F. Supp. 1104 (M.D. Fla. 1991).

Statutes

Sherman Act, 15 U.S.C. §§ 1–3 (2005).

Other Sources

Anon. (2005, September 2). Leading tennis doubles players bring antitrust suit against Association of Tennis Professionals. PR Newswire US. Retrieved June 14, 2009, from LEXIS-NEXIS.

Anon. (2006, January/February). The world according to Martina Navratilova. Tennis, p. 18.

Arcella, C. F. (1997). Note: Major League Baseball's disempowered commissioner: Judicial ramifications of the 1994 restructuring. Columbia Law Review, 97, 2420–2469.

Association of Tennis Professionals. (2004, July 23). Player suspended two years for doping offense. Retrieved October 7, 2005, from www.atptennis.com.

Friedman, A., & Much, P. J. (1997). 1997: Inside the ownership of professional sports teams. Chicago: Team Marketing Report.

International Tennis Federation. (2005). The tennis anti-doping programme. Retrieved June 14, 2009, from www.itftennis.com.

Ladies Professional Golf Association. (2009a). About the LPGA. Retrieved June 14, 2009, from www.lpga.com.

LPGA. (n.d.). Leading golf organizations come together for anti-doping. Retrieved June 14, 2009, from www.lpga.com/content_1.aspx?pid=12761&mid=4.

LPGA. (2009). LPGA 2009 tour schedule. Retrieved June 14, 2009, from www.lpga.com/tournaments_index.aspx.

Lentze, G. (1995). The legal concept of professional sports leagues: The commissioner and an alternative approach from a corporate perspective. Marquette Sports Law Journal, 6, 65–94.

Lite, J. (1999, May 13). DeBartolo, in complaint, demands rescission of 49ers sale to corporation. Associated Press State & Local Wire, Sports News. Retrieved January 8, 2006, from LEXIS-NEXIS.

McKeown, J. T. (2009). 2008 Antitrust developments in professional sports: To the single entity and beyond. Marquette Sports Law Review, 19, 363–393.

Professional Golfers' Association Tour. (2005). About us. Retrieved October 7, 2005, from www.pgatour.com.

Sanchez, R. J. (1994, September 30). MLB owes investors apologies, $6 million. USA Today, p. 11C.

Sirak, R. (2008, January 11). The truth about testing. Golf World. Retrieved June 14, 2009, from www.golfdigest.com/golfworld.

Walker, T. M. (2009, November 17). Goodell fines Titans owner $250,000 for gesture. *Associated Press*. Retrieved November 21, 2009, from http://news.lp.findlaw.com.

Women's Tennis Association. (2009). About the Sony Ericsson WTA Tour. Retrieved June 14, 2009, from www.sonyericsson.wtatour.com.

WEBSITE RESOURCES

www.itftennis.com/antidoping/ ▪ Antidoping policies, regulation of tours, and discipline of players have all made their way into the sports spotlight. The antidoping page on the International Tennis Federation's website lays out its policies, provides statistics and a list of prohibited substances, and gives updates on cases that involve member players.

http://www.lpga.com/content_1.aspx?pid=13555& mid=4 ▪ Organizations like the PGA and LPGA have the authority to regulate the rules of their sport and determine who can participate in it. In recent years, this has included the power to implement drug testing as part of antidoping measures. The LPGA website offers a collection of news updates related to antidoping efforts and information on the organization's drug-testing program, which began in 2008.

Governance Issues and Regulation of Participation in Olympic Sport

INTRODUCTION

T he purpose of the Olympic Movement is to contribute to world peace by educating youth through sport and by developing mutual understanding and a spirit of friendship and fair play. The Olympic Movement is also a moneymaker, generating more than $4 billion from broadcast rights, ticket sales, official sponsorships, and other marketing and licensing efforts during the 2001–2004 quadrennium (IOC, 2005). In the 2005–2008 quadrennium, broadcast revenue alone totaled $2.57 billion, and The Olympic Program (TOP) sponsorships generated $866 million (IOC, 2008). Governance of such a large and ongoing international undertaking is understandably complex. This chapter will examine the legal structure and relationships of the many governing bodies that participate in the Olympic Movement. It will also discuss the impact of the Amateur Sports Act of 1978, and the Ted Stevens Olympic and Amateur Sports Act of 1998, on Olympic governance within the United States. Finally, the authority of Olympic governing bodies to regulate events and participants will be examined. Exhibit 12.1 presents the management contexts, legal issues, and relevant law discussed in this chapter.

| EXHIBIT | 12.1 | Management contexts in which governance and regulation issues may arise, with relevant laws and cases. |

MANAGEMENT CONTEXT	MAJOR LEGAL ISSUES	RELEVANT LAW	ILLUSTRATIVE CASES
Authority of governing bodies	Personal jurisdiction	Civil procedure law	*Reynolds*
	Private right of action	Amateur Sports Act	*Sternberg*
	Judicial/arbitral review	Law of private associations	*Harding*
Regulation of events	Events included in program	Olympic Charter, antidiscrimination laws	*Martin*
	Team/nation participation	Constitution: review of political questions; Amateur Sports Act	*Spindulys, Ren-Guey, DeFrantz*
	Selection of host cities	IOC procedures	
	Sponsorship/advertising: use of Olympic trademarks	Olympic Charter, Amateur Sports Act, Lanham Act	*San Francisco Arts & Athletics, Intelicense*
	Security measures	4th Amendment	
Regulation of participants	Disputed competition outcomes	IOC rules	*Yang Tae-Young*
	Amateurism	Olympic Charter	
	Drug testing	WADA Code/IF rules	*R. v. IOC, C. v. FINA, USADA*
	Sex tests	IOC Medical Commission policy, sex discrimination laws	
	General competition rules	IOC rules	*Pistorius*
	Disciplinary action	Law of private associations	*Samoa NOC, Harding*

LEGAL STRUCTURE AND RELATIONSHIPS OF GOVERNING BODIES

T he governance of Olympic sport is quite complex because several layers of governing bodies are involved, some national and some international, as well as multiple governing bodies within each governance layer. The major governance layers are overseen by the following governing bodies: the International Olympic Committee (IOC), the national Olympic committees (NOCs), the international Olympic federations (IFs), the national governing bodies (NGBs), and the organizing committees for the Olympic Games (OCOGs). Their organizational relationships and governance responsibilities are illustrated in Exhibit 12.2 and are discussed in detail throughout the first section of this chapter. Information regarding the organizational structure of the Olympic Movement can be accessed at the IOC's website, located at www.olympic.org.

Legal Structure of Governing Bodies

International Olympic Committee

The governing body with overarching control over Olympic sport is the IOC, which is a nongovernmental, nonprofit organization. The Olympic Movement is comprised of organizations and individuals who agree to abide by the IOC's Olympic Charter, which codifies the by-laws and regulations of the IOC. The IOC consists of a maximum of 115 members elected from a list of nominees generated by the IOC Executive Board. The members are elected for renewable four-year terms. The Session, which is the general assembly of IOC members, meets annually (meetings have been open to the media only since reforms were enacted in 1999) and has the ultimate responsibility for amending and interpreting the Olympic Charter. A 15-member Executive Board oversees the administrative affairs of the IOC. The IOC President is elected by secret ballot of the IOC members for an eight-year term of office, which may be extended once for an additional four years (see www.olympic.org).

The IOC has exclusive ownership of all rights pertaining to the organization, marketing, reproduction, and broadcasting of the Olympic Games, and it may seek gifts and other resources needed to fulfill its mission. The IOC's regulatory decisions are final; however, the IOC has agreed to submit disputed decisions for final arbitration to the Court of Arbitration for Sport (CAS)—an international arbitral court originally created by the IOC in 1984. For enforcement of its decisions, the IOC relies primarily on courts and the NOCs.

International Olympic federations, national governing bodies, national Olympic committees, and organizing committees for the Olympic Games

The IFs, such as the International Association of Track & Field (IAAF) and the International Bobsleigh and Skeleton Association (FIBT), are independent, nongovernmental international organizations responsible for governing a particular Olympic sport or set of sports worldwide. Their regulatory activities, which must conform to the Olympic Charter, include establishing and enforcing competition rules and participant eligibility criteria for their sports, as well as providing

EXHIBIT   12.2   Organizational chart highlighting governance authority and responsibilities of sample Olympic governing bodies.

Court of Arbitration for Sport (CAS)

responsible to:
    International Council of Arbitration & Sport

responsible for:
    reviews legal disputes in international sport

International Olympic Committee (IOC)

responsible to:
    Olympic Charter, CAS review

responsible for:
    overarching control of all Olympic sport; controls all rights pertaining to Games, program of events

World Anti-Doping Agency (WADA)

responsible to:
    independent

responsible for:
    administers universal antidoping policy/testing

International Federation (IF)

example: International Judo Federation (IJF)

responsible to:
    Olympic Charter, CAS review

responsible for:
    governing judo worldwide competition, rules/eligibility, dispute resolution within judo/NGBs

International Paralympic Committee (IPC)

responsible to:
    IPC Constitution

responsible for:
    control of paralympic sport

National Olympic Committee (NOC)

example: United States Olympic Committee (USOC)

responsible to:
    IOC, Olympic Charter, laws of U.S., AAA review

responsible for:
    guiding Olympic movement in U.S., athlete selection to national teams, dispute resolution for NGBs/athletes, prevent violence/discrimination/substance abuse, control use of Olympic trademarks in U.S.

Organizing Committee for the Olympic Games (OCOG)

example: Atlanta Committee for the Olympic Games (ACOG)

responsible to:
    IOC Exec. Bd., Olympic Charter, contracts w/IOC, USOC, host city

responsible for:
    organizing and hosting Games, constructing venues & providing security for Games, preventing political disruptions of Games, ensuring adherence to competition rules

National Governing Body (NGB)

example: USA Judo

responsible to:
    Olympic Charter, USOC, IJFs competition/eligibility rules, U.S. laws

responsible for:
    governing judo within U.S., recommending athletes to USOC for selection to national team

internal dispute resolution procedures. The NGBs, such as USA Basketball, are the governing authorities for particular sports within each country. In addition to being subject to the laws of their respective countries, NGBs must comply with the Olympic Charter, the regulatory authority of their NOC, and the rules of the IF relevant to their sport(s).

The NOCs, such as the United States Olympic Committee (USOC), are charged with guiding the Olympic Movement within their respective countries. They are also independent, nongovernmental agencies and must comply with the Olympic Charter and the governing authority of the IOC, as well as being subject to the laws of their country. The NOCs select the athletes who will represent their countries at the Games, usually based on the recommendations of the NGBs. The NOCs are also responsible for preventing violence, discrimination, and participant use of substances banned by the IFs. As mentioned in Chapter 3, the American Arbitration Association provides information on its website concerning arbitration of Olympic athlete disputes.

An OCOG, such as the Organizing Committee for the Beijing 2008 Games (BOCOG), is formed by the NOC of the host city's country and is charged with organizing and carrying out the hosting of the Games. The OCOG must comply with the Olympic Charter, the IOC Executive Board's instructions, and its contractual agreements with the IOC, the NOC, and the host city. Among the OCOG's responsibilities are: constructing the facilities necessary for holding the Games, ensuring adherence to the competition rules of the IFs, preventing disruptive political demonstrations, and providing adequate security.

There are currently 205 NOCs distributed over five continents, and 33 IFs that govern sports on the menus for the Summer and Winter Games. Each NOC governs a wide array of NGBs (the USOC oversees 45 NGBs, for example). Additionally, as many as four OCOGs may be operating simultaneously, some in the planning stages, some in the operational phase, and some wrapping up the affairs of past Games.

Olympic Movement Partners

Two of the Olympic Movement Partners recognized by the IOC are important with respect to legal aspects of governance—the World Anti-Doping Agency (WADA) and the Court of Arbitration for Sport.

World Anti-Doping Agency

The WADA is an independent agency created in 1999 to implement a universal anti-doping policy that defines banned substances, drug-testing procedures, and penalties in order to harmonize the policies of the various IFs. The WADA Foundation Board is composed of representatives from the IOC, NOCs, and IFs, as well as Olympic athletes and representatives of governments from the five continents. More information about the WADA is presented later in the chapter in the section on drug testing.

Court of Arbitration for Sport

The Court of Arbitration for Sport was established by the IOC in 1984 and is based in Lausanne, Switzerland. Its purpose is to resolve legal disputes in international sport quickly through arbitration or mediation, using procedures adapted specifically to the needs of the international sport context. The intent is that the CAS provide a single adjudicating body that can bring consistency, and thus fairness, in applying the rules of the many international sport governing bodies. The IOC and all the Olympic IFs have agreed to be subject to the jurisdiction of the CAS, and the IFs require their NGBs and individual athletes to submit all disputes with the IF to the CAS. Parties must enter a written agreement to submit their dispute to the CAS for final resolution, and courts will generally enforce that agreement as final and therefore not subject to judicial review (see, e.g., *Raguz v. Sullivan,* 2000). Third parties, such as athletes whose interests may be affected by an arbitration ruling, are allowed to intervene in CAS proceedings. (The CAS website at www.tas-cas. org is a good source for information about topics covered in this section.)

Following allegations that the CAS was not sufficiently independent of the IOC to serve as a truly impartial arbiter, reforms were implemented in 1994. One of these was the establishment of the International Council of Arbitration and Sport (ICAS) to govern the operations of the CAS, manage its funds, and appoint its members, thereby removing these functions from the IOC. Also in 1994, the Code of Sports-Related Arbitration was promulgated to codify the operations and procedures of the CAS and ICAS.

This code provides for four different dispute resolution processes available under the auspices of the CAS:

1. Ordinary arbitration for legal disputes, such as a sponsorship contract dispute
2. Appeals arbitration for resolving appeals from final decisions of IFs
3. Consultation for advisory opinions on legal issues
4. Mediation

Parties in ordinary arbitration or appeals arbitration proceedings exchange written statements of the case and have an oral hearing before CAS arbitrators.

In all CAS proceedings, the parties may be represented by legal counsel and may choose who will hear their case from a pool of CAS arbitrators. Additionally, the parties may choose to agree on the rules of law to be applied by the CAS in their case. If none are so chosen, the proceedings are governed by Swiss law. CAS arbitration is final and binding, and it may be judicially enforced by courts in countries that have signed the New York Convention on the Uniform Enforcement of Foreign Arbitration Awards (see *Slaney v. IAAF,* 2001). The CAS may award damages and allocate legal costs. Finally, the CAS provides a three-person panel of arbitrators at each Olympic Games to enable resolution within 24 hours of disputes that arise onsite during the Games.

Significant recent decisions of the CAS are posted on its website at www. tas-cas.org. Archived cases are available for decisions rendered since 1986. Additionally, the website provides statistics for each year since the CAS was created that document numbers of filed arbitration requests, awards granted, and advisory opinions rendered. Also provided are annual numbers for ordinary arbitration and appeals arbitration cases filed compared to numbers decided. The numbers are always higher during the actual years the Games are held, but they jumped from 75 arbitration cases filed in the year 2000 and 83 in 2002 to 271 in 2004. Of those 271, 178 resulted in a CAS award decision or decision to terminate the case. In 2008, 311 requests for arbitration were filed and 92 had resulted in an award by the end of that year.

Relationships Among the Olympics-Related Governing Bodies

The multifaceted web of governing bodies creates major difficulties with regard to overlapping regulatory responsibilities, which are further complicated by differences in human rights and other laws among the participating nations. The resulting jurisdictional squabbles have often made it far from clear which governing body's "authority to regulate" in a given area is most legitimate and thus will be honored in a particular case. The jurisdictional problem is illustrated in *Reynolds v. International Amateur Athletic Federation* (1994), in which the IAAF, the USOC, and the U. S. federal courts all claimed conflicting authority to regulate in the area of athlete eligibility to compete.

In the case, Butch Reynolds, a 1988 Olympic medalist and world record-holding sprinter, tested positive in 1990 for the steroid Nandrolone, a substance banned by the International Amateur Athletic Federation (IAAF). As a result, the IAAF banned him from all international track events for two years, rendering him ineligible to compete in the 1992 Olympic Games in Barcelona. After suspending Reynolds, the IAAF, instead of notifying Reynolds of the situation, told the relevant NGB, The Athletics Congress of the United States (TAC, now USA Track & Field), to notify him and investigate the matter. To challenge his suspension, Reynolds requested relevant documents from the IAAF, but it told him he had to get them through TAC.

Reynolds immediately sued the IAAF, alleging that the drug test was administered negligently and that the results were erroneous. The U. S. District Court stayed his case after finding that he had not exhausted the administrative remedies provided in the Amateur Sports Act of 1978 or those provided by TAC. Reynolds then attempted to exhaust his administrative remedies by submitting his case to arbitration before the American Arbitration Association (AAA), as provided for by the Amateur Sports Act and the USOC Constitution. The AAA arbitrator found strong evidence that the tainted urine samples were not Reynolds' and exonerated him, but the IAAF refused to recognize this decision because the arbitration was not performed under its rules. Accordingly, it refused to remove the two-year suspension.

Reynolds then attempted to follow IAAF rules and appealed his suspension to TAC. The TAC Doping Control Review Board also exonerated him, finding the validity of the drug test to be suspect. The IAAF then decided to conduct an independent arbitration proceeding of its own. The IAAF arbitration upheld the validity of the drug tests and left Reynolds' suspension intact.

Reynolds again filed suit in his home state of Ohio alleging, among other things, breach of contractual due process and sought monetary damages and a temporary restraining order that would allow him to participate in track meets leading up to the U. S. Olympic trials to be held in June 1992. The IAAF refused to appear, arguing that the U. S. District Court in Ohio had no jurisdiction over the IAAF. The district court decided it did in fact have jurisdiction based on its determination that the IAAF and TAC had transacted business with Reynolds in Ohio. The court then issued a preliminary injunction ordering that Reynolds be allowed to participate in the Olympic trials.

The IAAF eventually responded by announcing that if Reynolds competed in the U. S. Olympic trials, every athlete who competed with him would be ineligible to compete in Barcelona. Finally, the USOC and the IAAF reached an agreement allowing Reynolds to participate in the trials, and he made the team as an alternate in the 400 meter relay. However, the IAAF refused to allow him to compete in the Barcelona Olympic Games, and so TAC removed him from the official team roster. Additionally, the IAAF increased the length of his suspension by four months to punish him for competing in the U. S. Olympic trials.

On the basis of these events, Reynolds filed a supplemental complaint with the district court, to which neither the IAAF nor TAC responded. The district court entered a default judgment in favor of Reynolds and awarded him over $27 million in damages, which included treble punitive damages against the IAAF for acting out of ill will, suppressing evidence, threatening Reynolds and other athletes, and vengefully extending Reynolds' suspension. The Sixth Circuit then reviewed the IAAF's motion to vacate the default judgment against it. The court reversed, holding—for several reasons—that the district court lacked jurisdiction over the IAAF.

THE AMATEUR SPORTS ACT OF 1978, AS AMENDED BY THE TED STEVENS OLYMPIC AND AMATEUR SPORTS ACT (OASA) OF 1998

The Amateur Sports Act of 1978 was enacted by Congress to revise the federal charter it originally granted to the USOC in 1950. To eliminate power struggles between American amateur sport governing bodies, the act vested the USOC with exclusive jurisdiction over participation and representation of the United States in the Olympic Games. The USOC has granted each NGB the exclusive right to determine athlete eligibility to participate in Olympic competition. Section 374 of the Amateur Sports Act grants authority to the USOC to resolve disputes involving the NGBs, amateur athletes, and amateur sports organizations, with the purpose of protecting the opportunities of athletes, coaches, and other relevant individuals to participate in amateur athletics.

The Supreme Court has ruled that the fact that Congress granted the USOC its corporate charter did not transform it into a **state actor.** A state actor is a government entity or an entity that, due to joint action or entwinement with government, may be said to act with the authority of the government. State action is a prerequisite to establishing that constitutional protection of individual rights has been violated, because the Bill of Rights protects citizens from government abuse, not mistreatment by private actors. Thus, constitutional protections of individual rights, such as freedom of expression, are not applicable to the USOC (*San Francisco Arts & Athletics, Inc. v. USOC*, 1987; see also *DeFrantz v. USOC*, 1980). Neither are NGBs considered state actors (*Behagen v. Amateur Basketball Association of the United States*, 1989; see also *Harding v. United States Figure Skating Association*, 1994).

In amending the Amateur Sports Act, the Ted Stevens Olympic and Amateur Sports Act (OASA) made a number of changes, one of which was expressly to locate responsibility within the USOC for governing U. S. activities related to the Paralympic and Pan-American Games. However, the Paralympics are not governed by the IOC and thus do not get a share of its revenue; instead, they are governed by the International Paralympic Committee. In contrast to the case in United States, in most countries, the Olympic NOC is not the same entity as the Paralympic NOC.

Section 220506 of the Stevens Act amendments also grants exclusive rights to the USOC to control the commercial use of Olympic trademarks within the United States, which may conflict with the IOC's ultimate right to its marks (see discussion of *USOC v. Intelicense Corp.*, 1984, later in this chapter). Further, § 220509 requires the USOC to establish regulations for resolving eligibility disputes and to employ an ombudsman who will provide cost-free advice to athletes and their attorneys in such disputes.

If an athlete is unhappy with the USOC's resolution, the act provides that the dispute may be submitted to the AAA for binding arbitration (§ 220529). This provision may conflict with the obligation to submit disputes to the CAS that NGBs and athletes have under the rules of the IFs. Therefore, an athlete who obtains a decision from the AAA may find to her dismay that the IF will choose to disregard that decision and insist that the athlete follows its rules by having the dispute arbitrated by the CAS. Refer to the *Reynolds* case for an example in which the IAAF disregarded the AAA's decision and conducted its own arbitration, which resulted in an outcome opposite to that of the AAA.

American courts have generally ruled that the OASA preempts judicial review in the form of state law challenges to USOC or NGB regulation of athlete eligibility (see *Slaney v. IAAF*, 2001; *Walton-Floyd v. USOC*, 1998), but they have upon occasion intervened in federal law race and gender discrimination claims (see *Sternberg v. USA National Karate-Do Federation, Inc.*, 2000; *Lee v. United States Taekwondo Union*, 2004). Courts also generally find that there is no **private right of action** under the statute, which means that individuals cannot use it to sue the USOC or NGBs for **injunctive relief** (i.e., a court order to rectify an injury) or damages (i.e., a monetary award to compensate them for an injury) (*DeFrantz v. USOC*, 1980). However, in a few cases courts have recognized a private right of action for federal law claims of race and sex discrimination. For a case to the contrary, see *Sternberg v. USA National Karate-Do Federation, Inc.*, 2000.

Given the complexity of international sport governance, courts have been reluctant to intervene in Olympic governing body decision making. However, in rare cases, courts are willing to review cases providing an athlete has first exhausted all administrative remedies (that is, she has pursued all internal and external grievance procedures mandated by the organization; see *Barnes v. IAAF*, 1993). Applying the law of private associations (also known as contractual due process; see also p. 266). U. S. courts are willing to rule on the issues of whether the USOC or an NGB met three conditions:

- followed its own rules
- provided appropriate due process
- was not arbitrary and capricious in applying its rules

(See *Lindemann v. American Horse Shows Association*, 1994; *Schulz v. United States Boxing Association*, 1997.)

For example, in *Harding v. U.S. Figure Skating Association* (1994), Tonya Harding's disciplinary hearing for her alleged misconduct in the incident that

Competitive Advantage

STRATEGIES

Relationships of Governing Bodies

If you work for an Olympic sport governing body, be sure you investigate and understand the interrelationships among the various governing bodies and their regulations. This will help to prevent you from inadvertently running afoul of important regulations that may apply to you simply by virtue of your organization's relationship with another governing body.

injured fellow Olympic skater Nancy Kerrigan was unfairly scheduled in contravention of the skating association's own by-laws. The court found that this procedural injustice justified judicial review. This case is discussed in more detail later in the chapter, in the section on disciplinary actions for rules violations.

REGULATION OF EVENTS

Authority to regulate the Olympic Games and its events varies by type of governing body. The following areas of authority to regulate events are discussed in this section: the program of sports and events offered; team/nation participation; determination of host cities, sponsorship, and advertising; and security measures.

Sports and Events Program for the Games

Under the Olympic Charter, the IOC retains the authority to decide which sports and specific events are included on the menu of events for the Summer and Winter Olympic Games. To have a chance for inclusion, a sport's IF must first petition for official recognition by the IOC and must adhere to the rules of the Olympic Movement's Anti-Doping Code. The IOC typically grants a two-year provisional recognition period in which it observes the IF in action, before making a decision as to whether to grant formal recognition. Then the recognized IF can petition to have its sport(s) included on the program of events for the Games. The IOC reviews the program of events after each Games to determine whether changes should be made. For example, in July 2005 the IOC voted to eliminate baseball and softball from the Olympic program after the 2008 Summer Games in Beijing (Wilson, 2005).

To be on the program for the Summer Games, a men's event must be practiced in at least 75 countries on four continents, and a women's event in at least 40 countries on three continents. For the Winter Games, an event must be practiced in at least 25 countries on three continents. Once the IOC has recognized the IF and deemed the sport's worldwide participation adequate, it considers such issues as number of potential competitors, spectator interest, and potential for revenue generation in deciding whether to support the new sport. For example, snowboarding was added in order to attract young viewers, as well as the promise of higher television ratings and increased sponsorship revenue that that target market brings (Hums & MacLean, 2009).

Sometimes politics is an important factor in determining the program of events. For example, ski jumping is currently the only Winter Olympics sport not open to women. When female ski jumpers asked to have their sport added to the program for the 2002 Salt Lake City Winter Olympics, the International Ski Federation did not support it, saying there were not enough competitors worldwide. Despite similar problems with the number of competitors, women's bobsledding was added in 1998 because many insiders were worried that the sport of bobsledding would be dropped from the Olympic program if it did not attract more competitors. The result of adding the women's bobsledding event was that many more women were attracted to participate (Boyce, 2002).

IOC authority to determine inclusion of events has rarely faced a legal challenge. In *Martin v. IOC* (1984), the Ninth Circuit refused to interfere in the IOC's decision not to include 5,000 and 10,000 meter track events for women, holding that the plaintiffs did not have a strong likelihood of success in proving a violation of state and constitutional antidiscrimination laws. Additionally, the court asserted that U. S. courts should be wary of applying state law to alter the content of an event conducted under an international agreement like the Olympic Charter.

In April 2009 the Supreme Court of British Columbia heard a lawsuit brought by women ski jumpers against the Vancouver Olympic Organizing Committee (VANOC), challenging the IOC's decision to exclude women's ski jumping from the 2010 Winter Games. The complaint alleged that VANOC's unwillingness to include the event (ostensibly due to budget constraints) influenced the IOC's decision, and that the exclusion violates the Canadian Charter of Rights and Freedoms by treating women differently from men (CBC Sports, 2008). The IOC's position was that there are insufficient competitors to support adding women's ski jumping to the Olympic menu. VANOC argued that the power to determine what events can be held resides solely with the IOC. The Supreme Court of British Columbia agreed that the exclusion discriminated against the women in violation of the Canadian Charter but ruled that the IOC was beyond its reach (Fong, 2009). The British Columbia Court of Appeals later agreed that neither VANOC nor the Canadian government had any authority to challenge the IOC policy, explaining that the gender equity section of the Charter was inapplicable because there is no law or government contract related to the Olympic Games that transferred control over the selection of events from the IOC to anyone in Canada (Keller, 2009).

Team/Nation Participation

As stated earlier, the OCOGs are charged with preventing political demonstrations at the Games. In *Spindulys v. Los Angeles Olympic Organizing Committee* (1985), certain groups from the countries of Estonia, Latvia, and Lithuania wished to participate in the opening ceremonies of the 1984 Los Angeles Olympics by performing dances in native folk costumes. At the time, these countries were part of the Union of Soviet Socialist Republics (USSR), which was the governmental entity recognized by the IOC. The plaintiffs wished to participate as recognized representatives of their own three countries to protest what they claimed was the Soviet Union's illegal annexation of their homelands. The Los Angeles Olympic Organizing Committee denied them the opportunity to participate, and they sued claiming discrimination on the basis of ancestry, national origin, and political beliefs under the state of California's Unruh Civil Rights Act.

The court ruled that the issue presented by the plaintiffs was a political issue for governments to handle and not a legal issue that the courts should decide. The New York courts made a similar decision when a Taiwanese athlete accused the Lake Placid Olympic Organizing Committee of discriminating against him by refusing to allow him to carry the flag of Taiwan in the opening ceremonies because Taiwan was not formally recognized by the U. S. government at that time (*Ren-Guey v. Lake Placid 1980 Olympic Games*, 1980).

A nation's NOC has the authority to determine whether that country sends a competitor or team to the Olympic Games. The *DeFrantz* case discusses the scope of the USOC's authority for such decisions under the Amateur Sports Act.

DeFrantz v. USOC

FACTS

In 1980, under considerable pressure from President Carter, the USOC voted to boycott the 1980 Moscow Olympic Games because the U. S. government felt that by sending a team to compete it would be communicating a message that it condoned the recent Soviet invasion of Afghanistan. The USOC's decision was challenged by the plaintiffs, who claimed that this decision exceeded the USOC's statutory authority and violated their constitutional rights to liberty, to self-expression, to travel, and to pursue their chosen occupation of athletics.

HOLDING

The U. S. District Court upheld the USOC's decision to boycott the Games as a legitimate exercise of its statutory authority.

RATIONALE

First, the court found that the USOC was not a state actor; hence, there was no violation of the Constitution. Next, it found that the Olympic Charter granted the right to the NOCs to determine their nation's participation and that the language of the Amateur Sports Act of 1978 defining the USOC's authority did not contradict the Charter. The plaintiffs had pointed to language in § 374 of the act that directed the USOC to provide for speedy resolution of disputes between amateur sports organizations and to protect the participation opportunities of any amateur athlete. They argued that this duty to protect participation opportunities would be breached by the elimination of opportunities inherent in a decision to boycott. The court looked to the legislative history of the act and construed § 374 to mean only that participation opportunities were protected against the effects of interorganizational conflicts between amateur sports governing bodies. Hence, the USOC's authority to decide whether to send a team was not threatened by this provision of the Amateur Sports Act, and its decision to boycott was upheld.

Selection of Host Cities

The NOCs are responsible for conducting a selection process in their own countries for cities that wish to bid to host the Olympic Games. They then nominate the winner to the Executive Board of the IOC to be considered for official candidacy to become the host city. The Executive Board conducts a Candidature Acceptance Procedure to determine which cities will become official candidates. These cities then submit a candidature file to an Evaluation Commission composed of representatives from IFs and NOCs, IOC members, representatives of the IOC Athletes' Commission and the International Paralympic Committee, and other experts. The Evaluation Commission submits a final report to the Executive Board, which compiles a slate of candidates for an election held during the appropriate IOC Session. The host city election is typically held seven years prior to the Games. The IOC thus has ultimate decision-making authority

Timeline of the selection procedure for the host city for the 2014 Winter Olympic Games.	EXHIBIT **12.3**

STEPS IN CANDIDATURE ACCEPTANCE PROCESS	DEADLINE
NOCs to inform IOC of the name of an Applicant City	28 July 2005
Signature of the Candidature Acceptance Procedure	16 August 2005
Payment of the Candidature Acceptance Fee (USD 150,000)	16 August 2005
Creation of a logo to represent the application	N/A
IOC information seminar for 2014 Applicant Cities	27–30 September 2005, Lausanne
Submission of Application File and guarantee letters to IOC	1 February 2006
Examination of replies by the IOC and experts	February–June 2006
Olympic Winter Games Observer Programme—Torino 2006	February 2006
IOC Executive Board meeting to accept Candidate Cities for the XXII Olympic Winter Games in 2014	21–23 June 2006
Creation of an emblem to represent the candidature	N/A
Submission of Candidature File to the IOC	January 2007
Report of the 2014 IOC Evaluation Commission	June 2007
Election of Host City of the XXII Olympic Winter Games in 2014	July 2007 (119th IOC Session, Guatemala City)

Adapted from a document retrieved from the IOC's website at http://multimedia.olympic.org/pdf.en_report_945.pdf.

to select the host city. See Exhibit 12.3 for the timeline of the selection procedure for the 2014 Winter Olympic Games.

Following allegations of bribery of IOC officials to influence the selection of the host cities of Nagano and particularly Salt Lake City, in 1999 the IOC enacted reforms to the host city selection process. Among the changes were:

- A new policy prohibiting visits by IOC members to candidate cities
- Opening the IOC Session meetings to the media
- Mandatory publication of sources of revenue and expenditures

Sponsorship and Advertising

Article 17 of the Olympic Charter provides that the IOC has exclusive ownership of all rights to the symbols of the Olympic Games, although it permits the NOCs to use and license Olympic trademarks for nonprofit Olympic fundraising and related activities. The NOCs are also charged with protecting against the unauthorized use of Olympic marks. In several instances, American courts have upheld the right of the USOC to protect against unauthorized use of the name "Olympics." For example, in *San Francisco Arts & Athletics, Inc. v. USOC* (1987), the Supreme Court upheld the USOC's right to prevent a nonprofit organization from using the title "The Gay Olympic Games" to host its own athletic competition. The Court also ruled that the Amateur Sports Act incorporated the civil liability remedies of the Lanham Act, but not its defenses, so the USOC is not required to show that unauthorized use is likely to cause consumer confusion as to the source of the goods or services. This has made it easier for the USOC to bring successful claims of trademark infringement against unauthorized users of the Olympic marks. (Trademark infringement actions are discussed more fully in Chapter 19.)

Although the Olympic Charter reserves exclusive ownership of the Olympic symbols to the IOC, § 220506 of the Ted Stevens Olympic and Amateur Sports Act of 1998 grants to the USOC the exclusive right to control the commercial use and licensing of the Olympic trademarks in the United States. In the *Intelicense* case below, the court had to address a perceived conflict in the rights to control the use of the Olympic symbols.

USOC v. Intelicense Corp.

737 F.2d 263 (2nd Cir. 1984), *cert. denied,* 469 U.S. 982 (1984)   **CASE OPINION**

[FACTS

In 1979, Intelicense Corp. entered into two agreements with the IOC under which Intelicense was granted the exclusive worldwide rights to be the marketing agent for the official pictograms of the IOC. These pictograms are designs of athletes in various sports portrayed against a background that includes the Olympic symbol of the five interlocking rings. Under the agreements, Intelicense was to receive 60% of the licensing revenues, and the IOC would get the remaining 40%. Finally, the agreements provided that Intelicense was required to obtain the approval of each NOC prior to any commercial use of the symbol in the respective countries.

During the next year, Intelicense sought permission from the USOC to use the mark in the United States. The USOC refused to grant permission, asserting that the Intelicense proposal to market the pictograms would diminish the USOC's ability to obtain corporate sponsorships critical to the support of the U. S. Olympic Movement. Intelicense proceeded to license the use of the pictograms on products marketed in the United States without USOC permission. The USOC then filed suit, requesting an injunction forbidding Intelicense to contact corporate sponsors in the United States. The U. S. District Court entered a permanent injunction under § 380 of the Amateur Sports Act requiring Intelicense to stop its commercial use of the Olympic symbol in the United States without the consent of the USOC.]

HOLDING

The 2nd Circuit affirmed the permanent injunction entered by the District Court.

RATIONALE

An understanding of this case is predicated largely upon a complete appreciation of the language and purpose of The Amateur Sports Act of 1978. This statute, enacted in 1978, empowers the USOC to exercise exclusive jurisdiction over all matters pertaining to the participation of the United States in the Olympic Games. The Act further vests the USOC with the responsibility of financing the participation of the United States in the Olympic Movement. Because the USOC is the only NOC that does not receive formal financial assistance from the Government, financing the United States Olympic team poses unique obstacles. Consequently, the marketing of the Olympic symbol in the United States assumes great importance.[3] Protecting the value of the Olympic symbol was, therefore, a significant factor that led to passage of the Act.

The relevant portions of § 380 so essential to a determination of this case follow:

---

[3]Indeed, during the period of 1980–1982, the USOC received 45% of its income from its 44 corporate sponsors. Under the USOC's corporate sponsorship program, each participant is authorized to use the USA Olympic emblem which contains the Olympic rings in exchange for a minimum guaranteed monetary contribution to the USOC. As the trial court concluded, if the USOC could not grant exclusive rights to market the Olympic symbol, the number of corporate participants would greatly be reduced and the USOC would find itself unable to raise the funds required for participation in the Olympic Movement.

(a) Without the consent of the [USOC], any person who uses for the purpose of trade, to induce the sale of any goods or services, or to promote any theatrical exhibition, athletic performance, or competition—

(1) the symbol of the IOC, consisting of five interlocking rings; or . . .

(3) any trademark, trade name, sign, symbol, or insignia falsely representing association with, or authorization by, the IOC or the [USOC] . . . shall be subject to suit in a civil action by the [USOC] for the remedies provided in the . . . Trademark Act.

It is clear that the Congressional intent in enacting § 380 was to promote the United States Olympic effort by entrusting the USOC with unfettered control over the commercial use of Olympic-related designations. This would facilitate the USOC's ability to raise those financial resources from the private sector that are needed to fund the United States Olympic Movement.

* * *

Intelicense claims, however, that because it is not falsely associated with the IOC, its conduct falls outside the proscriptive ambit of subsection (a)(3) and, therefore, cannot be reached by the remaining provisions of § 380. But, such a construction constitutes a patent misreading of the statute and would render § 380(a)(1), as well as the other subsections, superfluous. The view urged is contrary to this Circuit's established rules of statutory construction (a statute should be construed to give force and effect to each of its provisions rather than render some of them meaningless). Accordingly, a violation of § 380 can properly be grounded upon a violation of subsection (a)(1) alone, notwithstanding Intelicense's exhortations to the contrary.

When viewed against the factual landscape present in the instant case coupled with Congress's intent in enacting § 380 and the plain statutory language of subsection (a)(1), we cannot imagine a more blatant violation of the Act. Indeed, it is uncontroverted that Intelicense made commercial use of the Olympic symbol to induce the sale of goods in the United States, without having secured the consent of the USOC. This is all that subsection (a)(1) requires.

* * *

Intelicense alternatively posits that it has standing to assert a taking claim on behalf of the IOC, as its authorized agent. We find that such a claim is belied by the evidence adduced at trial. Indeed, in a letter from the IOC's director, Monique Berlioux, to Intelicense's director, Stanley Shefler, on October 13, 1980, the IOC explicitly accepted the authority vested in the USOC by § 380 to control marketing of the Olympic symbol in the United States. And in a subsequent letter dated November 5, 1982, Berlioux advised Shefler that "any and all licensing activities should cease in the United States."

It is clear . . . that [the Olympic] Charter [does not] govern . . . this action because of the doctrine of preemption, under which a clear and unambiguous Congressional statutory command is controlling. The IOC Charter is not a treaty ratified in accordance with constitutional requirements . . .[7]

Moreover, the United States did not intend to be bound by the IOC Charter. Indeed, at a 1981 diplomatic conference in Kenya, the United States cast the lone dissenting vote against a treaty that was to give the IOC worldwide control over the use of the Olympic symbol. The United States opposed the treaty precisely because it would contravene the thrust of § 380. Accordingly, the United States' position on the licensing of the Olympic symbol is unequivocal and is encapsulated in § 380, and, as such, cannot be overborne by the terms of . . . the IOC Charter.

Congress expressly chose to safeguard the United States Olympic movement by enacting § 380. We hold that Intelicense has violated both the letter and spirit of § 380 by commercially marketing the pictograms in the United States without the consent of the USOC. Accordingly, we affirm the district court's permanent injunction.

Questions

1. Who asserted that the IOC's rights to control commercial use of the Olympic symbol should outweigh the seemingly conflicting rights granted to the USOC by the Amateur Sports Act?

2. Why did the USOC refuse to grant permission to Intelicense to market the Olympic symbol within the United States?

---

[7]If the IOC Charter were in fact a treaty, the Constitution states that treaties and acts of Congress are of equal force. *See* U.S. Const. Art. VI, cl. 2.

3. What canon of statutory interpretation did the court use to rule that the Amateur Sports Act did in fact grant unequivocal authority to the USOC to control the use of Olympic symbols in the United States?

4. Besides the statutory interpretation analysis, what other argument did the court make for why the Amateur Sports Act should outweigh any potentially conflicting "right to control" provided to the IOC by the Olympic Charter?

5. Isn't the USOC bound by the Olympic Charter? What action did the IOC take that might have rendered the charter less relevant in this case? Would Intelicense have had a stronger case if there had been no provision in the IOC-Intelicense agreements that required consent of the NOCs to use the symbols in their countries?

Security Measures

The NOCs create the OCOGs, which are responsible for the nuts-and-bolts preparations for and conduct of the Games, including security procedures. The IOC evaluates the overall emergency response and security plans to ensure that acceptable standards have been met. The NOC and OCOG determine the specific security procedures regarding access to venues, security of the Olympic Village, searches for weapons and other unauthorized possessions, and so forth.

At the 2002 Salt Lake City Winter Olympic Games, facial-recognition video technology, capable of screening spectators' images against databases of known criminals and terrorists, was installed in the ice arena, but officials decided at the last minute not to use it (Balint, 2003). It is arguable that the use of such a procedure, combining highly invasive surveillance technology with information-gathering functions to search sports spectators on a mass, suspicionless basis is an illegal search under the Fourth Amendment (Claussen, 2006).

Conceivably, a spectator attending a future Games hosted on American soil might challenge similar search procedures as a violation of his Fourth Amendment right to be free from unreasonable searches. To establish state action, the following facts would be considered:

- Whether security personnel included local and federal police, intelligence, and armed forces personnel, as well as volunteers
- The fact that the OCOG has a contractual relationship with the host city
- The fact that the OCOG's executive body consists of the IOC member(s) of the host country, the President and Secretary General of the NOC, at least one representative from the host city, and, usually, a few governmental representatives

The involvement of the police, military, city, and governmental officials might serve to establish the OCOG as a state actor in its function of providing security measures.

The question would then be whether an American court faced with a Fourth Amendment unreasonable search claim would insist on applying the Constitution or would follow the pattern of judicial deference to the decision making of Olympic governing bodies we have seen in other contexts. Should American citizens be forced to give up their constitutional right to be free of unreasonable searches simply because they choose to attend an international sports event hosted in their own country? Should host countries be expected to suspend some of their laws simply because the

Olympic Games is an international event? The Italian government resisted pressure from the IOC athletes' commission to suspend its law treating doping as a criminal offense during the 2006 Winter Olympic Games in Torino (Dampf, 2005; Wilson, 2005). The Olympic regulations classify doping as a sports infraction and impose only suspensions and disqualifications rather than criminal punishment. During the Torino Games, Italian police participated in a raid on the living quarters of the Austrian ski team, and confiscated a large amount of doping paraphernalia (Hohler, 2006). In June 2009, the team's coach, Walter Mayer, and the five athletes involved were indicted for violating Italy's antidoping laws. The athletes have also been banned for life from the Olympics ("Ten Austrians indicted," 2009).

> **Competitive Advantage**
> # STRATEGIES
>
> **Contracts with Olympics-Related Governing Bodies**
>
> If you work for an organization like Intelicense that has a contract with an NOC or an NGB, find out how the Amateur Sports Act and other laws, as well as the interrelationships among Olympics-related governing bodies, may affect your business decisions.

REGULATION OF PARTICIPANTS

I n addition to regulating events, Olympic sport governing bodies possess varying degrees of authority to regulate the behavior of participants, including athletes, coaches, and officials. This section discusses the authority to regulate participants in six areas: disputed competition outcomes, amateurism, drug testing, sex testing, general competition rules, and disciplinary actions for rules violations.

Disputed Competition Outcomes

The Olympic Charter grants to the IFs the authority to regulate the competition of their sport(s) worldwide, including regulating the fairness of the competition. Olympic judges and officials are approved by the IFs, and the IFs have the authority to suspend them for violating rules or ethical codes of conduct. For example, during the 2002 Winter Olympic Games in Salt Lake City, the French judge for the pairs figure skating event accused the French skating federation president of pressuring her to vote for the Russian pairs team (Berezhnaya and Sikharulidze), which had made some technical errors, over the Canadian skaters (Sale and Pelletier), who had performed without a mistake. As a result, the Russian team won the gold medal by a 5–4 judges' vote. The IF (International Skating Union) suspended both the judge and the French skating federation president for three years including the 2006 Winter Games in Torino (Shipley, 2002). Similarly, in the men's all-around gymnastics event in the 2004 Athens Olympics, the judges incorrectly scored Korean gymnast Yang Tae-Young's performance, causing American Paul Hamm to be erroneously awarded the gold medal. As a result, the International Gymnastics Federation (FIG) suspended the three judges responsible for the error (Gardner, 2004).

Despite suspensions of judges that acknowledge flawed competition results, the affected athletes do not always get the relief they seek. Because of the improprieties involved in the pairs skating judging, the Russian skaters were allowed to keep their gold medals, and Sale and Pelletier were awarded duplicate gold medals. However, in the gymnastics situation above, the IOC refused to issue gold medals to both

STRATEGIES

Regulation of Participants

- Become familiar with your sport governing body's rules for submitting protests and appeals, so that you make your complaint or appeal at the proper time and file it with the correct person or office. A sample set of protest and appeals rules, from the International Skating Union (ISU), is provided in Exhibit 12.4.

- Familiarize yourself with the decision-making standards of the Court of Arbitration for Sport. This knowledge will stand you in good stead if the Olympic sport governing body for which you work becomes a party in a CAS arbitration, by giving you a framework for determining the best approach to preparing your case.

- From the perspective of a sport manager at an NGB or IF, it would seem important to communicate to coaches the message that their athletes can and will be punished for doping—even for accidental consumption. Coaches would then be on notice that they need to be careful when providing food to their athletes, because the CAS nearly always rules that even accidental consumption will result in disqualification from an upcoming event, and it may also result in suspensions depending upon the severity of the offense. Coaches should also be instructed to educate their athletes about the CAS strict liability approach so that the athletes themselves can be cautious about what they ingest.

- If you work for a recognized Olympic Movement organization, advise any staff you may supervise, such as coaches and trainers, about which governing bodies may have the authority to regulate their conduct, as well as that of participating athletes, and in what areas of conduct.

Hamm and Yang Tae-Young, indicating that it would reallocate the medals upon the request of the FIG. The FIG, however, declined to make such a request because of a procedural technicality—the Korean Olympic Committee (KOC) had not filed a timely protest to the appropriate referee on its gymnast's behalf. Instead, the FIG requested that Hamm voluntarily relinquish his gold medal, but the USOC rejected that request. Yang Tae-Young and the KOC then petitioned the CAS to correct the judging error and reallocate the gold medal (Gardner, 2004).

The CAS typically does not overrule competition judges' decisions, unless they were made as a result of corruption, fraud, or arbitrariness, or in violation of the law. Here, the CAS refused to correct an error in scoring identified in hindsight, stating that the error might have cost the Korean the gold medal, but it also might not have. According to the court, he had one more apparatus on which to perform after the scoring error, and it is anyone's guess as to whether he would have risen to the occasion or crumbled under pressure if he had been the leader at that point instead of being (albeit mistakenly) in third place (*Yang Tae-Young v. International Gymnastics Federation*, 2004).

Furthermore, according to the CAS panel, there are certain issues that are not the proper province of the law. The court's refusal to second-guess competition results would

> contribute to finality. It would uphold, critically, the authority of the umpire, judge, or referee, whose power to control competition, already eroded by the growing use of technology such as video replays, would be fatally undermined if every decision taken could be judicially reviewed. And, to the extent that the matter is capable of analysis in conventional legal terms, it could rest on the premise that any contract that the player has made in entering into a competition is that he or she should have the benefit of honest "field of play" decisions, not necessarily correct ones.

* * *

> While in this instance we are being asked, not to second guess an official but rather to consider the consequences of an admitted error by an official . . . we consider that we should nonetheless abstain from correcting the results. . . . An error identified with the benefit of hindsight, whether admitted or not, cannot be a ground for reversing a result of a competition. We can all recall occasions where a video replay can show that a . . . critical . . . call was mistaken. . . . However, quite apart from the consideration . . . that no one can be certain how the competition in question would have turned out had the official's decision been different, for a Court to change

Excerpts from the protest and appeals rules of the International Skating Union. (The actual document is longer; omissions are indicated by asterisks.)*	EXHIBIT	12.4

1. **Protests**

    Protests based on alleged violation of rules may be lodged provided that they are not forbidden by this or another rule. The Referee decides upon all protests. Protests must be filed with the Referee in writing and within the stated time limit.

    * * *

2. **Persons entitled to file a protest**

    Protests may be lodged only:

    a) by a competitor (team captain in Synchronized Skating), or competitors entered for the competition concerned or a Team Leader accredited for the competition concerned;

    b) with the approval of such competitor, competitors, coach (for Speed Skating only) or Team Leader, by members of the committee organizing the competition or by official representatives of those Members or affiliated clubs that have entered competitors.

3. **Time limits for filing protests**

    a) Protests concerning the participation of a competitor must be filed before the competition starts. If an immediate decision cannot be reached, the competitor is permitted to start, but the announcement of the result and the distribution of the prizes shall be deferred until a decision has been reached.

    b) Protests concerning the composition of the panel of Officials must be filed within one hour of its announcement.

    c) Any other protests, except cases covered by subparagraph d) below, must be filed with the Referee immediately, however, not later than 30 minutes after the completion of the competition concerned. . . .

    * * *

    d) Protests against incorrect mathematical calculation may be filed until 24 hours after the completion of the competition concerned. (See also paragraph 4. A. (iii) below.) If the Referee is not available in person at the site or hotel, the Protest shall be sent by fax or email to the ISU Secretariat which will forward it to the Referee concerned.

    * * *

*The full text of the rules can be found on www.isu.org.

Source: International Skating Union, www.isu.org. Reprinted with permission.

the result would . . . still involve interfering with a field of play decision. Each sport may have within it a mechanism for utilizing modern technology to ensure a correct decision is made in the first place . . . or for immediately subjecting a controversial decision to a process of review . . . but the solution for error, either way, lies within the framework of the sport's own rules; it does not license judicial or arbitral interference thereafter.

The CAS panel also said that sometimes referees make mistakes, as do players, and that that is an inevitable fact of life that all sports participants must accept. Therefore, it refused to reallocate the medals, and Hamm retained the gold.

Amateurism

The principle of amateurism has been embedded in the Olympic Movement since the beginning, but as sport modernized in the twentieth century, the line separating true amateurism from professionalism became increasingly blurred. In response, the IOC voted in 1974 to delete the word "amateurism" from the Olympic Charter. However, the change was not implemented until 1986, when the 91st IOC Session decided to permit professional ice hockey players to participate in the Winter Games, subject to the approval of the relevant IF, the International Ice Hockey Federation (IIHF). Subsequently, professional tennis players were allowed to play beginning with the Seoul Summer Games in 1988, and in 1992 professional basketball players first participated in the Summer Games in Barcelona.

The IOC completely abandoned the amateurism principle when former President Juan Samaranch opened participation in the Games to professional athletes, stipulating only that they cannot receive any money during the Games, either for taking part or for winning (IOC, 2002). Additionally, Rule 41 of the Olympic Charter prohibits participants (including athletes, coaches, and trainers) from allowing their "person, name, picture or sports performance to be used for advertising purposes during the Games." Thus, while no longer strictly adhering to the principle of amateurism, the IOC still retains some authority to regulate the economically motivated conduct of participants during the Games.

Drug Testing

In general, the IFs have the authority to promulgate antidoping and drug-testing rules, which are then investigated and enforced by the respective NGBs. In practice, this has led to inconsistency in antidoping efforts. In 1999, the World Anti-Doping Agency was formed with the purpose of promoting a uniform and equitable drug-testing policy for international sport athletes, one that would include common standards for doping control. In 2003, the World Anti-Doping Code was approved by nearly 80 national governments and virtually all the IFs, thus rendering adherence to the code mandatory for their respective NGBs and athletes. This code established a uniform system of drug-testing procedures and possible sanctions for rules violations. The code was revised in 2009 and is available on WADA's website at www.wada-ama.org. U. S. professional athletes who are subject to collective bargaining agreements are not bound by the code unless they give their express consent to be so bound.

The United States Anti-Doping Agency (USADA), formed in 2000, serves as the drug-testing agency for Olympic sports in the United States. It is not subject to the control of the USOC, but independently conducts drug-testing, investigation, and adjudication functions. If the USADA finds evidence of a doping violation, it proposes sanctions in accordance with the relevant IF's disciplinary rules. The athlete may accept those sanctions or request an arbitration hearing before a panel of the American Arbitration Association consisting of individuals who are also members of the North American CAS pool of arbitrators. Either party, the athlete or the IF, may appeal the AAA decision to the CAS, whose decision will be considered final and binding on the parties. Information about the USADA can be found on its website at www.usantidoping.org.

The CAS generally applies a principle of strict liability (see Chapter 15) when it finds a valid positive test for banned substances. In this context, strict liability means that even if an athlete can prove he was not at fault, he will be automatically disqualified from competition. The CAS believes such a policy is best, even though it seems unfair to the disqualified athlete, because it would be unfair to all the other athletes in the event to allow the (albeit inadvertently) performance-enhanced athlete to compete with a drug-induced advantage. To rebut the presumption of guilt on the part of one who has tested positive, the athlete would have to provide evidence establishing with near certainty that he was not at fault. Although the athlete would still be disqualified to prevent competitive unfairness, proof of lack of fault would mitigate additional penalties, such as suspension from future competition.

As part of its strict liability framework for deciding drug-testing appeals, the CAS insists that

- IOC and IF antidoping policies provide clear notice of the rules to athletes.
- The testing procedures be designed to be reliable.
- The procedures be followed.

Thus, in a case where the rules of the IOC and the International Ski Federation (FIS) did not clearly ban marijuana, the CAS overturned the IOC's decision to strip the gold medalist in the giant slalom event at Nagano of his medal after he tested positive for that drug (*R. v. International Olympic Committee,* 1998).

In addition to disqualification, the World Anti-Doping Code authorizes the IOC to impose sanctions for doping violations that include

- Issuing a warning to the athlete.
- Imposing a ban on competition.
- Imposing a fine.
- Imposing a suspension from participation.

Although an athlete's ability to provide evidence of lack of fault will not normally prevent disqualification, it will mitigate against imposition of further penalties. The CAS has indicated that instead of the fixed penalty structure adopted by some IFs, it prefers to impose penalties based on the proportion of fault attributable to the athlete (*C. v. Federation Internationale de Natation Amateur,* 1996).

The hypothetical case below helps to illustrate how the CAS applies strict liability in the case of inadvertent consumption of a banned substance.

considering . . .   STRICT LIABILITY

B. K. Stroker, an Olympic swimmer, tested positive for a stimulant on the list of prohibited substances. FINA, the IF for swimming, investigated and decided to expel Stroker from her event later that day and suspend her from international competition for two years. She appealed within the IF, but her appeal was denied, so she is now appealing to the CAS for a final decision. Stroker has evidence that she did not knowingly ingest the stimulant. She avers that 30 minutes before every race she relinquishes control over her food and drink choices to her coach. Her coach admitted that in this instance he inadvertently gave Stroker a capsule of the stimulant when providing her with food and drink before her race. Stroker has a reputation for unimpeachable moral integrity and generally exemplary conduct.

Questions

- Will the CAS apply a strict liability approach to Stroker's case, or will it decide in her favor and overturn her suspension?
- If the CAS finds Stroker to bear very little of the blame, will it reduce the severity of the penalty imposed by FINA, or is proportion of blame irrelevant to CAS decisions?

Note how you would answer the questions and then check your responses using the Analysis & Discussion at the end of this chapter.

The CAS arbitrated a dispute between the USADA and American track and field athlete Tim Montgomery in a case in which Montgomery never tested positive for prohibited substances (*USADA v. Montgomery*, 2004). The USADA, however, charged him with participating in the doping activities aided by the Bay Area Laboratory Cooperative (BALCO) and particularly with using prohibited substances in violation of IAAF rules. Although the USADA had no positive drug tests to use as evidence against Montgomery, it presented other types of evidence, such as one witness's testimony that Montgomery admitted to her that he had used a banned substance, tetrahydrogestrinome (THG), and documentary evidence showing abnormalities in various blood test results. According to the USADA, these pieces of evidence, taken together, established that Montgomery had indeed used a prohibited substance. The CAS asserted that it was able and willing to find him guilty as charged based on the witness's testimony alone, particularly since her evidence was not controverted by Montgomery. The USADA asked for a four-year suspension, but the CAS found that the offense warranted only a two-year suspension. Additionally, Montgomery was stripped of all his results, rankings, and awards as of the date in 2001 when he admitted to the witness that he had used THG.

Sex Testing

Sex tests to ensure that competitors in Olympic women's events were in fact female were first conducted in 1968 in the Grenoble Winter Games and the Mexico City Summer Games. The purpose of these tests was to ensure that males were not entering women's events and thus automatically disadvantaging the female entrants, who were presumably less capable than males. Since that time, sex reassignment operations have become more frequent, and concerns about discrimination against transsexual individuals have increasingly been voiced. Nevertheless, gender verification tests were endorsed by the IOC as recently as the 2000 Sydney Games. Occasionally, some athletes were allowed to compete under their new gender, but those cases were handled by the individual's sport federation on a case-by-case basis without any clear rules (IOC Medical Commission, 2003).

In 2004, the IOC Executive Board approved the following recommendations of the IOC Medical Commission regarding the eligibility of athletes who have undergone sex reassignment surgery:

- Individuals who underwent sex reassignment from male to female or female to male before puberty are regarded as persons of their reassigned sex.

- Individuals who undergo sex reassignment from male to female after puberty are eligible to participate in female or male competitions if the surgical anatomical changes are complete, legal recognition of their reassigned sex has been conferred by the appropriate authorities, and hormonal therapy for the reassigned sex has been utilized in a verifiable manner and for a sufficient period of time to minimize sex-related competitive advantages. Furthermore, eligibility does not begin until two years after the gonadectomy.

The IOC policy requires a confidential, case-by-case evaluation to determine whether the eligibility requirements have been met. Additionally, it grants to the medical delegate of the relevant sport governing body the authority to take all appropriate measures to determine the sex of a competitor once it has been questioned (IOC, 2004).

General Competition Rules

Per the Olympic Charter, the IFs determine the general rules of competition for their particular sport(s) worldwide. These rules would include, for example, rules defining how the sport is to be played, scoring methods to be used, criteria for disqualification, and specifications for legal equipment. Oscar Pistorius, an elite South African sprinter who runs with the aid of prostheses on both legs, sought to compete in international track events against able-bodied competitors. The case that follows illustrates how the Court of Arbitration for Sport (CAS) handled this unprecedented issue.

Pistorius v. Int'l Ass'n of Athletics Federations (IAAF)

CAS 2008/A/1480 Pistorius v/IAAF   **FOCUS CASE**

FACTS

Oscar Pistorius is a world-class sprinter who had both legs amputated below the knee when he was eleven months old. He wears a prosthetic device, known as the Cheetah Flex-Foot, on both legs when he runs. At the time of this court's decision, Pistorius held the Paralympic world record in the 100-, 200-, and 400-meter races, and his time in the 400-meter event was only 1.01 seconds slower than the Olympic qualifying standard. He wished to continue to compete in IAAF-sanctioned track meets, which would allow him the chance to qualify to compete in the Olympic Games against able-bodied competitors. Pistorius had been allowed to compete in such events in 2004 and 2007, but in March 2007 the IAAF adopted Rule 144.2(e) that carried a new prohibition:

> Use of any technical device that incorporates springs, wheels or any other element that provides the user with an advantage over another athlete not using such a device [is prohibited.]

In June 2007 the IAAF president stated in a press conference that Pistorius would not be excluded from IAAF track events unless the IAAF received scientific evidence that demonstrated that his prostheses gave him an advantage over able-bodied athletes. One month later, the IAAF arranged for an Italian sports laboratory to videotape a race run by Pistorius for the purpose of analyzing whether his stride length and time of ground contact differed significantly from other runners, and they did not. The tape also showed that while Pistorius ran his fastest 100-meter splits on the straightaways, the able-bodied runners' fastest splits were in the first and second 100 meters. Pistorius was slower than the other runners off the starting blocks, during the first 50-meter acceleration phase, and around the first curve.

The IAAF later requested that the Institute of Biomechanics and Orthopaedics at the German Sport University in Cologne conduct tests designed to determine whether the Cheetah Flex-Foot prosthesis gave Pistorius any biomechanical or metabolic advantages over other athletes, and Pistorius agreed to be tested. The German scientists reported that Pistorius received significant biomechanical advantages and benefited from a lower metabolic cost due to the use of the prostheses. Based on these findings, in January 2008 the IAAF determined that Pistorius' use of the Flex-Foot contravened Rule 144.2(e) and declared him immediately ineligible to compete in IAAF-sanctioned events. Pistorius appealed the IAAF Council's decision to the Court of Arbitration for Sport (CAS). The three issues ruled upon *de novo* by the CAS were:

1. Was the IAAF's decision-making process procedurally unsound?
2. Did the IAAF's decision constitute unlawful discrimination on the basis of disability?
3. Was the IAAF wrong in determining that Pistorius' use of the Cheetah Flex-Foot contravenes Rule 144.2(e)?

HOLDING

The CAS overturned the decision of the IAAF Council, clearing Pistorius to compete.

RATIONALE

The CAS found it likely that the new rule was introduced with Pistorius in mind. It also found that the testing protocol commissioned by the IAAF instructed the Cologne lab only to test Pistorius while he was running in a straight line after the acceleration phase (it was known by then that this was the stage of a race when he would usually run his fastest). In the court's view, these instructions created a distorted view of his advantages and disadvantages by failing to consider the effect of the device on his performance over all stages of the race. The CAS concluded that this distortion rendered dubious the validity and relevance of the Cologne lab's test results.

The CAS further found that the scientist nominated by Pistorius to participate in the Cologne tests declined because he was going to be allowed to do so only as an observer, with no input on the testing protocol or data analysis. Additionally, IAAF officials failed to provide the IAAF Council with any scientific data other than their own summary of the Cologne analysis, which was later criticized by the Cologne scientists as inaccurate.

In addition to other procedural problems associated with unfairness in the voting process, IAAF officials announced to the press prior to the Council's vote that Pistorius would be banned from IAAF-sanctioned events.

The CAS concluded that there was sufficient procedural unsoundness to give rise to the impression that the IAAF had predetermined that they would try to prevent Pistorius from competing in international IAAF-sanctioned events, regardless of the outcomes of scientific testing. However, the CAS stated that its finding of procedural unsoundness made little difference to the outcome of Pistorius' appeal since its panel was considering the appeal *de novo*.

The CAS found that Monaco (the home of the IAAF) had neither signed nor ratified the United Nations' Convention on the Rights of Persons with Disabilities. Even if it had, the Convention only encourages signatory states to promote the participation of people with disabilities in sports on an equal basis with able-bodied participants. Therefore, according the CAS, the Convention did not help Pistorius in this appeal because whether he was competing on an equal basis with other athletes was precisely what this appeal sought to determine. In other words, if he had no artificial advantage, then the IAAF would have allowed him to compete, but if the prostheses did give him an advantage, then the Convention would not apply. The CAS thus rejected Pistorius' claim of disability discrimination.

The CAS rejected the IAAF's view that Rule 144.2(e) prohibited use of a technical device that provided an athlete with *any* advantage over others, however small, regardless of any compensating disadvantages. The court found that proper interpretation of the rule required proof that the device provided the user with an *overall net advantage* over nonusers. According to the CAS, "If the use of the device provides more disadvantages than advantages, then it cannot reasonably be said to provide an advantage over other athletes, because the user is actually at a competitive disadvantage." The CAS concluded that the testing protocol followed by the Cologne lab was thus inadequate because it assessed only the advantages of using the device.

Pistorius presented his own scientific evidence from tests conducted by a lab in Houston that showed the Flex-Foot provided him no metabolic advantage over nonusers. The CAS requested that the two scientific teams cooperate in producing for the court a list of scientific findings summarizing points on which they agreed and disagreed. Upon review of this list, the CAS found that the experts agreed that neither group had quantified all the possible advantages and disadvantages of Pistorius' use of the device in a 400-meter race, thus an overall net advantage had not been proven by the IAAF. The court also found that the scientists acknowledged that current knowledge in the field of biomechanics was inadequate on the issue of whether Pistorius' flatter running gait was an advantage or disadvantage, as well as on the issue of whether energy spared by a prosthetic ankle could be effectively transferred to other parts of the body. Thus, based on current scientific knowledge, the experts were unable to say whether the Flex-Foot prosthesis provided more of a spring effect than a human ankle and lower leg. Moreover, the experts agreed that a mechanical advantage provided by a prosthetic device would be expected to create a concomitant metabolic advantage, and neither lab had been able to find one. Finally, the court took notice of the fact that the same device had been in use by other runners for 10 years, and no one except Pistorius had run fast enough to compete effectively against able-bodied runners.

On these grounds, the CAS concluded that the IAAF failed to carry its burden of proof (on the balance of probability) that Pistorius' use of the Cheetah Flex-Foot violated Rule 144.2(e). In closing, the CAS clarified that its decision on this appeal was specific to the facts of this case and would have no application to any other athlete, any other version of the same device, or any other type of prosthetic limb. Further, this decision would not exclude the possibility that further advances in scientific knowledge and a more relevant testing protocol that assessed overall net advantage might lead to the IAAF's future ability to prove this device does give Pistorius an unfair advantage after all.

QUESTIONS

1. Did the actions taken by the IAAF appear to you to be aimed at reaching an objective and fair decision about whether to allow Pistorius to compete in sanctioned track events? What fears or concerns might have been behind some of the actions taken by IAAF officials?
2. How did the CAS determine that Pistorius had not suffered discrimination on the basis of his disability?
3. Do you think the CAS reached the right decision in this case and for the right reasons? If so, why? If not, why not?
4. What are the practical implications of the *Pistorius* decision for future decisions regarding the use of new technology by athletes with disabilities in order to compete with able-bodied athletes?

For a discussion of the distinction between allowable new technology and forbidden artificial aids relative to the full-body drag-diminishing LZR Racer swimsuits, see Brown (2008).

Disciplinary Actions for Rules Violations

NGBs typically have the authority to impose disciplinary sanctions when international federation rules against misconduct have been violated. The Court of Arbitration for Sport has demonstrated a willingness to overturn NGB and IF sanctions if they appear arbitrary or if the organization fails to follow its rules. In one case, a Samoan Olympic weightlifter was accused of statutory rape and suspended for one year by his NGB, which would have prevented him from competing in the Sydney 2000 Games. This penalty was then endorsed by the International Weightlifting Federation (IWF), even though no criminal charges had been brought and no arrest made. As an NGB, the Samoan Weightlifting Federation (SWF) was subject to Samoan law, and the Samoa Supreme Court overturned the SWF's suspension. The IWF, however, refused to lift its endorsement of the suspension to Sydney officials.

The CAS ruled that once the Samoa Supreme Court invalidated the SWF's suspension based on a presumption of innocence until proven guilty, the IWF could no longer sustain its decision because it was now considered to be based on an invalid prior decision by the Samoan NGB. Therefore, the CAS set aside the IWF's arbitrary suspension and allowed the weightlifter to compete (*Samoa NOC and Sports Federation, Inc. v. International Weightlifting Federation*, 2000).

In *Harding v. United States Figure Skating Association* (1994), the U.S. District Court found that the NGB violated its own due process rule requiring that upon receipt of the athlete's reply to the disciplinary charges against her, it must set a time and place for a disciplinary hearing that is reasonably convenient for both parties. The U.S. Figure Skating Association (USFSA) had set Tonya Harding's hearing date before it received her reply to the charges, and set it for only three days after her reply was filed. The court found this unreasonable because she would not have had enough time in those three days to prepare an adequate defense to the charges against her. Thus, because the NGB had not followed its own rules, the court would have upheld an earlier injunction delaying the disciplinary hearing for three and a half months, had it not dismissed the case for other reasons.

Although the court in *Harding* would have upheld an injunction delaying the hearing out of concern for the plaintiff, in other situations quick resolution of a dispute is what the plaintiff needs so that she can meet approaching deadlines for qualifying events or compete in scheduled events at the Games themselves. However, § 220509(a) of the Ted Stevens Olympic and Amateur Sports Act prohibits any court from granting relief to an athlete regarding an eligibility dispute with the USOC that occurs within 21 days of the beginning of the Games, as long as the USOC has provided a written statement saying it cannot resolve the dispute in time. The purpose of this provision is to prevent courts from infringing on the regulatory authority of the USOC when it does not have time to implement fully its dispute resolution procedures.

CONCLUSION

Governance and regulation of Olympic sport is quite complex due to the multilayered governance structure with its many participating governing bodies, as well as the international scope of the enterprise. Jurisdictional conflicts between Olympic sports governing bodies are common, although efforts to create shared standards, such as those espoused by the WADA and the CAS, are showing some success. With improved governance, the regulation of events and participant conduct will become more effective and, ideally, more responsive to the needs of those whose interests have been harmed.

discussion questions

1. Do you think the CAS perspective on strict liability for doping violations is fair? Why or why not?

2. Is it always in athletes' best interest to have a governance and regulatory scheme that requires them to exhaust all administrative remedies before seeking review from the judicial system? Why do you think such a requirement exists? Is this consistent with the IOC's statement that one of its major purposes is to promote the well-being of athletes?

3. Can you think of any negative aspects related to an international arbitration body, such as the CAS, being the final avenue of appeal on athlete participation eligibility and disciplinary issues?

4. Who benefits from the Amateur Sports Act prohibition of judicial review for eligibility disputes against the USOC that occur within 21 days of the Games? Does it help or hinder most athletes who might have a dispute? With this statutory provision in place, would it be wiser for an American athlete to submit a dispute to the CAS ad hoc division that is onsite at the Games instead of to an American court? Why or why not?

5. Respond to the following question regarding the hypothetical situation presented on p. 313: If you were a sport management professional working for

FINA, what might you learn from such rulings as Stroker's? What would you communicate to elite swimming coaches?

learning activities

1. Explore the International Olympic Committee website. Follow the links to find out about the specialized IOC commissions that are part of the organizational structure of the IOC. In particular, examine the information on the IOC Athletes' Commission. The IOC Athletes' Commission exerted pressure on Italy to relax its criminal laws pertaining to doping for the 2006 Winter Games in Torino (Wilson, 2005). In what current governance issues is this commission playing a significant role?

2. Access the Olympic Charter on the IOC's webpage and locate the provisions relating to the criteria for inclusion of a sport or event in the Olympic program.

3. Choose an NGB or IF that is of particular interest to you and visit its website to examine its regulations governing disciplinary procedures applicable to participants who violate rules.

4. Visit the websites of the IOC and the OCOG for the upcoming Summer or Winter Olympic Games and try to discover what kinds of security measures they are planning to implement.

5. Visit the website of the Court of Arbitration for Sport and read one of the cases featured in the case law section. If it is a doping case, analyze whether the CAS followed a strict liability approach in reaching its decision.

CASE STUDY

Roquet Legues, competing for France, was awarded the silver medal in the women's 100 meter speed skating race in the Winter Olympic Games. Her time was 0.0009 seconds slower than the winning time of Kuhl Brieze, the German competitor who was awarded the gold medal. However, in conflict with the time clock results from the photo finish, television video appeared to show Legues as the winner, suggesting the possibility of mechanical error by the official race camera. Based on the videotape evidence of possible error in the results and the minuscule time difference involved, Legues and the French NGB requested that the IOC award gold medals to both Legues and Brieze. Due to a delay in obtaining the videotape from the television network, their appeal was not filed until just before the medal ceremony, which occurred three hours after the race. The IOC declined to change the medal awards, and Legues appealed that decision to the CAS.

1. What are the major issues presented here that the CAS will have to address?

2. How has the CAS ruled on these issues in past cases?

3. Should it make a difference to the CAS that the results challenged here were obtained by high-tech equipment rather than by human judges or officials?

4. Here, the event was completed, unlike the *Yang Tae-Young* case, in which the gymnasts had more performance rounds to complete after the judging error occurred. Should this fact affect the decision of the CAS?

5. In your opinion, how should the CAS rule in this case?

considering . . .   ANALYSIS & DISCUSSION

Strict Liability (p. 313)

First, yes, the CAS will approach this case energetically wielding the club of strict liability. Although Stroker took the stimulant accidentally and unbeknownst to her, to allow Stroker to compete later in the day with a performance-enhancing substance in her system would be to impose a purposeful unfairness on all the rest of the competitors while trying to remedy an accidental unfairness to one. Therefore, under strict liability the CAS will exclude her from competing in her upcoming event and will probably uphold at least part of the suspension. Second, if the CAS finds Stroker's case credible and thus that she bears little blame for her positive drug test, it will reduce the severity of the penalty imposed by FINA to a length of suspension that it believes is just.

REFERENCES

Cases

Barnes v. International Amateur Athletic Fed'n, 862 F. Supp. 1537 (S.D. W.Va. 1993).

Behagen v. Amateur Basketball Ass'n, 884 F.2d 524 (10th Cir. 1989).

C. v. Federation Internationale de Natation Amateur, Arbitration CAS 95/141 (1996).

DeFrantz v. USOC, 492 F. Supp. 1181 (D.D.C. 1980).

Harding v. United States Figure Skating Ass'n, 851 F. Supp. 1476 (D. Or. 1994), *vacated on other grounds*, 879 F. Supp. 1053 (D. Or. 1995).

Lee v. United States Taekwondo Union, 331 F. Supp. 2d 1252 (D. Haw. 2004).

Lindemann v. American Horse Shows Ass'n, 624 N.Y.S.2d 723 (N.Y. Sup. Ct. 1994).

Martin v. IOC, 740 F.2d 670 (9th Cir. 1984).

Pistorius v. Int'l Ass'n of Athletics Federations (IAAF) CAS 2008/A/1480 Pistorius v. IAAF (2008).

R. v. IOC, Arbitration CAS ad hoc Division (O.G. Nagano 1998) 002, in Digest of CAS awards 1986–1998 at 419. (Reeb, ed. 1998).

Raguz v. Sullivan, 2000 NSW LEXIS 265 (Supreme Ct. NSW, Ct. of Appeal 2000).

Ren-Guey v. Lake Placid 1980 Olympic Games, 1980 N.Y. App. Div. LEXIS 9699 (N.Y. App. Div. 1980), *aff'd*, 403 N.E.2d 178 (N.Y. 1980).

Reynolds v. International Amateur Athletic Fed'n, 23 F.3d 1110 (6th Cir. 1994).

Samoa NOC v. International Weightlifting Fed'n, Arbitration CAS ad hoc Division (O.G. Sydney 2000) 042 (2000).

San Francisco Arts & Athletics, Inc. v. USOC, 483 U.S. 522 (1987).

Schulz v. United States Boxing Ass'n, 105 F.3d 127 (3rd Cir. 1997).

Slaney v. IAAF, 244 F.3d 580 (7th Cir. 2001).

Spindulys v. Los Angeles Olympic Organizing Comm., 1985 Cal. App. LEXIS 2824 (Cal. Ct. App. 1985).

Sternberg v. USA National Karate-Do Fed'n, Inc., 123 F. Supp. 2d 659 (E.D.N.Y. 2000).

USADA v. Montgomery, Arbitration CAS 2004/O/645 (2004).

USOC v. Intelicense Corp., 737 F.2d 263 (2nd Cir. 1984), *cert. denied*, 469 U.S. 982 (1984).

Walton-Floyd v. USOC, 965 S.W.2d 35 (Tex. Ct. App. 1998).

Yang Tae-Young v. International Gymnastics Federation, Arbitration CAS 2004/A/704 (2004).

Statutes

Amateur Sports Act of 1978, 36 U.S.C. §§ 371 *et seq.*

Ted Stevens Olympic and Amateur Sports Act of 1998, 36 U.S.C. §§ 220501 *et seq.*

Other Sources

Anon. (2009, June 6). Ten Austrians indicted in Turin Olympics doping probe. *Deutsche Press-Agentur.* Retrieved June 14, 2009, from LEXIS-NEXIS.

Balint, K. (2003, January 20). San Diego police say no to face scanning technology for Super Bowl security. *The San Diego Union-Tribune,* p. E1.

Boyce, N. (2002, January 21). Flying economy: As the country prepares for the Winter Olympics, some are asking why women can't (ski) jump. *U.S. News & World Report,* p. 51.

Brown, G. (2008, October 2). Slick suits cause sticky issue for swimming rules makers. *NCAA News.* Retrieved October 9, 2008, from www.ncaa.org.

CBC Sports. (2008, November 18). Frustrated ski jumpers to have case heard in April. Retrieved June 14, 2009, from www.cbc.ca/Canada/british-columbia/story/2008/11/18/ski-jumpers-court.html?ref=rss.

Claussen, C. L. (2006). The constitutionality of mass searches of sports spectators. *Journal of Legal Aspects of Sport, 16,* 153–175.

Dampf, A. (2005, October 19). Italian senators oppose doping law moratorium for Turin Olympics. Associated Press, Sports News section. Retrieved March 5, 2006, from LEXIS-NEXIS.

Fong, P. (2009, November 14). Female ski-jumpers lose Olympic bid; won't be competing after B.C. court dismisses their appeal. *The Toronto Star,* p. A02.

Gardner, C. F. (2004, October 22). Winner and still champion: Court rules that Hamm should keep his gold medal. *Milwaukee Journal Sentinel,* p. C1.

Hohler, B. (2006, February 21). Austrian officials decry Mayer; actions by central figure of raid are 'inexcusable.' *The Boston Globe,* p. D2. Retrieved March 5, 2006, from Lexis-Nexis.

Hums, M. A., & MacLean, J. C. (2009). *Governance and policy in sport organizations,* 2nd ed. Scottsdale, AZ: Holcomb Hathaway.

IOC. (2002). The Olympic Winter Games: Fundamentals and ceremonies. Retrieved October 3, 2005, from http://multimedia.olympic.org/pdf/en_report_267.pdf.

IOC. (2004). IOC approves consensus with regard to athletes who have changed sex. Retrieved October 3, 2005, from www.olympic.org/uk/organisation/commissions/medical/.

IOC. (2005). Marketing revenue: Revenue generation 2001-2005. Retrieved October 3, 2005, from www.olympic.org.

IOC (2008). IOC Marketing Media Guide, Beijing 2008. Retrieved June 14, 2009, from www.olympic.org.

IOC Medical Commission. (2003). Explanatory note to the recommendation on sex reassignment and sports. Retrieved October 3, 2005, from www.olympic.org.

Keller, J. (2009, November 21). Court explains why women ski jumpers excluded; says IOC is only body that can decide which events are at Olympics. *The Toronto Star,* p. A25.

Reuters. (1998, February 4). Oly: Expert says progress in campaign against sex tests. Retrieved October 4, 2005, from LEXIS-NEXIS.

Shipley, A. (2002, May 1). 2 French skating officials banned: Olympic scandal prompts decision. *The Washington Post,* p. A01.

Wilson, S. (2005, October 26). IOC to review process for determining sports program. Associated Press, Sports News section. Retrieved January 11, 2006, from LEXIS-NEXIS.

WEBSITE RESOURCES

www.tas-cas.org ▪ Visit this site to access current and archived decisions of the Court of Arbitration for Sport (CAS) since 1986.

www.olympic.org ▪ Visit this site to get the most current information on the financing and governance structure of the IOC, as well as links to NOCs, IFs, and other affiliated organizations.

www.isu.org ▪ Visit IF sites like this one for the International Skating Union to access rules, history, and news pertinent to the sport(s) regulated by the IF.

www.usantidoping.org ▪ At this site for the U.S. Anti-doping Agency you will find the list of prohibited substances, as well as news and other resources, such as FAQs on doping in sport.

www.wada-ama.org ▪ Here you will find the World Anti-doping Agency's anti-doping code, news, and information about antidoping educational programs.

Governance Issues in High School and College Athletics

INTRODUCTION

W hen athletics programs were first introduced on high school and college campuses in the late 1800s, they were student-directed activities. Quickly, however, concerns about injury rates, recruiting abuses, professionalization, and commercialization provided the impetus for the creation of governing bodies that would establish rules and enforcement mechanisms to address these issues. The National Collegiate Athletic Association was established in 1906 to govern college athletics, and there are now more than 1,000 member institutions. The National Association of Intercollegiate Athletics (NAIA), originated in 1937, is the governing body for nearly 300 smaller institutions. Other governing bodies in college sport include the National Christian College Athletic Association (NCCAA), the United States Collegiate Athletic Association (USCAA; an organization that governs athletics for approximately 50 very small colleges), and the National Junior College Athletic Association (NJCAA).

At the high school level, all but three states had their own state high school athletic associations by 1923, and in that year the entity that evolved into the National Federation of State High School Associations (NFHS) was formed (Swanson & Spears, 1995). The NFHS now oversees the interscholastic athletics participation of more than seven million high school students from more than 17,000 high schools (NFHS, n.d.).

In this chapter, we first explore governance and regulatory authority in high school athletics and then do the same for college athletics. Important governance issues discussed include the relationship of governing bodies with their member institutions, in terms of governance structure and functions, and the scope of regulatory authority of governing bodies. Exhibit 13.1 lists the management contexts, legal issues, and relevant law discussed in this chapter.

GOVERNANCE AND SCOPE OF REGULATORY AUTHORITY IN HIGH SCHOOL ATHLETICS

T his section briefly describes the areas in which high school athletic associations typically assert regulatory authority, for example, eligibility to participate. However, our primary focus is on judicial review of high school athletic association decision making. Administrators working in interscholastic athletics will be at a competitive disadvantage if they do not understand the limits on their regulatory authority. By understanding these limits they will reap the twin benefits of being better able to administer their programs in a fair and equitable manner, thus providing a positive experience for all stakeholders, and also avoiding costly and time-consuming litigation.

High School Athletic Association Governance

Authority to govern interscholastic athletics within a state is granted to the state association by the state legislature or by judicial decision. Each state's high school athletic association is responsible for implementing and enforcing regulations governing interscholastic athletics participation of the member high schools. Most have adopted the NFHS playing rules for the various sports. Member high schools

| | EXHIBIT | 13.1 |

Management contexts and legal issues pertaining to interscholastic and intercollegiate athletics governance, with relevant laws and cases.

MANAGEMENT CONTEXT	MAJOR LEGAL ISSUES	RELEVANT LAW	ILLUSTRATIVE CASES
High school governance	Home/charter schools	State association rules	*McNatt, Davis*
	State actor status and due process in enforcement	Case law and Due Process Clause	*Brentwood Academy*
	Judicial deference to policy	Law of voluntary associations	*Letendre*
College governance	State actor status and due process in enforcement	Case law and Due Process Clause	*Tarkanian, Cohane*
	NCAA rules infractions	NCAA rules	
	Athlete eligibility	Law of voluntary associations; Antidiscrimination laws; Antitrust laws; and ADA	*Bloom, Pryor, Smith, Bowers*
	Coaching compensation	Antitrust laws	*Law v. NCAA*
	Restrictions on athletics-based aid	Antitrust laws	*White v. NCAA*
	Restricted postseason play	Antitrust laws	*NIT v. NCAA*
	Business of other organizations	Antitrust laws	*NCAA v. Board of Regents, Adidas*
	NCAA certification	NCAA rules	
	Athletics reform	Equity in Athletics Disclosure Act	
	Athletic conference contracts	Contract law	*Big East Conference*
	NCAA tax-exempt status	Federal tax law	*Internal Revenue Service*

are typically permitted to determine their own general participation policies, as long as they also abide by the state association's rules, which are designed to create a level playing field for all member schools within that state. These rules are voted into being by representatives from the member institutions.

Scope of High School Athletic Association Regulatory Authority

The following sections discuss the areas that high school athletic associations typically regulate, as well as the limits of their authority to regulate.

Typically regulated areas of interscholastic athletics

Typically, high school athletic associations regulate eligibility to participate, which includes such issues as academic eligibility, transfer between schools, age limits, athlete conduct and discipline, and dress/grooming. Other areas of regulation typically include recruiting practices and drug testing of athletes. Exhibit 13.2 provides a summary of areas in which state high school athletic associations typically assert regulatory authority, using the Utah High School Activities Association (UHSAA) as an example.

| EXHIBIT | 13.2 | Areas of interscholastic athletics regulated by the UHSAA. |

Eligibility to participate

Academic eligibility	Transfer between schools	Age limits
Athlete conduct and discipline	Charter school students	Homeschoolers
Dress/grooming		

Recruiting practices

Drug testing of athletes

Racial taunting

Home-schooled students. A relatively new and still unsettled area of regulation is the eligibility of home-schooled students to participate in public school interscholastic athletics programs. Some of the major concerns voiced by opponents of allowing participation are that it would: (1) detract from using limited resources for enrolled students; (2) allow homeschoolers to play without having to comply with all of the school rules; (3) dilute school spirit; (4) encourage recruiting of star athletes. In 25 states, the legislature has enacted a law requiring public schools to allow home-schooled and private school students to try out for sports ("Home school rule," 2009). The role of the legislatures is vital for homeschoolers who want to expand their base of supportive states, because the courts have been fairly consistent in rejecting homeschoolers' claims of a constitutional right to participate in athletics in the public schools (Batista & Hatfield, 2005). (See, e.g., *McNatt v. Frazier School District*, 1995—denial of participation did not violate Equal Protection Clause; but see, e.g., *Davis v. Massachusetts Interscholastic Athletic Association*, 1995—under Equal Protection Clause, distinguishing in-school-building students from out-of-school-building students was not rationally related to state high school athletic association's legitimate goal of prohibiting total nonattenders from participating in extracurricular activities.)

Racial taunting. A new area in which state high school athletics associations are beginning to regulate is dealing with racist taunting by athletes and spectators. In 2007, the Oregon School Activities Association (OSAA) requested a former judge to investigate this problem in their state, and she issued a 17-page report, including nine recommendations for OSAA policy changes. These recommendations included the following: adopting minimum standards for student conduct to be applied consistently across all leagues in Oregon; review of the state's

Competitive Advantage

STRATEGIES

Governance and Regulatory
Authority in High School Athletics

- If you work in high school athletics administration, become familiar with the home school and charter school movements. If your state or school district has not yet formulated policies to address the issue of athletics participation for students in these situations, be proactive. Find out what other school districts or states have done and try to determine what the best policy would be for your state or school district. Then work on formulating and implementing that policy.

- If you are an administrator of interscholastic athletics, be sure that your waiver and enforcement processes are followed in a fair and rational manner, so that a court cannot find that you acted in an arbitrary and capricious manner and thereby overturn your decisions. Careful and judicious decision making in these areas can prevent much ill will, negative publicity, and costly litigation.

discrimination policy; revision of ingress and egress procedures for pedestrian and vehicular traffic; implementing a security staffing plan that adjusts numbers of security staff relative to the number of spectators in attendance; and establishing a better communication protocol between the staffs of competitor schools (Schmidt, 2007). Schools are also beginning to formulate policies to address online taunting between athletes from rival schools (Kocian, 2006).

High school athletic associations as state actors

Because their authority to regulate interscholastic athletics is granted to them by the state and because public officials typically serve as staff or officers in the state high school athletic associations, the courts have traditionally viewed these organizations as state actors for purposes of constitutional issues. As discussed in Chapter 12, only state actors are constrained by the constitutional protections of individual fundamental freedoms. As state actors, state high school athletic associations must be careful not to infringe on the civil liberties of athletes and other constituent groups, including rights protected by the First, Fourth, and Fourteenth Amendments. A very important concern here is that these associations provide appropriate **due process** (that is, fairness in administrative procedures—see Exhibit 13.3) when enforcing their rules.

The traditional view that state high school athletic associations are state actors was affirmed by the Supreme Court in *Brentwood Academy v. Tennessee Secondary School Athletic Association* (2001). In that case, the Court held that the Tennessee Secondary School Athletic Association was a state actor due to "the pervasive entwinement of public institutions and officials in [the] composition and workings" of the association (p. 298). Let's take a closer look at the *Brentwood* case to get an idea of the Court's reasoning.

Definition of due process and the *Mathews v. Eldridge* (1976) test for determining whether sufficient procedural due process was provided.   EXHIBIT **13.3**

Under the Fourteenth Amendment's Due Process Clause, a state actor is obligated to provide procedural due process (that is, fundamental procedural fairness) when deciding whether to deprive someone of life, liberty, or property. Usually, notice of a hearing, a fair opportunity to present one's own case, and an opportunity to hear and confront the opposing evidence will suffice in cases of minimal deprivation. As the severity of the deprivation increases, so do the expectations for more stringently controlled fairness of procedure—for example, a trial with rules of evidence that must be followed. In *Mathews v. Eldridge* (1976), the Supreme Court established a balancing analysis to determine whether procedural safeguards should be required in a given case. It requires balancing three competing factors:

1. The private interest that will be affected by the official action
2. The probable value, if any, of additional or substitute procedural safeguards
3. The government's interest, including the fiscal and administrative burden that the additional or substitute procedural requirements would entail

Brentwood Academy v. Tennessee Secondary School Athletic Association

FACTS

In 1997, the Tennessee Secondary School Athletic Association (TSSAA) determined that Brentwood Academy, a private school member of the TSSAA, had violated a rule prohibiting certain types of recruiting practices. The recruiting rule in question prohibited member high schools from using "undue influence" in recruiting middle school student-athletes. The purpose of the rule was three-fold: one, to prevent the exploitation of children; two, to ensure that academics take precedence over athletics; and three, to promote fair competition among member schools.

Brentwood Academy's football coach had sent a letter inviting several eighth-grade boys to attend spring high school football practices. The recruiting letter contained statements indicating that football equipment would be distributed, and that "getting involved as soon as possible would definitely be to your advantage." It was also signed "Your Coach." The TSSAA believed this to be an example of "undue influence" in recruiting that violated its rule, and decided to sanction Brentwood Academy.

This decision was preceded by an investigation, several meetings, exchanges of correspondence between relevant parties, written notice of an adverse decision, and two hearings at which the school was represented by counsel and given the opportunity to respond to the evidence against it. However, during the TSSAA Board's deliberations, it also heard additional evidence that an AAU coach had encouraged talented kids to attend Brentwood Academy—ex parte evidence to which Brentwood Academy did not have a chance to respond. The TSSAA then placed the athletic program on probation for four years, declared the boys basketball and football teams ineligible to compete in the playoffs for two years, and imposed a fine of $3,000. At the time of the enforcement decision, all the voting members of TSSAA's board of control and the legislative council were administrators in the public schools. There was also evidence of animosity between the private and public school members of the TSSAA.

Brentwood Academy responded to the sanctions by suing the TSSAA, claiming its enforcement action violated the First and Fourteenth Amendments. The district court found in favor of the school, holding that the TSSAA was a state actor that was thus bound by the Constitution. The Court of Appeals for the Sixth Circuit reversed, finding no state action, and Brentwood appealed to the Supreme Court.

HOLDING

The Supreme Court, in a 5–4 vote, reversed the decision of the Sixth Circuit, holding that the TSSAA was indeed a state actor, and remanded the case for further proceedings consistent with this holding.

RATIONALE

The Supreme Court found that 84 percent of the TSSAA's membership was composed of public schools and that public school officials serving as member school representatives in the TSSAA overwhelmingly performed all but the most routine functions of the TSSAA—that, indeed, they "were" the TSSAA. Additionally, State Board of Education members were assigned as ex officio members of the TSSAA's board of control (enforcement arm) and legislative council. Also, the TSSAA's staff were treated as state employees, due to their eligibility to participate in the state retirement system.

According to the Court, these facts constituted an unmistakably high degree of entwinement of the TSSAA with the state sufficient to establish that the TSSAA acts as an arm of the state. The Court bolstered its holding with a statement that every circuit court to face the question of whether state high school athletic associations are state actors had found them to be so; therefore, its decision was in harmony with the majority of the circuit courts.

Upon remand, the district court concluded that the TSSAA had violated the Due Process Clause and enjoined it from enforcing the sanctions it had imposed on Brentwood Academy (*Brentwood Academy v. TSSAA*, 2003).

The Court's reliance on a fact-specific inquiry in finding state action may have left open a judicial loophole for a school in another jurisdiction to challenge the state actor status of its state high school athletic association. However, for now, the majority position is that state high school athletic associations are considered state actors. This means that administrators working for those organizations must be careful to provide procedural due process in any disciplinary action. Thus, state actor status imposes an important limit on the regulatory authority of state high school athletic associations—one that helps to ensure that governance decisions are fair to those governed by them. A discussion of the Due Process Clause and First Amendment claims in this case is provided in subsequent court opinions (*TSSAA v. Brentwood Academy*, 2007; *Brentwood Academy v. TSSAA*, 2008).

Judicial deference to educational policy

Another limit on the state association's authority to regulate interscholastic athletics is the perspective of the judiciary. If an association rule is broken or challenged, the association's investigation and enforcement mechanism usually must be used before the aggrieved party may seek redress in the courts. Even then, courts are historically reticent to intervene in educational institution decision making concerning academic issues, unless the procedures followed were arbitrary and capricious or the institution failed to follow its own policies. This judicial deference to educational institution policy making is less noticeable when a fundamental right is at issue, but even then it plays a role. This point is illustrated in the *Letendre* case.

Letendre v. Missouri State High School Activities Association

86 S.W.3d 63 (Mo. Ct. App. 2002)   **CASE OPINION**

[FACTS

Plaintiff was a swimmer who had practiced and competed for her private swim club three hours a day for six days a week since the age of five. As a high school sophomore, she joined her school's swim team. The Missouri State High School Activities Association (MSHSAA), which governs interscholastic athletics in the state of Missouri, had a rule (by-law 235) prohibiting a student-athlete from practicing or competing in organized nonschool events in the same sport during the interscholastic sport season. Although aware that violating this rule would make her ineligible to participate in school swimming, Letendre chose to practice with her swim club rather than her school team. When the MSHSAA proceeded to enforce by-law 235, Letendre sued for injunctive relief, claiming a violation of the Equal Protection Clause and the First Amendment freedom of association. The trial court denied her request for an injunction, and she appealed.]

HOLDING

The court affirmed the judgment of the lower court denying the plaintiff's request for an injunction.

RATIONALE

The power of a court to review the quasi-judicial actions of a voluntary association is limited to determining: (1) whether there are inconsistencies between the association's charter and by-laws and any action taken in respect to them; (2) whether the member has been treated unfairly, i.e., denied notice, hearing, or an opportunity to defend; (3) whether the association undertakings were prompted by malice, fraud or collusion; and (4) whether the charter or by-laws contravene public policy or law.

* * *

It is only upon the clearest showing that the rules have been violated by a decision of the association's tribunal that courts should intercede.

Claire [the plaintiff] agrees that the Association has acted consistently with its rules, given her due process and did not act out of malice. But instead argues that by-law 235 is against public policy because it is arbitrary, capricious and violates her constitutional rights to equal protection and free association as guaranteed by the Fourteenth Amendment of the United States Constitution.

The specific inequity she claims is that by-law 235 is internally inconsistent in that it does not affect those who wish to participate in non-athletic activities both in and outside of school; it does not affect those who participate in one sport in school and another sport outside of school; and it does not apply to athletes who participate in national or Olympic development competitions during a sport season. She maintains that the prohibition of simultaneous same-sport competition is irrational and unrelated to any legitimate goal of the association and asks us to declare by-law 235 unconstitutional as applied to her.

The Fourteenth Amendment guarantees that no person shall be denied equal protection of the law. It assures all individuals fair treatment if fundamental rights are at stake. It also eliminates distinctions based on impermissible criteria such as race, age, religion, or gender. Where there is no suspect classification or impingement on a fundamental right explicitly or implicitly protected by the U.S. Constitution, Equal Protection claims are reviewed by this Court under the "rational relationship" standard.

* * *

Claire's claim is not based upon a suspect classification, such as race, religion, national origin, or gender. Nor is it based upon a claim that her fundamental rights were violated, because she recognizes there is no fundamental right to play high school athletics. Accordingly, our inquiry is confined to whether there is a "rational relationship" between by-law 235 and any legitimate interest of the MSHSAA.

* * *

At trial the Executive Director of the MSHSAA identified several reasons for the adoption of by-law 235, including: (1) preventing or reducing interference with a school's academic program; (2) preventing interference with athletic programs by organized non-school athletics; (3) promoting and protecting competitive equity; (4) avoiding conflicts in coaching philosophy and scheduling; and (5) encouraging students not to overemphasize athletic competition.

The director of the MSHSAA testified that the association's 76 years of experience allowed them to conclude that the potential for harm is not as great in activities such as music, speech, debate and academics as in extracurricular sports.

* * *

The issue for us, then, is not whether we agree with the Association, but whether the challenged rule bears a rational relationship to a reasonable goal of the MSHSAA.

* * *

We conclude that there are reasonable grounds for by-law 235 because a reasonable person could believe that a legitimate goal of the Association is furthered by the rule. [To determine reasonableness under Missouri law] . . . the court must determine if the action is so willful and unreasoning, without consideration of the facts and circumstances, and in such disregard of them as to be arbitrary and capricious. Where there is room for two opinions on the matter, such action is not "arbitrary and capricious," even though it may be believed that an erroneous conclusion has been reached.

. . . In 1975, the Association identified outside competition during the school year as one of the "principal areas of problems facing high schools and state associations." A reasonable person could conclude that it is not in the best interest of the majority of high school students to compete in the same sport at the same time on two different teams, with different coaches, different rules, different practice schedules, and different competition schedules. . . . Here there is substantial evidence to conclude that by-law 235 is rationally related to the legitimate goal of protecting that interest. Claire's Equal Protection argument must fail.

Claire's second argument is that by preventing her from simultaneously competing on her school and swim club teams the MSHSAA has violated her right to free association. The First Amendment assures the freedom of expression, including the implied right of association. . . .

The Court has made clear that the right of association encompasses only two distinct cases: (1) those involving "intimate" human relationships fundamental to personal liberty and (2) those involving activities expressly protected by the First Amendment such as speech, assembly, petitioning for redress of grievances and the exercise of religion. By-law 235 does not impinge upon intimate human relationships nor core First Amendment freedoms. There is, consequently, no First Amendment right for a high school student to associate simultaneously with both a school and a non-school swim team.

* * *

While we might personally believe that a better rule could be drafted, one that would allow a student athlete who is getting good grades, such as Claire, to compete simultaneously on both her school and non-school swim teams, the law does not permit us to interject our personal beliefs in the name of the Constitution. Claire's constitutional challenges must fail because by-law 235 is rationally related to the MSHSAA's purpose of drafting rules that protect the welfare of the greatest number of high school athletes possible. The judgment of the trial court is, therefore, affirmed.

Questions

1. What was the essence of Letendre's due process claim—that the MSHSAA had harmed her by not providing her with procedural fairness in enforcing by-law 235? Or that their rule making had denied her due process because by-law 235 was itself arbitrary and capricious (and thus unfair)?

2. In the opinion, it appears as though the court gave Letendre's case a full review. However, at the beginning the court stated that it could review decisions of voluntary associations like the MSHSAA only under four specific circumstances. Were any of those identified by the court before it proceeded to review the case?

3. Why did the court dovetail the plaintiff's due process claim with its analysis of her Equal Protection Clause claim?

4. Did the court feel compelled to establish that the MSHSAA was a state actor before it began making decisions about violations of the Constitution, or did it simply assume state action existed? If the latter, why did the Supreme Court seem to struggle so much with the idea in its 5–4 decision in the *Brentwood Academy* case?

GOVERNANCE AND SCOPE OF REGULATORY AUTHORITY IN COLLEGE ATHLETICS

This section focuses on the NCAA because it is the most visible and powerful, as well as the most litigated, of the national sport governing bodies. As we consider the scope of regulatory authority possessed by the NCAA, we will examine challenges to that authority in the areas of due process concerns, eligibility of athletes to participate, compensation of coaches, restricted postseason play, and business affairs of nonmembers. Additionally, this section will discuss the NCAA certification process and the tax-exempt status of the NCAA. Finally, the reform roles of the Knight Foundation's Commission on Intercollegiate Athletics (Knight Commission) and the Equity in Athletics Disclosure Act are briefly addressed.

Intercollegiate athletics administrators, whether they work within a university athletics department, in a conference office, or for the NCAA, are well served by a working familiarity with the potential legal ramifications of governance decisions. Not only does such an understanding help in avoiding litigation, it can also assist administrators in keeping their organizational efforts running smoothly and effectively, and in maintaining a strong and positive public image. As part of the educational enterprise, interscholastic and intercollegiate athletics play an integral role in shaping young people's lives. Athletics administrators who abide by appropriate limits on their authority to regulate athletics will provide a more positive and edifying educational experience for the athletes who participate in their programs.

National Governance: The National Collegiate Athletic Association

Most of the principles of governance discussed in the section on interscholastic athletics also apply to the governance of intercollegiate athletics, with the notable exceptions of the lack of a state-granted authority to regulate and the related issue of whether the Constitution is available for the protection of individual rights.

The NCAA is considered by the courts to be a private, voluntary membership organization. That is, members are free to join or not, and there is no statutory or judicial grant of authority from any particular state that delegates the power to regulate athletics to the NCAA. This is one way in which the NCAA differs from state high school athletic associations. Another difference is that the heavy representation of public university officials in the NCAA governance structure and rule-making process is not considered by the Supreme Court to be pervasive entwinement or joint action sufficient to consider the NCAA to be a state actor. The Court's position on the state actor status of the NCAA was established in *NCAA v. Tarkanian* (1988).

State action and the NCAA

Prior to the *Tarkanian* case, nearly all the lower courts that addressed the issue had ruled that the NCAA was a state actor for purposes of the Constitution. They based their decisions on prevailing Supreme Court precedent that required a finding of joint action between a private actor and the state. If the court found that the private actor performed a public function in such a way that it wielded the authority of the state, or that the state had delegated its authority to the private actor to act on its behalf, joint action could be said to exist. Or, if there was a sufficient nexus of entanglement between the state and the private actor, a court could find joint action. Under these tests, courts uniformly found that the NCAA was a state actor, asserting that public institutions had delegated their authority to govern intercollegiate athletics to the NCAA, that the NCAA performed the public function of governing intercollegiate athletics nationally, and that the high representation of public institutions as NCAA members (it was the members who actually enacted the rules) constituted a sufficient nexus of entanglement.

However, shortly before the *Tarkanian* case, the Supreme Court decided a trilogy of cases in which it narrowed the grounds for finding state action. The language now endorsed by the Court is that the action in question must be *fairly attributable to the state* for it to be considered joint, and therefore state, action. The *Tarkanian* case shows how the Court applied its new theory of state action to the NCAA.

NCAA v. Tarkanian

| 488 U.S. 179 (1988) | **FOCUS CASE** |

FACTS

After the NCAA found the University of Nevada, Las Vegas (UNLV) guilty of 38 rules infractions, including 10 involving its men's basketball coach Jerry Tarkanian, it placed the basketball team on probation for two years and ordered the university to show cause why it should not impose further penalties unless UNLV suspended Tarkanian for the same two-year period. At the NCAA's request, UNLV had conducted an investigation of Tarkanian, which it completed with the assistance of the Attorney General of Nevada. After receiving the results of the university's investigation exonerating Tarkanian, the NCAA's Committee on Infractions conducted a four-day hearing at which counsel for both Tarkanian and UNLV presented their views and challenged the credibility of the NCAA investigators and informers. During the hearing on whether UNLV should impose the NCAA's recommended sanctions, the NCAA was not represented, so Tarkanian had no chance to confront his accusers in that hearing. The day before his suspension was to begin, Coach Tarkanian filed suit against UNLV in Nevada state court claiming he had been denied due process. He later added the NCAA as a defendant. The trial court ruled in favor of Tarkanian, finding that the NCAA was a state actor and that it had acted arbitrarily and capriciously in the disciplinary actions against him. It enjoined UNLV from disciplining the coach and enjoined the NCAA from conducting any further proceedings against the university and from enforcing its "show cause" letter against UNLV. On appeal, the Nevada Supreme Court affirmed. The NCAA then appealed to the United States Supreme Court.

HOLDING

The Supreme Court, in a 5–4 decision, reversed, holding that the NCAA is not a state actor and therefore was under no constitutional obligation to provide due process to Tarkanian.

RATIONALE

According to the Court, the NCAA was in an adversarial relationship with UNLV regarding termination (because the university wanted to keep its winning coach) and thus could not be seen as engaged in joint action with UNLV. Furthermore, agreement by the collective NCAA membership to rule making and to be subject to NCAA rules enforcement could not be fairly attributable to the state of Nevada. Also, the NCAA's principle of institutional control of athletics showed that member institutions had not delegated their authority to regulate athletics to the NCAA. Finally, the voluntary nature of membership meant that the NCAA did not have ultimate control over intercollegiate athletes, because institutions could simply choose not to be members. For all these reasons, the NCAA could not be considered as acting with the power of the state, and therefore it was not bound by the Constitution and did not have to afford due process to Tarkanian.

As stated earlier, this decision followed the Court's narrowing of the state action doctrine and reversed a long line of federal court decisions that had treated the NCAA as a state actor and found constitutional protections for athletes. As a result, ever since the *Tarkanian* case, the NCAA has enjoyed immunity from constitutional attacks on its policies and practices. Hence, most of the current sport-related litigation against the NCAA is based on federal statutes instead, such as Title VI, Title IX, the Americans with Disabilities Act, and the antitrust laws.

In 2007, however, the Second Circuit ruled that the district court in New York erred in interpreting *Tarkanian* to mean that the NCAA could never be a state actor. In this case, plaintiff Cohane was terminated from his position as head men's basketball coach at SUNY–Buffalo after the NCAA investigated him for major rules violations. He sued the NCAA under the Fourteenth Amendment, claiming he had been defamed and deprived of his liberty interest in working in his chosen profession without proper due process of law. Cohane alleged that, in order to placate the NCAA, the university had colluded with the NCAA in denying him a fair hearing. The district court granted the NCAA's motion to dismiss, but the Second Circuit reversed, stating that under facts like these it is conceivable that a plaintiff could prove that the state university willfully engaged in joint action with the NCAA to deprive him of his liberty interest. According to the court, Cohane might be able to prove that without the state's assistance and coercive power, the NCAA would not have been able to issue the defamatory report and impose sanctions on him. The court concluded that the district court had erred in holding categorically that the NCAA could never be a state actor when it conducts an investigation of a state school (*Cohane v. NCAA*, 2007).

NCAA structure and the regulatory process

In 1997, the NCAA restructured and moved from a one institution–one vote rule-making process to a structure that uses a representative form of governance. Interestingly, in 1985 the NAIA, seeking to add a more democratic dimension to decision making, abandoned a representative governance system and adopted a one institution-one vote process instead. The current NCAA representative governance structure, including functions of the various boards, committees, and councils, is set forth in Exhibit 13.4.

The NCAA Division I Manual (NCAA, 2008a) documents the structure and functions of its governance layers. Focusing first on Division I, the Leadership Council and the Legislative Council each have 31 members, who are university or conference athletics administrators, faculty athletics representatives, or other institutional administrators assigned duties relevant to athletics.

Among the duties of the Division I Leadership Council are reviewing issues related to the interests of ethnic minority and female student-athletes, recommending fiscal policy to the Board of Directors, and coordinating strategic planning

NCAA governance structure.

EXHIBIT **13.4**

EXECUTIVE COMMITTEE

Responsibilities

A. Approval/oversight of budget.
B. Appointment/evaluation of Association's president.
C. Strategic planning for Association.
D. Identification of Association's core issues.
E. To resolve issues/litigation.
F. To convene joint meeting of the three presidential bodies.
G. To convene same-site meeting of Division I Legislative Council and Division II and Division III Management Councils.
H. Authority to call for constitutional votes.
I. Authority to call for vote of entire membership when division action is contrary to Association's basic principles.
J. Authority to call special/annual Conventions.

Members

A. Eight FBS members from Division I Board of Directors.
B. Two FCS members from Division I Board of Directors.
C. Two Division I members from Division I Board of Directors.
D. Two members from Division II Presidents Council.
E. Two members from Division III Presidents Council.
F. Ex officio/nonvoting—President.[1]
G. Ex officio/nonvoting—Chairs of Division I Leadership Council and Division II and Division III Management Councils.

[1]*May vote in case of tie.*

ASSOCIATION-WIDE COMMITTEES

A. Committee on Competitive Safeguards and Medical Aspects of Sports.
B. Honors Committee.
C. Minority Opportunities and Interests Committee.
D. Olympic Sports Liaison Committee.
E. Postgraduate Scholarship Committee.
F. Research Committee.
G. Committee on Sportsmanship and Ethical Conduct.
H. Walter Byers Scholarship Committee.
I. Committee on Women's Athletics.
J. Foreign Student Records (Divisions I and II).
K. NCAA committees that have playing rules responsibilities.

DIVISION III PRESIDENTS COUNCIL

Responsibilities

A. Set policy and direction of division.
B. Delegate responsibilities to Management Council.

Members

A. Institutional presidents or chancellors.

DIVISION III MANAGEMENT COUNCIL

Responsibilities

A. Recommendations to primary governing body.
B. Handle responsibilities delegated by primary governing body.

Members

A. Presidents or chancellors.
B. Athletics administrators.
C. Faculty athletics representatives.
D. Student-athletes.

DIVISION II PRESIDENTS COUNCIL

Responsibilities

A. Set policy and direction of division.
B. Delegate responsibilities to Management Council.

Members

A. Institutional presidents or chancellors.

DIVISION II MANAGEMENT COUNCIL

Responsibilities

A. Recommendations to primary governing body.
B. Handle responsibilities delegated by primary governing body.

Members

A. Athletics administrators.
B. Faculty athletics representatives.

DIVISION I BOARD OF DIRECTORS

Responsibilities

A. Set policy and direction of division.
B. Adopt legislation for the division.
C. Delegate responsibilities to leadership and legislative council.

Members

A. Institutional presidents or chancellors.

DIVISION I LEGISLATIVE COUNCIL

Responsibilities

A. Recommendations to primary governing body.
B. Handle responsibilities delegated by primary governing body.
C. Adopt legislation for the division.

Members

A. Athletics administrators.
B. Faculty athletics representatives.

DIVISION I LEADERSHIP COUNCIL

Responsibilities

A. Recommendations to primary governing body.
B. Handle responsibilities delegated by primary governing body.

Members

A. Athletics administrators.
B. Faculty athletics representatives.

Source: 2008–09 NCAA Division I Manual, available at www.ncaa.org

(NCAA Constitution, Article 4.5.2). The Legislative Council's duties include serving as the primary legislative authority, with its actions subject to possible review by the Board of Directors, and making interpretations of the by-laws (NCAA Constitution, Article 4.6.2).

The Division I Board of Directors has 18 members, who are presidents and chancellors from member universities. The duties of the Board of Directors include:

1. At its discretion, ratifying, amending, or defeating legislation adopted by the Legislative Council
2. Reviewing and approving policies and procedures pertaining to the enforcement program
3. Establishing a strategic plan and directing general policy
4. Approving an annual budget (NCAA Constitution, Article 4.2.2)

The Executive Committee is composed of 16 voting and 4 nonvoting members. Among the many duties of the Executive Committee are providing strategic planning for the overall organization, overseeing the NCAA's budget, and initiating and settling litigation on behalf of the NCAA (NCAA Constitution, Article 4.1.2).

Each NCAA division may adopt operating by-laws and regulations pertaining to the administration of college athletics by its member institutions, the administration of NCAA championships and enforcement procedures for NCAA rules, and adoption of rules of play (NCAA Constitution, Article 5.2.2). Changes to the Division I rules must be supported by a two-thirds majority vote of the Legislative Council. Any such changes will be considered adopted unless the Board of Directors amends or defeats them at their next meeting. If at least 30 member institutions or an athletic conference provides a written request to override a piece of legislation, a five-eighths majority vote of the full membership will result in the rescission of that piece of legislation (NCAA Constitution, Article 5.3). Otherwise, members are obligated to apply and enforce NCAA legislation or be subject to enforcement procedures (NCAA Constitution, Article 1.3.2).

NCAA rules enforcement mechanism

The purpose of the enforcement program is to investigate rules infractions and enforce the rules by imposing appropriate penalties. Under by-law 19.01.3, all representatives of member institutions are obligated to cooperate fully with the NCAA in these processes. Full cooperation includes full and complete disclosure of relevant information requested by NCAA investigation and enforcement personnel. The NCAA Committee on Infractions (COI) is charged with investigating allegations of rules violations and with determining disciplinary actions, with the exception of suspension or termination of membership (by-law 19.1.2). Before imposing any penalties, the COI must provide the member institution with notice of the charges that will be brought against it, as well as an opportunity for a hearing before the committee (by-law 19.3.1). The process for a typical infraction investigation is shown in Exhibit 13.5. The NCAA Infractions Appeals Committee reviews actions taken by the COI on major violations that are appealed by a member institution (by-law 19.2.1.3). For a critique of the COI's functioning written by a former COI chair, see Marsh (2009).

```
Information indicating possible violation received      →   Information is not substantiated.
and evaluated by NCAA enforcement staff.                    No further review is warranted.
                                                                      (END)
              ↓
Information determined to be reasonably substantial.
Institution is notified that preliminary investigation will
be conducted by enforcement staff.
```

```
Staff determines that case should be closed    Violation is confirmed, and it is believed    Violation is confirmed, and it is determined
for lack of evidence. Decision is reviewed     by staff to be major in nature. The institution  to be secondary in nature. An appropriate
and approved by Committee on Infractions.      and enforcement staff discuss the summary      penalty is determined by the enforcement
Institution is notified that case is closed.   disposition process.                           staff and/or approved by a designated
                                                                                              Committee on Infractions member. Institution
(END)                                                                                          is notified of the penalty, if any, and may
                                                                                              appeal to Committee on Infractions.

                                                                                                        (END)
```

```
Institution, in consultation with enforcement
staff and other involved parties, determines
its position on possible violations.

              ↓
A summary-disposition report is written and accepted
by all involved parties and forwarded to Committee
on Infractions for its review in private.
```

```
Committee does not        Committee accepts findings    Committee accepts findings and proposed
accept findings.          but not proposed penalties.   penalties. Infractions report is released.

                                                                  (END)
```

```
An official inquiry with statements of allegations
is forwarded to institution and involved parties.

              ↓                                         Expedited hearing is held concerning
Institution and involved parties conduct investigation  penalties only, or full hearing concerning
(if necessary) and prepare written responses to notice  findings and penalties is held.
of allegations or elect summary-disposition process.

              ↓                                                       ↓
Committee on Infractions conducts hearing (to     →    Committee on Infractions' report is forwarded
determine findings and penalties) involving institution's  to institution and involved parties including
representatives, involved parties, enforcement staff.     findings and proposed penalties.
```

```
Follow the steps for processing   ←   Institution (or involved party) indicates    Institution (or involved party) indicates it will
of a typical NCAA Infractions         it will appeal certain findings or penalties   accept findings and penalties in infractions report.
Appeals Case.                         to the appropriate appeals committee.
                                                                                              (END)
```

Scope of NCAA regulatory authority

The NCAA regulates nearly every aspect of the conduct of intercollegiate athletics, from the conduct of university personnel to the conduct of athletes. Article 1.2 of the NCAA Constitution stipulates that one of the purposes of the NCAA is to legislate in any area of athletics administration that is of general concern to the membership (NCAA, 2008a). A review of the contents of its operating by-laws reveals that the NCAA regulates in the areas shown in Exhibit 13.6.

NCAA regulation of these aspects of intercollegiate athletics is generally accepted as legitimate by the member institutions that choose to join and thereby consent to the scope of these regulations. However, there are limits to the scope of the NCAA's regulatory authority, including internally and externally imposed constraints.

Institutional control of athletics. An internally imposed constraint is found in Article 2.1 of the NCAA Constitution. This provision establishes the NCAA's position that member institutions must maintain control of and responsibility for their own intercollegiate athletics programs, although such control must be in conformity with NCAA regulations. Article 6.01.1 adds the idea that athletic conferences also have responsibility for controlling the conduct of their member universities' athletics programs (NCAA, 2008a). Universities are expected to self-monitor for compliance with eligibility requirements, Title IX, and other applicable laws and NCAA regulations.

Occasionally, the NCAA brings an action against a member institution for failure to control its athletics program if it appears that university officials failed to take corrective action once aware of questionable practices. The authority to do so appears to place ultimate control of intercollegiate athletics in the hands of the

EXHIBIT 13.6	Aspects of intercollegiate athletics regulated by the NCAA.

Ethical conduct

Conduct and employment of athletics personnel

Amateurism

Recruiting

Academic eligibility

Financial aid

Athletes' benefits and expenses

Playing and practice seasons

Championship events

Enforcement policy

Division membership

Athletics certification

Academic performance program (penalizes programs that do not demonstrate satisfactory academic progress of their student-athletes)

NCAA, which seems contrary to the principle of institutional control. However, an institution that disagrees with a rule or a sanction against it could choose to withdraw its membership and thus retain institutional autonomy with regard to athletics governance. As you will recall, the Supreme Court in *NCAA v. Tarkanian* (1988) used a member institution's option to withdraw from NCAA membership to support its view that the NCAA does not have the coercive power of a state actor. It would be rare indeed, though, to find a university willing to withdraw its membership from the NCAA, thus giving up, for example, the opportunity to participate in NCAA championships postseason play.

NCAA provision of due process. The threat of external constraints has at times pushed the NCAA to adopt rules of its own accord that further limit its regulatory authority. The Supreme Court held in *Tarkanian* that the NCAA was not a state actor and so was not required to provide due process when it investigated and sought to enforce rules violations against UNLV and its men's basketball coach. In response, several states, including Nevada, introduced legislation that would have required any national collegiate athletics association to provide fair procedures in its enforcement process when conducted within the state. Many of the procedures required by the Nevada statute were not included in the NCAA enforcement program. For example, the NCAA did "not provide the accused with the right to confront all witnesses, the right to have all written statements signed under oath and notarized, the right to have an official record kept of all proceedings, or the right to judicial review of a Committee decision" (*NCAA v. Miller,* 1993).

The Nevada statute further provided that a state district court could enjoin any NCAA proceeding that violated the statutory provisions. Furthermore, an institution that successfully challenged the NCAA would have been entitled to costs, attorneys fees, and compensatory damages. Finally, the NCAA would have been prohibited from impairing the rights or privileges of membership of any institution on the basis of rights conferred by the statute. Thus, the NCAA would not have been able to avoid compliance simply by expelling its Nevada members (*NCAA v. Miller,* 1993).

In *NCAA v. Miller* (1993), the NCAA successfully challenged the Nevada law as a violation of the Commerce Clause of the U. S. Constitution. The Supreme Court's Commerce Clause analysis prohibits states from passing laws that cannot be enforced equitably across different states. According to the court, laws like the Nevada statute could result in several states having differing due process requirements that would force inconsistent obligations on the NCAA, which would in turn lead to the inequitable application of its enforcement mechanism across different states—results that the Commerce Clause prohibits. Despite this decision in its favor, the NCAA subsequently revised its by-laws to strengthen due process protections in its enforcement scheme. Among the changes was the creation in 1993 of the Infractions Appeals Committee, as well as revised notice, evidentiary, and conduct of hearings procedures.

External constraints on NCAA authority to regulate. Federal statutes and case law serve as external constraints on the NCAA's authority to regulate intercollegiate athletics. Court challenges to the NCAA's authority to regulate athletics usually arise under three areas of the law: (1) the law of voluntary associations, (2) federal antidiscrimination statutes, and (3) antitrust laws. In this section, the application of these areas of law is explored in the following areas of athletics regulated by the NCAA: athlete eligibility, compensation of coaches, restrictions on postseason play, and business affairs of non-NCAA members.

Athlete eligibility. Several challenges to the NCAA's authority to regulate athlete eligibility are of particular interest. The *Bloom* case illustrates the application of the law of voluntary associations, in which the courts traditionally defer to the decision making of those entities unless they have acted in an arbitrary and capricious manner or failed to abide by their own policies.

Bloom v. NCAA

FOCUS CASE   93 P.3d 621 (Colo. Ct. App. 2004)

FACTS

The NCAA prohibited Jeremy Bloom, a U. S. Olympic team skier, from earning endorsement and modeling money to finance his ski training if he wished to remain eligible to play football at the University of Colorado. The NCAA's decision was based on its by-laws prohibiting student-athletes from accepting payment for endorsing products. These by-laws were enacted to further its goal of preserving the distinction between amateur and professional athletics. When the university sought a waiver of these rules on Bloom's behalf, it was denied by the NCAA. Bloom filed suit, claiming that denying him a waiver of these rules was arbitrary and capricious. He sought an injunction against NCAA enforcement of its rules pertaining to his endorsement and paid media opportunities. The trial court found that he was not likely to succeed on the merits of his claims and refused to enter the requested injunction. Bloom appealed.

HOLDING

The Colorado appellate court affirmed the denial of Bloom's request for a preliminary injunction, finding that the NCAA had not been arbitrary or capricious in enforcing its rules and denying a waiver of those rules for Bloom.

RATIONALE

According to the court, Bloom failed to provide adequate evidence that the NCAA's enforcement of its rules was arbitrary and capricious. The court found that Bloom's reliance on NCAA by-law 12.1.2, which states that "[a] professional athlete in one sport may represent a member institution in a different sport," was misplaced. Bloom had argued that, because a professional is one who "gets paid" for a sport, a student-athlete is entitled to earn whatever income is customary for his professional sport, which, in the case of professional skiers, primarily comes from endorsements and paid media opportunities.

In the court's view, other NCAA by-laws written to protect the amateurism principle express a clear and unambiguous intent to prohibit student-athletes from engaging in endorsements and paid media appearances, without regard to: (1)

when the opportunity for such activities originated; (2) whether the opportunity arose or exists for reasons unrelated to participation in an amateur sport; and (3) whether income derived from the opportunity is customary for any particular professional sport. The court felt it could not disregard the clear meaning of the by-laws simply because they might disproportionately affect those who participate in individual professional sports. The court concluded that although student-athletes have the right to be professional athletes, they do not have the right to engage in endorsement or paid media activity and simultaneously maintain their eligibility to participate in amateur competition. Further, the court found ample evidence that this interpretation was consistent with both the NCAA's and its member institutions' construction of the by-laws.

Finally, the court found that the bylaws bore a rational relationship to the NCAA's legitimate goal of preserving the distinction between amateur and professional sport. Additionally, it ruled that the NCAA had not applied its waiver review process unreasonably in Bloom's case. The court concluded that the NCAA had not acted in an arbitrary and capricious manner and affirmed the decision of the trial court.

For an example of how the law of voluntary associations was applied to the eligibility of a baseball player who used a lawyer in contract negotiations, see *Oliver v. NCAA* (2009).

Another set of cases deals with eligibility regulations that might implicate federal antidiscrimination statutes. One such case was a Title VI challenge alleging that the NCAA intentionally discriminated on the basis of race by raising the initial eligibility requirements when it adopted Proposition 16 (*Pryor v. NCAA*, 2002). (See Chapter 14 for an in-depth discussion of the race discrimination issue raised in *Pryor*.) Another was a Title IX challenge alleging that the NCAA granted more waivers of eligibility restrictions to male athletes than to females (*Smith v. NCAA*, 2001), and yet another was a Rehabilitation Act § 504 challenge to the NCAA's core course requirement as applied to a student with a learning disability (*Bowers v. NCAA*, 2000).

These cases are grouped together here because the federal statutes mentioned apply only to recipients of federal funds. Thus, the ability to restrict the NCAA's authority to regulate in ways that might infringe on student-athletes' rights to be free from discrimination on the basis of race, gender, and disability depends in part upon the answer to the question of whether the NCAA is a recipient of federal funds. The courts in all three cases addressed this question but never resolved it because, for various reasons, none has proceeded to a full trial on the merits of the statutory issues.

In *NCAA v. Smith* (1999), the Supreme Court ruled that dues payments to the NCAA by member institutions that have received federal funds do not suffice to make the NCAA qualify as a recipient of federal funds, because that was not a sufficiently direct recipient relationship. However, the Court left open the issue of the applicability of these federal statutes if it were proven that the NCAA receives federal funds for its National Youth Sports Program (NYSP) program. Two federal courts have concluded that the NCAA is a recipient of federal funds because of the extensive control it exercises over the NYSP and its National Youth Sports

Program Fund (which receives grant monies from the U. S. Department of Health and Human Services; see *Bowers v. NCAA,* 2000 for a list of the ways in which the NCAA controls the NYSP; also see *Cureton v. NCAA,* 1999).

In sum, existing case law suggests that the courts think there may be sufficient evidence to support a finding that the NCAA is a recipient of federal funds due to its relationship with the NYSP and NYSP Fund, but as of yet no definitive ruling on this issue has been made. The NCAA has taken steps to divorce itself from administering the NYSP, which might result in eliminating any support for federal funding recipient status for the NCAA (Benson, 2006; Minutes of the NCAA Executive Committee, 2000). Moreover, all the cases mentioned are unlikely to be pursued further, either because the plaintiffs have died or graduated (and were unable to certify a class action that would enable the claim to survive a ruling of mootness caused by graduation), or because the NCAA took subsequent actions to eliminate the basis for a claim.

For example, following the ruling in *Pryor,* the NCAA revised its initial eligibility standards once again, eliminating the elevated Proposition 16 minimum standardized test score by implementing a sliding scale in which a lower test score is allowable so long as it is balanced with a higher high school grade point average. Now that the offensive portion of the eligibility standard has been removed, a plaintiff would find it very difficult to establish proof of the alleged intentional discrimination on the part of the NCAA.

Other federal statutes are not limited to federal funding recipients. For example, when athletes with learning disabilities have challenged the NCAA's eligibility requirements as applied to them, the courts have generally agreed that Title III of the Americans with Disabilities Act (ADA) applies. The NCAA, due to its control of athletic events at university facilities, has been ruled to be a place of public accommodation for purposes of the ADA (see, e.g., *Bowers v. NCAA,* 2000; *Ganden v. NCAA,* 1996; *Matthews v. NCAA,* 2001; *Tatum v. NCAA,* 1998). Thus, the ADA has successfully been used to place limits on the NCAA's ability to regulate eligibility of athletes with learning disabilities.

Another example of a federal statute that does not require federal funding recipient status is the Sherman Act antitrust law; however, it has been held to have limited application to the NCAA's activities. In *Smith v. NCAA* (1998), the plaintiff alleged that the NCAA rule restricting postbaccalaureate eligibility to the same school at which the athlete earned her undergraduate degree constituted an unreasonable restraint of trade under the Sherman Act. The Third Circuit stated that the purpose of the antitrust laws is to prevent unreasonable restraints in business and commercial transactions. It cited several U. S. District Court opinions in support of its conclusion that the antitrust laws generally apply to the NCAA's business or commercial activities, but not to its promulgation of eligibility requirements (*College Athletic Placement Service, Inc. v. NCAA,* 1974; *Gaines v. NCAA,* 1990; *Jones v. NCAA,* 1975; but compare *McCormack v. NCAA,* 1988).

Compensation of coaches. A context in which the antitrust laws *do* apply to the regulatory actions of the NCAA is when it is involved in regulating business activities, for example, restricting compensation of coaches. Some universities have the wherewithal to hire the maximum allowable number of assistant coaches, but some do not. In 1992, in an attempt to cut escalating hiring costs in such a way as to maintain competitive balance among competing universities, the NCAA implemented a restricted earnings coach position for Division I sports (excluding football). A restricted earnings coach was limited by NCAA rules to a total annual compensation amount of $16,000.

The following academic year, men's basketball assistant coaches affected by the new rule filed a class action suit alleging that the rule constituted an unreasonable restraint of trade under the Sherman Act (*Law v. NCAA,* 1998). The Tenth Circuit found that the restricted earnings rule was **horizontal price fixing** (i.e., an agreement between parties to eliminate competitive pricing), which is normally an automatic antitrust violation. However, the U. S. Supreme Court had earlier found that the sports industry requires some horizontal restraints (i.e., agreements between competitors that restrain economic competition) in order to provide its product successfully; therefore, horizontal restraints should not be deemed illegal per se in the sport context (*NCAA v. Board of Regents of the University of Oklahoma,* 1984). The *Law* court followed that precedent and applied the rule of reason analysis normally reserved for anticompetitive business practices that have counterbalancing procompetitive effects. (See Chapter 11 for a more detailed discussion of rule of reason analysis.)

In holding that the restricted earnings salary cap violated the antitrust law, the court found that the anticompetitive effect of preventing experienced coaches from earning market value salaries outweighed any procompetitive effects identified by the NCAA, such as holding down rising athletic program costs and retaining entry-level coaching positions. In fact, the court found no evidence that these salary restrictions helped to hold down overall spending or that the restricted earnings coach positions were typically filled by entry-level applicants. Thus, the Tenth Circuit found an antitrust violation and affirmed the lower court's granting of the coaches' motion for summary judgment. In a court-approved settlement, the NCAA agreed to pay $54.5 million to be apportioned among the plaintiff coaches (*Law v. NCAA,* 2000).

Restrictions on athletics-based aid to students. In 2008, the U. S. District Court in Los Angeles approved a settlement of the *White v. NCAA* class action suit, which claimed that the NCAA's limiting of athletics-based aid to tuition, books, housing, and meals was an unreasonable restraint of trade in violation of antitrust law. Per the settlement agreement, the NCAA must create a $10 million fund to which former athletes may apply to get assistance in covering educational expenses. The settlement also facilitates greater flexibility for athletes in accessing $2.8 million in the NCAA's existing Special Assistance and Academic Enhancement funds (Elfman, 2008).

Restrictions on postseason play. The antitrust laws have also been used to challenge the NCAA's efforts to regulate member institution participation in postseason tournament play. The NCAA has a long-standing rule that requires colleges invited to its NCAA Championship Men's Basketball Tournament to accept that invitation over invitations to any others. The National Invitational Tournament (NIT) is a competing postseason tournament that is a year older than the NCAA Championship Tournament and that used to be a bigger event. In 1962, the NIT agreed to let the NCAA invite its teams first (Neumeister, 2005). Since then, the NCAA tournament has steadily increased in popularity. In 2001, the NIT sued under the antitrust laws, alleging that the NCAA was attempting to establish a monopoly and put it out of business. In 2005, the parties settled, with the NCAA agreeing to pay $56.5 million for the rights to both the preseason and postseason NIT tournaments (O'Connell, 2005). As part of the settlement agreement, the NCAA's invitation acceptance rule was retained, according to its lawyer, in order to prevent someone from luring the top teams to abandon the tournament for a more lucrative made-for-TV event (Neumeister, 2005).

Business affairs of other organizations. Two cases illustrate the NCAA's attempts to regulate business affairs of other organizations. We look first at the *NCAA v. Board of Regents of the University of Oklahoma* case to see how the Supreme Court applied antitrust law in this situation.

NCAA v. Board of Regents of the University of Oklahoma

FOCUS CASE   468 U.S. 85 (1984)

FACTS

In 1981, the NCAA entered into exclusive multiyear contracts with the ABC and CBS television networks—contracts that were designed to limit the number of college football games that were televised. The NCAA's stated purpose was to prevent televised football from adversely affecting live spectator attendance at games.

The College Football Association (CFA), a separate organization comprised of major football powers within the NCAA, then negotiated its own contract with NBC in order to get more of its members' games televised. In response, the NCAA threatened disciplinary action against any CFA member university that honored the CFA's contract with NBC. Two CFA members, the University of Oklahoma and the University of Georgia, sued the NCAA under § 1 of the Sherman Act, arguing that the NCAA's plan caused an unreasonable restraint of trade on teams that could otherwise obtain more television exposure. The district court found that the NCAA's television plan was illegal horizontal price-fixing and output limitation. The NCAA appealed, the Tenth Circuit affirmed, and the NCAA appealed again.

HOLDING

The Supreme Court affirmed, holding that the NCAA's plan violated § 1 of the Sherman Act.

RATIONALE

The Court found that the NCAA had provided no convincing evidence that its television plan promoted competitive balance among member institutions any more effectively than would restrictions on alumni donations or any other revenue-producing activity. It also would not protect live attendance because it allowed games to be broadcast at all hours during which the games were played. Applying the rule of reason analysis, the Court concluded that any procompetitive effects were outweighed by the anticompetitive effects—most particularly that fewer games would be telecast under the plan than in a free market, significantly suppressing consumption by television-viewing fans.

The second case is *Adidas America, Inc. v. NCAA* (1999). In this case, adidas sued under the Sherman Act alleging that the NCAA's by-law 12.5.5, which limited the number and size of manufacturers' trademarked logos on athletes' uniforms, was an unreasonable restraint on the market for promotional rights. This time, the court held in favor of the NCAA. It found that the logo restriction rule did not provide the NCAA with any commercial advantage that could be construed as restraining trade. It further found that by-law 12.5.5 had a threefold purpose: (1) to support the NCAA's amateurism principle by protecting student-athletes from commercial exploitation; (2) to preserve the integrity of intercollegiate sports by preventing universities from turning their student-athletes into billboards in the pursuit of advertising revenues; and (3) to avoid excessive advertising that could interfere with the immediate identification of the athlete's number and team to teammates and to game officials. The court concluded that, similar to the NCAA's eligibility rules, the purpose and effect of by-law 12.5.5 was noncommercial in nature. Following the majority position that antitrust law is meant to apply only to commercial activity, the court held that the antitrust laws were inapplicable and denied adidas' request for an injunction against NCAA enforcement of its rule.

NCAA certification process

In 1991, the Knight Foundation's Commission on Intercollegiate Athletics (discussed in more detail in the next section) published a report documenting the need for major reform in intercollegiate athletics. One of the recommendations urged by the Knight Commission was a process whereby university athletics programs would be evaluated for certification of compliance with key principles by objective, independent examiners. In response to the Knight Commission's report, in 1993 the NCAA adopted legislation creating its Division I Certification Process. According to by-law 22.2 in the Division I Manual (NCAA, 2008a), the purpose of this process is to evaluate and verify the integrity of member institutions' athletics programs with regard to three topics:

1. Effective governance/commitment to rules compliance
2. Academic integrity
3. Gender equity, diversity, and student-athlete well-being

Every 10 years, each member institution must submit a self-study report evaluating itself on the three topical areas. Then the self-study is to be evaluated and verified through an external peer review process. Finally, the NCAA's Committee on Athletics Certification (CAC) will render a certification decision based on the peer review report, the institution's response to the peer review report, the institution's self-study report, and any evidence presented at in-person interviews or hearings before that committee (by-laws 22.2 and 22.3).

According to by-law 22.3, the CAC may reach one of three decisions:

1. To certify the institution as being in substantial conformity with the operating principles identified for the three topical areas in by-law 22.2
2. To certify with conditions, meaning that the institution is in substantial conformity with by-law 22.2 pending fulfillment of certain corrective actions within a specified reasonable time period

3. Not to certify, based on substantial nonconformity with the by-law 22.2 operating principles, and to require corrective action within a specified reasonable time period

If an institution fails to meet the requirements for corrective action, the NCAA may place it in a restricted-membership category. An institution may appeal a certification decision to the Management Council.

According to the NCAA, serious sanctions will be imposed on universities that do not make a concerted effort to correct problems identified during the certification process, including ineligibility for NCAA championships and eventual removal from active membership (NCAA, n.d.). However, during round one of the certification process, 254 of the 288 institutions that had completed the process by December 2, 1999, were certified, 33 were certified conditionally, and only one was not certified (NCAA, 1999). The second certification cycle spanned the academic years 1999–2000 through 2007–08. As of June 2009, with 14 schools still lacking final decisions, 319 of 335 had been certified, two were certified with conditions, and none were not certified (M. Colman, personal communication, June 15, 2009). Such results have led to criticism that the process is somewhat toothless, but the NCAA's response has been that the purpose of certification is not to punish but to motivate athletics departments to change their practices when necessary (Brand, 2003).

The Knight Foundation's Commission on Intercollegiate Athletics

The Knight Commission, established in 1989 and composed of a group of university administrators concerned about the integrity of intercollegiate athletics, serves as a constraint on NCAA governance by being an influential advocate for reform. In May of 2005, the commission met and agreed to urge the NCAA to be firm in enforcing its new academic standards promulgated in the Academic Performance Program. Under this plan, the NCAA calculates an Academic Progress Rate (APR) for each member institution's athletics program that takes into account eligibility, graduation, and retention data. Failure to meet the NCAA's cut-off score can result in a university's loss of athletic scholarships or exclusion from postseason play (Carey, 2005).

The NCAA appears to be serious about using the APR to achieve reform. As of May 2009, 177 teams from 107 institutions faced penalties under the past year's review, most in the form of scholarship reductions, and at least two universities were banned from postseason play. In 2010, universities with four straight years of inadequate APR scores could face the NCAA's most severe penalty, which is restricted Division I membership for the school's entire athletics department (Marot, 2009). The APR appears to be working, because the number of teams penalized in 2009 (177) is down from 213 at 123 universities in 2008 (Lederman, 2008).

The commission also agreed to support a resolution by the NCAA's Board of Directors to petition the U.S. Department of Education to withdraw a Title IX Policy Clarification issued in March 2005. The policy clarification would allow schools to use email interest surveys of enrolled students to help prove they are meeting the interests and abilities of female students (Carey, 2005). The use of interest surveys is discussed further in Chapter 14.

Equity in Athletics Disclosure Act— 20 U.S.C. §§ 1092(e) and (g) (2005)

In 1994 Congress enacted the Equity in Athletics Disclosure Act, a statute that affects the governance of intercollegiate athletics by requiring university athletics programs to prepare, make available to the public, and submit to the U. S. Department of Education an annual report. This report is to contain information about such things as graduation rates, athletic scholarships, participation opportunities, revenues and expenditures, and coaches' gender and salaries. Because of this law, the public as well as the NCAA can better monitor member schools' progress toward improving the graduation rates of athletes and achieving gender equity.

"Regional" Governance: Intercollegiate Athletics Conferences

Athletics conferences comprise another significant layer in the governance of intercollegiate athletics. These conferences are organized to provide regular competition among relatively similar universities within loosely defined geographic regions. The member institutions pay a fee to join the athletics conference, as well as regular membership dues, and they agree to abide by the conference constitution and regulations. The athletics conferences comprised of NCAA member institutions are themselves members of the NCAA, so these conferences require their member institutions' athletics programs to abide by NCAA regulations unless the conference rules are more stringent (see, e.g., Conference Regulations—Article 3 of the *Western Athletic Conference [WAC] Code Book*, 2008). Each intercollegiate athletics conference has its own set of athletics regulations, which may cover the areas listed in Exhibit 13.7 (see, for example, the 2008–09 *WAC Code Book*).

Areas of athletics typically regulated by intercollegiate athletic conferences.	EXHIBIT 13.7

- ■ Governance policies and procedures
- ■ Conference membership requirements
- ■ Rules compliance and enforcement procedures
- ■ General athletics regulations
  - ● Eligibility
  - ● Financial aid
  - ● Recruiting
  - ● Sportsmanship
  - ● Control of relationships with the broadcast media
  - ● Scheduling of competitions
  - ● Procedures for hosting conference championships
  - ● Crowd control policies
  - ● Ticket distribution policies

Because athletics conferences are voluntary, private membership organizations (like the NCAA), the courts would consider them nonstate actors and would probably grant a level of judicial deference in ruling on challenges to the application of conference regulations, similar to the deference that they accord the NCAA.

An athletics conference's constitution is considered a contract between the member universities of the conference. (See Chapter 4 for more information on contracts.) This principle was highlighted in *Trustees of Boston College v. The Big East Conference* (2004). When several universities chose to defect from the Big East Conference to join the Atlantic Coast Conference (ACC), the Big East attempted to prevent their departure by amending its constitution to quintuple the penalty for withdrawal from $1 million to $5 million. The court applied contract law principles in holding that the Big East's constitutional amendment had not been adopted in accordance with its own constitutional procedures. Therefore, it ruled that Boston College was entitled to withdraw from the conference upon payment of the $1 million withdrawal fee found in the original contractual agreement (the constitution). The court further ruled that, until the effective date of its withdrawal, Boston College was entitled to retain the same rights and benefits provided to all other members of the Big East conference, with the exception of voting rights.

Taxation of College Athletics Governance Organizations

Intercollegiate and interscholastic athletics governing bodies are generally structured as nonprofit, tax-exempt organizations. Nevertheless, questions have been raised as to whether taxes may be imposed on some aspects of their activities. For a discussion of recent federal income tax issues relative to amateur and professional sport, see Musselman (2003).

The NCAA's tax-exempt status

The NCAA is a nonprofit, tax-exempt membership organization that is also a multimillion-dollar business that has a $6.2 billion 11-year television contract with CBS Sports and ESPN (Brown, 2005; NCAA, 2004; Smith & Dempsey, 1997). Exhibit 13.8 depicts the NCAA's income and expenses for 2007–2008. The amount of revenue over expenses for that year was $23,348,866.

On the expense side of the ledger, approximately 77 percent was returned to member institutions or spent on Division championships and programs. Spending on association-wide services included such services as student-athlete welfare programs, youth programs, and membership programs (e.g., membership education and outreach, enforcement, championship services, legal services and insurance, branding and communications, membership services and governance). Approximately 23 percent of expenses went to the costs of running the association. The projected budget for the 2008–2009 year increased to $661 million (NCAA, 2009b).

Because of such figures, many have questioned whether the NCAA should be allowed to retain its tax-exempt, nonprofit status. However, compared to Nike's 2004 revenue of $12.2 billion, which was 25 times that of the NCAA, the

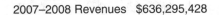

Revenues and expenses of the NCAA for fiscal year 2007–2008.   EXHIBIT   **13.8**

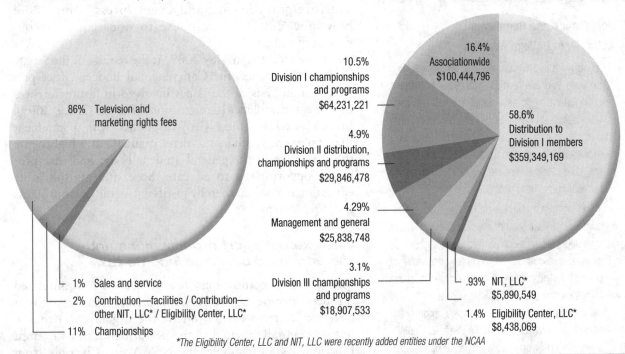

2007–2008 Revenues $636,295,428

86%   Television and marketing rights fees

1%   Sales and service

2%   Contribution—facilities / Contribution—other NIT, LLC* / Eligibility Center, LLC*

11%   Championships

10.5%
Division I championships and programs
$64,231,221

4.9%
Division II distribution, championships and programs
$29,846,478

4.29%
Management and general
$25,838,748

3.1%
Division III championships and programs
$18,907,533

2007–2008 Expenses $612,946,562

16.4%
Associationwide
$100,444,796

58.6%
Distribution to Division I members
$359,349,169

.93%   NIT, LLC*
$5,890,549

1.4%   Eligibility Center, LLC*
$8,438,069

*The Eligibility Center, LLC and NIT, LLC were recently added entities under the NCAA

NCAA looks like it is making pocket change (Brown, 2005). In 1988, the NCAA underwent an extensive IRS audit covering a three-year period, and the IRS did not challenge the organization's tax-exempt status (Smith & Dempsey, 1997). According to Smith and Dempsey, the NCAA Executive Director's salary is held within the range earned by CEOs of national nonprofit organizations with similar operating budgets. Also, the relocation packages that the NCAA offers prospective employees are considered a common recruitment tool for higher-education CEOs, and other perks for NCAA employees are reported annually to the IRS as individual taxable income. Moreover, NCAA employees' perks and fringe benefits are reportedly typical of those provided by other tax-exempt entities of comparable size to the NCAA. Thus, representatives of the NCAA have concluded that its financial practices are consistent with those of similar nonprofit organizations.

Nevertheless, in the fall of 2006, the U. S. House of Representatives Ways and Means Committee requested information from the NCAA about how intercollegiate athletics fits the tax-exempt status of the NCAA as a nonprofit educational organization. Of particular concern to the Committee were issues of amateurism and the sincerity of the NCAA with regard to academic integrity (Alesia, 2006). NCAA President Myles Brand wrote a lengthy response endorsing the NCAA's commitment to the educational enterprise and attempting to dispel

Competitive Advantage

STRATEGIES

Governance and Regulatory
Authority in College Athletics

- If you work in an intercollegiate athletics setting, be sure you are familiar with your national collegiate athletic association's rules and regulations, in particular its waiver procedures and infractions investigation and rules enforcement processes. If you are a high-level administrator, take steps to ensure that your staff is also familiar with these processes.

- If you work in management for a company like adidas and your business is negatively affected by a sport organization's rules, you may consider seeking a remedy under the antitrust laws. If you do so, work closely with your lawyer to arrive at an appropriate interpretation of whether the sport organization's rule regulates commercial activity so that you can make the best decision about whether you have a likelihood of success in court. With a justifiable argument that the rule has a commercial purpose and effect, the court will be less likely to reject your claim before it even begins to apply the rule of reason analysis.

- If you work in collegiate athletic administration, become familiar with the NCAA's certification process so that you can work proactively to improve your athletics program. By doing so, you will provide a better college athletics experience for student-athletes and be better able to satisfy the certification requirements without reservation.

- If your organization is considering sponsoring a sports or recreational event, consult a tax advisor about decisions with regard to sponsorship payments vs. advertising payments. A tax advisor should be knowledgeable about how the IRS interprets the tax law pertaining to the sponsorship benefits that will qualify for exclusion from the UBIT and those that will be considered advertising instead.

public misconceptions about the academic performance of most student-athletes and about the profitability of most athletics programs. The full text of his response to the Committee is available on the NCAA's website at www2. ncaa.org/portal/media_and_events/press_room/2006/ November/20061115_response_to_housecommitteeon- waysandmeans.pdf.

More recently, in May 2009, at the request of the Senate Finance Committee, the Congressional Budget Office prepared an analysis of the issues involved in tax preferences for collegiate athletics (Congressional Budget Office, 2009). In a news release, the NCAA responded with a statement that, on average, student-athletes graduate at a higher rate than students in the general student body, and that providing opportunities to educate those students fulfills its educational mission, thereby justifying its tax-exempt status (NCAA, 2009a).

Tax-exempt sport organizations and the unrelated business income tax

Tax-exempt organizations are subject to an **unrelated business income tax** (UBIT) for income generated by a trade or business carried on by the organization that is not substantially related to the performance of its exempt function. As an example, the NCAA earns income from the sale of advertising space in its basketball championship tournament programs. In 1982, the NCAA did not report $55,926.71 in income from its tournament program advertising revenue, and the IRS tax commissioner determined that it was liable for $10,395.14 in unrelated business income tax on the unreported income.

In *NCAA v. Commissioner of Internal Revenue* (1990), the Tenth Circuit found that the program advertisements were distributed over a period of less than three weeks and only once per year. The court held that this distribution occurred so infrequently that it could not be considered a regularly carried on business of the NCAA, and thus the NCAA was not subject to the UBIT that the tax commissioner had levied. Therefore, because of its status as a tax-exempt nonprofit organization, the NCAA was able to earn a significant amount of tax-free income from the sale of advertising in its tournament programs. The IRS disagreed with this decision of the Tenth Circuit and indicated that it would continue to litigate the issue in future cases (Internal Revenue Service, 1991a). No further litigation seems to have occurred, however.

The relationship of the UBIT to college sports was also challenged in 1991. Mobil Oil Corporation had paid over $1 million to the Cotton Bowl in a sponsorship agreement in exchange for naming rights to the event; signage on the scoreboard and field; public address system announcements of Mobil advertisements; and hospitality suites, hotel rooms, game tickets, and tickets to event-related activities. The IRS ruled that this payment constituted advertising revenue that was not substantially related to the exercise of the Cotton Bowl Athletic Association's tax-exempt function and thus was subject to the UBIT (Internal Revenue Service, 1991b).

Subsequently, section 513(i) of the Internal Revenue Code was enacted as part of the Taxpayer Relief Act of 1997. It specifically excludes "soliciting and receiving qualified sponsorship payments" from the definition of unrelated trade or business, which prevents such payments from being subject to the UBIT. A qualified sponsorship payment is defined in the act as "any payment . . . with respect to which there is no arrangement or expectation . . . [of] any substantial return benefit other than use or acknowledgment of the [sponsor's] name or logo (or product lines)" by the organization paid.

Payments for advertising the sponsor's services or products and payments contingent upon attendance, broadcast ratings, or similar factors are both excluded from the definition of a qualified sponsorship payment and thus would be considered taxable unrelated business income. A sponsor is allowed to make separate payments for the sponsorship and for advertising so that the advertising payment can be taxed without affecting the sponsorship payment's exemption from the UBIT. Thus, a carefully drafted sponsorship agreement should be able to avoid rendering the payment received by the sport organization subject to the UBIT. The following hypothetical case shows how this ruling would apply in a sport sponsorship situation.

considering . . . SPONSORSHIP AGREEMENTS

Big Buns Burgers, Inc. is negotiating a sponsorship agreement with Hip Hop Hoops, a three-on-three basketball tournament event organizer. In exchange for $10,000, Big Buns Burgers will be the title sponsor of next year's Hip Hop Hoops statewide championship tournament in Idaho. Big Buns Burgers is also interested in having signage on the scoreboard and public address announcements advertising their burgers during the game. Hip Hop Hoops is willing to agree to provide all of this for the $10,000. That is the amount they need, and they have no other potential sponsors waiting in the wings.

Question

- Should Hip Hop Hoops sign this sponsorship contract?

Note how you would answer the question and then check your response using the Analysis & Discussion at the end of this chapter.

CONCLUSION

Sports governing bodies have asserted broad authority to regulate inter-scholastic and intercollegiate athletics. The NCAA's status as a nonstate actor has insulated it from legal attack in many areas. Nevertheless, public visibility keeps the pressure on the NCAA to enact reform measures that minimize image problems resulting from the public perception of injustice. In contrast, state high school athletic associations (the majority position is that they are state actors) operate under greater restrictions because constitutional protections of rights and civil liberties apply to them. Additionally, federal and state statutory laws (including antidiscrimination laws, antitrust laws, and tax laws) function to limit the regulatory authority of the NCAA, athletic conferences, and state high school athletic associations. Other factors influencing the governance of college athletics include the Knight Commission and the Equity in Athletics Disclosure Act, both of which serve as agents of reform. In the final analysis, governing bodies in interscholastic and intercollegiate athletics are frequently granted judicial deference to their rule-making and enforcement decisions and thus are able to exercise broad regulatory authority.

discussion questions

1. After the *Tarkanian* decision, public universities can, by acting collectively through the NCAA, regulate areas that they might not be able to regulate on their own. For example, the NCAA can conduct drug testing of student-athletes without having to face scrutiny under the Fourth Amendment prohibition of unreasonable searches. But if a public university implemented its own drug-testing program, the Fourth Amendment would apply (see Chapter 14 for a fuller explication of this issue). Can you make a rational argument for why this is just? How about for why it is unjust?

2. In Sherman Act antitrust cases, the commercial activities of sport organizations are treated differently from those of other types of businesses. Why is this so?

3. Does the *Tarkanian* case provide another example of a situation where some sport organizations are different from other types of business organizations? That is, should courts consider the special nature of sport organizations and carve out an exception to the state action doctrine for collective membership organizations like the NCAA? Or should constitutional issues be treated differently than antitrust issues?

4. Why do you think the Knight Commission pushed for a regularly recurring external objective review of university athletics programs?

5. Do you think the NCAA certification process is structured in a way that enables it to accomplish fully what the Knight Commission intended? If not, what changes would you recommend?

learning activities

1. Using an online database such as LEXIS-NEXIS or WESTLAW, locate the *McNatt* (1995) and *Davis* (1995) decisions about whether home-schooled students should be allowed to participate in interscholastic athletics. From those cases, distill the arguments for and against allowing such students to participate.

2. Go to the website for the Knight Commission (www.knightcommission.org) and write a two-page summary of the Commission's most recent recommendations for reforming college athletics.

3. Ask your university athletics department if you can borrow a copy of its most recent self-study report for the NCAA certification process. Review it and try to determine what the major strengths and weaknesses of the athletics program were at the time of the most recent review.

4. Locate a copy of the complete opinion from *Bloom v. NCAA* (2004). Read it with the following question in mind: Are individual sport professional athletes treated unfairly by the NCAA's amateurism rules compared to team sport professional athletes? Next, assume you are a member of the NCAA's Division I Management Council. Write a two-page rationale for why you would or would not consider proposing a rules change after seeing the result in Jeremy Bloom's case.

CASE STUDY

The reconfiguration of the governance structure of the NCAA in 1997 occurred several years after the *Tarkanian* (1988) case was decided. A law review article by W. Burlette Carter questions whether the courts should continue to consider the NCAA a nonstate actor given the nature of the new governance structure (Carter, 2000). The nonstate actor status of the NCAA is also questioned in an article by Otto and Stippich (2008). The *Brentwood Academy* decision in 2001 has also raised the question whether *Tarkanian* ought to be overturned or limited to its particular facts. Read the articles by Carter and by Otto and Stippich and, based on those and the Court's reasoning in *Brentwood Academy*, write a position paper articulating a rationale for whether the courts should reconsider the *Tarkanian* decision.

considering . . .   **ANALYSIS & DISCUSSION**

Sponsorship Agreements (p. 351)

Not if they want to reduce their unrelated business income tax. Following the IRS decision in the Mobil Oil–Cotton Bowl case, Hip Hop Hoops should be careful to separate true sponsorship benefits from advertising practices. According to the IRS, a sponsorship payment that is exempt from the UBIT is one in which the only substantial return benefit is Hip Hop Hoops' use or acknowledgment of Big Buns Burgers' name or logo. In this hypothetical, Hip Hop Hoops should only grant Big Buns Burgers the right to be the title sponsor in exchange for its sponsorship payment. If the scoreboard signage and public address ads are included, the $10,000 payment will be considered advertising revenue that is subject to the UBIT.

A wise move for Hip Hop Hoops management would be to reduce the amount of the sponsorship payment by the cost of the signage and public address ads and require that Big Buns Burgers make a separate payment for those. Then only the smaller payment for the signage and ads would be subject to the UBIT, and Hip Hop Hoops will still get most of the $10,000 it was seeking.

REFERENCES

Cases

Adidas America, Inc. v. NCAA, 40 F. Supp. 2d 1275 (D. Kan. 1999).

Bloom v. NCAA, 93 P.3d 621 (Colo. Ct. App. 2004).

Bowers v. NCAA, 118 F. Supp. 2d 494 (D.N.J. 2000).

Brentwood Academy v. Tennessee Secondary Sch. Athletic Ass'n, 531 U.S. 288 (2001), *remanded* to 304 F. Supp. 2d 981 (M. D. Tenn. 2003).

Brentwood Academy v. Tennessee Secondary Sch. Athletic Ass'n, 2008 U.S. Dist. LEXIS 55312 (M.D. Tenn. 2008).

Cohane v. NCAA, 2007 U.S. App. LEXIS 1841 (2nd Cir. 2007), *cert. denied,* 2007 U.S. LEXIS 12179 (2007).

College Athletic Placement Serv., Inc. v. NCAA, 1974 U.S. Dist. LEXIS 7050 (D.N.J. 1974).

Cureton v. NCAA, 37 F. Supp. 2d 687 (E.D. Pa. 1999).

Davis v. Massachusetts Interscholastic Athletic Ass'n, 1995 Mass. Super. LEXIS 791 (Mass. Super. 1995).

Gaines v. NCAA, 746 F. Supp. 738 (M.D. Tenn. 1990).

Ganden v. NCAA, 1996 U.S. Dist. LEXIS 17368 (N.D. Ill. 1996).

Internal Revenue Service. (1991a, July 3). Action on Decision 1991-015, NCAA v. Comm'r, (1991 AOD LEXIS 50).

Jones v. NCAA, 392 F. Supp. 295 (D. Mass. 1975).

Law v. NCAA, 134 F.3d 1010 (10th Cir. 1998).

Law v. NCAA, 108 F. Supp. 2d 1193 (D. Kan. 2000).

Letendre v. Missouri State High Sch. Activities Ass'n, 86 S.W.3d 63 (Mo. Ct. App. 2002).

Mathews v. Eldridge, 424 U.S. 319 (1976).

Matthews v. NCAA, 179 F. Supp. 2d 1209 (E.D. Wash. 2001).

McCormack v. NCAA, 845 F.2d 1338 (5th Cir. 1988).

McGowan v. Maryland, 366 U.S. 420 (1961).

McNatt v. Frazier Sch. Dist., 1995 U.S. Dist. LEXIS 21971 (W.D. Pa. 1995).

NCAA v. Board of Regents of the Univ. of Okla., 468 U.S. 85 (1984).

NCAA v. Commissioner of Internal Revenue, 914 F.2d 1417 (10th Cir. 1990).

NCAA v. Miller, 10 F.3d 633 (9th Cir. 1993), *cert. denied,* U.S. LEXIS 2914 (1994).

NCAA v. Smith, 525 U.S. 459 (1999).

NCAA v. Tarkanian, 488 U.S. 179 (1988).

Oliver v. NCAA, Case No. 2008-CV-0762, Ct. of Common Pleas, Erie County, OH (2009).

Pryor v. NCAA, 153 F. Supp. 2d 710 (E.D. Pa. 2001), *aff'd in part, rev'd in part, and remanded,* 288 F.3d 548 (3d Cir. 2002).

Smith v. NCAA, 139 F.3d 180 (3d Cir. 1998).

Smith v. NCAA, 266 F.3d 152 (3d Cir. 2001).

Tatum v. NCAA, 992 F. Supp. 1114 (E.D. Mo. 1998).

Tennessee Secondary Sch. Athletic Ass'n v. Brentwood Academy, 551 U.S. 291 (2007).

Trustees of Boston College v. The Big East Conference, 2004 Mass. Super. LEXIS 298 (Mass. Super. 2004).

Statutes

Equity in Athletics Disclosure Act of 1994, 20 U.S.C. §§ 1092(e) and (g) (2005).

Internal Revenue Code, § 513(i) (1982).

Taxpayer Relief Act of 1977, Pub. L. No. 105-34, § 965(a), 111 Stat. 788, 893–94 (1977).

Other Sources

Alesia, M. (2006, October 5). Panel questions NCAA's tax status. *Indianapolis Star.* Retrieved October 10, 2006, from www.indystar.com.

Anderson, R. J. (2009, May 18). Commission all ears on spending fears. *Athletic Management Weekly Blog.* Retrieved May 26, 2009, from www.athletic management.com/2009/05/knight-commission-on-financial.html.

Batista, P. J., & Hatfield, L. C. (2005). Learn at home, play at school: A state-by-state examination of legislation, litigation and athletic association rules governing public school athletic participation by homeschool students. *Journal of Legal Aspects of Sport, 15,* 213–255.

Benson, M. (2006, April 9). NYSP lives precariously in budget cross hairs. *The NCAA News.* Retrieved June 14, 2009, from www.ncaa.org.

Brand, M. (2003, August 4). Consider certification a compliance vaccine. *The NCAA News.* Retrieved September 28, 2005, from www.ncaa.org/news/2003/20030804/editorial/4016n42.html.

Brown, G. T. (2005, August 29). Is college sports big business? *The NCAA News Online.*

Carey, J. (2005, May 24). Commission urges strict academic enforcement. *USA Today,* p. 8C.

Carter, W. B. (2000). Student-athlete welfare in a restructured NCAA. *Virginia Journal of Sports and the Law, 2,* 1–103.

Congressional Budget Office. (May 2009). *Tax Preferences for Collegiate Sports.* A CBO Paper, Pub. No. 3005.

Elfman, L. (2008, August 8). NCAA to provide former student-athletes with benefits. *Diverse Online.* Retrieved August 18, 2008, from www.diverseeducation.com/artman/publish/printer_11535.shtml.

Home-school rule. (2009, February 24). *The Salt Lake Tribune* (editorial opinion). Retrieved June 14, 2009, from LEXIS-NEXIS.

Internal Revenue Service. (1991b, August 16). Technical Advice Memorandum 91-47-007. *Cited in* Hill, F. R. (Fall 1995/Spring 1996). Corporate sponsorship in transactional perspective: General principles and special cases in the law of tax exempt organizations. *University of Miami Entertainment & Sports Law Review, 13,* 5–90.

Kocian, L. (2006, August 31). Teams take aim at online taunting. *The Boston Globe.* Retrieved September 7, 2006, from www.boston.com/news/local/articles/2006/08/31.

Lederman, D. (2008, May 7). Progress and more potent penalties. *Inside Higher Ed.* Retrieved May 15, 2008, from www.insidehighered.com/layout/set/print/news/2008/05/07/ncaa.

Marot, M. (2009, May 7). NCAA schools finding academic costs are priceless. *The Associated Press.* Retrieved June 14, 2009, from LEXIS-NEXIS.

Marsh, G. A. (2009). A call for dissent and further independence in the NCAA infractions process. *Cardozo Arts & Entertainment Law Journal, 26,* 695–717.

Minutes of the NCAA Executive Committee. (2000, August 11). Retrieved June 14, 2009, from www.ncaa.org.

Musselman, J. L. (2003). Recent federal income tax issues regarding professional and amateur sports. *Marquette Sports Law Review, 13,* 195–212.

NCAA. (n.d.). The purpose of athletics certification. Retrieved June 14, 2009, from www1.ncaa.org/membership/membership_svcs/athletics_certification/purpose.

NCAA. (1999). Division I athletics certification: Changes and issues for the second cycle. Retrieved September 28, 2005, from www.ncaa.org/databases/regional_seminars/guide_rules_compliance/other_topics/oth_09.html.

NCAA. (2008a). 2008–09 NCAA Division I Manual. Indianapolis, IN: NCAA Publications.

NCAA. (2008b). 2008 NCAA Membership Report. Retrieved June 14, 2009, from http://web1.ncaa.org/web_video/membership_report/2008/.

NCAA. (2009a, May 20). NCAA responds to May 2009 Congressional Budget Office report titled "Tax Preferences for Collegiate Sports." *NCAA News Release.* Retrieved June 14, 2009, from www.ncaa.org.

NCAA. (2009b). The NCAA revised budget for fiscal year ended August 31, 2009. Retrieved June 14, 2009, from www.ncaa.org/wps/ncaa?ContentID=4.

Neumeister, L. (2005, August 16). Tentative settlement announced in *NIT vs. NCAA* case. *Associated Press State and Local Wire.* Retrieved September 26, 2005, from LEXIS-NEXIS.

NFHS. (n.d.). About the NFHS. Retrieved February 19, 2006, from www.nfhs.org.

NFHS. (2005). 2004–05 NFHS High School Athletics Participation Survey. Retrieved February 19, 2006, from www.nfhs.org.

O'Connell, J. (2005, August 18). NCAA purchases NIT for $56.5 million to end legal fight. *Associated Press State and Local Wire.* Retrieved September 26, 2005, from LEXIS-NEXIS.

Otto, K. A., & Stippich, K. S. (2008). Revisiting *Tarkanian:* The entwinement and interdependence of the NCAA and state universities and colleges 20 years later. *Journal of Legal Aspects of Sport, 18,* 243–308.

Schmidt, B. (2007, April 26). Inquiry: OSAA needs stronger policies. *The Oregonian.* Retrieved May 7, 2007, from www.oregonlive.com.

Smith, S. H., & Dempsey, C. W. (1997, October 20). Editorial—Newspaper failed to tell whole story. Comment in *The NCAA News.* Retrieved September 26, 2005, from www.ncaa.org/news/1997/19971020/comment.html.

Swanson, R. A., & Spears, B. (1995). *History of sport and physical education in the United States,* 4th ed. Dubuque, IA: W.C. Brown.

Western Athletic Conference (WAC). (2008). *Western Athletic Conference Code Book,* 2008–09. Retrieved January 10, 2009, from www.wac.org.

WEBSITE RESOURCES

www.kgw.com/news/pdf/basketballreport.pdf ▪ Here you can read the full report from an investigation into accusations of racial taunting that involved high school spectators at a basketball playoff game in Oregon. The Oregon School Activities Association (OSAA) requested the investigation, and the recommendations near the end of the report show how responsibility for student conduct and incident prevention can be an important part of an organization like OSAA.

www.knightcommission.org ▪ The Knight Foundation's Commission on Intercollegiate Athletics advocates for reform in intercollegiate athletics. A 1991 report led to the development of the Division I certification process. The Commission's website offers extensive information on academic and fiscal integrity in athletics, including research, polls, policy statements, and reports. Go to "Academics Integrity" and select "Commission Reports" to see the 1991 report, among others.

www.ncaa.org ▪ The NCAA is the largest governing body in college sports. At this website you can find news, archives of the discontinued print publication *The NCAA News,* information on the NCAA's governance structure, NCAA rules, and a lot of other information related to intercollegiate athletics.

http://ncaa.org/wps/ncaa?key=/ncaa/NCAA/Legislation%0and%20Governance/Compliance/Certification%20and%20TrainingAthletics%20Certification/index-d1_ath_cert_prog ▪ The NCAA requires its Division I members to complete a certification self-study report every ten years in order to evaluate rules compliance, academic integrity, and student-athlete well-being. The report and the subsequent evaluation result in the program either being certified or put at risk for sanctions. At this page on the NCAA website, the organization lists resources for the certification process, provides a handbook for universities, and offers its measurable standards. For the full text of former Executive Director Myles Brand's comments on NCAA certification, go to www.ncaa.org/news/2003/20030804/editorial/4016n42.html.

www.nfhs.org ▪ This is the website for the National Federation of State High School Associations, the governing body that oversees interscholastic athletics for more than seven million high schools. Under the "Sports" tab, the organization provides rules, regulations, resources, and more for each recognized high school sport.

www.wacsports.com ▪ At websites of intercollegiate athletics conferences like this one, you will find news, conference rules, information about the conference governance structure, among other things.

Regulation of Participation in Private Clubs and High School and College Athletics

INTRODUCTION

P rivate clubs are designed to be exclusive with regard to membership, but this exclusiveness can result in unfairness in access to sport for women and ethnic minorities. High school and college athletics programs create opportunities for people of diverse backgrounds to join together as equals in the pursuit of common goals. However, they also create opportunities for discrimination to occur. Just as in the employment context discussed in Chapters 6 and 7, participants in interscholastic and intercollegiate athletics may face discrimination on the basis of gender (including sexual harassment), race, and disability, as well as unfair treatment based on expression—whether political or religious. Additionally, student-athlete behavior with regard to sexual activity, drug and alcohol use, and other delinquent conduct is often regulated by coaches and schools by means of "good conduct" rules. When efforts to regulate conduct are extreme, they may violate athletes' individual rights.

Managers of private country clubs, as well as high school and college athletics administrators, can use the information in this chapter to avoid creating discriminatory participation conditions for their members and students. Allegations of discriminatory policies or conduct can be very damaging to a club or school's reputation, thereby discouraging potential members from joining or students from participating or enrolling. Current participants might also be discouraged from continued participation or membership. Thus, organizations that are not careful in this area will be at a disadvantage compared to those that carefully craft and implement equitable policies. Athletics administrators will also benefit from the good public and community relations that ensue from fair and just implementation and enforcement of rules that regulate the behavior of athletes.

Exhibit 14.1 outlines the management contexts, legal issues, and relevant law discussed in this chapter.

SPORT PARTICIPATION IN PRIVATE CLUBS

A ugusta National Golf Club in Georgia and the Shoal Creek Country Club in Alabama are well-known examples of private clubs that have denied membership to women and to Blacks, respectively. In 1990, Shoal Creek was scheduled to host a PGA Tournament. When protests arose concerning its exclusionary membership policy, negative publicity and withdrawal of support by some of the tournament sponsors (including IBM, Honda, Toyota, and Delta Airlines) caused the club to change its policy, and within a few weeks it accepted its first Black member (Rothenberg, 1990). However, Augusta, host of the prestigious Masters tournament, continues to defy pressure to accept women.

Some country clubs admit women as "restricted" members without full voting rights or limit their access to the golf course or tennis courts to weekdays so that men can have the prime weekend times. They may also restrict women's access to the grill or bar. The issue for members of ethnic minority groups and for women is whether they have a legal right to membership, and all the privileges associated with it, or whether a club has the right to exclude them.

| Management contexts and legal issues pertaining to regulation of amateur participation in private clubs and in interscholastic and intercollegiate athletics, with relevant laws and cases. | | EXHIBIT | 14.1 |

MANAGEMENT CONTEXT	MAJOR LEGAL ISSUES	RELEVANT LAW	ILLUSTRATIVE CASES
Private clubs	Truly private/public accommodation	Title II CRA	Lansdowne
	Race discrimination	§ 1981; § 1983; Title II	Gibbs-Alfano
	Sex discrimination	§ 1983; public accommodation	Wanders, Borne, Barry
	Sexual orientation discrimination	First Amendment; public accommodation	Boy Scouts
	Disability discrimination	Title III ADA	Kuketz, PGA Tour, Williams
High school and college athletics	Gender equity	Title IX and regulations	Cohen, Kelley, Mercer
	Pregnancy	Title IX	Brady
	Sexual harassment	Title IX	Morrison, Jennings
	Race discrimination	Title VI	Pryor
	Disability discrimination	§ 504; ADA	Knapp, Dennin, Matthews
	Discipline issues	"Arbitrary and capricious" standard; Due Process Clause; Equal Protection Clause	Bunger, Palmer, Pegram, Long
	Transfer rules	Due Process Clause	Yeo
	Drug testing	Fourth Amendment	Derdeyn, Vernonia, Earls
	Dress/grooming codes	First Amendment; Equal Protection Clause; Due Process Clause	Stephenson, Stotts, Dunham, Menora, Moody, Liberty U.
	Pre-game prayer	First Amendment	Santa Fe, Chandler

Race Discrimination

In cases where access to country clubs is denied on the basis of race, a plaintiff may sue under Title II, § 1981, or § 1983 of the Civil Rights Act of 1964.

Title II of the Civil Rights Act

Title II of the Civil Rights Act of 1964 prohibits intentional discrimination on the basis of race, color, religion, or national origin in places of public accommodation. To prevail on a Title II claim, a plaintiff must prove discrimination on the part of a place of public accommodation. Section 2000(a) of Title II defines **place of public accommodation** to include places that affect interstate commerce and are facilities "principally engaged in selling food for consumption on the premises," as well as sports arenas, stadiums, and other places of exhibition or entertainment. There is a statutory exemption from the requirements of Title II for private clubs. The courts have generally held that sport facilities are places of entertainment under Title II, because the Supreme Court has found that both direct sport participation and spectatorship are entertainment (*Daniel v. Paul,* 1969). Hence, the real issue for plaintiffs suing country clubs is whether the club is truly private.

EXHIBIT	14.2	The *Lansdowne* eight-factor analysis for determining whether a club is truly private (*United States v. Lansdowne Swim Club*, 1989).

1. Genuine selectiveness regarding membership
2. Membership control over operations
3. History of the organization
4. Nonmember use of the facility
5. Purpose of the club's existence
6. Advertisement for members
7. Organization as a for-profit or nonprofit
8. Formalities observed, such as by-laws, meetings, and so forth

The courts have identified eight factors to be weighed in determining whether a club is truly private (see Exhibit 14.2). These factors are weighed on a case-by-case basis, and there is no magic number of factors that must be satisfied in order for a country club to establish its status as truly private. Let's examine the *Lansdowne* case to see how the court applied the eight-factor analysis.

United States v. Lansdowne Swim Club

FOCUS CASE   713 F. Supp. 785 (E.D. Pa. 1989), *aff'd*, 894 F.2d 83 (3rd Cir. 1990)

FACTS

A Black family that met all the qualification requirements applied several times for membership to the Lansdowne Swim Club and was ignored or denied each time. Over the preceding 19 years, every White applicant had been admitted, and there had been only one non-White member. The plaintiffs sued under Title II, claiming that the Swim Club was not a truly private club that was exempt from coverage of the statute; rather, it was a place of public accommodation that had engaged in race discrimination by failing to admit them to membership.

The district court held in the plaintiff's favor, finding that the club was not a truly private club exempt from Title II. In so doing, it identified eight factors to consider in making the determination as to whether a club is truly private (see Exhibit 14.2 for a list of these factors). The court further found that the club was a place of public accommodation within the coverage of the statute, and that it had engaged in a pattern and practice of intentional discrimination in its membership admission practices over the years. Finally, it found that the individual plaintiffs proved, under the *McDonnell Douglas* analysis (described in detail in Chapter 6), that they were also victims of that pattern and practice of racial discrimination. The Swim Club appealed.

HOLDING

The Third Circuit affirmed the decision of the trial court in all the respects mentioned above.

RATIONALE

The court found that three of the eight factors used to evaluate truly private status applied to the Lansdowne Swim Club. First, it found that the club's membership process was not genuinely selective. The fact that admission required a majority vote of the membership was not enough to establish exclusiveness in selecting members. Second, the history of the organization showed that it was intended to provide a service as a community swimming pool available to the public. Third, there was ample evidence that the facility was used regularly by nonmembers for certain events, including pool parties, swim meets, and volleyball and basketball played on courts in its parking lot. Finding that three of the eight factors failed to indicate private status was sufficient in the eyes of the court for it to conclude that the club was not truly private.

Furthermore, since some of the swimming pool equipment and beverages sold at the snack bar had moved in interstate commerce, and the club was a place of entertainment and had a regular food service, the court found that the club was a place of public accommodation under Title II. Finally, it held that the membership selection process that had been used over the years established a pattern and practice of race discrimination, and that the plaintiffs had been intentionally discriminated against by the application of that membership process in their cases. The court entered an injunction against the use of a discriminatory membership process.

§ 1981 of the Civil Rights Act

Section 1981 of the Civil Rights Act prohibits intentional racially discriminatory acts in the making or enforcement of a contract. There is no exemption for private clubs in § 1981, and the courts have generally held that the Title II exemption should not be read into a § 1981 analysis, because Congress did not see fit to do so when it made amendments to the law in the 1991 Civil Rights Act (see *Cook v. Twin Oaks Country Club*, 2000; *Crawford v. Willow Oaks Country Club*, 1999). An example of a § 1981 case is *Gibbs-Alfano v. Ossining Boat & Canoe Club, Inc.* (1999). In that case, the plaintiff, who was Black, had been suspended twice for using foul language and for improper behavior. The second suspension was never lifted, resulting in her effectively being expelled from membership. She claimed the suspensions were racially motivated and intended to negatively affect her contractual relationship with the club. The court found that she had alleged sufficient facts to support the pleadings and denied the club's motion to dismiss.

§ 1983 of the Civil Rights Act

To state a claim under § 1983, a plaintiff must allege that a right found in the Constitution or other federal law was violated and that the person who violated that right was acting under color of state law (i.e., engaged in state action). The plaintiff in the *Gibbs-Alfano* case discussed in the previous section also brought a § 1983 claim, which alleged that her First Amendment right to association was violated by the boat club and also alleged a property deprivation (loss of membership) without due process. The court ruled that state action existed because the boat club and the town of Ossining were in a symbiotic relationship due to a license agreement in which the club paid only a nominal annual fee to use the town's land; all improvements to the property were paid for by the boat club and became the property of the town immediately upon construction; and the boat club provided insurance coverage to the town, as well as legal defense and indemnification against all claims relating to use of the licensed property. The court further found that the boat club performed a public function by agreeing to serve as a place of public accommodation and to promote water and boating safety. Thus, the court concluded that the boat club was a state actor, so § 1983 would apply and protect the plaintiff's constitutional rights. The parties eventually settled out of court.

Gender Discrimination

Sex is not a protected category under Title II, so plaintiffs bringing gender discrimination claims have to rely on § 1983 or state public accommodation statutes instead.

§ 1983 of the Civil Rights Act

In *Citizens Council on Human Relations v. Buffalo Yacht Club* (1977), the court found that a private yacht club's relationship with the city of Buffalo made it a state actor, and denied a motion to dismiss § 1983 claims against both the yacht club and the city for excluding plaintiffs from membership on the basis of their sex.

State public accommodation statutes

State public accommodation statutes are often broader in scope than federal antidiscrimination laws. For example, unlike Title II, which only provides protection on the basis of race, color, religion, and national origin, most of the state laws protect women from discrimination in access to places of public accommodation. Additionally, many of the state statutes protect people in a range of other categories as well, including sexual orientation, marital status, age, and disability. Exhibit 14.3 provides an example of this additional breadth.

Wanders v. Bear Hill Golf Club, Inc. (1998) is an example of a case in which a state public accommodation statute was used in a gender discrimination claim. The golf club had denied plaintiffs the opportunity to play in weekend golf tournaments solely because of their sex. After finding that the club qualified as a place of public accommodation under the Massachusetts public accommodation statute and that the women golfers had been treated in a discriminatory fashion, the court found for the plaintiffs.

EXHIBIT	14.3	Wisconsin public accommodation statute—protected classes (Wis. Stat. § 106.04(9)(a)2).

[No person may:]

Give preferential treatment to some classes of persons in providing services or facilities in any public place of accommodation or amusement because of sex, race, color, creed, sexual orientation, national origin or ancestry.

A similar result was reached in *Borne v. Haverhill Golf & Country Club, Inc.* (2003). In *Borne,* the court found that the country club was a place of public accommodation that had manipulated membership categories to systematically exclude women, limit women's access to the golf course by restricting their tee times, and attempted to restrict their access to the grill and the card room. The court ordered the club to change its policies and upheld the jury's award to the nine plaintiffs of $1.9 million in compensatory and punitive damages.

In contrast to *Wanders* and *Borne,* a Wisconsin court ruled that the Maple Bluff Country Club qualified as a truly private club under the *Lansdowne* eight-factor analysis (see Exhibit 14.2). First, it found that the membership policy was truly selective. The club had a well-defined plan, requiring nomination, interviews, and a unanimous vote of approval by the members, and this plan was consistently employed in determining membership. Second, there was a high degree of member control over the operations of the club, in that the membership owned the club's property and its elected board made the decisions as to what programs and facilities would be provided and the hours of use. Third, the historical purpose of the club had always been that of a private country club established to provide social and recreational services and facilities to its members and their guests.

The fact that the club had entered into a lease agreement with the Village of Maple Bluff that permitted limited use of the swimming pool, tennis courts, and golf course did not, in the court's view, overcome the weight of the *Lansdowne* factors it found applicable. The court stated that the provisions of the lease did not mean that most village residents would be admitted to membership. Thus, when a female member brought suit alleging that the club had engaged in sex discrimination by favoring male over female members in its provision of services and opportunities, the court held that the club was truly private and did not have to comply with the state public accommodations law (*Barry v. Maple Bluff Country Club,* 2001).

Discrimination on the Basis of Sexual Orientation

Several state and city human rights laws prohibit discrimination on the basis of sexual orientation as well as the usual protected categories. As future cases arise, these laws might be used to challenge club policies that discriminate on this basis. However, much depends upon whether a

Competitive Advantage
STRATEGIES

Participation in Private Clubs/ Places of Public Accommodation

■ If operating a club that is intended to be truly private, you should carefully examine the cases that apply the *Lansdowne* factors and structure your policies regarding membership and use by nonmembers accordingly. Remember, a court might rely on only two or three of the *Lansdowne* factors to rule that a club is not truly private but functions instead as a place of public accommodation. Thus, it would be important for a club desiring to be truly private to address as many of those factors as possible in developing and implementing policy.

■ If operating a club that functions as a place of public accommodation, avoid implementing policies restricting playing time or access to dining areas and bars on the basis of race or gender.

■ If operating a truly private club that differentiates on the basis of race and/or gender in access to membership, programming, or facilities, be aware that while the club may be beyond legal challenge, negative publicity about prejudicial practices could result in considerable damage to organizational success.

■ Plan for the inclusion of athletes with disabilities in all programs and services where feasible.

■ Implement training sessions to educate staff about the needs of people with different types of disabilities and to change attitudes about the value of providing equal sport and recreation participation opportunities for people with disabilities.

■ Create and implement written policies and procedures to be used when an individual with a disability requests an accommodation.

EXHIBIT 14.4   Legal analysis of an ADA Title III claim.

To analyze a Title III claim, the steps are as follows:

1. Does the individual have a covered disability?
2. Does that impairment substantially limit a major life activity?
3. Was the individual discriminated against solely on the basis of that disability?

Under the third prong, Title III discrimination includes:

(i) the imposition or application of eligibility criteria that screen out or tend to screen out an individual with a disability or any class of individuals with disabilities from fully and equally enjoying any goods, services, facilities, privileges, advantages, or accommodations, unless such criteria can be shown to be necessary for the provision of the goods, services, facilities, privileges, advantages, or accommodations being offered;

(ii) a failure to make reasonable modifications in policies, practices, or procedures, when such modifications are necessary to afford such goods, services, facilities, privileges, advantages, or accommodations to individuals with disabilities, unless the entity can demonstrate that making such modifications would fundamentally alter the nature of such goods, services, facilities, privileges, advantages, or accommodations. (42 U.S.C. § 12182(b)(2)(A), 2005)

country club that is sued for excluding homosexuals can defend itself by showing that the club is engaged in expressive association under the First Amendment. In *Boy Scouts of America v. Dale* (2000), the Supreme Court found that part of the Boy Scouts' mission is to instill their moral values in young people (including the view that homosexuality is inconsistent with those values) and that therefore the Scouts regularly engaged in expressive activity.

The Court held that applying the New Jersey public accommodation statute to require the Boy Scouts to admit an openly gay scoutmaster would violate their expressive association rights by interfering with their choice not to endorse a perspective contrary to their beliefs. It would be more difficult to argue that membership in a country club, the primary purpose of which is sport and social entertainment, constitutes expressive activity. However, as mentioned above, the *Gibbs-Alfano* court hinted, without explanation, that the Ossining Boat Club might have violated the plaintiff's right to expressive association by terminating her membership.

Discrimination on the Basis of Disability

Title III of the Americans with Disabilities Act protects people with disabilities from discrimination by private entities operating as places of public accommodation. Exhibit 14.4 details the typical Title III analysis once it has been determined that the defendant is a place of public accommodation.

The *Kuketz* case illustrates how a court applied Title III in an athletic club setting.

Kuketz v. Petronelli

821 N.E.2d 473 (Mass. 2005)

FACTS

Plaintiff Kuketz was a nationally ranked wheelchair racquetball player whose athletic club denied him permission to play in the club's Men's "A" Level Tournament League against able-bodied competitors. He had asked for two accommodations as part of his request to participate: (1) that he be allowed to play in his wheelchair; and (2) that he be allowed two bounces to hit the ball rather than one. Kuketz sued under Title III of the Americans with Disabilities Act. The trial court granted summary judgment for the defendant club, holding that the requested "two-bounce" rule modification would fundamentally alter the nature of the racquetball competition. Kuketz appealed, and the Massachusetts Supreme Court transferred the case to itself.

HOLDING

The Supreme Judicial Court of Massachusetts affirmed, holding that the requested accommodation was unreasonable because it would have fundamentally altered the game of racquetball.

RATIONALE

The court followed the analysis established by the U. S. Supreme Court in the *PGA Tour, Inc. v. Martin* (2001) case, which requires a three-part inquiry in Title III claims as to whether a requested accommodation should have been granted:

1. Was the accommodation necessary in order to provide the disabled individual the full and equal enjoyment of the services or facilities?
2. Was the accommodation reasonable?
3. Would the accommodation fundamentally alter the nature of the competition?

According to the court, Kuketz clearly had the ability to be an "A" League player except for his paraplegia, so for him to participate at that level it would be necessary for the club to provide the requested accommodations. With regard to reasonableness, the court said that there was disputed evidence about whether safety concerns were reasonable as to whether the wheelchair posed a significant risk of injury to others. There was also some disagreement about whether the rule modification would fundamentally alter the nature of the game. The court concluded that allowing Kuketz two bounces would fundamentally alter the nature of the game, so it did not feel compelled to go any further into the reasonableness of the safety concerns.

On the issue of fundamental alteration, the court applied the test used by the Supreme Court in the *PGA Tour, Inc. v. Martin* (2001) case. In *PGA Tour*, the Court articulated a two-pronged test for recognizing a fundamental alteration of a sport organization's rules or policies. According to the Court, a modification is a fundamental alteration if one of the following is true:

1. It affects an essential, rather than peripheral, aspect of the organization's policies or programs.
2. It is a minor change that nevertheless gives the disabled individual an advantage over other participants.

In the *PGA Tour* case, Casey Martin, who suffers from a severe circulatory disorder in his legs that makes it very painful and indeed dangerous for him to walk very far, had sued the PGA Tour for denying his request for a waiver of the "must walk" rule so he could ride in a cart in professional tournaments.

The Court held that the PGA Tour had to grant his request because it was a reasonable accommodation; that is, allowing Martin to ride in a cart would not fundamentally alter the game of golf, the essence of which is shotmaking. How one gets to the ball is peripheral, said the Court. The Court further found that granting a waiver of the "walking" rule would not give Martin a competitive advantage, because he would probably still experience more fatigue walking from the cart to his ball and back than would the other competitors who had to walk the entire course. Additionally, some professional golfers testified that walking the entire course was actually an advantage because it gave them time to focus their thoughts and allowed them to get a better feel for the course and playing conditions.

In applying the *PGA Tour* analysis, the judge in *Kuketz* found that the two-bounce rule modification was different from Martin's request to ride in a golf cart because the two-bounce rule would change the essence of racquetball, which is hitting a moving ball before the second bounce. The court also acknowledged testimony that such a rule would affect the speed, strategy, positioning, and movement of the players.

The court noted that the U. S. Racquetball Association (USRA) had promulgated separate rules for wheelchair racquetball that allowed two bounces but that no set of rules addressed play by a wheelchair player against an able-bodied player. The court concluded that it was within the athletic club's authority to adopt whatever rules it wanted to govern whatever style of play it wanted to allow. Nothing in the ADA required the adoption of rules that would fundamentally alter the nature of racquetball competition as defined by the USRA's Official Rules.

The court recognized that allowing the two-bounce rule modification might also constitute the second type of fundamental alteration by giving Kuketz an unfair advantage over other players. However, since summary judgment was supported by the fundamental alteration analysis, the court did not decide this issue.

The *Kuketz* case illustrates how one state court analyzed a case where an athlete with a physical disability sued for the right to compete in "elite" sport with able-bodied athletes. A case addressing this issue in the context of youth sport is *Williams v. Wakefield Basketball Association* (2003). In this case, plaintiff Williams, a 7-year-old confined to a wheelchair, sued the Wakefield Basketball Association after it refused to let him play in a league with his friends because his wheelchair would be dangerous to the other players. The district court, in an unreported decision, held that the rules modifications necessary to permit Williams to play would be so extensive as to fundamentally alter the essence of the game of basketball. Additionally, the court found that Williams' wheelchair would pose a direct threat to the safety of other players, particularly in the activities of setting picks and rebounding, which involve the potential for physical contact. According to the court, the safety considerations involved would also create a competitive disadvantage for the opposing team.

HIGH SCHOOL AND COLLEGE ATHLETICS

Many laws are implicated by efforts to regulate participation in high school and college athletics. This section focuses on legal issues concerning regulation of participants in the areas of gender equity, race and disability discrimination, discipline issues, transfer rules, drug testing, dress and grooming codes, and discrimination on the basis of religion.

Gender Equity—Title IX

Gender inequities in interscholastic and intercollegiate athletics have coexisted for many years with sex discrimination in other educational contexts, such as admissions policies. In 1972, Congress passed Title IX as a remedial statute intended to address sex discrimination throughout the whole spectrum of educational offerings, not just athletics (refer back to Exhibit 6.5 for the actual language of Title IX). As a result, many educational opportunities have been created for women in diverse areas such as in law and medical schools, as well as in competitive athletics. In high schools, the number of girls participating in athletics has risen from 294,000 in 1971 to over 3 million in 2007–08 (NFHS, 2008). When Title IX was enacted, only 15 percent of intercollegiate athletes were female, compared to 43 percent in 2006–07, nearly a three-fold increase (NCAA, 2008).

Nevertheless, inequities continue, even as women constituted approximately 57 percent of the overall undergraduate student body nationwide by Fall 2005 (Women's Sports Foundation, 2008). The Women's Sports Foundation estimates that 80 percent of all universities remain out of compliance (Dunnavant, 2002). In light of the great value Title IX has proven to be for females who want to compete, as well as the huge expense to an institution of being found in violation of Title IX, prudent athletics administrators should make every effort to act in good faith with respect to *all* their student-athletes and aggressively move toward Title IX compliance if they have not yet done so.

Enforcement process and remedies

Under Title IX, individual athletes who have experienced sex discrimination may bring suit for monetary damages and injunctive relief. Additionally, individuals and organizations (such as the Women's Sports Foundation or the National Women's Law Center) may file claims with the U. S. Department of Education's Office for Civil Rights (OCR), which then must investigate. Finally, the OCR itself may initiate investigations into Title IX compliance. In addition to court orders to improve opportunities for women and monetary damages awards to successful plaintiffs, punitive damages may be awarded when the discrimination is found to have been intentional. Another very threatening remedy, which to date has never been used, is that a school could be punished with a complete loss of its federal funding, which would mean losses in the millions of dollars for some universities that receive research dollars from large federal grants.

Title IX regulations

The U. S. Department of Education is charged with enforcing the athletics regulations promulgated under Title IX (see Exhibit 14.5). When the OCR investigates a school for lack of compliance, it evaluates the program as a whole. It does not simply rule a university noncompliant if, for example, the university fails to provide adequate resources for one item in the list of athletics benefits and opportunities, such as publicity.

EXHIBIT	14.5	Title IX athletics regulations.

34 C.F.R. § 106.37(c) Financial Assistance

(c) *Athletic scholarships.* (1) To the extent that a recipient awards athletic scholarships or grants-in-aid, it must provide reasonable opportunities for such awards for members of each sex in proportion to the number of students of each sex participating in interscholastic or intercollegiate athletics.

(2) Separate athletic scholarships or grants-in-aid for members of each sex may be provided as part of separate athletic teams for members of each sex to the extent consistent with this paragraph and § 106.41.

34 C.F.R. § 106.41 Athletics

(a) *General.* No person shall, on the basis of sex, be excluded from participation in, be denied the benefits of, be treated differently from another person or otherwise be discriminated against in any interscholastic, intercollegiate, club or intramural athletics offered by a recipient, and no recipient shall provide any such athletics separately on such basis.

(b) *Separate teams.* Notwithstanding the requirements of paragraph (a) of this section, a recipient may operate or sponsor separate teams for members of each sex where selection for such teams is based upon competitive skill or the activity involved is a contact sport. However, where a recipient operates or sponsors a team in a particular sport for members of one sex but operates or sponsors no such team for members of the other sex, and athletic opportunities for members of that sex have previously been limited, members of the excluded sex must be allowed to try-out for the team offered unless the sport involved is a contact sport. For the purposes of this part, contact sports include boxing, wrestling, rugby, ice hockey, football, basketball and other sports the purpose or major activity of which involves bodily contact.

(c) *Equal opportunity.* A recipient which operates or sponsors interscholastic, intercollegiate, club or intramural athletics shall provide equal athletic opportunity for members of both sexes. In determining whether equal opportunities are available the Director will consider, among other factors:

(1) Whether the selection of sports and levels of competition effectively accommodate the interests and abilities of members of both sexes;

(2) The provision of equipment and supplies;

(3) Scheduling of games and practice time;

(4) Travel and per diem allowance;

(5) Opportunity to receive coaching and academic tutoring;

(6) Assignment and compensation of coaches and tutors;

(7) Provision of locker rooms, practice and competitive facilities;

(8) Provision of medical and training facilities and services;

(9) Provision of housing and dining facilities and services;

(10) Publicity.

Unequal aggregate expenditures for members of each sex or unequal expenditures for male and female teams if a recipient operates or sponsors separate teams will not constitute noncompliance with this section, but the Assistant Secretary may consider the failure to provide necessary funds for teams for one sex in assessing equality of opportunity for members of each sex.

Athletics scholarships and scheduling of sports seasons

Claims have been filed with the OCR against several universities for their failure to provide scholarship dollars to female athletes in proportion to the percentage of athletes who are female (Jenkins, 2002). At the high school level, with regard to the "laundry list" of athletics benefits and opportunities, the Michigan High School Athletic Association recently lost a lawsuit on the issue of inequities in sport season schedules for girls versus boys. Certain girls sports had been scheduled as fall or spring sports when the more appropriate season would have been the other one given the college recruiting seasons for those sports. The boys' teams, however, were scheduled in seasons appropriate for their sports. Thus, the girls' sports had been treated unfairly so that the boys' teams could have the facilities in the season most advantageous to them. The district court found that the inequitable scheduling system violated Title IX and the Equal Protection Clause (*Communities for Equity v. Michigan High School Athletic Association,* 2001). The Sixth Circuit later affirmed with regard to the equal protection claim and so did not find it necessary to reach a decision on the Title IX claim (2004). On similar facts, the Second Circuit found a Title IX violation (*McCormick v. School District of Mamaroneck,* 2004).

Participation opportunities

Most of the athletics-related Title IX litigation so far, though, has centered on the issue of participation opportunities. The defining case on this issue is *Cohen v. Brown University* (*Cohen IV,* 1996), which was the first case in which a federal appellate court adopted the three-part test (see Exhibit 14.6) that has become the standard test for compliance in participation opportunities.

Three-part test for equity in participation opportunities.	EXHIBIT **14.6**

THE THREE-PART TEST FOR COMPLIANCE REGARDING EQUITY IN PARTICIPATION OPPORTUNITIES (1979 OCR POLICY INTERPRETATION)

In effectively accommodating the interests and abilities of male and female athletes, institutions must provide both the opportunity for individuals of each sex to participate in intercollegiate competition, and for athletes of each sex to have competitive team schedules which equally reflect their abilities.

a. Compliance will be assessed in any one of the following ways:

(1) Whether intercollegiate level participation opportunities for male and female students are provided in numbers substantially proportionate to their respective enrollments; or

(2) Where the members of one sex have been and are underrepresented among intercollegiate athletes, whether the institution can show a history and continuing practice of program expansion which is demonstrably responsive to the developing interest and abilities of the members of that sex; or

(3) Where the members of one sex are underrepresented among intercollegiate athletes, and the institution cannot show a continuing practice of program expansion such as that cited above, whether it can be demonstrated that the interests and abilities of the members of that sex have been fully and effectively accommodated by the present program.

Let's examine the decision in *Cohen v. Brown University* to see how the court applied the three-part test.

Cohen v. Brown University (Cohen IV)

FOCUS CASE   101 F.3d 155 (1st Cir. 1996)

FACTS

In 1993–94, Brown University offered 32 varsity sports, 16 of which were women's teams. Although women comprised 51 percent of the undergraduate student body, only 38 percent of the athletes were female. In response to a university-wide order to cut the budget, the athletic department decided to demote two men's sports (water polo and golf) and two women's sports (volleyball and gymnastics) to club sport status. As a result, the demoted teams received lower priority in scheduling practice times and in access to athletic training services, and they lost admissions preferences in recruiting freshmen. Additionally, the coaches of the demoted women's teams lost their office space, long-distance telephone access, and clerical support (*Cohen v. Brown University [Cohen I]*, 1992). Members of the demoted women's gymnastics and volleyball teams brought suit under Title IX, claiming that Brown's action exacerbated the university's existing failure to provide women with equitable opportunities to participate in varsity-level intercollegiate athletics. The district court applied the three-part test it found in the 1979 Policy Interpretation issued by the Office for Civil Rights and held that Brown University was not providing equitable participation opportunities in violation of Title IX. The university appealed.

HOLDING

The U. S. Court of Appeals for the First Circuit affirmed the decision of the district court, holding that an institution violates Title IX if it ineffectively accommodates its students' interests and abilities in athletics, regardless of its performance relative to the other areas of concern listed in the athletics regulations (the "laundry list"). The First Circuit ruled that under this analysis Brown University had violated Title IX and thus would have to adhere to a court-ordered compliance plan, which included reinstating the demoted women's teams to varsity status. As part of its decision, the court explicitly adopted the three-part compliance test enumerated in the OCR's 1979 Policy Interpretation.

ISSUES DISCUSSED BY THE COURT

1. The validity of the Policy Interpretation's three-part test
2. The validity of Brown's quota argument
3. The meaning of full accommodation of interest and ability
4. The validity of Brown's relative interest argument

RATIONALE

Issue #1: Affirmation of the Validity of the Policy Interpretation's Three-Part Test

Brown University challenged the appropriateness of the district court's adoption of the three-part test for equity in participation opportunities that OCR had introduced in its 1979 Policy Interpretation. In affirming the district court's adoption of that test, the First Circuit stated that it is well-settled law that when Congress has expressly delegated authority to an administrative agency to promulgate regulations to implement a statute, the courts should grant substantial judicial deference and accord those regulations controlling weight unless they are arbitrary, capricious, or clearly contrary to the statute. Here, the court found that the Policy Interpretation reflected OCR's interpretation of Title IX and its implementing regulations regarding athletics, and thus the policy supported the intent of the statute.

Issue #2: Rejection of Brown University's Quota Argument

Brown University argued that the compliance test establishes a quota of participation slots that must be provided for women—a quota that disregards what they referred to as women's lesser interest in sport compared to men—and therefore gives preferential treatment to women when there are many more male students who would be interested in participating if there were more opportunities for them. Section 1681(b) of the statute does state that the law does not

> require any educational institution to grant preferential or disparate treatment to the members of one sex on account of an imbalance which may exist with respect to the total number or percentage of persons of that sex participating . . . in comparison with the total number or percentage of persons of that sex in any community, State, section or other area.

That portion of the law provides, however, that subsection (b) "shall not be construed to prevent the consideration in any . . . proceeding under this chapter of statistical evidence tending to show that such an imbalance exists." Therefore, using statistical evidence to measure compliance with the law is permitted by the statute.

What is not permitted is granting *preferential treatment* to the underrepresented sex on the *sole* basis of a statistical imbalance in participation numbers. In the words of the court:

> . . . the three-part test is, on its face, entirely consistent with § 1681(b) because the test does not require preferential or disparate treatment for either gender. [It does not mandate] statistical balancing; rather, the policy interpretation merely creates a presumption that a school is in compliance . . . when it achieves such a statistical balance. (*Kelley v. Board of Trustees*, 35 F.3d 265 (7th Cir. 1994))

If a school is unable to satisfy prong one of the test to create such a presumption, it can still use the second or third prong to demonstrate compliance with the law. Thus, the test does not depend solely on statistical balancing.

In dismissing Brown's argument that Title IX is a quota system, the First Circuit court stated,

> Brown's approach fails to recognize that, because gender-segregated teams are the norm in intercollegiate athletics programs, athletics differs from admissions and employment [situations] in analytically material ways. In providing for gender-segregated teams, intercollegiate athletics programs necessarily allocate opportunities separately for male and female students, and, thus, any inquiry into

a claim of gender discrimination must compare the athletics participation opportunities provided for men with those provided for women.

... Rather than create a quota or preference, this unavoidably gender-conscious comparison merely provides for the allocation of athletics resources and participation opportunities between the sexes in a non-discriminatory manner.

... In contrast to the employment and admissions contexts, in the athletics context, gender is not an irrelevant characteristic. Courts and institutions must have some way of determining whether an institution complies with the mandate of Title IX ... and some way of fashioning a remedy.

Additionally, the court stated that OCR could have required that the women's programs have exactly the same teams as the men's, including women's football, for example, which would have made it easy to assess compliance in the provision of participation opportunities. Instead, OCR opted to allow schools flexibility in offering differing sports to men and women, which means that compliance must be measured by other criteria, such as percentages of participation slots and differences in dollar amounts allocated.*

In sum, prong one of the compliance test does universities a favor by providing them with a clear and measurable way of knowing they are safely in compliance with the law; they do not have to guess whether a court would find that they had satisfied the other prongs of the test, which are inherently less objective ways to measure compliance. Quoting *Kelley* again, the court stated that:

... if compliance with Title IX is to be measured through this sort of analysis, it is only practical that schools be given some clear way to establish that they have satisfied the requirements of the statute. The substantial proportionality contained in Benchmark 1 merely establishes such a safe harbor. (*Kelley*, 35 F.3d at 271)

Issue #3: Defining the Meaning of Full (and Effective) Accommodation of Interest and Ability

The First Circuit court determined that prong three "demands not merely some accommodation, but full and effective accommodation. If there is sufficient interest and ability among members of the statistically underrepresented gender, not slaked by existing programs, an institution necessarily fails this prong of the test." Where, as in this case, a university has demoted or eliminated viable women's teams, clearly existing interest and ability are no longer being fully accommodated.

---

*The OCR has provided additional guidance on acceptable disparities between numerical goals and reality in the recognition that the student body gender ratios and athlete gender ratios will fluctuate slightly from year to year at any given school. For example, the OCR's 1996 Policy Interpretation states:

As another example, over the past five years an institution has had a consistent enrollment rate for women of 50 percent. During this time period, it has been expanding its program for women in order to reach proportionality. In the year that the institution reaches its goal—i.e., 50 percent of the participants in its athletic program are female—its enrollment rate for women increases to 52 percent. Under these circumstances, the institution would satisfy part one.

In a case where there has been no such demotion or elimination, but female athletes have requested a new varsity team or elevation of a club team to varsity status, the *Cohen II* court stated that

> the mere fact that there are some female students interested in a sport does not *ipso facto* require the school to provide a varsity team to comply with the third benchmark. Rather, [the third prong would require granting such a request] . . . when, and to the extent that, there is "sufficient interest and ability among the members of the excluded sex to sustain a viable team and a reasonable expectation of intercollegiate competition for that team." (*Cohen II* at 898)*

Issue #4: Rejection of Brown University's Relative Interest Argument

In disputing its failure on prong three, Brown University argued that the third prong should be interpreted to require allocating participation opportunities on the basis of the ratio of interested and able females versus interested and able male students. For example, if Brown surveyed its student body and found that 80 percent of its male students would participate in athletics if the opportunity existed versus only 40 percent of the females, then twice as many participation opportunities should be given to males because twice as many males were interested. Given women's lesser interest in participating in sports, Brown argued, affording them fewer opportunities based on the relative interests of the two sexes would still effectively accommodate existing interest and ability under prong three.

Brown's relative interest argument was resoundingly rejected by the court, which stated that such an approach "reads the 'full' out of the duty to accommodate 'fully and effectively.'" Indeed, measuring effective accommodation of interest using the relative interest method would cause the law itself to limit program expansion for women to the status quo level of interest. The court recognized that women's lower participation rate reflects an historical lack of opportunities and encouragement to participate in athletics. In the court's words, "Interest and ability rarely develop in a vacuum; they evolve as a function of opportunity and experience." The court concluded that "even if it can be empirically demonstrated that, at a particular time, women have less interest in sports than do men, such evidence, standing alone, cannot justify providing fewer athletics opportunities for women than for men."

Brown University's approach would have contravened the whole purpose of Title IX because it does not permit a "court to remedy a gender-based disparity in athletics participation opportunities. Instead, this approach freezes that disparity by law. . . . Had Congress intended to entrench, rather than change, the status quo—with its historical emphasis on men's participation opportunities to the detriment of women's opportunities—it need not have gone to all the trouble of enacting Title IX." The court found that the explosive growth in women's participation in sport since the enactment of Title IX was evidence that interest is closely related to opportunity.

---

*The Second Circuit court found Colgate University to have violated prong three when, over a nine-year period, it refused four student requests to elevate the women's ice hockey club team to varsity status (*Cook v. Colgate University*, 1993). Additionally, the women's rowing club team sued Baylor University for failing to grant its request to be elevated to varsity status after Baylor had promised to do so by the year 2003 and later put off the promised date to 2006 (Harrer, 2004).

Competitive Advantage
STRATEGIES

Gender Equity in High School and College Athletics

- Strongly consider adding or elevating a women's sport to varsity status if the requesting female athletes can show evidence of interest and ability to compete and a reasonable expectation of competitive opportunities for the team.

- In keeping with the spirit of the law, try to consider alternatives to dropping men's sports when attempting to move toward Title IX compliance. However, recognize that Title IX does not mandate that schools create more opportunities or spend more money on women's sports; instead, it leaves the choice of method for achieving compliance up to the individual school—until it is successfully sued.

- Know that when boosters or alums give money in support of a sex-specific program, the Title IX regulations require that the school balance that money with an equal amount of financial support for the other gender's programs. A good way to handle this is to make clear in fundraising campaigns and literature that the law requires you to do this type of balancing, so that a large gift could actually hurt the overall athletics program unless it is not restricted by sex.

- Remember that Title IX applies to club sports and intramurals as well as to varsity sports, so be sure to evaluate the compliance status of those types of programs too.

- Consider capping the number of walk-ons allowed in men's sports.

- Consider supporting the Women's Sports Foundation's proposal that the NCAA reduce the number of football scholarships from 85 to 60 and limit the total number of football players, including walk-ons, to 80 per team.

(continued)

In March 2005, the Office for Civil Rights issued another Policy Clarification, focused on the third prong of the three-part test. Its "Dear Colleague" cover letter states the following:

> An institution will be found in compliance with part three unless there exists a sport(s) for the underrepresented sex for which *all* three of the following conditions are met: (1) unmet interest sufficient to sustain a varsity team in the sport(s); (2) sufficient ability to sustain an intercollegiate team in the sport(s); and (3) reasonable expectation of intercollegiate competition for a team in the sport(s) within the school's normal competitive region. Thus, schools are not required to accommodate the interests and abilities of all their students or fulfill every request for the addition or elevation of particular sports, unless all three conditions are present. In this analysis, the burden of proof is on OCR . . . or on students . . . to show by a preponderance of the evidence that the institution is not in compliance with part three.

The 2005 Clarification also endorses the use of interest surveys of enrolled students to assess interest and ability. In support of this endorsement, the Policy Clarification is accompanied by a "User's Guide to Developing Student Interest Surveys Under Title IX," which permits the lack of student response to an interest survey to be interpreted by an institution as a lack of interest in athletics participation. Under any circumstances, attempting to extract substantive meaning from a failure to respond is a highly problematic approach to survey research. It is especially troubling here, given that the Office of Civil Rights found that in the past most of the institutions it investigated had reported their response rates as low or failed to report them at all (U. S. Dept. of Education, 2005). In fact, the OCR reported that "few if any institutions made an effort to obtain high response rates" (U. S. Dept. of Education, 2005, p. 6). Scholars have consistently questioned the use of interest surveys to assess interest and ability for several reasons, including the fact that they are distributed to the existing student body, which is not where most intercollegiate athletes "come from" (Claussen, 1997; Samuels & Galles, 2003). As a result, Title IX advocates are extremely concerned that this 2005 Policy Clarification will set back progress toward gender equity in university athletics programs.

Reverse discrimination and the contact sport exemption

The federal courts have uniformly followed the *Cohen IV* court's analysis when deciding subsequent cases pertaining to gender equity in participation opportunities. Other issues that demand mention here are: claims by male athletes that the application of a Title IX remedy constitutes reverse discrimination against men and claims alleging discrimination under the contact sport exemption in the regulations.

Reverse discrimination. In several cases, the courts have made it clear that Title IX and its application do not constitute reverse discrimination against male athletes. For example, in *Kelley v. Board of Trustees, University of Illinois* (1994), the Seventh Circuit held that when the University of Illinois terminated its men's swimming program but retained its women's swimming program, it did not violate Title IX because even after doing so, the percentage of athletes who were male outstripped the percentage of males in the undergraduate student body. See also *Miami University Wrestling Club v. Miami University* (2002). In both *Kelley* and *Miami University Wrestling Club*, the courts also ruled that the elimination of men's teams did not violate the Equal Protection Clause.

Contact sport exemption. The Title IX regulations require that where a particular sport is offered to one sex but not the other, persons of the excluded sex must be allowed to try out for the existing team. So, for example, if there is a men's tennis team but no women's team, a woman who wants to play tennis must be allowed to try out for the men's team. However, an exemption to this requirement is made if the sport is a contact sport (34 C.F.R. § 106.41(b)).

Some are of the view that the contact sport exemption is paternalistic and based on outdated notions of female frailty and thus should be removed from the regulations (Furman, 2007).

With regard to the contact sport exemption, an important case is *Mercer v. Duke University* (1999). Here, Heather Sue Mercer was a placekicker who had made the Duke football team. When she was subsequently treated in a discriminatory fashion based on her sex, she sued. Duke argued that the contact sport exemption found in the regulations (see Exhibit 14.5, 34 C.F.R. §106.41(b)) means that Title IX is simply inapplicable to contact sports, and thus the football coach's actions (dropping her from the team because of her sex and making gender-biased remarks to her) did not violate Title IX.

The court saw things differently and held that Mercer's claim was valid because the contact sport exemption merely means that a school need not allow a female to try out

Competitive Advantage
STRATEGIES

Gender Equity in High School and College Athletics, continued

- Be sure to consider the "laundry list" of athletics benefits found in the Title IX regulations whenever making decisions about the items listed there, such as, expenditures on publicity, hiring coaches, creating or upgrading facilities, and scheduling practices.

- Ensure that the gender ratio of dollars spent on athletics grants-in-aid mirrors the gender ratio of participating athletes.

- Conduct training seminars for coaches and players that provide guidance on avoiding behavior and comments that could be construed as sex discrimination.

- Be wary of inviting a negligence lawsuit by taking shortcuts to Title IX compliance that would increase the numbers of female athletes but do so in an unsafe manner or increase the risk of injury by not ensuring adequate facilities and coaching supervision.

- Invite Title IX consultants to campus to assist with program evaluation and development of compliance strategies.

- Reallocate resources in a more equitable fashion by identifying ways to reduce unnecessary or extravagant costs.

- Plan fund-raising efforts to increase resources available for sports for females, including corporate sponsorships.

- Do not become reliant on soft money as part of your regular athletics budget, but put donated money into interest-bearing accounts that will continue to generate income in perpetuity.

- Conduct a self-evaluation of your program by utilizing checklists available on the website of the National Women's Law Center: www.nwlc.org.

for a contact sport. If and when they do, however, the general antidiscrimination provisions still apply, and the athlete must be treated in a gender equitable manner. The trial court awarded Mercer one dollar in compensatory damages (connoting a moral victory) and $2 million in punitive damages, finding that the university had engaged in intentional discrimination. The Fourth Circuit later vacated the punitive damages award, holding that punitive damages are not available as a remedy in private Title IX actions. In January of 2004, Mercer was awarded $349,243 in attorneys' fees (*Mercer,* 2004).

Pregnancy and Participation—Title IX

Individuals may use Title IX to seek a remedy for discrimination suffered due to pregnancy. Pregnancy-based discrimination falls under Title IX because it is considered a form of gender-based discrimination—because only women get pregnant, and, historically, becoming pregnant has led to unfavorable treatment with regard to holding jobs and participating in sport.

Some athletic departments have written policies informing student-athletes that they could lose their grant-in-aid if they become pregnant (Iacobelli, 2007). There is evidence that some student-athletes respond by choosing to terminate their pregnancy to avoid losing their grant-in-aid or their participation opportunity (Ulrich, 2007).

Some of the myths used to justify differential treatment based on pregnancy include the idea that pregnancy poses huge health risks to a working or playing woman and her fetus, the idea that pregnant women and new mothers will be distracted and not perform up to expectations on the job or on the court, and the idea that to be pregnant as a high school- or college-age student is scandalous and will represent a major distraction for the rest of the team or student body.

The last notion was present in the case of *Brady v. Sacred Heart University,* which was settled out of court in 2003 (*Chronicle of Higher Education,* 2003). Tara Brady was the starting center on Sacred Heart University's basketball team during her sophomore year. In June of that year, she discovered she was pregnant and notified her coach. When her athletic scholarship for the following year was rescinded, Brady sued the university under Title IX, alleging that her coach had discriminated against her based on her pregnancy in telling her she would be a "distraction" and "an insurance risk," and by deciding that Brady would be dismissed from the team and lose her scholarship for the following year.

According to Brady, she repeatedly sought a hardship waiver that is commonly given to allow athletes a medical redshirt year so they can retain their scholarship and not lose eligibility. These requests were denied until her parents complained to an NCAA compliance officer. Finally, Sacred Heart reinstated Brady's scholarship and told her she would be reinstated to the basketball team; however, she alleged that her coach made it clear that he still did not want her to play on the team. Brady then withdrew from Sacred Heart and transferred to West Chester University, where she played out her senior year. After years of pressure to address the issue of student-athlete pregnancy, the NCAA issued new guidelines, approved in January 2008, that, among other things, ensure that pregnant athletes will not lose their grant-in-aid during the affected year ("After long battle," 2008).

Sexual Harassment/Abuse in the Context of Sport Participation—Title IX

The Title VII legal theories underlying quid pro quo and hostile environment sexual harassment claims were explained in detail in Chapter 7. Sexual harassment that occurs in an educational institution may also be litigated under Title IX. The Supreme Court has upheld the use of monetary damages under Title IX as a remedy for sexual harassment (*Franklin v. Gwinnett County Public Schools,* 1992). Whereas employers may be strictly liable for sexual harassment under Title VII whether or not they knew the harassment was occurring, a successful Title IX harassment claim requires that school officials with authority to intervene have known that harassment was occurring and through deliberate indifference failed to stop it (*Davis v. Monroe County Board of Education,* 1999). Thus, a student-athlete who is being sexually harassed by a peer or a coach must report the problem to the appropriate school officials in order to obtain judicial relief.

To date, few sexual harassment lawsuits have been brought by players against their coaches, but two cases may be representative of a growing trend. Two female athletes used Title IX to sue Northern Essex Community College on the grounds that the college had noticed that its women's basketball coach was sexually harassing his players but allowed him to continue to coach for seven years and then for three more years following a four-year suspension for misbehavior. These two basketball players claimed that the coach had asked for massages, grabbed their breasts, made jokes about their breasts, and benched them for rejecting his advances. Both players reported the problem to university officials, including the associate dean and the sexual harassment counselor of the college, and both eventually withdrew from the college.

The college argued that it had allowed the coach to resume coaching after his four-year suspension because it had received no further complaints of harassment. Therefore, argued the college, it had not acted with deliberate indifference to the current plaintiffs. The court ruled that knowledge of harassment of the current plaintiffs was not necessarily required since the college already had notice of previous harassment of other student-athletes. Thus, the court felt there was a reasonable question of fact as to whether the college knowingly failed to respond to sex discrimination in its athletics program. The court vacated the lower court's grant of summary judgment for the defendant and remanded the case back to the trial court for reconsideration (*Morrison v. Northern Essex Community College,* 2002).

Competitive Advantage

STRATEGIES

Avoiding Sexual Harassment Claims

- An athletic department should develop and implement a sexual harassment policy that includes a reporting process and appeals procedure, and include this information in its student-athlete handbook. Refer to Chapter 7 for information on essential elements of a sexual harassment policy and guidance on where to find a sample policy.

- Publicize and review your existing sexual harassment policy with student-athletes, coaches, and athletics department staff and administrators.

- Sensitize all constituents to the fact that sexual harassment is not just an issue of men harassing women—males can also be victims and females can also be harassers.

- Ensure that the hostile environment type of harassment is understood, because it is often perpetrated unintentionally by those who are insensitive to the issue. Thus it is often preventable if those individuals are educated about the problem.

- Establish and disseminate a reporting procedure that encourages nonvictims who observe sexual harassment to report it.

- Investigate allegations of harassment promptly so you do not appear to be indifferent to the problem, and take immediate corrective action if you find it has indeed occurred.

- Hold orientation sessions for teams planning to compete internationally that inform athletes and coaches about the university's drinking and sexual harassment policies. Require these individuals to sign a statement acknowledging that all policies that govern on-campus behavior also apply while they are abroad.

In another case, two female soccer players filed a $12 million lawsuit against their coach, Anson Dorrance, and the University of North Carolina at Chapel Hill, alleging that he sexually harassed them by creating a hostile environment. Additionally, one of the athletes claimed that Dorrance retaliated against her for filing this lawsuit by intentionally interfering with her attempt to be selected for the 1999 U. S. national soccer team, resulting in a loss of income and recognition for her because she was denied the opportunity to participate when the 1999 team won the World Cup.

UNC Chapel Hill's defense was that Dorrance's conduct was simply the teasing that typically occurs in a college athletics environment and does not rise to the level of inappropriate conduct that would constitute sexual harassment. The university moved to dismiss the Title IX claim, but the court ruled that the plaintiffs had alleged sufficient facts to allow the claim to go forward (*Jennings v. University of North Carolina*, 2002). Subsequently, UNC settled out of court with one of the plaintiffs, agreeing to pay her $70,000 and requiring Coach Dorrance to attend a year of sensitivity training. The other plaintiff continued to pursue the lawsuit, and, in 2004, a federal judge dismissed the case, finding that the coach's behavior was not severe and pervasive enough to constitute hostile environment sexual harassment ("Judge throws out," 2004). Eventually, the Fourth Circuit, sitting en banc, decided this controversy as described in the Focus Case below.

Jennings v. University of North Carolina

FOCUS CASE   482 F.3d 686 (4th Cir. 2007)

FACTS

Anson Dorrance, arguably the most acclaimed collegiate women's soccer coach in the country, repeatedly asked prying personal questions about his players' sex lives, using vulgar and sexually explicit language. He also made inappropriate gestures and advances, made comments about his players' bodies that objectified them as sex objects, discussed his sexual fantasies about players with other players—and did all this on a regular basis. While Jennings was only directly targeted two or three times because she made every effort to "fly beneath the coach's radar" and avoid his abuse, she claimed she was further traumatized by watching it happen repeatedly to her teammates. In addition to Jennings, several teammates testified as to how uncomfortable and "dirty" his conduct made them feel and also testified that they put up with it so that he would continue to let them play.

When Jennings was cut from the team after her sophomore year, she sued under Title IX, claiming that Coach Dorrance had created a hostile, sexually harassing environment. She also sued UNC's legal counsel, Susan Ehringhaus, using a theory of supervisor liability under § 1983 because, when she had reported the coach's misconduct to Ehringhaus, Ehringhaus took no action and advised Jennings to "work it out" with Dorrance.

HOLDING

The Fourth Circuit vacated the summary judgment that the district court had awarded to the defendants on both the Title IX claim and the § 1983 claim, and remanded the case back to the district court.

RATIONALE

The court identified four elements necessary for a plaintiff to establish a Title IX sexual harassment claim:

1. plaintiff was a student at an educational institution receiving federal funds
2. plaintiff was subjected to harassment based on sex
3. the harassment was sufficiently severe or pervasive to create a hostile (or abusive) environment in an educational program or activity
4. grounds existed for imputing liability to the institution

Clearly, Jennings satisfied the first element of proof. As to the second, the court found that Dorrance's sexually charged comments went far beyond ordinary teasing—even of the nature that often occurs in a sport environment—and were persistently degrading and humiliating to his players as women, thus constituting sex-based harassment. Third, the court found that a jury could objectively conclude that the two incidents (which occurred over a two-year period) of direct harassment of Jennings were more abusive due to the general pattern of sexual abuse that instilled "fear and dread" in many of the players. Thus, the incidents of abuse were not considered trivial and isolated but instead were severe and pervasive events. The evidence that several other players experienced similar discomfort and humiliation supported the court's conclusion that Jennings was objectively reasonable in perceiving the environment to be hostile and abusive.

The court relied on an earlier Supreme Court Title IX harassment decision in *Davis v. Monroe County Board of Education* (1999), which stipulated that a plaintiff must prove she had been effectively denied equal access to educational benefits or opportunities, or that the harassment had had "a concrete, negative effect on her ability to participate." Here, the court concluded that the humiliation and anxiety caused by the coach's sexual harassment concretely and negatively affected Jennings' academic performance and ability to participate on the soccer team. With respect to institutional liability, the court concluded that the university's legal counsel acted with deliberate indifference (the required Title IX standard for institutional liability) when Ehringhaus took no action on Jennings' complaint.

Ultimately, this case was settled, the coach issued a formal apology, and Melissa Jennings was awarded $385,000, mostly in attorney's fees. Anson Dorrance remains employed as the head coach of women's soccer at UNC (Beard, 2008).

In a few cases, Title IX has been used successfully to challenge same-sex peer sexual harassment. The rationale used by these courts is that harassment based on sexual orientation violates Title IX because Title IX prohibits harassment based on gender nonconformity (Women's Sports Foundation, 2008; *Theno v. Tonganoxie Unified Sch. Dist.*, 2005; *Montgomery v. Indep. Sch. Dist. No. 709*, 2000; *Schroeder v. Maumee Bd of Educ.*, 2003; *Ray v. Antioch Unified Sch. Dist.*, 2000).

Another relatively new issue is one raised when college athletics teams travel to other countries for preseason play and sexual harassment occurs. Often, the drinking age in other countries is 18, and the likelihood of inappropriate sexual conduct increases with excessive alcohol consumption. In a lawsuit against Eastern Michigan

University (EMU; since settled out of court), a U. S. District Court judge ruled in a pretrial motion that Title IX applies when students who are U. S. citizens are harassed in foreign countries while participating in study abroad programs. One of the alleged harassers was an associate professor who was an assistant to the trip leader. EMU had argued that Title IX applies only to students in the United States (Young, 2002). The following hypothetical case considers a similar situation in the context of sport.

considering . . .   SEXUAL HARASSMENT OCCURRING ABROAD

An assistant coach of the Middle America University women's basketball team sexually harasses a student-athlete on multiple occasions during a 10-day team trip to Europe where they are playing four games against European teams. When the team returns to Kansas, the athlete reports the harassment to the athletic director. The director tells the player that, if it happens again on American soil, the player should come back and report it and she will take action. She will not, however, take further action on this first complaint because it did not happen in the United States.

Questions

- If the judge in the Eastern Michigan study abroad case was correct, did the athletic director handle the problem correctly?
- If not, how should she have dealt with the player's complaint?

Note how you would answer the questions and then check your responses using the Analysis & Discussion at the end of this chapter.

Finally, a female student who has been sexually assaulted on campus should not give in to pressure from coaches or athletic department personnel to refrain from reporting the incident to the police. After a female basketball player at La Salle University was allegedly raped by a member of the men's basketball team, news reports claimed that the coaches persuaded her not to report it to the authorities. A cover-up of this sort would be a violation of the 1990 Jeanne Clery Act, which requires college officials to report such incidents (Byrne, 2004).

Race Discrimination—Title VI

Although for decades sport sociologists have trained their floodlights on race discrimination in sport, there has been next to no litigation over this issue. If the problem looms as large as the sociologists claim, why haven't there been court battles over ethnicity equity, as there have been over gender equity? The best answer is probably that when racism affects sport participation, it is much more subtle and less overt than gender discrimination. Because we don't intentionally separate Black teams from White, as we do female teams from male, any race discrimination that occurs on the part of coaches or administrators is much more difficult to perceive and even more difficult to prove.

However, in *Cureton v. NCAA* (1999) and *Pryor v. NCAA* (2002), African American student-athletes brought suit against the NCAA, alleging that the initial eligibility standards unfairly discriminated against them on the basis of race. Both cases centered on Proposition 16. Proposition 16 is the name of the standard for determining initial eligibility that was implemented in 1992 because the NCAA wanted to improve the graduation rates of student-athletes. It placed the student's high school GPA and SAT or ACT test score on a sliding scale that allowed a student to qualify with a lower standardized test score if she had a higher GPA, and vice versa. It replaced Proposition 48, which had required a minimum high school GPA of 2.0 and a minimum SAT score of 700. Proposition 16 placed greater emphasis on the standardized test score than its predecessor by setting the minimum test score at 820 for students with a 2.5 GPA and requiring a 1010 for students with a 2.0 GPA.

When the NCAA was in the process of evaluating whether Proposition 16 would achieve its goal of improving graduation rates, it considered three other standards and determined that, of the four, Proposition 16 would promote the largest increase. As part of this analysis, the NCAA obtained data on the effect that the four proposed standards would have on initial eligibility of Black student-athletes. The projections found that Proposition 16 would raise the graduation rates of all athletes and would raise the graduation rates of African Americans the most. However, it would also have the effect of excluding a greater number of Black athletes at the outset than would the other three proposed standards. Knowing this, the NCAA membership went ahead and voted to adopt Proposition 16 anyway.

In *Cureton v. NCAA* (1999), the plaintiffs brought suit under Title VI of the Civil Rights Act of 1964 (see Exhibit 14.7) alleging that Proposition 16 had a discriminatory disparate impact on African Americans. (See Chapter 6 for a detailed discussion of the difference between a disparate impact claim—which alleges that a neutral rule has an unfair effect on a protected group of people—and a disparate treatment claim—which alleges intentional discrimination.) The *Cureton* case was never fully heard, having been voided by a later Supreme Court case in which the Court ruled that there is no private right to bring a disparate impact claim under Title VI (*Alexander v. Sandoval*, 2001).

In contrast, the plaintiffs in *Pryor v. NCAA* (2002) claimed that the NCAA engaged in intentional race discrimination when it adopted Proposition 16, thus violating Title VI. The Third Circuit found that because the NCAA had researched the likely effects of Proposition 16 and thus knew the rule would disproportionately impact the initial eligibility of Black student-athletes, the plaintiff had alleged sufficient facts to support a claim of intentional discrimination.

Title VI of the Civil Rights Act of 1964, 42 U.S.C. § 2000d (2005).   EXHIBIT **14.7**

No person in the United States shall, on the ground of race, color, or national origin, be excluded from participation in, be denied the benefits of, or be subjected to discrimination under any program or activity receiving federal financial assistance.

Race Discrimination in High School and College Athletics

■ Persons with influence on rule-making should avoid establishing eligibility standards that place a lot of weight on data that may be racially biased (such as standardized test scores).

■ Policy makers should be aware of the distinction between a policy that has a negative effect on members of an ethnic minority group "because of" their ethnicity and one that does so "in spite of" their ethnicity. Evidence that the policy makers had prior knowledge (*"Pryor* Knowledge"?) that a rule or policy would probably have a disproportionately negative effect on an ethnic minority group will be scrutinized closely by a court to determine whether it was implemented "because of" the likelihood of that negative effect.

In the aftermath of the decision in *Pryor* to let the plaintiffs' claims proceed, the NCAA revised the initial eligibility standards to de-emphasize the standardized test score. The rule change took the wind out of the sails of the *Pryor* case. Effective in 2003, the revised standard requires only a minimum SAT score of 400, as long as the student has a high enough GPA (3.55) to balance that out on the sliding scale. Although a higher incoming GPA is required, instead of placing so much weight on initial eligibility, these new rules have tightened up the requirements for continuing eligibility. Student-athletes must accrue 24 semester hours before entering their second academic year and must maintain a minimum load of 18 hours each academic year and six hours per semester. Additionally, under rule 14.4.3.2 student-athletes in four-year programs must complete 40 percent of their credits by the end of their second year and 60 percent by the end of year three, and 80 percent must be completed by the end of the fourth year (NCAA, 2008b).

Discrimination on the Basis of Disability—§ 504 and the ADA

The question of whether and how to provide fair opportunities for individuals with disabilities to participate in high school and college athletics presents numerous difficult issues. First, should an athlete with a disability be accommodated when sport, after all, is all about superior physical and mental ability? If so, what kinds of accommodations are reasonable? Should courts be in the business of deciding when the rules of sports governing bodies are to be applied or cast aside?

All individuals differ in ability, and yet we make the majority play according to one standard—for example, a 6'3" basketball player may be assigned to guard a 6'6" player, placing the shorter person at a competitive disadvantage—and yet no law attempts to accommodate the fact that he is "height-challenged." So why should we allow the law to require that a person with a severe circulatory disorder in his legs be allowed to ride a golf cart during his college days instead of being required to walk like all the rest of the golfers?

What exactly constitutes a disability when it comes to sports participation? Should a 5'6" athlete be considered disabled if he wants to play college basketball? Should a 6'9" female be considered disabled if she wants to be a gymnast? What about obesity due to a thyroid disorder? Should a person with that type of obesity be considered disabled if she wishes to compete in cross-country running?

If it would be unfair to try to integrate individuals with disabilities onto existing teams, should we require athletics departments to provide them with separate teams, for example, a varsity wheelchair basketball team? Is it fair to provide resources and support for elite able-bodied competition without providing the same level of support for competitive opportunities for individuals with disabilities? Is sport participation considered a major life activity, thus bringing it within the purview of § 504 of the

Rehabilitation Act or the Americans with Disabilities Act? These are some of the difficult questions that arise when one begins to consider how to prevent discrimination against individuals with disabilities who want to participate in athletics.

Prior to the enactment of § 504, courts routinely upheld rules excluding people with disabilities from participation based on the risk posed to the participant and to others. But the passage of § 504 signaled a new era in which the courts began to recognize that overprotecting athletes with disabilities did not comport with the intent of the disabilities laws, which was to support the idea that individuals with disabilities are entitled to live as full a life as possible. Based on the principle of rejecting paternalism, several cases were then decided in which the courts held that high school athletes who were disabled should be allowed to participate in contact sports if they choose to do so. For example, in *Poole v. South Plainfield Board of Education* (1980), the court held that a student with only one functional kidney must be allowed to participate on the school wrestling team even though he would risk grave consequences. The court said that a sport like wrestling entails taking the risk of serious injuries, and thus students with disabilities must be allowed to take risks because risk-taking is part of living life to the fullest.

Several lawsuits have been filed against schools by athletes alleging discrimination on the basis of having either a physical or a learning disability. These lawsuits are brought under § 504 of the Rehabilitation Act, Title II of the ADA (which provides a remedy for discrimination by public entities), or Title III of the ADA (which provides recourse against private entities that are considered places of public accommodation). The legal analysis under Title II of the ADA is the same as that under § 504 (see Exhibit 14.8). (For a more complete statement of these laws and an in-depth description of the legal analysis, refer to Chapter 6, where these concepts were first introduced.)

Lawsuits against public entities—§ 504 and Title II of the ADA

Physical disabilities. A case of a student who wanted to play basketball at the college level, despite a heart abnormality, will serve to illustrate the application of § 504 to an athletics situation. The court in *Knapp v. Northwestern University* (1996), however, took a position contrary to that of prior cases like *Poole* on the issue of whether the plaintiff's disability substantially limited a major life activity.

Legal analysis under § 504 and Title II of the ADA.	EXHIBIT 14.8

The plaintiff must prove that she or he is:

1. Disabled
2. Otherwise qualified
3. Excluded solely on the basis of disability

To prove she or he is disabled, the plaintiff must prove that she or he has a:

1. Physical or mental impairment
2. Which substantially limits
3. One or more major life activities

Knapp v. Northwestern University

FOCUS CASE   101 F.3d 473 (7th Cir. 1996)

FACTS

Plaintiff Knapp had been recruited to play basketball on an athletics grant-in-aid for Northwestern University (NU). However, once the school found out that Knapp had a heart abnormality that had triggered cardiac death and required him to have a defibrillator implanted in his heart, they refused to allow him to play. The NU team doctors ruled Knapp medically ineligible because the implanted defibrillator had never been tested under the intense conditions of elite college basketball, and thus Knapp would be exposed to what they determined was an unacceptable level of risk. These doctors based their decision on published guidelines from medical conferences as well as consultations with other doctors.

NU admitted that Knapp had been excluded solely on the basis of his heart problem. Knapp sued the university, claiming he had been discriminated against on the basis of disability in violation of § 504 of the Rehabilitation Act. The district court found the university in violation of § 504 and entered a permanent injunction barring the university from excluding Knapp from the team for any reason related to his heart condition. NU appealed.

HOLDING

The Seventh Circuit reversed and entered summary judgment for Northwestern University, holding that Knapp was not disabled under the law.

RATIONALE

The central issue for the court was whether Knapp's physical impairment substantially limited a major life activity. The court ruled that playing basketball is itself not basic enough to constitute a major life activity (as compared to standing, breathing, or hearing). Nevertheless, they considered whether playing intercollegiate basketball implicated learning, which is generally considered to be a major life activity for purposes of this law. According to the *Knapp* court, although playing an intercollegiate sport may be part of the learning experience at a university, not being able to play does not render a person unable to get a satisfactory education. Therefore, the court held that Knapp was not disabled under the law, because his impairment did not substantially limit the major life activity of learning.

Moreover, according to the court, NU had not excluded Knapp based on stereotypes about people with disabilities, but rather had acted reasonably in relying on competent, case-specific medical evidence. The court further ruled that even if Knapp were considered to have met the criteria for being disabled, he was not otherwise qualified to participate. This is because there was a significant health risk, and significant risk can disqualify a person when that risk cannot be reduced by a reasonable accommodation—which in this case it could not. The court concluded that NU's decision was not illegal under § 504.

The decision in *Knapp* appears to have redefined sport participation as not being a major life activity. It also seems to stand for the proposition that doctors should be allowed to determine what are acceptable versus unacceptable risks for potential participants with disabling conditions. Instead of blithely allowing any athlete with a disability to take any and all risks associated with participation in her preferred sport, such a stance probably comports well with the case-by-case, fact-specific approach of disability law. It would also seem to provide schools with protection from negligence liability as long as they act reasonably in relying on the advice of appropriate medical personnel.

Learning disabilities. Learning disabilities have posed an even more difficult challenge for the courts. Athletes with learning disabilities may run afoul of several eligibility rules, such as the age-limit rule for high school participation, the longevity rules in high school participation that limit the number of semesters of eligibility, or academic standards and progress rules in college.

Many high school athletic associations have a rule limiting interscholastic athletics participation to students age 18 and under. The federal courts have been divided on the issue of whether such an age limit violates the disabilities laws when applied to students whose educational progress has been delayed (thus making them over the age of 18 by the time they graduate) due to a learning disability. This same type of analysis is pertinent to the alleged violation of longevity rules, since they also are concerned with keeping the playing field fair so that older and more mature students do not gain an unfair advantage in participation.

The Sixth and Eighth Circuit Courts have ruled that to grant a waiver of the age-limit eligibility rule to a learning disabled student over the age of 18 would constitute an undue administrative burden by requiring too much case-by-case analysis on the part of the school and would constitute a fundamental alteration of the interscholastic sports program by allowing older students to participate (creating an unlevel playing field and an unsafe one because of severe mismatches in size, weight, and strength) (*Sandison*, 1995; *Pottgen*, 1994).

However, several U. S. district courts have ruled to the contrary, holding that a case-by-case analysis is exactly what Congress intended when it passed § 504 and the ADA. They contend that such an analysis is not an undue burden and is necessary to enable a court to determine whether a waiver in the individual case would work a fundamental alteration in the competitive sports program. The *Dennin* case provides an example.

Dennin v. Connecticut Interscholastic Athletic Conference

913 F. Supp. 663 (D. Conn. 1996)   **FOCUS CASE**

FACTS

Plaintiff Dennin was a 19-year-old with Down Syndrome who was a member of the swim team. He had been held back a year in middle school due to his special educational needs, with the result that he was 19 years old during his senior year in high school. He was thus denied eligibility for his senior year under the Connecticut Interscholastic Athletic Conference (CIAC) age-limit rule. His request for a waiver of the rule was denied, but because his participation on the team was written into his individualized education plan, the CIAC said they would allow him to continue to participate as a nonscoring exhibition swimmer on his relay team. This meant that his relay team could not earn any points for the overall team. Dennin sued under § 504 and the ADA.

HOLDING

The court found in favor of Dennin, holding that it would be a reasonable accommodation for the CIAC to grant a waiver in his case.

RATIONALE

According to the court, allowing Dennin to participate only as an exhibition swimmer would be to treat him differently on the basis of his disability, thus potentially damaging his self-esteem and his willingness to attempt to function in the larger community. This, said the court, would violate the goal of the disabilities laws to enable the full and equal participation of persons with disabilities. In contrast, granting Dennin a waiver of the age-limit rule would not impose an undue burden on the CIAC because they already conduct similar individualized assessments for a waiver process for transfer students. The occasional difficulties caused by doing these assessments did not rise to the level of an undue burden.

Furthermore, in the eyes of the court, granting such a waiver did not create a fundamental alteration in the conduct of interscholastic athletics. The court found there were five purposes behind the age-limit rule:

1. To prevent a competitive advantage for older, stronger athletes
2. To protect younger, less mature athletes from injury
3. To discourage athletes from delaying the completion of their education for athletics purposes
4. To prevent coaches from redshirting athletes to gain a competitive advantage
5. To avoid having younger athletes lose out on participation opportunities due to the greater physical prowess of older athletes

Because Dennin was always the slowest swimmer in the pool, the court found that none of the competitive advantage purposes of the age-limit rule would be undermined by granting him a waiver, and Dennin's older age would not pose an injury risk to others because swimming is not a contact sport. The court concluded, therefore, that granting a waiver would not fundamentally alter the nature of the interscholastic swimming program.

In this case, the CIAC also argued that their age-limit rule was a neutral rule neutrally applied, and thus Dennin was not excluded from participation solely because of his disability. Instead, he was excluded because the passage of time simply made him too old to participate during his senior year. The court found that this argument ignored the reality that he was too old solely due to his disability.

Other courts have disagreed with the *Dennin* rationale. These courts have held that age-limit rules are neutral rules, and have taken the position that the fact that plaintiffs like Dennin were allowed to participate during their first three years is evidence that they had not been discriminated against solely because of their disability. Instead, they were excluded simply because they became too old during their senior year (see, e.g., *Sandison*, 1995).

Lawsuits against places of public accommodation—Title III of the ADA

Athletes may sue a sport governing body under Title III of the ADA, which allows litigation against private entities that own, lease, or operate places of public accommodation. Title III litigation has primarily been used in lawsuits against the NCAA, which has been deemed a private entity by the courts since the 1988 Supreme Court decision in *NCAA v. Tarkanian*. Initially, the federal courts were divided on whether Title III applied to suits against the NCAA, because the statute and its regulations seem to suggest that a place of public accommodation refers to a place with an actual physical being, and of course the NCAA does not conduct events within any facility of its own.

However, in *PGA Tour, Inc. v. Martin* (2001), the Supreme Court ruled that the PGA Tour operates places of public accommodation when it conducts its professional golf tournaments at various golf courses around the country. In that case, the Court held that a place of public accommodation is not limited to the spectator areas during the golf tournaments, but also extends to the competitive area of the golf course. It is true that the PGA Tour actually leases and operates each golf course during a given professional tournament, whereas the NCAA rarely does such a thing. Nevertheless, following the *Martin* decision, most federal courts have ruled that, for purposes of ADA Title III litigation, the NCAA is a private entity operating a place of public accommodation. In drawing that conclusion, they reason that a strong enough nexus exists between the university's athletics program and the NCAA by virtue of the control the NCAA exerts over access to participation through its eligibility requirements and requirements of compliance with its other rules (*Matthews v. NCAA*, 2001; *Ganden v. NCAA*, 1996; *Tatum v. NCAA*, 1998; *Bowers v. NCAA*, 1998). Once it was determined that Title III of the ADA applies to the NCAA, the courts could proceed with the merits of the Title III claim (see Exhibit 14.4).

The *Matthews* case provides an example of how Title III of the ADA applies to the NCAA.

Matthews v. NCAA

| 179 F. Supp. 2d 1209 (E.D. Wash. 2001) | FOCUS CASE |

FACTS

Plaintiff Matthews was a football player at Washington State University who suffered from severe learning disabilities with respect to reading comprehension (he had scores in the 6th to 10th percentile) and written expression, and whose IQ was in the 13th percentile. In his first year, he had been granted a waiver of the NCAA's full-time student credit hour rule and the 75/25 rule that prohibited student-athletes from completing more than 25 percent of their yearly credit hour requirement in summer school. The NCAA denied Matthews' request for a second waiver of the 75/25 rule the following year, declaring him academically ineligible and asserting that his failure to meet the 75/25 rule was due to his lack of effort and poor class attendance (offering evidence that he had attended only half of the lectures in his criminal justice class) rather than to his learning disability. Matthews sued the NCAA under Title III of the ADA.

HOLDING

The district court held that: (1) the plaintiff's learning disability was a covered disability, citing the federal regulations promulgated under the ADA that state that mental impairments include "any mental or psychological disorder such as mental retardation, organic brain syndrome, emotional or mental illness, and specific learning disabilities," 28 C.F.R. § 36.104 (2005); (2) Matthews' learning disability substantially limited his ability to learn (learning is included in the regulations' list of covered major life activities); and (3) Matthews was discriminated against by the NCAA's denial of his request for a second year's waiver of the 75/25 rule.

RATIONALE

The NCAA argued that the ADA should not protect Matthews because playing football is not a major life activity (this is similar to the argument successfully used in the *Knapp* case, discussed earlier). However, the court decided that playing football was not the major life activity in question—instead, learning was. According to the court, the NCAA's action against Matthews resulted from an impairment affecting his ability to learn—not from a physical impairment affecting his physical capability of playing football. Thus, the ADA protected Matthews from discrimination based on eligibility requirements that discriminated against him based on his learning disability.

The court also felt that the requested waiver was a reasonable accommodation of his learning disability, especially given the fact that the NCAA had granted him a similar waiver the year before. Thus, granting this waiver could not be construed as modifying an essential part of the NCAA's policies and so would not constitute a fundamental alteration of the NCAA's purpose of promoting student-athlete development. According to the court, the NCAA has plenty of other rules to ensure a focus on academics.

Furthermore, the court asserted (without explanation) that granting this waiver would not give Matthews an unfair advantage over other student-athletes. Therefore, the court would have granted in part Matthews' motion for summary judgment. However, the court also recognized the potential validity of the NCAA's argument that Matthews' failure to meet the 75/25 rule was due to lack of effort, not disability, and found a sufficient question of fact to deny in part Matthews' motion for summary judgment. The case as a whole was rendered moot and dismissed because Matthews had since transferred to Eastern Washington University and played out his eligibility, and the court was thus left with no remedy to grant him, since under Title III money damages are not available to plaintiffs—the only remedy is injunctive relief.

High school/college athletics teams for disabled participants

Another issue for consideration is whether high schools and universities are legally obligated to provide separate interscholastic, intercollegiate, or intramural teams for athletes with physical disabilities. Occasionally, such athletes have competed on varsity teams, including Aimee Mullins, a female sprinter with artificial legs on the track team at Georgetown University, and Casey Martin, who rode a cart in varsity golf play for Stanford University (Suggs, 2004a). As another example, in 2006, a court issued a temporary injunction ordering a Maryland school district to allow Tatyana McFadden, a two-time Paralympic Games medalist in 2004, to compete in interscholastic middle-distance races in a wheelchair alongside able-bodied competitors ("Wheelchair athlete disqualified," 2007). However, no school has yet created entire teams of people with disabilities, such as a wheelchair basketball team, and fully supported them as varsity teams.

Despite the uncertain legal obligations, some universities are beginning to provide such opportunities in a qualified manner. The University of Illinois offers a men's and a women's wheelchair basketball team, both coached by the same coach, and the athletes get scholarships, varsity letters, and access to tutoring and academic services for athletes. But they do not get dedicated practice facilities, assistant coaches, or publicity support. In 2004, the University of Missouri's recreation department hired a coach and began awarding $50,000 in scholarships for a wheelchair basketball team that is to function as a varsity team, but not under the auspices of the athletic department (Suggs, 2004a). At present, nine schools offer participation opportunities on wheelchair basketball teams (sanctioned by the National Wheelchair Basketball Association), three of which also have women's teams ("Wheelchair athletes earn," 2006).

> ### Competitive Advantage
> # STRATEGIES
>
> **Avoiding Disability Discrimination Claims**
>
> - Consider offering special teams, such as wheelchair basketball or sledge ice hockey, for people with disabilities.
>
> - Always make an individualized assessment of each request for accommodation. The individualized inquiry should include informing potential participants of their rights and assuring them a prompt and fair review if questions arise concerning eligibility or safety issues (Grady & Andrew, 2003).
>
> - Establish an internal complaint procedure for resolving ADA and § 504 disputes that includes the following:
>
>   - Procedures for filing written complaints
>   - A timeline for resolution of complaints
>   - Procedures for tracking complaints
>   - Resolutions
>   - Accommodations offered and implemented
>   - Policies regarding the retention of dispute files (Grady & Andrew, 2003)

Discipline Issues

Athletes, like any other students, are subject to various disciplinary penalties when they violate school rules governing appropriate behavior. Such rules, often termed "conduct rules," have been challenged for unfairness under three different causes of action:

1. The law of private associations "arbitrary and capricious" standard
2. The Due Process Clause
3. The Equal Protection Clause

Conduct rules and the arbitrary and capricious standard

In *Bunger v. Iowa High School Athletic Association* (1972), the Iowa Supreme Court struck down a rule that rendered a student-athlete ineligible for athletic participation because he had knowingly been in a car that contained alcoholic beverages when that car was stopped by the police. The court acknowledged that it was reasonable to punish athletes with ineligibility if they consumed, possessed, or transported alcohol during any part of the school year, even outside of their particular competitive season. However, this school's "beer rule" was ruled arbitrary and unreasonable because it was too broad. For example, it would have allowed punishment of an athlete who caught a ride home with an adult who had just come from the grocery store with alcohol among the purchased items. (Refer to the section titled "Judicial Deference to Educational Policy" and the *Letendre* case, both in Chapter 13, for an explanation of the "arbitrary and capricious" standard and an illustration of how it is applied in educational contexts.)

Conduct rules and the Due Process and Equal Protection Clauses

In eligibility cases, an issue has often been whether a student has a right to participate in athletics that cannot be taken away without appropriate due process (usually fair notice and a hearing; see Exhibit 13.3). Some courts have found a protected property interest in an athletic scholarship or a liberty interest in one's reputation as a star athlete, but that is not the majority position. Most courts have held that athletic participation is a privilege, not a right that would be protected by the Due Process Clause.

Beer rules have also been challenged under the Due Process and Equal Protection Clauses of the Constitution. In *Palmer v. Merluzzi* (1988), a high school football player was suspended from the team for 60 days, in addition to receiving a 10-day suspension from school, for consuming marijuana and beer on campus. The football suspension was challenged under the Due Process Clause because the athlete had had no notice that this penalty existed, nor had he received a hearing before he was suspended from the team. The district court followed the majority of states in ruling that there is no due process liberty or property interest that generates a right to participate in school athletics; instead, participation is a privilege, and therefore the student had no right to receive due process.

Sometimes, however, an unduly lengthy suspension from athletics will trigger a court to find that a student-athlete was entitled to due process. In *Pegram v. Nelson* (1979), a high school student received a 10-day suspension from school and a four-month suspension from extracurricular activities. The court ruled that although the opportunity to participate was not in itself a property right, "total exclusion from participation . . . for a lengthy period of time could . . . be sufficient deprivation to implicate due process." This decision appears to be based on the idea that such a lengthy suspension deprived the student of too large a portion of the overall education process—a process that is partly comprised of extracurricular activities.

As stated above, a minority of other jurisdictions in older cases have found a protectable property interest in school athletics participation based on the notion that such participation could lead to a valuable college athletic scholarship without which a student might be unable to attend (*Boyd v. Board of Directors*, 1985;

Duffley v. New Hampshire Interscholastic Athletic Association, 1982). The courts justified these decisions partly on the basis of the high skill level of the athletes. However, the Texas Supreme Court recently held that an athlete's high level of skill and earning potential did not overcome the speculative nature of her interest in future financial opportunities based on her reputation in her sport (*NCAA v. Yeo,* 2005). This case is discussed later in the chapter in conjunction with transfer rules.

Disciplinary rules have also been challenged under the Equal Protection Clause. (To refresh your memory on the strict scrutiny, intermediate scrutiny, and rational basis review tests used in Equal Protection Clause analysis, refer back to Exhibit 6.6 and the accompanying text.) In *Palmer v. Merluzzi* (1988), the court was asked to decide whether the school's good conduct rule unfairly singled out athletes as its focus by subjecting them, and not other students, to punishment if they had not "demonstrated good citizenship and responsibility." Because the category "athletes" is not a suspect classification, the court applied the easiest test—rational basis review—and upheld the use of suspensions as a reasonable means of achieving the school's legitimate goal of enforcing compliance with its drug and alcohol policy.

Conduct rules, delinquency, and the disability laws

Sometimes athletic participation is used as a rehabilitation tool for delinquency or as part of a required individualized education plan (IEP) for students with certain disabilities. For plaintiffs in these types of circumstances, courts have occasionally been willing to make exceptions to enforcement of conduct rules (*Florida High School Athletic Association v. Bryant,* 1975—a juvenile delinquent needed basketball for rehabilitation; *Bercovitch v. Baldwin School, Inc.,* 1998—a school's misconduct suspension of a student with attention deficit–hyperactivity disorder ran afoul of the requirement to reasonably accommodate his disability; see also *Hoot by Hoot v. Milan Area Schools,* 1994).

However, in *Long v. Board of Education District 128* (2001), the court went the other way. Here, a high school athlete with manic depression was suspended from all extracurricular activities upon being arrested for behavior that also violated the school's code of conduct. Based on the fact that extracurricular activities were a part of his IEP, the student requested that the suspension not be enforced so he could play lacrosse and football for his school as a "reasonable accommodation" for his disability. When the school denied his request, he brought suit under the ADA, § 504 of the Rehabilitation Act, and the Individuals with Disabilities in Education Act. The court balanced the interest of the school in consistent enforcement of its code of conduct against the interest of the student in following his IEP, and concluded that the school's interest in retaining its authority to enforce its disciplinary rules was stronger. It found that any harm to the plaintiff caused by his suspension could be minimized by participation in summer athletics programs outside of school.

Transfer Rules

Both high school athletic associations and college athletic associations have rules in place regulating the circumstances under which athletes may transfer to other schools or colleges. The intent of transfer rules on the high school level is to regulate the behavior of school districts that might attempt to entice a star athlete to move from one school district to another. Transfers should be based on reasons other than athletic competition. For example, in the case of *Indiana High School Athletic Association v. Wideman* (1997), the Indiana High School Athletic Association (IHSAA) had decided that a student who transferred to another school district should be ineligible for a year of competition in her sport. The IHSAA rule penalized students who transferred "primarily for athletic reasons," but the court held that the IHSAA clearly ignored the evidence concerning why this student transferred. Her parents moved their residence because of caretaking responsibilities for a sick relative which, of course, had nothing to do with "athletic reasons." The court found in favor of the student since it held that the IHSAA had acted "arbitrarily and capriciously."

On the college level, the transfer rules are an attempt to ensure competitive balance. A student who transfers from one four-year college to another is prohibited by NCAA rules from participating in athletic competition for a year, but this restriction may be waived under certain circumstances. The following Focus Case deals with a transfer rule.

NCAA v. Yeo

FOCUS CASE   171 S.W.3d 863 (Tex. 2005)

FACTS

Joscelin Yeo from Singapore was a world-class swimmer when she was recruited to swim at the University of California at Berkeley. She was an All-American swimmer while at Berkeley and was a member of a world-record-setting relay team in 1999.

Yeo's coach at Berkeley left for employment at the University of Texas (UT), and Yeo then transferred to UT. The NCAA transfer rule prohibited her from swimming at UT for a full academic year unless Berkeley agreed to waive this restriction. Berkeley would not waive it, so Yeo was ineligible for an academic year.

Yeo did not enroll in classes in that fall semester so that she could compete in the 2000 Olympics. She enrolled in classes in the spring but did not compete. UT mistakenly believed that the Fall 2000 semester counted toward the time Yeo had to sit out, and so she was allowed to compete in the fall of 2001. Berkeley complained about this, and the NCAA determined that the Fall 2000 semester did *not* count toward satisfying the transfer rule because of the way in which they interpreted another rule related to her having competed in the Olympics that semester. Therefore, the NCAA ruled that Yeo had to sit out more events in the Spring 2002 semester to complete her inactive year.

The end result was that Yeo would not have been able to participate in the Spring 2002 NCAA national swimming and diving championship. More than once during this string of rules interpretations pertaining to Yeo's eligibility, UT made adverse eligibility decisions without telling her in time for her to present her side of the story. Because of this, Yeo sought an injunction against UT, claiming a due process violation. She won, and she was permitted to compete in the championship event. After a trial, the lower court decided that UT had denied her procedural due process by depriving her, without fair process, of a protected liberty interest in her reputation and a property interest in her endorsement offers. The state court of appeals affirmed, and the NCAA and UT appealed.

HOLDING

The Texas Supreme Court reversed, holding that Yeo was not entitled to due process because she had no protected interest in college athletics participation.

RATIONALE

The court noted that the overwhelming majority of jurisdictions hold that students do not possess a constitutionally protected interest in their participation in extracurricular activities. Thus, participation alone does not rise to the level of a protectable property or liberty interest.

In this case, Yeo had argued that her case should be treated differently because of her unique reputation as a world-class swimmer, especially in her native land of Singapore and because of her earning potential in the sport of swimming. Yeo contended that it is the *degree* of her interests, and not merely the *character* of those interests, that should bring them within constitutional protection.

The court disagreed, however, and stated that whether an interest is protected by due process depends upon the nature of the interest, not its weight. The nature of one's interest in a good reputation is the same no matter how good the reputation is. Further, Yeo's claimed interest in future financial opportunities was too speculative to deserve due process protection. Thus, Yeo had no constitutionally protected interests.

The *Yeo* case reinforces the majority position that athletes have no property or liberty interest in athletic participation. Further, simply because an athlete has a stellar reputation, that reputation is not entitled to more constitutional protection than a more modest reputation. Finally, the prospect of having a professional career in a sport or of having future endorsement opportunities is too speculative to translate into a current property interest.

Drug Testing of Athletes

A March 2004 survey of California high school students (283 males and 203 females) found that 33 percent of the girls and 52 percent of the boys knew someone who was using performance-enhancing drugs or supplements. Also, 18 percent of the boys knew of coaches or other athletic department staff members who were promoting their use (Popke, 2004). A federal study found that 2.7 percent of high school seniors have used steroids (Keys, 2008). Witnesses at a 2004 hearing before the U. S. Senate's Caucus on International Narcotics Control testified that steroid abuse is rampant in intercollegiate athletics (Suggs, 2004b). It is widely perceived that there is a drug problem in school sports.

"We need to protect the health and safety of student-athletes." "We need to make sure that student-athletes are good role models for the other students who look up to them." "We need to maintain a level playing field for athletes." "We need to preserve the integrity of athletic contests against those who would cheat by using drugs." These are the most common reasons that schools, universities, and sport governing bodies give when justifying their drug-testing programs. Arguments commonly raised by athletes against drug-testing programs include: "It's an embarrassing invasion of my privacy"; "it's an unreasonable search and seizure because urinalysis can detect all sorts of other private medical conditions, like epilepsy, diabetes, and pregnancy"; "it's unfair to single out athletes from the rest of the student body for drug testing"; "it's unfair to *force* me to 'consent' to drug testing in order to retain my opportunity to play."

Who is right—the student-athlete plaintiffs or the drug-testing defendants? The Colorado Supreme Court asserted that we should not strip individuals of their dignity and privacy when "after all, it is only athletic games we are concerned with here. . . . A government that invades the privacy of its citizens without compelling reason no longer abides by the constitutional provisions essential to a free society" (*University of Colorado v. Derdeyn*, 1993). In contrast, columnist George Will wrote that "A society's recreation is charged with moral significance. Sport—and a society that takes it seriously—would be debased if it did not strictly forbid things that blur the distinction between the triumph of character and the triumph of chemistry" (Will, 1988). It would indeed be a tragedy to watch sport deteriorate into a clash between competing drugs and methods of preventing their discovery instead of a fair contest between worthy, noncheating opponents. And yet, what cost to individual privacy is justified in the effort to maintain drug-free sport?

The primary legal analysis in drug-testing cases involves application of a balancing test to evaluate the reasonableness of a search under the Fourth Amendment (see Exhibits 14.9 and 14.10).

Student-athletes in both high school and college settings are routinely subjected to random selection for mandatory drug testing. To determine whether such procedures are legal, courts apply the balancing test for reasonableness depicted in Exhibit 14.10, and they apply it similarly to drug-testing policies in both settings. The only major difference is that middle school and high school athletes are minors, which reduces their constitutional protection somewhat. The doctrine of *in loco parentis* gives the school extra authority to regulate students because the school is responsible for the well-being of those students in the absence of the parents. This point is explicitly acknowledged in the *Vernonia* case, and it may partly explain the conflicting decisions reached in a college drug-testing case (*Derdeyn*, 1993) and *Vernonia* (1995), a middle school drug-testing case. Nevertheless, a comparison of the two cases illustrates that courts applying the balancing test can reach widely divergent conclusions about the reasonableness of essentially the same drug-testing policy. In this section, we compare the courts' application of the balancing test in *Derdeyn* and *Vernonia*.

EXHIBIT   14.9   Fourth Amendment.

Amendment IV, United States Constitution

The right of the people to be secure in their persons, houses, papers, and effects, against unreasonable searches and seizures, shall not be violated, and no warrants shall issue, but upon probable cause, supported by oath or affirmation, and particularly describing the place to be searched and the persons or things to be seized.

| | EXHIBIT 14.10 |

Legal analysis of a drug-testing search under the Fourth Amendment.

Legal Analysis

In general, the issues in a student-athlete drug testing case proceed as follows:

1. Was there state action? If so,
2. Does the complained-of activity constitute a search and/or seizure? If so,
3. Was the search reasonable?

   a. Was it justified at its inception? (by probable cause, reasonable suspicion, exigent circumstances, or random searches based on other special governmental needs, e.g., airport searches)

   b. Was it reasonable in scope?

   (1) Individual's reasonable expectation of privacy

   (2) Nature and degree of the intrusion

   balanced against

   (1) Government's interest in conducting the search

   (2) Efficacy of the search in meeting the government's goal

4. If the search was reasonable, the Fourth Amendment was not violated.

University of Colorado v. Derdeyn

863 P.2d 929 (Colo. 1993)

FOCUS CASE

FACTS

The NCAA requires a mandatory random drug test that is visually monitored in order to ensure "ownership" of an untampered-with urine sample. In this case, the University of Colorado (CU) had implemented a drug policy nearly identical to that used by the NCAA. CU then amended the policy to require that testing be based on reasonable suspicion rather than random selection of athletes and to make it less intrusive by requiring only aural, and not visual, monitoring of the sample collection. However, the consent form continued to indicate that athletes were required to consent to *random* suspicionless testing. The trial court issued a permanent injunction prohibiting CU from enforcing its drug-testing policy, finding a lack of genuine consent on the part of student-athletes, and the appeals court generally affirmed. CU appealed again.

HOLDING

The Colorado Supreme Court held that the testing procedure was an unreasonable search under the Fourth Amendment.

RATIONALE

After acknowledging that random searches in the school context could be justified by special needs (i.e., to combat widespread drug use by students), the court conducted the balancing test for reasonableness, weighing the intrusiveness of the search against the university's need to conduct it.

First, the court examined whether the athletes had a reasonable expectation of privacy. The university argued that the athletes had a diminished expectation of privacy because:

1. They routinely provide urine samples as part of their annual preparticipation physical examinations.
2. They submit to extensive regulation of their behavior, including diet, conditioning, academic performance, and so forth.
3. They are already subject to the NCAA's drug-testing protocol.
4. The consequence of refusing to provide a urine sample is not severe because they only lose their opportunity to participate in athletics (in contrast to losing one's job, for example).
5. Positive test results are kept confidential and are not provided to criminal law enforcement authorities.

The court responded to these arguments as follows:

1. Athletic department personnel were involved in the sample collection process, rendering it less private than if it had been conducted by "strangers" in a medical setting.
2. None of the other behavioral regulations imposed on the athletes entailed an extensive invasion of their privacy.
3. Although submission to the NCAA's drug-testing program might seem to render submission to CU's program less intrusive, the athletes testified that CU's policy was more intrusive because it transformed otherwise trusting relationships between athletic trainers and athletes into untrusting and confrontational interactions.
4. Although most college athletes will never turn pro, many athletes who could not otherwise afford to attend college do so by means of their athletic scholarship, thus increasing their future earning potential—so it is not just the chance to have fun playing that is lost by those who refuse to be tested.
5. While there is no risk of criminal penalties, there is also no warrant or probable cause impediment to these mandatory searches that would provide the same protection against abuse to athletes that is provided to criminal suspects.

Overall, the court felt that CU's arguments did not successfully establish a strongly reduced expectation of privacy on the part of student-athletes.

In assessing the intrusiveness of the search procedure itself, the court found that while aural monitoring is indeed less intrusive than visual monitoring, the university had admitted that under certain circumstances it might return to a policy of visual monitoring. This lack of assurance of lower intrusiveness combined with a finding that the athletes had a reasonable expectation of privacy led the court to conclude that CU's policy permitting random, suspicionless drug testing was significantly intrusive.

This high level of intrusiveness then had to be balanced against the university's interests in conducting the drug-testing program. According to CU, they needed to test in order to: (1) prepare their athletes for undergoing NCAA drug testing during postseason play; (2) promote the integrity of their intercollegiate athletics program; (3) deter drug use by other students who view athletes as their role models; (4) ensure fair competition; and (5) protect the health and safety of the athletes. In the court's view, all of these interests were commendable, but the only one that rose to the level of an important governmental concern was the need to protect the health and safety of the athletes.

The court then assessed the governmental need to search by comparing the case at bar to the large body of nonathletics related case law, in which a majority of courts have required the government to have truly compelling interests to justify having a testing policy, such as preventing public transportation safety disasters or protecting national security. In this case, concluded the *Derdeyn* court, the university's interests simply were not comparable to those established precedents. Thus, CU's need to search athletes did not outweigh the significant intrusiveness of its drug-testing program; therefore, the drug-testing procedure constituted an unreasonable search.

Finally, the university argued that even if its policy was determined to be unreasonable under the Fourth Amendment, it should not be considered to violate the Constitution because the student-athletes gave their voluntary consent to be tested. The court acknowledged that a warrantless search is generally considered reasonable if an individual has consented to it. However, the court went on to quote from a U.S. Supreme Court decision in which consent was defined as "a consent intelligently and freely given, without any duress, coercion or subtle promises or threats calculated to flaw the free and unconstrained nature of the decision" (*Schneckloth v. Bustamonte*, 1973). Applying this definition, the *Derdeyn* court concluded that in this case the athletes' "consent" was clearly coerced because they could not participate without a signed consent form.

Let's contrast the *Derdeyn* case with *Vernonia*.

Vernonia School District 47J v. Acton

115 S.Ct. 2386 (1995)	FOCUS CASE

FACTS AND HOLDING

The U. S. Supreme Court decided 6 to 3 to uphold a school district's athlete drug-testing policy after it was challenged by a seventh grade football player. The only relevant factual differences between *Derdeyn* and *Vernonia* are that in this (the latter) case: (1) the athletes were minors; (2) the sample collection was monitored aurally, except that the boys were sometimes watched from behind; and (3) the Vernonia school district claimed the existence of a large-scale drug abuse crisis led by athletes.

RATIONALE

Justice Scalia, writing for the majority in *Vernonia*, applied the usual balancing test to determine the reasonableness of the search. In contrast to the Colorado court's analysis in *Derdeyn*, the Supreme Court found that the athletes did indeed have a diminished expectation of privacy for four reasons: (1) in choosing to participate, they submitted themselves to a higher degree of regulation than other students and thus should expect intrusions on normal rights and privileges; (2) they regularly engage in a state of "communal undress" in the locker room; (3) they routinely undergo preparticipation physical examinations; and (4) they are minors, so schools standing in the shoes of the parents (*in loco parentis*) while children are in their care possess a degree of control that exceeds what could be exercised over adults. The Court considered the *in loco parentis* factor as central to its analysis of the students' expected level of privacy.

Having concluded that the student-athletes did have a diminished expectation of privacy, the Court went on to characterize the intrusiveness of the search as minimal. Because it was aurally monitored, because the test assessed only the presence of banned drugs and not other medical conditions, and because disclosure of the results was limited and not used for criminal law enforcement, the Court concluded that the invasion of student privacy was insignificant.

On the other hand, the government's interest in conducting the drug-testing program was found to be strong, based on the school district's evidence of student-athlete involvement in a disciplinary rebellion of "epidemic proportion" that was fueled by drug and alcohol abuse. Additionally, the Court asserted the importance of deterring drug use by the nation's schoolchildren, and particularly among students for whom drug use would pose immediate risks of harm, such as athletes. In rejecting the argument that suspicion-based testing would accomplish the deterrence objective just as efficaciously as random testing but less invasively, the Court asserted that parents would be less likely to accept it due to its potential for appearing accusatory, which might "transform . . . the process into a badge of shame."

Additionally, the Court thought that teachers and coaches might abuse a nonrandom testing process by imposing testing arbitrarily on troublemakers who were not necessarily likely drug users. Finally, the Court said that suspicion-based testing would, because of its accusatory nature, require that more due process be provided, and would place teachers and coaches in the role of being drug abuse spotters—a role for which they are not well-prepared. Thus, concluded the Court, the school district's interests in continuing to conduct random drug testing of athletes outweighed the minimal intrusion on student privacy that it created.

As you can see, the *Vernonia* Court reached the opposite conclusion from the *Derdeyn* court on the reasonableness of nearly identical drug-testing policies. Once again, while this difference may be partly explained by the age difference in the populations tested, a comparison of the courts' analyses of the reasonableness factors highlights the inherent subjectivity of the inquiry.

More recently, the Supreme Court has extended the constitutionality of drug testing from being limited to student-athletes to encompassing all students who participate in extracurricular activities, including cheerleaders, the band, the choir, the Academic Team, and the Future Farmers of America (*Board of Education of Independent School District No. 92 of Pottawatomie County v. Earls,* 2002). In a 5–4 decision, the Supreme Court dismissed the idea that individualized suspicion should be required to justify a search, saying that "special needs" are inherent in the public school setting.

Moving on to examine the nature of the students' privacy interest, the Court followed *Vernonia* in finding an expectation of privacy diminished by the *in loco parentis* stature of public schools and by the highly regulated nature of participation in extracurricular activities. As to the nature of the intrusion, because the school district's policy only required aural monitoring from outside a closed bathroom stall, the Court found this procedure even less intrusive than the one in *Vernonia*.

With regard to the governmental need for the testing program, the *Earls* Court refused to second-guess the district court's finding that the school district had a drug problem, and also asserted that it was unwilling to force a school district to wait until a crisis developed before it could implement a deterrence procedure. The efficacy of the policy in deterring drug use by students did not, according to the Court, require a close nexus between the groups tested and those most likely to use drugs.

The importance of the *Earls* case is that, in its analysis, the Court ignored the facts that nonathletic extracurricular activities differ in significant ways from athletics. Compared to sport activities, the nonsport activities lack the same type of safety concerns, do not all involve preparticipation physical exams and "communal undress," and do not have the concern as to fairness or integrity of competition. These factors were an important part of the Court's justification for the result it reached in the *Vernonia* case. The Court's willingness to ignore this is a cause for concern. Bereft of mooring in the special context of athletics, the *Earls* decision allows the Court to drift toward the possibility that the next step will be to allow drug testing of *all* secondary school students—not just participants in extracurricular activities.

Competitive Advantage

STRATEGIES

Drug Testing of Athletes

- Consider whether the monetary costs and the costs to individual privacy are outweighed by the deterrent value of implementing a drug-testing program. Steroid-and-stimulant screening can cost up to $50 per test (Shipley, 2003).

- Minimize the intrusiveness of the search by only requiring aural monitoring by a same-sex monitor from outside a closed bathroom stall.

- Limit consequences of positive test results to restrictions on participation opportunities and requiring the student to undergo treatment or rehabilitation. Avoid involvement of criminal law enforcement.

- Maximize anonymity and accuracy in the sample collection and testing processes, as well as confidentiality in the reporting and data storage processes.

- Provide opportunities for retesting samples to verify positive results.

- Arrange for sample collection to be performed by nonathletic department personnel.

A final point that needs to be made is this: the NCAA's drug-testing program is beyond the reach of the Constitution, but public universities that choose to supplement the NCAA's program with their own drug-testing procedures are subject to constitutional restraints. This has created an interesting twist for drug-testing law, because it means that virtually identical drug-testing procedures could be held unconstitutional if administered by a public university but be untouchable if administered by the NCAA. This scenario is, in fact, close to the reality of current law, as you can see by comparing the NCAA's drug-testing situation with the situation at the University of Colorado following the *Derdeyn* decision.

The situation is also complicated by state court interpretations of state constitutions as applied to drug testing of athletes. Sometimes state constitutions protect civil liberties more rigorously than does the U. S. Constitution (see *Hill v. NCAA*, 1994). At least two states have relied on their state constitutions in deciding drug testing cases (*Hill v. NCAA*, 1994; *York v. Wahkiakum Sch. Dist. No. 200*, 2008).

Expression Issues

Sometimes student-athletes are subjected to discipline for engaging in expressive activity, such as wearing their hair, clothing, or a tattoo in such a way as to violate a grooming or dress code. Failure to comply with such codes is often grounds for suspension from the team or from school. Students have challenged the application of these kinds of rules, claiming either a liberty interest in self-expression protected by the Due Process Clause or a First Amendment right to freedom of expression or freedom of religion. Additionally, athletes have claimed that dress or grooming codes have unfairly singled them out from the rest of the student body in violation of the Equal Protection Clause.

The federal courts are split on the issue of whether dress and grooming codes violate the First Amendment right to freedom of expression. Some courts have upheld such codes, ruling that grooming (e.g., hairstyle, makeup) and dress choices (e.g., jewelry, clothing styles) are simply a type of individual self-expression that does not rise to the type of valuable speech that the First Amendment was designed to protect (see, e.g., *Zeller v. Donegal School District,* 1975; *Davenport v. Randolph County Board of Education,* 1984). Other courts have struck down such codes as unconstitutional, ruling that First Amendment protection does extend to such low-value expression (see, e.g., *Dunham v. Pulsifer,* 1970; *Long v. Zopp,* 1973).

A new issue is whether the First Amendment will prevent athletics departments from enforcing their social networking policies with penalties like suspension or expulsion for student-athletes who post prohibited content on sites such as Facebook and Twitter (Orland, 2009; Wilson, 2009).

Freedom of expression and the Due Process and Equal Protection Clauses

In a nonsport-related tattoo case, a high school threatened to suspend a student if she did not get removed a tattoo of a cross that they said violated a rule forbidding the display of symbols of gang activity. The court found that her tattoo was merely a form of self-expression that did not rise to the level of important communication the First Amendment was designed to protect. However, it also found that there is a liberty interest in determining one's personal appearance and that the rule in question was too vague about defining what constituted a symbol of gang activity to have provided the student with clear notice of what was prohibited (*Stephenson v. Davenport Community School District,* 1997).

In an unreported decision, the U. S. District Court for the Central District of Illinois upheld a high school basketball team's grooming rule. Plaintiff Jeff Stotts was suspended from the team for getting a tattoo of a dragon on his back in violation of the rule, and he sued under the First Amendment and the Equal Protection Clause. The district court denied his request for an injunction prohibiting the school district from enforcing the rule, finding that Stotts had little likelihood of succeeding on the merits of his claim. On appeal, the Seventh Circuit dismissed the claim as moot because Stotts had by then graduated and a decision by the court could have no practical impact (*Stotts v. Community Unit School District No. 1,* 2000).

A high school tennis player used the Equal Protection Clause successfully to challenge a grooming code that specified acceptable hair length for athletes

(*Dunham v. Pulsifer*, 1970). Here, the court found that choice of hairstyle was a fundamental right, and thus the school could not regulate it without the rule passing strict scrutiny. In finding a fundamental right to determine one's appearance, the court relied on precedent that had been fairly unanimous in finding such a right, although grounding it in various provisions of the Constitution. Additionally, the court stated the following:

> Whether hairstyles be regarded as evidence of conformity or of individuality, they are one of the most visible examples of personality. . . . Furthermore, the cut of one's hair style is more fundamental to personal appearance than the type of clothing he wears. Garments can be changed at will whereas hair, once it is cut, has to remain constant for substantial periods of time. In addition to manifesting basic personality traits, hair style has been shadowed with political, philosophical and ideological overtones and as such has to be afforded a measure of the protection given these underlying beliefs. (p. 419)

Although agreeing that maintaining team discipline was a compelling interest, the court ruled that requiring compliance with a grooming code that was unrelated to any performance objective was unreasonable and thus violated the Equal Protection Clause.

Freedom of religion

A dress code violation prompted a freedom of religion lawsuit in *Menora v. Illinois High School Association* (1982). A Jewish basketball player wanted to wear his yarmulke while playing in order to honor his religious beliefs. But the athletic association enforced its "no headgear rule," asserting that loose headgear could create a safety hazard on the basketball court. The court ruled in favor of the athletic association, holding that this rule was a neutral rule with a legitimate purpose and was not an attempt to target Judaism for suppression. The court did, however, suggest that the athletic association modify its rule to allow secure headgear to be worn in order to accomplish their safety objective without unnecessarily burdening students with similar religious practices.

In *Moody v. Cronin* (1980), the court ruled in favor of two Pentecostal plaintiffs who were suspended for refusing to attend coeducational physical education classes in which they would have been required to wear shorts in violation of their religion's stance on appropriate public modesty. They sued under the First Amendment, claiming their right to freely exercise their religion was being infringed upon.

Other forms of religious discrimination might include treating student-athletes differently with respect to playing opportunities due to their religion, or imposing

---

Competitive Advantage

STRATEGIES

Athletics Policies That Do Not Infringe on the Bill of Rights

- Coaches and school authorities who wish to impose dress or grooming codes for their athletics teams will probably be fine. To be on the safe side, dress or grooming choices of student-athletes that involve important communication of the sort the First Amendment was designed to protect should probably be avoided. Having a sport-performance-related objective for a dress code would aid in its justification.

- School administrators should avoid creating and implementing pre-game prayer policies. If a pre-game solemnizing message is desired, the policy should be carefully worded to avoid giving the impression that there is any religious intent, and it should ensure that the selection of messages and speakers is administered by the students. If the students still choose to include religious content in their speech, it might be wise not to censor it because a court may consider this protected freedom of speech.

team penalties for religious expression. For example, the NCAA has a "Celebration Rule" for football that prohibits self-aggrandizing acts of celebration after a good play or a touchdown and limits celebration to sportsmanlike behavior directed at celebrating as a team. One of the end zone celebrations originally banned was taking a knee as an act of prayer. When Liberty University threatened to sue the NCAA for religious discrimination in a place of public accommodation under Title II of the Civil Rights Act of 1964, the NCAA quickly removed the prayer action from its list of prohibited celebration behaviors (Rhoden, 1995).

Pre-game prayer

The issue of pre-game prayer impacts students' freedom of religion and speech rights as spectators and participants. Found in the First Amendment, the Establishment Clause and the Free Exercise Clause protect the freedom of religion. The Establishment Clause prohibits the government from establishing a preferred, government-endorsed religious faith or practice, while the Free Exercise Clause prohibits the government from impermissibly targeting a religious faith or practice for suppression. Taken together, these two clauses are meant to protect religious liberty. The freedom of speech provision in the First Amendment protects individuals' right to engage in religious speech as well as political speech and other valued types of speech. The general rule is that the government may not impose content-based restrictions on speech unless it has a compelling reason and the restriction can pass a strict scrutiny test. If the restriction on speech is content-neutral, the government may impose reasonable time, place, and manner restrictions on the speech activity as long as the content of the message is not thereby suppressed.

The Supreme Court has used three different tests to identify violations of the Establishment Clause—the endorsement test, the coercion test, and the *Lemon* test (*Borden v. Sch. Dist. of the Township of East Brunswick*, 2008). The endorsement test asks whether a reasonable observer would perceive the practice in question to be a government endorsement of religion. The coercion test looks at whether the government's action might have the effect of coercing anyone to support or participate in religion. And *Lemon v. Kurtzman* (1971) established a three-pronged test examining whether the government's conduct (1) lacks a secular purpose, (2) has the primary effect of advancing or inhibiting religion, or (3) fosters an excessive government entanglement with religion.

In 2000, the Supreme Court rendered the *Santa Fe Independent School District v. Doe* decision, which ruled that a pre-game prayer was an unconstitutional establishment of religion. Prior to 1995, an elected student council chaplain regularly delivered a prayer over the public address system before each home football game. Then, in response to the initiation of litigation in this case, the school district adopted a new policy that permitted, but did not require, student-initiated prayer at football games. The policy authorized a student election to determine whether an "invocation and/or message" should be delivered and a second election to determine which student would deliver it. The stated purpose of the invocation or message was to promote sportsmanship and safety, to establish the appropriate social environment for the competition, and to solemnize the event. In the school district's view, this policy permitted private student speech that could be religious or nonreligious in content. Hence it did not promote government speech endorsing religion but instead promoted speech protected by the freedom of speech and free exercise of religion clauses of the First Amendment. The school district also considered the policy to be neutral because it did not endorse or favor any particular religion and had a secular purpose of promoting good sportsmanship.

The Supreme Court, however, found that the words "solemnize" and "invocation" conveyed the idea that religious messages were encouraged and that this idea matched the students' actual understanding of the policy. The Court also found relevant that the pre-game prayers were delivered over the public address system, as part of a larger pre-game ceremony clothed in the indicia of school-sponsored sports events (e.g., school colors and insignia, uniforms, involvement of band and cheerleaders) and structured as part of a school-sponsored event held on school property. It concluded that, instead of private speech, the pre-game prayer was a public expression of the view of the majority of students that was delivered with the approval of the school administration. In the Court's view, therefore, this policy represented an improper state endorsement of religion.

The Court also was persuaded that the election policy structured by the school district was designed to permit the majority preference for pre-game prayers to continue to prevail. Because the policy required that only those messages considered appropriate under the policy (solemnization, sportsmanship, etc.) were delivered, the majoritarian election process ensured that the views of the minority would not have a chance to be voiced. Thus, the election process was so dictated by the school district that it did not remove entanglement of the government with religious activity. In fact, the Court implied that the policy was a sham instituted to preserve the practice of pre-game prayer. While the choice of the speaker was the students', the decision to hold the elections and the structure and mandated purpose of the "invocation and/or message" was a choice attributable to the state.

The Court also stated its view that while spectator attendance at the football games was voluntary, certain people (e.g., band members, cheerleaders, athletes) were required to be there, making them a captive audience. Furthermore, the Court felt that the delivery of a pre-game prayer over the public address system impermissibly coerced all those present to participate in an act of religious worship—which some might find offensive—and thus the policy would not pass the coercion test.

In addition to the endorsement and coercion tests, the Court applied the *Lemon* test for analyzing Establishment Clause violations (*Lemon v. Kurtzman*, 1971). It concluded that the policy's affirmative sponsorship of prayer violated the Establishment Clause because of its religious purpose, as well as the school district's continuing entanglement with structuring religious activity.

The dissent argued that the policy gave students a choice about the nature of the message to be delivered; therefore, the policy had a plausibly secular purpose and potentially secular effect. It noted that Establishment Clause jurisprudence does not mandate complete neutrality of content, so a policy may tolerate religion without endorsing it. The dissent also argued that the election process succeeded in disentangling the school district from religion by permitting the students to engage in private, as opposed to state-orchestrated, religious speech.

The Eleventh Circuit, in *Chandler v. James* (1999) (*Chandler I*), reached a different conclusion about a pre-game prayer policy than the Supreme Court did in *Santa Fe*. The *Chandler* case explicates the complex interaction between the freedoms of speech and religion and the Establishment Clause. This case is summarized in the following Focus Case.

Chandler v. James (Chandler I)

FOCUS CASE   180 F.3d 1254 (11th Cir. 1999)

FACTS

In 1993, Alabama enacted a statute that explicitly permitted nonsectarian, non-proselytizing student-initiated prayer during school-related events, including sports events. In 1996, Chandler sued, challenging the statute and its application as unconstitutional. The district court ruled the statute unconstitutional as a violation of the Establishment Clause and issued a permanent injunction against its enforcement. In addition to prohibiting the schools from organizing or officially sanctioning prayer and other religious activities, the permanent injunction prohibited the schools from permitting all vocal prayer that might have occurred at school events and required school officials to forbid students from praying aloud while at school-related events.

HOLDING

The Eleventh Circuit vacated the permanent injunction and remanded the case back to the district court, holding that the lower court could not constitutionally enjoin the school system from permitting student-initiated religious speech in its schools.

RATIONALE

The court reviewed a number of school prayer cases and concluded that what rendered the relevant prayer policies unconstitutional was not that they had permitted religious speech but that they had required that the speech be religious. The court went to great length to explain that the principle of government neutrality toward religion has been misunderstood and often misapplied by the courts, and elaborated on the necessity for striking the appropriate balance between the prevention of an impermissible establishment of religion and the protection of the free exercise of religion. In support of this position, the court quoted from the Supreme Court in the case of *School District of Abington Township v. Schempp* (1963) as follows:

> untutored devotion to the concept of neutrality can lead to invocation or approval of results which partake not simply of that noninterference and noninvolvement with the religious which the Constitution commands, but of a brooding and pervasive dedication to the secular and a passive, or even active, hostility to the religious. Such results are not only not compelled by the Constitution, but . . . are prohibited by it. (p. 306)

The Eleventh Circuit concluded that the exclusion of religion from the public sphere marginalizes and sends a message of disapproval of religion. In the court's view, true neutrality means tolerance of belief and disbelief alike, not the establishment of atheism as the government's preferred belief about religion.

Furthermore, the court emphasized that student speech is not state speech but is the speech of private actors. In the words of the court,

> Permitting students to speak religiously signifies neither state approval nor disapproval of that speech. The speech is not the State's—either by attribution or adoption. The permission signifies no more than that the State acknowledges its Constitutional duty to tolerate religious expression. Only in this way is true neutrality achieved.
>
> Because genuinely student-initiated religious speech is private speech endorsing religion, it is fully protected by both the Free Exercise and the Free Speech Clauses of the Constitution. (p. 1261)

The court went on to quote from another Supreme Court case, *Lee v. Weisman* (1992), as follows:

> We do not hold that every state action implicating religion is invalid if one or a few citizens find it offensive.... We know that sometimes to endure social isolation or even anger may be the price of conscience or nonconformity. (p. 597)

According to the Eleventh Circuit, a person who does not agree with a speaker's religious belief is free not to listen or participate. On this point, the opinion states,

> Accommodation of religious beliefs we do not share is . . . a part of everyday life in this country. . . . Respect for the rights of others to express their beliefs, both political and religious, is the price the Constitution extracts for our own liberty. This is a price we freely pay. It is not coerced. Only when the speech is commanded by the State does it unconstitutionally coerce the listener. (p. 1263)

The court went on to say that a school must not participate in or actively supervise otherwise genuinely student-initiated speech. The mere presence of a teacher or coach is not, in the court's view, unconstitutional coercion. Additionally, a school may impose reasonable time, place, or manner restrictions on religious student speech only to the same extent it would for nonreligious student speech. To treat religious speech differently would be to engage in viewpoint discrimination, which is the most egregious form of a freedom of speech violation because it is censorship.

A year later, the Supreme Court decided the *Santa Fe* case discussed earlier. It then vacated the judgment in *Chandler v. James* and remanded it back to the Eleventh Circuit for reconsideration in light of the holding in *Santa Fe*. Upon review, the Eleventh Circuit concluded that its earlier decision did not conflict with *Santa Fe* and reinstated it (*Chandler v. Siegelman*, 2000 [*Chandler II*]). According to the court, "*Santa Fe* condemns school sponsorship of student prayer. *Chandler* condemns school censorship of student prayer . . . the cases are complementary rather than inconsistent" (p. 1315). The court reiterated its view that "It is not the public context that makes some speech the State's. It is the entanglement with the State. . . . Remove the sponsorship, and the prayer is private" (p. 1316). Further, "A policy which tolerates religion does not improperly endorse it" (p. 1317).

CONCLUSION

After reading this chapter, you should understand that regulating amateur sport participation in country clubs and school settings involves a myriad of issues, from various forms of discrimination, to application of eligibility and athlete conduct rules, to drug testing, and to religious expression, among others. A good manager will be able to use this knowledge to recognize a potential legal problem ahead of time and take steps to prevent it from blossoming—before finding herself on the defensive because someone has filed a complaint or a lawsuit.

discussion questions

1. Why do some country clubs work hard at being truly private? If you were the assistant manager at a fairly ritzy country club in New Orleans where the membership wants to continue to exclude White people as it has always done since it started business in 1963, what advice would you give about how to ensure that a court will view the club as truly private? What laws do you need to consider as part of your analysis for the club?

2. If someone sues a university under § 504 or the ADA for its failure to provide equal participation opportunities to individuals with disabilities, the decision will probably turn on whether the athlete with a disability is considered a "qualified" person with a disability. Does qualified mean qualified to compete with and against able-bodied athletes? Or could it also mean qualified to compete as a wheelchair-bound athlete on a team for wheelchair athletes?

3. If adding disabled athletes to able-bodied competitions would require accommodations that constituted a fundamental alteration of the sport, as was the case in *Kuketz,* would a reasonable accommodation be to create separate teams for athletes with disabilities instead? Is this what we have done in creating separate teams for female athletes?

4. The court in *Cohen v. Brown* (*Cohen IV*) explicitly addressed the argument that the first prong of the three-part test for compliance in participation opportunities constitutes an impermissible quota. In your own words, what were the court's reasons for rejecting that argument? Was the court's reasoning on this issue persuasive to you? If so, why? If not, why not?

5. After *Earls,* we are now in the strange position of having the Colorado Supreme Court and the U. S. Supreme Court in virtual agreement that there is little difference between the privacy expectations of athletes and other types of students—but one court uses that argument to strike down drug testing, and the other uses it to allow drug testing of even wider groups of students. Or is there an argument that the *Derdeyn* and *Earls* cases can be logically reconciled?

6. Can you draw a meaningful distinction between the two free exercise of religion cases, *Moody* and *Menora?*

7. Consider a hypothetical case of an intercollegiate basketball player who turns her back to the flag during the pregame playing of the national anthem in order to protest U. S. involvement in a current war. Would a court be more likely to decide that the First Amendment protected this student than the student with the tattoo in *Stephenson* or in *Stotts?*

8. Why do you suppose Liberty University did not also threaten a First Amendment Establishment Clause claim with regard to its challenge to the NCAA's Celebration Rule?

9. Iowa State University recently stirred controversy by considering appointing a "life skills assistant" to serve as a spiritual advisor to its football team. As proposed, the advisor would report to the athletic director; serve those athletes who sought out spiritual counsel; would not "pressure, coerce or proselytize" athletes; and would have access to practices and games. Any prayer led during mandatory team functions would have to be student-initiated and student-led. Based on *Santa Fe* and *Chandler II*, as well as the *Borden* case discussed in Chapter 7, do you think this policy would be considered constitutional?

learning activities

1. Make a copy of the eight-factor *Lansdowne* analysis (Exhibit 14.2) for determining whether a club is truly private, and add a few explanatory details or examples for each factor based on the cases referenced in this book. Then take the list to a nearby country club and ask them how they would assess whether they are truly private based on *Lansdowne* factors. Be sure to have a conversation with them after they scribble on your list so you can ask clarifying questions. Write a one-page summary detailing your opinion about whether the club is truly private.

2. Engage in role-reversal. If men's athletics were to receive only what the women have, would the men be satisfied? If not, there is still a problem. Identify the changes you think the athletic program at your university needs to make in order to make you happy in this "new perspective" position.

3. On the Web, visit the site of the National Women's Law Center (www.nwlc.org) or the Women's Sports Foundation (www.womenssportsfoundation.org) and discover what kinds of Title IX educational aids are available there.

4. Retrieve the *Feeney* case (*Personnel Administrator of Massachusetts v. Feeney*, 99 S.Ct. 2282 (1979)) and *Pryor* (discussed earlier), and compare the factual situations in the two cases. Can you see a difference in the facts that led the courts in these two cases to reach different results? Write a paragraph explaining this difference. Then write a paragraph arguing that there is *no* significant difference between the facts in *Feeney* and *Pryor.*

5. On the Web, visit the site of the Women's Sports Foundation (www.womenssportsfoundation.org) and evaluate the WSF's position statement on athletics competition for individuals with disabilities.

6. Visit the NCAA's website (www.ncaa.org) and evaluate the guidelines pertaining to pregnant student-athletes.

CASE STUDY

The ACLU recently filed an internal grievance at New World State University (NWSU; a public university in Colorado) alleging that the NWSU football coach engaged in religious discrimination against a Muslim student-athlete. The grievance claims that Coach Al West violated the First Amendment by repeatedly questioning his running back Mohammed Ahman about Islam and its ties to al-Qaeda and by requiring the team to recite the Lord's Prayer after each practice.

Additionally, some evidence suggests that religious discrimination played a role in Ahman's release from the team after six games. Ahman had begun the season at the top of the depth-chart. He started the first game and rushed for 21 yards in seven carries. He did not start the next game, however, and was not even included on the roster for the next four games prior to his release. The coach claims that Ahman's release was performance-related, as his replacement is now one of the leading rushers in the SMAC Conference. Ahman claims he learned of his release via a message left on his cell phone by an assistant coach. He also claims that his requests to meet with the coaching staff to discuss it have been denied. Two other Muslim players were also released from the team under similar circumstances.

In response to the grievance, NWSU hired a law firm to investigate the allegations, and it reported finding no evidence of religious discrimination. The ACLU has questioned the impartiality of the investigation. Ahman's father has stated that the family intends to pursue the complaint in federal court. Meanwhile, Ahman has petitioned the NCAA for a hardship waiver to allow him to transfer to Coastal California State University without having to lose a year of eligibility.

(These facts are based on an actual situation. See "Former Aggie to Transfer to Portland State," reported by the Associated Press on December 16, 2005.)

1. Could Ahman bring a claim for religious discrimination under Title II of the Civil Rights Act? If so, what would the analysis look like? If not, why not?

2. Could Ahman bring a religious discrimination claim under the First Amendment Free Exercise Clause? Refer to Chapter 7 for detailed information on the religion clauses in the First Amendment to help you describe what Ahman's freedom of religion argument would be under the First Amendment.

3. Could Ahman bring an Equal Protection Clause claim? If so, on what grounds? What level of review would a court give such a claim?

4. Could Ahman bring a Title VI claim for race discrimination? If so, what would his arguments be? If not, why not?

5. Could Ahman bring a Due Process Clause claim? If so, on what grounds?

considering . . .   ANALYSIS & DISCUSSION

Sexual Harassment Occurring Abroad (p. 380)

The athletic director erred. She should have investigated the complaint because she has been put on notice that sexual harassment has occurred. If the athlete were to be harassed again back in the United States, a court could find that the university knew that harassment had occurred previously but was deliberately indifferent in failing to act to prevent it from happening again. In that case, the student could be awarded monetary damages.

R E F E R E N C E S

Cases

Alexander v. Sandoval, 121 S.Ct. 1511 (2001).

Barry v. Maple Bluff Country Club, Inc., 629 N.W.2d 24 (Wis. Ct. App. 2001).

Bercovitch v. Baldwin Sch., Inc., 133 F.3d 141 (1st Cir. 1998).

Board of Educ. of Indep. Sch. Dist. No. 92 of Pottawatomie County v. Earls, 122 S.Ct. 2559 (2002).

Borden v. Sch. Dist. of the Township of East Brunswick, 2008 U.S. App. LEXIS 8011 (3rd Cir. 2008).

Borne v. Haverhill Golf & Country Club, Inc., 791 N.E.2d 903 (Mass. App. Ct. 2003).

Bowers v. NCAA, 9 F. Supp. 2d 460 (D.N.J. 1998).

Boy Scouts of America v. Dale, 530 U.S. 640 (2000).

Boyd v. Board of Dirs., 612 F. Supp. 86 (E.D. Ark. 1985).

Bunger v. Iowa High Sch. Athletic Ass'n, 197 N.W.2d 555 (Iowa 1972).

Chandler v. James, 180 F.3d 1254 (11th Cir. 1999) (*Chandler I*).

Chandler v. Siegelman, 230 F.3d 1313 (11th Cir. 2000) (*Chandler II*).

Citizens Council on Human Relations v. Buffalo Yacht Club, 438 F. Supp. 316 (W.D.N.Y. 1977).

Cohen v. Brown Univ. (*Cohen I*), 809 F. Supp. 978 (D.R.I. 1992), *aff'd*, (*Cohen II*) 991 F.2d 888 (1st Cir. 1993), *on remand*, (*Cohen III*), 879 F. Supp. 185 (D.R.I. 1995), *aff'd*, (*Cohen IV*) 101 F.3d 155 (1st Cir. 1996), *cert. denied*, 117 S. Ct. 1469 (1997).

Communities for Equity v. Michigan High Sch. Athletic Ass'n, 178 F. Supp. 2d 805 (W.D. Mich. 2001), *aff'd*, 377 F.3d 504 (6th Cir. 2004).

Cook v. Colgate Univ., 992 F.2d 17 (2nd Cir. 1993).

Cook v. Twin Oaks Country Club, 122 F. Supp. 2d 1064 (W.D. Mo. 2000).

Crawford v. Willow Oaks Country Club, 66 F. Supp. 2d 767 (E.D. Va. 1999).

Cureton v. NCAA, 198 F.3d 107 (3rd Cir. 1999).

Daniel v. Paul, 395 U.S. 298 (1969).

Davenport v. Randolph County Bd. of Educ., 730 F.2d 1395 (11th Cir. 1984).

Davis v. Monroe County Bd. of Educ., 119 S.Ct. 1661 (1999).

Dennin v. Connecticut Interscholastic Athletic Conference, 913 F. Supp. 663 (D. Conn. 1996).

Duffley v. New Hampshire Interscholastic Athletic Ass'n, 446 A.2d 462 (N.H. 1982).

Dunham v. Pulsifer, 312 F. Supp. 411 (D. Vt. 1970).

Florida High Sch. Athletic Ass'n v. Bryant, 313 So.2d 57 (Fla. Dist. Ct. App. 1975).

Franklin v. Gwinnett County Pub. Sch., 112 S.Ct. 1028 (1992).

Ganden v. NCAA, 1996 U.S. Dist. LEXIS 17368 (N.D. Ill. 1996).

Gibbs-Alfano v. Ossining Boat & Canoe Club, Inc., 47 F. Supp. 2d 506 (S.D.N.Y. 1999).

Hill v. NCAA, 865 P.2d 633 (Cal. 1994).

Hoot by Hoot v. Milan Area Sch., 853 F. Supp. 243 (E.D. Mich. 1994).

Indiana High Sch. Athletic Ass'n, Inc. v. Wideman, 688 N.E.2d 413 (Ind. Ct. App. 1997).

Jennings v. University of N.C., 240 F. Supp. 2d 492 (M.D.N.C. 2002) 482 F.3d 686 (4th Cir. 2007, *en banc*); *cert. denied*, 128 S.Ct. 247 (2007).

Kelley v. Board of Trustees, Univ. of Illinois, 35 F.3d 265 (7th Cir. 1994).

Knapp v. Northwestern Univ., 101 F.3d 473 (7th Cir. 1996).

Kuketz v. Petronelli, 821 N.E.2d 473 (Mass. 2005).

Lee v. Weisman, 112 S.Ct. 2649 (1992).

Lemon v. Kurtzman, 91 S.Ct. 2105 (1971).

Long v. Board of Educ. Dist. 128, 167 F. Supp. 2d 988 (N.D. Ill. 2001).

Long v. Zopp, 476 F.2d 180 (4th Cir. 1973).

Matthews v. NCAA, 179 F. Supp. 2d 1209 (E.D. Wash. 2001).

McCormick v. School Dist. of Mamaroneck, 370 F.3d 275 (2nd Cir. 2004).

Menora v. Illinois High Sch. Ass'n, 683 F.2d 1030 (7th Cir. 1982).

Mercer v. Duke Univ., 190 F.3d 643 (4th Cir. 1999) *on remand,* 301 F. Supp. 2d 454 (M.D.N.C. 2004).

Miami Univ. Wrestling Club v. Miami Univ., 302 F.3d 608 (6th Cir. 2002).

Montgomery v. Indep. Sch. Dist. No. 709, 109 F. Supp. 2d 1081 (D. Minn. 2000).

Moody v. Cronin, 484 F. Supp. 270 (C.D. Ill. 1980).

Morrison v. Northern Essex Cmty. Coll., 780 N.E.2d 132 (Mass. App. Ct. 2002).

NCAA v. Tarkanian, 488 U.S. 179 (1988).

NCAA v. Yeo, 171 S.W.3d 863 (Tex. 2005).

Palmer v. Merluzzi, 689 F. Supp. 400 (D.N.J. 1988).

Pegram v. Nelson, 469 F. Supp. 1134 (M.D.N.C. 1979).

Personnel Adm'r of Mass. v. Feeney, 99 S.Ct. 2282 (1979).

PGA Tour, Inc. v. Martin, 532 U.S. 661 (2001).

Poole v. South Plainfield Bd. of Educ., 490 F. Supp. 948 (D.N.J. 1980).

Pottgen v. Missouri State High Sch. Athletic Ass'n, 40 F.3d 926 (8th Cir. 1994).

Pryor v. NCAA, 288 F.3d 548 (3rd Cir. 2002).

Ray v. Antioch Unified Sch. Dist., 107 F. Supp. 2d 1165 (N.D. Cal. 2000).

Sandison v. Michigan High Sch. Athletic Ass'n, 64 F.3d 1026 (6th Cir. 1995).

Santa Fe Indep. Sch. Dist. v. Doe, 120 S.Ct. 2266 (2000).

Sch. Dist. of Abington Township v. Schempp, 374 U.S. 203 (1963), Harlan, J., concurring.

Schneckloth v. Bustamonte, 93 S.Ct. 2041 (1973).

Schroeder v. Maumee Bd. of Educ., 296 F. Supp. 2d 869 (N.D. Ohio 2003).

Stephenson v. Davenport Cmty. Sch. Dist., 110 F.3d 1303 (8th Cir. 1997).

Stotts v. Community Unit Sch. Dist. No. 1, 230 F.3d 989 (7th Cir. 2000).

Tatum v. NCAA, 992 F. Supp. 1114 (E.D. Mo. 1998).

Theno v. Tonganoxie Unified Sch. Dist., 377 F. Supp. 3d 952 (D. Kansas 2005).

United States v. Lansdowne Swim Club, 713 F. Supp. 785 (E.D. Pa. 1989), *aff'd,* 894 F.2d 83 (3rd Cir. 1990).

University of Colo. v. Derdeyn, 863 P.2d 929 (Colo. 1993).

Vernonia Sch. Dist. 47J v. Acton, 115 S.Ct. 2386 (1995).

Wanders v. Bear Hill Golf Club, Inc., 1998 Mass. Super. LEXIS 650 (Mass. Super. 1998).

Williams v. Wakefield Basketball Ass'n, CA-01-10434-DPW (unreported decision) (D. Mass. 2003).

York v. Wahkiakum Sch. Dist. No. 200, 178 P.3d 995 (Wash. 2008).

Zeller v. Donegal Sch. Dist., 517 F.2d 600 (3rd Cir. 1975).

Constitution

U.S. CONST. amend. I.

U.S. CONST. amend. IV.

U.S. CONST. amend. XIV.

Statutes and Regulations

Americans with Disabilities Act of 1990, 42 U.S.C. § 12101 *et seq.*

Americans with Disabilities Act Regulations, 28 C.F.R. § 36.104 (2005).

Civil Rights Act of 1964, 42 U.S.C. § 1981.

Civil Rights Act of 1964, 42 U.S.C. § 1983.

Individuals with Disabilities Education Act, 20 U.S.C. § 1400 *et seq.*

Rehabilitation Act of 1973 (§ 504), 29 U.S.C. § 701 *et seq.*

Title II of the Civil Rights Act of 1964, 42 U.S.C. § 2000a.

Title VI of the Civil Rights Act of 1964, 42 U.S.C. § 2000d (2005).

Title IX of the Education Amendments of 1972, 20 U.S.C. §§ 1681(a) (2009).

Title IX Athletics Regulations, 34 C.F.R. § 106.41 Athletics.

Title IX Athletics Regulations, 34 C.F.R. § 106.37(c) Financial Assistance.

Wisconsin Public Accommodations Statute, Wis. Stat. § 106.52(3)(a)2 (2005).

Other Sources

AB Editors. (2009, March 25). Baseball and softball aren't comparable, association says. *Athletic Business*. Retrieved March 31, 2009, from http://athleticbusiness.com/articles/default.aspx?a=2025&template=print-article.htm.

"After long battle, NCAA publishes guidelines to protect pregnant athletes." *Chronicle of Higher Education* News Blog, November 14, 2008. Retrieved April 2, 2010, from http://chronicle.com/article/After-Long-Battle-NCAA-Pub/41946/. The NCAA's manual *Pregnant and Parenting Student-Athletes: Resources and Model Policies* may be retrieved from the NCAA's website at www.ncaa.org.

Beard, A. (2008, January 14). Sexual harassment suit settled, N. Carolina's Dorrance can move on. *The Associated Press*. Retrieved June 20, 2009, from LEXIS-NEXIS.

Byrne, R. (2004, August 6). 2 La Salle U. coaches quit amid allegations of rapes by players. *Chronicle of Higher Education*, p. A34.

Chronicle of Higher Education. (2003, November 7). Sacred Heart U settles pregnancy suit, p. A43.

Claussen, C. L. (1997). Measuring women's interest in participation in intercollegiate athletics: A critique. *Journal of Legal Aspects of Sport*, 7(1), 5–11.

Dunnavant, K. (2002, June 17–23). Landmark Title IX still a work in progress 30 years later. *SportsBusiness Journal*, pp. 23, 32.

Former Aggie to transfer to Portland State. (2005, December 16). *The Associated Press & Local Wire, Sports News*.

Furman, B. L. (2007). Gender equality in high school sports: Why there is a contact sport exemption to Title IX, eliminating it, and a proposal for the future. *Fordham Intellectual Property, Media and Entertainment Law Journal*, 1169.

Grady, J., & Andrew, D. (2003). Legal implications of the Americans with Disabilities Act on recreation services: Changing guidelines, structures, and attitudes in accommodating guests with disabilities. *Journal of Legal Aspects of Sport*, 13(3), 231–252.

Harrer, K. M. (2004). Baylor rowers seek better opportunities—for everyone. *Women's Sports Foundation Newsletter*, p. 14.

Iacobelli, P. (2007, August 3). Awareness key issue for pregnant athletes. *South Florida Sun-Sentinel.com*. Retrieved August 8, 2007, from www.sun-sentinel.com/sports/.

Jenkins, S. (2002, June 24). Title IX opponents a bunch of sad sacks. *Washington Post*, p. D01.

Judge throws out sexual harassment suit against UNC coach. (2004, October 28). *Associated Press, Sports News*. Retrieved January 18, 2006, from LEXIS-NEXIS.

Keys, P. (2008, July 28). UIL to expand steroid testing. *Beaumont Enterprise*. Retrieved August 6, 2008, from www.beaumontenterprise.com.

Martin, N. (2008, January 21). Court upholds Pasternak ruling. *Winnipeg Free Press Live*. Retrieved February 6, 2008, from www.winnipegfreepress.com.

National Federation of State High School Associations. (2008). *2007–08 NFHS High School Athletics Participation Survey*. Retrieved June 14, 2009, from www.nfhs.org.

NCAA. (2008a). *1981–82–2006–07 NCAA Sports Sponsorship and Participation Rates Report*. NCAA Publications.

NCAA. (2008b). *2008–09 NCAA Division I Manual*. Indianapolis, IN: NCAA Publications.

Orland, R. (2009, July 10). Socially unacceptable; NCAA tries to stay a step ahead of networking sites. *The Washington Times*, p. C01.

Popke, M. (2004, July). Juice barred? *Athletic Business*, 34.

Rhoden. W. C. (1995, September 14). On Football: Celebration, jubilation cause tribulation. *New York Times*, p. B22.

Rothenberg, R. (1990, August 10). Corporate response to Shoal Creek: More caution by sponsors after Shoal Creek furor. *The New York Times*, p. A17.

Samuels, J., & Galles, K. (2003). In defense of Title IX: Why current policies are required to ensure equality of opportunity. *Marquette Sports Law Review*, 14, 11–47.

Shipley, A. (2003, May 30). NCAA initiates EPO testing, extends existing drug protocols. *Washington Post*, p. D03.

Suggs, W. (2004a, February 13). "Varsity" with an asterisk. *Chronicle of Higher Education*, p. A35.

Suggs, W. (2004b, July 23). Steroids are rampant among college athletes, a Senate panel is told. *Chronicle of Higher Education*, p. A33.

Ulrich, L. (May 2007). Probing pregnancy participation policies. *The Training-Conditioning.com blog*. Retrieved October 16, 2007, from www.training-conditioning.com/2007/05.

U.S. Department of Education. (1979). *The three-part test for compliance regarding equity in participation opportunities* (1979 OCR Policy Interpretation).

U.S. Department of Education. (1996). Clarification of intercollegiate athletics policy guidance: The three-part test (1996 OCR Policy Clarification).

U.S. Department of Education. (2005). Additional clarification of intercollegiate athletics policy: Three-part test—part three (2005 OCR Clarification).

Wheelchair athlete disqualified at state meet. (2006, May 28). *WTOP News*. Retrieved June 13, 2006, from www.wtopnews.com.

Wheelchair athletes earn sports scholarships. (2007). *Houston Chronicle*. Retrieved July 17, 2007, from www.chron.com.

Will, G. (1988, October 2). Why the chemistry has to be right. *Newsday*, p. 9.

Wilson, C. (2009, October 30). School sued for punishing teens over MySpace pix. *Brattleboro Reformer* (Vermont). Retrieved November 27, 2009, from LEXIS-NEXIS.

Wolohan, J. T. (2003, April). Hostile witness: Administrators risk plenty by failing to acknowledge and combat sexual harassment. *Athletic Business*, pp. 28–32.

Women's Sports Foundation. (2008a). 2008 statistics: Gender equity in high school and college athletics: Most recent participation and budget statistics. Retrieved June 14, 2009, from www.womenssports foundation.org.

Women's Sports Foundation. (2008b). Title IX and discrimination based on sexual orientation. Retrieved June 14, 2009, from www.womens sportsfoundation.org.

Young, J. R. (2002, October 4). When trips go bad: A recent ruling extends sex-discrimination protections beyond U.S. borders. *Chronicle of Higher Education*, pp. A49–50.

WEBSITE RESOURCES

www.ncaa.org/wps/portal/ ▪ The NCAA's Drug Testing program was created to protect the health and safety of student-athletes and to ensure that no one participant might have an artificially induced advantage or be pressured to use chemical substances. The documents on this site provide general information as well as drug testing consent forms, drug education and testing videos, frequently asked questions, and supporting information.

www.ncaa.org/titleix ▪ The NCAA website includes an educational and interactive page detailing What Does Title IX Mean to You? It is part of a year-long conversation on the personal impact of Title IX on a variety of athletes; the testimonies were designed to highlight truths and misconceptions of the law. This page also includes links to a number of news stories and press releases on the subject of Title IX.

www.nfhs.org ▪ On this National Federation of State High School Associations site, one can use the publication index to locate information on NFHS High School Athletics Participation Survey History, the *National High School Sports Record Book,* and *A Guide for College-Bound Student-Athletes and Their Parents, Updated.*

www.nwlc.org ▪ The mission of the National Women's Law Center is "to protect and advance the progress of women and girls at work, in school, and in virtually every aspect of their lives." The site turns a spotlight on the 35th anniversary of Title IX and offers tools to help readers discover if schools are providing equal opportunities to girls. Students can conduct a self-evaluation of their university's program by using checklists available on the site.

www.womenssportsfoundation.org ▪ The Women's Sport Foundation aims to " advance the lives of girls and women through sport and physical activity" in many different ways. Go to the Issues and Action section to see reports on Title IX, sexual harassment, sport psychology, health and fitness, and more.

PART IV | **Operations Management**

INTRODUCTION TO THE LAW
IN OPERATIONS MANAGEMENT

Your sport/recreation programs and your facilities are the cornerstones of your organization. Providing safe and beneficial participation opportunities is a critical facet of sport and recreation. Enhancing the viewing experience of spectators is also a critical aspect. Ensuring that your facility is operated within the parameters of the law is critical to successful and competitive sport/recreation operations.

If you perform any of the diverse responsibilities related to the operations of your sport/recreation facilities or programs, you will encounter a number of legal issues. You and your organization can be much more successful with a fundamental understanding of some of the legal areas implicated in the operations management function of a sport organization.

LEGAL PRINCIPLES AND THE
OPERATIONS MANAGEMENT FUNCTION

Many legal areas are implicated in operations management. Chapter 15 focuses on negligence law as related to the participants in the programs you develop and oversee. In Chapter 16 you will learn about the legal issues relating to operating a sport/recreation facility and managing a sporting event. This chapter also focuses on negligence law as it pertains to responsibilities to spectators and liability for premises defects. Chapter 17 provides you with an understanding of how waivers may be used in your sport/recreation organization. Finally, Chapter 18 explores legal issues related to participant violence, including assault, battery, and hazing.

The operational issues described in these chapters will require you to be knowledgeable in a variety of legal theories so that you can develop effective policies to protect and enhance the welfare of participants in your programs and spectators of your events. The following chapters explore each of these areas and their application in sport and recreation organizations.

Participant Liability Issues

INTRODUCTION

U nderstanding the law related to negligence and the prevalent liability issues in your sport organization is critical in gaining a competitive advantage in the sport marketplace. This chapter discusses the law of negligence as it applies to those who are athletes or participants in the activities or sports you offer in your sport organization. Your participants are important stakeholders in your organization, and the success of your organization is directly tied to making the participant experience more enriching. Understanding the liability concerns related to participants can help you reframe potential liabilities as opportunities to make your programs safer and less prone to litigation.

This chapter first introduces you to the concept of negligence, discussing the elements of negligence as a legal cause of action and the applicable defenses. The remainder of the chapter is devoted to discussing those areas that are most likely to lead to participant liability concerns: lack of supervision, improper instruction or training, equipment concerns, medical care, and transportation. A discussion of products liability law is also included. Facilities issues related to participants and spectators are discussed in Chapter 16. See Exhibit 15.1 for an overview of the managerial contexts, major legal issues, relevant laws, and illustrative cases pertinent to this chapter.

EXHIBIT   15.1   Management contexts in which participant liability issues may arise, with relevant laws and cases.

MANAGEMENT CONTEXT	MAJOR LEGAL ISSUES	RELEVANT LAW	ILLUSTRATIVE CASES
Oversight of sport/recreation program	Pleading a case in negligence	Elements of negligence	
		Duty	*Davidson*
		Causation	*Bellinger*
	Defenses in negligence case	Negligence defenses	
		Government immunity	*Tippett, Feagins*
		Charitable immunity	
Oversight of land opened for recreational use	Defining recreational use	Recreational use statutes	*Marks*
Supervision of activities/programs	Lack of supervision	Negligence law	*Garman*
Administration of sport/recreation program			
Coaches, instructors	Improper instruction/training	Negligence law	*Scott*
Coaches, equipment managers, administrators	Provision of safe equipment	Negligence law	*Elledge, Bello*
Athletic trainers, team physicians, coaches, administrators	Medical care	Negligence law	
		Fraudulent concealment	*Krueger*
Administration of organized sport program	Liability for transportation	Negligence law	*Clement*
Provision of sports equipment	Liability for defective equipment	Products liability law	*DeRienzo*
Oversight of outdoor activities	Assume risks of activity outlined in statutes	Shared responsibility statute/sport safety acts	*Lanzilla*

GENERAL PRINCIPLES OF NEGLIGENCE LIABILITY

N egligence is conduct that "falls below the standard established by law for the protection of others against unreasonable risk of harm" (Restatement [Second] of Torts § 282). As an unintentional tort, negligence appears at the opposite end of the intent spectrum from torts such as battery and assault (discussed in Chapter 18). The defendant in a negligence action has allegedly acted in an unreasonable fashion but did not intend to commit the act or to cause the harm. Therefore, because the law recognizes that the defendant in a negligence action simply failed to act reasonably, no punitive damages may be awarded. In most cases of negligence, the defendant acted in a careless or inadvertent fashion; this conduct is far removed from the type of conduct in which a defendant intends to commit an act and to cause harm and which may lead to an award of punitive damages.

Elements of Negligence

The cause of action of negligence has four elements that must *all* coexist to enable the plaintiff to go forward. These elements are: (1) duty, (2) breach of duty, (3) causation, and (4) damages. These elements are discussed below.

Duty

The first element in a negligence case is **duty**, which means that the defendant must have some obligation, imposed by law, to protect the plaintiff from unreasonable risk. Duty is a question of law for the court to ascertain and is a foundational issue. The legal concept of duty is based on policy considerations that lead courts to say that a particular plaintiff is entitled to protection from a particular defendant. Absent duty, there is no cause of action in negligence. For example, let's assume that two strangers pass each other on a trail in a national park. One of the strangers steps on the edge of the trail and begins to slide down a steep slope. Will the law impose a duty of care on the second stranger to help this person who is in peril? No: there is no legal duty to help here; the parties have no relationship such that one party is legally obligated to help the other. Of course, morality would dictate otherwise, and presumably on this basis the second stranger would help.

Ascertaining whether a duty of care exists often becomes quite complex. In the context of higher education, for example, courts need to find some policy justification for imposing a duty of care for the student-athlete, since the student is an adult. In contrast, it is relatively simple to find that a duty of care exists between the K–12 teacher and student or coach and athlete, since the courts use the theory of *in loco parentis* (standing in the place of a parent) and acknowledge that the custodial relationship of a teacher or coach with a minor student or athlete should lead to a duty of care.

In a few cases courts have found a duty of care to exist for the college student-athlete on the basis of a special relationship. The following case addresses this issue.

Davidson v. University of North Carolina

FACTS

The plaintiff was a junior varsity cheerleader at the defendant university. While warming up before a basketball game, the plaintiff fell from the top of a two-one-chair pyramid, approximately 13 feet to the wood floor. She suffered permanent brain damage as a result of the fall. The spotters were unable to prevent the plaintiff from hitting the floor.

The cheerleading squad did not have a coach, and they taught themselves how to perform stunts. The squad members made their own decisions about what stunts to perform, and they were not given any training to evaluate when they were ready to perform certain stunts. Although the varsity cheerleaders were sent to a summer camp where they learned techniques and safety information, the junior varsity squad was not provided that opportunity. The university did provide the squad with uniforms, transportation to away games, and access to university facilities and equipment. The squad cheered at junior varsity basketball games, women's basketball games, wrestling events, and represented the university at a trade show.

The plaintiff filed a claim against the university under the state tort claims act alleging negligence for failing to provide supervision and training for the cheerleaders. The North Carolina Industrial Commission's deputy commission heard the claim and ruled for the plaintiff. However, the full commission reversed, as it found that the university owed no duty to the plaintiff.

HOLDING

The North Carolina appellate court reversed and remanded the case for further consideration of the evidence.

RATIONALE

The primary issue before the court in this case was whether the university owed a duty of care to a student-athlete who is a member of a school-sponsored intercollegiate team. In this situation, one which is based on allegations that the school failed to provide necessary supervision and training, a special relationship must be found in order to establish a duty of care.

The court noted that the relationship between a student-athlete and the university is different from the university's relationship with the general student body. With an athlete, there is a situation of mutual dependence—the university received benefits from the cheerleaders' appearances and the cheerleaders were provided uniforms, transportation, and equipment. Second, the court commented on the degree of significant control exerted by the university over the participation of the cheerleaders. Third, the court found the precedent of *Kleinknecht v. Gettysburg College* (1993) persuasive, as it held that there was a special relationship between the college and the members of the lacrosse team who were recruited by the college to play in intercollegiate competition.

Based on the above policy factors and legal precedent, the court held that there was a special relationship in this situation in which the plaintiff was injured while practicing as part of a school-sponsored intercollegiate team. The court specifically noted that this finding of a special relationship cannot be extended to a university's students generally or even to other members of student groups, clubs, intramural teams, or organizations. In this situation, therefore, the university did owe the plaintiff a duty of care.

As the *Davidson* case points out, cheerleading can often be a very risky sport. The National Center for Catastrophic Sports Injury Research reported that in the past 25 years there have been 80 direct catastrophic injuries to high school female athletes and cheerleading accounted for 65.1 percent of those. Therefore, it is very important to hire a competent cheerleading coach who has the background to supervise a squad properly and to ensure appropriate safety measures are taken (McMannon, 2008).

In a case in which a court might generally find that there is no duty of care, if the defendant nonetheless assumes the duty of care, then the defendant must meet the appropriate standard of care. In the following hypothetical case, a university assumes a duty of care and is therefore bound to act reasonably.

considering . . .   DUTY OF CARE

As a part of her course of study for a degree in sport management, Jill Lefour, age 22, must complete a university-mandated internship program at a site specifically approved and suggested by the university. Lefour was assigned to complete her internship at a fitness club about 15 minutes from the university. One evening after her internship duties were completed, Lefour was abducted from the fitness club's parking lot and assaulted.

The fitness club was located in a dangerous part of town. The university personnel who assigned Lefour to this location were aware of other criminal incidents that had occurred in the fitness club's parking lot.

Question

■ If Lefour attempts to sue her university, does she have any arguments that the university has a duty of care to her in this circumstance?

Note how you would answer the question and then check your response using the Analysis & Discussion at the end of this chapter.

The foregoing hypothetical case is based on the case of *Nova Southeastern University v. Gross* (2000), in which the Florida Supreme Court held that a university may be liable in tort when it assigns a student to an internship site that it knows to be unreasonably dangerous but gives no warning to the student and the student is injured during the internship. Although the student is an adult, the university assumed the duty to assign the student to a reasonably safe location.

In most of the cases we will study, however, the duty of care is quite evident, and the courts do not focus on this aspect of the case. There is a duty of care between teacher or coach and student or athlete on the K–12 level and between facility owner and spectator. Schools have custodial and tutelary responsibilities for the minors in their care.

In the cases that we discuss in this chapter, the courts have ascertained that duty exists. For our purposes, therefore, we will pay more attention to the second element, whether there was a breach of the duty of care.

Breach of duty

There is a **breach of duty** if the defendant has failed to meet the standard of care required. The **standard of care** is ascertained by asking what a reasonably prudent person would have been expected to do in the same or similar circumstances. You can see from this that the law of negligence is closely tied to the factual circumstances. There can be no breach of duty in the abstract; whether a breach of duty exists is always relative to the particular circumstances.

To assist in ascertaining whether a breach of duty has occurred, the courts have developed an objective standard, the **reasonably prudent person.** This legal fiction is used as the standard against which an actual defendant is held. If the defendant acts in a way consistent with the actions of the fictional reasonable prudent person, then the defendant has not breached the duty of care; thus, element number two of the cause of action is not met. However, if the actions of the defendant fall below what would have been expected of the reasonable prudent person, then the defendant has breached the duty of care.

If the defendant possesses knowledge that is superior to the ordinary person, then the defendant is accountable for the care that is reasonable in light of the person's special skills, knowledge, or training. Thus, a coach with a master's degree in physical education who has coached for ten years and who has special certifications pertinent to coaching will be held to a standard of care based on that special skill and knowledge.

How does a jury decide what the reasonably prudent person should have been expected to do in a particular context? Juries do not have the expertise to ascertain the standard of care on their own. The parties to a lawsuit use expert witnesses to attempt to convince the jury what standard of care is applicable in a particular circumstance. Standards or recommendations or best practices usually arise from an organizational mandate or "suggestion." These organizations range from independent bodies such as the Consumer Product Safety Commission (CPSC) to sports or fitness organizations such as the American College of Sports Medicine (ACSM) and the National Federation of State High School Associations (NFHS) (Cohen, 2008). Expert witnesses are familiar with these standards and will present them to the jury as evidence of the "standard of care" that is applicable. In many cases, the expert witnesses called by the plaintiff may disagree with the expert witnesses called by the defendant. It is up to the jury to decide which experts to believe, since this is a question of fact within the purview of the jury.

In some circumstances expert testimony may not be needed to establish that the standard of care was breached. If, for example, the defendant fails to meet a statutory requirement that was established for the safety of participants, that failure is considered to be a breach of the standard of care. This is called **negligence per se.** The breach of the statutory standard is itself indicative of the breach of the standard of care, and the plaintiff has only to establish causation and damages to prevail in such a case. The following hypothetical case demonstrates this concept.

considering . . .

You are the aquatics manager for a health and fitness club in Maricopa County, Arizona. The federal government has passed the Pool and Spa Safety Act that requires antivortex drain covers to be installed in all pools ("Operators face hurdles in Pool Act compliance," 2009). This law was passed in December 2007 for safety reasons after the U. S. Consumer Product Safety Commission reported that there were 147 entrapment incidents in pools, of which 26 were fatal, between January 1985 and March 2002 (Popke, 2004).

Your club has just built a new pool, but the owners of the club chose not to adhere to the law's requirements due to cost. One of your patrons has just lost a limb after becoming entangled in the pool drain. This result would not have occurred if the new pool met the law's requirements.

Question

■ If the patron sues your club, does the plaintiff have a negligence per se case?

Note how you would answer the question and then check your response using the Analysis & Discussion at the end of this chapter.

Causation

The third necessary element of a negligence cause of action is **causation,** a causal connection between the breach of duty and the resulting injury. When an act or failure to act directly produces an event, and the event would not have occurred otherwise, this is known as **proximate causation** (or legal cause). Causation addresses the essential question of whether a party should be held accountable for the consequences of an action. It encompasses both the notion of causation in fact and the policy question of whether a court should hold someone accountable for an injury based on the notion of foreseeability (57A Am. Jur. 2d *Negligence* § 412).

Causation in fact depends on whether a particular outcome would have taken place even if the breach of duty had not occurred. The concept here is that if something would have occurred anyway, then the breach of duty cannot be said to have caused the outcome, and hence the requisite element of causation is lacking. The following Focus Case illustrates this point.

Bellinger v. Ballston Spa Central School District

871 N.Y.S.2d 432 (App.Div. 2008)

FOCUS CASE

FACTS

A fifth grader was playing one-hand touch football at recess when she collided with a teammate as both players ran toward the opponent. The teammate's head hit the girl in the mouth and she lost three teeth. The girl's mother sued the school district on her behalf and alleged that there was negligent supervision. The trial court denied the defendant's motion for summary judgment.

HOLDING

The New York appellate court reversed.

RATIONALE

The court noted that even if the plaintiff could show that there was inadequate playground supervision, the negligent supervision must be shown to be the cause of the injuries. In this case, there was a spontaneous and accidental collision between players. There was no history of bad behavior or rough play. In this case, no amount of supervision could have prevented the collision. Therefore, there is no causation.

In addressing causation, courts also look to another aspect of proximate causation that speaks to the issue of whether the defendant should be legally responsible for the injury, even if there was causation in fact. This issue is primarily a question of law for a court to address, and it often relates to the question of foreseeability. This means that courts often decide that the scope of liability should extend only to those risks that are foreseeable ones.

Damages

Damages, the final element of negligence, exist when some actual loss or damage has been sustained as a result of the breach of duty. The threat of future harm is not sufficient damage.

Defenses Against Negligence

Once the elements of the cause of action are established, the question becomes whether the defendant, in whole or in part, can avoid liability. The defendant's first recourse is always to argue that one or more of the elements of the cause of action have not been established. However, if all the elements do exist, the defendant must raise defenses. The most common defenses are the statute of limitations, act of God, contributory and comparative negligence, assumption of risk, and immunity.

Statute of limitations

The defense that the cause of action has not been filed in a timely fashion is known as raising the **statute of limitations.** This defense is a procedural one, not a substantive one. This means that, regardless of the merits of the plaintiff's case, the cause of action may be dismissed if the complaint has not been filed in a timely manner. Each state has legislation that specifies the time period for bringing a certain cause of action. Generally, if the action is not brought within that designated time period, the action may be dismissed. For example, many states provide that an action in negligence must be brought within two years from the time the tort occurred.

Act of God

An **act of God** defense rests on the idea that a person has no liability if an unforeseeable natural disaster resulted in injury to the plaintiff; the defendant's negligence, therefore, did not cause the injury. There are two aspects to this defense that must coexist:

1. There must truly be an act of God—some natural disaster such as a storm, lightning, earthquake, flood, or hurricane that caused the injury.
2. This act of God must have been unforeseeable. If it was foreseeable, the defendant may still have liability since the defendant did not act reasonably in protecting the plaintiff from the disaster.

The following hypothetical case illustrates this defense.

 considering . . . THE ACT OF GOD DEFENSE

The baseball coach at High River Academy is running the last practice before the playoffs. He is determined to have all the players get their turns at bat. Storm clouds appear in the sky above, and there is lightning nearby. Practice continues. The third baseman is hit by lightning and killed.

Question

- Does the coach have a viable act of God defense?

Note how you would answer the question and then check your response using the Analysis & Discussion at the end of this chapter.

Contributory and comparative negligence

Contributory and comparative negligence are also defenses against negligence. In discussing the elements of negligence, we have used the legal fiction of the reasonably prudent person to set the standard for whether the defendant breached the duty of care. With **contributory negligence,** we ask whether the plaintiff acted as a reasonably prudent plaintiff. With a child plaintiff, we ask whether the child exercised the level of care that should be expected of a child of like age, knowledge, judgment, and experience (*Clay City Consolidated School District Corp. v. Timberman,* 2008). We use the legal fiction of the **reasonably prudent plaintiff** to determine what the plaintiff should have done in a particular circumstance to protect his or her own safety. If the plaintiff's conduct falls below the standard of care, then the plaintiff is said to be contributorily negligent. If a court uses the contributory negligence theory, any conduct that is unreasonable by the plaintiff results in no recovery for the plaintiff.

The rule of contributory negligence is rather harsh; any negligence by the plaintiff completely bars recovery. Therefore, most states have adopted a rule of **comparative negligence,** where any negligence by the plaintiff is compared to the degree of negligence by the defendant. There are two forms of comparative negligence:

1. Under **pure comparative negligence,** a plaintiff's damages are reduced in proportion to the plaintiff's fault, so that even if the plaintiff's proportion of

negligence is greater than the defendant's proportion, the plaintiff will still recover something.

2. Under **modified comparative negligence,** a plaintiff's negligence will bar recovery completely if it is a specified proportion of the total fault.

The legislatures of each state decide which form of comparative negligence will be used in that state. The following hypothetical situation illustrates variations of the two forms of this defense.

considering . . .   COMPARATIVE NEGLIGENCE

Bob Bright has brought a negligence action against Rock On, a company that offers indoor rock-climbing instruction. Bright suffered a fractured leg while he was climbing the wall. Bright failed to follow some of the safety rules that were explained to him prior to his climb. The jury heard all the evidence and decided that Bright failed to act as a reasonably prudent plaintiff in violating safety rules and that his behavior, in part, contributed to his injury. The jury also decided that Rock On was also negligent. The jury heard evidence relating to damages as well and ascertained that the damages should be $100,000.

Question

- If the jury ascertains that Bright was 60 percent responsible for his own injury, what amount of damages will he receive?

Note how you would answer the question and then check your response using the Analysis & Discussion at the end of this chapter.

Assumption of risk

Assumption of risk is the defense that is most prevalently discussed in contexts of physical activity and sport. Assumption of risk is frequently discussed as being either primary or secondary; these distinctions are important.

Primary. **Primary assumption of risk** means that a plaintiff understands and voluntarily agrees to accept the inherent risks of an activity. If a plaintiff is "coerced" into attempting an activity, there is no assumption of risk. For example, in the case of *Calouri v. County of Suffolk* (2007), a 40-year-old student was injured in a community college backpacking class while attempting to do an agility drill. The court held that, as a neophyte, she was in the position of following the directions of the gym instructor, her superior whose direction she was obliged to follow. The court concluded that the jury should decide whether her participation was "voluntary" under the circumstances. Also, in the case of *Smith v. J. H. West Elementary School* (2008), a child was injured when he tripped and fell during a "backward" relay race. In the lawsuit based on negligence, the court held that assumption of risk did not apply because the plaintiff raised the issue of whether there was "inherent compulsion" in participating in the race.

The inherent risks of an activity are those risks that are obvious and necessary to the conduct of the activity. With primary assumption of risk, the defendant has no duty of care toward the plaintiff to protect the plaintiff from the particular risk of harm that caused injury, since the plaintiff agreed to encounter the risks that are common to that activity. For example, in power lifting, an experienced competitor assumes the risks related to the bar falling and injuring him, including the risk that a spotter may fail to catch the bar quickly enough to prevent injury (*American Powerlifting Association v. Cotillo*, 2007).

The plaintiff does not agree, however, to accept risks that are beyond those inherent in the activity; the plaintiff does not assume the risk of the negligence of the coach or instructor in enhancing the inherent risks of an activity. This concept arises in the following hypothetical situation.

considering . . .   ASSUMPTION OF RISK

A skydiver breaks his ankle upon landing in a field. This is an inherent risk of skydiving, since some impact with the ground is both obvious and necessary for the activity. There is no way to make the landing without risk; sometimes the force of landing may cause a broken or sprained ankle, for example. Likewise, perhaps the wind comes up suddenly after the jump is made and the skydiver is injured because he cannot avoid a tree. This is a risk inherent in the very nature of skydiving, and it would therefore be an assumed risk.

Questions

- If a skydiver is killed because neither of his parachutes opened, is the failure of the parachutes an inherent risk?
- Is the failure of the parachutes an obvious and necessary risk of the activity?

Note how you would answer the questions and then check your responses using the Analysis & Discussion at the end of this chapter.

The concept that the negligence of instructors is not an inherent risk of an activity is an important one. In the case of *Morganteen v. Cowboy Adventures, Inc.* (1997), the plaintiff was on a trail ride. Her horse began to skitter, and the plaintiff alleged that the wrangler told her to "pull on the reins," which is bad advice in this situation. Although the court eventually decided the case based on the exculpatory agreement signed by the plaintiff, the court did note that negligent trail guidance is not an inherent risk of a trail ride.

In California, an interesting series of cases has come about that, in some circumstances, provides that a coach is not liable for his or her own negligence. In the case of *Kahn v. East Side Union High School* (2003), the California Supreme Court held that a high school swimming coach would not be liable unless his or her actions were reckless. Essentially, this means that an athlete assumes the risk of negligence by a coach or instructor. The following two California cases have both interpreted the *Kahn* case with different outcomes.

Schweichler v. Poway Unified School District

FOCUS CASE   2005 Cal. App.Unpub. LEXIS 1553 (App. Div. 2005)

FACTS

A high school student was injured during wrestling practice. The assistant coach demonstrated a wrestling move with the student, and the student's ankle was severely injured when the coach incorrectly positioned the student for the move and then incorrectly performed the move on the student. The negligence action was dismissed by the trial court as it held that the action was barred by primary assumption of the risk.

HOLDING

The California appellate court affirmed the trial court's decision.

RATIONALE

The court noted that generally each person has a duty to use ordinary care and is liable for a failure to exercise reasonable care. The court further noted that in the context of active sports, this duty is limited by the doctrine of primary assumption of the risk. However, using the *Kahn* precedent, the court opined that a cause of action against a coach cannot be based on negligence. It must be shown that the coach "acted with intent to cause the injury or acted recklessly so that the coach's conduct was totally outside the range of the ordinary activity involved in teaching or coaching the sport" (*Kahn,* p. 1011). This standard has been adopted to avoid inhibiting vigorous participation or to prevent altering the nature of the activity.

   In this case, there is no claim that the coach intentionally injured the student. The injury occurred as the coach was demonstrating a wrestling move and thus was within the ordinary activities in teaching a sport. There is no basis for finding that the coach acted recklessly. Therefore, the doctrine of primary assumption of risk applies and the plaintiff's action was properly dismissed.

   However, contrary to *Schweichler,* the court in the following Focus Case declined to use the *Kahn* precedent in a case against a middle school instructor.

Hemady v. Long Beach Unified School District

FOCUS CASE   49 Cal. Rptr. 3d 464 (Ct. App. 2006)

FACTS

A middle school student was hit in the face with a golf club, which was swung by another student in a physical education golf class. The student alleged that the instructor was negligent in the way that he structured the class, so the students were unsure about when they could hit or when they were to watch. This disorganization and confusion led to the injury in question, and the injured student alleged that the instructor was negligent and sued the instructor and the school district. The trial court granted summary judgment in favor of the defendants on the basis that there was an assumption of the risk by the student.

HOLDING

The California appellate court reversed and remanded the case to the trial court for further proceedings.

RATIONALE

The court declined to use the *Kahn* limited duty of care standard. Instead the court deemed it appropriate to use the prudent person duty of care standard. The *Kahn* standard was developed to prevent a fundamental alteration of certain sports and to guard against chilling a coach's role in certain sports settings.

However, being hit in the head by a club is not an inherent risk of playing golf, especially in a physical education golf class for seventh graders. Application of the reasonably prudent person standard will not require a fundamental alteration of the game of golf nor will it chill a coach's role to challenge student-athletes. This case presents none of the factors identified in *Kahn* that would support the application of the limited duty standard of care. The reasonably prudent person analysis must be used, and the case is remanded to proceed using that standard of care.

contributory negligence

Secondary. Secondary assumption of risk means that a plaintiff deliberately chooses to encounter a known risk and that the plaintiff, in doing so, acts unreasonably. For example, if a plaintiff fails to follow the safety rules for an activity and that failure leads to plaintiff's injury, at least in part, that plaintiff has acted unreasonably. In many jurisdictions, this concept of secondary assumption of risk has been subsumed by the concept of comparative negligence, discussed above. The underlying notion of secondary assumption of risk is the same as comparative negligence, that is, the plaintiff acted unreasonably in behaving as he or she did.

Immunity

Defenses related to immunity are different from the defenses discussed above in that if a defendant is held to have **immunity**, this precludes a suit from being brought. The notion is that even if a defendant has engaged in tortious behavior, the status of the defendant is of such social importance that the defendant may escape liability for that behavior.

Governmental immunity. Historically, the concept of governmental immunity is rooted in the idea that "the king can do no wrong." Of course, that idea was erroneous; kings can do wrong, and, in our system of government, states and the national government also may do wrong. However, the notion of granting governmental entities freedom from suit grew out of this notion of the sovereign as deserving of immunity.

Today the federal government has allowed itself to be sued for certain tort claims arising under the Federal Tort Claims Act (FTCA; 28 U.S.C. §§ 1346 *et seq.*). This statute gives a general consent to be sued in tort, although there are several restrictions placed upon the lawsuit. One important aspect of this act provides for an exception to the waiver of immunity in cases involving discretionary functions. The gist of this concept is that there are certain governmental activities that should not be subject to suit because the government is acting in ways that involve policy judgments pertinent to the government's legislative or executive functions. When the government is acting in ways to further those functions, tort liability should not be imposed. The following Focus Case illustrates the discretionary function analysis in a suit brought under this Act.

Tippett v. United States

FOCUS CASE   108 F.3d 1194 (10th Cir. 1997)

FACTS

The plaintiff was a member of a guided snowmobile tour exploring Yellowstone National Park. As his group exited the park, a moose blocked the road. A park ranger directed the plaintiff's group to go around the moose on the right. As the plaintiff attempted to do so, the moose charged the snowmobile, kicking the windscreen and breaking the plaintiff's neck.

The plaintiff brought a negligence claim under the Federal Tort Claims Act based on the alleged negligence of the park ranger in directing the plaintiff to pass the moose. The district court dismissed the claim, finding that the claim was barred by the discretionary function exception to the act.

HOLDING

The Tenth Circuit Court of Appeals affirmed the dismissal.

RATIONALE

Under the FTCA, the United States waives its sovereign immunity with respect to certain injuries caused by governmental employees acting within the scope of their employment. However, there is an exception to this waiver of immunity if the claim is based upon the performance of a "discretionary function or duty" by the employee. The discretionary function exception exists to allow a measure of tort liability against the government, but not if the government is engaged in a discretionary act.

A two-part analysis is used to ascertain whether the action should be considered to be discretionary. First, is the action one of choice for the employee? Second, is the judgment one of the kind that the discretionary function exception was designed to shield?

In this case, the court noted that the park ranger did have discretion in how he chose to implement the policy directive that stated that "the saving of human life will take precedence over all other management actions." The general goal of saving human life was not a specific mandatory directive that allowed the ranger no discretion.

In terms of the second part of the analysis, the court held that there was a public policy interest at stake in balancing the interest of conserving wildlife versus the opportunity for public access to national parks. The regulations of the park service allowed discretion in these types of situations. There are no specific regulations dealing with confrontations between wildlife and vehicles. It is up to the park employee to use his discretion in dealing with such confrontations.

Therefore, the court held that the discretionary function exception to the FTCA applied and the claim was barred.

There are also state statutes providing immunity for certain actions taken by state employees. The following Focus Case illustrates this concept as it pertains to a coach's action.

Feagins v. Waddy

978 So.2d 712 (Ala. 2007)

FOCUS CASE

FACTS

Tamesha Feagins was an eighth-grade middle school student who participated on the school's track and field team. Tamesha arrived late at the citywide track meet on April 12, 2003, and her coach told her she had to perform in the high jump, an event that Tamesha had never done. Tamesha told her coach that she did not know how to high jump and did not want to do it. However, her coach told her she could do it. Tamesha tore a ligament in her knee as she attempted a practice jump. Tamesha, through her mother, sued the coach, the athletic director, and the school system for negligence and willful and wanton misconduct. The trial court entered a summary judgment in favor of the coach and athletic director on the basis that they had "state-agent" immunity.

HOLDING

The Alabama Supreme Court affirmed the trial court's decision as it upheld immunity.

RATIONALE

Under Alabama law, a state agent is immune from civil liability when the conduct in question is based on an agent's exercise of judgment in the administration of a department or agency of government. In a previous Alabama case, a baseball coach was immune from liability as he hit a baseball too hard and injured a player in practice. The coach was protected by state-agent immunity because he hit the ball within the intended nature or scope of his practice drill. In this case, the coach was discharging his duties in educating students by coaching the track team. By selecting which athletes would participate in which events, the coach was exercising his judgment in the discharge of his duties and is entitled to state-agent immunity.

Charitable immunity. Historically, U. S. courts established a doctrine that charitable entities were immune from tort liability. However, most contemporary courts have repudiated this idea of complete immunity for charities. A few states retain a limited version of charitable immunity, and this can be ascertained by checking state statutes related to immunity.

Good Samaritan statutes. You will recall from the discussion of duty that the law does not impose a duty upon a stranger to act to help another stranger in distress. Under common law, if a person assumes the duty of aiding another, that person is liable for a failure to act reasonably in assisting the injured person. However, as a matter of social policy we would like to encourage individuals to come to the aid of others who are in distress, even absent a legal duty to do so.

Therefore, all states have adopted some version of the **Good Samaritan statutes,** which generally provide that persons who act in good faith to help others in distress by providing emergency medical aid may not be sued for ordinary negligence based on their efforts to assist. This type of legislation furthers the social policy of encouraging people to assist others by immunizing them from liability for negligence should they make an error in providing medical aid to another. Some jurisdictions extend immunity to all persons administering emergency care; other states limit immunity to specified medical personnel or to physicians (57A Am. Jur. 2d *Negligence* § 193).

Recreational use statutes. All states have adopted some type of **recreational use statute** that provides a level of immunity for landowners who open their property to recreational use by the public with no fees charged. This type of legislation represents an attempt to encourage landowners to give property access to the public so that more land will be available for recreational purposes. The state statutes are available online at http://www.nationalaglawcenter.org/assets/recreationaluse/index.html.

In some jurisdictions, the recreational use statute has been extended to apply to school recreational facilities. The following Focus Case addresses this issue.

Marks v. Kansas Board of Regents

FOCUS CASE 157 P.3d 1129 (Kan. Ct. App. 2007)

FACTS

Nicole Marks, a student at the University of Kansas, was enrolled in a lifeguard training class. She injured her elbow and her side when she slipped and fell on her way from the locker room to the pool in the education and recreation center on campus. This building is used for classes, for athletic teams, for campus recreation, and for community events. Marks sued the school for negligence.

The defendant university moved for summary judgment under the recreational use exception to the Kansas Tort Claims Act, which provides that a governmental entity or an employee acting within the scope of the employee's employment shall not be held liable for damages resulting from "any claim for injuries resulting from the use of any public property intended or permitted to be used as a park, playground or open area for recreational purposes, unless the governmental entity or such employee thereof is guilty of gross and wanton negligence proximately causing such injury" (Kan. Stat. Ann. § 75-6104(o)). The trial court granted summary judgment for the defendant holding that the recreational use exception applied in this case.

HOLDING

The Kansas appellate court affirmed the trial court's decision.

RATIONALE

The court noted that the statutory language "intended or permitted" to be used for recreational purposes should be read broadly. The issue is whether the "location" is intended or permitted to be used for recreational purposes; the injury itself need not arise from recreation. In this case, the facility is both intended and permitted to be used for recreational purposes by university constituencies as well as the community. The university encourages groups to rent the facilities. Therefore, this facility is a recreational facility within the meaning of the statutory exception, and the defendant has immunity from the plaintiff's negligence suit.

Volunteer immunity statutes. Unfortunately, we live in a litigious climate where people may sometimes sue others at the slightest provocation. Many of our sport-related activities for youth could not exist without the generous participation of volunteers to serve as coaches, instructors, supervisors, and so forth in these activities. To encourage people to volunteer in these capacities certain legislation, federal and state, has been passed.

The U. S. Congress passed the Volunteer Protection Act of 1997 (42 U.S.C. §§ 14501 *et seq.*) to encourage volunteers to offer their services to nonprofit entities, including youth sport organizations. The legislation essentially provides that no volunteer of a nonprofit organization or a governmental entity shall be liable for harm caused by the volunteer due to negligence, providing that the volunteer was "properly licensed, certified or authorized by the appropriate authorities for the activities" (§ 14503). This legislation preempts state laws on this matter, unless the state law provides more protection for the volunteer. This act provides protection only for the volunteer, not for the organization or governmental entity.

Some states have statutes providing similar protection for volunteers. Some of the statutes are broad ones, protecting volunteers in any type of nonprofit setting. Other statutes are more specific and provide protection specifically for those who volunteer in sport and recreation settings. A complete listing of the state liability laws for charitable organizations and volunteers is available online at www.non profitrisk.org/library/state-liability.shtml.

Sport safety acts. In many states, a variety of outdoor activities are important to the state's economy, primarily in terms of tourism dollars. These activities may range from skiing to horseback riding to whitewater rafting. Many state legislatures have chosen to protect this sector of the economy by passing some version of a sport safety act or **shared responsibility statute.** The essence of this type of statute is to provide that participants in an activity assume the risk of hazards inherent in the activity (the inherent hazards are listed in the statute). These hazards are those that a participant should expect to confront in that activity. If the participant chooses to assume those risks, the activity provider does not owe a duty of care to the participant relative to those risks, under the concept of primary assumption of risk.

However, many of these statutes were enacted when some activities that we enjoy today did not even exist, e.g., snowboarding or snow tubing. Courts now have to interpret statutes to ascertain what protection should be given to these newer activities. The following Focus Case illustrates that concept.

Lanzilla v. Waterville Valley Ski Resort

FOCUS CASE   517 F. Supp. 2d 578 (D. Mass. 2007)

FACTS

On February 19, 2004, Paul Lanzilla and his family visited the Waterville Valley Ski Resort. Lanzilla's youngest child could not ski and no lessons were available, so Lanzilla took this child snow tubing. Because of the curvature of the slope, people at the top of the slope could not see the bottom. Lanzilla took a few runs with his daughter without incident, but, on a subsequent run, Lanzilla came around a curve to find an adult walking up the slope pulling two tubes with children. Lanzilla swerved, hit the embankment, and the tube went into the air. Lanzilla's left leg hit a metal pole that held snow fencing and his tibia and fibula were shattered.

Lanzilla sued, alleging that his injuries were due to the negligent operation and maintenance of the tubing slope. The defendant ski resort moved for summary judgment asserting that Lanzilla's claims were precluded by the state statute (N.H. Rev. Stat. Ann. §225-A:24) that provides that there is no liability for a ski resort when someone is injured in the "sport of skiing."

HOLDING

The federal district court of New Hampshire, applying state law, granted summary judgment for the defendant.

RATIONALE

When the state statute was originally passed in 1978, there was no reference to any sport except skiing since other activities did not exist. In 2005 the state legislature amended the statute to include "snowboarding, snow tubing, and snowshoeing" as covered activities. However, the question remained as to whether this language added in 2005 should be applied retroactively to the plaintiff's claim, which arose in 2004. The federal district court deferred to a 2007 decision addressing this issue. In the case of *Cecere v. Loon Mountain Recreation Corp.* (2007), the Supreme Court of New Hampshire held that the 2005 amendments clarified, rather than changed, the meaning of the 1978 statute, and, therefore, the claims on behalf of a person fatally injured in snowboarding were precluded. The legislative intent of the immunity statute in 1978, therefore, encompassed snow tubing injuries and Lanzilla's claims were precluded by the statute.

COMMON LIABILITY ISSUES REGARDING PARTICIPANTS

There are many ways in which a plaintiff may allege that a defendant sport or recreation program provider may be negligent. This section discusses a number of frequently occurring allegations, including: (1) a lack of supervision, (2) improper instruction or training, (3) the unsafe use of equipment, (4) improper medical care, and (5) negligence in transportation.

Lack of Supervision

Many liability concerns relating to participant injuries occur because of a failure of supervision. Proper supervision of participants means that the person(s) entrusted with this responsibility are competent to oversee the participants (quality of supervision) and that there are sufficient supervisors to fulfill the duty of care (quantity of supervision). The obligation to supervise does not mean that there is a duty of instruction, but it does mean that supervisors must be able to recognize dangerous behaviors and stop them.

Quality of supervision

The issue of quality of supervision involves the competence of the supervisor. Even if there is a one-to-one ratio of supervisors to participants, the supervision may be inadequate if a supervisor does not have the competence to identify dangerous behavior and, therefore, to intervene to stop the behavior. For example, supervision was allegedly improper in the case of *Garman v. East Rochester School District* (2007). During a field trip to an obstacle course a district employee allowed a high school student to climb on another participant's back while swinging across an obstacle. The student fell off and landed on her head. Swinging in tandem, according to the physical education chairperson's testimony, should not have been permitted. A warm body is not the equivalent of competent supervision; a supervisor must know enough about the activity in question to identify danger. The following hypothetical case illustrates this principle.

Competitive Advantage
STRATEGIES

Supervision

- Make sure that all employees who have supervisory responsibilities are competent to identify unsafe behaviors within the activity or sport they are supervising.

- Develop supervisory plans that have an appropriate ratio of supervisors to participants, considering such factors as
  - the nature of the activity,
  - the age and maturity of participants,
  - the skill level of participants, and
  - any limitations posed by the type of activity area or facility.

- Develop supervisory plans that designate certain areas of the activity area for each supervisor. You may have a reasonable number of supervisors, but if they all congregate together, you will not have proper coverage.

- Ensure that all supervisors are trained to identify and stop rowdy behavior.

considering . . .   **QUALITY OF SUPERVISION**

Tim Jones has just been hired at the campus recreation center as an activity supervisor. He has been assigned to supervise the campus weight room, although he has no background or training in weightlifting. He received no orientation from the campus recreation program, and he has been told just to check student identification cards and to make sure that the room does not become too crowded according to the legal capacity.

On Jones' first night on the job, Harry Hulk came into the facility. Harry ignored all the safety rules related to proper lifting, which were posted on the wall. Tim said nothing to Harry because Tim did not have the proper training to know that Harry was engaging in dangerous behavior. Harry then injured Sam Goodheart through Harry's carelessness with the weights.

Question

■ Can Sam sue Tim (and thus the university vicariously as Tim's employer) alleging a failure of supervision?

Note how you would answer the question and then check your response using the Analysis & Discussion at the end of this chapter.

Quantity of supervision

The question of quantity of supervision is whether the number of competent supervisors is sufficient relative to the number of participants—whether the ratio of supervisors to participants is reasonable.

Whether the ratio is proper is a question that cannot be answered in the abstract. There is no "magic number" that is proper for all occasions. The type of activity must be factored in; obviously, an activity such as gymnastics, with more risk than table tennis, would suggest that the ratio of supervisors to gymnasts must be lower than it is for table tennis players. The age and maturity of the participants must also be considered. Generally, youthful participants require more supervisors than adults. If a particular group has shown a propensity for rowdy behavior, then this must be taken into consideration when assigning the number of supervisors. If the participants have any physical or mental disability that makes them more prone to injury, more supervisors will be necessary. There may be concerns related to the facility or area in which an activity is taking place. For example, more supervisors are necessary if the participants are more spread out or if a supervisor cannot make visual contact with all participants because of the way the area is configured.

A manager should consider all of the above factors when making decisions about the number of supervisors to assign. All of these issues bear on the essential question: what number of competent supervisors is reasonable in this setting, at this time? Further, supervisory plans should delineate not just the number of supervisors but also the specific areas of supervision. Designating specific areas of supervision is necessary because supervisors may tend to cluster together, thereby leaving certain areas without supervisory coverage.

Improper Instruction or Training

The question of proper instruction or training in the context of physical activity and sport has more severe liability implications than it has in other educational contexts. Of course, we would hope that an English teacher would properly instruct students that the author of *The Inferno* is Dante and not Shakespeare, but the student will not suffer physical injury as a result of such an error. However, if a physical educator, coach, or activity instructor fails to act reasonably

---

Competitive Advantage
STRATEGIES

Instruction and Training

■ Develop criteria to assess whether a person is competent to serve as an instructor or coach for an activity.

■ Have all instructors attend risk management workshops that cover the principles of safe instruction.

■ As part of the introduction to any activity, make sure that specific risk information is shared with participants.

■ Emphasize that the proper progression of activities or skills must be followed.

■ Discuss the dangers of mismatch based on size, maturity, or skill.

in the way she teaches a physical skill, serious consequences may ensue, including severe physical injury or death. Competent instruction has many aspects. The following discussion focuses on a number of critical issues in instruction.

Selection and supervision of properly qualified instructors

The first issue related to instruction is whether the instructor has the appropriate competence to provide instruction. In some cases, administrators who are selecting instructors or coaches may be able to rely upon a teaching certificate or other accepted credential to ensure that the person has the level of competence necessary for the activity. In cases where there is no credentialing process, the employer must be more actively engaged in ascertaining what the proper competence for a position entails and whether the applicant possesses those credentials. If the person doing the hiring does not act as a reasonably prudent person in choosing someone who is competent for the position, then there may be liability for negligent hiring, as discussed in Chapter 5.

In the fitness industry, those who hire personal trainers should be aware of the controversy surrounding certification programs. Since there are numerous "certification" programs for personal trainers and no nationwide standard as to competency, some states have introduced legislation to license or otherwise regulate personal trainers. There is a great deal of discussion about this, however, and a number of experts in the fitness industry believe that the answer is not licensing but rather a good formal education in exercise science. Further, some professionals believe that the language in many of the pending state bills is not helpful in meeting the stated goals of consumer protection (Goldman, 2009; Herbert, 2008). Fitness professionals should stay current with the discussion relating to the certification of personal trainers.

The responsibility to supervise instructors in a reasonable fashion remains, regardless of the instructors' qualifications. What qualifies as reasonable supervision will vary depending upon an instructor's experience levels. Regardless of the instructor's expertise, a complete abdication of supervisory responsibility is unacceptable and may lead to liability for negligent supervision, as discussed in Chapter 5.

Adequacy of instruction

Instruction must be suitable for the intended audience. The language used must be understandable by the participants based on their age and familiarity with the activity. Also, since verbal instruction of physical skills is often accompanied by physical demonstration, the language used must be congruent with the demonstration. There cannot be an incongruence between what is conveyed to the participant verbally and what is shown to the participant. Demonstration of an activity must also be done safely. In *Murphy v. Polytechnic University* (2009), a softball coach hit a player in the face while he was demonstrating a batting technique to her. The coach swung the bat while the player stood close enough to be hit with the bat. This was determined to be negligent behavior.

If participants are relatively young and immature, important instructional concepts will need to be repeated more frequently than with a more mature audience. Also, younger groups tend to be very literal as they listen to instruction, so certain departures from instruction may be foreseeable. For example, in the case of *Glankler v. Rapides Parish School Board* (1992), a group of kindergarten children was taken on a field trip to a very large park with many types of playground equipment. This park had 47 adult swings, which were very heavy and were quite dangerous to small children. The children were told that they were not to push the swings. However, they were not forbidden to climb up on the swings, which led to dangerous behavior because the children's feet could not touch the ground as they sat in the swings. It is foreseeable that children will take action to get the swing to move. Expert testimony established that the children should have been told not to play on the swings at all.

Instructors and coaches should always follow the practices that have been widely accepted by experts in the activity. This is true because courts will give great deference to the standards that have been developed by those persons or organizations that have expert knowledge about the activity. Therefore, instructors should exercise great caution in developing drills or methods that vary from widely accepted practices. Even if a certain method seems to make sense, it is advisable to explore the issue and choose a method that is endorsed widely in the sport or activity. Coaches and instructors should attend workshops and seminars to ensure that the most current practices are being used.

Proper progression of skill

A culminating activity should not be attempted unless the proper lead-up activities are presented and practiced. Physical skills are often taught in a sequential manner, and no shortcuts can be taken if the participant is to be properly prepared for actually engaging in the final outcome. In *Scott v. Rapides*, the court defined proper preparation to include:

1. An explanation of basic rules and procedures
2. Suggestions for proper performance
3. Identification of risks

Teachers and coaches should include these three elements in their instruction for culminating physical activities. Let's look more closely at this case.

Scott v. Rapides Parish School Board

FOCUS CASE   732 So.2d 749 (La. Ct. App. 1999)

FACTS

The plaintiff, Zwireck Scott, was a high school student who injured his knee during a physical education class as he attempted a long jump and landed improperly. On the day he was injured, Scott was attempting to do the long jump for the first time while running full speed. He hoped to try out for the track team, and the team's coach was the class instructor.

Scott had been jumping in the sand pit for several days, but he had never before run full speed and attempted a jump while going "all out." The teacher/coach gave him no instruction. He had not spoken to Scott about proper landing or control in the air, nor did he discuss any risks involved in the long jump.

The trial court found liability for improper instruction and awarded damages in the amount of $207,000.

HOLDING

The Louisiana appellate court affirmed the judgment.

RATIONALE

The appellate court noted that "when an activity is potentially dangerous a student should not be required to attempt such activity without first receiving proper instruction and preparation, including an explanation of basic rules and procedures, suggestions for proper performance, and identification of risks" (p. 753). In this case, the court held that the coach had a duty to provide Scott, who was unfamiliar with the long jump, instruction that would permit him to complete the long jump successfully and safely under the maximum effort conditions. Long jumping is a skilled sport, and there must be a reasonable amount of preparatory instruction before students are permitted to attempt a maximum-effort jump.

Dissemination of safety rules and warnings

An important component of learning any activity is knowing what aspects could be dangerous to oneself or others. Safety rules and procedures should be discussed and reinforced on a frequent basis. The reason for the safety rules should also be shared with participants. Every practice session should have some time devoted to safety, and the safety rules and warnings pertinent to each activity should be given proper attention. Instructors should warn participants about the specific risks of each activity and discuss the possible adverse consequences if safety rules are not followed.

Participants are entitled to rely upon the safety procedures that have been identified and shared with them. For example, in the case of *Rosania v. Carmona* (1998), a karate student was injured during a proficiency test match when he was kicked in the face by the instructor. The student alleged that the safety rules of the dojo identified the head as an illegal target area. These no-contact karate rules were mandatory, and the student relied upon these rules when he chose to study at this dojo. Therefore, the violation of these rules was negligence, since the inherent risks of the sport, as practiced at that dojo, prohibited the type of contact encountered in this situation.

The safety rules pertinent to an activity must be both shared and enforced. The following hypothetical case addresses this point.

considering . . .   ENFORCEMENT OF SAFETY RULES

Roberta Roche is the softball coach of an elite junior team (members aged 13–17). The team has been very successful in the past, and the team must win today's game to advance to the regional tournament.

Dixie Winn, one of Roche's players, is a runner on third base. Roche calls for a suicide squeeze, and Winn runs over the opposing catcher, scoring the winning run. Although Winn's behavior is reckless and dangerous and Roche did not teach this dangerous strategy in practices, Roche does not chastise Winn because Winn has just scored the winning run.

On the next weekend at the regionals, Winn is again on third base and Coach Roche again calls for the suicide squeeze. Winn attempts to run over the opposing catcher again, but this time Winn is catastrophically injured, becoming a quadriplegic.

Question

- If Winn's parents sue Roche, alleging negligent training and instruction, will they win?

Note how you would answer the question and then check your response using the Analysis & Discussion at the end of this chapter.

Dangerous behaviors *must* be penalized, and coaches must be consistent in trying to stop these behaviors by penalizing players every time they do them—even if the unsafe behavior resulted in a good consequence for the team.

Mismatch of opponents

Competitive situations will almost always pit opponents who are not exactly equal in size, strength, or competency. In some cases, it is not reasonably prudent to allow competition between those who are so different in size, strength, or competency that those disparities may result in injury beyond what is accepted as inherent in the activity itself. Often, there may be formal guidelines established by a league or governing body to address this. For example, the age and weight restrictions for youth football represent an attempt to level the playing field.

In some cases, participants may be equal in terms of size but so different in skill level that it is imprudent for them to be matched up. The following hypothetical situation illustrates this point.

 considering . . .   MISMATCH OF OPPONENTS

Over the winter break, Coach Rogers asks some of his former wrestlers to come back and wrestle in practice with members of his current high school wrestling team. One of his former wrestlers, Bobby Bonecrusher, is now one of the top wrestlers in the country in his weight class at the Division I level. Bonecrusher, a college senior, has accepted the coach's invitation to return and wrestle with the current team.

Rogers pairs Bonecrusher with freshman wrestler Cory Lewis. Although Bonecrusher and Lewis are in the same weight class, Bonecrusher, due to his vastly superior skills, pins Lewis and Lewis suffers a separated shoulder.

Question

- If Lewis' parents sue Coach Rogers, what would be the outcome?

Note how you would answer the question and then check your response using the Analysis & Discussion at the end of this chapter.

Unsafe Use of Equipment

Part of instructional and coaching responsibilities is to provide necessary equipment that is proper and safe for an activity. If necessary protective equipment cannot be provided, the activity should be discontinued—the courts do not view lack of funds as a legal defense. In the case of *Moose v. Massachusetts Institute of Technology* (1997), the court found liability for the failure to provide supplemental padding for a pole vault landing pit since the coaches were aware that vaulters bounced off the pit mattress and landed out of the pit. Necessary equipment means equipment that is essential to do the activity; it does not mean that state-of-the-art equipment must be purchased, so long as what is provided reasonably meets the participants' needs. Protective equipment must be in good condition. For example, in the case of *Fithian v. Sag Harbor Union Free School District* (2008) a student alleged that the school district was negligent in providing him with a cracked batter's helmet. The equipment must also fit properly. A football helmet that is in good shape, for example, but falls over the eyes of the wearer does not meet the criterion of acceptable equipment. Players should be taught how to fit equipment properly and how to inspect the equipment prior to each use.

The equipment provided must meet the standards mandated for that type of equipment. For example, pertinent standards for pole vaulting equipment have been promulgated by the National Federation of State High School Associations as well as by the NCAA. Football helmet standards are set by the National Operating Committee on Standards for Athletic Equipment (NOCSAE). Playground equipment standards are found in Consumer Product Safety Commission (CPSC) guidelines and in the American Society for Testing and Materials (ASTM) standards. The following Focus Case deals with playground equipment.

Competitive Advantage

STRATEGIES

Equipment Use

- Provide equipment that is in good condition and maintain the equipment properly.
- Teach participants how to check for equipment problems prior to each use.
- Make sure equipment meets all pertinent specifications.
- Make sure instruction is given on the proper use of all equipment.

Elledge v. Richland/Lexington School District

| 534 S.E.2d 289 (S.C. Ct. App. 2000) | **FOCUS CASE** |

FACTS

A nine-year-old child slipped and fell while playing on the school's playground. She fell from monkey bars that had been modified by the school. The child was walking across the bars after a light rain when her foot slipped and her right leg became trapped between the bars. The child suffered a severe fracture to her femur.

The suit against the school alleged that it was negligent in its modification of the playground equipment, making it unsafe. The trial court refused to allow evidence of the industry guidelines for playground safety, and the jury returned a verdict for the school district.

HOLDING

The appellate court reversed and remanded as it held that the evidence of playground standards should have been presented to the jury.

RATIONALE

The court first noted that evidence of industry standards, customs, and practices is often quite helpful in ascertaining the standard of care. In this case, the fact that the school district did not adopt the CPSC guidelines or the ASTM standards did not mean that the standards are not relevant to establishing the standard of care. Even if the standards are not imposed by statute or otherwise made mandatory, national standards may be considered in setting the applicable standard of care. Therefore, the evidence of plaintiff's expert regarding those standards should have been admitted.

Proper instruction about how to use equipment should also be given. If equipment is used for a nontraditional use, information about how to use the equipment in that context should be given. The following Focus Case illustrates that concept.

Bello v. Fieldhouse at Chelsea Piers

FOCUS CASE   795 N.Y.S.2d 24 (App. Div. 2005)

FACTS

A 10-year-old girl, Natalie Bello, attended a birthday party at the defendant's facility. An employee of defendant instructed the children how to walk on a balance beam, and Natalie had no problem with this.

Then the employee set up an obstacle race for the children and the balance beams were used as obstacles. The children were instructed to climb over the first beam and under the second, alternating in this fashion through all the beams. Natalie fractured her arm as she fell while trying to climb over a balance beam during the race. Natalie's parents sued alleging that the instructor was negligent in explaining how to use the equipment.

The trial court dismissed the complaint finding that the defendant had met its duty of care.

HOLDING

The New York appellate court reversed.

RATIONALE

An instructor has a duty to explain how to use athletic equipment properly. In this case, the instructor explained the use of the balance beam properly as to the traditional use of walking on the beam. However, there was no instruction given as to the nontraditional use of the beam in the obstacle course. The 10-year-old plaintiff may not have been able to appreciate how to use this apparatus in an unfamiliar way without instruction on that point.

Improper Medical Care

Medical care issues related to participants in sport and recreation programs are important to address. In some cases, you may have an obligation to screen for health problems or monitor the well-being of athletes. In all cases, you have an obligation to develop a protocol for and provide emergency medical care. Issues related to medical malpractice and fraudulent concealment are also important to understand.

Preventive health concerns

In organized sport settings, there is usually a screening mechanism to ensure that players are healthy enough to compete in activities. On the high school level, most states have a standardized medical history form for student-athletes provided by or overseen by the state high school athletic federation. These forms are filled out by the student, parents, and family doctors.

Whether schools should use echocardiograms to screen athletes for heart problems is a subject of debate. Cardiac conditions that may lead to sudden death in young athletes may conceivably be discovered with this type of exam. However, some physicians believe that this type of screening will not be effective in identifying all who may be at risk for cardiac death, and the exams may therefore give a false sense of security (Popke, 2003).

Coaches and administrators should also be aware of the health issues related to eating disorders. According to Wilson (2003), approximately 25 percent of college female athletes suffer from amenorrhea, a condition in which women do not get their menstrual periods, which will compromise bone density. This condition stems primarily from an imbalance between activity level and nutritional intake and is frequently an indicator of an eating disorder. The need to monitor for amenorrhea and eating disorders should be addressed with athletes and athletic trainers. There is also support to institute a screening program to identify students at risk of eating disorders (Scholand, 2009).

For male athletes, rapid weight loss has led to a number of problems, such as wrestlers trying to lose weight to compete at a certain weight class. In response to this issue, the National Federation of State High School Associations Wrestling Rules Committee mandated that every state implement a weight management program by the beginning of the 2006–07 season. This program assesses each athlete to ascertain that person's safe minimum weight and mandates that the athlete cannot fall below that weight ("NFHS approves new weigh-in rules," 2005).

Another current critical issue is preventing an outbreak of MRSA, methicillin-resistant *Staphylococcus aureus*. This bacterium is a type of staph that is immune to many common antibiotics and thus is medically dangerous. MRSA can lead to serious and potentially fatal complications. MRSA is becoming increasingly prevalent in athletic settings, and it is prudent to set up a preventive plan to deal with the cleaning of facilities and equipment to prevent the spread of this infectious disease. According to the Centers for Disease Control and Prevention (CDC), MRSA has been linked to nearly 20,000 deaths nationally (Scholand, 2009). The CDC and the NCAA have developed protocols dealing with MRSA, www.cdc.gov/MRSA and www.ncaa.org/health-safety, respectively.

Emergency medical care

Two major issues are associated with the provision of emergency medical care to participants: (1) making sure that qualified personnel are available to render emergency first aid and CPR, and (2) ensuring that there is a protocol to get outside medical personnel to the site as quickly as possible.

Availability of qualified personnel to render emergency medical care. Whether you are dealing with a team situation or with participants at a fitness club, for example, you have a duty to provide emergency medical care to participants. This also applies to other recreational facilities (see *Spotlite Skating Rink, Inc. v. Barnes*, 2008; this case dealt with a failure to render emergency medical care at a roller skating rink). In a team situation, if you do not have the luxury of a qualified athletic trainer at all your practices, your coaches should be certified in CPR and first aid. You cannot rely upon calling the training room for a first responder to a severe injury, if an emergency arises. Time is of the essence, particularly in a cardiac or respiratory emergency. First responders should only respond in accordance with their training; they should not attempt to diagnose or treat an injury as if they were physicians.

In regard to the emergency personnel issue as it pertains to high school sport, the state of Kentucky passed legislation in 2009 that requires all prep coaches to complete a new 10-hour sports safety course. After completing the course, which focuses on medical and other safety issues, the coaches must pass a test. The course is intended to be taught by a certified athletic trainer, physician, nurse, or physician's assistant. (Due to funding issues, however, it is currently offered online.) The course addresses issues related to emergency planning; heat-related illnesses; head, neck, and facial injuries; and first aid. This legislation was passed as a response to the heat-related death of a high school football player in the summer of 2008 (Popke, 2009). Other states are sure to follow since this is a critical issue in educational sport.

In a fitness club, each shift should be staffed with multiple individuals who are trained to respond to medical emergencies. It is not prudent to have just one person per shift who is trained in emergency first aid and CPR. When that person leaves the building to go to lunch or calls in sick, the club is left in a precarious position.

Clear protocol for outside emergency personnel. All employees should go through an orientation on their first day at work that familiarizes them with how emergency help is summoned. In one particularly unfortunate occurrence, a death occurred at a city recreation swimming pool because the employees did not realize that they had to dial 9 for an outside line before dialing 911. By the time the employees realized the problem, the delay in getting the EMTs to the location resulted in the death of the swimmer. In another case, the delay in getting medical assistance to a student who had suffered a head injury allowed a blood clot to enlarge from the size of a walnut to the size of an orange. A $2.5 million judgment was rendered against the school district (*Barth v. Board of Education*, 1986). The Learning Activities for this chapter include an activity for developing an emergency action plan (EAP) for medical emergencies in your organization.

With experience, sport and recreation organizations have become better at dealing with medical emergencies. However, the matter of heat-related injuries, especially related to summer football conditioning, continues to be problematic.

In an early case (*Mogabgab v. Orleans Parish School Board*, 1970), a high school football player suffered heat stroke and the coaching staff simply allowed his condition to worsen by putting him in the locker room, where he did not have access to medical assistance for over two hours. This is egregious conduct, but similar scenarios are repeated across the country every year.

In fact, the National Center for Catastrophic Sport Injury Research reported in 2008 that there were 26 heat stroke deaths in football in the last 10 years (www.unc.edu/depts./nccsi/AllSport.pdf). As the Center points out, heat stroke injuries are avoidable, for the most part, if logistical aspects are considered, such as scheduling water breaks, implementing shorter practice sessions, or moving the practice to cooler times of the day. However, often coaches become so focused on using the heat as a test of players' prowess that precautions relating to the prevention of heat stroke are ignored.

The case of Korey Stringer is an unfortunate example of the "no pain, no gain" mentality of football at the professional level. Stringer was an offensive lineman for the Minnesota Vikings. On July 30, 2001, after practicing in extreme heat and humidity, Stringer left practice complaining of exhaustion, and his line coach allegedly called Stringer a "big baby." The next day at practice—in a heat index of 110 degrees—Stringer vomited three times and collapsed. The trainer gave Stringer water but did not measure his vital signs. Stringer went into the training tent for about 45 minutes and then lay down on the ground and was unresponsive when a cart was called to take Stringer back to practice. At this point, the trainer applied ice towels to Stringer. When he arrived at the hospital his temperature had reached 108.8 degrees, and he died early the next morning.

Stringer's widow brought a wrongful death suit, but the litigation was unsuccessful, primarily because the Minnesota workers' compensation statute severely limited her possible avenues of recovery. (See Chapter 8 for a discussion of workers' compensation.) It is, however, instructive to look at the allegations made by Ms. Stringer as they relate to the culture of the sport. The complaint alleged that the NFL culture is one that "unreasonably subjects players to heat-related illness during practices, ostensibly out of the twisted belief that players benefit from being subjected to such working conditions" (Charnley, 2005, p. 92). The complaint also called the NFL training camps "modern-day sweat shops" and alleged that the NFL culture is a "perverse and deadly culture that the League tolerates, fosters, and even markets" (p. 55). This "no pain, no gain" mentality, common at all levels of football, is a prime contributor to the prevalence and seriousness of heat-related injuries and should be an important point of discussion between athletic directors and football coaches prior to summer practice.

Three other cases also raise the specter of the "no pain, no gain" mentality. At the University of Missouri a freshman football player, who had sickle cell symptoms,

Competitive Advantage

STRATEGIES

Medical Care

- Make sure that one or more persons with first aid and CPR training are always readily available to deal with emergency medical conditions.

- Develop a protocol to contact outside emergency medical assistance quickly. Make sure all employees understand this protocol.

- Try to eliminate any conflict of interest issues in medical treatment by giving the team physician the final authority as to whether a player is medically able to play. The coach should not have the prerogative to override competent medical opinion.

- Always provide full disclosure to players regarding their injuries.

died during a summer workout in 2005. The university settled the lawsuit for $2 million after a number of problems came to light, including the sports medicine director's refusal to examine the player even after he had blurry vision and collapsed. The department personnel also were unfamiliar with exercise-induced complications arising from the sickle cell trait (Scherzagier, 2009). At the University of Central Florida, football player Ereck Plancher died in March 2008, during offseason conditioning drills, and a lawsuit was filed in March 2009. Plancher also had the sickle cell trait, which exacerbated the likelihood of distress during fatigue. In this case, the trainers and coaches allegedly ignored Plancher's exhaustion, dizziness, shortness of breath, and collapse (Fainaru-Wade, 2009). Finally, in a well-publicized high school case, a Kentucky high school football player died after running sprints in the summer of 2008 in 94-degree weather. This situation resulted in reckless homicide charges being brought against the football coach (Popke, 2009). These tragedies are preventable with good risk management protocols. There is no acceptable reason for these types of injuries and fatalities to occur as they do.

Medical malpractice

As stated previously, commentators have often noted that the culture of sport perpetuates the "no pain, no gain" mentality.

For example, Ted Johnson, a linebacker for the New England Patriots, asserted that his coach, Bill Belichick, forced him to return to practice while he was suffering from a concussion. During this practice, Johnson suffered another concussion. Belichick admitted that he made a mistake in forcing Johnson to return, and Johnson stated that he felt that Belichick did not realize the danger of putting Johnson back into action so soon (Davis, 2008).

The risks of a concussion and returning a player to competition too soon after the athlete has suffered a concussion have also been raised by a number of parties in regard to high school athletes. The Center for Injury Research and Policy in Columbus, Ohio, conducted a study that found as many as 40.5 percent of high school athletes who have suffered concussions return to competition too early, thus risking further concussions or death. Further, in the sport of football, which accounts for the highest number of concussions, 16 percent of players who suffered concussions returned to play the same day they lost consciousness. This is directly contrary to all medical advice on this condition (Lloyd, May 5, 2009). In Washington, legislation was passed as a direct response to a severe injury suffered by a 13-year-old football player who was permitted to play after an undiagnosed concussion and then suffered a second concussion. The player was in a coma for 37 days and is still unable to walk. The legislation, known as Zachary's Law, provides that parents and athletes be informed of concussion risks and symptoms. If a young athlete is suspected to have a concussion, the athlete must be removed from play and not allowed to play again until a health professional gives approval (Lloyd, May 28, 2009).

Fraudulent concealment

Claims of improper treatment or medical malpractice in situations such as those discussed above are predicated upon allegations of mere negligence: that a physician failed to act as a reasonably prudent physician in either diagnosing or treating an injury. **Fraudulent concealment,** however, is founded upon allegations of intentional wrongdoing: that either the physician or team officials, or both, knowingly withheld information from a player concerning his injury, in an effort to urge the player to continue participating to the detriment of the player's health.

In the *Stringer* lawsuit, the complaint alleged that the NFL condoned a "deadly culture," one that pressured players into performing with pain or injury (Charnley, 2005). In another lawsuit, brought by former NHL player Dave Babych against the Philadelphia Flyers and team doctor Arthur Bartolozzi, Babych claimed that not only were his serious foot injuries mistreated by Bartolozzi but that there was "improper and fraudulent medical advice motivated by a corporate strategy of pressuring injured players to return to the ice" ("Former Flyers player sues team," May 2002). Allegations of this nature have also arisen in collegiate sport. In the case of *Gathers v. Loyola Marymount University,* a tragic situation arose in which a college basketball player with a congenital heart defect died. Gathers was undergoing treatment for the defect to allow him to continue to participate. The complaint alleged that Gathers was "sacrificed on the altar of basketball for the sole benefit" of various defendants, including the coach and athletic director, who would benefit financially and professionally from the continued play of the team's star, Hank Gathers (Complaint, *Gathers v. Loyola Marymount Univ.*, p. 49).

The seminal case for this type of claim is *Krueger v. San Francisco Forty Niners.*

Krueger v. San Francisco Forty Niners

| 234 Cal. Rptr. 579 (Ct. App. 1987) | **FOCUS CASE** |

FACTS

Charlie Krueger, a defensive lineman, began playing in the NFL with the Forty Niners in 1958 and played with them until his retirement in 1973. During his career, Krueger played despite numerous injuries, including multiple fractures. Krueger also had problems with his left knee, which became the focus of the lawsuit. While in college Krueger had surgery on his left knee to repair a torn meniscus. Then in 1963 a Forty Niners team physician operated on the knee after Krueger tore his medial collateral ligament. The physician told Krueger that it was a good repair despite the fact that the physician realized that Krueger was missing the anterior cruciate ligament in that knee. Thereafter Krueger had continuous severe pain and swelling in that knee, which was treated by repeated injections of steroids. At no time was he told about the adverse effects of continuing to play on a knee that was missing a ligament or of the adverse effects of repeated steroid injections, which caused serious deterioration of the knee. In 1970 he suffered a game injury in which part of his left knee broke off, but he was given codeine and told to return to the game.

Krueger retired in 1973, and only in 1978 was he advised that his knee had chronic and permanent disability. He suffered from traumatic arthritis and a crippling degenerative process in the left knee. Krueger could not stand for prolonged periods, nor could he run. The condition is irreversible.

Krueger sued the team physicians and the Forty Niners for fraud and deceit. He alleged that, had he known of the severity of the problems with his knee, he would not have continued to play football. He alleged that the medical information dealing with the adverse effects of his knee injury as well as the serious consequences of the steroid treatment given was withheld from him so that he would continue to play football for his employer.

The trial court rendered a judgment for the defendants.

HOLDING

The appellate court reversed and remanded.

RATIONALE

In finding for Krueger, the court noted that although Krueger knew that his injury was serious, he relied upon the physicians to advise him truthfully of the seriousness of the injuries. It was perfectly reasonable for a player to accept and act upon the medical advice given.

The court held that the evidence clearly demonstrated that the defendants, in their desire to keep Krueger on the playing field, consciously failed to make full, meaningful disclosure to Krueger respecting the magnitude of the risk he took in continuing to play a violent contact sport with a profoundly damaged left knee. Krueger was entitled to full professional warnings, and the deliberate failure to disclose is fraudulent concealment.

Negligence in Transportation

The transportation of participants is a critical function, and when an organization assumes the duty to provide transportation, it must be provided in a reasonably safe manner. There are four primary issues related to transportation:

1. The selection of competent drivers
2. The selection of a safe mode of travel
3. The proper maintenance of vehicles
4. The proper training of drivers

Selection of competent drivers

In many cases, an organization may choose to contract with an outside agency for the provision of transportation services. As we discussed in Chapter 5, this contract would, most likely, be structured as an independent contractor relationship to allow the organization to avoid vicarious liability for the negligent acts of drivers. However, due care must be taken with the selection of the independent contractor: the credentials of the transportation agency must be scrutinized to ensure that the agency and its drivers can provide reasonably safe transportation. If the organization selects a transportation agency without reviewing the fitness of the agency to provide these services and the agency, if scrutinized, would not have been chosen because of its safety record, a possible cause of action against the employing organization may arise under the principles of negligent selection (see Chapter 5).

If the organization chooses to have its own employees serve as drivers, care must be taken to ensure that the drivers possess the necessary credentials for this purpose. If vans or buses are to be driven, the state usually mandates that the driver possess a type of chauffeur's license. The organization should implement a policy to ensure that drivers have proper, current credentials.

Selection of a safe mode of travel

Many athletic programs use passenger vans to transport athletes. In 2005 the National Highway Traffic Safety Administration issued a consumer advisory stating that 15-passenger vans are three times more likely to roll over when they are used to carry 10 or more passengers (www.nhtsa.gov). In view of this disclosure, many schools have invested substantially in other types of vehicles, particularly motor coaches.

Although motor coaches would seem to be a better choice, there has been some concern that some universities may be using charter bus companies that do not meet federal safety standards. ESPN disclosed that at least 85 Division I universities during 2007 and 2008 used charter bus companies with one or more deficient federal safety scores (Holtzman, 2009). This emphasizes the need to research bus companies and to choose those with proven safety records that meet federal safety standards. There is also guidance available from the NCAA (www.ncaa.org/sports_sciences/safety_in_student_transportation.pdf).

With regard to air travel, the National Transportation Safety Board (NTSB) provided the NCAA with a safety recommendation on January 21, 2003, after the NTSB investigated the crash of an airplane carrying members of the Oklahoma State University (OSU) basketball team. The team was traveling in three planes that had been donated for this purpose. OSU's air travel policy at the time of the crash required approval of charter companies providing transportation but did not require coordination pertaining to donated flights. The crash was caused by pilot error.

Although the NTSB stated that OSU's transportation policy did not cause the accident, it recommended that OSU revamp its policy to ensure better oversight and coordination of all air travel, even if the flights are donated. OSU did revamp its policy to ensure more control over weather-related situations, specific criteria for aircraft, and airplane maintenance. The revised OSU policy is appended to the NTSB Safety Recommendation report and is available at http://www.ntsb.gov/recs/letters/2003/A03_01.pdf.

Proper maintenance of vehicles

Many lawsuits in the area of vehicle maintenance have arisen because vehicles were neither inspected nor properly maintained prior to use. Maintenance personnel must have experience dealing with the types of vehicles used and must know the proper air pressure for tires, ensure that headlights and wiper blades are in

Competitive Advantage
STRATEGIES

Transportation

- As a part of your risk management plan, appoint a transportation coordinator to develop and oversee this critical aspect of your program.
- Ensure that all drivers are properly credentialed.
- Drivers should obtain a certification from an Emergency Vehicle Operator's Course in the type of vehicle they will be operating (NTSB, 2003).
- A qualified, paid driver should be used if participants are traveling farther than 350 miles one way or if the trip is expected to extend later than 2:00 a.m. or overnight (NTSB, 2003).
- Twelve-passenger vans should be loaded with no more than eight passengers and equipment. Fifteen-passenger vans should be loaded with no more than 10 passengers and equipment (NTSB, 2003).

good shape, and check all fluids for proper levels. Underinflated tires may result in blowouts, which are quite dangerous on the open road. An inspection checklist should be filled out each time a vehicle is checked out for use.

Proper training of drivers

Not only must an organization use properly credentialed drivers, it must have and enforce safety policies for all drivers. Drivers should have the knowledge to conduct a vehicle inspection and know the specifications for each type of vehicle. Drivers should also undergo a safety orientation and learn how to react to emergency situations, such as icy roads or a tire blowout. Finally, it is critical that drivers have proper rest before beginning a lengthy drive and that they take rest stops at reasonable intervals.

The following Focus Case addresses three of the above issues.

Clement v. Griffin

FOCUS CASE   634 So.2d 412 (La. Ct. App. 1994)

FACTS

This negligence action arose from a single-vehicle accident that occurred in Mississippi. A van carrying 13 members of the Delgado Community College baseball team rolled over after a tire blowout occurred. The driver, a student coach, was unable to control the van after the blowout, and several of the passengers were ejected from the vehicle. The driver did not hold a chauffeur's license, which was mandated by the state to operate a van and required under college rules. Further, the college's president testified that he was not aware that student drivers were being used and that he considered this to be inappropriate.

The driver testified that he was never given instructions regarding the speed of the vehicle nor any safety instructions of any kind. He was not given any direction on how to control the van if a blowout occurred.

As to the inspection and maintenance of vehicles, the tires were routinely maintained at 45 p.s.i. rather than the recommended 75 p.s.i. Several experts testified that the underinflation of the tires contributed greatly to the blowout.

The case included products liability claims against Goodyear Tire & Rubber Company, manufacturer of the van's tires, and Ford Motor Co., manufacturer of the van. These claims are not discussed here.

HOLDING

The Louisiana appellate court affirmed the trial court judgment holding the college liable for the accident.

RATIONALE

The court held that the college had duties to the plaintiffs to (1) properly maintain the vehicle, (2) select a qualified driver for the vehicle, and (3) properly train the driver. The court found that the evidence supported a finding that the college breached all of the above.

In regard to improper maintenance, the court noted that the mechanic in charge of maintenance did not know the proper tire pressure for the van since he had never seen the owner's manual for the van. Thus the tires were consistently underinflated, leading to a safety issue, i.e., the blowout.

In regard to the selection of a qualified driver, the student driver did not have the proper credential to operate this vehicle. In fact, the college violated its own policy in allowing someone without a chauffeur's license to drive the van. Further, it violated the university's policy to allow a student to drive the van.

Finally, the court noted that the driver was not trained properly. He never received any safety information, and that failure was detrimental since he was not able to take appropriate action after the blowout occurred.

Since there was evidence to support the above, it was appropriate to find the college liable. There was also vicarious liability based on the negligence of the student driver.

PRODUCTS LIABILITY

M alfunctioning sports equipment can cause injury without any negligent action on the part of an instructor or participant. When this occurs as a result of some defect in the equipment, the injured party may sue under products liability law.

Two types of product defects may be the cause of injury—design defects and manufacturing defects. A **design defect** exists when the very design of the product is flawed so as to render that product unsafe. In contrast, a **manufacturing defect** is the result of an error in the manufacturing and production process that flaws one or more of the manufactured items, even though the design itself is a safe one. When a factory-installed bolt on a weight machine curl bar broke, causing the user to fall backward and injure his spine, the court found that the bolt had been weakened due to a manufacturing defect (*Diversified Products Corp. v. Faxon*, 1987). Compare this case to *Dudley Sports Co. v. Schmitt* (1972), which presents an example of a design defect. In *Dudley Sports Co.*, a baseball-pitching machine injured a custodian when he bumped the unplugged machine and the throwing arm snapped through unexpectedly. The court held that the pitching machine was defective because it had been designed without a protective guard around the throwing arm.

Potential Causes of Action Under Products Liability Law

A person injured by a defective product has three potential causes of action under products liability law:

1. Negligence
2. Strict liability
3. Breach of warranty

If the facts support it, two of these or all three claims may be joined in one lawsuit.

Negligence claims

A manufacturer, seller, or supplier may be sued for negligence in design, manufacturing, or distribution of a defective product, or for negligent failure to warn about an unobvious (and therefore unreasonable) risk presented by the product.

Negligent design. The baseball-pitching machine case described earlier is an example of a case in which a court found the manufacturer liable for negligently designing a product that proved unsafe because it lacked a safety feature that would have protected against an unobvious danger.

Negligent failure to warn. In *Dudley Sports Co.,* the court also found that the manufacturer had been negligent in failing to provide an adequate warning about the danger. The only warning provided with the machine was a label that read as indicated in Exhibit 15.2.

The court ruled that the manufacturer should have provided a more specific warning about the propensity of the throwing arm to snap forward even when the machine was not plugged in.

Another failure to warn case illustrates the principle that manufacturers must also provide a warning if a defect is discovered after a product has gone on the market. Riddell, Inc. was held liable for failing to warn that its football helmets did not protect as well as other helmets on the market in a "crown impact" situation, a danger that was not obvious to ordinary consumers (*Arnold v. Riddell, Inc.,* 1995).

Additionally, some courts have held that failure to warn about the inherent risks of using sports equipment may establish product liability even when there is no underlying manufacturing or design defect. In *Prince v. Parachutes, Inc.* (1984), the court ruled that the plaintiff, who became a quadriplegic as a result of a skydiving collision, had a legitimate claim for failure to warn. He admitted that there was nothing wrong with his parachute, claiming instead that the cause of the collision was his inability to control the chute, which was too advanced for his skill level. The court agreed that he would not have used such an advanced piece of equipment if a warning about such a risk had been sewn into the parachute itself, instead of only being provided in a detailed user's manual that came with the chute, and thus found the warning inadequate. Finally, courts have held that

EXHIBIT 15.2 Product warning label in baseball-pitching machine case (*Dudley Sports Co. v. Schmitt,* 1972).

WARNING! SAFETY FIRST.

READ INSTRUCTIONS BEFORE ROTATING MACHINE EITHER ELECTRICALLY OR MANUALLY.

STAY CLEAR OF THROWING ARM AT ALL TIMES.

DON'T REMOVE THIS PACKING BLOCK UNTIL YOU FULLY UNDERSTAND THE OPERATION OF THE THROWING ARM AND THE DANGER INVOLVED.

manufacturers have a duty to warn consumers, not just about dangers inherent in a product's normal use, but also about dangers associated with foreseeable misuses (van der Smissen, 1990).

Defenses to negligence claims. Defenses to a negligence products liability claim include:

- The defect or failure to warn was not the proximate cause of the injury.
- The plaintiff was contributorily negligent.
- The plaintiff assumed any increased risk created by the defect that was beyond the inherent risk of the activity itself.
- The danger was open and obvious.
- The product was not in fact defective.
- An adequate warning was provided.

Strict liability

A manufacturer or seller may be strictly liable for an injury caused by a defective product even if it was reasonably careful in designing and manufacturing the product. Strict liability for defective products is based on a public policy rationale that responsibility for unreasonably dangerous products ought to be placed where it will most effectively reduce the risks to consumers. Because products often pose dangers beyond the contemplation of ordinary consumers but foreseeable to the manufacturer or seller, responsibility is placed on them through the strict liability cause of action, thus relieving the consumer of the difficult challenge of having to track down hard-to-find evidence of corporate negligence. Policymakers also reason that manufacturers and merchants are in the best position to spread the costs of consumer safety and litigation by building them into the prices of their products. Additionally, exposure to strict liability is thought to motivate businesses to take consumer safety seriously (Garrett, 1972; Nader, 1972; Plant, 1957).

Prevailing in a strict liability claim. To prevail in a strict liability claim, a plaintiff must establish that the product was indeed defective by proving that the defect was present at the time the product left the manufacturer's control, and that it was unreasonably dangerous to consumers. Traditionally, a product would be considered unreasonably dangerous if the ordinary consumer would be unaware of the nature and extent of the danger, or if an economically feasible safer design existed. Recently, however, several jurisdictions have begun to adopt the relatively new position recommended in the Restatement (Third) of Torts (1997) that courts should use a risk–utility balancing test to determine the unreasonableness of the danger. If, on balance, the social utility of the product outweighs the risk to the consumer, then it will not be considered unreasonably dangerous. The factors to be weighed include those presented in Exhibit 15.3.

 Wallach v. American Home Products Corp. (2001) illustrates the application of risk–utility balancing in a case where the plaintiff, who was an experienced treadmill jogger, was injured when he fell off the back of a treadmill. He sued the manufacturer in strict liability, claiming that the treadmill's design was unreasonably dangerous because it had no side handrails and because the front motor cover forced him too far back to be able to reach the front handrail when he lost his

EXHIBIT | 15.3   Factors in the risk–utility balancing test (Restatement [Third] of Torts, 1997).

Magnitude of the danger

Likelihood of injury

Obviousness of the danger

Cost and technological
feasibility of a safer design

Adequacy of warnings

Desirability and usefulness
of the product as designed

Level of consumer
awareness of the risk

SOCIAL UTILITY CONSUMER RISK

balance. The court found that, while there is always a risk of falling off, this product's risk was minimal because it provided the user with complete control of grade, speed, and stride. Additionally, the court disagreed that a safer design was feasible, because it found no evidence that side rails were safer than front rails; indeed, there was evidence that normal human reaction time would not have enabled the plaintiff to grab a side rail before he was thrown off after suddenly losing his balance. Thus, the lack of side rails, while not decreasing the likelihood of injury, did not increase it either. Finally, the court concluded that the danger of falling off the treadmill was open and obvious, particularly to an experienced user like Wallach, who thus could be held to have assumed the risk. Balancing these risk factors against the social utility of the treadmill, which allows users to get cardiovascular exercise without undue exposure to bad weather, traffic, or unsafe surfaces, the court held that the utility of the treadmill outweighed the risks to the consumer, and thus the product was not unreasonably dangerous. Therefore, Wallach's strict liability claim was rejected.

Defenses to a strict liability claim. Defenses available to the manufacturer or seller include:

- Unforeseeable misuse by the consumer
- Alteration of the product after it left the manufacturer's control
- Predictable deterioration of an aging product
- Provision of an adequate warning
- Secondary assumption of the risk by the consumer
- Social utility that outweighs the consumer risk so that product is not unreasonably dangerous

It should be noted that in those jurisdictions that have adopted risk–utility balancing, provision of a warning is only one factor in determining the reasonableness of the risk and will not serve as a complete defense sufficient in itself to defeat a strict liability claim (Sanborn, 1998).

The predictable deterioration defense would be used when a product malfunctions due to its age. Because all products eventually wear out, it would be unfair to hold the manufacturer responsible for an injury caused by predictable deterioration. The defense of unforeseeable misuse by the consumer might be used by a golf club manufacturer who has been sued by a plaintiff who was injured by breaking her club when she smashed it against a tree in frustration over her poor play. If golf clubs had to be designed to withstand such forces, they would not be well suited for hitting a golf ball with appropriate distance and accuracy. In another example of the unforeseeable misuse defense, a court found for the defendant in holding that the plaintiff's consumption of 125 ephedrine tablets per day was an unforeseeable misuse of that nutritional supplement (*Green v. BDI Pharmaceuticals*, 2001).

Breach of warranty claims

A **warranty** is an assertion of fact or promise made by a manufacturer or seller that is relied upon as part of the consumer transaction. Several warranties may be involved in the sale of sports equipment. When such warranties are found to be false, a breach of warranty claim may be brought. Breach of warranty claims are contract-based actions, so **privity of contract** (a direct contractual relationship between user and provider) may be required in some states; however, many states do not require privity for breach of warranty claims in personal injury actions.

Express warranty. An **express warranty** is one that is explicitly made by a manufacturer or seller, either orally or in writing, or as a visual image (for example, in a catalog or advertisement). This type of warranty is intended to induce a purchase by making an assertion of fact or a promise regarding the quality of the goods. An example of the breach of an express warranty is found in *Hauter v. Zogarts* (1975). In this case, a golf training device had been packaged with language that encouraged the user to "drive the ball with full power," and that said "Completely Safe Ball Will Not Hit Player." When the cord attached to the ball wrapped around the user's golf club, causing the ball to hit him in the head, the plaintiff sustained a serious injury and sued the manufacturer. The court found that the language on the packaging constituted an express warranty that materially misrepresented the facts and held that the manufacturer had breached that warranty.

Implied warranties. There are two implied warranties that can create a claim for breach of warranty—the implied warranty of merchantability and implied warranty of fitness.

The **implied warranty of merchantability** is an implied promise that the product is fit for its ordinary intended use and thus is merchantable (or saleable). It accompanies any sale of goods by a merchant in the regular course of their business. Such a warranty accompanying a purchase of catcher's masks would imply that those masks would protect a pretty face as well as any ordinary catcher's mask on the market.

The **implied warranty of fitness** accompanies a sale when the seller has reason to know the particular purpose of a purchase and the buyer relies on the seller's expertise in providing a product appropriate for that purpose. A breach of the implied warranty of fitness is illustrated in *Filler v. Rayex Corp.* (1970). In this case, an advertisement for sunglasses purchased by a high school for its baseball team indicated that the sunglasses were made for playing baseball and that the players' eyes would be protected by the "scientific lenses" that guaranteed "instant eye protection." Additionally, inside the box the company had provided a lifetime guarantee that the lenses were unbreakable. After a baseball hit a player's sunglasses and they shattered, causing him to lose an eye, the court found that the glasses were not fit for the advertised particular purpose of playing baseball because the lenses were not made with plastic or shatterproof glass. Thus, the manufacturer had breached the implied warranty of fitness made in its advertisement.

Defenses to breach of warranty claims. Defenses to breach of warranty claims include:

- Lack of privity between user and provider (depending on state law)
- Provision of an adequate disclaimer (such as a statement indicating that the item is "For Sale—As Is")
- Unforeseeable misuse by the consumer

Differences in Exposure to Liability for Different Types of Defendants

The purpose of products liability law is to provide a legal remedy against parties involved in the production and distribution of defective products—so manufacturers and sellers are the typical defendants. Manufacturers have a duty to inspect or test their products for hidden dangers that would present an unreasonable risk to ordinary consumers. Sellers have a lesser duty to make a cursory inspection of sample items for sale in order to determine that they are undamaged and fit to sell. Sellers and other product suppliers, such as athletics departments or fitness centers that purchase sports equipment for their teams or members, can also be found negligent for providing defective equipment when they knew or should have known of the defect (*Everett v. Bucky Warren*, 1978). Strict liability, however, is typically limited to manufacturers and merchants.

Organizations that rent sports equipment are subject to the same types of liability as sellers because consumers place similar reliance on lessors to provide equipment that is fit for its intended use. Thus, in *Perton v. Motel Properties* (1998), a motel that rented bicycles to its guests was found liable for breach of warranty when a guest was injured while riding one of the bikes, which turned out to be defective. In contrast, service providers that are not lessors or regular merchant sellers will not be subject to strict liability. When a member of a fitness center was injured while using a defective squat machine, the court ruled that strict liability is intended to apply only to manufacturers and sellers, not to organizations that purchase and use equipment simply to provide a service (such as the opportunity for a fitness workout; *Bhardwaj v. 24 Hour Fitness*, 2002). When, however, a service provider, such as a swimming pool construction company, also sells an optional product—such as a diving board—as a regular feature of its construction service, if that product is defective and causes injury, the service provider can be held liable (*Anthony Pools v. Sheehan*, 1983). When the product is *not* a regular feature of a service but is provided as a *de minimis* part of a service contract, no liability will be imposed on the service provider. For example, a company that constructed a basketball court, including installation of the basketball goals, would not have been liable for defective rims when they did not provide goals as a regular or substantial part of their regular construction business (*Traub v. Cornell University*, 1998).

Strict liability has occasionally been imposed on repair service companies (see, e.g., *Gentile v. MacGregor Mfg. Co.*, 1985). However, a reconditioning service was held to have no liability for a brain injury caused by a football helmet that it had reconditioned. The court reasoned that the helmet was defective in design, and the reconditioning company had no duty to redesign a helmet made by another company. Remarkably, though, the court also found no strict liability on the part of the helmet manufacturer because the helmet had been altered by the reconditioning service after it left the control of the manufacturer (*Rodriguez v. Riddell Sports, Inc.*, 2001). Rulings like this suggest that caution be exercised in deciding whether to use reconditioned equipment, because, when a cause of action in strict liability is unavailable, plaintiffs are left with the difficult challenge of gathering evidence sufficient to support an alternative claim for negligence.

An equipment manufacturer that is also a sport sponsor may not avoid liability for a defective product by relying on a waiver that releases it from liability in its role as a sponsor. In *Curtis v. Hoosier Racing Tire Corp.* (2004), a tire blew out during a stock car race at the Talladega Super Speedway, resulting in serious injury to the driver. Hoosier Racing Tire Corp. was the manufacturer of the defective tire and was also a major sponsor of the race. Prior to the race, the driver had signed a form releasing the sponsors and promoters from liability for any injury suffered while participating in the event. The court ruled that this release did not reach Hoosier Racing Tire in its role as manufacturer and therefore allowed the plaintiff's strict liability claim to proceed. Earlier, the Sixth Circuit reached a similar result on this issue of liability of a sponsor that is also a manufacturer (*Mohney v. USA Hockey, Inc.*, 2001).

Competitive Advantage STRATEGIES

Products Liability

- Think twice about using reconditioned sports equipment, because a court may reject a strict liability claim, leaving you with a negligence cause of action, which is typically more difficult to prove.

- To protect your sponsors who are also equipment manufacturers, use a waiver that explicitly encompasses their dual roles. That way, a court cannot misconstrue the waiver as applicable to them only in their role as sponsors.

- Avoid language in your advertising or packaging that uses such terms as "safe" or "foolproof." Such assertions are construed liberally in favor of plaintiffs (*Hauter v. Zogarts*, 1975) and will very often prove untrue due to the high potential for injury given varying skill levels of sports and recreation participants.

- Ensure that your employees know that they should avoid negligently purchasing sports equipment that they know or should know is defective.

Multiple Products Liability Claims and Multiple Defendants

Occasionally, the facts permit a products liability plaintiff to join all three causes of action in one lawsuit. A good example is the *DeRienzo* mountain biking case.

DeRienzo v. Trek Bicycle Corp.

376 F. Supp. 2d 537 (S.D.N.Y. 2005)   **FOCUS CASE**

FACTS

Plaintiff David DeRienzo was severely injured when his Trek model Y5 bicycle frame broke as he landed following a nine-foot mountain biking jump off a rock. DeRienzo was the second owner of the bike, and both he and the original owner had replaced several components, such as brakes and shocks, prior to the crash. In particular, the first owner had replaced the front shocks with a Rock Shox fork designed to handle stronger forces, such as jumping, than the original shocks. The Rock Shox fork was listed as being installed on several similar Y model bikes, although not on the Y5.

DeRienzo sued Trek, the manufacturer of the bike frame, in products liability, joining claims of strict liability, negligent failure to warn, and breach of warranty. He alleged that jumping is a normal use of a mountain bike and that he performed the jump in a manner that would have resulted in a successful landing had the frame not failed. He also alleged that Trek knew that the Y5 bike was regularly used by mountain bikers for jumping, but that it failed to warn consumers that the Y5 was not designed for that use.

Trek moved for summary judgment on all three claims. The company alleged that DeRienzo had landed improperly and that his history of misusing the bike for jumping had weakened the frame. Trek further argued that it had not marketed the Y5 for jumping, that it had indeed provided an adequate warning against such a use, and that DeRienzo's failure to read the warning was not the company's fault.

HOLDING

The district court denied Trek's motion for summary judgment, finding that the facts were sufficient to support a full trial on all three claims.

RATIONALE

The court accepted the expert testimony of a metallurgist who conducted tests on the broken frame and determined that a manufacturing defect had occurred during the process of welding the frame. He further testified that fatigue cracks due to such a defect would often be invisible to the naked eye. The court also accepted the testimony of a cycling expert that jumping is a foreseeable and expected use of a mountain bike, and that it was also foreseeable that a user would modify such a bike by adding shocks that would make it more suitable for jumping. The court further found that the Trek catalog pictured Y model bikes (although not the Y5) being jumped. Finally, it found that two different user's manuals had been issued by Trek during the time frame that the bicycle was purchased, one of which warned against jumping, while the other simply advised jumpers to inspect the frame visually for signs of weakening. Moreover, said the court, these warnings could have been viewed as inadequate in both manuals because they were inconspicuous, given that over half the pages of both manuals consisted of various warnings.

With respect to the strict liability claim, the court concluded that a jury could reasonably find as follows:

1. That jumping is a normal use of a mountain bike
2. That a defective weld could have existed that could have caused the frame failure, which could have caused the injury
3. That this manufacturing defect was unreasonably dangerous because it would not have been obvious to the user upon visual inspection of the frame

Relative to the negligent failure to warn claim, the court held that a jury could reasonably find that Trek knew that jumping was a normal use of the bike and that mountain bikers would be likely to modify such bikes to make them more suitable for jumping. Therefore, if the Y5 was not designed to withstand such forces, a jury could find that Trek owed a duty to provide an adequate warning to that effect and that Trek had breached that duty by providing inconsistent or inadequate warnings. Finally, as to the breach of warranty claim, the court found that the Trek catalog pictures of airborne Y model bicycles could be interpreted as evidence that Trek had in fact marketed the bikes as suitable for jumping, but the company's expert witness had testified that the Y5 was not designed for that use. Therefore, a jury could reasonably conclude that Trek had breached the warranty of merchantability. The court thus allowed DeRienzo to proceed to a full trial on all three claims.

CONCLUSION

U nderstanding negligence liability is critical for managers in sport organizations. This chapter addressed the legal theory of negligence and applicable defenses. This chapter also discussed the most prevalent liability claims against sport organizations relating to participants. Increased knowledge of liability issues should translate into better preventive efforts to enhance participants' experience by making it safer and more enriching. Satisfied participants lead to better competitive success in the sport marketplace.

discussion questions

1. What are the elements of negligence? Define and discuss each.
2. Explain the concept of negligence per se.
3. Explain the act of God defense. What two elements must exist to use this defense?
4. What is the core concept for both contributory and comparative negligence? What is the difference between the two?
5. Based on your understanding of an inherent risk being one that is "obvious and necessary," list a number of activities or sports and then identify some inherent risks for each activity or sport. Do you think that inherent risks may change as technology and rules change in sport? Explain.
6. What is the difference between primary assumption of risk and secondary assumption of risk?
7. What is the purpose of Good Samaritan statutes?
8. Discuss a number of aspects of competent instruction or training. Give examples of poor instruction in a sport or physical activity of your choice.
9. Explain the difference between a claim based on medical malpractice and one based on fraudulent concealment.
10. Discuss whether or not having a cause of action in strict liability for defective products makes good sense. Why is it fair to hold manufacturers strictly liable for defective products without regard to how careful they were in designing and manufacturing those products? What is the benefit to consumers of having the option to pursue a strict liability claim?

learning activities

1. Do an Internet search and find five agencies or companies that offer "certification" for personal trainers. Compare and contrast the rigor of each certification. What are the criteria for becoming certified? What type of education is required? Assess whether any of these certifications ensure that a personal trainer you might hire is sufficiently qualified for the position.

2. Do an Internet search to locate a sample emergency action plan for a sport or recreation program of your choice. For example, the NCAA has developed criteria for an EAP in intercollegiate sport in its *NCAA Sports Medicine Handbook, Guideline 1c Emergency Care and Coverage,* found at http://www.ncaapublications.com/Uploads/PDF/2007-08_sports_medicine_handbook 6786d571-ad07-492e-85cc-075cb4c74e51.pdf. EAP criteria for youth sports can be found at www.sportssafety.org/articles/emergency-action-plan/.

3. Review the Oklahoma State University revised transportation policy that is appended to the NTSB report mentioned in the transportation section of this chapter. It is available at www.ntsb.gov/recs/letters/2003/A03_01.pdf. Discuss the aspects of the OSU policy that you would include in your policy if you were the athletic director of a major college athletic program.

4. Using LEXIS-NEXIS, retrieve the *Traub v. Cornell University* case. For each defendant, write a paragraph summarizing why they were found to be liable in products liability or not liable for the plaintiff's injury.

CASE STUDY

In the case of *Rostai v. Neste Enterprises,* 138 Cal. App. 4th 326 (2006), a client alleged that he suffered a heart attack in his first training workout because of the negligence of the personal trainer in failing to investigate the cardiac risk factors of the client. The appellate court stated that the trainer's function is to challenge a participant, and "inherent in that process is the risk that the trainer will not accurately assess the participant's ability and the participant will be injured as a result." The court, therefore, held that the client had assumed the risk of this erroneous advice and assessment.

1. Compare the rationale in this case to the one used by the court in the *Schweichler* case that you read earlier in the chapter.

2. Compare the rationale in this case to the one used by the court in the *Hemady* case that you read earlier in the chapter.

3. What are the consequences of using the "reckless disregard" standard in cases involving a teacher, coach, or personal trainer?

4. As a matter of policy, discuss whether it makes sense to essentially "immunize" a coach, teacher, or personal trainer from the consequences of their failure to act as a reasonably prudent professional.

considering . . . ANALYSIS & DISCUSSION

Duty of Care (p. 419)

Yes, Lefour will argue that the university assumed a duty of care in this case. When the university assumed the obligation of assigning students to internship sites, it assumed the duty to act with reasonable care in choosing sites that did not create a foreseeable zone of risk for the students.

Negligence Per Se (p. 421)

Yes, this plaintiff could win this case based on negligence per se. The plaintiff would not have to call a swimming pool design expert to testify that this pool was unsafe. The pool was not constructed in accordance with the pool law, and the provisions of that law were there specifically to prevent the type of entrapment incident that occurred here. Thus, the violation of the law establishes a breach of the standard of care, and all the plaintiff has to show is causation, established by the fact that this incident would not have happened if the pool law had been followed.

The Act of God Defense (p. 423)

Although lightning is "an act of God," the lightning was foreseeable. The storm was imminent and lightning was close. The coach continued to practice and ignored the danger. In this case, the coach could not use the act of God defense successfully because the natural disaster was foreseeable.

Comparative Negligence (p. 424)

If a pure comparative negligence model is applicable, then Bright will receive $40,000 in damages, since his award of $100,000 will be reduced by the percentage of fault attributable to his behavior (60 percent), even though the percentage of fault attributable to his behavior exceeds the percentage of fault attributable to the defendant's conduct. Under pure comparative negligence Bright would recover damages even if he were found 99 percent negligent, in the amount of $1,000 ($100,000 minus $99,000).

In a jurisdiction that uses a modified comparative negligence rule of "50/50 not greater than," Bright will receive nothing, since the percentage of fault attributable to his behavior exceeds 50 percent. If the jury had found, for example, that Bright was 49 percent responsible for his own behavior, under this model, Bright would receive $51,000 ($100,000 minus $49,000).

Assumption of Risk (p. 425)

The answer to both questions is no, because the failure of the parachutes to open was caused by the negligence of the person who packed the chute or by the malfunction of the chute itself. In either case, these were not risks assumed by the skydiver; they are risks beyond what the skydiver anticipated when he began the jump. In this latter scenario, there is no primary assumption of risk.

Quality of Supervision (p. 433)

Yes: An important aspect of supervision is the ability to recognize dangerous behavior by participants and to stop this behavior. Tim breached his duty of care because he did not have the competence to supervise this activity. Tim's supervisor also breached his or her duty of care by placing Tim in this situation when he was incompetent to serve as a supervisor.

Enforcement of Safety Rules (p. 437)

Most likely, they can prevail. Although Roche taught the proper sliding techniques at practice, she ignored Winn's previous dangerous behavior when she ran over the catcher for the first time. Ignoring dangerous behavior can lead to a repetition of that behavior, since players will often repeat behaviors that have been successful and have not been punished by their coach. Roche, in allowing the dangerous behavior to continue, has failed to act as a reasonable prudent coach.

Mismatch of Opponents (p. 438)

Coach Rogers failed to act as a reasonably prudent coach in allowing Bonecrusher to wrestle with Lewis. The imprudent mismatch resulted from Bonecrusher's greatly superior expertise and experience at the elite level. Coach Rogers was negligent in allowing this mismatch to occur.

REFERENCES

Cases

American Powerlifting Ass'n v. Cotillo, 934 A.2d 27 (Md. 2007).

Anthony Pools v. Sheehan, 455 A.2d 434 (Md. 1983).

Arnold v. Riddell, Inc., 882 F. Supp. 979 (D. Kan. 1995).

Barth v. Board of Educ., 490 N.E.2d 77 (Ill. App. Ct. 1986).

Bellinger v. Ballston Spa Cent. Sch. Dist, 871 N.Y.S.2d 432 (App. Div. 2008).

Bello v. Fieldhouse at Chelsea Piers, 795 N.Y.S.2d 24 (App. Div. 2005).

Bhardwaj v. 24 Hour Fitness, Inc., 2002 Cal. App. Unpub. LEXIS 3288 (2002).

Calouri v. County of Suffolk, 841 N.Y.S.2d 598 (App. Div. 2007).

Cecere v. Loon Mountain Recreation Corp., 923 A.2d 198 (N.H. 2007).

Clay City Consol. Sch. Dist. Corp. v. Timberman, 896 N.E.2d 1229 (Ind. Ct. App. 2008).

Clement v. Griffin, 634 So.2d 412 (La. Ct. App. 1994).

Curtis v. Hoosier Racing Tire Corp., 299 F. Supp. 2d 777 (N.D. Ohio 2004).

Davidson v. University of No. Carolina, 543 S.E.2d 920 (N.C. Ct. App. 2001).

DeRienzo v. Trek Bicycle Corp., 376 F. Supp. 2d 537 (S.D.N.Y. 2005).

Diversified Prods. Corp. v. Faxon, 514 So.2d 1161 (Fla. Dist. Ct. App. 1987).

Dudley Sports Co. v. Schmitt, 279 N.E.2d 266 (Ind. Ct. App. 1972).

Elledge v. Richland/Lexington Sch. Dist., 534 S.E.2d 289 (S.C. Ct. App. 2000).

Everett v. Bucky Warren, Inc., 380 N.E.2d 653 (Mass. 1978).

Feagins v. Waddy, 978 So.2d 712 (Ala. 2007).

Filler v. Rayex Corp., 435 F.2d 336 (7th Cir. 1970).

Fithian v. Sag Harbor Union Free Sch. Dist., 864 N.Y.S.2d 456 (App. Div. 2008).

Garman v. East Rochester Sch. Dist., 850 N.Y.S.2d 306 (App. Div. 2007).

Gathers v. Loyola Marymount Univ., Complaint in Superior Ct. of Cal., County of Los Angeles.

Gentile v. MacGregor Mfg. Co., 493 A.2d 647 (N.J. Super. Ct. Law Div. 1985).

Glankler v. Rapides Parish Sch. Bd., 610 So.2d 1020 (La. Ct. App. 1992).

Green v. BDI Pharmaceuticals, 2001 La. App. LEXIS 2390 (2001).

Hauter v. Zogarts, 534 P.2d 377 (Cal. 1975).

Hemady v. Long Beach Unified Sch. Dist., 49 Cal. Rptr. 3d 464 (Ct. App. 2006).

Kahn v. East Side Union High Sch., 75 P.3d 30 (Cal. 2003).

Kleinknecht v. Gettysburg College, 989 F.2d 1360 (3rd Cir. 1993).

Krueger v. San Francisco Forty Niners, 234 Cal. Rptr. 579 (Ct. App. 1987).

Lanzilla v. Waterville Valley Ski Resort, 517 F. Supp. 2d 578 (D. Mass. 2007).

Marks v. Kansas Bd. of Regents, 157 P.3d 1129 (Kan. Ct. App. 2007).

Mogabgab v. Orleans Parish Sch. Bd., 239 So.2d 456 (La. Ct. App. 1970).

Mohney v. USA Hockey, Inc., 2001 U.S. App. LEXIS 3584 (6th Cir. 2001).

Moose v. Massachusetts Inst. of Tech., 683 N.E. 2d 706 (Mass. App. Ct. 1997).

Morganteen v. Cowboy Adventures, Inc., 949 P.2d 552 (Ariz. Ct. App. 1997).

Murphy v. Polytechnic Univ., 850 N.Y.S. 2d 339 (Supreme Ct., 2007).

Murphy v. Polytechnic Univ., 872 N.Y.S. 2d 505 (App. Div., 2009).

Nova Southeastern Univ. v. Gross, 758 So.2d 86 (Fla. 2000).

Perton v. Motel Properties, Inc., 497 S.E.2d 29 (Ga. Ct. App. 1998).

Prince v. Parachutes, Inc., 685 P.2d 83 (Alaska 1984).

Rodriguez v. Riddell Sports, Inc., 242 F.3d 567 (5th Cir. 2001).

Rogers v. Ingersoll-Rand, 144 F.3d 841 (D.C. Cir. 1998).

Rosania v. Carmona, 706 A.2d 191 (N.J. Ct. App. 1998).

Schweichler v. Poway Unified Sch. Dist., 2005 Cal. App. Unpub. LEXIS 1553 (Ct. App. Feb. 23, 2005).

Scott v. Rapides Parish Sch. Bd., 732 So.2d 749 (La. Ct. App. 1999).

Smith v. J. H. West Elementary Sch., 861 N.Y.S. 2d 690 (App. Div. 2008).

Spotlite Skating Rink, Inc., v. Barnes, 988 So.2d 364 (Miss. 2008).

Tippett v. United States, 108 F.3d 1194 (10th Cir. 1997).

Traub v. Cornell Univ., 1998 U.S. Dist. LEXIS 5530 (N.D.N.Y. 1998), proceedings later stayed pending interlocutory appeal of denial of defendants' motion for summary judgment on assumption of risk issue, 1999 U.S. Dist. LEXIS 5315 (N.D.N.Y. 1999).

Wallach v. American Home Products Corp., Case Index #25642-97 (S.Ct., Nassau Cty., 2001), aff'd, 2002 N.Y. App. Div. LEXIS 12729 (N.Y. App. Div. 2002).

Statutes

Federal Tort Claims Act, 28 U.S.C. §§ 1346 et seq.

Pool and Spa Safety Act, 15 U.S.C. §§ 8001 et. seq.

Volunteer Protection Act of 1997, 42 U.S.C. §§ 14501 et seq. (PL 105-19).

Other Sources

57A Am. Jur. 2d Negligence § 193, § 412.

Charnley, K. B. (2005). Comment: Is the football culture out of bounds? Finding liability for Korey Stringer's death. Villanova Sport and Entertainment Law Journal, 12, 53–96.

Cohen, A. (2008, April). Objection! Athletic Business, 60–66.

Davis, T. (2008, Spring). UMKC sports law symposium: Emerging legal issues affecting amateur & professional sport: Tort liability of coaches for injuries to professional athletes: Overcoming policy and doctrinal barriers. UMKC Law Review, 76, 571–596.

Fainaru-Wade, M. (2009, March). Plancher's parents sue Central Florida. Retrieved June 9, 2009, from http://sports.espn.go.com/ncf/news/story?id=3973607.

Former Flyers player sues team and doctor over medical advice. (2002, May). Sports Lawyers Association Update, 5(1), 6–7.

Garrett, M. C. (1972). Allowance of punitive damages in products liability claims. Georgia Law Review, 6(3), 613–630.

Goldman, S. (2009, May). License to train. Fitness Business, 35–38.

Herbert, D. L. (2008, December). Certification for personal trainers. Fitness Management, 50.

Holtzman, B. (2009, March 31). Bus safety an issue for colleges. Retrieved June 9, 2009, from http://sports.espn.go.com/espn/otl/news/story?id=3997988.

Lloyd, J. (2009, May 5). High school athletes face serious concussion risks. USA Today, p. 7D.

Lloyd, J. (2009, May 28). Zachary's law aims to make a difference. USA Today, p. 4D.

McMannon, C. (2008, Oct/Nov). Support needed. Athletic Management, 51–55.

Nader, R. (1972). Unsafe at any speed: The designed-in dangers of the American automobile. New York: Grossman.

National Transportation Safety Board. (2003, January 21). Safety recommendation. Found at www.ntsb.gov/recs/letters/2003/a03%5F01.pdf.

NFHS approves new weigh-in rules. (2005, August/September). Athletic Management, 14–15.

NHTSA report on 15 passenger vans. (2005). Retrieved June 9, 2009, from www.nhtsa.dot.gov.

Operators face hurdles in Pool Act compliance. (2009, March). Fitness Business, 10–11.

Plant, M. L. (1957). Strict liability of manufacturers for injuries caused by defects in products: An opposing view. *Tennessee Law Review, 24*(7), 938–951.

Popke, M. (2003, December). Bill of health. *Athletic Business, 27,* 32–36.

Popke, M. (2004, July). Under water. *Athletic Business, 28,* 74–82.

Popke, M. (2009, June). Emergency response. *Athletic Business,* 15–17.

Restatement (Second) of Torts § 282, § 402A (1965).

Restatement (Third) of Torts § 2 and related comments (1997).

Sanborn, H. V. (1998, October). Manufacturer beware: A warning on a product may not bar liability, two courts hold in decisions citing the new Restatement. *ABA Journal,* pp. 30–31.

Scherzagier, A. (2009, April 14). Documents show Missouri missteps in O'Neal death. Retrieved June 9, 2009, from http://news.lp.findlaw.com/scripts/printer_friendly.pl?page=ap_stories/s/2060/04-14-2009.

Scholand, G. (2009, February/March). An ounce of prevention. *Athletic Management,* 63–67.

van der Smissen, B. (1990). *Legal liability and risk management for public and private entities.* Cincinnati, OH: Anderson Publishing.

Wilson, S. (2003, April/May). An ignored epidemic. *Athletic Management,* 47–53.

WEBSITE RESOURCES

www.aacca.org. ▪ This is the website for the American Association of Cheerleading Coaches and Administrators, an educational association for cheerleading coaches in the United States. There is a link to its safety course.

www.cdc.gov/MRSA. ▪ This is the Centers for Disease Control and Prevention website on MRSA. It provides the latest information on preventing MRSA infections.

www.ncaa.org/health-safety. ▪ This is the NCAA's link for health and safety issues for student-athletes. If you click on the link for "MRSA Poster Series," you can find a number of resources regarding MRSA.

www.ncaa.org/sports_sciences/safety_in_student_transportation.pdf. ▪ This is a lengthy resource guide for colleges and universities developed in May 2006 and entitled "Safety in Student Transportation."

www.poolsafetycouncil.org. ▪ This is the website for the Pool Safety Council, which provides information regarding the federal Pool & Spa Safety Act passed in December, 2008.

www.unc.edu/depts/nccsi. ▪ The National Center for Catastrophic Sport Injury Research provides information about its 25th annual report.

www.ncaapublications.com/Uploads/PDF/2007-08_sports_medicine_handbook6786d571-ad07-492e-85cc-075cb4c74e51.pdf. ▪ This website presents the criteria the NCAA has developed for an emergency action plan in intercollegiate sport in its *NCAA Sports Medicine Handbook, Guideline 1c Emergency Care and Coverage.*

www.sportssafety.org/articles/emergency-action-plan/. ▪ This website presents emergency action plan criteria for youth sports.

http://nonprofitrisk.org/library/state-liability.shtml. ▪ A free PDF listing of state liability laws for charitable organizations and their volunteers is available here. Since many sport-related activities function thanks to the help of volunteers, it is important to know how to minimize risk and harm due to negligence.

www.nationalaglawcenter.org/assets/recreationaluse/index.htm. ▪ This site features a listing of state statutes regarding the level of immunity for landowners when it comes to recreational use of their land. These statutes are in place to encourage landowners to allow their land to be used for recreational purposes.

www.ntsb.gov/recs/letters/2003/A03_01.pdf. ▪ This site contains the NTSB safety recommendation report. Appended to this report is the revised OSU transportation policy after the plane crash carrying members of the OSU basketball team.

Premises Liability and Sport Facility/Event Issues

INTRODUCTION

T his chapter first focuses on the legal responsibilities of owners of land and facilities to those who use the land and facilities. We will, therefore, address the general principles of premises liability law that hold property owners and possessors of property liable for injuries that occur on the property.

The second focus of this chapter is the variety of legal issues pertinent to facilities and events. We address legal issues relevant to the financing and construction of sport facilities. Next, legal issues related to several operational functions of a facility or an event will be discussed. These operational functions include contractual agreements commonly associated with facility and event operations and those associated with spectators/visitors, such as compliance with the Americans with Disabilities Act and spectator searches.

Facility operation, maintenance, and policies and procedures are often the foundation of a sport or recreation enterprise. In many cases, the only contact someone will have with an organization is by visiting its facility. To be competitive in the sport business, therefore, it is critical to be familiar with the legal principles applicable to this area. You may have many opportunities to develop policies and procedures for your facility that will minimize exposure to liability relative to the concerns addressed in this chapter. See Exhibit 16.1 for an overview of the managerial contexts, major legal issues, relevant laws, and illustrative cases pertinent to this chapter.

GENERAL PRINCIPLES OF PREMISES LIABILITY

W hen we refer to premises liability, we are discussing your legal responsibilities to those who use your land and facilities. We discussed the general principles of negligence in Chapter 15. Premises liability is predicated upon negligence principles; however, in most jurisdictions, your duty of care depends upon how the courts characterize those who are injured. Thus, the legal status of the injured person is critical to this type of lawsuit.

Status of the Person upon the Premises

In most jurisdictions, the duty owed by a facility owner or operator is dependent upon the status of the person who is on the premises. That is, the scope of the duty owed varies depending upon whether the person is on the property with permission or without permission. The duty also varies depending upon whether a person who is there with permission brings an economic benefit to the property owner. A minority of jurisdictions have abolished these status distinctions, in whole or in part, so the law of the state in which an incident occurred must be consulted. You should discuss these laws with your attorney.

Invitee

A person whose status is that of **invitee**—a person on the property with the permission of the landowner—is owed a duty of reasonable care by the premises owner. A **business invitee** is on the premises with the permission of the landowner and brings some economic benefit to the landowner. If I pay an admission charge to attend a sporting event, for example, I would be considered to be a business

| Management contexts in which issues related to premises liability and sport facilities and events may arise, with relevant laws and cases. | | EXHIBIT | 16.1 |

MANAGEMENT CONTEXT	MAJOR LEGAL ISSUES	RELEVANT LAW	ILLUSTRATIVE CASES
Maintenance of sport/ recreation facility	Determining duty owed to person on property	Negligence law	
	Defenses in premises liability case	Open and obvious danger	*Barbato*
		Distraction doctrine	*Lowe*
Owner of unimproved land	Recreational use statute	State statutes	*Prokop*
Sport/recreation facility planning	Duties to invitees to design facility safely	Negligence law	
Facility maintenance/ operation	Duty to warn	Negligence law	
	Duty to inspect		
	Duty to repair dangers		
Facility operation	Duty to provide emergency medical assistance	Negligence law	
		AED statutes	*Mayer, Rotolo*
Game/event management	Spectator injuries/crowd control	Foreseeability	*Bearman*
		Prior similar incidents rule	
	Spectators injured by players	Negligence law	
	Spectator hit by projectile	Limited duty rule	*Sciarrotta, Turner*
		Assumption of risk	
Financing proposals	Use of public funds for new sport facilities	State statutes and constitutions	*Rowe*
			Kelly
			King County
Team relocation	Long-term tenant agreements with professional teams	Contract law	*Minnesota Twins*
			City of Seattle
Property acquisition	Government condemnation of private lands for stadium projects	Fifth Amendment	*Berman*
			Kelo
Lease agreements	Lessor and lessee rights and responsibilities	Contract law negotiations	
Tickets	Ticket holder rights	Contract law/licenses	
Game contracts	Nature of rights and responsibilities for game contests	Contract law	*University of Louisville*
Access for people with disabilities	Avoiding discrimination against patrons with disabilities	Americans with Disabilities Act	*PGA Tour, Inc.*
			Miller
			Feldman
			Celano
			Clark
Spectator searches	Searching spectators prior to entry to facility	Fourth Amendment	*Katz*
			Johnston

invitee. If you are a university student, you would be considered a business invitee when you use the university's recreation facility. Even if you do not pay a fee on a per-use basis, you have paid for this amenity in your student fees. **Public invitees** are persons who are legally on public land. When you attend a community event at a local public park, for example, you are a public invitee.

In the case of *Yates v. Johnson County Board of Commissioners* (2008), a woman, after attending a circus, was injured on stairs leading from the school property. The circus was held on school property, and even though the school was not receiving any financial benefit from the circus, the circus attendee was considered to be a public invitee due to the implied invitation to the general public to enter the property to attend the circus.

Invitees are owed a duty of *reasonable care*. You should be familiar with this concept from the discussion of negligence and its elements in Chapter 15. In terms of premises liability, the duty of reasonable care means that the facility owner must make the facility reasonably safe for the use of invitees (see discussion later in this chapter).

Licensee

Unlike an invitee, a **licensee** is a person who is on the premises with the consent of the owner but who *does not bring any economic benefit to the property owner*. A person who is invited to your house for a party, for example, would be considered to be a licensee. According to Restatement (Second) of Torts § 342, the scope of duty owed to a licensee is considerably less than that owed to an invitee. There is no duty of inspection due to the licensee, and the landowner is liable for harm due to defects or dangers on the property only if the owner has knowledge of the danger and the licensee does not.

Trespasser

A **trespasser** is one who is on the premises without permission. In this situation, the landowner's scope of duty is diminished even further. The only duty is to refrain from wantonly inflicting injury upon that person (Restatement [Second] of Torts § 333). For example, you cannot protect your racing yacht from trespassers' intrusions by setting up a trapdoor that sends the intruders to the depths of the ocean should they step into the cabin.

This general rule relating to the duty owed to trespassers, however, is altered when the trespasser is a child. If the **attractive nuisance doctrine** is applicable, a duty of ordinary care is created when ordinarily there would be none. This doctrine provides that there is an affirmative duty on landowners to use reasonable care to protect child trespassers who may be attracted to the property because of some manmade or artificial feature of the land that poses some serious danger to a child (e.g., a swimming pool).

Defenses Available in a Premises Liability Case

As with any claim based on negligence, there are defenses to consider. Two prevalent defenses are that the danger is open and obvious, and recreational use statutes.

Danger is open and obvious

In a premises liability case, the plaintiff will not be able to recover if the danger complained of is **open and obvious.** According to the Restatement (Second) of Torts § 343A, "A possessor of land is not liable to invitees for physical harm caused to them by any activity or condition on the land whose danger is known or obvious to them, unless the possessor should anticipate the harm despite such knowledge or obviousness." If the danger is one that a plaintiff should be or actually is aware of, then the plaintiff has assumed the risk of that danger or defect. The defendant, therefore, will have no liability. The following Focus Case illustrates this point.

Barbato v. Hollow Hills Country Club

789 N.Y.S.2d 199 (App. Div. 2004)   **FOCUS CASE**

FACTS

The plaintiff was an experienced golfer who had played the defendant's golf course on several occasions. He was injured as he slipped and fell while descending a green. He admitted that he had seen that a sprinkler adjacent to the green was watering the area.

The trial court denied the defendant's motion to dismiss the complaint.

HOLDING

The New York appellate court reversed and dismissed the complaint.

RATIONALE

The court noted that the evidence showed that the plaintiff voluntarily assumed the risk of injury by playing on the wet surface. The plaintiff was fully aware of the condition of the grass; the wet grass was an open and obvious condition. Therefore, the plaintiff cannot prevail in his suit against the golf course.

There is an exception to the "open and obvious" condition defense, known as the **distraction doctrine.** This doctrine provides that, in some cases, even though a condition appears to be open and obvious, the plaintiff may somehow be distracted from appreciating the danger. For example, a person who is engaged in playing a game of basketball may know that a tire filled with concrete is being used as a base for the goal. However, the plaintiff may not be able to avoid coming down on that tire if he is focused on the game itself. In such a case, the distraction doctrine overcomes the open and obvious rule. See *Menough v. Woodfield Gardens* (1998). This doctrine applies in spectator situations as well. If a mascot is distracting fans during play and as a result a spectator fails to get out of the way of a ball, the fan has been distracted by the mascot and the open and obvious nature of the foul ball is secondary to the distraction. The following Focus Case provides an example of the distraction doctrine as applied to spectators.

Lowe v. California League of Professional Baseball

56 Cal. App. 4th 112 (App. Ct. 1997)   **FOCUS CASE**

FACTS

John Lowe was seriously injured when struck on the left side of his face by a foul ball while attending a professional baseball game. The game was being played at

"The Epicenter," the home field of the Rancho Cucamonga Quakes, a Class A, minor league baseball team. The Quakes, at their home games, feature a mascot called "Tremor." He is a caricature of a dinosaur, standing seven feet tall with a tail that protrudes from the costume. Tremor was performing his antics in the stands just along the left field foul line. Tremor was behind plaintiff and had been touching him with his (Tremor's) tail. Lowe was distracted and turned toward Tremor. In the next moment, just as Lowe returned his attention to the playing field, he was struck by a foul ball before he could react to it. Very serious injuries resulted from the impact. As a result, the underlying action was commenced against the California League of Professional Baseball and Valley Baseball Club, Inc., which does business as the Quakes. The case was resolved in the trial court by summary judgment entered in favor of defendants.

HOLDING

The court of appeals reversed.

RATIONALE

The Quakes were able to persuade the trial court, under the doctrine of primary assumption of the risk (*Knight v. Jewett,* Cal. 1992), that defendants owed no duty to the plaintiff, as a spectator, to protect him from foul balls. Such rationalization was faulty. Under *Knight,* defendants had a duty *not to increase* the inherent risks to which spectators at professional baseball games are regularly exposed and which they assume. As a result, a triable issue of fact remained, namely whether the Quakes' mascot cavorting in the stands and distracting plaintiff's attention, while the game was in progress, constituted a breach of that duty—that is, whether it constituted negligence in the form of increasing the inherent risk to plaintiff of being struck by a foul ball. The California Supreme Court has stated (in the context of injuries to participants) that a defendant generally has no duty to eliminate or protect a plaintiff from risks inherent to the sport itself, but has only a duty not to increase those risks. A mascot is not integral to the sport of baseball.

In other words, the key inquiry here is whether the risk that led to plaintiff's injury involved some feature or aspect of the game that is inevitable or unavoidable in the actual playing of the game. In the first instance, foul balls hit into the spectators' area clearly create a risk of injury. If such foul balls were to be eliminated, it would be impossible to play the game. Thus, foul balls represent an inherent risk to spectators attending baseball games. Under *Knight,* such risk is assumed. Can the same thing be said about the antics of the mascot? The court decided no.

Recreational use statutes

All states have passed a type of statute that confers immunity upon a landowner in certain situations. As discussed in Chapter 15, these statutes are designed to encourage landowners to open portions of their unimproved land to the general public to use for recreational purposes, free of charge. Although this is the common intent of the statutes, they vary widely in interpretation from state to state. The following is a representative case from Minnesota.

Prokop v. Independent School District #625

FACTS

A father was injured during a recreational team batting practice with his son. The practice was being held on a public school field. The father was hit in the face by the baseball when the L-screen, a piece of equipment used to protect the pitcher in batting practice, failed, allowing the ball to hit the father. The L-screen had plainly visible holes, gaps, and repair knots. No one had complained to the school district about the condition of the L-screen. The father sued, alleging negligence by the school district. The trial court, however, granted summary judgment to the district as it held that the district was protected by recreational use immunity.

HOLDING

The Minnesota appellate court affirmed.

RATIONALE

First, the court noted that under Minnesota law the question of whether recreational use immunity is applicable is based not on the activity being performed by the injured person but on the intended recreational function of the property. In this case, the L-screen was covered by recreational use immunity because it facilitated the use of the property for recreational use.

Second, the trespasser liability exception is not applicable. This exception to recreational use immunity applies if the landowner engaged in conduct that would entitle a trespasser to damages against a private person. In this case, to find the exception applicable, there would have to be evidence that the school district had actual knowledge of the dangerous condition posed by the L-screen. The court noted that there had been no complaints or repair requests made concerning the L-screen. Absent actual knowledge of the danger, there can be no trespasser liability exception.

DUTIES OWED TO INVITEES

A facility owner or operator has the duty of reasonable care for the safety of invitees. This section discusses a number of these obligations, including the duty to design a safe facility, the duty to warn of dangers, the duty to inspect for defects, the duty to repair dangers promptly, and the duty to provide emergency medical assistance.

Duty to Design the Facility Safely

There is a duty to design a facility safely for its intended uses. This, of course, should be done in conjunction with an architectural firm that has expertise in the type of facility being constructed. It is a fact of life that construction budgets are often overrun and initial plans are often modified. Care must be taken, however,

Duty to Inspect

- Develop an inspection protocol for all land and facilities. Use inspection checklists to make sure that the inspection is thoroughly completed.

- Ensure that the persons who do facility inspections are properly trained to identify dangerous conditions.

- Make sure that inspections are done as often as necessary based on the type of facility and the use of the facility.

to ensure that cost-saving modifications do not affect safety issues.

If mandatory safety standards are in force, you must ensure that these standards are adhered to. A failure to do so may result in negligence per se (discussed in Chapter 15). Even if a standard is only a "recommendation" or a "suggestion," experts use these to set the standard of care, and courts give great deference to national association standards even if they are voluntary in nature.

Playgrounds and pools offer special challenges in this regard (Brown, 2008). Stadium escalators and bleachers also pose design issues (Steinbach, April, 2008; Steinbach, June, 2008).

Duty to Warn

The courts have held that there is a duty to warn invitees about hidden dangers—those dangers that would not be obvious to an average user. Hidden dangers are ones that the user is not able to discover with a casual inspection.

For example, you own a private beach and you charge admission for users to sunbathe and swim there. From the beach, the water looks calm and inviting. An average user of the area would not realize that there is a severe undertow in the water not far from shore. You have an obligation to post a warning sign concerning this danger since it is not obvious to the average swimmer using your beach.

Duty to Inspect

The facility possessor has the duty of reasonable inspection to discover dangers. What is reasonable inspection depends upon the frequency and type of use of the area. For example, an infrequently used area may reasonably be inspected less often than a high-use area in a facility.

Since landowners are responsible to remedy defects of which they, as reasonably prudent landowners, should have been aware, as well as defects of which they are actually aware, it is imperative to have a regular protocol for inspection. **Actual notice** implies that the landowner knows of a danger through inspection by employees. **Constructive notice** means that a court will hold a landowner responsible for dangers that the landowner should know about if reasonable inspections were undertaken. (See the *Bearman* case, discussed later, regarding the concepts of actual and constructive notice.)

Duty to Repair Dangers

- Develop a system for reporting dangerous conditions so that all employees know how to report a facility problem promptly. Make sure that the reports are conveyed promptly to the persons who can actually remedy them.

- Make sure that warning signs are placed in plain view and that they remain legible.

Duty to Repair Dangers

After a property owner has notice of a danger, the danger must be repaired or remedied within a reasonable period of time. As with all questions of reasonableness, that becomes a question of fact for a jury to decide. In some cases, reasonable behavior may mean that a danger cannot be repaired quickly but that users are kept away from the dangerous area (by roping it off, using cones to warn of the danger, etc.). The following hypothetical case illustrates this concept.

considering . . .   DUTY TO REPAIR DANGERS

Mary King is the athletic director at New River High School. She is responsible for overseeing all school athletic events. One evening at a home volleyball match a spectator spills a soda as she climbs the bleachers. The person who is walking immediately behind her slips and falls because of the spill.

Question

■ Is the school liable?

Note how you would answer the question and then check your response using the Analysis & Discussion at the end of this chapter.

Duty to Provide Emergency Medical Assistance

Under Restatement (Second) of Torts § 314A at 118 (1965), "a possessor of land who holds it open to the public is under a similar duty to members of the public who enter in response to his invitation." The "similar duty" is to "give them first aid after the landowner knows or has reason to know that they are ill or injured, and to care for them until they can be cared for by others." This duty owed to the business invitee generally means that there is an obligation to provide emergency first aid and to have a protocol to get further medical assistance in a timely manner (see Chapter 15). The following Focus Case concerns whether this duty extends to the provision of defibrillators.

L.A. Fitness International v. Mayer

| 980 So.2d 550 (Fla. Dist. Ct. App. 2008) | FOCUS CASE |

FACTS

A patron at a health club died while using a stepping machine at the defendant's club. The patron died from hypertrophic cardiomyopathy. The decedent's estate sued the club, alleging negligence for failing to have an automated external defibrillator (AED) on its premises for use in medical emergencies. When this incident occurred in 2003, the club was not required by law to have an AED on the premises. A jury found the club to be 85 percent negligent and awarded damages.

HOLDING

The appellate court reversed and remanded the matter to enter judgment for the club.

RATIONALE

According to the court there is no common law or statutory duty to have an AED on the defendant's premises. The Florida legislature does not require that an AED be placed on the premises. The court also cited cases from California, Illinois, and New York, which found no common law duty by a health club to have an AED on the premises. Therefore, there was no breach of duty in failing to have an AED, and the health club met its duty of care by summoning paramedics within a reasonable time.

The *Mayer* case by no means settles this question for all jurisdictions. For example, in the case of *Fowler v. Bally Total Fitness* (2008), a Maryland circuit court held that a health club, even in a state that does not mandate the presence of an AED in a health or fitness club, may be seen as grossly negligent for a failure to have an AED for its patrons' medical emergencies. According to the court, the failure to have such life-saving equipment shows indifference to the welfare of its patrons (Wolohan, 2008).

In the following Focus Case, the issue was whether a venue that had installed an AED had a duty to inform the users of the facility of its availability.

Rotolo v. San Jose Sports and Entertainment

FOCUS CASE   151 Cal. App. 4th 307 (2007)

FACTS

During an ice hockey tournament game held at the defendant's venue, a 17-year-old player suffered sudden cardiac arrest. Two event bystanders who were trained in medical emergencies began to administer CPR. Two other individuals, including one employee from the venue, called 911. None of the tournament participants, including coaches and referees, was aware that an automated external defibrillator (AED) was located on the wall near the penalty box of the rink where the player collapsed. Despite the efforts of those giving CPR, the player died. The parents of the deceased brought a negligence action against the venue alleging that it had a duty of care to notify all invitees of the existence and location of the AED unit. The trial court entered judgment in favor of the defendant.

HOLDING

The California appellate court affirmed the judgment.

RATIONALE

The court first addressed the legislation that the state of California passed regarding AEDs. The California statutes encourage the availability of AEDs by providing immunity from liability for those who acquire the devices. The statutes do not require venues to acquire AEDS; the legislation simply provides immunity for those who do provide them if the venue meets certain requirements regarding maintenance, testing, and notice to tenants. The court reasoned that there was nothing in the language of the statute to require a building owner to give notice concerning the AEDs to members of the public expected to use the building. Although the statutes reflect a legislative recognition that AEDS can save lives, the court declined to add a duty to notify building users when the legislature declined to add that type of obligation statutorily.

In terms of common law duty, although there is a special relationship between the building owner and invitees, the venue did nothing in this case to maintain the facility unsafely or unreasonably increase the risk that a player would succumb to cardiac arrest. But the common law does not require a duty imposed upon a sport property owner to provide notice to those who are using the facility of the availability of medical devices upon the premises. There is no duty in this case and therefore, no liability.

All states have some law or regulation in force requiring the availability of automated external defibrillators (AEDs) in a number of types of public buildings, including apartment buildings, public schools, some transportation centers, some office complexes, and other facilities in which sudden cardiac arrest may often occur. Eleven states have passed legislation mandating the use of AEDs in health clubs; some also provide immunity for ordinary negligence in the use of the equipment (Goldman, 2009). See Exhibit 16.2 for an example of such a statutory provision.

Rhode Island statute regarding health clubs and use of AEDs.	EXHIBIT **16.2**

R.I. GEN. LAWS § 5-50-12 (2009)

§ 5-50-12. Defibrillators.

(a) Every health club registered with the department of attorney general pursuant to this chapter shall have at least one automated external defibrillator (AED) on the premises. The AED will at all times be deployed in a manner which best provides accessibility to staff, members and guests. At least one employee per shift must be properly trained by the American Heart Association or comparable state recognized agency in cardiopulmonary resuscitation (CPR) and AED, and must be on duty during hours of operation.

(b) Any facility that has a health club on premises that currently complies with all parts within this act shall be exempted from duplication.

(c) A cause of action against a health club or its employees, in connection with the use or nonuse of an AED, shall not exist except in cases where the health club has failed to purchase an AED as required under this act and in cases of willful or wanton negligence.

(d) A knowing or willful violation of this section by a health club may result in suspension or revocation of its registration.

(e) Any health club that operates a facility on a pass key basis with no attending employee on duty is exempt from the trained employee on duty requirement set forth in subsection (a) of this section.

Competitive Advantage
STRATEGIES

Duty to Provide Emergency Medical Assistance

- Prior to purchasing an AED, make sure you have a comprehensive system to manage the program and a quality assurance program to make sure that you keep proper records, maintain the devices, and review your program as necessary.

- Make sure that you know all relevant state law pertaining to the use of AEDs in your facility.

- Make sure that your AED program is developed with the assistance of qualified medical personnel.

- Ensure that your employees are trained properly in the use of the AED through recognized programs (such as the American Heart Association).

- Integrate the use of the AED into your overall emergency medical protocol.

This is an area in which the standard of care is evolving, and owners must exercise vigilance to ensure that their organizations are in compliance with state statutes (Connaughton, Spengler, & Zhang, 2007). The status of state legislation is available at www.ncsl.org/IssuesResearch/Health/LawsonCardiacArrestandDefibrillatorsAEDS/tabid/14506/default.aspx. Also, in June 2006, the National Athletic Trainers' Association issued recommendations for high school and college athletic programs that access to defibrillators occur within three to five minutes of cardiac arrest (Mihoces, 2006).

There is also a duty to have emergency response plans in place to deal with states of emergency in a facility, whether the emergency arises from medical disasters, fire, bomb threats, power loss, or weather-related circumstances. Evacuation plans should be developed, and an emergency response team should be formed to deal with all types of emergency situations within a facility.

SPECTATOR INJURIES

Generally, spectators at a facility or event are invitees, and the owner has a duty of reasonable care for their safety. This section discusses a number of issues relating to spectator injuries: crowd control, injuries related to alcohol consumption, injuries caused by projectiles from the playing area, and other spectator injuries.

Crowd Control

In tort law, there is generally no duty to protect others from the actions of a third party. However, a landowner has the duty to keep a facility reasonably safe for spectators. As a part of this duty, "a landowner who opens his property to the public for business purposes has a duty to exercise *reasonable care* to protect the public from physical harm caused by the accidental, negligent, or intentionally harmful acts of third persons" (Restatement [Second] of Torts § 344). What is reasonable care is predicated on the question of what is foreseeable. The following is a seminal case regarding this proposition.

Bearman v. University of Notre Dame

FOCUS CASE   453 N.E.2d 1196 (Ind. Ct. App. 1983)

FACTS

Christenna Bearman attended a Notre Dame football game in 1979. She left the game before it ended and walked through a parking lot toward her car. She saw two men who appeared to be drunk and fighting and did not walk toward the altercation. The two fighters walked away from each other, and then one of the men pushed the other, falling into Bearman from behind, breaking her leg. There were no security personnel from Notre Dame in the area when the injury occurred.

Bearman sued, alleging that she, as a business invitee, should have been protected by Notre Dame from the act of this third party. Notre Dame argued that it had no liability absent any actual notice of a particular danger to a patron.

The trial court granted Notre Dame's motion for summary judgment.

HOLDING

The Indiana Court of Appeals reversed and remanded.

RATIONALE

In this case Notre Dame argued that it had no duty of care regarding the third party actions because it had no actual knowledge of a particular disturbance in the parking lot. However, the court noted that actual knowledge is not the only concern here; a facility owner may also have liability if it has constructive knowledge of a danger. If Notre Dame should reasonably anticipate careless or criminal conduct by third parties, it may be under a duty to take precautions against this conduct.

The court then built a logical chain of foreseeability from the fact that the university was fully aware of the tailgating that occurred before and during games in university parking lots. The university was fully cognizant that tailgating often includes the consumption of alcoholic beverages, which results in some patrons becoming intoxicated. Those inebriates then pose a general threat to the safety of other patrons. The court concluded, therefore, that Notre Dame had a duty to take reasonable precautions to protect those who attend its football games from injury caused by the acts of third parties.

The *Bearman* case is important because it emphasized that a facility owner is responsible to deal not only with dangers of which the owner has *actual knowledge*—for example, when facility employees know that a brawl is occurring—but that the owner has a duty to exercise care regarding dangers of which the owner should, as a reasonably prudent facility owner, be aware—that is, *constructive knowledge*. This point is crucial because it puts a duty of inspection and/or awareness upon a facility owner. Whether the danger is one of sagging bleachers or rowdy fans, courts expect facility owners to act reasonably in ascertaining whether a danger may exist. If the danger is reasonably foreseeable, there is a duty to exercise care in taking precautions against that danger.

For example, in the case of *Lane v. Saint Paul's College* (2008), a college basketball player traveled with her team to another school for a conference contest. During the game the player was assaulted by a player on the opposing team, and a number of spectators joined in the assault. The player sued the conference, Central Intercollegiate Athletic Association (CIAA), on the basis that the CIAA oversaw the event and was responsible for the management of the event including security. The court overruled the motion to dismiss by the CIAA on the basis that the CIAA knew that assaults had happened before at the defendant school. The CIAA had been informed of a specific imminent risk, and additional security should have

STRATEGIES

Crowd Control

- Develop crowd control plans based on factors specific to a contest, such as whether there is a rivalry, whether there has been prior violence, whether alcohol will be served, and what the demographics of a contest are likely to be. Use all information available to determine what crowd behaviors may be foreseeable.

- At football games, consider whether you will attempt to keep fans off the field or simply control their access to goalposts. Consider the use of goalposts that can be lowered quickly, either mechanically or manually, to avoid fan injury during postgame celebrations.

- For youth sports, consider having parents sign an agreement to cheer only in ways that are positive and that support the goal of good sportsmanship.

been added to prevent a foreseeable risk. In contrast, in the case of *Uzun v. Oakwood Sports Center of Hamden* (2008), a soccer player was pushed and intentionally forced to the ground by an opposing player. In the suit against the venue for negligence in security, the court held that the assault was not foreseeable since the participant had not demonstrated any violent behavior during the game or in past games.

Unfortunately, fighting and the use of weapons at sporting events are becoming more prevalent. Many high schools have developed plans to deal with violence and unsportsmanlike conduct, often instituting a zero tolerance policy for any bad behavior (Scholand, 2006). The NCAA issued a report on crowd control issues (www.ncaa.org/Sportsmanship/SportsmanshipFanBehavior/report.pdf). Also, the NFL has developed a new code of conduct regarding fan behavior in an effort to reduce disruptive behavior during games (Wood, 2008).

Injuries Due to Alcohol Consumption

Alcohol consumption is tied to the spectator experience in sport. Tailgating is very common, and many tailgaters begin their consumption of alcohol hours prior to a contest, sometimes setting up more than five hours before game time (River of Dreams, 2005). At Louisiana State University (LSU), the football stadium holds 91,600 but typically approximately 100,000 people show up, leaving nearly 10,000 individuals to engage in tailgating with no hope of entering the stadium. The LSU athletic department has characterized the tailgating as a "real Mardi Gras" (Steinbach, 2003, p. 30). The *Bearman* case showed the importance of foreseeability in crowd control liability. The prevalence of tailgating and the ever-present possibility of the overconsumption of alcohol make it foreseeable to a facility owner that some misbehavior due to alcohol will occur. Thus a facility owner or operator must act reasonably to have sufficient personnel to deal with the prospect of rowdy, inebriated fans.

There is another liability issue associated with alcohol. **Dram shop acts** provide for liability against those who commercially serve alcohol to minors or to persons who are visibly intoxicated when the inebriate subsequently injures third parties. When a person who has overconsumed alcohol drives drunk and injures or kills an innocent motorist, the person (and entity) who served the alcohol may be liable.

A landmark judgment in the amount of $135 million was awarded against Aramark, the liquor concessionaire at Giants Stadium. The jury included punitive damages of $75 million because they believed that Aramark had sold beer to a person who was visibly intoxicated (Dvorchak, 2005). Although the judgment was reversed on evidentiary grounds, a substantial settlement was reached

(Gottlieb, 2008). The patron, Daniel Lanzaro, left the stadium in his truck with a blood alcohol level 2.5 times the legal limit and collided with a family in a car. The child in the car, two-year-old Antonia Verni, became a quadriplegic (Southall & Sharp, 2006). This award may cause stadium concessionaires to reevaluate some of their business practices. Alcohol management is a constant challenge (Steinbach, October 2008).

Injuries Caused by Projectiles from the Playing Area

Spectators at baseball or hockey games are frequently hit by batted balls, broken bats, or hockey pucks. It is part of the excitement for spectators at such events to be as close to the action as possible with an unimpeded view. However, such closeness to the action carries certain risks, since balls, bats, and pucks do find their way into the stands and can be dangerous projectiles. Some courts have chosen to resolve the tension by applying the "limited duty" rule in these circumstances. The **limited duty rule** provides that a facility owner "is not liable for injuries to spectators that result from projectiles leaving the field during play if safety screening had been provided . . . and there are a sufficient number of protected seats to meet ordinary demand" (*Benejam v. Detroit Tigers, Inc.,* 2001, p. 219). Let's look at a case that illustrates this principle.

Competitive Advantage
STRATEGIES

Injuries Due to Alcohol Consumption

- Develop alcohol management policies regarding tailgating and, if applicable, service of alcohol.

- Do not allow patrons to return to the parking lot during the game or after the end of the game to continue their tailgating.

- Enforce all alcohol management policies consistently and fairly.

- Educate patrons regarding what constitutes responsible drinking.

- Give incentives to "designated drivers" to encourage this practice.

- If you use an independent contractor as your liquor concessionaire, select a concessionaire that has a strong safety record and that uses recognized training techniques, such as TIPS and TEAM.

Sciarrotta v. Global Spectrum

944 A.2d 630 (N.J. 2008)	FOCUS CASE

FACTS

The plaintiffs, Denise and Peter Sciarrotta, attended an East Coast Hockey League game on January 4, 2003, at the Sovereign Bank Arena. They were seated in the sixth or seventh row above the ice, near the center of the arena, and above the Plexiglas barriers. During the teams' warm-up session, Denise Sciarrotta was struck in the head by a puck that hit the side of the goal post and ricocheted into the stands. During warm-ups, there are dozens of pucks on the ice being passed and shot toward the goal. The plaintiffs sued the defendant arena alleging that a dangerous condition existed. The trial court granted the defendants' motion for summary judgment.

The appellate court reversed, as it held that the injured plaintiff could have great difficulty attending to the multiple pucks flying all over the arena during warm-up. The measures that may be adequate to protect a spectator during a game may not be adequate during warm-ups. This "heightened vulnerability" suggests that the business invitee rule of liability should be used here instead of the limited duty rule.

HOLDING

The New Jersey Supreme Court reversed.

RATIONALE

First, the court identified the essence of the limited duty rule. Essentially, a sport venue has satisfied its duty of care to patrons regarding the perils of objects leaving the field of play and injuring spectators in the stands if the venue owner provides screened seating in the most dangerous section of the stands sufficient for those spectators who desire protected seats on an ordinary occasion. In this situation, the court had to decide whether the limited duty rule should apply to the warm-up period before the game is played. In regard to this point, the court noted that the plaintiff argued that the limited duty rule should not apply to warm-ups because there were so many pucks flying around. However, the court noted that there was no factual, logical, or legal reason to restrict the scope of the limited duty rule to "the temporal limits of the game itself" (p. 637). The court ruled that "to demand separate and distinct duties of care in respect of the same peril in the same area based solely on the temporary goings-on on the field of play is impractical and not grounded in reason" (pp. 637–638).

Competitive Advantage
STRATEGIES

Injuries by Projectiles from the Playing Area

- At baseball or hockey games, make sure that patrons who wish to be seated in protected areas are given the opportunity to do so.

- Make sure that mascots do not distract patrons from the field of play while the game is ongoing.

- At baseball games, make sure that spectators are protected from foul balls while they are purchasing food or beverages from mobile concessions areas.

Another recent case from Nevada, *Turner v. Mandalay Sports Entertainment* (2008), extended the limited duty rule to a situation in which a patron had her nose broken by a foul ball as she ate in the beer garden, a concessions area located several hundred feet from home plate on the top viewing level of a minor league baseball park. The patron chose not to sit in a protected area of the park, and the beer garden, according to the court, did not pose "an unduly high risk of injury" from foul balls. Therefore, the limited duty rule was applicable and the patron was unable to prevail.

The analyses in *Sciarrotta* and *Turner* focused on the limited duty rule, which was satisfied by the venues in these cases. Other courts have analyzed the same type of factual situation and come to the same result by determining that the defense of primary assumption of risk should apply. For example, in the case of *Rees v. Cleveland Indians Baseball Company, Inc.* (2004), the plaintiff was hit in the face by a broken bat that flew into the stands behind third base. The Ohio Court of Appeals found that there was no liability here since the plaintiff was familiar with the stadium, knew the game of baseball, and knew that she was unprotected from objects that might enter the stands. The court found that the defense of primary assumption of risk applied and that no duty was owed to the plaintiff.

FACILITY FINANCING AND CONSTRUCTION ISSUES

I n this section we explore legal issues related to facility financing proposals, team relocation, and property acquisition for new stadiums and arenas. We have witnessed significant changes in facility financing over the past 90 years. Prior to the 1960s, facilities like Chicago's Wrigley Field and Boston's Fenway Park were funded primarily or entirely by teams and their owners. A funding shift began after World War II, whereby public rather than private financing was used to pay for most or all of a facility. State and local governments viewed the stadiums and arenas as a benefit not only to the teams but the larger communities where the facilities were located. From 1962 to 2003, over $15 billion was spent on stadiums and arenas for professional sports teams located around the United States, and almost half of the funding was provided by state and local governments (Howard & Crompton, 2005).

Starting in the mid-1980s, taxpayers began to push back on public financing, particularly as teams and owners demanded new facilities to replace seemingly suitable ones already in existence. Although the share of public funding has decreased, the overall amount has increased because of the high rate of stadium construction (Brown et al., 2010). Requests were also made for single-use facilities rather than hosting two sports in the same multipurpose stadium. Additionally, the teams and owners asked for new amenities like luxury boxes and club seats in order to increase their revenue from the sale of such seats. The luxury amenities have caused the building costs of the new facilities to skyrocket. The average facility cost jumped from $87 million during the 1970s and early 1980s to $220 million by the late 1990s (Howard & Crompton, 2005). Costs continue to escalate. For example, the Dallas Cowboys recently built a new football stadium for a staggering $1.2 billion. The City of Arlington, Texas, where the facility is located, contributed $325 million through increases in sales, hotel, and car taxes. The team provided an additional $150 million, and team owner Jerry Jones agreed to pay the remaining costs with personal funds (Ballparks, 2010). The Cowboys and their owner were asked to pay a sizable portion of the construction costs, but the public investment of funds was still substantial. Despite a few examples of strong public opposition or cost sharing, support for new sport stadiums continues to grow in the United States. The New York Yankees $1.3 billion baseball stadium is funded largely by New York City and the state of New York, with over $200 million in government subsidies and close to $1 billion in tax-exempt bonds (Farley, 2008).

Financing Plans and Proposals

With the taxpayers bearing the bulk of the cost, it has become fairly common for new stadium proposals involving public financing to be challenged in the courts. The legal issues raised often include

- whether a voting referendum is necessary (i.e., whether the public must be allowed to approve or reject the financing proposal at the polls)
- whether a city, county, or state is authorized to issue bonds to finance the construction (e.g., whether a city can increase its debt to or beyond certain levels)
- whether public money can be used to assist private parties (i.e., whether a new stadium is in the public interest) (Greenberg, 2004)

Lawsuits filed by stadium opponents raise complex constitutional and statutory issues that are beyond the scope of this text, but the underlying policy arguments will certainly impact sport managers who are involved in the planning, financing, and construction of new sport facilities. The basic argument a stadium manager will encounter is whether the use of taxpayer money to construct private sport facilities with no guarantee of financial repayment is an appropriate or permitted use of public funds.

From the mid-1980s through the end of the 1990s many opponents of stadium plans raised legal challenges. For example, in *Rowe v. Pinellas Sports Authority* (1984), opponents challenged the new dome in St. Petersburg, Florida, on statutory and constitutional grounds, but the Florida Supreme Court held that state sunshine laws and the Florida Constitution were not violated. Similarly, in *Kelly v. Marylanders for Sports Sanity, Inc.,* in 1987, opponents sued to force a referendum for the financing plan for Oriole Park at Camden Yards in Baltimore, Maryland, but the Maryland Court of Appeals held that the appropriation was proper. And finally, in *King County v. Taxpayers* (1997) opponents of the Seattle Mariners financing plan argued that the plan was an unconstitutional gift of public money and that legislative authority had been unconstitutionally delegated to the public facilities district, but the Washington Supreme Court upheld the financing plan and said the stadium project served a valid public purpose.

Even though opponents of public financing of sports stadiums have not been particularly successful in their opposition, the legal challenges can pose a threat to new stadium financing proposals in terms of the litigation costs and delays in the projects themselves when challenged.

Team Relocation

While most legal challenges involving stadium projects relate to the financing plan, additional legal challenges have resulted after a stadium has been financed and built because a team threatens to leave for another city with an even newer stadium or arena.

As mentioned previously, as player salaries and team operating costs continue to escalate, professional sport teams seek new facilities as a way to increase revenues. Many new stadiums which are operated by a professional sports team have turned to high-priced features like luxury boxes, club seats, and personal seat licenses to increase revenue (*SportsBusiness Journal,* 2010). Typically, in a new sports stadium with a major league sports team, the team is the primary tenant and is responsible for the operation of the stadium. These lease agreements are usually very advantageous to the team in that the team pays little if any rent and retains a large share of revenue streams from concessions, advertising, luxury suites, club seats, naming rights, and ticket sales. However, cities also recognize that the benefits bestowed upon the team represent a significant investment of public funds and trust such that the team's commitment to stay in the city is critical for the city to reap the economic rewards of its investment. Since the Baltimore Colts loaded their Mayflower moving vans under cover of darkness on a cold, snowy morning on March 28, 1984, to relocate to Indianapolis, cities have struggled with how to ensure that their coveted professional sport franchises remain loyal to their city.

To this day, even though Baltimore has since acquired a new NFL franchise with the Ravens, Baltimore fans still harbor resentment toward the NFL team located in Indianapolis, Indiana (Hybl, 2010).

Cities often use the lure of a new stadium to attract a major league sports franchise even though the sport franchise is already committed to a long-term lease agreement in its home city. Since it is likely that the home stadium was primarily funded with public monies, many communities seek to prevent the sport franchise from leaving. A few cities have exercised their contractual rights under the stadium or arena lease agreements to either prevent the team from leaving or at least slow its departure. The City of Minneapolis was successful in forcing the Minnesota Twins to honor its lease agreement with the city when Major League Baseball announced plans to buy the team and then eliminate it from the league or relocate the franchise (*Metropolitan Sports Facilities Commission v. Minnesota Twins Partnership,* 2002). This case is important because the court required the Twins to play its final season in Minnesota, pointing out that a lease agreement with a professional sport franchise creates a different relationship than a standard commercial lease agreement. The relationship is more than just a landlord/tenant relationship because a professional sport franchise is a limited and valuable right, the facility it occupies is largely paid for with public dollars, and a franchise is a community asset.

Another recent example involved the City of Seattle and the Seattle Sonics NBA franchise. The City of Seattle sued to enforce the Sonics' Key Arena lease and sought a court order forcing the team to play out its lease at the Key Arena through September 2010. The City argued that a cash settlement from the NBA franchise to leave early would not be an adequate remedy. The Sonics tried to force the dispute to arbitration. However, the lease expressly said that disputes between the city and the team over the "term" or length of the lease were not subject to arbitration (Brunner, 2007). The case was suddenly settled during trial in Oklahoma City, which paved the way for the franchise to move to Oklahoma City. The Sonics owner Clay Bennett agreed to pay the City of Seattle $45 million, plus another $30 million in five years if the NBA had not agreed to place another franchise in Seattle. The City of Seattle also retained the Sonics name and the team's green and gold colors (Alberg, 2008).

Despite the pain of losing a team to another city, cities and fans usually have few legal remedies to prevent a team from relocating and abandoning the city.

Stadium Location and Property Acquisition

The next common legal issue associated with new stadiums and arenas relates to securing a desirable location. Some stadium or arena projects simply involve tearing down or imploding the old stadium or arena and building the new one. However, more frequently stadium and arena projects involve much more than just the stadium and arena. It is now common for these construction projects to include hotels, restaurants, shopping malls, and other related commercial facilities. In these types of projects, more land is needed; thus both commercial and residential properties surrounding these stadium projects are vulnerable to what is known as a "taking" by the city or county so that the land can be used for the stadium project.

Competitive Advantage
STRATEGIES

Facility Financing and Construction

- Stadium financing is a highly specialized area. Whether representing teams and leagues, state and local governments, or citizen interest groups, sport managers need legal counsel to prepare contracts with public partners and to anticipate potential lawsuits, as well as to advise the parties on important tax and property law issues.

- Anticipating legal challenges or public criticism of a project in advance enables the parties to resolve disputes more quickly and perhaps less publicly.

- Potential delays due to legal challenges should be taken into consideration in setting financing and construction timelines.

Naturally, government taking of privately owned commercial and residential properties is controversial and subject to legal challenges under the Fifth Amendment to the Constitution and most state constitutions as well. The Fifth Amendment limits the power of the government to interfere with private property rights and expressly states: ". . . nor shall private property be taken for public use, without just compensation." When a government agency seizes private land for public use, it exercises its eminent domain or condemnation powers to condemn land while providing its previous owners with fair market value (Garner et al., 2004). Historically, the government used eminent domain powers only for projects such as the construction of new roads, bridges, dams, or utilities that were considered a public use of the private land taken. However, beginning in the 1950s the Supreme Court expanded the concept of public use to include a public purpose. The Supreme Court unanimously ruled that private property could be condemned and resold to another private party because the redevelopment plan served a public purpose to improve a blighted neighborhood even though the land being taken was being used productively by the property owners and was not blighted (*Berman v. Parker*, 1954).

More recently, in 2000, the City of New London, Connecticut, implemented a redevelopment project to increase tax revenues and improve the economic conditions within its municipality. Although the 115 residential and commercial lots within the 90 acres to be acquired and redeveloped were not "blighted," the city eventually utilized its eminent domain power to acquire 15 parcels owned by citizens who refused to sell to the redevelopment corporation (*Kelo v. City of New London*, 2005). Kelo and other owners argued that seizing one party's private property in order to transfer ownership to another private entity—strictly for the economic benefit of the community—did not qualify as proper public use or purpose (*Kelo v. City of New London*, 2005). On June 23, 2005, the Supreme Court (5–4) held for the city of New London. The Court reasoned that, under Connecticut state law, public benefits, such as the economic growth and increased taxes likely to result from the city's redevelopment plans, qualified such condemnation and seizure of private property as a permissible "public use" under the Fifth Amendment's Takings Clause.

Use of eminent domain or condemnation powers for an overall public purpose also permits economic development as a rationale for taking property of one private citizen and selling it to another private citizen to redevelop for the benefit of the public. Some critics suggest the *Berman* decision "forged an unholy alliance between cities strapped for cash and entrepreneurs promising economic bounty" (Greenberg, 2005). The Institute for Justice documented over 10,000 eminent domain cases from 1998–2002 in which local governments attempted to condemn real estate for private redevelopment (Greenberg, 2005).

Sport organizations, particularly those operating in large facilities, are no strangers to the use of eminent domain and condemnation for construction of new sport stadiums. Recent eminent domain controversies involved the Dallas Cowboys (Joyner, 2005; Mosier, 2008), Florida Marlins ("SB 4 and Eminent Domain News," 2005), Washington Nationals (Natarajan & O'Connell, 2007), Oklahoma State University ("Oklahoma State wins," 2009), and the Atlantic Yards project in Brooklyn (Bagli, 2009).

Eminent domain has often assisted a team's new stadium construction. In 1990, eminent domain was the legal rationale for seizing 13 acres from the Mathes family, who refused to sell their parcel to the Texas Rangers (Bryce, 1997). Although the Mathes were unsuccessful in fighting the eminent domain proceedings, they were successful in suing the city, which had failed to provide adequate compensation for the taking. The family was eventually awarded $7.5 million by a Tarrant County jury. A similar suit was filed in 2008 against the City of Arlington over a large number of rental houses that were demolished for the new Dallas Cowboys stadium. The city agreed to pay landowners $1.8 million initially and ultimately paid another $868,250 to settle the suit ("Stadium eminent domain," 2008).

Acquiring adequate contiguous acreage from disparate parcels to build a new stadium can be difficult and potentially expensive, especially in a large metropolitan area. This urban environment reality resulted in eminent domain–related discussions in nearly half of all new major professional sport construction projects in the 1990s (McGraw, 2005). The government is an important partner with most stadium or arena projects, thus sport managers need to be well versed in working in this public environment and have an understanding of the legal issues surrounding acquiring new property for stadium expansion or construction projects.

This section has illustrated how securing and financing new sport facilities or trying to relocate a team from one city to another can involve a complex array of financing and lease agreements, ticketing agreements, voter approval, and political red tape. The complexity of these activities will naturally create a number of legal issues, as discussed above, surrounding the financing, construction, or location of a stadium or arena. However, sport facility managers face additional legal issues associated with operating the facility. These issues are explored in the next section.

FACILITY OPERATIONS AND CONTRACTUAL AGREEMENTS

T he operation of a sport stadium or arena raises additional questions for sport managers. This section examines the importance of common contractual agreements used in stadium operations, including lease, ticket, and game agreements.

As mentioned previously, new stadiums and arenas involve agreements with a primary tenant, often a professional or collegiate team. These teams depend on many revenue streams such as luxury suites, personal seat licenses, naming rights, concessions, broadcasting, licensing, and sponsorships. Of these new revenue streams, the personal seat license is perhaps the most controversial. Consumers may resent paying higher prices or may be simply priced out of the market. The New York Yankees have reported difficulties with selling tickets to fans who have balked at paying as much as $2,500 for a single game (Sandomir, 2009). In some cases, fans and community residents have responded by refusing to pay the higher prices. They have also filed lawsuits against the sports organizations for what they have viewed as a breach of contract as well as breach of fan loyalty and trust.

Thus a solid understanding of contract law is essential for facility owners and operators. Persons working for sport facilities must navigate a myriad of agreements. Each of these agreements creates unique challenges for sport managers. Below we examine some of these agreements in greater detail.

Lease Agreements

Lease agreements are important both to the facility owner and operator (**lessor**) and also to the **lessee** (the person or entity that rents or leases the facility). As with any contract, the **lease agreement** defines the rights and responsibilities of the parties and typically addresses such issues as how much rent must be paid, when access will be provided, what physical areas may be used, what services are provided by the facility owners (such as utilities, promotional assistance, ticket sales, security, and concessions), how to handle radio or television broadcasts, and a host of other issues that may arise.

To examine some of the key components of a lease agreement, let's consider a typical scenario in the sport industry. The local sports commission, Charleston Sports Council, has helped to attract a major event to the city, and the event will need a facility to use. Thus, the event promoter, ABX Sports, Inc. wants to enter into a lease agreement with the local stadium authority, Charleston Sports Property Management (CSPM), to lease the 25,000-seat arena owned by the City of Charleston and operated by CSPM. A standard lease agreement would include the following key elements.

Right to use and occupy. The lease will grant ABX Sports the right to use the facility and occupy certain spaces. Such spaces must be clearly and specifically defined, such as field and court area, all seating areas, press box, ticket booths, and parking lots. The duration of the right to use and occupy must also be clearly and specifically defined. For example, the lease may provide that the lessee is entitled to use and occupy the premises from 8:00 A.M. on the tenth day of July until 4:00 P.M. on the fourteenth day of July. See the hypothetical case on p. 486 demonstrating the importance of the right to use and occupy clause.

Specifying the exact time access is permitted is important so that the event organizers have ample time to set up and prepare for the event. A lease may also contain a clause that permits access (as opposed to occupancy) for a certain number of hours before and a certain number of hours after the lease term begins or ends for setup, deliveries, and teardown.

Rental fees. The rental fees represent the consideration for the contract, and they should be clearly expressed. A facility may demand a flat rental fee plus a percentage of gross ticket sales. A golden rule in facility management is "Always Take a Percentage." Most facility operators will want a percentage of the gate or ticket sales. Of course, the amount of that percentage is negotiable, and it may be structured to apply only when ticket sales reach a certain point or to vary as ticket sales meet or exceed certain targets. A portion of the fee may be required in advance as a nonrefundable fee or deposit.

Fee for additional services. The facility may provide a number of additional services that the lessee will have to agree to pay for, such as event security, merchandise sales, ushers, parking attendants, ticket takers, labor for setup and teardown, audio, maintenance, and administrative assistance. The lease may stipulate a fixed amount for these services, or a schedule of available services and their corresponding costs could be attached as an addendum to the lease agreement. Thus, the lessee is not required to use the facility's services, but if it does, it agrees to pay the stated fees.

Revenue sharing. The lease will provide whether the various revenues that will be generated from the event from concessions, merchandise sales, and parking are to be shared between the parties. Most facility operators either take or give a percentage of those revenue streams depending on how the lease agreement is structured. Most large multipurpose sports facilities retain all these revenue streams for themselves, but they may be willing to share a small percentage of net sales with the lessee. In a smaller facility, the operator may be more willing to negotiate those revenues.

Kitchen sink provisions. The lease will include a number of provisions that, while they are generic or common to most contracts, are also very important in defining the potential liability of the parties. These provisions include the following:

- A *nonassignment clause* preventing the lessee from assigning its rights to another person or organization.
- A *choice of law clause* designating that the lease will be governed by the law of a particular state.
- A *hold harmless clause* stating that one party, usually the lessor, will be held harmless by the second party, usually the lessee, for any tort liability of the lessor that arises out of the business activity referenced in the contract. In essence, the lessee is simply agreeing in advance that it will assume responsibility (legal liability) for any negligent acts, errors, or omissions of the lessor.
- An *indemnification clause* protecting the lessor in the event the lessee causes an injury to a guest that results in a lawsuit against the lessor. To try to shift potential liability to the lessee, most lessors will require that the lessee promise to "indemnify" the lessor. Under such an agreement, the lessor cannot recover

Competitive Advantage

STRATEGIES

Facility Operations Issues

- Facility managers should carefully examine all contractual agreements to determine if those agreements are both clear and comprehensive. Agreements should be readily understandable and address all questions that are likely to arise between the parties.

- While it is important to maximize revenue from ticket sales, it is equally important to avoid costly litigation or disenfranchising ticket holders and fans. Ticket policies and purchase agreements must be clear, and special attention should be paid to resolving customer complaints. Nowhere is customer service as important as in ticket sales and facility operations. Effective customer service procedures and trained customer service personnel help avoid lawsuits and disputes.

- If your organization is experiencing a high number of ticket holder complaints, it may be time to contact the sport management or marketing department at a local university to conduct customer service quality studies for your organization.

until it has actually suffered a loss. The scope of the indemnification should be spelled out and normally includes compensatory damages, punitive damages, and litigation costs and attorneys' fees (van der Smissen, 1990, § 25.21).

- An *insurance clause* requiring the lessee to buy insurance and provide proof of insurance before it will be permitted to occupy the facility.
- A *force majeure* (literally meaning "greater force") *clause* excusing or relieving a party from having to perform under the lease agreement due to natural disasters or other "acts of God," war, or the failure of third parties—such as suppliers and subcontractors—to perform their obligations to the contracting party. Force majeure clauses excuse a party only if the failure to perform could not be avoided by the exercise of due care by that party.
- A *damage clause* holding the lessee financially responsible for any damage it may cause to the building, premises, furnishings, or equipment.

This list includes only the main areas for negotiation that must be included in a facility lease agreement. The sophistication and complexity of the agreement will vary considerably from one event to the next depending upon the event and the amenities and services available at the facility. If a facility has convention or meeting space, restaurants, or luxury suites, those items may be part of the lease transaction.

The following hypothetical case demonstrates the importance of clearly identifying when access to the facility is granted.

considering . . .   FACILITY LEASE AGREEMENTS

Sally is the competition director for the local organizing committee (LOC) of the USA Team Handball Exhibition Tour, which is responsible for assisting the USA Team Handball Federation (USATHF) in a nationwide exhibition tour leading up to the world championships. One of the tour stops is in Sally's city, and the event will be held at the local downtown arena, Waterfront Arena, for six matches played over three days. The first two matches are scheduled for April 10 at 6:00 P.M. and 8:00 P.M. The organizing committee entered into a lease with the Waterfront Arena Authority on January 15 that included a provision stating, "This lease is for three days beginning at 12:01 A.M. on April 10 and ending at midnight on April 12."

Sally has been contacted by the USATHF operations crew to confirm the arrival times of the competition floor and goals. The competition floor is a prefabricated, thermofused vinyl sheet product that is rolled up for transport between venues. When rolled up for transport and storage, the floor is made up of four separate rolls that are 60 feet long and 49 inches in diameter. The setup for this product requires that the floor be rolled out and lay flat for 24 hours in order for it to relax and rebound sufficiently to adhere to the floor surface for soldering of the seams and marking. Thus, naturally, the USATHF operations crew needs to gain access to the arena floor no later than 4:00 P.M. on April 9 to install the floor, but the Waterfront Arena is booked on the evening of April 9 for a concert and will not be available until 11:00 P.M. at the earliest.

Questions

- What type of clause should the local organizing committee have negotiated into this lease to assure adequate time for setup and teardown for the event?
- What additional provisions could have been made in the lease agreement to provide some protection for Sally and the organizing committee?
- What strategies would you recommend to Sally to solve this dilemma?

Note how you would answer the questions and then check your responses using the Analysis & Discussion at the end of this chapter.

Ticket agreements

Ticket sales raise some interesting legal issues for sport managers. First, as with any contract, issues will arise as to what rights or benefits a fan has obtained when he or she purchases a ticket. The courts have consistently held that a ticket constitutes a revocable license. A **license** is defined as a privilege to go on the premises for a certain purpose, but it does not operate to confer on the licensee any title or interest in the property (*Black's Law Dictionary*, 2004). Thus, a **revocable license** is a license that may be revoked, withdrawn, or canceled. Typically, when a fan purchases a ticket to a sporting event, that ticket represents a privilege to access the premises according to the terms and conditions of the license. The ticket itself generally contains a number of restrictions and conditions. For example, on the back of the ticket the following may appear:

> This ticket is a revocable license. Failure of the ticket holder to comply with any of the following conditions will automatically terminate this license. Coolers, kegs, bottles, cans, alcoholic beverages, food, fireworks, illegal substances, weapons, umbrellas, horns, or other noisemakers may not be brought into the stadium. Smoking is prohibited. Consuming alcohol in sections 111 and 211 is prohibited. Throwing objects onto the playing field is strictly forbidden. Unless specifically authorized in advance by the licensor, this ticket may not be offered in a commercial promotion or as a prize in a sweepstakes or contest.

If the ticket holder violates any of these conditions, the license may be revoked. Many sport organizations impose further restrictions on season ticket holders, such that if the ticket holder violates any rules of the stadium or conditions of the ticket, he forfeits the right to buy tickets in the future. For example, a fan who interfered with New York Yankees outfielder Gary Sheffield during a game in Boston on April 18, 2005, lost his season ticket privileges for the season. A second spectator, not a season ticket holder, who spilled beer on Sheffield was also banned from buying Red Sox tickets for the rest of the 2005 season. In revoking season ticket privileges, the Red Sox cited the season ticket agreement, which states that "interfering with the play of the game in any way will not be tolerated and will be grounds for ejection from the premises, legal prosecution, rescission of tickets, and cancellation of subscription privileges" ("Boston fan has tickets revoked," 2005).

However, New York City paid over $10,000 in damages and $12,000 in attorneys' fees to settle a federal lawsuit on behalf of a spectator from Queens who was ejected from Yankee Stadium after walking toward the restroom during the playing of "God Bless America." The Yankees admitted they had no policy prohibiting fans from moving around during the playing of patriotic songs (Chan, 2009).

Thus, sport managers working in sales and ticket operations must pay close attention to season ticket holder agreements and back of ticket language to address those situations where the sport organization, as licensor, may properly revoke the ticket privilege.

Game Contracts

Many large public facilities do not host their own events (events that they create and operate). Instead, many major multipurpose public sport facilities are primarily in the business of renting or leasing space, providing support services, and serving the public interest by attracting visitors to the community, producing a positive economic impact for the community, and enhancing the image of the community. Other sport facilities are owned or operated by actual users of the facility, such as collegiate athletic teams, professional sports teams, high schools, and private training facilities. In these facilities, the owner is often also a user of the facility.

For example, a college basketball team will host another college in a contest and use its home arena to play the game. In these circumstances, the visiting team is not going to enter into a lease agreement to use the arena. Of course, the host team does not need a lease to use its own facility. Thus, instead, the two colleges will enter into a game contract, which will identify the particular rights and responsibilities related to the contest. Consider the following situation. You will notice that some provisions are similar to those involved in a lease agreement.

You are the athletic director for Victory University (Victory), and you want to play a nonconference powerhouse, University of Pigskin (Pigskin), in football in 2013 as a home game. You know that you can fill your 60,000-seat stadium if Pigskin agrees to the game. You are also confident that ESPN will also want to broadcast the game. What are the key components that must appear in this game contract?

1. **Location, date, and time of the event.** The location, date, and time of the game must be set forth. You may have to make the exact time of the game dependent upon your contract with ESPN.

2. **Financial arrangements.** The financial arrangements must be delineated. How much will you pay Pigskin for playing you at home? You may pay Pigskin a guarantee (a set amount), a percentage of the net revenue for the game, or a combination of the two. If you choose to share the revenue, you must define exactly what constitutes net revenue. For example, does revenue include only ticket sales, or are other revenue items included as well, such as concessions, parking, and broadcasting fees? You must also set a date on which you will disburse the payment to Pigskin. It is to your advantage to delay this date until the very end of the season so that you can have use of the money until then. Pigskin, however, will try to negotiate to have the compensation disbursed as soon after the game as possible. Pigskin may also negotiate an audit provision in the contract so that if Pigskin disagrees with your calculations about how much money you owe, an independent third party can have access to your financial records for this game to settle the dispute.

3. **Eligibility and game rules.** Since this is a nonconference game, a provision must set forth what conference's eligibility and game rules will apply. A provision will also define which party chooses the officials and from what conference(s) the officials will be chosen.

4. **Termination provision.** Since this event has the potential to generate a great deal of revenue, it is very important to negotiate a termination provision that protects Victory's interest. Sometimes schools do breach a game contract because a better opportunity comes along. Therefore, as part of your "worst case" scenario mentality, you would want to incorporate a liquidated damages clause. We discussed the worst case concept in Chapter 4 in the context of a coaching contract. You will also recall from Chapter 4 that this type of clause provides that the breaching party must pay an amount to the nonbreaching party that is a reasonable estimate of the damages to be sustained. In this case, assume that Victory could sustain approximately $500,000 in damages if Pigskin breached the agreement. We cannot state an exact number since attendance cannot be predicted with absolute certainty, but we can be close in our approximation. Therefore, Victory would try to negotiate a clause providing that Pigskin would pay $500,000 in liquidated damages if it breached the agreement. The *University of Louisville v. Duke University* Focus Case that follows further illustrates the importance of a carefully crafted liquidated damages clause.

5. **Force majeure.** The contract should include a force majeure clause, as in a facility lease. This clause provides that neither party is in breach of the contract if the game cannot be played due to an act of God such as a hurricane, an earthquake, or some unforeseen event beyond the control of the parties. For example, when hurricane Katrina devastated the Gulf Coast in 2005, any number of high schools, colleges, and professional sport teams found themselves without facilities and resources. A force majeure clause would have excused these organizations' nonperformance without making them liable for breach of contract. When negotiating a force majeure clause, make sure that the clause applies equally to all parties to the agreement. It is helpful if the clause sets forth some specific examples of acts that would excuse performance under the clause, such as wars, natural disasters, and other major events that are clearly outside a party's control. Inclusion of examples will help to clarify that the clause is not intended to apply to failures to perform for reasons within the control of the parties.

6. **Broadcast rights provision.** The contract should include a provision that discusses broadcast rights. Television and radio rights generally belong to the home team, unless a conference agreement takes precedence. However, as an inducement to Pigskin, Victory may offer to split the broadcast revenues, or at least share a percentage of the broadcast revenues with Pigskin.

7. **Insurance and indemnification provisions.** The contract should include insurance and indemnification provisions, as discussed in the previous section on leases.

8. **Complimentary tickets.** The contract should include a provision dealing with the number of complimentary tickets allocated to Pigskin. It is very common for a university to provide complimentary tickets for VIPs and donors who may travel with the team. Additionally, issues relating to sideline passes and

admission of the visiting team's staff, band, and cheerleaders must also be addressed. These individuals will need access to secured areas of the facility; thus proper credentials will be needed.

9. **Promotional rights.** The game contract should acknowledge that the colleges have exclusive sponsorship agreements that must be complied with. For example, Victory may have an exclusive sponsorship agreement with Gatorade, while Pigskin has an exclusive sponsorship agreement with Powerade. Victory would want to assure its sponsor that no Powerade logos will be affixed or displayed in any areas within the facility. Thus, if Pigskin brought its own water coolers and sport drink coolers and those coolers bore the logos of Powerade, Victory may want the right to cover those logos or require Pigskin to use coolers provided by the facility so that competing logos would not be visible to the live or television audience.

Now consider the following dispute between the University of Louisville and Duke University involving a game contract. This case is a good example of both the importance of a liquidated damages provision and the importance of clearly and carefully defining the terms of the liquidated damages provision.

University of Louisville v. Duke University

FOCUS CASE Case No. 07-CI-1765 (Franklin County Circuit Court, Commonwealth of Kentucky, 2008)

FACTS

On June 23, 1999, the University of Louisville and Duke University entered into an athletic competition agreement. The agreement provided that Louisville and Duke would play four football games between 2002 and 2009. Specific dates were provided as follows:

- October 5, 2002, in Durham, NC
- October 6, 2007, in Louisville, KY
- October 4, 2008, in Durham, NC
- October 3, 2009, in Louisville, KY

The 2002 game was eventually scheduled for September 7, 2002, at Durham, NC, and played on that date. On March, 24, 2003, Duke notified the University of Louisville that it was cancelling the remainder of the agreement. The University of Louisville then requested liquidated damages of $150,000 per contest remaining and also alternatively indicated it would accept a suitable replacement team from the Atlantic Coast Conference for the canceled games. Duke contended that it did not owe any liquidated damages unless the University of Louisville was unable to find a replacement team of similar stature to Duke. The agreement provided the following liquidated damages provision: "If this agreement is breached by the Visiting Team, and no contest occurs between the Home Team and the Visiting Team, and if no contest with a team of similar stature is scheduled by the Home Team to replace the one canceled because of the breach, then the Visiting Team shall pay the Home Team a liquidated sum of $150,000."

The University of Louisville sued Duke for breach of contract to enforce the liquidated damage provision.

HOLDING

University of Louisville's complaint was dismissed.

RATIONALE

Louisville argued that it had used its best efforts to find a suitable replacement, but it had been unable to find a team of similar stature. Louisville also argued that the liquidated damages clause was ambiguous and that a team of similar stature for purposes of the damage provision should be interpreted to mean a team from a conference with an automatic berth in the Bowl Championships Series. Duke argued that the term "similar stature" was not ambiguous and simply meant a team of similar status or quality. The Franklin County District Court in Kentucky observed that nothing in the language of the agreement suggests an in-depth analysis of the relative strength and weaknesses of the team in question. No particular conference or even a particular division of the NCAA had been stipulated. The court concluded that a "team of similar stature" meant any team that competes at the same level of athletic performance as the Duke football team. The court even accepted Duke's argument that in finding a replacement for Duke, the threshold could not be any lower since Duke had won only one football game and lost 11 games during the 2007 season.

This section presented three examples of contractual agreements commonly used by facility managers, including the basic lease agreement, ticket agreements, and a game contract. In addition to clearly and carefully defining the nature of the facility rights and responsibilities in our contractual agreements, we also must consider how our operating policies and practices create legal issues, which is the subject of the next section.

FACILITY OPERATIONS AND SPECTATOR/GUEST ISSUES

I n this section we discuss spectator/guest issues. We first explore legal issues surrounding the application of the Americans with Disabilities Act (ADA) to sports facilities, including large public access stadiums or arenas as well as private sport-related businesses such as a sporting goods retail store. Lastly, this section examines operating policies that directly affect guests and spectators such as spectator search policies and conduct or ejection policies.

Accessibility and the Americans with Disabilities Act

As discussed in Chapters 6 and 14, the Americans with Disabilities Act is a comprehensive civil rights law that prohibits discrimination on the basis of disability (ADA, 2005). The ADA ensures that people with disabilities will be able to gain equal access to employment (Title I, discussed in Chapter 6), state and local government facilities (Title II), and places of public accommodation (Title III, discussed in Chapter 14). For purposes of this chapter we focus again on Title III of the ADA, dealing with places of public accommodation. First let's consider what qualifies as a place of public accommodation.

Defining places of public accommodation

Places of public accommodation include several types of sport facilities, including gymnasiums, health spas, bowling alleys, golf courses, and stadiums (see Exhibit 16.3). More important, the general categories of places that are deemed places of public accommodation under the ADA encompass virtually all sport facilities. Essentially any facility or place that is a place of exhibition, entertainment, exercise, or recreation is covered by the ADA. Thus, parks, fitness clubs, sports museums, arenas, stadiums, training centers, recreation centers, and so on are all places of public accommodation. In addition, within a single facility, separate elements or areas also are places of public accommodation, such as restaurants, museums, galleries, day care centers, bars, convention centers, and auditoriums; these are also subject to the ADA.

The ADA has a broad mandate and has been interpreted broadly by the courts in its application to sport facilities. For example, the Supreme Court in *PGA Tour, Inc. v. Martin* had to determine whether the PGA Tour *competition* was a place of public accommodation subject to the ADA. The PGA Tour admitted the ADA applied to the golf course at which it held its events in terms of spectator access but drew a line

---

EXHIBIT 16.3 Definition of a "public accommodation" under the ADA, with sport- and recreation-related examples.

A public accommodation is defined as the following private entities if the operations of such entities affect commerce—

(A) an inn, hotel, motel, or other place of lodging, except for an establishment located within a building that contains not more than five rooms for rent or hire and that is actually occupied by the proprietor of such establishment as the residence of such proprietor;

(B) a restaurant, bar, or other establishment serving food or drink;

(C) a motion picture house, theater, concert hall, stadium, or other place of exhibition or entertainment;

(D) an auditorium, convention center, lecture hall, or other place of public gathering;

(E) a bakery, grocery store, clothing store, hardware store, shopping center, or other sales or rental establishment;

(I) a park, zoo, amusement park, or other place of recreation;

(J) a nursery, elementary, secondary, undergraduate, or postgraduate private school, or other place of education;

(L) a gymnasium, health spa, bowling alley, golf course, or other place of exercise or recreation. (42 U.S.C. § 12181(7))

between being able to access the physical golf course and being able to participate as part of the tour competition. The PGA Tour instead argued that the "opportunity to compete in its event" was not a "place" as that term is used under the ADA. The Court disagreed as follows:

> Petitioner's golf tours and their qualifying rounds fit comfortably within the coverage of Title III. The events occur on "golf courses," a type of place specifically identified by the Act as a public accommodation. In addition, at all relevant times, petitioner "leases" and "operates" golf courses to conduct its Q-School and tours. As a lessor and operator of golf courses, then, petitioner must not discriminate against any "individual" in the "full and equal enjoyment of the goods, services, facilities, privileges, advantages, or accommodations" of those courses. Certainly, among the "privileges" offered by petitioner on the courses are those of competing in the Q-School and playing in the tours; indeed, the former is a privilege for which thousands of individuals from the general public pay, and the latter is one for which they vie. Martin, of course, is one of those individuals. (*PGA Tour, Inc. v. Martin*, 2001, p. 677)

Thus, it is now clear that the reach of the ADA is not limited only to physical spaces and facility access issues. Instead, the best practice for sport managers is to understand that the ADA applies to the entire facility and all programs and services offered within that facility.

Since the ADA's mandate does not stop at the physical structure, nor is it limited only to spectators at stadiums and arenas, facility managers and operators of sport competitions must review their eligibility policies, competition rules, and other operating practices to determine if those policies or practices are having the effect of denying equal access to people with disabilities. Now that we know all sport facilities will need to comply with Title III of the ADA, let's consider how to understand ADA requirements with regard to the physical structure or property itself, and then we will look at how the ADA impacts operating policies.

The ADA and physical structures

We are concerned with two primary issues related to the physical structure of sport facilities: (1) access to the facility; (2) access to the services offered by the facility, which may involve the number of seats available for patrons with disabilities, sightlines for patrons using wheelchairs, and additional amenities required for disabled patrons.

Access to a facility. Undoubtedly, the ADA requires owners and operators of places of public accommodation to make sure that persons with disabilities can gain entry to their physical structures and move within those structures. A few common examples of this type of accessibility are wheelchair ramps, automatic doors, elevators, and directional signage posted in Braille. The ADA requires that newly constructed and renovated places of public accommodation be readily accessible to and usable by individuals with disabilities. The ADA requires that all new construction (and to the maximum extent feasible, all alterations) be designed and constructed to be accessible to and usable by people with disabilities. This covers buildings and facilities covered by Title II (state and local governments) and Title III (places of public accommodation and commercial facilities). The ADA also requires places of public accommodation to remove "architectural barriers . . . in existing facilities built prior to 1992 . . . where such removal is readily achievable." Removal is "readily achievable" when it is "easily accomplishable and able to be carried out without much difficulty or expense." Examples include the simple ramping of a few steps, the installation of grab bars where only routine reinforcement of the wall is required, the lowering of telephones, and similar modest adjustments. Thus, all places of public accommodation must comply with the ADA in some fashion regardless of the age of the building.

Alterations to a place of public accommodation covered by Title III of the ADA that are undertaken after January 26, 1992, are required to ensure that, to the maximum extent feasible, the altered portions of the facility comply with the ADA Accessibility Guidelines (ADAAG) adopted by the Department of Justice as current federal ADA standards. The ADA standards set minimum requirements for accessibility in alterations. Each element or space that is altered must meet the technical criteria for new construction where feasible. Where an entire room or space is altered, the room or space must be made fully accessible. Comprehensive renovations will trigger more of the ADA standards than limited small-scale projects. The ADA standards apply to all building repairs that are considered alterations. An alteration is defined as a change that affects usability. Certain improvements, such as re-roofing, painting, or changes to mechanical and electrical systems, are excluded (unless they affect the usability of the facility).

If the alteration affects an area of primary function—a principal use area—of the building, it may be necessary to include other improvements. If alterations are made to an area containing a primary function, an accessible "path of travel" is required, which means a continuous route connecting the altered area to an entrance. Phones, restrooms, and drinking fountains that, where provided, serve the altered area are also required to be accessible. Since this may involve modifications outside the intended alteration, compliance is required to the extent it is not "disproportionate" to the cost of alterations to the primary function area. "Disproportionality" is defined by the Department of Justice as costing more than 20 percent of the costs of the alteration to the primary function area.

For a facility built prior to 1992, the ADA distinguishes between "alterations" and "repairs" and would require a different standard of compliance. If the project involves an "alteration" of an existing facility, the areas being altered must be made accessible to the maximum extent possible as described above. If the project is merely a repair, the space should be made accessible if "readily achievable."

So for example, if a YMCA built in the 1970s began a project to repair its swimming pool and replace the pool filters and drainage systems, that project would likely fit under the definition of a "repair." Assuming the pool deck is elevated and accessible only through the locker rooms and involves several narrow walkways and a series of concrete steps, the YMCA may not be required to modify the space to make the pool area wheelchair accessible since the widening of the walkways, removal of the concrete steps, and installation of wheelchair access ramps may not be readily achievable. However, if the YMCA began a project to upgrade its entire pool facility, including those same repairs to the pool area, it is likely this project would be considered an "alteration," which would require the YMCA to make the space accessible to the maximum extent possible.

Managers should ensure that individuals with disabilities are generally able to access a sports facility and that they have access to and use of the various amenities offered within the facility. For example, in a large stadium, in addition to having access to the venue, a person with a disability would also need to be able to access parking, concession areas, restrooms, shopping areas, restaurants, and so on. In a recreation facility such as a YMCA or a fitness club, managers need to make sure all areas within the facility are accessible, such as parking spaces, exit routes, doors, assembly sections, and toilet and bathing facilities.

In addition, all areas of sport activities must be accessible. The ADA defines the *area of sport activity* as that portion of a room or space where the play or practice of a sport occurs. This includes but is not limited to basketball courts, baseball fields, running tracks, soccer fields, and skating rinks. For example, football fields are defined by boundary lines. In addition, a safety border is provided around the field. Players may temporarily be in the space between the boundary lines and the safety border when they are pushed out of bounds or momentum carries them forward when receiving a pass. Thus, in football, that space is used as part of the game and is included in the area of sport activity. Accessible routes must connect each area of sport activity. Some provisions are not required inside of the area of sport activity, since they may affect the fundamental nature of the sport or activity. For example, an accessible route is required to connect to the boundary of a soccer field, but there is no requirement to change the surface of a field to an accessible surface.

Access to and enjoyment of facility services and amenities. In addition to making the physical elements of a facility accessible, sport managers must also ensure that the programs and services offered are accessible by people with disabilities. Section 12182(a) of the ADA provides a general prohibition against discriminating against an individual with a disability in the full and equal enjoyment of goods, services, facilities, and privileges of any place of public accommodation. Several issues arise related to assuring full and equal enjoyment of patrons with disabilities. A few of these issues include the number and placement of wheelchair-accessible seating, comparable lines of sight for wheelchair patrons, and assistive devices for the hearing impaired.

Number and placement of wheelchair accessible seating. For stadiums built or renovated after January 26, 1992, the ADA requires that 1 percent of the total available seats be wheelchair accessible and those seats must be dispersed throughout the stadium. As mentioned in the previous section, for a facility built prior to 1992, the ADA distinguishes between "repairs" and "alterations" and would require a different standard of compliance. If the project involves an alteration of an existing facility built prior to 1992, the areas being altered would be subject to the 1 percent accessible seating requirement.

The University of Michigan recently encountered this issue when it began a $226 million renovation of its football stadium. A disabled veterans group sued, claiming wheelchair users were being denied equal access to the stadium and that the University of Michigan was avoiding compliance with the ADA requirements regarding the number and location of wheelchair seating in stadiums. The renovation would add luxury suites, 3200 club seats, and widen seating and aisles for the 107,501-seat stadium. Before the renovation, the stadium had 90 wheelchair accessible seats divided equally within each end zone of the stadium. The disabled veterans group claimed that the University of Michigan tried to label its renovation as a "repair" instead of an "alteration" so that they could avoid compliance with the ADA, which would require 1 percent, or 1,000 wheelchair accessible seats. Based on the university renovation plan, the stadium would increase its wheelchair accessible seats to 282 dispersed throughout the stadium including the outdoor and indoor club seat areas, and one wheelchair accessible seat would be located inside each new luxury suite, and companion tickets would be offered for some seats as well.

Since the stadium was originally built in 1927, it did not have to meet the same guidelines prior to the renovation as newly constructed facilities. This case raised an important question as to when a stadium renovation is extensive enough to be considered an alteration and thus requires full compliance with the ADA (Associated Press, 2007). In addition to the negative publicity surrounding the University of Michigan's renovation plan, the Department of Education also accused the university of violating disability laws (Wolverton, 2007; "U. of Michigan to increase," 2007). Ultimately, the University of Michigan signed a consent agreement with the U. S. Department of Justice and the disabled veterans group to resolve the lawsuit. By 2010, the stadium should have total wheelchair seating of 329, including companion seats and seats in multiple locations throughout the stadium (Gershman, 2008).

Comparable lines of sight. In late 2004, the Architectural and Transportation Barriers Compliance Board (the "Access Board") released a suggested amendment that requires wheelchair users be provided a choice of seating locations and viewing angles that are substantially equivalent to, or better than, those available to all other spectators. The Department of Justice (DOJ) revised Title III of the ADA, effective January 2005, to include the Access Board's suggested amendment. However, this amendment only applies to new construction and altered facilities. According to the Department of Justice, "Without question the single most prevalent issue that arises in new stadium projects involves the lines of sight afforded to patrons who use wheelchairs and sit in the stadium's wheelchair seating locations. The ADA's Standards for Accessible Design—the architectural requirements applicable to new stadiums—require that wheelchair seating areas provide people with disabilities with lines of sight comparable to those for members of the general public. Thus, we believe that facilities like sports stadiums, where spectators can be expected to stand during the event, must provide wheelchair locations with lines of sight over those standing spectators" (DOJ, 1996).

Several lawsuits have been filed against movie theaters and stadiums alleging violations of the ADA for failure to provide comparable sight lines for patrons in wheelchairs. Recently, in *Miller v. California Speedway Corp.* (2008), Robert Miller, a NASCAR fan who is a quadriplegic and uses a wheelchair, attended three to six events a year at the California Speedway in Fontana. Miller's view of the track and the cars from his viewing area in the grandstand was regularly blocked by fans standing immediately in front of him. Unable to fully enjoy his spectator experience, Miller filed suit, claiming that the Speedway had violated Title III of the ADA. A 1994 DOJ supplement stated,

> In addition to requiring companion seating and dispersion of wheelchair locations, ADAAG requires that wheelchair locations provide people with disabilities lines of sight comparable to those for members of the general public. Thus, in assembly areas where spectators can be expected to stand during the event or show being viewed, the wheelchair locations must provide lines of sight over spectators who stand.

The Ninth Circuit held that it must give controlling weight to an agency's interpretation of its own regulations unless it is plainly erroneous or inconsistent with the regulation. The court of appeals held that it is perfectly reasonable to interpret the term "lines of sight comparable to those for members of the general public" as requiring lines of sight that are comparable in the actual conditions under which a facility operates. If spectators are widely expected to stand during the key moments of an event—from the singing of the national anthem to the fourth quarter—it does not take a fertile legal imagination to understand that relatively immobile patrons will not have a comparable line of sight.

Despite the Ninth Circuit's decision in *Miller,* courts are divided over whether the ADA standards require lines of sight not blocked by standing spectators (Wolohan, 2009). The Oregon federal district court (*Independent Living Resources v. Oregon Arena Corp.,* 1997) and the Third Circuit (*Caruso v. Blockbuster-Sony Music Entertainment Centre at the Waterfront,* 1999), concluded that the DOJ regulations do not require lines of sight over standing spectators. However, the D. C. Circuit (*Paralyzed Veterans of America v. D.C. Arena L.P.,* 1997) and the Minnesota federal district court (*United States v. Ellerbe Becket Inc.,* 1997) and now the Ninth Circuit in *Miller* found that the DOJ's regulations do require lines of sight over standing spectators.

The best advice for facility managers in new or altered stadiums is to investigate the possibility of improving lines of sight for wheelchair patrons. Take into consideration that spectators seated in front of the designated accessible seating may stand and potentially block the sightlines from accessible seating area. If those sight lines are blocked by standing spectators, the facility should make necessary modifications to provide an unobstructed view for its wheelchair patrons.

Assistive devices for the hearing impaired. The DOJ's guidelines for accessible stadiums also address assistive listening devices. The guidelines provide that when audible communications are integral to the use of a stadium, assistive listening systems are required for people who are hearing impaired (DOJ, 2009). These systems amplify sound and deliver it to a special receiver that is worn by the spectator, or to the spectator's hearing aid, depending on the type of system that is used. The stadium must provide receivers for the assistive listening system. The number of available receivers must equal 4 percent of the total number of seats. Signs must be provided to notify spectators of the availability of receivers for the assistive listening system. Given that new stadiums are frequently multipurpose facilities that also host concerts, conventions, and other events, stadium managers must be aware that the ADA Standards require any facility to have a permanently installed assistive listening system.

Closed-captioning is a recent trend demonstrating how a facility can further assist its hearing-impaired patrons to more fully enjoy the services and experiences of attending a sporting event. Closed-captioning can be made available on video boards and concourse televisions. In 2006 patron Shane Feldman sued the Washington Redskins at FedEx Field for not providing captioning at their football games. Prior to the 2006 football season, FedEx Field did not caption any announcements made over its public address system. The Redskins had always offered listening devices to fans who requested one; however, Feldman did not benefit from an assistive listening device. In September 2008, the Maryland federal district court ruled that the ADA requires facility operators to provide deaf or hearing-impaired fans equal access to the aural information broadcast over the stadium public address system (*Feldman v. Pro-Football, Inc,* 2008). This information includes music with lyrics, game commentary, advertisements, referee calls, and safety and emergency information.

These few examples illustrate the importance of being a proactive facility manager to comply with the ADA. Many components of the facility can serve as barriers to people with disabilities. Simply considering the availability and placement of seating, sight lines, and closed-captioning may serve to address many, if not most, requests made by patrons with disabilities.

The ADA and operating policies

The previous sections discussed how the ADA impacts physical access, enjoyment of services, and responsibility for compliance, but it is also important to realize that one of the more unique aspects of the ADA is how it impacts access to *participation opportunities* by both elite and recreational athletes. The ADA's mandate does not stop at the physical structure, nor is it limited only to spectators at stadiums and arenas. Instead, facility managers and operators of sport competitions must review their eligibility policies, competition rules, and other operating practices to determine if those policies or practices are having the effect of denying equal access to people with disabilities. For sport organizations staging athletic competitions in stadiums, arenas, and other sport facilities, the *Martin v. PGA Tour, Inc.* case confirmed that the applicability of the ADA is not limited to the accessibility of the physical location for the event but also includes access to the competition itself. Rules affecting eligibility and access to programming services connected to a facility also came under scrutiny in *Matthews v. NCAA* (2001), which was discussed in Chapter 14. You may recall in that case the court held that the NCAA and its eligibility rules were subject to the ADA because it exercises an extreme amount of control over student-athletes' access to the playing field of competitive collegiate sports.

Consider another example where the Ohio High School Athletic Association (OHSAA) had a rule requiring football players to wear shoes, thigh pads, and knee pads. Game officials prevented a high school football player who did not have legs from playing in a football game based upon the above rule, despite the fact that he had been cleared to play by a physician and had been deemed eligible to play by the OHSAA ("OHSAA says mistake was made," 2005). In this situation the rule should have been modified to permit participation.

The *PGA Tour, Inc. v. Martin* case is a rare case because it involved an elite athlete with a disability who sought to compete alongside other athletes in a professional sports competition. More commonly, recreational activities at parks, golf courses, swimming pools, and ski resorts raise ADA challenges. The following Focus Case explores how operating policies may discriminate against people with disabilities seeking access to recreational sport opportunities.

Celano v. Marriott International, Inc.

U.S. Dist. LEXIS 6172 (N.D. Cal. 2008)   **FOCUS CASE**

FACTS

The plaintiffs filed suit under the ADA, alleging that the defendant failed to provide "accessible" or "single-rider" golf carts in violation of the ADA. The plaintiffs sought a declaration that Marriott's policies were unlawful and an injunction requiring the defendant to provide single-rider carts at each of its golf facilities. Due to varied mobility disabilities, the plaintiffs all require a single-rider cart to play golf. A single-rider cart is a specially designed golf cart that allows individuals with mobility impairments to hit the golf ball while seated in the cart on a rotating swivel seat. The carts also contain hand brakes and accelerators to allow mobility-impaired users to drive them. Marriott owns and operates 26 golf courses throughout the United States. The plaintiffs contacted several Marriott golf resorts expressing an interest in playing at the resort's golf courses and requesting a single-rider golf cart. Each plaintiff was told that Marriott does not maintain single-rider carts at its courses and that it was not required by current ADA rules to do so. Marriott informed the plaintiffs that they could bring their own single-rider carts to its courses.

HOLDING

The court found that Marriott's policy of not providing single-rider carts was a violation of the ADA.

RATIONALE

The plaintiffs' ADA claim rested on Title III of the ADA, which prohibits discrimination against disabled individuals in any place of public accommodation and provides injunctive relief against private entities that discriminate against the disabled. The determination as to whether a particular modification is "reasonable" and "necessary" involves a fact-specific, case-by-case inquiry that considers, among other factors, the effectiveness of the modification in light of the nature of the disability in question and the cost to the organization that would implement it. The plaintiffs argued that this modification was reasonable because it would enable each of the plaintiffs to play at Marriott courses that they were otherwise unable to. Financially the modification was reasonable given Marriott's operational budget. Marriott contended that it does not discriminate against disabled golfers because it allows them to bring their own accessible carts. The plaintiffs responded that this policy is discriminatory because it places disabled golfers in a distinctly unequal situation from their able-bodied counterparts.

Title III of the ADA outlaws not just intentional discrimination but also certain practices that have a disparate impact upon persons with disabilities even in the absence of any conscious intent to discriminate. Thus, a public accommodation may not "utilize standards or criteria or methods of administration that have the effect of discriminating on the basis of disability, or that perpetuate the discrimination of others who are subject to common administrative control. The ADA requires more than merely refraining from active discrimination. . . . As a general rule, the objective of Title III is to provide persons with disabilities who utilize public accommodations with an experience that is functionally equivalent to that of other patrons, to the extent feasible given the limitations imposed by that person's disability."

Marriott's policy did not provide the plaintiffs with an experience equivalent to that of other patrons. Because Marriott's policy put the plaintiffs in a distinctly unequal situation, as compared to their able-bodied counterparts, it was in violation of the ADA. The court held that providing accessible golf carts at Marriott's courses was both reasonable and necessary to accommodate the plaintiffs' disabilities.

Persons responsible for ADA compliance

Another issue frequently raised in ADA cases relates to who has the responsibility for compliance with the ADA. This issue was raised in the following Focus Case, *Clark v. Simms*. This case helps to illustrate not only the scope of the ADA, but also the relationships between owners, lessees and lessors, and operators of places of public accommodation. The following Focus Case also reminds us that the ADA is applicable to many places related to the sport industry other than just stadiums and arenas.

Clark v. Simms

FOCUS CASE | 2009 U.S. Dist. LEXIS 29027 (W.D. Va. 2009)

FACTS

On January 16, 2009, the plaintiff Robert Clark filed suit against the defendants Dennis and Mildred Simms under the ADA, alleging the existence of certain architectural barriers to access on the defendants' property. The Simms are co-owners of a building and surrounding property located in Gum Spring, Virginia. The building is currently leased to two other individuals who operate a hunting store called the "Hunt 'N' Shack." Clark is a quadriplegic and uses a power wheelchair for mobility. Clark alleged that he attempted to access the Hunt 'N' Shack in September 2008 but was unable to achieve full and equal access because of several architectural barriers on the property, including the lack of handicap-accessible parking spaces and a handicap-accessible route from the parking lot to the store. Because he wanted to patronize the store, Clark asked the court to (1) find that the Hunt 'N' Shack is in violation of the ADA; (2) order the defendants to alter the Hunt 'N' Shack so that it is readily accessible to and usable by individuals with disabilities to the full extent required by the ADA; (3) direct the defendants to evaluate and neutralize their policies, practices, and procedures toward individuals with disabilities. The Simms argued that the plaintiff's claim should be dismissed because the complaint failed to allege that they "operate" the store.

HOLDING

The complaint should not be dismissed.

RATIONALE

The Simms implied that they could not be held liable as owners of the property because they gave over their responsibilities for compliance with the ADA to the lessees who operate the Hunt 'N' Shack. Title III of the ADA prescribes, as a general rule, that "[n]o individual shall be discriminated against on the basis of disability in the full and equal enjoyment of the goods, services, facilities, privileges, advantages, or accommodations of any place of public accommodation by any person who owns, leases (or leases to), or operates a place of public accommodation." By its plain terms, the statute applies to those who own, lease, or lease to others a place of public accommodation. In no way does the language of the statute suggest that a person must both own and operate a place of public accommodation to be held liable. As the owners and the lessors of the property on which the Hunt 'N' Shack is located, the Simms may be held liable under the ADA.

Furthermore, the Simms may not assign their responsibilities for compliance with the ADA to the tenants who operate the Hunt 'N' Shack because "a landlord has an independent obligation to comply with the ADA that may not be eliminated by contract." Allowing a landlord to assign all responsibility for ADA compliance to his tenant, for example, could leave injured individuals without recourse in the event that compliance measures are not "readily achievable" for the tenant. The landlord is free to seek indemnification from the tenant if the terms of their lease agreement so allow.

As mentioned previously, the congressional mandate of the ADA is very broad, not only as to the types of places that are considered a public accommodation, but also the scope of persons responsible for ADA compliance. Any owner, operator, lessor, or lessee has a responsibility to ensure ADA compliance and can be sued under Title III for noncompliance.

Resources for ADA compliance

Sport managers have a number of tools and resources available to them to aid in complying with the ADA. When the ADA was enacted, the United States Attorney General was instructed to establish standards to guide businesses, service providers, employers, and governmental entities in complying with Title III of the statute. Congress further provided that these implementing regulations must be consistent with the minimum guidelines issued by the Architectural and Transportation Barriers Compliance Board ("the Access Board"), an independent federal agency charged with issuing guidelines to ensure that public accommodations are accessible to individuals with disabilities. The U.S. Department of Justice uses the Access Board guidelines to develop formal ADA standards, and the ADA standards issued by the DOJ are the legally enforceable standards at this time.

The Access Board's ADA guidelines are available for designers and operators to ensure that a sport facility is accessible and compliant with the ADA (United States Access Board, 2003). In addition, the Access Board has published ADA accessibility guidelines for recreation facilities (36 C.F.R. Part 1191, 2002) by facility type, available at www.access-board.gov/recreation/guides/index.htm. Both the Department of Justice and the Access Board provide technical manuals and guidance documents on their website. The guidelines and technical manuals may be used for guidance in areas where no accessibility standard exists (such as recreation facilities and play areas) or for those provisions that exceed the current ADA standards.

The Access Board revised its guidelines in 2004, and while the current guidelines do not have the force of law, they are still very helpful to sport managers in evaluating their ADA compliance. Plus, the guidelines are still persuasive to courts considering ADA claims.

Elements of an ADA discrimination claim

Even though there are a number of resources available to sport managers to aid in ADA compliance, one may not always be able to avoid litigation. Thus, it is important to understand the basic elements of an ADA discrimination claim under Title III and explore a few key cases that have identified some unique issues related to ADA discrimination claims arising in the sport context. Exhibit 16.4 identifies what a plaintiff must prove to establish discrimination under the ADA. If the plaintiff makes such a showing, the defendant must make the requested modification unless it proves that doing so would alter the fundamental nature of its business. The exception has become known as the *fundamental alteration* exception or defense. The basic idea is that while the requested modification is necessary (Element (4)(b) in Exhibit 16.4), it is not reasonable (Element (4)(a) in Exhibit 16.4) to require a modification that would fundamentally alter the nature of the provider's business.

EXHIBIT 16.4 The elements of an ADA discrimination claim.

An individual alleging discrimination under Title III must show that:

(1) he is disabled as that term is defined by the ADA;

(2) the defendant is a private entity that owns, leases, or operates a place of public accommodation;

(3) the defendant employed a discriminatory policy or practice; and

(4) the defendant discriminated against the plaintiff based upon the plaintiff's disability by

   (a) failing to make a requested reasonable modification that was

   (b) necessary to accommodate the plaintiff's disability.

This defense is often raised when it is undisputed that the plaintiff is a person with a disability and the defendant is operating a place of public accommodation. So the main issue remaining is whether the plaintiff is being discriminated against on the basis of his disability and being denied a reasonable accommodation.

The United States Supreme Court first considered a case involving an ADA claim in the sport industry in *PGA Tour, Inc. v. Martin* (2001), which we have mentioned previously. The PGA Tour argued that Casey Martin's requested modification would fundamentally alter the nature of the PGA Tour competition and therefore was not a reasonable modification. The "walking rule" required all PGA Tour elite golfers to walk the course during competition. Read the following Focus Case to see how the court evaluated the **fundamental alteration** defense asserted by the PGA Tour.

PGA Tour, Inc. v. Martin

532 U.S. 661 (2001) **FOCUS CASE**

FACTS

Casey Martin was a participant in a professional golf event operated by the PGA. The PGA Tour hosted its events at public and private golf courses throughout the United States. Both the events and the competition were open to the general public. The PGA Tour, when it was hosting tour events, was a place of public accommodation. Martin is an individual with a disability. Martin has a degenerative bone disease that causes atrophy in one leg. He is very limited in his ability to walk and to bear weight on the affected leg. As a college athlete he requested and received a reasonable accommodation from the NCAA and the PAC-10 Conference that permitted him to use a golf cart during competition to transport him from one shot location to another. When Martin earned a place on the PGA Tour, he requested a similar accommodation and was denied. The PGA Tour contended that permitting Martin to ride in a golf cart would be a fundamental alteration of its event, which is an elite professional golf contest.

HOLDING

Martin's requested modification was not a fundamental alteration of the tour competition.

RATIONALE

Section 12182(b)(2)(A)(ii) identifies the elements and evidentiary burdens for a discrimination claim. Martin was required to and offered competent evidence that he was an individual with a disability, that a modification was requested, and that the modification requested was reasonable. The burden then shifted to the PGA to demonstrate that the requested modification would fundamentally alter the nature of the PGA Tour event. The PGA argued that walking was a fundamental aspect of the game of golf and that the purpose of its rule requiring competitors to walk at all times during the competition was to inject the element of fatigue into the competition. The district court found that, assuming the purpose of the rule was to inject fatigue into the competition, such purpose was not being fundamentally altered by permitting Martin to participate with the aid of a cart due to his individual circumstances and the severity of his disability.

The Supreme Court upheld the district court's conclusion that when evaluating accommodation requests under Title III, the court must conduct an **individualized inquiry,** a fact-specific inquiry relative to the stated purpose of a rule and a person's individual disability and circumstances, to determine whether a requested modification of the rule is reasonable. The PGA had argued that only the nature of the public accommodation or its programs should be examined to determine whether a modification of a rule or policy would result in a fundamental alteration, and that substantive rules of a competition could not be waived without fundamentally altering the nature of the competition. Thus, in essence the PGA's argument was that once a rule is designated as a substantive rule, any modification would result in a fundamental alteration. However, Section 12182 provides that "reasonable modification in policies, practices, or procedures" must be made. The statute does not say that only policies, practices, or procedures that are not substantive are subject to modification.

The Supreme Court developed a two-step analysis to determine whether a modification of a substantive rule of competition would result in a fundamental alteration of the competition. First, the requested modification must not fundamentally alter the essence of the sport. Second, the requested modification must not give the disabled athlete a competitive advantage. The Court held that walking was not a fundamental part of the sport of golf—golf tests one's shot-making skills, not walking skills. The Court concluded that given Martin's individual circumstances, affording him the use of a cart would not give him a competitive advantage.

After the *Martin* decision was released, some critics speculated that it would open a floodgate of modifications requests. However, it has not had that effect. Few rule modifications would satisfy the two-part inquiry. An example of a rule modification that would satisfy the two-part inquiry is using a blinking light instead of a starting gun to signal the start of a race for a hearing-impaired swimmer. Clearly the essential nature of the competition, which is swimming, has not been altered, nor has the hearing-impaired athlete been given a competitive advantage.

This section focused on the application of the ADA to the operation of sport facilities. We discovered that all sport facilities are subject to the ADA in some fashion, and the ADA's mandate extends to accessing the building and its amenities as well as the programs and services offered by the owner or operator of the facility. We also discovered that both the owner and an operator of a facility have responsibility for ADA compliance. In the next section, we examine sport facility operations related to spectator searches.

Spectator Searches

In Chapter 14, the limitations imposed on the government by the Fourth Amendment to the Constitution were discussed in the context of drug-testing programs in state schools and universities. The issue there was whether a drug test represented a search and whether such a search was reasonable under the Fourth Amendment. Issues related to searches and seizures also arise in the context of facility and event management. The policies or procedures used by a stadium or arena to screen or limit access to the facility can implicate the Fourth Amendment also.

As was discussed in Chapter 14, a Fourth Amendment analysis generally asks three questions.

1. Is there state action? If so,
2. Does the challenged activity constitute a search and/or seizure? If so,
3. Was the search reasonable, i.e., does the state have probable cause and a warrant or some other acceptable justification for the search without a warrant?

The Supreme Court has consistently held that under the Fourth Amendment "a search conducted without a warrant issued upon probable cause is 'per se unreasonable . . . subject only to a few specifically established and well-delineated exceptions'" (*Katz v. United States,* 1967). A few exceptions to the probable cause and warrant requirements have been recognized by the courts. For example, in the school drug-testing situation, "special needs" of the public schools substituted for probable cause and relieved the public school of the requirement to obtain a warrant before conducting a drug test.

However, in the context of public venues such as stadiums and arenas the court has only recognized a few exceptions such as airports and courthouses. Prior to the terrorist attacks on September 11, 2001, the courts had considered only a few cases involving screening and spectator searches at stadiums, arenas, and theaters. In these cases, the courts focused on the reasonableness of the search.

Reasonableness of the search

The analysis for determining reasonableness in the context of spectator searches at public venues requires that courts look at the "totality of the circumstances." Typically the analysis hinges on three factors:

1. *Need.* The analysis of "need" examines the nature of the threat, whether the threat is real or perceived, whether the threat is particularized. Also considered is the significance of the harm in terms of its scope and size and whether those likely to be injured are unsuspecting.
2. *Efficacy.* For a proposed search to meet the standard of being efficacious, the courts examine whether the search will likely avert the harm identified as part of the need.
3. *Nature of the intrusion.* Examining the nature and degree of intrusion involves both a subjective and objective component. The subjective component looks at the amount of stigma associated with the search, whether the search is a mass or individualized search, and whether the procedures that are being used could frighten or humiliate or merely annoy. Also taken into consideration is whether the search is being conducted by uniformed officers who may tend to frighten or inject a level of authority that plainclothes searchers do not. The objective component compares the search techniques to assess the scope of the intrusion. For example, visual inspections would be less intrusive than physical touching. Delaying a spectator for a few seconds to inspect a purse or bag would be less intrusive than detaining them for a full pat-down search or handheld scope.

Competitive Advantage
STRATEGIES

Spectator/Guest Issues

- The facility owner, operator, or lessee should establish procedures for regularly evaluating the accessibility of the facility and its programs and services. Seeking input from local disability groups will enable you to better understand and appreciate this user group and comply with the ADA mandate. It also is good public relations.

- Facility operators must carefully balance the need for conducting spectator searches with the potential intrusion imposed upon their customers. Any search should be effective at addressing a specific need for protection or safety, and should be as non-intrusive as possible to achieve those objectives.

In 2005, the National Football League implemented a new policy that requires the teams in its league to initiate and conduct pat-down searches at all NFL games. The policy was immediately challenged in several courts. Those cases have reached inconsistent results thus far. As an example, a Tampa Bay Buccaneer season ticket holder sued the Tampa Sports Authority and challenged the pat-down searches implemented in response to the NFL policy. The following discussion will help to identify how the district court analyzed this issue and how stadium and arena managers are responding as well. Next, the court of appeals decision is provided as a Case Opinion for you to contrast with the district court's decision.

In August 2005, the National Football League declared that all persons attending league games must be physically searched before entering any of the venues where games are played, aiming to prevent terrorist attacks in the stadiums. The Buccaneers implemented this directive at Raymond James Stadium. Gordon Johnston had been a Buccaneers season ticket holder for several years and had renewed his season tickets for the 2005 season at a cost of $869.20 plus $250.00 for stadium parking. At that time Johnston was not given notice that he would have to submit to a pat-down search before entering the stadium. When Johnston learned of this new policy, he contacted the Buccaneers to complain, but he was told that the Buccaneers would not refund his payment for the season tickets. Moreover, even if Johnston were permitted to return his 2005 tickets for a refund, he would lose the remainder of his seat deposit and be put at the bottom of a 100,000-person waiting list if he desired to purchase season tickets in the future. In *Johnston v Tampa Sports Authority*, (2006), Johnston sued the Tampa Sports Authority (TSA) seeking to enjoin them from conducting pat-down searches of every person who attended a Tampa Bay Buccaneers home football game. A primary issue before the district court was whether Johnston had consented to the searches.

Initially the district court found that the TSA was a state actor and subject to the Fourth Amendment to the U.S. Constitution. The Fourth Amendment restraint generally bars government officials from undertaking a search or seizure without individualized suspicion. The district court acknowledged that the sanctity of one's person is the starting point for a Fourth Amendment analysis. The TSA contended that Johnston consented to the search by repeatedly attending NFL games—knowing in advance that he would either be subjected to a pat-down search or denied entry to the stadium. The essence of this argument is that Johnston was not compelled to submit to the search but rather that he consented to it when he chose to attend the Buccaneers' games. The district court held that where the government conditions the receipt of a benefit (i.e., attending the event) on the wavier of a constitutional right (i.e., to be free from suspicionless searches), the implied consent is invalid as an unconstitutional condition. The doctrine of unconstitutional conditions prohibits terminating benefits if the termination is based on motivations that are unconstitutional. Johnston's interest in his season tickets and his right to attend games and assemble with other Bucs fans constitute a benefit or privilege that cannot be conditioned on relinquishment of his Fourth Amendment rights. The district court also held that, even without the unconstitutional conditions, Johnston's conduct did not constitute implied consent because it was not voluntarily given. The district court found that Johnston was not notified of the pat-down policy prior to purchasing his season tickets; once notified, he was informed he could not receive a refund; and even if a refund were available, he would have lost his ticket priority. Johnston verbally objected each time he was asked to submit to the pat-down search. Thus, the district court concluded that Johnston's consent was not voluntarily given. The TSA appealed to the Eleventh Circuit Court of Appeals, whose decision is as follows.

Johnston v Tampa Sports Authority

530 F.3d 1320 (11th Cir. 2008)   **CASE OPINION**

FACTS

Under a franchise agreement, the public sports authority adopted a professional football league's policy of patting down patrons entering the authority's stadium to attend league games. The sole purpose of the pat-downs was to protect patrons from terrorism in the form of improvised explosive devices. The ticket holder allowed himself to be patted down over objection three times. The district court found that the pat-downs violated both the Florida and U. S. Constitutions.

HOLDING

We conclude that Appellee Gordon Johnston consented to the searches.

RATIONALE

The United States Supreme Court has consistently held that "a search conducted without a warrant issued upon probable cause is 'per se unreasonable . . . subject only to a few specifically established and well-delineated exceptions.'" "It is equally well settled that one of the specifically established exceptions to the requirements of both a warrant and probable cause is a search that is conducted pursuant to consent."

Consensual Searches

Whether consent is voluntary is a fact question determined according to the totality of the circumstances and determined on a case-by-case basis. Both the federal and Florida courts have enumerated non-exhaustive lists of factors to be considered in performing the analysis. We have previously identified the following non-exhaustive factors to consider in determining voluntariness: (1) whether the person is in custody, (2) the existence of coercion, (3) the person's awareness of his right to refuse consent, (4) the person's education and intelligence, and (5) whether the person believes incriminating evidence will be found.

Florida courts look for the existence of express or implied consent and consider the following implied consent factors: (1) whether the defendant was aware his conduct would subject him to search; (2) whether the search was supported by a "vital interest"; (3) whether the searching officer had apparent authority to search and arrest; (4) whether the defendant was advised of his right to refuse; and (5) whether refusal would result in a deprivation of a benefit or right.

Consent is not voluntary if the government conditions receipt of a right or a benefit on the relinquishment of a constitutional right (*Bourgeois v. Peters*, 2004). Johnston knew well in advance that he would be subjected to a pat-down search by the Authority if he presented himself at an entrance to the Stadium to be admitted to a Buccaneers game. The factors above demonstrate the voluntariness of Johnston's consent. Johnston was not in custody at the time of the search, rather, he presented himself willingly at the search point. The screeners did not coerce Johnston, they merely performed the search to which Johnston submitted. Johnston was well aware of his right to refuse to submit to the pat-down search and did in fact express his objection to the searches to specific screeners and over the telephone to the Buccaneers before the searches were implemented. At the search point, Johnston pulled his shirt up (apparently to show that he was not wearing an IED) and asked not to be patted down. When screeners insisted on the pat-down before permitting Johnston to enter, Johnston elected to be patted down and thereby gain entrance to the Stadium. Johnston appears from the record to be a man of heightened intelligence and well-educated. The record shows he did not believe that the search would disclose incriminating evidence, as shown by his attempt to show screeners he was not carrying any suspicious devices under his shirt.

Johnston also impliedly consented to the search under the factors for implied consent developed by Florida courts. Johnston was well-aware his insistence in entering the Stadium would cause him to be subject to a search. The record also reflects that Johnston was aware of his ability to refuse to be searched and leave the Stadium. There is no evidence that the Authority would have detained Johnston if he refused, or that Johnston otherwise believed the searches to be compulsory.

Doctrine of Unconstitutional Conditions

The district court found that the consent exception did not apply in this case, in part, because of the "unconstitutional condition" doctrine developed by federal and Florida courts. "The doctrine of unconstitutional conditions prohibits terminating benefits, though not classified as entitlements, if the termination is based on motivations that other constitutional provisions proscribe." ("This is a classic 'unconstitutional conditions,' in which the government conditions receipt of a benefit or privilege on the relinquishment of a constitutional right.") The district court erred in its application of the unconstitutional conditions doctrine because in this case the condition for entry was imposed by the NFL and the Buccaneers, both private entities, and not the government.

As we noted, Johnston did not have any right or entitlement to enter the Stadium. His purchase of a ticket granted him at most a revocable license

to a seat. As is typical of sporting events, the NFL and the Buccaneers explicitly retained the right to exclude him from the Stadium for any reason. The NFL chose to impose a pat-down as a condition for entry. Although the Authority acquiesced to the NFL's requests by hiring screeners to conduct pat-downs, the conclusion that this policy was the NFL's—and not the Authority's—condition for entry is reinforced by the Authority's security measures at other non-NFL events at the Stadium, including collegiate football games, where the Authority does not conduct pat-downs. In other cases where we have used the unconstitutional conditions doctrine to invalidate consent, we found that it was the government imposing the condition and performing the search.

In this case, the government had no role in formulating or mandating the pat-down policy. The policy exists solely because of the NFL's mandate. Because the condition for entry was imposed by a private party, Johnston was not forced by the government to choose between assertion of his constitutional rights and obtaining a benefit to which he was entitled. The NFL's condition does not invalidate Johnston's voluntary consent to the pat-downs. Considering the totality of the circumstances, the Court concludes that Johnston voluntarily consented to pat-down searches each time he presented himself at a Stadium entrance to attend a game.

Questions

The Supreme Court denied Johnston's Petition for Certiorari on January 21, 2009 (*Johnston v. Tampa Sports Authority,* 2009). The *Johnston* case presents an excellent opportunity to review Fourth Amendment issues in the context of stadium operations. It is important to note, however, that the Eleventh Circuit Court of Appeals reversed the district court, focusing almost exclusively on the issue of implied consent. Consider the following discussion questions to compare and contrast the two decisions.

1. How do the factors for determining voluntariness and those used to evaluate implied consent differ?

2. Based on the district court's decision, how did the principle of unconstitutional conditions apply to Johnston as a season ticket holder seeking to gain entry to the event? How did the court of appeals address this issue?

CONCLUSION

This chapter applied numerous legal principles in the context of the sport facility. Specifically, we examined the duty of care owed by the stadium owner or operator to the spectator and the major contract considerations related to lease agreements, ticket agreements, and game contracts. We also examined the application of the Americans with Disabilities Act to places of public accommodation, specifically to stadiums and arenas. Lastly, we explored the constitutional law issues that arise when operators of public stadiums seek to conduct searches of spectators without suspicion. A solid understanding of the varied legal issues presented in this chapter will enable you to be a more effective facility owner or operator.

discussion questions

1. Define the terms "invitee," "licensee," and "trespasser." What difference do these classifications make in the scope of duty owed by a facility owner or operator?

2. When does a plaintiff assume the risk of a dangerous condition on the property? Discuss the open and obvious doctrine and give an example. What is the distraction doctrine? Give an example.

3. What is the purpose of the recreational use statutes?

4. Compare and contrast the concepts of actual notice and constructive notice. Give an example of each.

5. Explain the limited duty rule applied to spectators who are hit by foul balls at baseball games.

6. Explain the importance of clearly identifying the areas to be leased and the duration of a lease in a standard sport facility lease.

7. How is an "alteration" defined under the ADA?

8. Explain the Department of Justice's basis for requiring facilities to provide people with disabilities comparable lines of sight.

9. Explain the rationale for applying the ADA to owners, operators, and lessees of places of public accommodation.

10. What is a revocable license? Assuming tickets are revocable licenses, how does that benefit the sport facility or sport organization that sells the tickets?

11. Explain why spectators attending sporting events may be legally subject to pat-down searches before they are permitted to enter the stadium or arena.

learning activities

1. Do an online search for your state statutes that mandate emergency medical protocols at sport facilities. For example, is there legislation mandating automated external defibrillators at fitness centers? Is there legislation providing

that an ambulance must be present at sporting events where the seating capacity of the facility exceeds a certain number?

2. Locate online the ADA technical assistance guide for accessible stadiums provided by the Department of Justice's Office of Civil Rights. What are two key features of accessible stadiums? What other accessible features are covered in the guidelines? What percentage of drinking fountains should be wheelchair accessible? Take the guidelines to a recreational facility in your area and evaluate how well the facility meets the accessibility criteria.

CASE STUDY

Northern City is building a new 28,000-seat multipurpose facility downtown. The facility is owned and operated by the Northern City Sports Development Board. The arena will be the home of the University of Northern City's men's and women's basketball teams. The arena should be completed by October 1, 2013. Southern University hosts an invitational basketball tournament in December each year and usually plays at its home stadium in Southville. What are some of the major issues that would need to be included in a contract between Southern University and the Northern City Sports Development Board for use of the new arena for the 2013 Southern Invitational?

considering . . .   **ANALYSIS & DISCUSSION**

Duty to Repair Dangers (p. 471)

In this case, the answer is most likely no. Since virtually no time passed between the time of the spill and the time of the fall, it was not unreasonable for the school personnel to be unable to react to the spill and clean it up. If we change the facts to suggest that the spill had been there since a game held the week prior, that period of time is clearly unreasonable.

Facility Lease Agreements (p. 486)

First, Sally and the LOC needed to understand fully the exact needs of the event in order to evaluate the appropriateness and availability of the facility spaces before negotiating the lease agreement. Ideally the lease agreement would have begun a day earlier, on April 9. This would certainly have increased the event costs, but it would have avoided the problem. Had the lease agreement included a clause that granted access to all the lease spaces 24 hours prior to the start of the lease term, the LOC would also have been protected. However, it is unlikely that a facility would provide for that much advance access without additional fees.

As a compromise position or solution, the LOC may have negotiated access to an adjacent exhibition hall or practice court without incurring additional rental costs, thus permitting the Waterfront Arena Authority to lease the main arena for the concert on the day before the team handball event. Access to this adjacent exhibition hall or practice court would have allowed the USATHF operations crew the opportunity to roll out the floor in advance so that it would relax and rebound. The main lesson for Sally and for any event or operations director is to communicate space, equipment, and installation needs clearly to the person or persons negotiating the lease agreements. This hypothetical case also emphasizes the importance of the "right to use" clause in defining when the lessee will be permitted to gain access to the premises.

REFERENCES

Cases

Barbato v. Hollow Hills Country Club, 789 N.Y.S.2d 199 (App. Div. 2004).

Bearman v. University of Notre Dame, 453 N.E.2d 1196 (Ind. Ct. App. 1983).

Benejam v. Detroit Tigers, Inc., 635 N.W.2d 219 (Mich. Ct. App. 2001).

Berman v. Parker, 348 U.S. 26 (1954).

Caruso v. Blockbuster-Sony Music Entertainment Centre at the Waterfront (3rd Cir. 1999).

Celano v. Marriott International, Inc., U.S. Dist. LEXIS 6172 (N.D. Cal. 2008).

Clark v. Simms, 2009 U.S. Dist. LEXIS 29027 (W.D. Va. 2009).

Disabled Rights Action Comm. v. Las Vegas Events, Inc., 375 F.3d 861 (9th Cir. 2004).

Feldman v. Pro Football, Inc, 579 F. Supp. 2d 697 (S.D. Md., 2008).

Fowler v. Bally Total Fitness, Case no. 07 L 12258 (Md. Circuit Court 2008).

Independent Living Resources v. Oregon, 982 F. Supp. 698 (D. Ore. 1997).

Johnston v Tampa Sports Authority, 530 F.3d 1320 (11th Cir. 2008).

Johnston v Tampa Sports Authority, 442 F. Supp. 2d 1257 (M.D. Fla. 2006).

Katz v. United States, 389 U.S. 347 (1967).

Kelly v. Marylanders for Sports Sanity, Inc., 530 A.2d 245 (Md. Ct. App. 1987).

Kelo v. City of New London, 545 U.S. 469 (2005).

King County v. Taxpayers, 949 P.2d 1260 (Wash. 1997).

L.A. Fitness International v. Mayer, 980 So.2d 550 (Fla. Dist. Ct. App. 2008).

Lane v. Saint Paul's College, 2008 Va. Cir. LEXIS 133 (October 1, 2008).

Lowe v. California League of Prof'l Baseball, 56 Cal. App. 4th 112 (App. Ct. 1997).

Maisonave v. Newark Bears Prof'l Baseball Club, 881 A. 2d 700 (N.J. 2005).

Matthews v. NCAA, 179 F. Supp. 2d 1209 (E.D. Wash. 2001).

Menough v. Woodfield Gardens, 694 N.E.2d 1038 (Ill. App. Ct. 1998).

Metropolitan Sports Facilities Comm'n v. Minnesota Twins P'ship, 638 N.W.2d 214 (Minn. Ct. App. 2002).

Miller v. California Speedway Corp., 536 F.3d 1020 (9th Cir. 2008).

Paralyzed Veterans of America v. D.C. Arena, L.P., 117 F.3d 579 (D.C. Cir. 1997).

PGA Tour, Inc. v. Martin, 532 U.S. 661 (2001).

Prokop v. Independent Sch. Dist. #625, 754 N.W.2d 709 (Minn. Ct. App. 2008).

Rees v. Cleveland Indians Baseball Co., Inc., 2004 Ohio App. LEXIS 5580 (Ohio Ct. App. Nov. 18, 2004).

Rotolo v. San Jose Sports and Entertainment, 151 Cal. App. 4th 307 (2007).

Rowe v. Pinellas Sports Auth., 461 So. 2d 72 (Fla. 1984).

Salte v. YMCA of Metro. Chicago Found., 814 N.E.2d 610 (Ill. App. Ct. 2004).

Sciarrotta v. Global Spectrum, 944 A.2d 630 (N.J. 2008).

Turner v. Mandalay Sports Entertainment, 180 P.3d 1172 (Nev. 2008).

United States of America v. Ellerbe Becket, Inc., 976 F. Supp. 1262 (D. Minn. 1997).

University of Louisville v. Duke University, Case No. 07-CI-1765 (Franklin County Circuit Court, Commonwealth of Kentucky, 2008).

Uzun v. Oakwood Sports Center of Hamden, Inc., 2008 Conn. Super. LEXIS 2650 (October 21, 2008).

Yates v. Johnson County Bd. of Comm'rs, 888 N.E.2d 842 (Ind. Ct. App. 2008).

Statutes

Title III of the Americans with Disabilities Act, 42 U.S.C. § 12181 et seq. (2005).

United States Constitution, Fifth Amendment.

Other Sources

Alberg, A. (2008, July 2). *USA Today*. Retrieved April 1, 2010 from www.usatoday.com/sports/basketball/nba/sonics/2008-07-02-seattle-trial_N.htm

Americans With Disabilities Act (ADA) Accessibility Guidelines for Buildings and Facilities; Recreation Facilities, 36 C.F.R. Part 1191 (2002).

Associated Press. (2007, April 17). Disabled vets challenging Michigan stadium upgrades. *Sports Illustrated*. Retrieved June 12, 2009, from http://www.callsam.com/bernstein-media-center/richard-bernstein-news-fighting-for-justice/fighting-for-disabled-veterans-rights/disabled-vets-challenging-michigan-stadium-upgrades.

Bagli, C. V. (2009, November 24). Ruling lets Atlantic Yards seize land. *The New York Times*, Retrieved February 16, 2010, from http://www.nytimes.com/2009/11/25/nyregion/25yards.html?_r=1.

Black's law dictionary. (2004). St. Paul, MN: West Publishing Co.

Boston fan has tickets revoked for interference. (2005, April 19). *Washington Post*, p. D10. Retrieved February 27, 2006, from www.washingtonpost.com/wp-dyn/articles/A64520-2005aprl18.html.

Brown, M. T., Rascher, D. A., Nagel, M. S., & McEvoy, C. D. (2010). *Financial management in the sport industry*. Scottsdale, AZ: Holcomb Hathaway.

Brown, N. (2008, August). Pool rules. *Athletic Business*, 58–68.

Brunner, J. (2007, September 25). Blame flies as city sues Sonics. *The Seattle Times*. Retrieved April 1, 2010, from http://seattletimes.nwsource.com/html/localnews/2003900552_sonics25m0.html

Chan, S. (2009, July 7). On Yankee Stadium restroom dispute, the city settles. *The New York Times*. Retrieved January 20, 2010, from http://cityroom.blogs.nytimes.com/2009/07/07/on-yankee-stadium-restroom-dispute-the-city-settles/.

Connaughton, D., Spengler, J. O., & Zhang, J. J. (2007, Winter). Symposium: Risk management issues in sports: An analysis of automated external defibrillator implementation and related risk management practices in health/fitness clubs. *Journal of Legal Aspects of Sport, 17*, 81–101.

Department of Justice. (1996, October 22). Letter to Commissioner Allan Selig, Major League Baseball.

Dvorchak, R. (2005, April 3). $135 million jury award forces new look at high costs of sports and drinking. *Post-gazette.com*. Retrieved July 27, 2005, from www.post-gazette.com/pg/05093/481516.stm.

Garner, B. A., et al. (2004). *Black's law dictionary* (8th ed.). St. Paul, MN: Thompson.

Gershman, D. (2008, October 29). Disabled fans cheer new handicapped seating at Michigan Stadium. *Ann Arbor News*. Retrieved June 12, 2009, from http://www.mlive.com/news/ann-arbor/index.ssf/2008/10/disabled_fans_cheer_new_handic.html.

Goldman, S. (2009, January). One step at a time. *Fitness Business, 29*–37.

Gottlieb, H. (2008, December 4). Court orders unsealing of settlement in stadium beer vendor liability case. Retrieved June 10, 2009, from http://www.law.com/jsp/LawArticleFriendly.jsp?id=1202426456825.

Greenberg, G. (2005, January/February). The condemned. *Mother Jones*. Retrieved March 22, 2007, from http://www.motherjones.com/news/feature/2005/01/01_407.html.

Greenberg, M. J. (2004). Sports facilities financing and development trends in the United States. *Marquette Sports Law Review, 15*(1), 93–174.

Hybl, D. (2010, January 15). Is it time for Baltimore's ultimate revenge on the Colts? *Baltimore Sports Then and Now*. Retrieved April 13, 2010, from http://baltimore.sportsthenandnow.com/2010/01/is-it-time-for-baltimore%e2%80%99s-ultimate-revenge-on-the-colts/

Joyner, J. (2005, June 25). Eminent domain ruling affects Dallas Cowboys stadium. *Outside the Beltway*. Retrieved February 16, 2010, from http://www.outsidethebeltway.com/archives/eminent_domain_ruling_affects_dallas_cowboys_stadium/.

McGraw, D. (2005, May). Demolishing sports welfare. *Reason online*. Retrieved October 1, 2006, from http://www.reason.com/0505/fe.dm.demolishing.shtml.

Mihoces, G. (2006, June 15). Trainers stress preparedness. *USA Today*, p. 10C.

Mosier, J. (2008, September 10). Court case challenges eminent domain for Dallas Cowboys stadium. *The Dallas Morning News*. Retrieved February 16, 2010, from www.dallasnews.com/sharedcontent/dws/news/localnews/cowboysstadium/stories/091108dnmetstadium.616aec1e.html.

Natarajan, P., & O'Connell, J. (2007, October 5). Fight for land near Nats' stadium goes to extra innings. *Washington Business Journal*. Retrieved February 16, 2010, from http://washington.bizjournals.com/washington/stories/2007/10/08/story2.html.

OHSAA says mistake was made in benching legless player. (2005, October 7). *Sports Litigation Alerts, 2*(16), 17.

Oklahoma State wins eminent domain case. (2009, December 10). *Inside Higher Ed.* Retrieved February 16, 2010, from http://www.insidehighered.com/news/2009/12/10/qt/oklahoma_state_wins_eminent_domain_case.

Ove, T. (2005, February 11). Judge benches fan's lawsuit against Steelers and NFL. *Pittsburgh Post-Gazette.* Retrieved February 4, 2006, from www.post-gazette.com/pg/05042/456085.stm.

Popke, M. (2003b, January). Playground confidential. *Athletic Business,* 9–10.

Restatement (Second) of Torts (1965).

River of Dreams. (2005, April 3). *Tailgating stats.* Retrieved July 26, 2005, from www.tailgating.com/Stats.htm.

SB 4 and eminent domain news. (2005, June 23). Retrieved October 1, 2006, from http://newballpark.blogspot.com/2005/06/sb-4-and-eminentdomain-news.html.

Scholand, G. (2006, Apr/May). Getting tough. *Athletic Business,* 28–35.

Southall, R. M., & Sharp, L. A. (2006). The National Football league and its "culture of intoxication": A negligent marketing analysis of *Verni v. Lanzaro. Journal of Legal Aspects of Sport, 16,* 121–147.

SportsBusiness Journal. (2010, January 25). Five questions for the facilities industry. p. 18.

Stadium eminent domain. (2008, February 11). *Settlements and Verdicts.* Retrieved February 16, 2010, from http://www.lawyersandsettlements.com/case/football-stadium-eminent-domain.html.

Steinbach, P. (2003, August). Party lines. *Athletic Business,* 30–34.

Steinbach, P. (2008, April). A step further. *Athletic Business,* 68–69.

Steinbach, P. (2008, June). The rise and fall of stadium escalators. *Athletic Business,* 14–16.

Steinbach, P. (2008, October). Cold beer here! *Athletic Business,* 20–24.

U. of Michigan to increase wheelchair-accessible seating in stadium. (2007, November 19). *The Chronicle of Higher Education.* Retrieved June 12, 2009, from http://chronicle.com/news/article/3458/u-of-michigan-to-increase-wheelchair-accessible-seating-at-stadium.

United States Access Board. (2003, June). Accessible sports facilities: A summary of accessibility guidelines for recreation facilities. United States Access Board. Retrieved February 27, 2006, from http://www.access-board.gov/recreation/guides/sports.htm

van der Smissen, B. (1990). *Legal liability and risk management for public and private entities.* Cincinnati, OH: Anderson Publishing.

Wolohan, J. T. (2008, May). Aftershocks. *Athletic Business,* 28–31.

Wolohan, J. T. (2009, September). An unobstructed view. *Athletic Business.* Retrieved February 16, 2010, from http://www.athleticbusiness.com/articles/article.aspx?articleid=2573&zoneid=31.

Wolverton, B. (2007, October 31). Education Department accuses U. of Michigan of broad violations of disabilities law in stadium changes. *The Chronicle of Higher Education.* Retrieved June 12, 2009, from http://chronicle.com/daily/2007/10/557n.htm.

Wood, S. (2008, Sept. 12). Code of conduct to control fans gone wild gets early thumbs up. *USA Today,* p. 11C.

WEBSITE RESOURCES

http://www.ncaa.org/Sportsmanship/SportsmanshipFanBehavior/report.pdf ▪ This is a report generated by the NCAA regarding the best practices in crowd management.

www.nata.org/newsrelease/archives/000416.htm ▪ This relates to the "Recommendations on Emergency Preparedness of Sudden Cardiac Arrest in High School and College Athletic Programs" released by the National Athletic Trainers Association in June 2006. The NATA recommended early defibrillation, i.e., within 3–5 minutes.

www.NCAA.org/health-safety ▪ Link to the 2008–09 Sports Medicine Handbook to find Guideline 1d entitled Lightning Safety for a statement that planned access to early defibrillation should be a part of any emergency plan.

www.ncsl.org/IssuesResearch/Health/LawsonCardiacArrestandDefibrillatorsAEDS/tabid/14506/Default.aspx. ▪ This link from the National Conference of State Legislatures provides information on the state laws pertaining to the use of AEDS.

www.sporteventsecurity.com ▪ This is the website for the National Center for Spectator Sports Safety & Security housed at the University of Southern Mississippi. The Center conducts workshops to train sport venue personnel in professional and college sports on issues related to risk management and security for sports venues.

www.access-board.gov/recreation/guides/index.htm ▪ An overview of accessibility guidelines for recreation facilities such as amusement rides, golf courses, and swimming pools put together by the United States Access Board. The organization is dedicated to accessible design, and this section of their site provides an overview of the legislation that affects different recreational areas, sample accessible routes, and descriptions of possible devices that can help accessibility.

www.accessgolf.org/ ▪ The National Alliance for Accessible Golf focuses on promoting golf for persons with disabilities and on increasing accessibility at golf facilities. The site offers studies and statistics as well as tool kits for golfers and golf course owners. The organization's GAIN program is offered for organizations wishing to implement an inclusive golf program.

www.resourcecenter.usga.org ▪ The United States Golf Association has compiled information for golfers with disabilities, creating the Resource Center for Individuals with Disabilities. There are databases of players, instructors, facilities, tournaments, and therapists, all of whom work with or can work with disabled golfers.

www.ncaonline.org ▪ The Department of Recreation, Park and Tourism Studies at Indiana University houses the National Center on Accessibility. Under "Access A to Z," they have real-world case studies of organizations and places that worked to become more accessible, in addition to research, recommendations, and news. The "Training and Education" tab provides listings of accessibility training courses across the country.

www.ncpad.org ▪ The site for the National Center on Physical Activity and Disability provides a wealth of resources on disabilities, physical activity, and health promotion. A large database of videos contains clips of exercise programs, recreational instruction, and stretches. The site also provides resources regarding accessibility and disabilities, including links to journals, magazines, books, and news reports.

Use of Waivers and Exculpatory Clauses

INTRODUCTION

The ways in which you communicate with sport and recreation participants affect many aspects of your managerial and legal relationship with them. As in any relationship, business or personal, what you say to people and how you say it become a cornerstone of the relationship. Use your communication mechanisms to convey and reinforce the message that you are concerned about the welfare of participants and that you are sharing information with them to make their participation experiences better and safer. The notion of using documents to avoid liability, such as the exculpatory clause, is only a secondary aspect. Using the law to attain a competitive advantage in the business of sport has particular application in the context of information exchange, since you and your organization have complete control over the messages you send to your participants. This philosophy should sound familiar to you—it represents the essence of the preventive law process as discussed in Chapter 2.

This chapter focuses on the types of information exchanges you may have with your participants, such as brochures, videos, other promotional materials, exculpatory agreements, and agreements to participate. We discuss the legal concerns relevant to each of these as well as the managerial implications of each for your business. See Exhibit 17.1 for an overview of this chapter's managerial contexts, major legal issues, relevant laws, and illustrative cases.

EXHIBIT	17.1	Management contexts in which issues related to waivers and exculpatory clauses may arise, with relevant laws and cases.

MANAGEMENT CONTEXT	MAJOR LEGAL ISSUES	RELEVANT LAW	ILLUSTRATIVE CASES
Oversight of any activity	Setting standard of care	Negligence	*Sunday*
Development of marketing materials	Accuracy of promotional materials	Breach of contract	
Oversight of youth sport programs Supervision of K–12 athletics	Validity of waivers signed by minors or parents	Contract law	*Hojnowski, Krathen*
Athletic directors of school sports or university sports	School sports as essential services	Contract law	*Wagenblast, Kyriazis*
Ski resort managers	Skiing as essential service	Contract law	*Silva*
Providers of commercial outfitters	Violation of statutory duty and waivers	Contract law Statute setting standard of care	*Murphy*
Oversight of any sport/ recreational activity	Public policy and waivers	Contract law	*Debell*
	Waiver language clarity	Contract law	*Zides, Cohen, Wang*
	Conduct beyond negligence	Contract law	*City of Santa Barbara*
	Agreements to participate	Assumption of risk	
		Comparative negligence	
		Failure to warn	

BROCHURES, VIDEOS, AND PROMOTIONAL MATERIALS

One of the principles discussed in Chapter 2 with regard to the preventive law process was to have a holistic approach to every aspect of the organization. Therefore, when you are developing brochures, videos, and promotional materials for your programs, you should involve not only the marketing and advertising employees but also your attorney. The attorney can advise you regarding the legal impact of certain words or phrases that you wish to use. The following Focus Case provides an example of this issue. In Chapter 20 you will study the concept of false advertising; here we are instead focused on the effect the language of your advertising may have in setting the standard of care to which your organization will be held accountable.

Sunday v. Stratton Corp.

| 390 A.2d 398 (Vt. 1978) | **FOCUS CASE** |

FACTS

A novice skier was seriously injured while he traversed a novice trail at a fast walk. He allegedly tripped over a small "bush or brush" on the trail that had been concealed by snow. The plaintiff became a quadriplegic. In the lawsuit the plaintiff alleged that the defendant ski resort negligently maintained its ski trails and failed to warn of hidden dangers. The defendant took the position that the "bush/brush" could not have existed because of the "perfection" of the surface. All the witnesses for the defendant testified that the resort tried to achieve a "perfect surface for skiing" (p. 401). Further, the trail was portrayed as a "complete new surface," like a "fairway, absolutely flat" (p. 401). The jury believed, however, that the "bush/brush" did exist, and the plaintiff was awarded $1.5 million.

HOLDING

The Vermont Supreme Court affirmed the judgment in favor of the plaintiff.

RATIONALE

The primary issue was whether the "bush/brush" should be considered to be an inherent risk of skiing. If it is an inherent risk, there is no liability since the plaintiff would have assumed this risk as a part of the activity.

First the court discussed an earlier case that held that a tree trunk was an inherent risk of skiing for an intermediate skier. The court noted, however, that the passage of time (the earlier case was 20 years prior to *Sunday*) and technology had altered the sport of skiing. Since the defendant asserted that it could groom the slopes "perfectly," then it was held to that standard of care. Therefore, anything (including the "bush/brush") that was on the trail should not have been there, was a breach of the standard of care, and was not an inherent risk. The court also commented upon how the resort marketed to encourage the "timorous" not to stay home, but rather to come to the resort and ski. In choosing to attract this population, the resort assumed a responsibility to provide novice trails suitable for their use.

Competitive Advantage
STRATEGIES

Brochures, Videos, and Promotional Materials

- Information exchange with your participants is a crucial aspect of your preventive law plan. Incorporate the preparation of all documents into this process.

- Draft all documents to support your corporate culture and your goal of fostering the well-being of your participants.

- Never promise "perfection" in your brochures or other advertising materials. Perfection is unattainable, and your promise may serve to set an unrealistic standard of care for your program.

- Never promise that an activity is "perfectly safe"; that is inaccurate because there are always inherent risks in any physical activity.

- Consult an attorney when developing your advertising and marketing materials to avoid using language that may be detrimental to your legal position.

The *Sunday* case illustrates the difficulty when your organization, in effect, sets its own standard of care at "perfection." Brochures and promotional materials should certainly stress the aspects of a program that are valuable for participants and that will increase the enjoyment level. However, they should avoid any absolute assertions. They should never describe anything as "perfect," and never portray that an experience will be "absolutely safe." After all, no matter how well run a program is, an activity always has inherent risks that cannot be completely eliminated. Do not state that your activity meets or exceeds industry standards unless that is the case—then specify exactly the standard or standards to which you are referring.

Language is not only a problem in terms of setting or raising the standard of care; an organization may also incur liability for breach of contract, fraud, misrepresentation, or a violation of a consumer protection statute if the language is inaccurate. For example, in the case of *Brooks v. Timberline Tours, Inc.* (1997), a mother was injured and her minor son was killed while they were participating in a snowmobile tour. The plaintiffs brought a breach of contract action in addition to their negligence action against the snowmobile tour company. The plaintiffs used an advertising brochure, a guide manual, and the defendant's agreement with the owner of the land used for touring as the basis of the contract claim. All of the documents you use must contain accurate information about the nature of the activity and the actual risks that participants may encounter.

EXCULPATORY AGREEMENTS

An **exculpatory agreement,** by definition, is a contract in which a person or entity that is legally "at fault" tries to excuse itself from fault. An **exculpatory clause** is defined as a "contractual provision relieving a party from any liability resulting from a negligent or wrongful act" (*Black's Law Dictionary,* 1999, p. 588). Often, in sport/recreation situations, the agreement is in the form of a waiver or a pre-injury release. The party signing the waiver or release agrees to give up his or her right to sue the party at fault. There are technical differences between a waiver and a release, but either may be used in the type of case we are discussing, in which someone gives up his or her right to sue someone prior to participating in a sport or an activity.

This area of the law becomes complex because courts are involved in a difficult balancing act between two pillars of the law—tort law and contract law. Under the principles of tort law, defendants are held accountable for tortious acts that injure others. Plaintiffs have the right to seek damages against defendants who have injured them in situations in which the courts give a remedy.

In contrast, contract law gives adults the right to engage in various undertakings, including giving up rights. A **waiver** is a type of contract in which one party gives up his or her right to sue the other party, thus, in effect, altering the outcome that would transpire under the usual tort law principles. If a court upholds a waiver or release, it is making a choice to give precedence to contract law instead of tort law. The Colorado Supreme Court summarized this conflict as it stated that a release exists "at the cross-roads of two competing principles: freedom of contract and responsibility for damages caused by one's own negligent acts" (*Heil Valley Ranch v. Simkin*, 1989, p. 784).

Often people remark to the effect that "waivers are not worth the paper they are written on." This remark is fallacious, particularly as it pertains to physical activities and sport, because waivers are often upheld when two criteria are met:

1. They are used in the right circumstances (*context*).
2. They are written properly (*content*).

We will explore each of these major concepts at length.

Context

Because of the competing considerations between tort and contract law, courts will not uphold waivers in all circumstances. Giving up one's right to sue is an important decision, and courts must be satisfied that the context is appropriate for doing so. There are two primary aspects to consider when looking at the context issues:

1. Whether the person giving up the right to sue is a minor
2. Public policy considerations

Minority

Since a waiver is a contract, the usual rules of contract law apply. As we discussed in Chapter 4, if a minor signs a contract, the minor might later disavow that contract. This is because the law considers minors to be under a legal disability in entering into contracts (Restatement [Second] of Contracts §§ 7 and 12, 1981). Therefore, the usual rule today is that contracts entered into by minors are voidable (42 Am. Jur. 2d *Infants* § 82, 2000).

Generally speaking, parents cannot give up their children's rights to sue, either. Read the following Focus Cases and consider which approach to this issue makes more sense to you. The first case is representative of the majority of courts that have addressed the parental release issue, and the second case is representative of the minority position.

Hojnowski v. Vans Skate Park

901 A.2d 381 (N.J. 2006)   **FOCUS CASE**

FACTS

A 12-year-old skateboarder fractured his femur as another aggressive skateboarder forced the minor off a ramp. The incident occurred at the defendant's skate park. On a previous visit to the facility, the minor's mother had executed a release on the minor's behalf. The minor and his parents sued the defendant skate park on the basis of negligence alleging negligent supervision and negligence in failing to provide a safe place. The defendant alleged that the claims were precluded by the waiver signed by the minor's parents. The trial court granted summary judgment in favor of the defendant. The appellate court affirmed summary judgment but held that the waiver of liability contained in the pre-injury release document signed by a parent was void.

HOLDING

The New Jersey Supreme Court affirmed the judgment of the appellate court.

RATIONALE

The New Jersey Supreme Court held that the waiver was unenforceable because (1) the best interests of a child are not fostered by allowing parents to waive claims and (2) allowing a commercial facility to get the benefit of waivers in this type of case removes a significant incentive for operators to take reasonable steps to protect their young patrons. In regard to the first point above, the court noted that if a parent is unable to pay for the care associated with the child's injuries, the child may be left with no resources to obtain the necessary care or support. The court also commented that a parent may not fully understand the consequences of signing the waiver or perhaps will not even read it before signing.

Krathen v. School Board of Monroe County, Florida

FOCUS CASE | 972 So.2d 887 (Fla. Ct. App. 2007)

FACTS

A high school student was injured during a cheerleading practice at her school. The student and her mother alleged that the school board was negligent in failing to adequately supervise the practice and in various other ways. The school board asserted that the student's claim was barred by a waiver signed by the student and her mother that released the school board from liability for "any injury or claim resulting from . . . athletic participation." The trial court upheld the waiver as it granted summary judgment for the school board.

HOLDING

The Florida appellate court affirmed the trial court's judgment.

RATIONALE

The primary issue before the court was whether a parent can bind his or her child to a waiver of liability. Based on precedent in Florida, the court opined that parents have the authority to decide whether to waive a child's litigation rights in exchange for participation in an activity that a parent feels is beneficial for the child. Parents should be free to make this decision since parents are presumed to act in the best interests of their child. In this case, the minor's parent thought that participation in cheerleading was beneficial for her child and the decision to sign the waiver was within the parent's authority to do so.

As the *Hojnowski* and *Krathen* cases show, courts are divided about the nature of the parent–child relationship and how much discretion should be vested in a parent to give up a child's right to sue. The *Hojnowski* case reflects the position of most courts, that public policy should protect minor children against possibly unwise decisions by parents. The *Krathen* case, in the minority, presumes that parents will act in the best interests of their children, even in this type of situation.

Public policy

The concept of public policy is rather nebulous, yet overarching. Courts address a number of considerations when ascertaining whether a waiver may be used and will not violate the public interest. The following concerns are often addressed in discussing public policy.

First, some jurisdictions hold that no waivers will be upheld, or the courts in those jurisdictions make it very difficult for waivers to be upheld. Some jurisdictions allow the use of waivers in certain limited circumstances. In some circumstances, federal law supersedes and no waivers are permissible.

Second, many courts address the public policy aspect by determining whether the situation concerns a provision of essential services. This means that parties providing services of great public importance will not usually be allowed to get the benefit of a waiver or release. An example is health care providers.

Third, the principle of **unfair dominance** provides that a waiver will not be upheld if the party getting the benefit of the waiver has so much power in the transaction that it is not a "fair deal." This principle is enforced in many types of consumer contracts. For example, the courts would never uphold an exculpatory clause in a contract with a very powerful seller. It would violate the notion of unfair dominance if, in your purchase agreement for a vehicle, you gave up your right to sue Ford Motor Company for negligence in manufacturing that car. This would not be a fair deal because a consumer has virtually no negotiating power in a transaction with a multibillion-dollar corporation. Similarly, if a person has no choice about whether to engage in an activity, a waiver will not be upheld, because that would be considered a "contract of adhesion" (discussed in Chapter 4).

Finally, on some occasions it is inappropriate to use a waiver because to do so would allow a provider of recreational services to violate a statutory duty of care imposed upon it.

Below we discuss these concepts at greater length.

Waivers disallowed or disfavored. A few states have resolved the conflict between principles of freedom to contract and responsibility for one's negligent acts by stating that no waivers will be allowed, regardless of the context. For example, in a Virginia case, the plaintiff became a quadriplegic after sustaining an injury in a recreational triathlon. The plaintiff, Hiett, struck his head on an underwater object in a lake during the swimming event. He had signed a release form prior to the event, but the Virginia Supreme Court held that, according to long-standing precedent, "the pre-injury release provision signed by Hiett is prohibited by public policy and, thus, it is void" (*Hiett v. Lake Barcroft Community Association, Inc.,* 1992, p. 897). One critic argued that this decision, which used broad and sweeping language, was wrongly decided in view of the trend across the country to uphold exculpatory contracts in athletic events (Espaldon, 1994). Two other jurisdictions, Montana and Louisiana, have also adopted this blanket prohibition against enforcing waivers (Wolohan, 2007), but most jurisdictions allow waivers.

A provider of recreational services that operates on federal land may not use an exculpatory agreement. Federal policies require the provider to use a "Visitor's Acknowledgment of Risks" form, if a form is used at all (Hansen-Stamp, 2003). Exhibit 17.2 provides an example.

In some jurisdictions there is no absolute prohibition on the use of waivers, but the courts have made it very difficult for waivers to be upheld in many circumstances. The following Focus Case from New York deals with the question of whether a release signed in a training session at a spa should be upheld.

Debell v. Wellbridge Club Management, Inc.

FOCUS CASE   835 N.Y.S.2d 170 (App. Div. 2007)

FACTS

The plaintiff, a spa client, suffered a herniated disc and a torn rotator cuff during a one-hour instructional session conducted by a trainer. The plaintiff was injured doing exercise on the "hang bar" despite the plaintiff's complaints that this exercise hurt his upper back, shoulders, and neck. The defendant sought to dismiss this case because the plaintiff had signed a release form contained in the spa's membership application. The plaintiff argued that the release form should be void as against public policy since there is a New York statute (N.Y. Gen Oblig. Law § 5-325) that voids releases that are used in "places of amusement or recreation." The lower court granted the defendant's motion to dismiss as it upheld the release.

HOLDING

The New York appellate court reversed the lower court's decision and held that the release was void.

RATIONALE

The appellate court found that the lower court was in error when it focused on whether plaintiff's activity was recreational or instructional. The focus should have been on whether the spa's purpose was recreational or instructional. In this regard, the court noted that the spa advertised itself as providing "the latest facilities and services in health and beauty." No mention was made of training or instruction. The training session in this case was ancillary to the recreational activities offered by the spa. Therefore, the waiver was void as against public policy since the spa was a place of recreation within the meaning of the statute.

Essential services. Some organizations owe a duty to serve the public, and the courts deem it inappropriate for that type of organization to gain the benefit of a waiver. You will never, therefore, see a waiver upheld in a health care setting. A patient may be asked to sign a document advising her of the inherent risks of

Federal "Visitor's Acknowledgment of Risks" form.   EXHIBIT   **17.2**

VISITOR'S ACKNOWLEDGMENT OF RISKS

In consideration of the services of _____, their officers, agents, employees, and stockholders, and all other entities associated with those businesses hereinafter collectively referred to as "_____," I agree as follows:

Although _____ has taken reasonable steps to provide me with appropriate equipment and skilled guides so I can enjoy an activity for which I may not be skilled, _____ _____ has informed me this activity is not without risk. Certain risks are inherent in each activity and cannot be eliminated without destroying the unique character of the activity. These inherent risks are some of the same elements that contribute to the unique character of this activity and can be the cause of loss or damage to my equipment, or accidental injury, illness, or in extreme cases, permanent trauma or death. _____ does not want to frighten me or reduce my enthusiasm of this activity, but believes it is important for me to know in advance what to expect and to be informed of the inherent risks. The following describes some, but not all, of those risks.

(Description of risks)

I am aware that _____ entails risks of injury or death to any participant. I understand the description of these inherent risks is not complete and that other unknown or unantici-pated inherent risks may result in injury or death. I agree to assume and accept full responsibility for the inherent risks identified herein and those inherent risks not specifically identified. My participation in this activity is purely voluntary, no one is forcing me to participate, and I elect to participate in spite of and with full knowledge of the inherent risks.

I acknowledge that engaging in this activity may require a degree of skill and knowledge different than other activities and that I have responsibilities as a participant. I acknowledge that the staff of _____ has been available to more fully explain to me the nature and physical demands of this activity and the inherent risks, hazards, and dangers associated with this activity.

I certify that I am fully capable of participating in this activity. Therefore, I assume and accept full responsibility for myself, including all minor children in my care, custody, and control, for bodily injury, death, or loss of personal property and expenses as a result of those inherent risks and dangers identified herein and those inherent risks and dangers not specifically identified, and as a result of my negligence in participating in this activity.

I have carefully read, clearly understood, and accepted the terms and conditions stated herein and acknowledge that this agreement shall be effective and binding upon myself, my heirs, assigns, personal representative, and estate and for all members of my family, including minor children.

_____   _____

Signature   *Date*

_____   _____

Signature of Parent or Guardian, if participant is under 18 yrs. of age   *Date*

EXHIBIT	17.3	The *Tunkl* factors used in developing public policy analysis, *Tunkl v. Regents of the University of California* (1963).

1. The agreement concerns an endeavor of a type generally thought suitable for public regulation.

2. The party seeking exculpation is engaged in performing a service of great importance to the public, which is often a matter of practical necessity for some members of the public.

3. Such party holds itself out as willing to perform this service for any member of the public who seeks it, or at least for any member coming within certain established standards.

4. Because of the essential nature of the service, in the economic setting of the transaction, the party invoking exculpation possesses a decisive advantage of bargaining strength against any member of the public who seeks the services.

5. In exercising a superior bargaining power, the party confronts the public with a standardized adhesion contract of exculpation, and makes no provision whereby a purchaser may pay additional reasonable fees and obtain protection against negligence.

6. The person or property of members of the public seeking such services must be placed under the control of the furnisher of the services, subject to the risk of carelessness on the part of the furnisher, its employees, or agents.

surgery or other medical procedure, but a waiver will not be upheld. Hospitals and medical personnel are expected to serve the public, so it would violate public policy to allow a patient to give up the right to sue if a hospital or physician acts negligently. The seminal case of *Tunkl v. Regents of the University of California* (1963) provides courts with a number of factors to use in developing the public policy analysis. These factors were used in the case of *Wagenblast v. Odessa School District No. 105-157-166J* (1988) (see Exhibit 17.3 and the excerpted case below).

Interscholastic or intercollegiate sport as essential service. Some courts have held that waivers or releases may be inappropriate in the context of interscholastic or collegiate sport since the extracurricular participation in sport flows from the educational mission of the school and education is an essential service. Since the school owes a duty to its students in offering education, it may not take away any of the participants' rights by using waivers. The excerpted case below explores how one court addressed this.

Wagenblast v. Odessa School District No. 105-157-166J

758 P.2d 968 (Wash. 1988)	**CASE OPINION**

[FACTS

The plaintiffs were students in the Odessa School District who wished to participate in interscholastic athletics. As a condition of participation, the defendant school district required students and parents to sign a release of liability form. It released the school district from "liability resulting from any ordinary negligence that may arise in connection with the school district's interscholastic activities programs" (p. 969).

The Seattle School District had a similar requirement and a similar form.

Students and parents in both districts objected to this practice on the basis that the release form violated public policy. The lower court in the Odessa case enjoined the school district from using the releases as it agreed with the plaintiffs that the release should be void as against public policy. The lower court in the Seattle case came to a contrary decision. These cases were consolidated upon appeal and heard by the Washington Supreme Court.]

HOLDING

The Washington Supreme Court held that the release requirements violated public policy, thereby affirming the lower court in the Odessa case and reversing the judgment in the Seattle case.

RATIONALE

Conclusion. We hold that the exculpatory releases from any future school district negligence are invalid because they violate public policy.

The courts have generally recognized that, subject to certain exceptions, parties may contract that one shall not be liable for his or her own negligence to another.

* * *

In accordance with the foregoing general rule, appellate decisions in this state have upheld exculpatory agreements where the subject was a toboggan slide, a scuba diving class, mountain climbing instruction, an automobile demolition derby, and ski jumping.

* * *

As Prosser and Keeton [legal commentators] further observe, however, there are instances where public policy reasons for preserving an obligation of care owed by one person to another outweigh our traditional regard for the freedom to contract. Courts in this century are generally agreed on several such categories of cases.

Courts, for example, are usually reluctant to allow those charged with a public duty, which includes the obligation to use reasonable care, to rid themselves of that obligation by contract.

* * *

Probably the best exposition of the test to be applied in determining whether exculpatory agreements violate public policy is that stated by the California Supreme Court. In writing for a unanimous court, the late Justice Tobriner outlined the factors in *Tunkl v. Regents of Univ. of Cal.* [citation omitted]: [The court then set forth the *Tunkl* factors; see Exhibit 17.3].

Obviously, the more of the foregoing six characteristics that appear in a given exculpatory agreement case, the more likely the agreement is to be declared invalid on public policy grounds. In the consolidated cases before us, all of the characteristics are present in each case. We separately, then, examine, each of these six characteristics as applied to the cases before us.

* * *

1. The agreement concerns an endeavor of a type generally thought suitable for public regulation.

* * *

Regulation of governmental entities usually means self-regulation. Thus, the Legislature has by statute granted to each school board the authority to control, supervise, and regulate the conduct of interscholastic athletics. In some situations, a school board is permitted, in turn, to delegate this authority to the Washington Interscholastic Activities Association (WIAA). . . . In the cases before us, both school boards look to the WIAA for regulation of interscholastic sports. The WIAA handbook contains an extensive constitution with rules for such athletic endeavors.

* * *

Clearly then, interscholastic sports in Washington are extensively regulated, and are a fit subject for such regulation.

2. The party seeking exculpation is engaged in performing a service of great importance to the public, which is often a matter of practical necessity for some members of the public.

This court has held that public school students have no fundamental right to participate in interscholastic athletics. Nonetheless, the court also has observed that the justification advanced for interscholastic athletics is their educational and cultural value. . . . [I]nterscholastic athletics is part and parcel of the overall educational scheme in Washington. . . . In sum, under any rational view of the subject, interscholastic sports in public school are a matter of public importance in this jurisdiction.

* * *

3. Such party holds itself out as willing to perform this service for any member of the public who seeks it, or at least for any member coming within certain established standards.

Implicit in the nature of interscholastic sports is the notion that such programs are open to all students who meet certain skill and eligibility standards. . . .

4. Because of the essential nature of the service, in the economic setting of the transaction, the party invoking exculpation possesses a decisive advantage of bargaining strength against any member of the public who seeks the services.

* * *

Not only have interscholastic sports become of considerable importance to students and the general public alike, but in most instances there exists no alternative program of organized competition. . . . While outside alternatives exist for some activities, they possess little of the inherent allure of interscholastic competition. . . . In this regard, school districts have near-monopoly power. And, because such programs have become important to student participants, school districts possess a clear and disparate bargaining strength when they insist that students and their parents sign these releases.

* * *

5. In exercising a superior bargaining power, the party confronts the public with a standardized adhesion contract of exculpation, and makes no provision whereby a purchaser may pay additional reasonable fees and obtain protection against negligence.

* * *

Both school districts admit to an unwavering policy regarding these releases; no student athlete will be allowed to participate in any program without first signing the release form as written by the school district. In both of these cases, students and their parents unsuccessfully attempted to modify the forms by deleting the release language. In both cases, the school district rejected the attempted modifications. Student athletes and their parents or guardians have no alternative but to sign the standard release forms provided to them or have the student barred from the program.

* * *

6. The person or property of members of the public seeking such services must be placed under the control of the furnisher of the services, subject to the risk of carelessness on the part of the furnisher, its employees or agents.

* * *

A school district owes a duty to its students to employ ordinary care and to anticipate reasonably foreseeable dangers so as to take precautions for protecting the children in its custody from such dangers. This duty extends to students engaged in interscholastic sports. As a natural incident to the relationship of a student athlete and his or her coach, the student athlete is usually placed under the coach's considerable degree of control. The student is thus subject to the risk that the school district or its agent will breach this duty of care.

In sum, the attempted releases in the cases before us exhibit all six of the characteristics denominated in *Tunkl v. Regents of Univ. of Cal.* [citation omitted]. Because of this, and for the aforesaid reasons, we hold that the releases in these consolidated cases are invalid as against public policy.

* * *

Questions

1. The *Wagenblast* court did a very thorough job of applying all six factors from the *Tunkl* decision. Comment specifically upon the court's view of interscholastic athletics as being a part of a service of great importance to the public. Do you agree with this view? Why or why not? Would this reasoning extend to intercollegiate athletics?

2. The court also noted that school districts possess a decisive bargaining advantage in this type of situation. Discuss the court's analysis that school districts possess a "near-monopoly power." This decision was written in 1988. Do you think that school districts today have more or less monopoly power?

3. Could the *Wagenblast* court have ended the controversy simply by using the principle that minors (all the high school students here) can disavow any contract they sign, including waivers? Why do you believe the court chose to address the public policy issue?

Many jurisdictions have yet to address the public policy issue of whether waivers should be upheld in the context of interscholastic sports. The court in the *Krathen* case, discussed earlier in this chapter, found nothing objectionable about waivers used in this setting. One commentator has suggested that the use of waivers in school settings may actually promote public policy, since without releases some schools could not afford to offer sports because of the financial risk that a large verdict or settlement could bring (Murr, 2002).

Similarly, only a few cases on the intercollegiate level have directly addressed the question of whether the provision of sport should be considered an essential service. The next Focus Case provides one court's view.

Kyriazis v. West Virginia University

450 S.E.2d 649 (W. Va. 1994)	**FOCUS CASE**

FACTS

As a condition of participating in the university's rugby club, participants had to sign a release. Jeffrey Kyriazis, a novice rugby player, signed the release and was injured playing in his first club match. Kyriazis left the game in the second half after he became dizzy and lost his balance. Later, medical tests ascertained that he had suffered a basilar-artery thrombosis. He sued the university for negligence, and the university contended that the release barred suit. The lower court granted the university's motion to dismiss.

HOLDING

The highest court in West Virginia, the West Virginia Supreme Court of Appeals, held that the release violated public policy, reversing and remanding the lower court's decision.

RATIONALE

The court primarily focused on whether participation in the rugby club was an essential or public service. To do so, the court reviewed the *Tunkl* criteria and found that "When a state university provides recreational activities to its students, it fulfills its educational mission, and performs a public service" (p. 655). Further "athletics are integral and important elements of the education mission at West Virginia University" (p. 655).

The court also noted that the release was signed with a decisive bargaining advantage by the university. University counsel prepared the release, whereas Kyriazis had no legal representation. Students had no choice but to sign the release if they wished to play.

Based on these two factors, the court held that the release was void as a matter of public policy.

A 2006 case, *Zides v. Quinnipiac University* (2006), which is discussed as a Focus Case on page 532, also noted that college-age students should not necessarily be characterized as "educated adults" since many of them are not experienced in the risks presented to them in daily life. The court also mentioned the *Wagenblast* decision (see the earlier Case Opinion) as indicative of the public policy concerns that may arise in the context of school waivers.

Nonschool sport and recreation as essential service. Most courts agree that, outside of the context of an educational institution, sport, recreation, fitness, and adventure activities are not essential services provided to the public. Therefore, the use of waivers or releases in those situations does not generally violate public policy. The following Focus Case is indicative of the reasoning used in these cases.

Silva v. Mt. Bachelor, Inc.

FOCUS CASE   2008 U.S. Dist. LEXIS 55942 (D. Or. July 21, 2008)

FACTS

The plaintiff, an avid skier, injured his knee while skiing in an ungroomed area of the defendant's ski resort. The plaintiff filed a claim based on negligence and premises liability asserting that the defendant failed to make the ski area reasonably safe. The defendant ski resort argued that the plaintiff's claims were barred by the release agreement, which was located on the back of plaintiff's ski pass. The ticket windows posted signs that stated "YOUR TICKET IS A RELEASE" and advised skiers to read the ticket. Patrons were urged not to ski at the resort unless they chose to be bound by the terms of the release. The plaintiff maintained that the release should not be enforceable because the parties did not negotiate at arm's length, and therefore the release violates public policy.

HOLDING

The Oregon District Court held that the release was enforceable and granted summary judgment for the defendant ski resort.

RATIONALE

The court found the plaintiff's arguments unpersuasive. First, the court noted that no Oregon court has held that a release from liability in a recreational, as opposed to a commercial context, offends public policy. Second, the release is not invalid as a contract of adhesion since the plaintiff voluntarily chose to ski at this resort and a ski resort does not provide essential public services.

Another case of note exemplifies the minority position, as the court held that health clubs do provide essential services. In *Schneeloch v. Glastonbury Fitness & Wellness, Inc.* (2009), a plaintiff was injured in an exercise class conducted at a health club. The court declined to uphold the waiver of liability provision because it opined that an exculpatory agreement that would excuse the potential negligence of a health club was in conflict with the public policy of encouraging participation in athletics and other recreational activities.

Principle of unfair dominance. In some circumstances, notions of fairness may be offended if the enforcement of a waiver is allowed. This is the case when there is a huge disparity in bargaining power or the person signing the waiver has no real choice about whether to participate in the activity—situations that may be found to involve coercion or a contract of adhesion, concepts addressed in Chapter 4.

For example, in the case of *Whittington v. Sowela Technical Institute* (1983), a nursing student had to participate in a field trip to an out-of-town hospital. There was no alternative assignment if a student chose not to attend. Each student was required to sign a release form prior to participating or the student was not permitted to go on the field trip. The plaintiff was injured in a vehicular accident, and the school argued that the release should be upheld. The court disagreed as it held that the student, under the circumstances, could not give her free and deliberate consent. The circumstances showed that the parties were not dealing upon an equal footing.

Another case involved a release signed by a student who wished to participate in a college-sponsored study abroad trip to Peru. In *Fay v. Thiel College* (2001), the plaintiff student had a medical emergency in Peru. The group supervisors left her at a clinic, and she underwent an unnecessary appendectomy. The surgeon and anesthesiologist also sexually assaulted her. The college asserted that the release should be upheld in regard to the college supervisors' alleged negligence. The court refused to uphold the release on the basis that it was a contract of adhesion, that is, the student had no bargaining power. If the student had refused to sign the release, she would not have been permitted to go on the trip. In this "take it or leave it" situation, the court refused to uphold the release.

However, some case law provides that if a student could choose another class to fulfill a curricular requirement, then the release may be upheld since it does not violate the adhesion contract prohibition. For example, in *Thompson v. Otterbein College* (1996), a college student signed a release prior to taking an equestrian course. She was injured when her horse was "spooked." The court upheld that release as it stated that the equestrian course was not a required course. Although this course could be used to fulfill the physical education requirement, there were a variety of other courses available for that purpose, not requiring a release to be signed. The plaintiff was not in an unequal bargaining position; hence, the release was enforceable.

Outside of the realm of education, the principle of unfair dominance does not mean that those who want to engage in commercial health, recreation, or fitness endeavors must have an opportunity to "negotiate" the content of the release. Although prospective participants should be given enough time to read the document before engaging in the activity, courts have consistently held that objections to the document do not have to be accommodated since participants are not taking part in an essential activity. Participants are free to choose not to go on the rafting trip or to use that health club. For example, in the case of *Schlobohm v. Spa Petite, Inc.* (1982), the court upheld an exculpatory clause in a membership contract for a health spa. The court stated that it was not a contract of adhesion since the services of the spa were not a public necessity and were available elsewhere.

It is essential, however, that the document be available to participants for prior review if they are traveling to a location specifically for an activity. Release documents should be provided to participants as soon as they register for the event or activity.

Use of waiver would violate statutory duty. In some cases, a provider of commercial recreation activities may be mandated by a state statute to meet a certain standard of care in providing the activities. In such a case, a court may find that it would be incongruent and unfair to allow a release to be upheld. The following Focus Case provides an example.

Murphy v. North American River Runners, Inc.

FOCUS CASE   412 S.E.2d 504 (W. Va. 1991)

FACTS

The plaintiff was injured while whitewater rafting as a paying passenger in defendant's raft. Plaintiff's guide attempted a rescue operation of another raft. When the plaintiff's raft bumped the other raft, she was thrown forcefully in her raft, injuring her knee and ankle. The plaintiff had signed a release prior to participating in the trip. The lower court upheld the release.

HOLDING

The Supreme Court of Appeals of West Virginia (the state's highest court) reversed and remanded.

RATIONALE

Under a provision of a West Virginia statute (W. Va. Code 20-3B-3 (b)), commercial whitewater guides must "conform to the standard of care expected of members of their profession" (p. 512). This statute, therefore, establishes a statutory safety standard for the protection of those who choose to go on whitewater rafting expeditions. The court stated that a release clause is unenforceable if its purpose is to exempt a party from tort liability based on a statutory standard of care. In this case, the release was unenforceable since it violated this principle.

A case decided by the New Mexico Supreme Court, *Berlangieri v. Running Elk Corp.* (2003), dealt with the effect of that state's Equine Liability Act on the effectiveness of a release. The plaintiff was injured during a trail ride. The court noted that most of the act explains the types of activities for which equine operators may be liable. The court held that the intent of the statute was to express a public policy that operators should be held accountable for their own negligence. Based on this interpretation of the statute and a review of the *Tunkl* factors, the court found that this release violated public policy and was not enforceable.

Also, in the case of *Capri v. L.A. Fitness International* (2006) a California court determined that a waiver signed by a health club patron was void as it pertained to a claim based on negligence per se (see Chapter 15). The plaintiff had slipped and fallen due to an accumulation of algae around the drain on the pool deck. This algae was indicative of a violation of the state health and safety code. The court declined to uphold the waiver because that would contravene section 1688 of the California Civil Code that stated it was against public policy to exempt a party from liability if the party had violated the law, in this case the health code.

Content

Most cases dealing with waivers in the recreation and commercial sport context pass scrutiny on the above factors, and the question then becomes whether the document is written properly. The focus shifts to the document itself and whether the document has the necessary language and format to be upheld. It is important to understand that each state varies regarding language that is absolutely necessary for a valid waiver. There are general principles, to be sure, but you should consult with an attorney who knows your state's specific requirements when you wish to implement a waiver in your setting.

Terms must be conspicuous

Something is conspicuous if it stands out, if it is easily spotted, like the proverbial sore thumb. Therefore, language in a document is conspicuous if it is called to the reader's attention. We can accomplish this by using a larger typeface, by putting the language in bold, or by putting the information in a location in a document that the reader will see and note easily. For example, if you have a multipage document, you would not "hide" the exculpatory clause at the end of the document in very small type. The courts recognize that your right to sue someone is a very important right; therefore, if you do give up this right, you must be cognizant of what you are doing. The requirement of conspicuousness ensures that the signer cannot miss this important information.

In the case of *Stokes v. Bally's Pacwest, Inc.* (2002), the language in an exculpatory agreement for a health club was in issue. The exculpatory clause was a part of the retail installment contract signed by the member. The document included a line reading, "WAIVER AND RELEASE: This contract contains a WAIVER AND RELEASE in Paragraph 10 to which you will be bound" (p. 165). Further, the referenced Paragraph 10 was entitled "WAIVER AND RELEASE." The court completely discounted the plaintiff's argument that he thought these sections pertained to his financial obligations under the contract. The court noted, "Reasonable persons could not disagree that the content of paragraph 10 is quite clearly a waiver and release of liability for negligence" (p. 165). The court held that the waiver and release provisions were conspicuously displayed.

However, in the case of *Atkins v. Swimwest Family Fitness Center* (2005), the Wisconsin Supreme Court found that a waiver contained in a guest registration card was not "distinguishable" enough to be conspicuous. The court noted that the form was printed on one card with the same

Competitive Advantage

STRATEGIES

Waivers and Exculpatory Agreements

- If you choose to use exculpatory agreements, consult with an attorney to understand your state's requirements for a valid waiver or release.

- Remember that in most jurisdictions, a minor may disavow a waiver. Also, in most jurisdictions, a parent cannot give up a minor's right to sue.

- Do not use an exculpatory clause if you know that it is not valid just to try to "persuade" people not to sue.

- Exculpatory clauses should be placed conspicuously within your documents. The typeface for this clause should be large and bold. If you have a multipage document such as a membership agreement, put the exculpatory clause on a separate page. *Draw attention to the exculpatory language.*

- The language of the exculpatory clause must be clear, unambiguous, and explicit. In some jurisdictions, you must specifically use the word "negligence" in the waiver. Consult with your attorney on this point.

- Instruct your employees to give participants adequate time to read the waiver before signing. If participants are traveling to your location to participate, send the waiver document to them ahead of time for their review.

- Do not use a "group" release form. Have a separate agreement for each participant, even if group members are engaging in the activity at the same time.

- Instruct your employees never to say that the waiver is "meaningless" or that it is "just policy." Participants are giving up their right to sue your organization, and that is a valuable right.

- The exculpatory agreement is not there just to avoid liability. It is there to share valuable information about the nature of the activity and the risk (Connell & Savage, 2003).

size print, font, and color. There was nothing to set apart the critical waiver language from the rest of the document.

Language must be clear, unambiguous, and explicit

Two aspects frequently arise when courts address whether the language of an exculpatory agreement is sufficiently clear, unambiguous, and explicit to be upheld. First, courts address whether it is evident from the language that the signer of the document is giving up his or her right to sue when the party getting the benefit of the agreement is engaging in "negligent" behavior. Some courts require that the "magic word" *negligence* appear in the exculpatory clause. The following Focus Case illustrates this concept.

Zides v. Quinnipiac University

FOCUS CASE   2006 Conn. Super. LEXIS 473 (Feb. 7, 2006)

FACTS

Andrew Zides was injured during practice for the college baseball team. He suffered a severe head injury when he was hit by a batted ball. Although he was pitching behind an "L-screen," which is meant to protect the pitcher from batted balls, the screen was allegedly in disrepair and broke upon impact with the batted ball. Zides claimed that he was injured due to the negligence of the coaches in failing to properly maintain the L-screen. Zides had signed a waiver of liability pertaining to participation in the college's athletic program. The document stated that the signer accepts the risks of injury inherent on the sport. The document also provided that the signer "understands even with the best of coaching, use of protective equipment, and strict observance of the rules, injuries are still a possibility." There was no mention of the word "negligence" in the waiver document.

HOLDING

The Superior Court in Connecticut denied the defendants' motion for summary judgment.

RATIONALE

The main issue before the court in regard to the waiver was whether that document should be upheld in view of the fact that the waiver did not explicitly mention the word "negligence." The court addressed precedent in this jurisdiction, the case of *Hyson v. White Water Mountain Resort* (2003), which held that a waiver must expressly use the word negligence to protect a ski resort from a suit arising from its own negligence. The defendants argued that this precedent, from a ski resort, should not be applicable in this situation, because a student, unlike those who visit a ski resort for an isolated recreational activity, make thoughtful decisions as an "educated adult" attending a university. The court disagreed with this characterization of young college students as "educated adults" since many of them are not experienced in the risks presented to them in daily life. The court also mentioned the *Wagenblast* decision (see the earlier Case Opinion) as indicative of the public policy concerns that may arise in the context of school waivers. Therefore, the court opined that the *Hyson* precedent should apply in the context of a college student in sports activities.

The waiver document, according to the court, can be construed as an affirmative representation that coaches would take every reasonable step to avoid student injury. No reasonable reader would conclude that signing the document waived the right to sue if the university or its agents were negligent. The *Hyson* court recognized that the law does not favor exculpatory provisions, so it must be very clear that a party is trying to relieve itself from liability for its own negligence. Therefore, the court declined to uphold the waiver.

The rest of the decision discussed the infliction of emotional distress claim, the coach's culpability, and whether the college president had any duty to the plaintiff in this situation.

The second aspect to consider is whether the scope of the release covers the activity that led to the injury in question. Essentially, the court looks at the language of the release and determines whether it is written in a way that would allow the signer to understand just what kinds of injuries might be related to the purpose of the release. Compare the following two Focus Cases on this aspect.

Cohen v. Five Brooks Stable

72 Cal. Rptr. 3d 471(Ct. App. 2008)   **FOCUS CASE**

FACTS

The plaintiff was injured while she was on a guided horseback ride in the Golden Gate National Recreational Area. The horses and guide were provided by the defendant stable. The plaintiff fell from her horse after the guide, without warning, suddenly caused his horse to gallop, which in turn made the plaintiff's horse gallop. Galloping was not permitted on this trail, and the guides were instructed not to increase gaits without obtaining the permission of the riders in their care. The plaintiff was unable to control her horse, and she fell from the saddle and was dragged across the ground. Before the ride the plaintiff had signed a release, and the trial court upheld the release on the grounds that the risk of a horse "running without warning and without apparent cause" was included in the release.

HOLDING

The California appellate court reversed, holding that the risk of the injury suffered in this incident was not within the scope of the release.

RATIONALE

First, the court noted the general principle that a release may relieve a defendant of negligence only if it does so in "clear, unambiguous, and explicit" language. California courts require a high degree of clarity and specificity in a release, and the express terms of the agreement must be applicable to the particular misconduct of the defendant. In this case, the release language was clear as to the inherent risks of horseback riding but was ambiguous about any negligence of the guide. In fact, the court noted that the word "negligence" was only used as it applied to the plaintiff and not to the defendant. The court declined to uphold the release since it was not clear that it applied to any negligence of the defendant or its employees connected with the trail ride.

Wang v. Whitetail Mountain Resort

FOCUS CASE | 933 A.2d 110 (Pa. Super. Ct. 2007)

FACTS

The plaintiff was injured at a resort while snow tubing. A resort employee instructed the plaintiff to exit the snow tube spillway in a direction that caused another snow tuber to collide with the plaintiff. She was injured and filed suit based on the negligence of the resort employee. The resort sought a dismissal of the complaint based on the release document plaintiff had signed prior to her snow tubing. The trial court dismissed the plaintiff's complaint.

HOLDING

The Pennsylvania appellate court affirmed the trial court's order.

RATIONALE

The issue before the court was whether the release of liability covered the negligent directives of employees. The language of the release stated that the resort was exonerated from "ALL LIABILITY RELATED TO INJURY, PROPERTY LOSS OR OTHERWISE RELATED TO MY USE OF THE TUBING FACILITY, REGARDLESS OF ANY NEGLIGENCE ON THE PART OF WHITETAIL". The court reasoned that the negligence of an employee in giving a directive was within the contemplation of the parties as evidenced by the clear and unambiguous language of the agreement. Therefore, the court concluded that the release was enforceable in this situation.

As these cases show, courts use contract interpretation guidelines to determine whether a reasonable person, trying to interpret the language in a release, would fully understand just what the purpose of the release was and what rights were being given up in signing the document. Any ambiguity in interpretation will be resolved against the drafter of the document since the choice of language is within the control of the one who writes the document.

Language cannot exonerate for conduct beyond negligence

Generally speaking, courts will not uphold releases that attempt to exonerate a party for behavior that is something beyond negligence, such as gross negligence, reckless behavior, or intentional torts. The following Focus Case illustrates this issue.

City of Santa Barbara v. Superior Court of Santa Barbara County

161 P.3d 1095 (Cal. 2007)

FOCUS CASE

FACTS

The city owned a recreational camp for developmentally disabled children. The application form contained a release of liability for "all acts of negligence" related to a child's participation in the camp. These forms were signed by parents or guardians of the children. A child drowned at the camp and her parents brought suit.

The California appellate court upheld the release as it pertained to "ordinary" negligence but held that a release of future claims for "gross" negligence is unenforceable.

HOLDING

The California Supreme Court affirmed the judgment of the appellate court.

RATIONALE

The issue on appeal was whether an agreement attempting to release liability for future gross negligence in the context of a sport or recreational program may be upheld. The court noted that the vast majority of jurisdictions find that such provisions are unenforceable as a matter of public policy. In California, "gross negligence" connotes a "want of even scant care" or "an extreme departure from the ordinary standard of conduct." After reviewing the precedent from other jurisdictions, the court adopted a "public policy to discourage" behavior that removes an obligation to adhere to even a "minimal" standard of care. Therefore, the court deemed the release in question to violate public policy and, therefore, to be unenforceable.

Decision to Use an Exculpatory Clause

Exculpatory clauses may not be upheld in some situations, as we discussed above. If your program participants are minors, exculpatory clauses will not be upheld. If parents sign a release in an attempt to give up a minor's right to sue, that parental release will be ineffective in most jurisdictions. If your program can be considered as offering an essential service, as may be the case in the realm of educational sport/recreation, courts may not uphold releases in that setting. Some states simply do not allow waivers to be used or are very restrictive in their use.

In addition, program administrators may opt not to use exculpatory agreements, even where the context is appropriate and courts would generally support the use of waivers. Even if the legal climate is favorable to the use of the waiver, it is up to you to ascertain whether the use of exculpatory clauses fits your mission and your organizational culture. You may feel that it is "unfair" or "unethical" to try to "escape" from your own negligence, even if it is legal to do so. You may feel that it sends a better message to participants if you choose not to take advantage of the legal mechanism to avoid liability. Whatever your decision, it should be congruent with your organization's mission and culture, as we discussed in Chapter 2.

AGREEMENTS TO PARTICIPATE

Even when you decide that it is not appropriate to use an exculpatory agreement, you need to disclose information, including the risks of the activity, to the participant. You may also want to inform the participant of his or her obligations in the undertaking. You can provide this information in an agreement to participate. Van der Smissen (1990) has identified three essential components of all agreements to participate:

1. The nature of the activity
2. The expectations of the participant
3. The condition of the participant

You may add an exculpatory clause to the agreement to participate, if the circumstances are appropriate.

In regard to the nature of the activity, you should describe the demands of the activity and the risks inherent in the activity. This serves three purposes:

1. It lets the participant know that you are doing whatever you can to communicate necessary and important information about a program.
2. The dissemination of risk information serves to ensure that the participant cannot bring a successful action against you for failure to warn, as discussed in Chapter 15.
3. This disclosure strengthens your ability to use the affirmative defense of primary assumption of risk, as discussed in Chapter 15, since the participant is voluntarily encountering the inherent risks of the activity with knowledge and understanding of those risks.

The next component of the agreement to participate is sharing your expectations for the participant's behavior. In every activity, participants must follow certain rules and regulations to try to minimize hazards to themselves and coparticipants. The statement of what is expected behavior and the participant's assent to behave in that way are at the core of this component. If the participant is injured because he or she violates these behavioral expectations, you have the defense of comparative negligence (discussed in Chapter 15). Since the participant knew what is reasonable behavior and deviated from that, the participant failed to act as a reasonably prudent participant.

The final component of the agreement to participate is the section in which you ask the participant to state that he or she has the appropriate skill level to participate and that he or she is in proper medical condition to engage in the activity. If the participant misrepresents this information, this may be viewed as unreasonable behavior leading to the participant's own injury—another way in which the defense of comparative negligence may be used. Exhibit 17.4 provides a sample agreement to participate.

Competitive Advantage

STRATEGIES

Agreements to Participate

- Even if you cannot or do not use an exculpatory agreement, you should always use an agreement to participate. This is important in sharing risk information with participants to avoid a failure to warn allegation.

- Having participants agree to follow the rules of conduct to make the experience enjoyable and safe for all also enables a comparative negligence defense should the participant endanger himself or herself by violating the rules of the activity.

Sample agreement to participate.   EXHIBIT   **17.4**

University of Oklarado
School of Sport and Exercise Science
Agreement to Participate in PE 124 Paddle Sports

Participation in all sports and physical activities involves certain inherent risks and, regardless of the care taken, it is impossible to ensure the absolute safety of the participant. *Paddle sports* is an activity requiring *moderate coordination and cardiovascular fitness*. It involves *deep and moving water and may require repetitive movement over long periods of time (i.e. paddling long or difficult river sections)*. Moreover, undue joint and muscle stress may occur, causing temporary pain or discomfort in the affected body regions. While it is a reasonably safe sport as long as safety guidelines are followed, some elements of risk cannot be eliminated from the activity.

A variety of injuries may occur to a *paddle sports* participant. Some examples of those injuries are:

1. Minor injuries such as *scrapes, bruises, strains, and sprains; sunburn, dehydration, burns, and cold weather injuries;*
2. More serious injuries such as *broken bones, cuts, concussions, and eye injuries (including loss of vision);*
3. Catastrophic injuries such as *heart attacks, near drowning, and death.*

These, and other injuries, sometimes occur in *paddle sports* as a result of hazards or accidents such as *capsizing, oncoming obstacles (e.g., rocks, strainers, holes, low head dams, debris, the boat), foot entrapment, being struck by lightning, encountering water-borne/insect-borne illnesses, or excessive stress placed on the cardiovascular and muscular systems.*

To help reduce the likelihood of injury to yourself and to other participants, participants are expected to follow the following rules:

- *All participants are expected to wear proper footwear.*
- *All participants are expected to wear proper clothing, including PFDs and helmets when required.*
- *All participants are expected to be "aware" of their environment (changing weather, etc.).*
- *All participants are expected to follow all posted safety rules as well as those associated with the rules of paddle sports.*
- *All participants are expected to maintain a positive attitude and to avoid injurious behavior.*

I agree to follow the preceding safety rules, all posted safety rules, and all rules common to the sport/activity of *paddle sports*. Further, I agree to report any unsafe practices, conditions, or equipment to the instructor.

I certify that (1) I possess a sufficient degree of physical fitness to participate safely in *paddle sports,* (2) I understand that I am to discontinue activity at any time I feel undue discomfort or stress, and (3) I will inform the instructor in writing of any health-related conditions that might affect my ability to participate in *paddle sports* and I will verbally inform the instructor immediately.

I have read the preceding information and it has been explained to me. I know, understand, and appreciate the risks associated with participation in *paddle sports* and I am voluntarily participating in the activity. In doing so, I am assuming all of the inherent risks of the sport/activity. I further understand that in the event of a medical emergency, the instructor will call DPS to render assistance and that I will be financially responsible for any expenses involved.

_____

Name of Participant (Print)   *Date*   *Signature*

CONCLUSION

Information exchange with participants is a critical aspect of any sport or recreation program, and it reinforces your commitment to making participation experiences enriching and safe. You communicate with your participants in many ways: (1) through brochures, videos, and promotional materials; (2) through exculpatory agreements; and (3) through agreements to participate. All of these documents must be drafted to meet your needs. All of the documents you use must contain accurate information about the nature of the activity and the risks inherent in that activity.

Exculpatory agreements epitomize the conflict between principles of tort law dealing with accountability for one's tortious acts and principles of contract law allowing people to fashion their own agreements. Therefore, exculpatory agreements must be used in the proper context and must be drafted so that the content of the document meets necessary legal criteria.

Agreements to participate are necessary tools to share risk information with participants. They are also useful in getting participants to agree to follow the safety rules and regulations of an activity.

The information exchange that you have with participants is an important component of your risk management plan. Use your documents purposefully and wisely.

discussion questions

1. A school district seeks your advice regarding its waiver form. All of the student-athletes are minors. Based on your knowledge of the law regarding minors and waivers, would you recommend that a waiver form be used? Of what use is a parental signature—can parents release their minors' claims in most jurisdictions? Regardless of the minority issue, what are the public policy issues that may arise when an educational institution attempts to use a waiver form? Use the *Wagenblast* decision as a guide in answering this last point.

2. After reviewing the *Hojnowski* and *Krathen* decisions, think about how you would answer the following questions to reinforce your understanding of parents' versus minors' rights: How far should parental rights extend regarding decision-making for one's children? Is there a need to protect minors even from the actions of parents, as the *Hojnowski* decision implied? Or should we empower parents to make this type of decision for children, just as we allow parents to make many other decisions for their offspring?

3. In regard to the *Kyriazis* decision, do you agree with the court's view that the provision of recreational activities to students is a part of a university's mission? That case dealt with "club" sport. How did the court in *Zides* extend its rationale to intercollegiate sport? How would you extend the rationale to intramural sport? In which case does the argument of an extension of "educational mission" make more sense?

4. Discuss the likelihood of a waiver not being upheld at a ski resort on the grounds that it violates public policy since the ski resort provides an "essential service." Remember the reasoning of the *Silva* case.

5. Discuss the concept of conspicuousness. What does this mean when you are developing your waiver form?

learning activities

1. Visit the websites of sport or recreation providers in your area or locate their brochures or other promotional materials. Look at the language and identify words or phrases that might convey inaccurate information about the activity. Identify whether the language in any way promises a "perfect" or "perfectly safe" experience. Suggest changes to the language where necessary.
2. Find out whether agreements to participate are being used in activity classes at your university. If so, review them in class. Do they have the necessary three components?

CASE STUDY

You are thinking of operating a summer camp for high school soccer players, and you want to use whatever documents will be helpful in dealing with liability issues.

First, review the law of the state in which you plan to operate and ascertain whether waivers will be upheld if signed by your camp participants, who are minors. Will the waiver be upheld if signed by the minor's parent or guardian?

Second, develop an agreement to participate that has the necessary components and may be used with the players at your camp.

REFERENCES

Cases

Atkins v. Swimwest Family Fitness Center, 691 N.W.2d 334 (Wis. 2005).

Berlangieri v. Running Elk Corp., 76 P.3d 1098 (N.M. 2003).

Brooks v. Timberline Tours, Inc., 127 F.3d 1273 (10th Cir. 1997).

Capri v. L.A. Fitness Internat'l, 136 Cal. App. 4th 1078 (2006).

City of Santa Barbara v. Superior Ct. of Santa Barbara County, 161 P. 3d 1095 (Cal. 2007).

Cohen v. Five Brooks Stable, 72 Cal. Rptr. 3d 471 (Ct. App. 2008).

Debell v. Wellbridge Club Mgmt., Inc., 835 N.Y.S.2d 170 (App. Div. 2007).

Fay v. Thiel College, 55 Pa. D. & C. 4th 353 (Pa. Com. Pleas Ct. 2001).

Heil Valley Ranch v. Simkin, 784 P.2d 781 (Colo. 1989).

Hiett v. Lake Barcroft Cmty. Ass'n, Inc., 418 S.E.2d 894 (Va. 1992).

Hojnowski v. Vans Skate Park, 901 A.2d 381 (N.J. 2006).

Hyson v. White Water Mountain Resort, 829 A.2d 827 (Conn. 2003).

Krathen v. School Bd. Monroe County, FL, 972 So.2d 887 (Fla. Ct. App. 2007).

Kyriazis v. West Va. Univ., 450 S.E.2d 649 (W. Va. 1994).

Murphy v. North Am. River Runners, Inc., 412 S.E.2d 504 (W. Va. 1991).

Schlobohm v. Spa Petite, Inc., 326 N.W.2d 920 (Minn. 1982).

Schneeloch v. Glastonbury Fitness & Wellness, Inc., 2009 Conn. Super. LEXIS 191 (Feb. 2, 2009).

Silva v. Mt. Bachelor, Inc., 2008 U.S. Dist. LEXIS 55942 (D. Ct. Or. July 21, 2008).

Stokes v. Bally's Pacwest, Inc., 54 P.3d 161 (Wash. Ct. App. 2002).

Sunday v. Stratton Corp., 390 A.2d 398 (Vt. 1978).

Thompson v. Otterbein College, 1996 Ohio App. LEXIS 389 (Ohio Ct. App. 1996).

Tunkl v. Regents of Univ. of Cal., 60 Cal. 2d 92 (Cal. 1963).

Wagenblast v. Odessa Sch. Dist. No. 105-157-166J, 758 P.2d 968 (Wash. 1988).

Wang v. Whitetail Mt. Resort, 933 A. 2d 110 (Pa. Super. Ct. 2007).

Whittington v. Sowela Technical Inst., 438 So.2d 236 (La. Ct. App. 1983).

Zides v. Quinnipiac Univ., 2006 Conn. Super. LEXIS 473 (Feb. 7, 2006).

Other Sources

42 Am. Jur. 2d, *Infants* § 82 (2000).

Black's Law Dictionary (7th ed. 1999). St. Paul, MN: West Publishing.

Connell, M. J., & Savage, F. G. (2003). Releases: Is there still a place for their use by colleges and universities? *Journal of College and University Law, 29*(3), 579–617.

Espaldon, K. M. (1994, Fall). Virginia's rule of non-waiver of liability for negligent acts: *Hiett v. Lake Barcroft Community Ass'n, Inc., George Mason Law Review, 2,* 27–52.

Hansen-Stamp, C. (2003). Risk management: A different perspective. *Recreation and Adventure Program Law and Liability* (pp. B-12–19). Vail, CO: CLE International.

Murr, A. (2002, January). Chalk talk: Sports waivers: An exercise in futility? *Journal of Law & Education, 31,* 114–120.

National Park Service. (2009). Visitor's acknowledgment of risk form. Retrieved May 12, 2009, from www.nps.gov/acad/parkmgmt/upload/risk_sample.pdf.

Restatement (Second) of Contracts (1981).

Restatement (Second) of Torts (1965).

van der Smissen, B. (1990). *Legal liability and risk management for public and private entities.* Cincinnati, OH: Anderson Publishing.

Wolohan, J. T. (2007, Oct.). Bad education. *Athletic Business, 32,* 34, 36.

WEBSITE RESOURCES

www.nirsa.info/know/2007/07/risk001.html ▪ This article discusses the use of electronic waivers in campus recreation. It provides a checklist to use when preparing an electronic waiver.

http://recsports.osu.edu/uploads/Climbing%20Waiver.pdf ▪ This website contains the waiver used by The Ohio State University for those who wish to use the climbing wall. It is a good model for a waiver used in that situation.

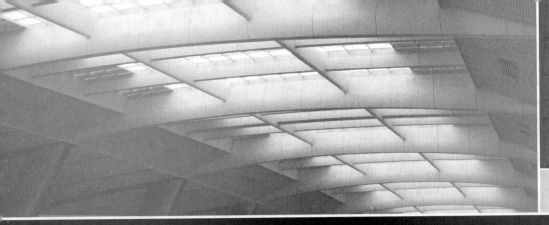
Participant Violence in Sport

541

INTRODUCTION

I magine you are taking a stroll around your campus on a beautiful spring day. As you meander down the sidewalk, you come upon a large individual who is blocking your way. You do not feel that it is appropriate that you should have to step off the walk to accommodate this person, and you yell, "Get out of my way." He does not respond to your request, and you have no space on the sidewalk to get around. Incensed by this breach of etiquette, you push the sidewalk blocker and begin pummeling him with your fists. You even swipe at his head with your shillelagh (Irish walking stick).

In this scenario, you are clearly violating norms of social behavior in your conduct. Even if you were miffed by this intrusion upon your rightful space, society would not tolerate your retaliation. We do not condone physical violence as a reaction to discourtesy. If we did, we would have a very uncivil society indeed.

If you transport the above participants, however, to an ice rink during a hockey game, society might condone and accept the same behaviors. In fact, pushing one's opponent with great force and sometimes using an implement (a hockey stick) to further intimidate the opposition is not uncommon. In many contact sports we allow a degree of contact that if found in a nonsporting context would subject the perpetrator of violence to criminal and/or civil sanctions.

It is important for you, as a prospective sport coach or sport/recreation program administrator, to explore the legal and social context of violence in sport. Many commentators have noted that the degree and kind of violence are escalating within sport, at all levels. We are all too familiar with the level of violence that exists in professional sport, but we are increasingly dealing with incidents of violence in the college, high school, youth league, and recreational sport contexts as well. A survey of athletes aged 9 to 15, coaches, and parents found that nearly 13 percent of the youth participants had tried to hurt an opponent. Further, according to the study, 8 percent of the coaches had encouraged their athletes to hurt an opponent ("Bad behavior," 2005). Those who administer sport and recreation must jointly decide and then enforce the standard for civility. What level of violence is permissible within the context of sport and recreational activities that necessitate some level of contact? What types of contact and aggression are necessary and intrinsic to activities themselves, and what types of contact are merely gratuitous violence and must be abolished? As one court stated, "Some of the restraints of civilization must accompany every athlete upon the playing field." Where do we draw those lines?

In our roles as event and game managers, as coaches, as league administrators, as program directors or athletic directors, we need to find solutions to stem the increase in violence on the playing fields. The development of strategies to make athletic contests displays of sportsmanship and prevent unnecessary displays of violence makes sense legally, and it makes our sport organizations more socially responsible and competitively sound.

To respond to the issues related to violence during competition, it is necessary to explore the legal frameworks that are used to deal with issues of player-to-player violence in sport participation. Spectator violence and crowd management, which are also critical issues, are discussed in Chapter 16. Exhibit 18.1 presents the management contexts, major legal issues, relevant laws, and illustrative cases for this chapter.

	EXHIBIT	18.1
Management contexts in which issues of participant violence may arise, with relevant laws and cases.		

MANAGEMENT CONTEXT	MAJOR LEGAL ISSUES	RELEVANT LAW	ILLUSTRATIVE CASES
Game management	Violence by sport participants	Criminal law	
Coaching		Assault	
League administration		Battery	
		Reckless misconduct	*Nabozny, Karas*
Supervision of athletic programs	Hazing	Criminal statutes	
	Organizational liability	Negligent supervision	*Reeves*
		Vicarious liability	*Tomjanovich*

VIOLENCE AND CRIMINAL LAW VERSUS CIVIL LAW

Criminal law concerns itself with societal harms. The legislature decides what is reprehensible conduct by society's members and passes statutes forbidding certain conduct. If someone allegedly violates a criminal statute, an action may be filed against that person on behalf of the government. In sport violence situations, if a criminal action is brought, it is usually predicated upon a criminal assault or criminal battery statute. Keep in mind that criminal statutes have their own elements that must be proven; the elements of a crime are not synonymous with the elements of a civil assault or a civil battery.

Unfortunately, largely due to the increasing violence in youth sport, over 20 states have adopted specific statutes providing for criminal penalties for those who assault sports officials (Berkowitz, 2009). Whether it is done by players, coaches, or fans, there is an increasing propensity to engage in "sports rage," and often the game officials become the target of that excessive violence. Much of this violence is perpetrated by unhappy "soccer moms" or "hockey dads" (Fiore, 2003).

In some cases, however, the same behaviors may result in a criminal proceeding or a civil case, or both. For example, in the scenario that began this chapter, the local prosecutor may wish to file a criminal complaint against you for your "pushing, pummeling, and swinging the shillelagh" behaviors. In your jurisdiction, these actions may be considered criminal assault (or perhaps assault with a deadly weapon if the shillelagh may be defined as such). If the prosecutor went forward with this case and you were found guilty, you would be subject to fines and/or imprisonment.

A civil case might also be brought against you; the sidewalk blocker would file this complaint. He would state that the "pushing and pummeling" conduct was battery and that "swinging the shillelagh" was assault. We discuss the civil causes of action in the next section. If the plaintiff prevailed against you in this lawsuit, you would pay damages to the plaintiff.

Although violent behavior is a common occurrence in sport, relatively few criminal cases have arisen. There are a number of reasons for this infrequency, including the reluctance of prosecutors to bring criminal actions based on conduct in a sporting contest. Prosecutors often have demanding workloads dealing with "real" crime, such as rape or homicide. Therefore, prosecutors may believe that it is a waste of taxpayer money to file criminal complaints based on sport violence; they need to use their resources to bring those who commit more egregious crimes to justice. There is also the belief that the sport leagues are in the best position to control violence through internal regulation and punishment, should they desire to do so.

Even if a criminal action is brought to trial, juries often have difficulty seeing "criminal" behavior by athletes. After all, coaches and teams often reward athletes for violent behavior. Some league administrators appear to condone violence, and they sometimes use violence as a marketing strategy. Why should members of society be offended by this behavior if the behavior is not reprehensible to those within the sport?

There are further legal difficulties in obtaining a guilty verdict in these cases. The defense of consent is often raised to assert that "an athlete implicitly consents to bodily contact permitted by a sport's rules or customs" (Samson, 2005). Athletes also try to argue that their aggressive actions were justified based on an apparent threat to themselves by other athletes—that is, self-defense. In criminal law, it is difficult to show the requisite intent to cause the harm (called *mens rea*).

In a case that illustrates the difficulty of attaining any real deterrence through criminal law, Todd Bertuzzi of the NHL Vancouver Canucks broke the neck of Steve Moore of the Colorado Avalanche in a game on March 8, 2004. Bertuzzi "sucker-punched" Moore in the head and then drove him to the ice causing multiple fractures in Moore's neck and a concussion. Despite this senseless and egregious violence, Bertuzzi, after being charged with assault causing bodily harm, accepted a plea bargain with the Vancouver prosecutor for a one-year probation with 80 hours of community service and no criminal record (Samson, 2005).

Due to the difficulties inherent in the current criminal system, one commentator has suggested that Congress pass a Sports Violence Act that provides for criminal sanctions for "purposefully, knowingly, or recklessly using physical contact to cause injury to an opposing player . . ." (Samson, 2005, p. 97). The proposed language would avoid the problem of proving "intent" and would be a consistent legal framework throughout the United States. Although some argue that the leagues are in the best position to "clean up" violence, this is a conflict of interest for leagues that profit from the violence in their product. The authors of one law review surveyed a number of trial court judges who felt very strongly that the problem of sports violence must be addressed by the courts and not by the professional leagues (Barry, Fox, & Jones, 2005).

VIOLENCE AND TORT LAW

As discussed earlier, in cases of player violence, there may also be legal recourse from civil law. As you will recall, civil law is concerned with individual wrongs. The state is not involved in civil cases; individual parties bring damage claims against each other. In sport violence situations, these claims are based in tort.

The law does not treat all tort claims the same. The distinctions made between types of torts are justifiable since there is a great difference between negligent behavior in which a plaintiff fails to act reasonably but does not intend to commit any harm and a situation in which a person intentionally acts in a way that is very likely to cause harm to someone. These latter actions, which are characterized as intentional torts, carry different consequences. For example, in negligence actions a plaintiff receives compensatory damages (discussed in Chapter 3), which means that the defendant pays damages in an effort to "make good" or replace the loss or injury sustained. If the plaintiff has suffered personal injury, then compensatory damages will pay for medical bills, lost wages, and pain and suffering. In this way, the plaintiff receives compensation, but there is no attempt to punish the defendant since the defendant's behavior was unintentional.

However, if the defendant commits an intentional tort, there may be punitive damages (also discussed in Chapter 3), which may be awarded in addition to the compensatory damages. Punitive damages are awarded, as you will recall, to punish the defendant and to deter that type of conduct from occurring again. Intentional torts are reprehensible to society, so courts are given the latitude in this situation to award damages that have the sole purpose of sending a message to the defendant not to repeat that type of behavior.

In the middle of this spectrum of tort law lie actions in which someone intends to commit an act, but not to cause harm. These actions may have different names in different jurisdictions, but they are often called reckless misconduct, gross negligence, or willful and wanton misconduct. A person acts recklessly when he or she realizes or should realize that there is a strong possibility that harm will result from the actions (Restatement [Second] of Torts § 500). Generally, compensatory damages are awarded in cases of reckless misconduct. Exhibit 18.2 presents the spectrum of tort law actions.

The next sections describe two intentional torts that arise in sport/recreation settings: assault and battery.

Assault

Assault is an intentional tort that often arises in the context of sport violence. The focus of this tort is on some type of menacing or threatening behavior (Restatement [Second] of Torts § 21). There is no contact involved in this tort; battery deals with contact. Three elements must be established by a plaintiff to plead a successful cause of action based on assault. They are:

1. Intent to cause immediate harm, which is menacing or threatening behavior
2. Apprehension of immediate harm by the plaintiff
3. Lack of consent

Distinctions between the types of torts. **EXHIBIT 18.2**

NEGLIGENT BEHAVIOR	RECKLESS MISCONDUCT/GROSS NEGLIGENCE/ WILLFUL AND WANTON MISCONDUCT	INTENTIONAL TORTS
No intent to harm	No intent to harm	Intent to harm
Compensatory damages	Compensatory damages (generally)	Compensatory damages and punitive damages

Intent to cause immediate harm

In regard to the first element, how do courts ascertain what is really intended by a defendant? If we look only at subjective intent, as evidenced by a defendant's motivation, it would be difficult ever to prove intent. For example, if we asked a person who had just hit someone with a baseball bat whether he meant to harm the person, most likely that defendant would disclaim any intent to hurt the person, in an effort to avoid the legal consequences. He would say that he didn't really "mean" any harm or that he was not "motivated" by any intent to injure the person.

Because of this difficulty, the law provides its own definition of "intent," one that allows courts to look objectively at the circumstances to determine what was intended. In the baseball bat example, the courts would look at what was actually done and from that determine intent based on what was "substantially certain" to happen from that act. In this case, hitting a person with a baseball bat is "substantially certain" to result in injury. Courts use the test of whether the consequences of an act are "substantially certain" to occur (Restatement [Second] of Torts § 8A) in order to fashion a more objective measure of intent.

Apprehension by the plaintiff

In regard to the second element, there are three aspects to remember. First, the plaintiff, in order to be apprehensive, must be aware of the threatening or menacing behavior. For example, if I raise my hand as if I were ready to strike A but I do so behind A's back and she cannot see my gesture, there is no apprehension and therefore no assault. Similarly, you cannot assault someone who is comatose or asleep.

Second, according to the view taken by the Restatement (Second) of Torts, apprehension is gauged through the eyes of the victim (plaintiff). If I threaten X with a water pistol, yet X believes it to be a real pistol and is therefore apprehensive, the second element is met. What is at issue is not the actual ability to carry out the threat; it is the apparent ability to do so as gauged by the plaintiff.

Third, there must be an "immediate" threat. If I threaten today to punch someone next Tuesday, this does not meet the elements of assault. There is no immediacy to my threat.

Lack of consent

The last element, lack of consent, becomes the crucial issue within the context of sport. The issue of lack of consent has been included in the elements of the tort to emphasize its importance. We could also look at consent as a defense to the tort.

The issue of consent is the crux of most discussions of sport violence. **Consent** may be defined as "the willingness that an act or invasion of an interest shall take place" (Restatement [Second] of Torts § 892). Consent need not be communicated overtly; it may also be customarily understood. In assault, we may have threatening behavior, and the plaintiff may be apprehensive, but there is no cause of action if we can find that the menacing behavior was somehow permitted within the sport context—that is, if we find consent.

How do we ascertain what is consented to within a sport setting? The following hypothetical case will provide a better understanding of this critical concept.

considering . . .

A major league baseball player intentionally throws a fastball at the batter's torso to "encourage" the batter not to crowd the plate. The ball zips past the batter, but the batter becomes upset at this affront and charges the pitcher's mound with bat in hand. The batter throws the bat at the pitcher and misses by a few inches.

Questions

- In the above scenario how many assaults, if any, do we have?
- Was either of these threatening situations consented to, thus negating the assault?

Note how you would answer the questions and then check your responses using the Analysis & Discussion at the end of this chapter.

As this hypothetical case shows, the issue of consent depends upon an understanding of the nature of the sport. From the starting point of the rules of the sport, we then analyze what continues to be acceptable behavior. We look at the culture of the sport and see what the sport has done to identify the parameters of permissible conduct.

Sport and recreation administrators are in control of the issue of consent and, by extension, the degree of permissible aggression and violence within sport. The courts do not decide, in a vacuum, what level of violence and intimidation is acceptable. Coaches, officials, rule makers, and administrators of leagues decide what the landscape of aggression and violence will look like in various sports. We define for the courts what behaviors are permissible within various sports and the different competitive levels of those sports. If we believe that levels of aggression are unacceptable, it is our responsibility to set those parameters, which will then be adopted by courts as they deal with civil cases of assault or battery.

Battery

In many cases, violence in sport occurs as actual physical contact, some of which may be well outside the rules or the acceptable levels of contact permitted within the sport. The intentional tort of battery differs from assault in that battery involves actual physical contact, not merely menacing or threatening behavior.

Elements of battery

The intentional tort of **battery** is defined as follows by the Restatement (Second) of Torts §§ 18 and 19. The elements of battery are:

1. Intent to cause harmful or offensive touching
2. Harmful or offensive touching
3. Lack of consent

Regarding the first element, remember that, like assault, battery is an intentional tort. As with assault, intent is defined in an objective manner; the question of motivation is irrelevant.

Also, note the word "touching" in the first element. Although the contact that becomes battery in sport often has a violent context, it is not technically necessary to have touching that causes bodily harm. The gist of this tort is unconsented touching; the contact need not be violent. For example, let's assume that a sport manager touched his assistant on the shoulder every morning when he stopped by the assistant's desk. Even though the assistant shies away from the contact (a clear message that this touching lacks consent), the manager continues to engage in this behavior. Technically, this is battery, since it meets the elements of the tort, regardless of the lack of physical injury.

In regard to the second element, the plaintiff does not have to be aware of the touching for a battery to occur. This is different from assault, where the plaintiff has to have been "apprehensive," denoting awareness. Battery can occur even if the plaintiff was sleeping or otherwise lacking in the ability to "feel" the contact. For example, if a surgeon performing a leg amputation removed the incorrect appendage, this is technically battery, even though (hopefully) the patient was unaware of the mistake as it occurred.

The actual touching may also occur through an instrumentality over which the defendant has control. If I hit you with a baseball bat or with a ball that I threw at you, that meets the requirement of "touching," even though I have not made direct physical contact with you.

As with assault, the critical element in most sport violence battery cases is consent. We must look to the culture and norms of a sport to ascertain what is acceptable contact (and therefore consented to) within that sport.

The following hypothetical case from sport addresses the important aspect of intent.

considering . . . INTENT

During an adult recreational softball league game, there is a runner on first base. When a ground ball is hit to the shortstop, the runner begins to run toward second base. The shortstop quickly fields the ground ball and tosses it to the second baseman, who tags second base and throws the ball to first to complete the double play. The second baseman, after throwing the ball to first, steps well away from second base toward the pitcher's mound. Although the double play has been completed, the runner from first veers out of the base path, continues to run at the second baseman, and hits the second baseman with great force. The runner did not slow down, and he also brought his arm up into the second baseman's chin, at the point of contact. The runner is a much larger man than the second baseman, outweighing him by at least 40 pounds. The second baseman suffers severe injury to his jaw.

Questions

- Is this a battery?
- What if the runner testifies at trial that he did not "mean" to hurt the second baseman?
- What if the runner alleges that he was not motivated by any desire to hurt a member of the opposing team?

- What are the natural and probable consequences of running at full speed and hitting a person in such a manner, considering the size disparity between the two men?
- What consequences were "substantially certain" to result from the runner making contact with the second baseman in this way?

Note how you would answer the questions and then check your responses using the Analysis & Discussion at the end of this chapter.

Privilege as a defense to battery

Two aspects of privilege are relevant as defenses to battery (Restatement [Second] of Torts § 10). The first pertains to a concept commonly known as **self-defense,** that is, a person may be entitled to use reasonable force to defend himself or herself from attack. To use self-defense, however, a person cannot be the initiator of contact.

The second aspect of privilege, which is relevant for those who teach or coach in an educational environment, is the privilege to use **reasonable force** to control, train, or educate a child (6 Am. Jur. 2d *Assault & Battery* § 104). To ascertain the reasonableness of a use of force, we look at a variety of factors, including those presented in Exhibit 18.3.

If the force used is excessive, then the privilege is defeated, and there is battery. The following hypothetical case addresses this aspect of privilege.

considering . . .   REASONABLE FORCE

At a junior high school football practice, the adult coach becomes displeased with a player's tackling technique. The coach yells loudly at the child, age 12, and then grabs the facemask on the child's helmet, twists the facemask, and throws the child to the ground. The child suffers a severe neck injury.

Question
- When the coach is sued for battery, can he use the defense of privilege to argue that this contact was necessary to train and discipline the young football player?

Note how you would answer the question and then check your response using the Analysis & Discussion at the end of this chapter.

Factors for ascertaining the reasonableness of the use of force with children (Restatement [Second] of Torts §§ 146, 150, 151, and 155).	EXHIBIT	18.3

1. The age, sex, and condition of the child
2. The nature of the offensive conduct
3. Whether force was reasonably necessary to compel obedience to a proper command
4. Whether the force was disproportionate to the offense or likely to cause serious injury

Reckless Misconduct

In many circumstances involving player violence, courts do not find that an intentional tort has occurred. However, a cause of action may nonetheless exist so that an injured player may receive compensation. **Reckless misconduct,** which is usually synonymous with *willful and wanton misconduct,* is defined as follows:

> The actor's conduct is in reckless disregard of the safety of another if he does an act or intentionally fails to do an act which it is his duty to the other to do, knowing or having reason to know of facts which would lead a reasonable man to realize, not only that his conduct creates an unreasonable risk of physical harm to another, but also that such risk is substantially greater than that which is necessary to make his conduct negligent. (Restatement [Second] of Torts § 500)

Familiarity with the evolution of the tort of reckless misconduct is important to understanding this concept. The case of *Nabozny v. Barnhill* is seminal.

Nabozny v. Barnhill

334 N.E.2d 258 (Ill. App. Ct. 1975)

CASE OPINION

[FACTS

A soccer match was held between two amateur teams at Duke Child's Field in Winnetka, Illinois. Plaintiff played the position of goalkeeper for the Hansa team. Members of both teams were of high school age. Approximately 20 minutes after play had begun, a Winnetka player kicked the ball over the midfield line. Two players chased the ball, and a Hansa player passed the ball to the plaintiff. The plaintiff went down on one knee to receive the pass and pulled the ball to his chest. The defendant player from Winnetka continued to run in the direction of the plaintiff and kicked the left side of the plaintiff's head, causing severe injuries.

Witnesses agreed that the defendant had time to avoid contact with plaintiff and that the plaintiff was in the "penalty area," an area in which the rules prohibit contact with the goalkeeper when he is in possession of the ball. Experts agreed that the contact in question should not have occurred.

In the action to recover damages for personal injuries, trial was before a jury. However, the trial court directed a verdict in favor of the defendant on the basis that, as a matter of law, the plaintiff had no cause of action against the defendant. The trial court found that no duty of care existed to benefit the plaintiff.

The plaintiff appealed this ruling.]

HOLDING

The appellate court reversed and remanded.

RATIONALE

The appellate court found a "dearth of case law involving organized athletic competition wherein one of the participants is charged with negligence."

* * *

This court believes that the law should not place unreasonable burdens on the free and vigorous participation in sports by our youth. However, we believe that organized athletic competition does not exist in a vacuum. Rather, some of the restraints of civilization must accompany every athlete on to the playing field. One of the educational benefits of organized athletic competition to our youth is the development of discipline and self-control.

* * *

For these reasons, this court believes that when athletes are engaged in an athletic competition; all teams are trained and coached by knowledgeable personnel; a recognized set of rules governs the conduct of the competition; and a safety rule is contained therein which is primarily designed to protect players from serious injury, a player is then charged with a duty to every other player on the field to refrain from conduct proscribed by a safety rule. A reckless disregard for the safety of other players cannot be excused. To engage in such conduct is to create an intolerable and unreasonable risk of serious injury to other participants.

* * *

It is our opinion that a player is liable for injury in a tort action if his conduct is such that it is either deliberate, willful or with a reckless disregard for the safety of the other player so as to cause injury to that player.

* * *

Questions

1. Based on this decision, is mere negligence actionable in player-to-player violence cases in contact sports? Cite language from the decision that supports your view.
2. Why would this court decline to set the standard of care at mere negligence? What effect would a negligence standard have upon "free and vigorous participation in sports"?
3. Why did the court decide that it was necessary to intervene at all in situations of player violence? Discuss what the notion that the "restraints of civilization must accompany every athlete on to the playing field" means in this context.

Nabozny is the seminal case in the realm of player-to-player violence. Most jurisdictions continue to follow the reckless disregard standard today. As one exception, Wisconsin courts adopted a negligence standard for player-to-player contact (*Lestina v. West Bend Mutual Insurance Co.*, 1993). In that state, however, the legislature acted in response to the courts' adoption of the negligence standard by passing a statute (Wisconsin Stat. §895.525 (4m)(a)) that provides immunity from negligence actions for participants in a recreational activity that involves physical contact between persons in an amateur sport. In a recent application of that statute the Wisconsin Supreme Court held that cheerleading participants were immune from a negligence action as it held that cheerleading was a "contact sport" for the purposes of this statute (*Noffke v. Bakke*, 2009).

There are essentially two policy reasons for adhering to the reckless disregard standard:

1. The promotion of vigorous participation in athletic activities
2. To avoid a flood of litigation that would ensue if the negligence standard were employed

The following 2008 case has set a different standard in cases in Illinois involving "full contact" sports such as ice hockey and football.

Karas v. Strevell

884 N.E.2d 122 (Ill. 2008)

FOCUS CASE

FACTS

On January 25, 2004, Benjamin Karas, a member of his high school's junior varsity ice hockey team, was injured as two members of the opposing team bodychecked Karas from behind, causing him neck and head injuries. The hockey league's rules prohibited bodychecking from behind, and every player's jersey had the word "STOP" on the back to remind players not to hit players from behind.

Karas's father filed suit on his son's behalf alleging that the two players who hit his son should be liable for their willful and wanton conduct. He also alleged that the hockey associations should be liable for their negligence and willful and wanton conduct in failing to enforce the bodychecking prohibition and for failing to instruct players properly regarding this rule. The trial court dismissed all claims. The appellate court affirmed dismissal of only the willful and wanton claim against the hockey associations.

HOLDING

The Illinois Supreme Court affirmed in part and reversed in part the appellate court judgment. The court affirmed the trial court judgment. The court remanded the matter to the trial court to permit the plaintiff to amend the complaint to plead facts to conform to the decision, if the plaintiff were able to do so.

RATIONALE

The court discussed the case of *Pfister v. Shusta,* 657 N.E.2d 1013 (Ill. 1995), the controlling precedent in Illinois, which adopted the exception to the standard of ordinary care for participants engaged in contact sports. Under this view a participant in a contact sport may not be held liable for negligent conduct that injures a coparticipant. Instead liability must be predicated upon behavior that is intentional or willful or wanton (essentially the *Nabozny* standard).

In this case, however, the court decided that the *Pfister* standard is unworkable in the context of ice hockey or football since bodychecking or tackling evinces a "conscious disregard for the safety of the person being struck" (p. 132). Physical contact in these "full-contact sports" is a fundamental part of the way the game is played, so it is problematic to adopt a standard that holds participants liable for consciously disregarding the safety of coparticipants. The traditional willful and wanton standard is not workable and is contrary to the *Pfister* rationale, which was developed in order to avoid a chilling effect upon the participants who are simply engaging in the inherent risks of an activity.

In this context, in which the bodycheck from behind violated a rule, the court recognized that some rules violations are inherent and anticipated in a sport and that not all rules violations, in themselves, are sufficient to impose liability. On the other hand, the court noted that, as the *Nabozny* court stated, "Some of the restraints of civilization must accompany every athlete on to the playing field" (p. 134). Therefore, the court concluded that, in sports such as ice hockey or football, a participant breaches a duty of care to a coparticipant only if the participant intentionally injures the coparticipant or engages in conduct "totally outside the range of the ordinary activity involved in the sport" (p. 134).

As currently pled in the complaint, the conduct by the two opposing players would not rise to the standard set forth by the court. Although the bodycheck was a rules violation, there were no allegations that it was deliberate or occurred after play had been stopped.

The court also addressed whether the organizational defendants (the hockey associations) should enjoy the benefit of the contact sports exception as well or whether they can be liable for negligence. The court held that it was within the spirit of the exception to apply it to the hockey associations. Therefore, to "successfully plead a cause of action for failing to adequately enforce the rules in an organized full-contact sport, plaintiff must allege that the defendant acted with intent to cause the injury or that the defendant engaged in conduct 'totally outside the range of ordinary activity'" (p. 137).

ORGANIZATIONAL ISSUES RELATING TO PLAYER VIOLENCE

Although the individual who actually engages in a violent act must answer for his or her own actions, there are also liability issues for the institutions that employ or are otherwise responsible for the actions of the person(s) acting violently. First we address the criminal and civil liability issues relating to hazing. Then we conclude with a discussion of how an institution may be vicariously liable for the violent actions of its employees.

Hazing

The behaviors that have traditionally been labeled as hazing run the gamut from the innocuous, such as having the "rookies" sing at training table, to humiliating, degrading, and physically dangerous behaviors, often accompanied by the consumption of alcohol. According to the results of a national survey on hazing known widely as the Alfred University study (Hoover, 1999), university student-athletes reported that 80 percent of them had been hazed, according to a listing of hazing behaviors, although only 12 percent of these athletes labeled those activities as hazing. More than half of the respondents stated that they had been involved in initiation activities involving alcohol. Further, 60 percent of the student-athletes stated that they would not report hazing to their school officials.

In March 2008, the initial findings of a subsequent survey of 11,480 college students at 53 universities were released. The investigators ascertained that 55 percent of college students involved in clubs, sport teams, and other student organizations have experienced hazing. Of the college students who did report being hazed, 95 percent did not inform school administrators. It appears that little progress has been made in the last decade in terms of preventing hazing (Allan & Madden, 2008).

These studies raise issues related to hazing that are pertinent to sport teams. First, there is confusion about what is actually hazing. The behaviors of **hazing** were defined in the Alfred University study as "any activity expected of someone joining a group that humiliates,

---

Competitive Advantage

STRATEGIES

Violence and Tort Law

- Organizations that offer competitive athletic competition should develop policies and procedures setting forth "zero tolerance" for excessive violence. Penalties for excessive violence should be severe and fairly administered.

- Coaches should be rewarded for teaching and implementing strategies that place a premium on skill and not on excessive violence. Coaches whose teams display bad sportsmanship and excessive violence should be sanctioned, as well as the players who engage in excessive violence.

- Youth leagues should hold preseason meetings for parents and players encouraging good sportsmanship for players and fans.

- Game officials should be instructed that your league has a "zero tolerance" policy for excessive violence, and officials should be encouraged to implement that philosophy in the way that games are called.

degrades, abuses, or endangers, regardless of the person's willingness to participate" (Hoover, 1999). In the 2008 study, however, the investigators reported that there was confusion about what constituted hazing and that administrators could not differentiate between bullying and hazing (Allan & Madden, 2008).

Second, there is a long-standing tradition of initiation rites in sport. It is a part of the socialization process to make newcomers engage in activities that indicate their willingness to belong to the team. Over the years many of these bonding experiences have become a part of the sport culture and often are not recognized as having unacceptable or dangerous components, such as hazing. The unwillingness to label behaviors as hazing is the first obstacle to eliminating this type of behavior. Because of the traditional aspect of "rites of passage," many involved in the sporting environment—including many coaches, players, and administrators—see no need to police or stop initiation or hazing rituals. Another difficulty in dealing with this issue is that much of the behavior is exacerbated by the consumption of alcohol, particularly in the college environment.

From a legal viewpoint, it is important to recognize the liability that hazing may impose, from individual accountability by those who haze to the liability of coaches, teachers, and administrators, as well as the vicarious liability of the employing university, school district, or other body.

Criminal liability

Currently, 44 states have antihazing laws ("State anti-hazing laws," n.d.). Most of these statutes identify hazing as a misdemeanor. The monetary penalties range from $10 to $10,000, and jail time ranges between 10 days and a year (Edelman, 2005).

A typical definition of hazing may be found in the statutes of Colorado. See Exhibit 18.4.

EXHIBIT 18.4   The definition of hazing found in Colorado Revised Statute 18-9-124.

(2) AS USED IN THIS SECTION, UNLESS THE CONTEXT OTHERWISE REQUIRES:

(a) **"Hazing"** means any activity by which a person recklessly endangers the health or safety of or causes a risk of bodily injury to an individual for purposes of initiation or admission into or affiliation with any student organization; except that **"hazing"** does not include customary athletic events or other similar contests or competitions, or authorized training activities conducted by members of the armed forces of the State of Colorado or the United States.

(b) **"Hazing"** includes but is not limited to:

(i) forced and prolonged physical activity;

(ii) forced consumption of any food, beverage, medication or controlled substance, whether or not prescribed, in excess of the usual amounts for human consumption or forced consumption of any substance not generally intended for human consumption;

(iii) prolonged deprivation of sleep, food, or drink.

There may be criminal liability for those who fail to notify authorities after observing hazing. Further, some statutes require public schools to develop and publicize antihazing policies ("State anti-hazing laws," n.d.).

Although 44 states have recognized hazing as a societal issue, as evidenced by the statutory protections, it cannot be said that, to date, the criminal statutes have provided much of a deterrent. Relatively few prosecutions have occurred under the statutes, partly because of the definitional difficulties in what is considered to be hazing and partly because some of the statutory penalties are not very severe. Some commentators have proposed that a federal hazing law be adopted to provide uniformity in protection from hazing (Sussberg, 2003; Edelman, 2005).

Civil liability

In the majority of states, there are also civil antihazing statutes, although their provisions vary widely from state to state. In some cases these statutes stem from their criminal counterparts, and in other jurisdictions the statutes exist independently. However, even in the states that have civil statutes, these statutes are not that effective for a variety of reasons, including the failure to extend liability to school personnel (Edelman, 2005).

Individual civil liability for hazing may also be predicated upon the theories of assault and battery that were discussed above in suits against the perpetrators. Tort liability of administrators, coaches, or teachers may be found under the theory of negligent supervision. A case based on negligent supervision would allege that the coach, teacher, or administrator failed to act as a reasonable prudent person in failing to intervene to stop dangerous hazing activities from taking place. Organizational liability may then be found under the usual principles of vicarious liability (see Chapter 5).

Some cases relating to hazing have been brought on the basis that hazing violates constitutional protections of a student's right to bodily integrity under the substantive aspect of the Fourteenth Amendment's Due Process Clause. Under current law, however, based on the Supreme Court's decision in *DeShaney v. Winnebago County Department of Social Services* (1989), governmental entities (school districts) do not have an affirmative duty to protect students from violence. An exception to this rule exists if the government has taken a person into custody. Courts have consistently held that students are not in custody for the purposes of the Fourteenth Amendment. Without this custodial aspect, there is no duty to protect and, thus, no cause of action under due process.

Competitive Advantage

STRATEGIES

Prevention of Hazing

■ Develop policies and procedures defining hazing, and implement steps to have coaches institute alternative "rites of passage" that are safe but serve the purpose of bonding and team cohesion.

■ If hazing has gone on for years at your school, advise your coaches to address previous incidents directly and forcefully with your teams at the beginning of a new season. Encourage students to report incidents of hazing (Smith, 2003).

■ Involve parents and community members to help develop and implement hazing policies.

■ Develop a culture of respect within your athletic department. Coaches should model respectful behavior to athletes, other coaches, administrators, and opponents. There should be no domination or humiliation based on power structures in your teams.

■ Encourage coaches to have mentoring programs that match older players with younger players to develop positive relationships (Popke, 2003).

The case of *Reeves v. Besonen* (1991) is consistent with the above principles. In that case, a high school football player was hazed on the school bus while returning from a game. The bus was driven by the football coach. The plaintiff was subjected to a "hit line" at the back of the bus and suffered a broken nose. In denying relief for the plaintiff on his substantive due process claim, the court held that the defendants did not deprive the plaintiff of any Constitutional rights because the plaintiff was voluntarily participating in football, and riding on the school bus could not be construed as incarceration or custody for the purposes of meeting the *DeShaney* standards. It is quite difficult to prevail on a Fourteenth Amendment claim relating to hazing.

Vicarious Liability for Violent Acts of Employees

As you will recall from Chapter 5's discussion of vicarious liability, generally employers are not found liable under *respondeat superior* principles for the intentional acts of their employees. In one noteworthy case, however, the Los Angeles Lakers organization was held liable for the actions of its player Kermit Washington. Washington, a known enforcer in the NBA, struck Rudy Tomjanovich of the Houston Rockets in a game in 1977. Tomjanovich suffered very serious injuries, including a broken nose and jaw, a fractured skull, facial lacerations, a concussion, and leakage of spinal fluid. One witness to the incident noted that the punch by Washington sounded as if a watermelon had been dropped onto a cement floor. In a jury trial, a judgment was rendered in the amount of $1,746,376.95 as actual damages and $1.5 million as punitive damages (*Tomjanovich v. California Sports, Inc.*, 1979).

The judgment was predicated upon vicarious liability under California law, which has arguably the most "expansive *respondeat superior* doctrine in the country" (Rubin, 1999, p. 282). However, regardless of California law, there could be vicarious liability under the theory that the act was foreseeable in view of the duties of the employee (Restatement [Second] of Agency § 245). In this situation, Kermit Washington was employed by the Lakers as an "enforcer"; his role on the team was to exert "muscle" against opponents. Therefore, it was certainly foreseeable that his anger and use of force could rise to the level of violence exerted against Tomjanovich.

Also, there is certainly an argument that the Lakers coach and general manager could be responsible under the theory of negligent retention or supervision (see Chapter 5). The coach and management retained Washington with full knowledge of his violent propensities. This retention was not reasonable behavior and posed a danger to opponents. This negligent behavior by the coach and general manager, who were acting within the scope of their employment with the Lakers, could be imputed to the Lakers organization under the usual rule of *respondeat superior*.

Competitive Advantage
STRATEGIES

Vicarious Liability for Actions of Employees

- Develop disciplinary policies to deter unsportsmanlike and violent behavior by athletes, and enforce them evenhandedly.

- Ensure that coaches know the difference between fair and competitive strategies and those that may instigate violence.

- Ensure that disciplinary sanctions for excessive violence are sufficient to deter that behavior.

Can there be liability by a college or university based on the violent acts of intercollegiate athletes? In the case of *Molina v. Christensen* (2001), there were allegations of the coach's direct instigation of violence. In this college baseball setting, a player from the University of Evansville, Anthony Molina, was in the on-deck circle prior to the start of the game. The opposing pitcher from Wichita State University, Benjamin Christensen, while warming up, was alleged to have deliberately thrown the ball at Molina, hitting him in the head and causing serious injuries. Christensen asserted that his actions were motivated by instructions from one of his coaches. The action against the coaches and university was dismissed, however, because of recreational use immunity (see Chapter 15 for a discussion of immunity). Molina failed to assert that the coach's actions amounted to gross and wanton negligence. If Molina had not made this error in pleading this case, the coaches should have been liable, if they had indeed instructed their pitchers to throw at opponents who were incapable of protecting themselves as they stood in the on-deck circle.

CONCLUSION

Sport managers must address many issues regarding sport violence. At all levels of participation, the degree and kinds of violence are escalating. Although there may be criminal and/or civil liability for individuals who engage in violent behavior, we have addressed the limitations of these legal remedies. There may also be organizational liability based on vicarious liability. It is incumbent upon sport and recreation administrators to realize that the responsibility for violent behavior falls on our shoulders. We must set the standards for permissible aggression within our sports and deter impermissible violence through our rule making and our stringent enforcement of those rules. As one jurist put it, "some of the restraints of civilization must accompany every athlete upon the playing field" (*Nabozny v. Barnhill*, 1975). Sport administrators must decide what those restraints should be.

discussion questions

1. An adult player in a recreational softball game strikes out. He becomes angry and throws his bat at the catcher, hitting the catcher and fracturing his nose. Do you think that a prosecutor would believe that this is criminal behavior and file charges against the batter? Why or why not? Regardless of the criminal aspect, what civil cause of action would the catcher have against the batter? Explain the elements of the cause of action.

2. How do you determine whether a certain contact was consented to within a game? Give examples of contact that might be consented to within professional football versus Pop Warner football.

3. Discuss the defense of privilege and give examples of its applicability.

4. What are some of the difficulties for administrators in addressing the issue of hazing among their teams?

learning activities

1. As a youth league administrator, you are concerned with the lack of sportsmanlike behavior shown by many parents who attend your games. Often, they make very rude comments to the game officials, and, on a couple of occasions, one of your supervisors has had to intervene before a parent physically attacked a referee. Research whether your state has a statute making the assault of a sports official a criminal offense. Then, prepare a memorandum to the parents identifying their possible liability for their interactions with game officials. If your state does not have such a specific statute, make your recommendations for parental conduct based on your state's definition of criminal assault generally.

2. Do an Internet search regarding the player violence that occurred on March 8, 2004, in an NHL game between Steve Moore of the Colorado Avalanche and Vancouver Canucks player Todd Bertuzzi. Ascertain what happened in this case, both as to the criminal charges that were filed against Bertuzzi in British Columbia and as to the civil case that was filed by Moore against Bertuzzi. Was the handling of this incident of violence consistent with what you learned in this chapter?

3. Play the role of athletic director at a high school. Research the laws regarding hazing in your state, and write a memorandum to your coaches explaining the legal ramifications of allowing hazing. Develop a policy regarding how your athletic department will try to prevent hazing among your teams and athletes.

CASE STUDY

In regard to the *Karas* decision discussed earlier, the court held that in sports it characterized as "full-contact sports" (specifically ice hockey and football) rules violations are an inherent part of the game and therefore, to hold a party liable for a violation of a rule, would "chill" participation in that sport. Discuss the ramifications of the new standard developed in the *Karas* decision as you write a memorandum opposing the *Karas* rationale to an association of youth ice hockey administrators. Remember that the ice hockey association in the *Karas* case had already deemed checking from the back to be dangerous behavior since the word STOP was on the back of all players' jerseys.

considering . . .   ANALYSIS & DISCUSSION

Consent (p. 547)

As we analyze the first two elements of assault, it seems clear that both elements are present. First, we do have menacing or threatening behavior in both the actions of the pitcher and the retaliatory behavior by the batter. Further, the batter would be apprehensive of a fastball thrown very close to his body. Likewise, the pitcher would be apprehensive of the behavior of the batter.

Therefore, we must address the issue of consent.

To ascertain consent, we first look at the rules of the sport to see what behaviors are prohibited. Rules prohibit the intentional throwing of pitches at batters. It is up to the umpire's judgment, of course, to determine the "intent" of the pitcher—but if an umpire does decide that a pitcher is throwing intentionally at the batter, there are consequences. There are also, of course, prohibitions against the type of behavior engaged in by the batter. If the rules of the sport were the only consideration in analyzing consent, then we would have two assaults in this scenario.

Consent, however, cannot be restricted to simply an analysis of the rules. We must look beyond the rules at the culture and context of the sport (Restatement [Second] of Torts § 50, comment b). In baseball, we know that players are taught, from very early ages, that pitchers must move batters away from the plate. When batters crowd the plate, they know that it is very likely that the pitcher will send a message by throwing a pitch at them. This behavior, even though it technically violates a rule of the sport, is consistent with the accepted norms of baseball. Any coach, player, or umpire would attest to the fact that throwing at batters is an accepted custom in baseball, that it is intrinsic to the nature of that sport. The pitcher's actions are consented to, based on the nature of the sport, and there is no assault by the pitcher.

On the other hand, even though we know of incidents in which the batter has "gone after" the pitcher, this rules violation is not treated as a custom or as part of the culture in the sport. Batters who engage in this retaliatory behavior are severely penalized by umpires and league sanctions; therefore, we can see that this type of behavior is not consented to within baseball. The behavior by the batter would be considered an assault.

Intent (p. 548)

Regardless of what the runner says about "intent," there *is* intent to cause a harmful contact. Intent to touch is evident as we look at what actually transpired, rather than what the runner tells us about his motivation.

As to the second element, we certainly have actual harmful contact. Finally, there is a lack of consent because this type of contact is forbidden by the rules and goes beyond what is acceptable within the custom of the sport. It is common for a runner to slide into a second baseman while the baseman is on or near the base, in an attempt to disrupt the double play. However, it is not permissible, after the play is over, to go well outside of the base path to make contact with an opposing player.

In this fact pattern, there is battery, and the jury may award punitive damages.

Reasonable Force (p. 549)

The question is whether the force used here can be considered a reasonable use of force. In this scenario, the coach will likely lose in his assertion that the contact (battery) was privileged. The child was young, and there was a considerable size difference between the adult coach and the player. The player was not being disruptive or unruly at practice; he simply was not tackling well. The force used was disproportionate to the offense, and serious injury ensued. This is a case in which the force used to discipline the player exceeded privilege. The coach is liable for battery.

REFERENCES

Cases

Bourque v. Duplechin, 331 So.2d 40 (La. Ct. App. 1976).

DeShaney v. Winnebago County Dep't of Social Services, 489 U.S. 189 (1989).

Karas v. Strevell, 884 N.E.2d 122 (Ill. 2008).

Lestina v. West Bend Mutual Ins. Co., 501 N.W.2d 28 (Wis. 1993).

Molina v. Christensen, 44 P.3d 1274 (Kan. Ct. App. 2001).

Nabozny v. Barnhill, 334 N.E.2d 258 (Ill. App. Ct. 1975).

Noffke v. Bakke, 760 N.W.2d 156 (Wisc. 2009).

Reeves v. Besonen, 754 F. Supp. 1135 (E.D. Mich. 1991).

Tomjanovich v. California Sports, Inc., 1979 U.S. Dist. LEXIS 9282 (S. D. Tex. Oct. 10, 1979).

Statutes

Hazing, Colo. Rev. Stat. § 18-9-124.

Immunity, Wisc. Stat. § 895.525 (4m)(a).

Other Sources

6 Am. Jur. 2d , Assault & Battery § 104.

Allan, E. J., & Madden, M. (2008). Hazing in view: College students at risk. Retrieved May 29, 2009, from www.hazingstudy.org.

Bad behavior cited in youth sports study. (2005, November 29). *USA Today*, p. 13C.

Barry, M. P., Fox, R. L., & Jones, C. (2005). Article: Judicial opinion on the criminality of sports violence in the United States. *Seton Hall Journal of Sports & Entertainment Law, 15*, 1–25.

Berkowitz, K. (2009, March 16). Confronting fan misbehavior. *Athletic Management*. Retrieved May 29, 2009, from www.athleticmanagement.com/2009/03/16/confronting_fan_misbehavior/index.php.

Edelman, M. (2005). Article: How to prevent high school hazing: A legal, ethical and social primer. *North Dakota Law Review, 81*, 309–341.

Fiore, D. K. (2003). Comment: Parental rage and violence in youth sports: How can we prevent "soccer moms" and "hockey dads" from interfering in youth sports and causing games to end in fistfights rather than handshakes? *Villanova Sports & Entertainment Law Journal, 10*, 103–129.

Hoover, N. C. (1999, August 30). *National survey: Initiation rites and athletics for NCAA sport teams*. Retrieved October 31, 2003, from Alfred University website at www.alfred.edu/news/html/hazing_study_99.html.

Popke, M. (2003, December). Uncivil rites. *Athletic Business, 27*, 101–107.

Restatement (Second) of Agency.

Restatement (Second) of Torts (1965).

Rubin, S. I. (1999, Fall). The vicarious liability of professional sports teams for on-the-field assaults committed by their players. *Virginia Journal of Sports and Law, 1*, 266–289.

Samson, C. (2005, Fall). Comment: No time like the present: Why recent events should spur Congress to enact a sports violence act. *Arizona State Law Journal, 37*, 949–972.

Smith, L. (2003, June/July). Hazing hits home. *Athletic Management*, 41–47.

State anti-hazing laws. (n.d.) Retrieved May 27, 2009, from www.stophazing.org//laws.html.

Sussberg, J. A. (2003, March). Note: Shattered dreams: Hazing in college athletics. *Cardozo Law Review, 24*, 1421–1491.

WEBSITE RESOURCES

www.hanknuwer.com ▪ Hank Nuwer, author of numerous articles and books on hazing, maintains this website to identify links to anti-hazing resources. It also provides some hazing videos and a map of hazing deaths across the United States.

www.hazing.cornell.edu ▪ This is a resource for students, faculty, and administrators at Cornell University setting forth the school's policies regarding hazing. It also provides a phone number for an antihazing hotline.

www.naso.org ▪ This is the website for the National Association of Sports Officials. Under the Government Relations link, you can find information on current state statutes relating to assault upon sports officials. There is also model legislation and an archive of articles relating to attacks upon sports officials.

www.NCAA.org/health-safety ▪ The NCAA has developed a comprehensive program to prevent hazing and to find alternative ways to foster camaraderie and team building. This is the program known as "Building New Traditions: Hazing Prevention in College Athletics."

PART V | **Marketing Management**

INTRODUCTION TO THE LAW
IN MARKETING ENVIRONMENTS

I ndividuals in sport marketing perform a wide range of services and functions that vary from one sport organization to another. For example, the responsibilities of a marketing director for a major league sports franchise and those of a marketing director for a local YMCA or a state university athletics program will naturally be quite different. Sport marketing will involve sales activities such as ticket sales, corporate sponsor sales, luxury suites sales, product sales, service agreement sales, and so forth. Retail and manufacturing sport organizations employ marketing people in product design and development as well as sales. Marketing directors are typically responsible for the creation and placement of advertising, conducting special promotions or game day promotions, coordinating Internet-based sales activities and advertising programs featuring the Internet, and creating and monitoring intellectual property rights.

If you perform any of these diverse responsibilities, you may encounter a number of legal issues. You can be much more successful with a fundamental understanding of the legal areas that are implicated in the marketing management function of a sport organization.

LEGAL PRINCIPLES AND THE MARKETING FUNCTION

M any legal areas are implicated in marketing management. The most constant and recurring legal area is that of contract law. All sport marketing activities require the negotiation, creation, drafting, modifying, execution, and performance of contractual obligations. Whether it is a corporate sponsor renewal, a family ticket package, a mascot appearance at a game promotion, a weekly newspaper advertisement, or a licensing agreement with a local retailer for merchandise, each and every activity represents a contractual agreement between the parties. Chapter 4 covered the basic contract principles you will need to use on a daily basis to perform your duties effectively. In addition to the general application of contract law to many functions of sport marketing, several other legal areas are implicated in marketing. Chapter 19 discusses the importance of intellectual property in the marketing and promotion of sports products and services. This naturally involves a discussion of trademark law and the law of copyrights. Chapter 20 addresses the legal issues faced by sport managers as they begin to operationalize marketing initiatives through advertising, sponsorship and broadcasting agreements, and monitoring the activities of competitors and consumers. Thus, Chapter 20 discusses false advertising, deceptive trade practices, consumer protection, publicity rights, ambush marketing, and defamation. Chapter 20 also revisits constitutional law issues arising from First Amendment protections of commercial speech and contract law issues related to sponsorship agreements, broadcasting agreements, and sales agreements.

19

CHAPTER

Development and Protection
of Intellectual Property

563

INTRODUCTION

T he term "intellectual property" is commonly used to refer to rights associated with patents, copyrights, trademarks, trade secrets, and trade dress. The primary goal of intellectual property law is to create and maintain an open and competitive marketplace. The various intellectual property laws both complement and challenge each other. For example, creators of original materials need to be rewarded for their creation and permitted to profit from their creativity. Creators of original works are granted an exclusive right to use and control the use of their works. However, a robust marketplace also needs vibrant competition and access to creative ideas. Thus, the duration or scope of the right is limited so that at some point the marketplace can gain free and continuing access to the invention, image, idea, or word. Intellectual property law is intended to provide a compromise between these competing goals so that a delicate balance is maintained.

Different areas of intellectual property law have overlapping protections and different purposes. For example, patent law and copyright law are intended primarily to protect inventions and creative works, while trademark law and unfair competition law are intended to protect consumers from confusing, deceptive, and misleading advertising and marketing practices. A single product could receive intellectual property protection for its design (patent), label (copyright), packaging (trade dress), and slogan (trademark), and for preventing false claims of competitors (unfair competition). The creation and protection of intellectual property (IP) rights is also one of the fastest-growing concerns for sport organizations. Often, many IP functions are performed by the marketing department staff. This chapter explores the law relating to trademarks and copyrights. Several additional legal issues are implicated by marketing functions, such as use of technology, cyber-squatting, and Internet domain name protection; these issues are also presented in this chapter. Since patents are a highly specialized area, we have elected not to provide detailed discussion of patent law. General information about patents is available from the United States Patent and Trademark Office's website, www.uspto.gov. Exhibit 19.1 provides an overview of the management contexts, major legal issues, and relevant laws and cases discussed in this chapter.

To begin our discussion, let's consider the following scenario. You are the marketing director for a minor league baseball team, the Hollyville Hornets. Some of your many functions are developing promotional ideas, creating and implementing marketing strategies, reviewing and approving advertisements, coordinating new merchandise designs, and communicating with the licensees and vendors who sell your team's merchandise. You will be better prepared to perform these functions effectively if you understand how to develop and protect the team's intellectual property. Let's begin with a new advertising campaign that you have created for the team to increase single game ticket sales: "Nothing Beats Hornets in the Summertime." This theme will emphasize to the local community that nothing is quite as enjoyable on a summer evening as going to the ballpark and watching the Hornets play. It will also allow you to emphasize the team's winning record. Your marketing mix will include radio, outdoor billboards, and newspaper advertisements, as well as the team website. You plan to develop a new logo with the team

	EXHIBIT	19.1
Management contexts in which issues of intellectual property may arise, with relevant laws and cases.		

MANAGEMENT CONTEXT	MAJOR LEGAL ISSUES	RELEVANT LAW	ILLUSTRATIVE CASES
Creating promotions and advertising campaigns/slogans	Creating a protectable property interest	Lanham Act	*Smack Apparel, University of Georgia Athletic Association, In re Seats*
	Registration of trademarks/ copyrights	Copyright Act of 1976	*NBA*
	Protection of trademarks/ copyrights through policing and infringement actions		
Using artwork and advertising messages from outside sources	Works made for hire and copyright ownership	Copyright Act of 1976	*Bouchat*
Merchandise sales and licensing	Permitted uses of protected trademarks and copyrights	First Amendment, free speech, Fair use	*World Wrestling*
	Limitations on uses		
	Response to infringing activities or noncompliant licensees	Copyright Act of 1976	
	Excessive licensing and potential abandonment of protected marks	Lanham Act	*Indianapolis Colts, USOC, Sinks*
Monitoring competitors' advertising and promotional activities; and media activities	Infringement of competing products or advertisements on protected trademarks/copyrights	Lanham Act	
	Knockoff products or advertising		
	Media and artist use of protected marks and copyrights	Visual Rights Act of 1990	*NASCAR*
	Permitted uses of protected marks/copyrights	First Amendment, free speech	*Campbell*
	Trademark dilution	Trademark Dilution Act	*Moseley, KST Electric*

mascot, Harley the Hornet, leaning back in his stadium seat wearing sunglasses, with a beverage in his hand.

The implementation of this marketing strategy will create a number of legal issues for you to consider. For example, can or should the slogan "Nothing Beats Hornets in the Summertime" be trademarked? If you are going to seek trademark registration, should it be state or federal registration? The same questions must be asked with regard to the new logo design with Harley in his stadium seat and sunglasses. Is the new logo sufficiently creative to warrant copyright protection as well as trademark protection? If one of your summer interns or another employee actually creates the new logo design, does he or she have any copyright interests to be considered? Below, we discuss the legal principles that will help you answer these questions and make sound management decisions.

THE LAW OF TRADEMARKS

T rademarks are used to identify the source or origin of a good or service. Essentially, trademarks serve to notify the consumer about where a product or service comes from, who provides or manufactures it, or what it is called or named. Many highly recognizable marks serve this purpose extremely well, such as those for Coca-Cola, Walt Disney, McDonald's, FedEx, and ESPN, just to name a few. A mark may consist of words, numbers, abstract designs, drawings, slogans, sounds, distinctive packaging, and virtually anything that can be used to identify the source or origin of a product or service. Logos and slogans are common examples of trademarks. However, distinctive colors, sounds, and scents can be trademarks as well. For example,

- Coca-Cola is a word used as a trademark for soft drinks.
- The Nike "swoosh" is a symbol used as a trademark for sports gear.
- The famous NBC chimes are a sound used as a trademark for television broadcast services.
- "Finger lickin' good" is a slogan used as a trademark for Kentucky Fried Chicken.
- The distinctive green and yellow color scheme on agriculture equipment and tractors are trademarks of the John Deere Company.

A **trademark** is defined as "a word, name, symbol, or device or any combination thereof adopted and used by a manufacturer or merchant to identify his goods and distinguish them from those manufactured or sold by others" (15 U.S.C. § 1127). If the word, name, or symbol relates to a good or product (e.g., Coca-Cola, adidas, Titleist, Nike), it is called a trademark. If the word, name, or symbol relates to a service (e.g., Ticketmaster, IMG, YMCA, Fogdog), then it is called a **service mark**. In addition, marks that are used to indicate membership within an organization, such as a professional players association, are called **collective marks** (e.g., Boy Scouts of America and National Football League Players Association). Another type of trademark is a certification mark, which indicates that a product meets certain certification standards, such as those maintained by Underwriters Laboratory, Inc. Here, we focus on federal trademark laws, and the term "trademark" or "mark" will be used to refer to any of the types of marks identified above. Exhibit 19.2 summarizes important definitions related to trademarks.

Purpose of Trademarks

A trademark can serve several functions or purposes. Following are five common purposes served by trademarks:

1. To identify the source or origin of a product or service and to distinguish it from others. For example, when a consumer purchases a T-shirt bearing the logo of adidas or Nike, the logo indicates the shirt comes from a single, identifiable source. For a trademark to function effectively, it should not be confused with the competition. Thus, distinguishing products from the competitors is also an important function of a trademark. It is not required the consumer know the company that owns the mark in order for the mark to perform this function.

Summary of trademark definitions.

EXHIBIT   19.2

Trademark—applied to commercial goods (e.g., "Coca-Cola," "Nike")

Service mark—applied to commercial services (e.g., "Weight Watchers," "YMCA")

Collective mark—applied to indicate membership in a group (e.g., "National Football League Players Association")

Certification mark—given to goods or services meeting certain qualifications (e.g., "UL")

Trade dress—the overall impression of a package or product produced by the shape and packaging (e.g., Hershey's Kiss)

Trade name—the mark given to a business (e.g., "Joe's Sports Bar and Grill")

2. To protect consumers from confusion and deception. The historical and primary purpose of the Trademark Act of 1946 (also known as the Lanham Act) is to serve as a consumer protection law. Thus, a critical function of a trademark relates to protecting consumers from being confused or deceived in the marketplace. Although businesses often perceive trademark law as protection for their marks and logos, protecting the trademark owner's rights is actually a secondary goal of federal trademark law. Interestingly, although consumer protection is the primary function of federal trademark law, consumers who are misled or confused cannot sue under the Lanham Act, nor is any government agency charged with enforcement of the Lanham Act. Rather, the Lanham Act is enforced by the trademark owners. Trademark owners have an affirmative duty to police their marks and to sue to enforce their rights against any misuse or unauthorized use.

3. To designate a consistent level of quality of a product or service. For example, the purchaser of a Mercedes automobile has a clear impression of a standard of quality associated with this automobile. However, the standard of quality does not have to be expensive or lavish for the trademark to function very effectively at creating a clear impression in the mind of the purchaser regarding the source of the product. For example, the WalMart brand also connotes a clear standard of quality, albeit a less expensive, more affordable standard. The function of the WalMart trademark is no less effective than the Mercedes mark.

4. To represent the goodwill of the owner or the owner's products and services. **Goodwill** has been defined as "the favor which the management of a business wins from the public" and "the fixed and favorable consideration of customers arising from established and well-conducted business" (*Black's Law Dictionary,* 2004). Goodwill also represents "a business reputation, patronage, and other intangible assets that are considered when appraising the business" (*Black's Law Dictionary,* 2004). An established trademark or service mark can be a symbol of goodwill, generating that "warm, fuzzy feeling" you get when you see a certain trademark that almost compels you to purchase that particular brand. For example, enormous amounts of goodwill are associated with the marks and images of Winnie the Pooh, such that Disney can put the Pooh family of marks on almost anything and make children and adults alike want to buy. The same can be said of many professional sports clubs as well, marks such as those of the Green Bay Packers and the New York Yankees. Goodwill is a key ingredient in a successful merchandising and licensing program for any sport organization.

5. **To signify a substantial advertising investment and business asset.** The functions identified here are not easily or automatically performed by a trademark. It may take a company many years and thousands, even millions of dollars to create effective and meaningful trademarks. The law recognizes this investment and treats trademarks as property connected with the goodwill of the company, capable of being sold, assigned, divided, licensed, or destroyed as the owner of the property chooses. The owner of the mark has the exclusive rights to the mark. The value associated with goodwill derived from trademark properties adds to the value of a company for purposes of taxation, licensing, estate valuation, and damage awards (McCarthy, 2001). If a company were to be purchased by another company, the intangible trademark property rights would be just as valuable as tangible property rights such as inventory, buildings, and furniture.

Creation of Trademarks

Clearly, not all trademarks are created equal. It is fair to say that the marks and logos of the Coca-Cola Company are stronger than those of Virgin Cola. Similarly, the marks and logos of ESPN (Entertainment and Sports Programming Network) are stronger and more distinctive than those of NESN (New England Sports Network). The value and effectiveness (*strength*) of a trademark or service mark relate to the *distinctiveness* of the mark and determine the level of protection that will be afforded the mark under the federal trademark laws. Marks are classified into various levels based upon their distinctiveness. The more distinctive the mark, the stronger it is considered for protection under the federal trademark laws.

Protection for Distinctive Trademarks

Trademarks can either be inherently distinctive or possess acquired distinctiveness. Inherently distinctive marks are classified as fanciful, arbitrary, or suggestive.

Fanciful marks

Fanciful marks, the most distinctive trademarks, are defined as coined words that have been invented for the sole purpose of functioning as a trademark. For example, Reebok, Pepsi, eBay, Kodak, and iPod are all fanciful marks since these words or names were created solely for the purpose of serving as a trademark. Fanciful marks are considered strong marks and are given a broad scope of protection (McCarthy, 2001).

Arbitrary marks

Arbitrary marks are also distinctive, but not as distinctive as fanciful marks. Arbitrary marks are defined as words, names, symbols, or devices that are in common linguistic use, but, when used with the goods or services, neither suggest nor describe any ingredient, quality, or characteristic of the goods or services. These marks would not ordinarily be associated with the product or service but for the advertising and marketing efforts of the owner. For example, Fathead, Maker's Mark, Hershey's, and Polo are actual words or names in the English language, but they do not describe or suggest characteristics of giant sports posters, bourbon, chocolate, or a clothing line. Many acronyms may belong in this category as well, such as ESPN, MLB, and the Y (YMCA). The full names, Entertainment and Sports Programming Network, Major League Baseball, and Young Men's/Women's Christian Association, are not arbitrary (see the discussion of descriptive marks below), but when a new logo is created from the acronym, it possesses greater distinctiveness.

Suggestive marks

The last category of inherently distinctive marks is suggestive marks. A **suggestive mark** subtly connotes something about the service or product but does not actually describe any specific ingredient, quality, or characteristic of the good or service. In other words, the consumer must use imagination to draw the association between the suggestive mark and the product or service. The more consumer imagination that is required to make the association between the mark and the actual product or service, the stronger the suggestive mark. For example, Nike and Louisville Slugger could be considered suggestive of some ingredient, quality, or characteristic of the goods or services sold. Nike, a Greek goddess, was the personification of victory in many arenas, not the least of which was athletics. "Nike" as a trademark for an athletic shoe clearly benefits from the suggested connection between athletic victory and wearing Nike shoes. Similarly, "Louisville Slugger" does not actually describe a baseball bat, but with a little imagination a consumer can appreciate the connection between a person considered a strong hitter (a slugger) and, of course, the place where the item was made, Louisville. Other suggestive marks may include LIDS, Players Inc., Sony's PlayStation, and Gatorade. Although a suggestive mark is not as distinctive or as strong as a fanciful or arbitrary mark, it still may be registered as a trademark or service mark.

Protection for Nondistinctive Marks

Marks can be termed nondistinctive because they are descriptive or generic.

Descriptive marks

Descriptive marks are not inherently distinctive and are not afforded any protection under the federal trademark laws. However, a descriptive mark may acquire the necessary distinctiveness to function as a trademark. **Descriptive marks** are defined as those marks that describe the intended purpose, function, or use of the goods; the size of the goods; the class of users of the goods; a desirable characteristic of the goods; or the end effect upon the user. Descriptive marks, while normally afforded no protection, can be entitled to trademark protection if they have acquired **secondary meaning.** Secondary meaning requires the mark to become associated in the mind of the public with a particular source or origin. Examples include Dick's Sporting Goods, the RCA Dome, Gold's Gym, Russell Athletic, and National Football League. All of these particular marks describe a characteristic of the goods or the intended purpose of the goods. As such they are not very distinctive. However, since these marks have a clear designation of origin recognizable to the consumer, they have acquired secondary meaning and are able to receive full protection under federal trademark laws.

Thus, secondary meaning is a way for descriptive marks to obtain protection that otherwise they would not be entitled to receive. The U.S. Supreme Court has held that color can function as a trademark (*Qualitex Co. v. Jacobson Products,* 1995; *see also NFL Properties, Inc. v. Wichita Falls Sportswear, Inc.,* 1982), so long as it possesses the basic legal requirements of a trademark: distinctiveness, source identification, and nonfunctionality.

The following Focus Case further explores whether sport teams color schemes and designs have acquired secondary meaning.

Board of Supervisors of LSU v Smack Apparel Company

FOCUS CASE | 438 F. Supp. 2d 653 (E.D. La 2006)

FACTS

Louisiana State University (LSU), the University of Oklahoma (OU), the Ohio State University (OSU), and the University of Southern California (USC) ("university plaintiffs"), along with their licensing agent, Collegiate Licensing Company (CLC), sued Smack Apparel Company for trademark infringement under the Lanham Act. The university plaintiffs owned trademark registrations for their names and commonly used initials. Additionally, more than a century ago, each university adopted a particular color combination as its school colors (LSU, purple and gold; OU, crimson and cream; OSU, scarlet and gray; USC, cardinal red and gold); since then, they have spent millions of dollars in marketing and promoting items bearing their initials and school colors.

The university plaintiffs alleged that Smack infringed upon their trademarks by selling T-shirts bearing the distinctive colors used by the respective universities, along with other symbols that identify the universities, as follows:

- OU (Two shirt designs): (1) "Bourbon Street or Bust" (with the "ou" in "Bourbon" in a different typestyle); (2) "Beat SoCal" (front), "And Let's Make it Eight!" (back). These shirts refer to the 2004 Sugar Bowl contest in New Orleans between OU and LSU.
- LSU (Two shirt designs): (1) "Beat Oklahoma" (front), "And Bring it Back to the Bayou!" and "2003 College Football National Championship" (back); (2) "2003 College Football National Champions" (front), colored circular depiction of game scores, with "2003 College Football National Champions" and "Sweet as Sugar" (back). These shirts also refer to the 2004 Sugar Bowl contest in New Orleans.
- OSU: "Got Seven?" (front), "We do! 7 Time National Champs," with a depiction of the state of Ohio and a marker noting "Columbus, Ohio" (back).
- USC: "Got Eight?" (front), "We Do! Home of the 8 Time National Champions!" and depiction of the state of California with a star marked "SoCal" (back).

Certain shirts also included some additional graphics or type, as well as scores of football games, and all the shirts bore the Smack logo.

HOLDING

The court found the universities had established "secondary meaning" in their particular color schemes, logos, and designs.

RATIONALE

Although the universities hold a number of registered marks, none of those exact marks were duplicated or used by Smack on its apparel. However, the universities also described their marks as color schemes for their school-themed merchandise marketed to fans. The court acknowledged that there is no question that a color scheme may be protected as a trademark. However, color is *not* protectible without proof of secondary meaning. Thus, the university plaintiffs must prove that their color schemes, logos, and designs on shirts referring to them or their accomplishments have attained a secondary meaning.

To support a finding of secondary meaning, the mark must denote to the consumer a single thing coming from a single source. The Fifth Circuit has adopted a seven-factor test for establishing secondary meaning:

1. length and manner of the use of the mark or trade dress
2. volume of sales
3. amount and manner of advertising
4. nature of use of the mark or trade dress in newspapers and magazines
5. consumer survey evidence
6. direct consumer testimony
7. the defendant's intent in copying the trade dress

The district court found that the universities had established secondary meaning in their particular color schemes, logos, and designs. The universities had used their color schemes for a long period of time (since the late 1800s), and they had marketed scores of items bearing their color schemes, logos, and designs, resulting in sales exceeding tens of millions of dollars. The universities also advertised items with the school colors in almost every conceivable manner and even used the colors to refer to themselves.

LSU markets scores of items bearing its color scheme, logos, and designs, and sales of these items exceed tens of millions of dollars. LSU advertises items with its school colors in almost every conceivable manner, and the record contains ample evidence that LSU's school colors have been referenced numerous times in magazines and newspapers, sometimes referring to the "Purple and Gold." Thus, the university plaintiffs' color schemes, logos, and designs have achieved secondary meaning.

The issue of distinctiveness will typically come up either during the registration process or during an infringement action. In the latter instance, one party may argue that no infringement has occurred because the marks either were not registered or are not capable of registration due to a lack of distinctiveness. This argument was raised by a beer distributing company when it was sued by the University of Georgia for producing a beer known as Battlin' Bulldog Beer, with a can that featured an English bulldog wearing a black sweater decorated with a large "G." (See *University of Georgia Athletic Association v. Laite,* 1985.)

The following Focus Case, *In re Seats, Inc.* (1985), presents the issue of distinctiveness raised during the trademark registration process.

In re Seats, Inc.

FOCUS CASE　757 F.2d 274 (Fed. Cir. 1985)

FACTS

Seats, Inc. appealed a decision of the Trademark Trial and Appeal Board (TTAB) in the United States Patent and Trademark Office refusing to register "SEATS" as a service mark for a computerized ticket reservation and issuing service. The TTAB rejected the registration application based on the grounds that the requested mark was descriptive. Seats, Inc. argued that the mark was suggestive and, even if descriptive, had acquired the necessary secondary meaning. The hearing examiner viewed the term SEATS as referring to a generic name of the end product of the applicant's services and ruled that it could never become distinctive with regard to those services. Seats, Inc. had customers' statements asserting that the name did indicate the origin of the services. Nevertheless, the TTAB concluded that SEATS was so descriptive as to render it incapable of designating origin.

HOLDING

The Federal District Court reversed, concluding that the TTAB never discussed whether SEATS was so descriptive *of the services themselves* as to be incapable of ever becoming distinctive.

RATIONALE

The district court observed that the TTAB did not find that SEATS was generic, nor could it have so found. The term "seats" may be generic in relation to chairs or couches or bleachers, but it clearly is not generic with regard to ticket reservation services. Seats, Inc. is not selling seats, but is selling a reservation service. It is equally clear that SEATS is not the common descriptive name of reservation services. Moreover, the issuance of registration would not deprive competitors from using such advertising phrases as "seats are available," "balcony seats—$12," and "reserve your seats through us." The court ruled that SEATS had acquired the necessary distinctiveness to be registered.

Generic marks

Another class of nondistinctive marks is generic marks. **Generic marks** are the common descriptive names of products or services and are considered part of the public domain. For example, words such as "gymnasium" and "arena" are the common names for these venues. Can you imagine Phillips Arena trying to prevent every other arena owner or operator from using the term "arena" to identify their venue? One commentator wrote, "no matter how much money and effort the user of a generic term has poured into promoting the sale of its merchandise and what success it has achieved in securing public identification, it cannot deprive competing manufacturers of the product of the right to call an article by its name" (Warren-Mikes, 1999). For example, an Internet company could not trademark "the net" and prohibit others from using that term. The Denver Broncos could not trademark the term "football team," and so on. In contrast, recently, the District Court for the Northern District of Texas rejected the defense of an Internet domain owner who operated www.marchmadness.com and asserted that the term "march madness" was generic and incapable of trademark protection. The court ruled instead that the term was descriptive and had acquired secondary meaning (*March Madness Athletic Association, L.L.C. v. Netfire, Inc.*, 2003).

It is possible for what once was a well-recognized trademark to become generic over time. For example, many once protected trademarks have become so identified with a particular product or service that all distinctiveness was lost. Aspirin, Nylon, YoYo, Cornflakes, Escalator, Raisin Bran, Dry Ice, and Trampoline were all protected trademarks at one time and have since lost that protection to "genericide" (In, 2002). Other marks may also be in danger of becoming generic, and companies must work diligently to protect the distinctiveness of their marks. For example, *Merriam-Webster's Dictionary* now defines "Kleenex" as both a facial or cleaning tissue and a registered trademark. However, in one edition *Merriam-Webster's* omitted the definition of Kleenex as a registered trademark. Kimberly-Clark Corporation, the owner of the Kleenex trademark, requested *Merriam-Webster's Dictionary* to correct its definitions as a preemptive strike against a claim of genericide. Once there is no distinction in the consumer's mind between a facial tissue and a Kleenex, then the mark is in jeopardy of becoming generic. Xerox, facing a similar problem, struck back with a nationwide media blitz to protect its brand.

The Zamboni ice resurfacing machine has been identified by many as very near genericide. Musicians have recorded songs about the Zamboni, and Zamboni races during intermission at hockey games are common. Such things have led to the Zamboni name becoming more of an identifier of the class of ice resurfacing machines, even though several other manufacturers of the machines are in the market, including Resurfice and Ice Master. The Frank J. Zamboni Company, producers of the resurfacers, prominently displays its marks on its website and reminds visitors that Zamboni is a protected trademark. The site contains the following statement:

> The ZAMBONI brand name is a valuable trademark which we must diligently protect. Like Coke, Kleenex, and Jeep, it has close identity in the public mind with a particular type of commodity—but the public doesn't always remember that it is a particular brand. . . . A trademark is always an adjective. Never a noun. So when referring to ZAMBONI, please use it in the correct context.

The machine is not "a Zamboni," it is a ZAMBONI ice resurfacing machine." (Zamboni, 2006)

Let's explore this issue in the following hypothetical situation.

considering . . .   GENERIC MARKS

Papa Joe's Pizza is conducting a special sales promotion during January called "The Biggest Pizza for the Big Game." Every person who purchases a new 24-inch extra large specialty pizza between January 1 and February 10 receives a special game card that permits him to visit Papa Joe's website and enter a sweepstakes to win 24 tickets to the NFL Super Bowl. The game cards contain visible disclaimers that the promotion is not in any way sponsored or endorsed by the National Football League.

Questions

- Would Papa Joe's use of the term "The Big Game" interfere with any rights of the NFL?
- Could Papa Joe's register "The Big Game" to prevent competitors from using the same promotion?

Note how you would answer the questions and then check your responses using the Analysis & Discussion at the end of this chapter.

Protection of Trade Dress

Trade dress can be protected under federal trademark laws. **Trade dress** primarily refers to distinctive packaging, including distinctive shapes in the appearance of a product or service. For example, if the trade dress creates a separate commercial impression and its use is primarily to identify or distinguish the product or service (i.e., its use is not just functional), then it is possible to register the trade dress and protect it under the Lanham Act. To recover for trade dress infringement under the Lanham Act, 15 U.S.C. § 1125(a), a plaintiff must prove by a preponderance of the evidence that

1. its trade dress has obtained secondary meaning in the marketplace;
2. the trade dress of two competing products is confusingly similar; and
3. the appropriated features of the trade dress are primarily nonfunctional.

As with descriptive marks, for trade dress to qualify as a distinctive identifier, it must have acquired secondary meaning.

Trade dress is the legal arena where patent and trademark laws collide. Unique product configurations should be able to obtain patent protection, and once that patent protection expires, the design becomes part of the public domain. This is consistent with a free market economy and vibrant competition in the marketplace. However, some companies attempt to seek trade dress protection for design configurations once the patents have expired in order to extend their monopoly beyond the length of time envisioned under patent law. Also, since trademarks are renewable indefinitely, such a strategy would effectively prevent the design from ever entering the free market and public domain. The courts cushion this collision between patent and trademark law with the functionality test and the requirement that the trade dress must have acquired secondary meaning. To establish that a design feature is not functional, it may be shown that the design feature is merely ornamental, incidental, or an arbitrary aspect of the device. Thus, if the design is not functional and has acquired secondary meaning, it may be approved for trade dress registration.

Protection of Trade Names

The Lanham Act affords no registration rights for trade names unless the trade name also is used in such a way as to function as a trademark or service mark. A **trade name** is "any name used by a person to identify his or her business or vocation" (15 U.S.C. § 1127). For example, a new sporting goods company may start doing business as Dunham's Sports, but if the company makes no effort to identify this name with this specific brand of sporting good stores (i.e., a unique combination of goods and services), it is not being used as a source identifier. Mark Johnson may open a sport marketing consulting business and use the trade name Johnson Sports Marketing, which would not be protectable as a federal trademark. Unless the trade name is also used to identify specific products or services, it cannot be registered under the Lanham Act. It is important to note that many states do allow the registration of a trade name; thus, sport managers should consult their state's laws for the trade name registration rules.

Registration of Marks

Once an individual or business has created a mark and is preparing to use the mark in commerce, it must decide whether to seek federal trademark registration or to rely on common law and state law protections.

Rights associated with trademarks can be divided into *rights to use* and *rights to register*. **Rights to use** are grounded in common law and are created when a mark is used in commerce to identify a product or service. A mark does not have to be registered before it may be used. The first to use the mark has the superior rights to the mark (this is known as **first use**). **Rights to register** are created by both state and federal statutes and provide certain benefits to the registrant. The law governing trademark registration at the federal level is found in the Trademark Act of 1946 (Lanham Act), 15 U.S.C. §§ 1051–1127. The United States Patent and Trademark Office (USPTO) is responsible for processing registration applications. The USPTO governs requests to register trademarks, service marks, collective marks, trade dress, and trade names. In addition, the USPTO resolves disputes related to *registration*. For example, if a mark is refused registration or if registration is challenged by another trademark holder, the Trademark Trial and Appeal Board would hear this dispute. Disputes related to the *use* of trademarks must be resolved by a court.

Applications for registration are typically one of two types: a *use application*, where the mark is already being used in commerce, or an *intent to use application*, used when the applicant is not yet using the mark in commerce but has a bona fide intention to use the mark. Registration is not required to create trademark rights; rather, those rights are created by the use of the mark in commerce.

Normally, if one is making a significant investment in a company name and logos, it is worthwhile to seek federal trademark registration. Federal registration carries with it substantial benefits and protections. Registration can be done without the assistance of counsel; however, it can be a complicated and technical process. An IP attorney can be very useful to assist in searching for potentially conflicting marks and navigating the USPTO registration procedures. Searching for conflicting marks prior to applying for registration is not required, but it is highly advisable since the application fee of $325 to $375 is nonrefundable. If a conflicting mark exists, the registration fee will not be refunded and the application will likely be denied. The USPTO does not conduct searches for the public, but it does provide a public library of marks and a searchable electronic database (USPTO, 2009). In addition, private search companies and IP attorneys can conduct searches for as little as $100.

If a federal trademark is obtained, the designation ® should always accompany the use of the mark. If federal trademark registration is either not sought or not yet obtained, then the designation ™ and ℠ should be used to provide notice that you are claiming the mark as a trademark and are asserting a property interest in it.

Trademark Infringement

The unauthorized use of another's mark is called *infringement*. **Trademark infringement** occurs when a person uses in commerce any *"reproduction, counterfeit, copy, or colorable imitation of a registered mark* in connection with the sale, offering for sale, distribution, or advertising of any goods or services on or in connection with which such use is *likely to cause confusion,* or to cause mistake, or to deceive"* without consent of the registrant (15 U.S.C. § 1114(1)(a)). The key elements of a trademark infringement claim are summarized in Exhibit 19.3.

As mentioned earlier, the federal trademark laws are enforced by the trademark owners. The Lanham Act provides for both injunctions and damages as remedies for infringement. In a typical infringement action, the trademark owner is trying to prevent the defendant (usually a direct competitor) from using identical or similar marks that would cause consumers to purchase the defendant's good or services instead of those of the actual trademark owner.

Proving trademark infringement

The owner of a mark has the burden to prove that the mark is being infringed upon. Federal registration helps to prove the first two elements of a claim (see Exhibit 19.3). If a mark is registered, then the owner can demonstrate that he or she is the only authorized user, and a valid registration is evidence of a protectable property interest. At this point, the owner need only prove that the unauthorized use is likely to confuse consumers.

The courts have identified a series of factors to consider in determining **likelihood of confusion.** No one factor is more important than the others, and not

Key elements of a trademark infringement claim.	EXHIBIT	19.3

1. An unauthorized use (*reproduction, counterfeiting, or copying*) of
2. A protectable property interest (*registered mark*) that creates
3. A likelihood of confusion (*likely to cause confusion*) among consumers as to the source or origin of the goods or services.

every factor must be shown to establish likelihood of confusion (*UGAA v. Laite*, 1985). These factors, first developed in the case of *Polaroid Corp. v. Polaroid, Inc.* (1963), have become known as *The Polaroid Test*. Other courts have added to or modified the factors over the years, and most courts today use the eight factors presented in Exhibit 19.4, or some combination of the factors, to determine whether likelihood of confusion has been proven.

Defenses to trademark infringement

In response to a trademark infringement claim, the defendant may raise a number of defenses. These defenses include fair use, parody, abandonment, and functionality.

The eight factors to prove the likelihood of confusion.	EXHIBIT	19.4

1. The strength of the plaintiff's mark—How distinctive is it? (fanciful, arbitrary, suggestive, descriptive with secondary meaning, or nondistinctive)
2. The similarity between the two marks—Often just a side-by-side comparison of appearance, size, shape, meaning, and impression.
3. The similarity of the products involved—Are the products quite similar, such as T-shirts and golf shirts, or seemingly dissimilar, such as tires and sailboats?
4. The market channels involved—Is the defendant in the same market? If not, how likely is it that he or she will enter a market that the plaintiff is in or that the plaintiff may enter in the future?
5. The distribution channels involved—Is the defendant using the same distribution channels as the plaintiff? If not, how likely is it that he or she will use distribution channels that the plaintiff is using now or that the plaintiff may use in the future?
6. Actual consumer confusion—To what extent are consumers actually confused by the defendant's use of the similar marks?
7. The intent of the defendant—To what extent is the defendant trying to capitalize on consumer recognition of the plaintiff's marks?
8. The sophistication of the potential buyers—To what extent can buyers protect themselves from being confused by the defendant's marks? More sophisticated buyers are presumed to be less likely to be misled, and children are often considered unsophisticated and unlikely to distinguish between similar marks.

Fair use. The fair use defense applies in situations involving comparative advertising, news and media usage, and parodies. Trademark rights are not absolute. The law allows the use of another's trademarks on or in connection with the sale of one's own goods or services so long as the use is not deceptive (Richman & Borden, 2003). Thus the use of a trademark in comparative advertising and on labeling for reconditioned or altered goods would also fall within the scope of permitted use. A fair use argument was successfully used against the manufacturer of Titleist and Pinnacle golf balls in its suit to enjoin a company that sold refurbished discounted golf balls (*Nitro Leisure Products, L.L.C v. Acushnet Co.*, 2003). Acushnet argued that Nitro's refurbishing process, which stripped off the outer coat of paint on the used golf ball, altered the product, such that when Nitro repainted the ball and reaffixed the Titleist or Pinnacle logo it was an unauthorized use. The court disagreed, opining that the use was permitted and that consumers understood that they were not purchasing the original, new golf ball but one that had been recovered and repaired.

Parody. Well-known companies can expect to be the object of parody and ridicule. Often times, highly recognizable marks and logos are an attractive target. When this happens, it is not uncommon for identical or substantially similar elements of the protected intellectual property to be used or incorporated into a third party's merchandise or advertising materials. It may be undisputed that the third party is using protected marks, but the third party will argue that such use is permitted under the fair use doctrine and/or commercial speech protections of the First Amendment.

It is important to note that using a protected trademark as a parody is not an affirmative defense to a trademark infringement action. In other words, there is not a special exception that allows one company to use another company's trademark so long as it is for purposes of parody. First Amendment principles cannot be used to usurp federal trademark law. In fact, trademark law permissibly regulates misleading commercial speech. Thus, the nature of the use (i.e., the parody) is considered as each likely confusion factor is analyzed by the court. If one employs a successful parody, the customer is not confused, but amused. The keystone of parody is imitation, but it must convey two simultaneous—and contradictory—messages: that it is the original, yet also that it is not the original but a parody instead. To the extent that it does only the former but not the latter, it is not only a poor parody but also vulnerable under trademark law, since the customer will be confused.

An example of a potential parody defense can be seen in an action brought by North Face Apparel Corporation against the South Butt Company in December 2009 (Salter, 2009). South Butt was started by a teenager in 2007 to help pay for college. The company produces a line of fleeces, T-shirts, and shorts. South Butt's product tag line "Never Stop Relaxing" is a parody of the North Face tagline, "Never Stop Exploring." North Face argues that South Butt is directly infringing and diluting North Face's famous marks. South Butt naturally defends its parody and suggests that the consuming public is insightful enough to know the difference between a face and a butt.

Abandonment. Another defense to trademark infringement is abandonment. Abandonment occurs when an owner of a mark discontinues its use and does not intend to resume using the mark within a reasonable amount of time. Typically, nonuse of a mark for three consecutive years is considered evidence of abandonment. For sport organizations, another significant form of abandonment is abandonment through excessive licensing and lack of supervision. If a sport organization fails to develop adequate safeguards in its licensing programs to supervise the use of its marks and to challenge unauthorized uses of its marks, the defendant could argue that the owner abandoned the mark and lost its trademark protection.

Two seminal cases reaching conflicting results are *Major League Baseball Properties, Inc. v. Sed Olet Denarius, Ltd., dba, The Brooklyn Dodger Sports Bar & Restaurant* (1993) and *Indianapolis Colts, Inc. v. Metropolitan Baltimore Football Club Ltd. Partnership* (1994). In the *Brooklyn Dodger* case, a district court in New York held that MLB had abandoned its trademark rights in the Brooklyn Dodgers by its nonuse for more than 20 years. The district court noted that in order for a trademark to remain active, it must actually be used. And since there was no likelihood that the Brooklyn Dodger restaurant would be confused with the Los Angeles Dodgers baseball club, the trademark was canceled. The opposite result was reached in the *Indianapolis Colts* case presented in the following Focus Case.

Indianapolis Colts v. *Metropolitan Baltimore Football Club*

34 F.3d 410 (7th Cir. 1994)   **FOCUS CASE**

FACTS

In 1984, the Colts left Baltimore for Indianapolis. Nine years later the Canadian Football League (CFL) awarded a franchise to the city of Baltimore. The new team was named the Baltimore CFL Colts, a name previously held by the Baltimore Colts of the National Football League. The Indianapolis Colts and the NFL brought a trademark infringement case against the new Baltimore club, arguing that consumers were likely to mistakenly link the Baltimore CFL Colts with the Indianapolis franchise or the NFL.

HOLDING

The CFL team was enjoined from using the name "Colts" since the use of the name would likely mislead consumers into believing the Baltimore CFL team was in some way associated with the Indianapolis franchise of the NFL.

RATIONALE

At the heart of the Seventh Circuit's decision was the issue of abandonment. The new Baltimore team argued that the Indianapolis franchise abandoned the name Baltimore Colts when they relocated. Once a mark is abandoned it becomes available for another organization to use, provided of course the mark does not suggest continuity with the former owner. In such cases, it is the responsibility of the new party to take measures to avoid consumer confusion. Relevant to the present case was the fact that the Baltimore CFL Colts offered the same primary service as the old Baltimore Colts NFL franchise. Because the name is likely to cause confusion between the two franchises, the Seventh Circuit held that the use of the mark by the new Baltimore club infringed on the current mark of the Indianapolis Colts.

Further, the Colts did not abandon the mark all together. The Indianapolis team is the same franchise as the original Baltimore club, just in a different city. The use of the mark by the new Baltimore club would confuse consumers about the products and services offered, the identity of the team, its sponsorship, and its league affiliation. The mere fact that the new Baltimore team is likely to conjure associations with the old Baltimore Colts is enough to justify the Seventh Circuit's decision.

Abandonment was also asserted by the United States Olympic Committee against the owner of the trademark "America's Team" in the USOC's petition to cancel the trademark.

United States Olympic Committee v. America's Team Properties, Inc.

FOCUS CASE   Cancellation Petition No. 92025167, Trademark Trial and Appeal Board (Sept. 30, 2003)

FACTS

America's Team Properties, Inc. (ATP) obtained the rights to the trademark "America's Team," registered in 1996. When ATP acquired the rights, the mark was already embroiled in litigation with the United States Olympic Committee, which was seeking to cancel the registration. The USOC argued that ATP had abandoned the mark through nonuse.

HOLDING

The appeal board found that ATP had not abandoned its mark.

RATIONALE

The appeal board found that the USOC had itself hampered ATP's ability to use the mark, since it commenced litigation against the owner of the mark almost immediately upon its registration. A mark is considered abandoned when "its use has been discontinued with intent not to resume such use." Nonuse for three consecutive years shall be prima facie evidence of abandonment. The statement of use was filed on January 31, 1995, and the USOC's petition to cancel was filed on June 3, 1996, less than three years after the statement of use was filed. While the mark had not been used for three consecutive years, the presumption of abandonment was rebutted due to excusable nonuse. In view of the USOC's demands and claims of superior rights, the respondent was justified in limiting or postponing its use of the mark pending the outcome of this proceeding.

Functionality. Another defense is functionality. A **functional mark** is one that does not describe or distinguish the product or service but that is necessary for the product to exist. For example, a baseball may be sold in a plastic cube. The cube is necessary for the company to sell the baseball product, but the cube itself does not fulfill any of the purposes served by trademarks in terms of source identification, goodwill, and so forth. The functionality defense was unsuccessfully raised against the Dallas Cowboys Cheerleaders when the defendant adult filmmaker, Pussycat Cinema, asserted that its depiction of an actress in a cheerleading uniform similar to those worn by the Dallas Cowboy Cheerleaders was not trademark infringement because the uniform design was not a trademark but rather a functionality of performing. The court disagreed and held that the unique design of the uniform could serve as a trademark and was not just a function of performing as a cheerleader. In rejecting the argument that the uniforms were merely functional, the court observed that the plaintiff did not claim a trademark in all clothing designed and fitted to allow free movement while performing cheerleading routines, but instead claimed a trademark in the particular combination of colors and collections of decorations that distinguish plaintiff's uniforms from those of other squads. Thus, the fact that an item serves or performs a function does not mean that it may not at the same time be capable of indicating sponsorship or origin, particularly where the decorative elements are nonfunctional (*Dallas Cowboys Cheerleaders, Inc. v. Pussycat Cinema*, 1979). Functionality was also raised as a defense in the following Focus Case.

University of Kansas v. Sinks

565 F. Supp. 2d 1216 (D. Kan., 2008)	FOCUS CASE

FACTS

The University of Kansas (KU) alleged various trademark claims including claims for trademark dilution against Larry Sinks and the other defendants collectively referred to as "Victory Sportswear." These claims involved the sale of certain T-shirts at the Joe-College.com retail store and website that reference KU. Victory Sportswear raised a number of affirmative defenses to KU's trademark claims, including functionality. KU sought summary judgment on Victory's affirmative defenses.

HOLDING

KU was granted summary judgment on Victory Sportswear's affirmative defenses of functionality.

RATIONALE

Under the functionality doctrine, a product feature cannot serve as a trademark "if it is essential to the use or purpose of the article or if it affects the cost or quality of the article, that is, if exclusive use of the feature would put competitors at a significant non-reputation-related disadvantage." Victory argued that KU's marks and colors lack distinctiveness and are merely a functional aspect of their merchandise; thus, it would be unfair to allow KU the exclusive right to use the color blue or the letters KU or the word "Hawks." The functionality doctrine forbids the use of a product's feature as a trademark where doing so will put a competitor at a significant disadvantage because the feature is "essential to the use or purpose of the article" or "affects [its] cost or quality." Courts have barred the use of black as a trademark on outboard boat motors (because black has the special functional attributes of decreasing the apparent size of the motor and ensuring compatibility with many different boat colors). The "ultimate test of aesthetic functionality is whether the recognition of trademark rights would significantly hinder competition." The court agreed with KU that there was no evidence that KU's marks are essential to the quality of T-shirts or affect how the T-shirts "work." Thus, the marks were deemed not functional and Victory's affirmative defense failed.

Cancellation of Marks

The USPTO has the authority to cancel a trademark. In an ongoing controversy, a group of Native Americans requested cancellation of the Washington Redskins trademarks. Suzan Harjo, on behalf of herself and six other Native Americans, sued the owners of the Washington Redskins football team, Pro-Football, Inc., contending that the "redskins" name and marks were disparaging to Native Americans and bring Native Americans into contempt or disrepute. The Trademark Trial and Appeal Board found that the marks were disparaging to Native Americans and recommended cancellation. Pro-Football, Inc. appealed to the U.S. District Court. The district court judge ruled that the finding of disparagement was not supported by the evidence and reversed the TTAB finding.

One commentator noted that the judge was well aware of the larger, ongoing controversy over the use of Native American names and symbols by sports teams and perhaps tried to distance herself from that controversy. The judge's ruling was based solely on the petitioners' failure to meet their burden of proof and their delay in seeking cancellation of the mark ("Washington Redskins win," 2003). The district judge specifically stated, "this opinion should not be read as making any statement on the appropriateness of Native American imagery for team names" (*Pro-Football, Inc. v. Harjo*, 2003, p. 144). This controversy continues, presenting both legal and public relations challenges for the Washington Redskins and other sport teams. Managers should consider the public relations and merchandising ramifications of this case and those similar to it.

Trademark Dilution and Famous Marks

The Lanham Act also prohibits trademark dilution. On January 16, 1996, the Federal Trademark Dilution Act of 1995 (Trademark Dilution Act; FTDA) became effective (Federal Trademark Dilution Act, 1996). Dilution was not previously recognized as a federal cause of action even though many states provided a state law dilution cause of action. Although the foundation of trademark protection is to protect consumers, the underlying purpose of adding a claim for dilution was to protect the value of the trademark to the trademark holder (Oswald, 1999). **Trademark dilution** is similar to trademark infringement, but it occurs when the defendant is *not* a direct competitor, when the defendant's use of a similar mark either tarnishes (*tarnishment*) the reputation of the plaintiff's mark or blurs (*blurring*) the ability of the plaintiff's mark to distinguish plaintiff's goods and services from those of the defendant.

The essence of a dilution claim is not that consumers are confused between the two marks, but rather that the defendant's use taints, damages, lessens, or weakens the exclusive association that the plaintiff has created between its mark and its products or services. Thus, the value of the mark is diminished or diluted. The Trademark Dilution Act defines dilution as "the *lessening of the capacity* of a *famous mark* to identify and distinguish goods or services, *regardless of* the presence or absence of (1) *competition* between the owner of the famous mark and other parties; or (2) the *likelihood of confusion,* mistake or deception" (Trademark Dilution Act of 1995, 15 U.S.C. § 1125(c)).

The scope of protection available under FTDA was somewhat limited when the U. S. Supreme Court held that a plaintiff must prove actual dilution or actual economic loss in order to prevail on a trademark dilution claim.

In *Moseley v. V Secret Catalogue* (2003), the owners of the Victoria's Secret retail chain and the Victoria's Secret trademark sought to compel a husband and wife, Victor and Cathy Moseley, to stop using the name "Victor's Little Secret" for their adult entertainment retail store in Kentucky. Victoria's Secret claimed trademark infringement, trademark dilution, and unfair competition under the Lanham Act. The U. S. Supreme Court held that relief under the FTDA requires objective proof of actual injury to the economic value of a famous mark, since the text of the FTDA unambiguously requires "actual dilution" rather than a likelihood of dilution (*Moseley v. V Secret Catalogue,* 2003). This was quite different from the burden of proof in a trademark infringement case, where the plaintiff need only prove a likelihood of confusion to prevail.

In response to the *Moseley* decision, Congress amended the FTDA in 2006 and replaced the actual dilution requirement with a "likelihood of dilution" requirement. Due to these amendments, now in order to recover monetary damages for trademark dilution, a trademark holder is only required to show a likelihood of dilution if the allegedly unlawful conduct began after October 6, 2006 (149 Pub. L. No. 109-312, 12-0 Stat. 1730 (amending Pub. L. No. 104-98, 109 Stat. 985 (1995)), codified at 15 U.S.C. § 1125(c)).

Only famous marks are protected under the Trademark Dilution Act. An essential ingredient of a famous mark is its value or selling power or strength. Thus, newly registered marks or weak marks with little or no instant recognition cannot be diluted. To determine whether a mark is famous under the Trademark Dilution Act, courts may consider the factors shown in Exhibit 19.5. As mentioned earlier, dilution typically takes one of two forms, either tarnishment or blurring.

Factors used by courts to determine whether a trademark is famous.	EXHIBIT	19.5

1. The distinctiveness of the mark
2. The duration of use
3. The duration and extent of advertising the mark
4. The geographical extent of the market area
5. The channels in which the goods or services are traded
6. The degree of recognition for the mark in the market area and advertising channels
7. The nature of use of the similar mark
8. Whether the mark has federal registration

Tarnishment

Tarnishment occurs when a similar mark is used in such a way as to disparage or harm the reputation of a famous mark. Most cases involving tarnishment claims involve a similar mark being used in connection with shoddy products or sexual, obscene, or socially unacceptable activities. For example, a dilution claim was successfully brought in *Anheuser-Busch, Inc. v. Andy's Sportswear, Inc.* (1996) to prevent the sale of T-shirts with the slogan "Buttwiser" and by Toys "R" Us, Inc. to shut down the use of an Internet site named adultsrus.com, at which sexual devices were sold (*Toys "R" Us, Inc. v. Akkaoui,* 1996).

Blurring

Blurring, the more traditional form of dilution, occurs when a mark that is similar to a famous mark is used by a *noncompetitor* in such a way that will, over time, diminish the famous mark's value by detracting from the exclusiveness of the famous mark. Blurring theory focuses on the diminishment of a trademark's ability to function as a unique identifier of the source or origin of goods and services. Remember, source identification is an essential purpose of a trademark. If one is permitted to use a mark similar to a famous mark, even though consumers may not be confused between the two marks or uses, eventually consumers will no longer *exclusively* associate the famous mark with the goods and services of the owner of the mark (Oswald, 1999). Dilution theory, particularly blurring, dates back to 1927, and protection has been justified as follows: "If you allow Rolls Royce restaurants, and Rolls Royce cafeterias, and Rolls Royce pants, and Rolls Royce candy, in 10 years you will not have the Rolls Royce mark any more" (Schechter, 1927).

The following Focus Case explains the test for determining whether a mark is "famous."

Board of Regents, The University of Texas System v. KST Electric

FOCUS CASE   550 F. Supp. 2d 657 (W.D. Tex. 2008)

FACTS

The University of Texas (UT) sued KST Electric (KST) for a number of state and federal trademark claims, including federal trademark dilution, alleging that several logos developed and used by KST infringed on UT's registered trademark, which depicts its mascot, a longhorn steer, in silhouette (referred to by UT as its "longhorn silhouette logo" or LSL). KST argued that it should be granted summary judgment on UT's federal dilution claim because UT has not provided any evidence that the longhorn silhouette logo is *famous* for purposes of the Trademark Dilution Revision Act ("TDRA").

HOLDING

KST was entitled to summary judgment on UT's trademark dilution claims.

RATIONALE

Dilution is a cause of action invented and reserved for a select class of marks—those marks with such powerful consumer associations that even noncompeting uses can impinge on their value. For example, such harm occurs in the hypothetical cases of "DUPONT shoes, BUICK aspirin, and KODAK pianos." This is true even though a consumer would be unlikely to confuse the manufacturer of KODAK film with the hypothetical producer of KODAK pianos. The TDRA specifically requires that a mark be *widely recognized by the general consuming public of the United States* as a designation of the source of the goods or services of the mark's owner."

Under the TDRA, four nonexclusive factors are relevant when determining whether a mark is sufficiently famous for antidilution protection:

1. The duration, extent, and geographic reach of advertising and publicity of the mark, whether advertised or publicized by the owner or third parties;
2. The amount, volume, and geographic extent of sales of goods or services offered under the mark;
3. The extent of actual recognition of the mark;
4. Whether the mark was registered under the Act of March 3, 1881, or the Act of February 20, 1905, or on the principal register.

KST's primary argument went to the third factor, the actual recognition of the mark, and contended that UT's mark was not sufficiently recognized on a national level to be famous. KST based this argument on their expert, Robert Klein, who conducted a national survey that demonstrated that only 5.8 percent of respondents in the United States "associated the UT registered longhorn logo with UT alone" and that merely 21.1 percent "of respondents in Texas associated the UT registered longhorn logo with UT alone." UT criticized the methodology of the Klein survey; however, despite this criticism, UT bore the burden of proof on the issue of fame. This meant that UT had to submit evidence to demonstrate that the LSL is famous.

UT offered evidence that UT football games are regularly televised nationally on ABC and ESPN, and the LSL is prominently featured as UT's logo during these broadcasts. Similarly, the men's college basketball team's games had been televised nationally 97 times in the past five seasons. UT pointed to the Bowl Championship Series (BCS) Rose Bowl national championship game, in which UT beat the University of Southern California. Over 35 million people watched it nationwide. The rest of UT's evidence similarly pointed to the success of its sports teams. The evidence submitted was deemed to be "niche" fame, which is a category of fame to which the TDRA explicitly does not apply.

The central problem for UT was that, with respect to the evidence, it was not at all clear that someone who wasn't a college football fan (or, to a much lesser extent, college baseball or basketball fan) would recognize the LSL as being associated with UT, since all of the evidence related to the logo as used at sporting events. The court was well aware that NCAA college football is a popular sport, but this hardly equals a presence with the general consuming public of the United States. Simply because UT athletics had achieved a level of national prominence does not necessarily mean that the longhorn logo is so ubiquitous and well-known as to belong in the same category as KODAK. Because UT's evidence failed to demonstrate the extremely high level of recognition necessary to show "fame" under the TDRA, summary judgment was granted to KST.

Competitive Advantage
STRATEGIES

Trademarks

- Have a coordinated plan to inventory all intellectual property and maintain up-to-date records of how such property is being used.

- Carefully develop a licensing program to provide a mechanism for monitoring the use of protected marks, as well as to build and enhance goodwill associated with the marks.

- Before beginning any new marketing activities, take the steps necessary to (a) identify whether any new IP rights are or will be created; (b) determine what level of protection should be pursued to protect your investment in the IP; and (c) seek and obtain the necessary protections before launching the campaign.

- Once a trademark has been registered, it must be used continuously; thus, its use must be monitored and documented in the event an abandonment claim is asserted.

- Develop an aggressive strategy to counter unauthorized use of your protected marks. Even if an infringement claim cannot be sustained,

(continued)

Trademarks and the Internet

The impact of the Internet upon marketing in the sport industry is no surprise to sport marketers. However, the wildfire growth of Internet-based businesses and marketing efforts has created legal challenges for sport organizations as well as organizations that use sport as a marketing tool. Legal challenges related to trademarks present two key issues for sport marketers. One is protecting an owner's trademark from being misused by a cyber-squatter. The second is how to know when an Internet domain name itself can function as a trademark.

Cyber-squatting and trademarks

A **cyber-squatter** is someone who registers a domain name for improper purposes such as extorting money from another. To understand cyber-squatting and the complex legal issues related to this activity, it is necessary to glance back at the history of the Internet. In the early days of the Internet, domain names were simple—first come, first served. If you were the first to register a particular domain name, it was yours. Not surprisingly, some individuals had a clearer vision than others of the potential of the Internet and the use of the Internet in business. For example, in 1994 Joshua Quittner was writing a story about domain names for *Wired* magazine when through his research he realized that mcdonalds.com was available as a domain name. Supposedly, Joshua contacted McDonald's Restaurants and warned them that anyone could register that domain name if they didn't. McDonald's did not respond, so Joshua registered www.mcdonalds.com. Eventually, McDonald's awakened to their lack of foresight, and Joshua transferred the domain name in return for a $3,500 donation to an elementary school (Grossman & Feinsilver, 2001).

Major League Baseball found itself in a similar situation when the law firm Morgan, Lewis, & Bockius had already registered www.mlb.com. Eventually, Major League Baseball and Morgan, Lewis negotiated a transfer of the domain name and issued a joint press release stating that the transfer was mutually agreed upon and in the best interests of both parties ("Morgan Lewis pitches web address," 2000).

Prior to the end of 1999, a trademark owner's remedy for alleged use of a trademark in a Web address was essentially limited to Lanham Act remedies for infringement and dilution. Now the landscape of relief is more diverse. Trademark owners can pursue remedies provided in the Anticybersquatting Consumer Protection Act (ACPA). The ACPA, enacted on November 29, 1999, protects trademark owners from **bad faith cyber-squatting**—instances where Internet domain names that are similar to trademarks are registered for the purpose of reselling the name or diverting consumers from their desired website to the cyber-squatter's site, rather than for the bona fide offering of goods and services. Under the ACPA, several remedies are available, including forfeiture or cancellation of the domain name, transfer of the domain name, and recovery of monetary damages.

Domain names as trademarks

Another trademark law issue related to the Internet is determining when a domain name or Web address can function as a trademark and receive trademark protection. To make this determination, we need only ask two questions: Is the domain name used as a trademark, and is the domain name distinctive (Kubiszyn, 2001)? The first question simply examines whether the domain name is performing the functions of a trademark—acting as a source identifier. For example, amazon.com actually identifies the source of the services provided and is not just a Web address. Conversely, the Web address for the University of Louisville, www.louisville.edu, is merely an address where one can find UofL's presence on the Internet.

If the domain name is being used as a source identifier, then the distinctiveness of the domain name must be analyzed to make the same determination of distinctiveness that we make for other trademarks—fanciful, arbitrary, suggestive, descriptive, or generic. If the domain name is either distinctive or descriptive with secondary meaning, then it can be registered as a trademark.

Trademark Law and the Olympics

Not surprisingly, the United States Olympic Committee owns several valuable trademarks. Unlike a typical business or sport organization, the USOC did not need federal registration under the Lanham Act in order to avail itself of the Lanham protections. Instead, the USOC's trademark ownership rights flow from the Amateur Sports Act of 1978 (ASA) and recent amendments to the ASA codified in the Ted Stevens Olympic and Amateur Sports Act of 1998 (OASA).

The ASA was enacted in part to protect the USOC's ability to produce funds necessary to support American athletes' participation in the Olympic Movement. The United States is one of the few countries that does not provide any direct governmental funding to its Olympic programs. Thus, the exclusive protections provided in the OASA allow the USOC to defend against ambush marketing activities as well as protect the value of a significant revenue stream through sponsorships and licensing. Several provisions grant the USOC exclusive rights within the United States to the words "United States Olympic Committee"; the symbols of the International Olympic Committee, including the five interlocking rings; and the words "Olympic" and "Olympiad," "Citius Altius Fortius," "Paralympic," "Paralympiad," "Pan-American," and "America Espirito Sport Fraternite," and any combination of those words. The USOC possesses the exclusive right to license the use of these marks. The OASA further provides that the USOC may pursue any remedies traditionally available for trademark infringement (e.g., under the Lanham Act) if any person uses the protected symbols "for the purpose of trade, to induce the sale of any goods or services, or to promote any . . . athletic performance, or competition."

Thus, the OASA extends to the USOC the same protections that the Lanham Act provides to traditional trademark owners. However, the elements of a trademark infringement action as identified in the Lanham Act have been modified by the courts for the USOC. In *USOC v. San Francisco Arts & Athletics, Inc.* (1987), the Supreme Court held that the USOC need not prove that the contested use of its marks is likely to cause confusion. Being relieved of this evidentiary burden has provided the USOC with broader protection than that available to ordinary trademark owners. An unauthorized user of USOC protected marks and symbols is often hit with a cease and desist order easily obtained by the USOC without any showing of consumer confusion. Essentially, to prevail in an infringement action under the OASA, the USOC need only show that the unauthorized user's marks are similar to the USOC's protected marks.

The USOC often ruthlessly uses this heightened or broadened trademark protection even when the unauthorized use seems benign and relatively insignificant. During the 2002 Winter Olympics, the Salt Lake Olympic Organizing Committee (SLOC) objected to a corn farmer who created crop circles in his field in the shape of the five interlocking rings, and demanded that the rings be removed. Similarly, during the 1996 Olympic games in Atlanta, several small, local businesses were taken to court by the Atlanta Committee for the Olympic Games (ACOG) for unauthorized use of Olympic marks and logos. Sometimes the USOC's or the local organizing committee's heavy-handed policing of Olympic marks and logos has been criticized. Such tactics, however, have generally been successful. In actuality, few alleged unauthorized users oppose the USOC or the local organizing committees, probably due in part to the heightened trademark protection and in part to the expense of litigating against an organization with such significant financial resources.

This section on trademark law has revealed important legal issues associated with trademarks. You should have a better understanding of the value of trademarks as part of a business's intellectual property portfolio, the requirements for registration of trademarks, and the protections afforded trademark owners. Next, we continue to explore intellectual property as we examine copyright law and its impact on sport marketing managers.

THE LAW OF COPYRIGHTS

"The Congress shall have Power . . . To promote the **Progress of Science** and useful Arts, by securing for limited Times to Authors and Inventors the exclusive Right to their respective Writings and Discoveries."

U.S. Constitution, Article I, § 8, cl. 8

If you are a sport enthusiast, you will either knowingly or unknowingly encounter copyrights in your daily life in a variety of ways—for example, through purchasing *Sports Illustrated* magazine or *Street & Smith's SportsBusiness Journal,* purchasing or downloading a music CD, watching or recording an ESPN broadcast, or playing an EA Sports video game. All of these are creative, original works that are protected by U. S. copyright laws. Copyright law is a compromise forged many years ago between the interests of authors of creative works and the public's interest in having access to those works. Copyright is a type of protection provided to authors of "original works," including literary, dramatic, musical, artistic, and others. Copyright law gives the holder a limited monopoly over a creative work to prevent others from using the work without the owner's permission.

You will recall that a trademark's main function is to serve as a source identifier for products and services, and it only represents a property interest to the extent that it is attached to a product or service. In contrast, a copyright represents a property interest from the moment a creative work is created and put into a tangible form. In the sport industry, copyright applies in numerous situations, such as product labels, website content and design, merchandise logo design, broadcasts of sporting events, sport novels, sport figure biographies, halftime performances by musical groups, the music played throughout an event, and paintings of sport celebrities and events. Certainly, trademarks tend to appear more prominently in the sport industry due to the emphasis placed on branding. Copyright, however, also has an important role and pervades many sport organizational decisions.

Purpose of Copyrights

The purpose of copyright law is to encourage creativity by extending protection to works of art, literature, and music, and other works of authorship. However, the goal of encouraging creativity competes with other laws seeking to foster a competitive marketplace and with First Amendment guarantees of free speech. Copyright law attempts to balance these competing goals in a variety of ways. To maintain this balance, the interests of the creator, the owner, and the public or users of the work must be considered. See Exhibit 19.6.

| Balancing competing interests in copyright law. | EXHIBIT | 19.6 |

Creator Rights
Copyright
Moral rights

Owner Rights
Works for hire
Licensing

Public Domain
Fair use
Time limits

Note: This figure represents the intersection and balance between competing interests related to copyrights. Although the image may also bear a resemblance to a famous and well-known copyrighted character, Mickey Mouse, such similarities are purely for educational and informational purposes. If Congress had not recently passed the Sonny Bono Copyright Term Extension Act, many images of Mickey Mouse would have passed into the public domain in 2003. Instead, the public will not have free and open access to these artistic creations until the year 2028.

On one hand, copyright law grants exclusive rights to the creator of an original work of authorship, but on the other hand, the law limits the duration of those rights and protects only the specific method used by the author to express his or her idea. Additionally, the law allows for *fair use* of copyrighted materials. Fair use practices together with time limits on copyright protections attempt to ensure a free and robust public domain for the expression of ideas, thereby balancing competing interests between authors or owners and the public domain or users. Similarly, laws relating to works for hire and protecting the moral rights of authors help to balance the competing interests of authors and owners.

The law does not protect an idea itself, but only an author's or artist's *fixed expression* of the idea. To illustrate, suppose you have an idea for a movie about an aging minor league baseball player and his relationship with a promising but erratic rookie pitcher. Both players become romantically involved with the same woman. This may sound like an idea for a great story, so you tell your friend about it. Unless and until you take your idea and write it down or otherwise put it into a tangible "fixed" form, it is not protected by copyright law. If you actually write a script telling the above story, at that point you have a copyright to the creative work. If your screenplay carries the name *Bull Durham,* the film version of your story would also be a separate creative work subject to copyright protection. The sheet music for a song is a different form of expression from an audio recording of a song. The public performance of a song that has not been written down or recorded represents the basic idea, not an expression of that idea. Thus, a performance cannot be copyrighted unless and until it is expressed in a copyrightable form. The same is true for an idea for a sport event. The idea is not copyrightable, nor is the live event. Instead, only the taped or recorded expression of the idea or event will ultimately be copyrightable.

Source of Copyrights

Copyright law is primarily provided for under the Copyright Act of 1976, as amended. In addition, the Digital Millennium Copyright Act (2003) provides copyright laws regarding digital creations and the Internet, and the Sonny Bono Copyright Term Extension Act (2003) extends the duration of previous limits on copyrights. Exhibit 19.7 identifies the duration of copyright protection for protected, creative works.

EXHIBIT 19.7	Duration of copyrights.

DURATION OF COPYRIGHT		DURATION OF MORAL RIGHTS
Author/artist creative works created prior to January 1, 1978	Author/artist creative works created after January 1, 1978	Artist's moral rights in fine arts created after June 1, 1991
Copyright protection lasts for 95 years from date of creation	Life of author + 70 years Works for hire: 95 years after first publication or 120 years after creation, whichever is earlier	Life of the author

Creation of Copyrights

Many types of materials and subject matter may receive copyright protection. The Copyright Act specifically includes the items shown in Exhibit 19.8. Essentially, to qualify for copyright protection, the material must meet two requirements: *originality* and *fixation*.

Originality requirement

Originality requires a work to be created by the author himself or herself and to contain some minimal amount of creativity. Words, short phrases, and familiar symbols or designs do not meet this requirement and may not be copyrighted. Remember, however, that many short phrases, words, symbols, and designs can be protected as trademarks so long as they are functioning to identify specific products and services.

Collections of data or facts do not meet the originality requirement and may not be copyrighted. For a collection of data or facts to be protected, it must possess some minimal amount of creativity or uniqueness. For example, the Supreme Court held that a listing of phone numbers in a phone book did not meet the originality requirement but was instead just a collection of data or facts (*Feist Publications, Inc. v. Rural Telephone Service Co.*, 1991). The Court noted that only minimal originality is required, but it must exist. The collection of phone numbers represented significant effort, but copyright does not reward effort. It rewards originality, which was lacking in an alphabetical listing of names, addresses, and phone numbers. This issue was discussed in *NBA v. Motorola, Inc.* (1997) when the court held that live sporting events are not original works of authorship. Congress specifically amended the Copyright Act of 1976 to extend copyright protection to broadcasts of live sporting events, but the underlying events and concepts for a game or event are not copyrightable. See *Anti-Monopoly, Inc. v. General Mills Fun Group, Inc.* (1979) (game concept cannot be copyrighted); *Affiliated Hosp. Prods., Inc. v. Merdel Game Mfg. Co.* (1975) (games that are in the public domain and the rules to those games are not copyrightable). Thus, the methods or rules of playing sports and games are not generally copyrightable. See *Nimmer on Copyright* § 2.18[H][3] ("no copyright may be obtained in the system or manner of playing a game or engaging in any other sporting or like activity"). In addition to originality, a work must be "fixed" in order to be protected by copyright law, as discussed next.

Materials and subject matter protected by the Copyright Act of 1976 (17 U.S.C. § 102).	EXHIBIT **19.8**

Literary works	Pictorial, graphic, and sculptural works
Musical works	Motion pictures and audiovisual works
Dramatic works	Sound recordings
Pantomimes and choreographic works	Architectural works

Fixation requirement

Fixation requires that the work be put into a tangible form—written down or recorded. This would include paper, fabrics, records, tapes, compact discs, portable drives, and DVDs. Consider the example of a Division I men's basketball game. The game itself is not tangible; it exists only in the moment. However, if the game is recorded, broadcast, or otherwise put into a tangible form, the fixed form of the game becomes copyrightable. Just writing down an idea for an event or game is not fixation of the expression of the idea or concept for purposes of copyright. For example, the court held in *Hoopla Sports & Entertainment, Inc. v. Nike, Inc.* (1996) that Hoopla had not complied with the necessary requisites to copyright its idea. Hoopla developed an idea for a United States versus the world basketball game featuring high school boys, called "Father Liberty Game" or "FLG." Even if a basketball game were copyrightable, Hoopla did not record or otherwise fix in any tangible medium of expression its idea for FLG. Thus, it did not possess a copyright in the FLG itself under the Copyright Act. It is a requirement of the Copyright Act that the expression must be fixed in a tangible medium before it can be copyrighted. Fixation is not merely a statutory requirement of the Copyright Act, but is required by the text of the Constitution itself, which protects only "writings," that is, tangible forms of expression. See *Nimmer on Copyright* § 2.03[B].

Notice that the *Hoopla* court did not determine whether a game or a sports contest was a copyrightable event. This issue was addressed in *NBA v. Motorola* (1997).

National Basketball Association v. Motorola, Inc.

| 105 F.3d 841 (2d Cir. 1997) | **CASE OPINION** |

[FACTS

The facts are largely undisputed. Motorola manufactures and markets the SportsTrax paging device while STATS supplies the game information that is transmitted to the pagers. The product became available to the public in January 1996, at a retail price of about $200. SportsTrax's pager has an inch-and-a-half by inch-and-a-half screen and operates in four basic modes: "current," "statistics," "final scores" and "demonstration." It is the "current" mode that gives rise to the present dispute. In that mode, SportsTrax displays the following information on NBA games in progress: (i) the teams playing; (ii) score changes; (iii) the team in possession of the ball; (iv) whether the team is in the free-throw bonus; (v) the quarter of the game; and (vi) time remaining in the quarter. The information is updated every two to three minutes, with more frequent updates near the end of the first half and the end of the game. There is a lag of approximately two or three minutes between events in the game itself and when the information appears on the pager screen.

SportsTrax's operation relies on a "data feed" supplied by STATS reporters who watch the games on television or listen to them on the radio. The reporters key into a personal computer changes in the score and other information such as successful and missed shots, fouls, and clock updates. The information is relayed by modem to STATS's host computer, which compiles, analyzes, and formats the data for retransmission. The information is then sent to a common carrier, which then sends it via satellite to various local FM radio networks that in turn emit the signal received by the individual SportsTrax pagers.]

* * *

HOLDING

The court ruled that the SportsTrax device and AOL reproduced only factual information and did not infringe on the NBA broadcast copyright.

RATIONALE

Copyrights in Events or Broadcasts of Events

The NBA asserted copyright infringement claims with regard both to the underlying games and to their broadcasts. Discussion of the infringement claims is necessary to provide the framework for analyzing the viability of the NBA's state law misappropriation claim in light of the Copyright Act's preemptive effect.

1. Infringement of a Copyright in the Underlying Games

In our view, the underlying basketball games do not fall within the subject matter of federal copyright protection because they do not constitute "original works of authorship" under 17 U.S.C. § 102(a). Section 102(a) lists eight categories of "works of authorship" covered by the act, including such categories as "literary works," "musical works," and "dramatic works." . . . The list does not include athletic events, and, although the list is concededly non-exclusive, such events are neither similar nor analogous to any of the listed categories.

Sports events are not "authored" in any common sense of the word. There is, of course, at least at the professional level, considerable preparation for a game. However, the preparation is as much an expression of hope or faith as a determination of what will actually happen. Unlike movies, plays, television programs, or operas, athletic events are competitive and have no underlying script. Preparation may even cause mistakes to succeed, like the broken play in football that gains yardage because the opposition could not expect it. Athletic events may also result in wholly unanticipated occurrences, the most notable recent event being in a championship baseball game in which interference with a fly ball caused an umpire to signal erroneously a home run.

What "authorship" there is in a sports event, moreover, must be open to copying by competitors if fans are to be attracted. If the inventor of the T-formation in football had been able to copyright it, the sport might have come to an end instead of prospering. Even where athletic preparation most resembles authorship—figure skating, gymnastics, and, some would uncharitably say, professional wrestling—a performer who conceives and executes a particularly graceful and difficult—or, in the case of wrestling, seemingly painful—acrobatic feat cannot copyright it without impairing the underlying competition in the future. A claim of being the only athlete to perform a feat doesn't mean much if no one else is allowed to try.

For many of these reasons, Nimmer on Copyright concludes that the "far more reasonable" position is that athletic events are not copyrightable. 1 M. Nimmer & D. Nimmer, Nimmer on Copyright § 2.09[F] at 2-170.1 (1996). Nimmer notes that, among other problems, the number of joint copyright owners would arguably include the league, the teams, the athletes, umpires, stadium workers and even fans, who all contribute to the "work." . . .

In claiming a copyright in the underlying games, the NBA relied in part on a footnote in *Baltimore Orioles, Inc. v. Major League Baseball Players Assn.,* 805 F.2d 663, 669 n. 7 (7th Cir. 1986), *cert. denied,* 480 U.S. 941, 94 L. Ed. 2d 782, 107 S. Ct. 1593 (1987), which stated that the "players' performances" contain the "modest creativity required for copyrightability." However, the court went on to state, "Moreover, even if the players' performances were not sufficiently creative, the players agree that the cameramen and director contribute creative labor to the telecasts." *Id.* This last sentence indicates that the court was considering the copyrightability of telecasts—not the underlying games, which obviously can be played without cameras.

We believe that the lack of caselaw is attributable to a general understanding that athletic events were, and are, uncopyrightable. Indeed, prior to 1976, there was even doubt that broadcasts describing or depicting such events, which have a far stronger case for copyrightability than the events themselves, were entitled to copyright protection. Indeed, as described in the next subsection of this opinion, Congress found it necessary to extend such protection to recorded broadcasts of live events. The fact that Congress did not extend such protection to the events themselves confirms our view that the district court correctly held that appellants were not infringing a copyright in the NBA games.

2. Infringement of a Copyright in the Broadcasts of NBA Games

As noted, recorded broadcasts of NBA games—as opposed to the games themselves—are now entitled to copyright protection. The Copyright Act was amended in 1976 specifically to insure that simultaneously-recorded transmissions of live performances and sporting events would meet the Act's requirement that the original work of authorship be "fixed in any tangible medium of expression" 17 U.S.C. § 102(a).

Congress specifically had sporting events in mind: The bill seeks to resolve, through the definition of "fixation" in section 101, the status of live broadcasts—sports, news coverage, live performances of music, etc.—that are reaching the public in unfixed form but that are simultaneously being recorded. H.R. No. 94-1476 at 52, reprinted in 1976 U.S.C.C.A.N. at 5665. The House Report also makes clear that it is the broadcast, not the underlying game, that is the subject of copyright protection. In explaining how game broadcasts meet the Act's requirement that the subject matter be an "original work of authorship," 17 U.S.C. § 102(a), the House Report stated:

> When a football game is being covered by four television cameras, with a director guiding the activities of the four cameramen and choosing which of their electronic images are sent out to the public and in what order, there is little doubt that what the cameramen and the director are doing constitutes "authorship." (H.R. No. 94-1476 at 52, reprinted in 1976 U.S.C.C.A.N. at 5665.)

Although the broadcasts are protected under copyright law, the district court correctly held that Motorola and STATS did not infringe NBA's copyright because they reproduced only facts from the broadcasts, not the expression or description of the game that constitutes the broadcast. The "fact/expression dichotomy" is a bedrock principle of copyright law that "limits severely the scope of protection in fact-based works." *Feist Publications,* *Inc. v. Rural Tel. Service Co.,* 499 U.S. 340, 350, 113 L. Ed. 2d 358, 111 S. Ct. 1282 (1991). "'No author may copyright facts or ideas. The copyright is limited to those aspects of the work—termed 'expression'—that display the stamp of the author's originality." *Id.* (quoting *Harper & Row, Inc. v. Nation Enter.,* 471 U.S. 539, 547–48, 85 L. Ed. 2d 588, 105 S. Ct. 2218 (1985)).

We agree with the district court that the "defendants provide purely factual information which any patron of an NBA game could acquire from the arena without any involvement from the director, cameramen, or others who contribute to the originality of a broadcast."

* * *

Questions

1. What characteristics of athletic events are used by the court to support its conclusion that sport events are not "authored" for purposes of copyright protection?

2. How does Congress' decision to entitle live broadcasts of sporting events to copyright protection hinder the NBA's arguments for protection of the games themselves?

3. How is the information used by Motorola similar to the information used by Rural Telephone Service in *Feist Publications, Inc. v. Rural Tel. Service* Co. (1991)?

Registration of Copyrights

Registration is not required for a copyright to exist. The copyright comes into existence as soon as the work is created and put into a tangible form. However, similar to trademark registration, registration of a copyright carries with it procedural benefits in the event of an unauthorized use. For example, an owner of a copyright may not sue for infringement unless the copyright is registered. Thus, if one does not register a copyright and the work is copied, the copyright must be registered before suit can be brought. Also, if a copyright is not registered prior to the alleged infringement, the amount of damages recoverable for the infringement is more limited. Thus, it is a wise business practice to submit creative works promptly for registration with the Copyright Office and always to include the claim of copyright on all creative works.

The U. S. Copyright Office regulates registration and deposit of copyrighted materials and has three basic functions. It registers copyrights, issues certificates of registration, and regulates and stores copyrighted material. If an author's work meets the originality and fixation requirements, then the author may register and deposit the work with the U. S. Copyright Office simply by paying a small registration fee ($35 in 2009). The Copyright Office provides resources for authors and online registration at its website, www.copyright.gov.

1. Registration is required to bring an infringement claim.
2. Failure to register can reduce damages recoverable for infringement.

The proper designation of a copyright contains three basic elements: the copyright symbol or word, the date, and the name of the author or copyright holder.

© 2012, Jane Doe
Copyright 2012, Jane Doe

All original works should include this designation. Although no longer required by law, this notification will provide additional evidence of a claim of copyright in the event of unauthorized use.

Determining Ownership of Copyrights

When a single author creates an original work comprised solely of new materials, determining ownership is fairly simple. Once the work is created in a fixed form, the single author immediately becomes the owner of the work *and* the copyright, unless he or she has entered into an agreement to the contrary. Determining ownership is more difficult when a work has joint authors, when a work is included within another work as part of a collection of works (collective works), and when a work is a work for hire.

Joint authors and collective works

The authors of **joint work** are co-owners of the copyright in the work unless they have entered into an agreement to the contrary. In addition, each separate contribution to a periodical or **collective work** represents a distinct copyright from the collective work as a whole. The copyright for each separate part of a periodical rests with the author of that part, while the copyright for the collective work rests with another. For example, a typical issue of *ESPN The Magazine* may contain a dozen articles written by different authors. Each individual article represents a separate copyright owned by the author of that article. The entire magazine, or collective work, represents another copyright work owned by ESPN, Inc. In addition, each photograph included in the magazine also represents a separate copyright, owned by the photographer.

Works for hire

A **work for hire** can result in two ways. First, a work made for hire may be a work prepared by an employee within the scope of his employment. For example, an intern in the Ohio State Athletic Department may create a new Media Guide for women's basketball. This work would be considered a work for hire, as a work prepared by an employee within the scope of her employment. Both the work and the copyright would be owned by Ohio State. Second, a work made for hire may be a *contracted work,* defined as a work specially ordered or commissioned for use as a contribution to a collective work, a part of a motion picture or other audiovisual work, a translation, a supplementary work, a compilation, an instructional text, a test, answer material for a test, or an atlas, if the parties expressly agree in a written instrument signed by them that the work shall be considered a work made for hire. For an employee to protect a creative work as his own, an express agreement must exist reserving those rights to the employee. Employee creations are presumed to belong to the employer. However, just the reverse is true for contracted works: the person commissioned to create the work is presumed to own the copyright unless a written agreement assigns those rights to the commissioning person or company.

Rights Granted with Copyright

The rights granted with a copyright can be categorized as either property rights or moral rights.

Property rights

A **property right** provides the creator or owner of a copyright the exclusive economic and property interests to the work. Property rights recognized under current copyright law grant to the owner of copyright the exclusive rights to do and to authorize any of the following:

1. To reproduce the copyrighted work in copies or phonorecords
2. To prepare derivative works based upon the copyrighted work
3. To distribute copies or phonorecords of the copyrighted work to the public by sale or other transfer of ownership, or by rental, lease, or lending
4. To perform the copyrighted work publicly (in the case of literary, musical, dramatic, and choreographic works, pantomimes, and motion pictures and other audiovisual works)
5. To display the copyrighted work publicly (in the case of literary, musical, dramatic, and choreographic works, pantomimes, and pictorial, graphic, or sculptural works, including the individual images of a motion picture or other audiovisual work)
6. To perform the copyrighted work publicly by means of a digital audio transmission (in the case of sound recordings) (17 U.S.C. § 106, 2009)

It is possible for the creator of a work and the owner of the work to be two different people or entities. For example, the creator may sell, assign, transfer, or license her rights to another, who becomes the owner of the copyright and the rights included with the copyright. Or the author may retain the copyright but transfer the exclusive distribution rights to another. For example, an artist may create an original painting depicting the winner of the Kentucky Derby, sell the painting to a collector, and license another company to create prints for mass distribution. The purchaser of the original is the owner of the painting but not the copyright. Similarly, the distribution company owns exclusive licensing and distribution rights but not the copyright itself, which is still owned by the artist.

Moral rights

Regardless of how an author chooses to dispose of her copyright, she will retain certain moral rights to a visual work even if the original copyright or work has been sold or transferred. The United States has recognized moral rights only since the Visual Arts Rights Act of 1990 (VARA, 1990, 2003). Moral rights attach to a copyright because authorship is an extension of an author's personality. Moral rights generally fall into two categories: right of attribution and right of integrity. The **right of attribution** prevents others from claiming authorship or attributing authorship falsely to an individual. The **right of integrity** prevents others from distorting, mutilating, or misrepresenting the author's work. See Exhibit 19.10.

VARA protects the rights of attribution and integrity of the author of a "work of visual art" (17 U.S.C. § 106A). Passed by Congress in 1990 to bring this country more in line with others in protecting certain "moral" rights of artists, the VARA, among other things, allows artists to claim authorship in certain works of art. Congress, however, recognized the problems inherent in expanding VARA protection too broadly, so it therefore went to extreme lengths to narrowly define the works of art to be covered by the act. As such, Congress decided that the VARA would protect only "works of visual art," as defined by the Copyright Act.

Very few cases have been decided on the merits under VARA. A sport artist, Daniel Moore, asserted a claim against the University of Alabama under VARA claiming that a university official had altered his artworks on its website, where jersey and helmet colors were changed from crimson to green. Moore's claims were dismissed by the district court ("Federal judge dismisses artist's claim," 2005). Another such case involves a dispute over attribution to the design of the trophy for the NASCAR Nextel Cup in *NASCAR v. Scharle* (2006). Scharle worked as an independent contractor for the Franklin Mint and was asked to help

---

The Visual Artist Rights Act of 1990.　　　　　　　　　EXHIBIT   **19.10**

Visual Artists Rights Act of 1990, 17 U.S.C. § 106A. Rights of certain authors to attribution and integrity

(a) Rights of attribution and integrity. Subject to section 107 [17 USCS § 107] and independent of the exclusive rights provided in section 106 [17 USCS § 106], the author of a work of visual art—

   (1) shall have the right—

      (A) to claim authorship of that work, and

      (B) to prevent the use of his or her name as the author of any work of visual art which he or she did not create;

   (2) shall have the right to prevent the use of his or her name as the author of the work of visual art in the event of a distortion, mutilation, or other modification of the work which would be prejudicial to his or her honor or reputation; and

   (3) subject to the limitations set forth in section 113(d) [17 USCS § 113(d)], shall have the right—

      (A) to prevent any intentional distortion, mutilation, or other modification of that work which would be prejudicial to his or her honor or reputation, and any intentional distortion, mutilation, or modification of that work is a violation of that right, and

      (B) to prevent any destruction of a work of recognized stature, and any intentional or grossly negligent destruction of that work is a violation of that right.

Competitive Advantage
STRATEGIES

Copyright

- Engage the services of an intellectual property attorney or other expert for sophisticated and complicated tasks such as trademark searches, copyright renewals, and digital rights management.

- Establish procedures for responding to instances of possible trademark or copyright infringement. Often, an innocent infringement can be curtailed by a simple letter notifying the infringer of your superior rights to a mark or copyright.

- To avoid finding itself in the position of the Baltimore Ravens and having to defend a copyright infringement case, a sport organization should have a firm policy prohibiting any employee from accepting creative works from outside sources. An internal policy to refuse to accept sample artwork, drawings, or other creative works from anyone who is not an employee of the organization will strengthen your defense to a copyright infringement case by making it more difficult for the plaintiff to prove "access."

- Include the copyright symbol, ©, on all sponsorship proposals or promotional ideas that you present to other businesses. This should serve to notify them that the promotional idea is your property and cause them to think before implementing your promotion without your permission.

- Webcasting is growing in popularity and may provide many college athletic departments with a much-needed revenue stream; thus, television broadcasting agreements should clearly reserve the webcasting rights to the university. It is, of course, likely that the broadcaster will prohibit simultaneous webcasting for high-profile events for fear of reducing the value of their broadcast rights.

design a new trophy to replace the Winston Cup. Scharle created numerous computer images for the trophy design and presented them to the Franklin Mint. When the new trophy was unveiled, the new trophy design was credited to the Franklin Mint, not Scharle. Scharle wanted attribution under VARA. The *Scharle* court carefully examined the definition of a "work of visual art" in the statute in reaching its decision. Among other things, a work of visual art does *not* include any "technical drawing, diagram, model, . . . merchandising item[,] or advertising [or] promotional . . . material." The court concluded that Scharle's works (computer images) did not exist in a single copy or a limited quantity of signed and numbered copies but instead as multiple attempts to arrive at the optimal design for the trophy. Because Scharle's drawings are not "works of visual art" as defined by the Copyright Act, they were not protected by the VARA.

Consider another example: Kyle Busch's destruction of the guitar trophy awarded to the winner of the Nationwide Series Federated Auto Parts 300 at a racetrack in Nashville. Would any action against Busch by longtime NASCAR artist Sam Bass who painted the Gibson guitar be covered by VARA? The Gibson guitar has become the symbol of Nashville Superspeedway. The one Busch smashed was the 30th designed by Bass, who said the trophy has come to be "a very revered piece of history . . . and revered by the fans here in Tennessee" (Gluck, 2009). Bass estimated that he and Gibson put "hundreds and hundreds of hours" of work into the guitar, which is so unique that "you can't just buy this thing right off the shelf."

Copyright Infringement

Copyright infringement occurs when someone makes an unauthorized use of a copyrighted work. To prove copyright infringement, the copyright owner must (1) prove ownership of a valid copyright and (2) prove copying of constituent elements of the work that are original. Even accidental or inadvertent copying constitutes infringement. Courts have adopted a substantial similarity test to satisfy the copying element of direct infringement. The test has two parts:

1. The defendant had access to the copyrighted work.
2. The allegedly infringing work is substantially similar to the copyrighted work.

In the case that follows, copyright infringement was raised by Frederick Bouchat against the Baltimore Ravens for the alleged copying of a logo design he created after it was announced that the NFL team, the former Cleveland Browns, was moving to Baltimore.

Bouchat v. Baltimore Ravens, Inc.

241 F.3d 350 (4th Cir. 2000)   **FOCUS CASE**

FACTS

The plaintiff, Frederick Bouchat, filed an action in federal district court seeking $10,000,000 in damages. He alleged that the Baltimore Ravens and National Football League Properties had infringed his copyright rights in a "shield logo." Bouchat is an amateur artist who works full-time as a security guard at the State of Maryland Office building in Baltimore. As public knowledge of the new team spread in 1995, Bouchat, on his own, created drawings and designs for his favorite possible team name—the Ravens. Bouchat put his design on a miniature football helmet and gave the helmet to Eugene Conti, a state official who worked in the state office building in late 1995. Thereafter, Conti set up a meeting between Bouchat and John Moag, the chair of the Maryland Stadium Authority.

In March 1996, Bouchat met Moag at Moag's law office. The office suite that held Moag's office also held the temporary offices of the Ravens and the team owner, David Modell. After learning of Bouchat's work, Moag urged Bouchat to send his drawings to him (Moag), and Moag stated that he would give them to the Ravens for consideration. On April 1 or 2, 1996, Bouchat faxed his drawings as requested. On April 2, 1996, Modell met with the NFL Properties design director to discuss the development of a team logo. In June of 1996, the Ravens unveiled their new logo, which Bouchat immediately recognized as his work. Bouchat copyrighted the drawing in August 1996 and later filed a copyright infringement suit against the Ravens and NFL Properties. A jury returned a verdict for Bouchat and the Ravens appealed.

HOLDING

The court of appeals ruled in favor of Bouchat.

RATIONALE

To prove copyright infringement, a plaintiff has to prove that the defendant copied protected elements of the work. The plaintiff may prove by circumstantial evidence that the alleged infringer had access to the work and that the supposed copy is substantially similar to the author's original work. In this case, to prove access, the plaintiff successfully showed that the NFL designers, the alleged infringers, had an opportunity to view Bouchat's drawings because Bouchat had evidence that he faxed the drawing to Moag, who shared an office with Modell. By proving that the drawings were sent to Moag and that Modell shared office space with Moag, the plaintiff proved that Modell had access to the drawing. Bouchat was not required to prove that Modell actually saw the drawings, merely that Modell had access to the drawings.

The court had to determine how the doctrine of striking similarity would be applied in this case. The court had two interpretations of the strikingly similar doctrine from which to choose. The Fifth Circuit has held that access need not be proven if there is a striking similarity. However, the Second and Seventh Circuits have held that striking similarity is only circumstantial evidence of copying that supports the inference of access. The Fourth Circuit adopted the rationale of the Second and Seventh Circuits and held that the striking similarity of the works was a proper factor for the jury to consider, with all other evidence, to determine whether the plaintiff had proven copying.

Defenses to Copyright Infringement

The Copyright Act provides for several exceptions to the exclusive rights granted a copyright owner. The defense most often used in the entertainment and sport industries is **fair use** discussed previously in the context of trademark law. The fair use defense as it relates to copyrights was originally created by the courts as an equitable rule of reason that permitted courts to avoid rigid application of a copyright statute if such application would stifle the very creativity that the law is designed to foster. This defense is now expressly included in the Copyright Act as follows:

> [T]he fair use of a copyrighted work . . . for purposes such as criticism, comment, news reporting, teaching (including multiple copies for classroom use), scholarship, or research, is not an infringement of copyright. In determining whether the use made of a work in any particular case is a fair use the factors to be considered shall include—
>
> (1) the purpose and character of the use, including whether such use is of a commercial nature or is for nonprofit educational purposes;
>
> (2) the nature of the copyrighted work;
>
> (3) the amount and substantiality of the portion used in relation to the copyrighted work as a whole; and
>
> (4) the effect of the use upon the potential market for or value of the copyrighted work. (17 U.S.C. § 107 [2003])

The line between infringement and fair use is not clearly drawn. A finding of a commercial purpose will not automatically defeat a fair use claim, and there is no magic portion or percentage calculation to use to determine substantiality. Cases raising fair use defenses are decided on a case-by-case basis. In general, if the new work substantially transforms the original one through comment, criticism, or additional materials, it is likely deserving of fair use protection and represents creative work on the part of its author. A parody is recognized as a fair use, as was reaffirmed by the Supreme Court in *Campbell v. Acuff-Rose Music, Inc.* (1994), where rap group 2 Live Crew released a song containing musical and lyrical elements very similar to the classic Roy Orbison song "Pretty Woman."

Now let's consider how fair use applies to protected copyrighted works in the following Case Opinion.

World Wrestling Federation Entertainment, Inc. v. Big Dog Holdings, Inc.

280 F. Supp. 2d 413 (W.D. Pa., 2003)

CASE OPINION

[FACTS

World Wrestling Federation Entertainment, Inc. (WWE) has been involved in the sports entertainment business for over twenty (20) years and has developed story lines based around numerous wrestling characters. WWE sued Big Dog for copyright infringement based on several characters featured on Big Dog products based on the persona of WWE's characters. Big Dog contends that its Big Dog character is intended to be irreverent, funny, and not afraid to make fun of "overinflated aspects of our society." Big Dog alleges that its t-shirts appeal to customers who enjoy mocking "over-promoted pop phenomena" that are prevalent in today's media. The Big Dog graphics ridicule, poke fun at, and mock these self-serious icons by characterizing them as dogs, particularly associating them with the Big Dog character, giving them humorous names, and "dogifying" them. A Big Dog graphic artist described "dogify" as a means "to satirize a given entity by giving him big floppy ears, a big silly tail, turning him into this variety of dog that we turn everything into." The dog graphic essentially is a caricature of the intended subject, copying elements of the subject so in satirizing a particular person or thing, it is recognizable to the public.]

HOLDING

Big Dog's graphics are parodies of the WWE property, entitled to fair use under the Copyright statute.

RATIONALE

Federal copyright law provides an exception to the prohibition on reproduction of a copyrighted work where the reproduction qualifies as "fair use." 17 U.S.C. § 107. The fair use doctrine was fashioned as a "guarantee of breathing space" within the confines of copyright that allows for new transformative works that further the public discourse and the free exchange of ideas in order to promote science and the arts. See *Campbell v. Acuff-Rose Music, Inc.*, 510 U.S. 569, 579, 127 L. Ed. 2d 500, 114 S. Ct. 1164 (1994). As Justice Story recognized, in truth, in literature, in science and in art, there are, and can be, few, if any, things which in the abstract sense are strictly new and original throughout. Every book in literature, science and art, borrows, and

must necessarily borrow, and use much which was well known and used before.

* * *

Big Dog argues that its graphics are entitled to a measure of protection under the fair use doctrine as parodies of the WWE property. Although the statute does not specifically list parodies among the categories of potentially "fair" uses, the Supreme Court has confirmed the applicability of the fair use doctrine to parodies. In *Campbell*, the Court initially noted that "parody may or may not be fair use," and "parody, like any other use, has to work its way through the relevant factors."

(1) The Purpose and Character of the Use

The first factor in this fair use analysis requires an examination of two aspects, the character and the purpose, of the Big Dog graphics. Prior to *Campbell*, courts overemphasized the purpose of the use, finding "every commercial use of copyrighted material [to be] presumptively an unfair exploitation of the monopoly privilege that belongs to the owner of the copyright." *Sony Corp. of America v. Universal City Studios, Inc.*, 464 U.S. 417, 451, 78 L. Ed. 2d 574, 104 S. Ct. 774 (1984). The Supreme Court in *Campbell*, however, has definitively held that a finding of *fair use is not barred by the commercial nature of the work*. In so holding, the Court stated "the statute makes clear that the commercial or nonprofit educational purpose of a work is only one element of the first factor enquiry . . ." There is no issue herein with regard to the commercial purpose of Big Dog's graphics.

A critical inquiry regarding this first fair use factor is whether the second work "adds something new, with a further purpose or different character, altering the first with new expression, meaning, or message; it asks, in other words, whether and to what extent the new work is 'transformative.'" With respect to parody, the Supreme Court concluded: Parody has an obvious claim to transformative value. Like less ostensibly humorous forms of criticism, it can provide social benefit, by shedding light on an earlier work and, in the process, creating a new one. The Big Dog graphics therefore must alter WWE's intellectual property with new expression, meaning or message. It is undisputed that in creating Big Dog's graphics, the artist used photographic references of WWE's wrestling characters. Specifically, the artist would get a series of pictures of the wrestlers, generally from magazines, and using all the pictures as a reference, the artist would sketch caricatures of the wrestlers and scan them into the computer for further design. Because the new work must reference the copyrighted material, a "parody needs to mimic an original to make its point, and so has some claim to use the creation of its victim's (or its collective victims') imagination . . ." Moreover, to qualify as a parody under the Supreme Court's definition, the newly created work must comment upon or criticize the original copyrighted work.

A visual examination of the graphics themselves is evidence of the humor, ridicule, and/or comment on the over-hyped world of professional wrestling. The graphics depict dogs in wrestling garb, with beards and goatees, one dog wearing an earring, with tattoos, wearing leather jackets and vests, wearing sunglasses, smashing each other with chairs, and in fact, wrestling. The merchandise can certainly be perceived as commenting, through mockery or derision, on " . . . the larger-than-life, intimidating, self-serious fierce and violent images and persona of WWF professional wrestling."

The threshold question when fair use is raised in defense of parody is whether the parodic character can be perceived. While the Court has no comment on the quality of the humor, it can certainly perceive the merchandise as commenting on, or criticizing, the original works. The Court will weigh the first factor in favor of Big Dog.

(2) The Nature of the Copyrighted Work

The second statutory factor, "the nature of the copyrighted works," 17 U.S.C. § 107(2), recognizes that some works are closer to the core of intended copyright protection than others, and therefore fair use is more difficult to establish when those works are copied. This Court certainly questions the originality and creativity of the WWE characters and storylines. The good guys against the bad guys certainly precedes the establishment of professional wrestling, and regarding wrestling's "original" characters. However, it is not disputed that WWE has spent time and effort on the development of its characters, storylines and personas, and the Court does not question its right to protection. Because "parodies almost invariably copy publicly known, expressive works," this factor provides little help in determining whether the parody is a fair use of

the original. Drawing all reasonable inferences from the facts in favor of WWE, the Court finds the second factor favors WWE, but only minimally.

(3) The Amount and Substantiality of the Portion Used in Relation to the Copyrighted Work as a Whole

The third factor asks whether "the amount and substantiality of the portion used in relation to the copyrighted work as a whole," 17 U.S.C. § 107(3), are reasonable in relation to the purpose of the copying. The Supreme Court has stated: "Parody's humor, or in any event its comment, necessarily springs from recognizable allusion to its object through distorted imitation. Its art lies in the tension between a known original and its parodic twin. When parody takes aim at a particular original work, the parody must be able to 'conjure up' at least enough of that original to make the object of its critical wit recognizable."

There is no dispute that Big Dog used actual photographs to copy the recognizable characteristics of THE ROCK and STONE COLD STEVE AUSTIN. The question is whether Big Dog took more than was reasonably required to "conjure up" the characters and persona of WWE's professional wrestling. The Supreme Court instructs, however, that a parodist's copying of more than is necessary to conjure up the original will not necessarily tip the third factor against fair use. Once Big Dog has taken enough to assure identification with the WWE property, the reasonableness of taking additional aspects of the original property depends on the extent to which the overriding purpose and character of the merchandise is to parody the original, as well as "the likelihood that the parody may serve as a market substitute for the original." Based on the foregoing, even if Big Dog has "copied every recognizable characteristic" of the WWE characters, this third factor carries very little, if any, weight against fair use when the first and fourth factors favor the parodist.

(4) The Effect on the Potential Market for or Value of the Copyrighted Work

The fourth fair use factor is "the effect of the use upon the potential market for or value of the copyrighted work." Because parody must be a transformative use, a parody is unlikely to serve as a market substitute for the original. "It is more likely that the new work will not affect the market for the original in any way cognizable under this factor. This is so because the parody and the original usually serve different market functions." Based on the foregoing, it is not difficult to determine that the balance in this instance markedly favors Big Dog.

Questions

1. What is the purpose of the fair use doctrine? Why is it an important exception to copyright protection?

2. Why must someone who is parodying another's work use a portion of the protected work in the parody?

3. What factors do the courts consider when determining whether the use of a copyrighted work qualifies as a "fair use"?

4. Which of the above factors carried the most weight in this case and why?

CONCLUSION

For sport organizations, effectively managing intellectual property is certainly becoming more complex. It requires the ability and knowledge to navigate technical statutory requirements for registering trademarks and copyrights, as well as the ability to understand and interpret court decisions explaining the scope of the rights and protections available. A successful sport manager must be able to integrate knowledge of these legal concepts with his or her daily decision-making strategies.

discussion questions

1. What are the five functions of a trademark?
2. Explain how fanciful, arbitrary, and suggestive marks differ and why they all are considered distinctive trademarks.
3. When is secondary meaning required to establish distinctiveness, and what is the seven-factor test for secondary meaning?
4. What are the elements of a trademark infringement claim? What is the most effective way to prove the first two elements?
5. Explain the parody defense to trademark infringement.
6. Explain the difference between trademark infringement and trademark dilution.
7. Explain the concepts of tarnishment and blurring.
8. According to *KST Electric*, when is a mark a famous mark?
9. What is the purpose of copyright law?
10. Explain the concept of fixation as it relates to copyrights.
11. Explain the concept of fair use and identify the four factors used when determining fair use as it relates to copyright.
12. Assume a city hosts an annual 10K run that originates at a local park, which contains a statue of a man, woman, and child. For purposes of decoration and promotion, the event organizers decide to fit each statue with an event T-shirt so when people walk or drive by they will be reminded of the upcoming event. Would this decoration violate the sculptor's moral rights (right of integrity) such that he or she could prevent the distortion of the artwork under the VARA?

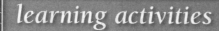

learning activities

1. Internet Assignment: Go to the website for the United States Patent and Trademark Office, www.uspto.gov, and search for trademarks of a popular sport organization or sport product, such as the New York Yankees, Dallas Cowboys, National Football League, or Reebok. See if you can find the following information about the marks: owner, date of first use, date of registration, registration number, description of the mark, and type of mark.

2. The rapid growth of Internet fantasy sports has again raised the question whether sports statistics are information in the public domain or copyrightable information. What characteristics of player profiles and performance statistics are most likely to be determined as copyrightable? Base your arguments on the *Motorola* and *Feist* cases discussed in the chapter.

CASE STUDY

Judy Garcia is co-owner and CEO of Jock & Judy's, a sports bar and sport memorabilia outlet. Garcia opened her first location about eight years ago and added two more stores in the last two years. The stores are located in Louisville, Cincinnati, and St. Louis. Judy has been using the following slogan in much of her print media for about a year: "Just Eat It—At J & J's Sports Bar."

Judy has just received a letter from an attorney for Nike, Inc. informing her that they consider Garcia's use of the slogan "Just Eat It" to be an infringement of their trademark slogan "Just Do It." Garcia cannot decide whether she should discontinue the use of the slogan or take on the giant corporation. If Garcia has to change her slogan now, she will have to cancel thousands of dollars of promotional material. She also is concerned that if she changes the slogan and advertising campaign, it will send a message that her business is unstable. (This activity was modified from the Dickson, Maxwell, and Kurtz, 2001, teaching case.)

1. What factors will a court consider in deciding whether Garcia's mark infringes on Nike's slogan?

2. What business factors will Garcia need to take into consideration in deciding how to proceed?

3. What should Garcia have done when she selected the slogan?

4. Create four potential new names for Garcia's business, including: (a) a fanciful name; (b) an arbitrary name; (c) a suggestive name; and (d) a descriptive name.

5. Using the USPTO's database, conduct a preliminary search for one of your potential names to see if it is available.

considering . . .   ANALYSIS & DISCUSSION

Generic Marks (p. 574)

Papa Joe's use of the term "The Big Game" would likely be considered a generic term; thus, Papa Joe's could not register the mark to prevent others from using it. The NFL would not be able to prevent Papa Joe's from referring to the Super Bowl with a generic term such as "The Big Game," even though the connection may be obvious to the average consumer.

R E F E R E N C E S

Cases

Affiliated Hosp. Prods., Inc. v. Merdel Game Mfg. Co., 513 F.2d 1183 (2d Cir. 1975).

Anheuser-Busch, Inc. v. Andy's Sportswear, Inc., 1996 U.S. Dist. LEXIS 15583 (N.D. Cal. 1996).

Anti-Monopoly, Inc. v. General Mills Fun Group, Inc., 611 F.2d 296 (9th Cir. 1979).

Board of Regents, The University of Texas System v. KST Electric, 550 F. Supp. 2d 657 (W.D. Tex. 2008).

Board of Supervisors of LSU v. Smack Apparel Company, 438 F. Supp. 2d 653 (E.D. La 2006).

Bouchat v. Baltimore Ravens, Inc., 241 F.3d 350 (4th Cir. 2000).

Campbell v. Acuff-Rose Music, Inc., 510 U.S. 569 (1994).

Dallas Cowboys Cheerleaders, Inc. v. Pussycat Cinema, 604 F.2d 200 (2d Cir. 1979).

Feist Publ'ns, Inc. v. Rural Tel. Serv. Co., 499 U.S. 340 (1991).

Hoopla Sports & Entertainment, Inc. v. Nike, Inc., 947 F. Supp. 347 (N.D. Ill. 1996).

In re Seats, Inc., 757 F.2d 274 (Fed. Cir. 1985).

Indianapolis Colts, Inc. v. Metropolitan Baltimore Football Club, Ltd., 34 F.3d 410 (7th Cir. 1994).

Major League Baseball Props., Inc. v. Sed Olet Denarius, Ltd., 817 F. Supp. 1103 (S.D.N.Y. 1993).

March Madness Athletic Ass'n, L.L.C. v. Netfire, Inc., 2003 U.S. Dist. LEXIS 14941 (N.D. Tex. 2003).

Moseley v. V Secret Catalogue, Inc., 123 S. Ct. 1115 (2003).

NASCAR v. Sharle, 184 Fed. Appx. 270, U.S. App. LEXIS 15254 (3rd Cir. 2006).

National Football League Props., Inc. v. Wichita Fall Sportswear, Inc., 532 F. Supp. 651 (W.D. Wash. 1982).

NBA v. Motorola, Inc., 105 F.3d 841 (2d Cir. 1997).

Nitro Leisure Prods., L.L.C. v. Acushnet Co., 341 F.3d 1356 (Fed. Cir. 2003).

Polaroid Corp. v. Polaroid, Inc., 319 F.2d 830 (7th Cir. 1963).

Pro-Football, Inc. v. Harjo, 284 F. Supp. 2d 96 (D.D.C. 2003).

Qualitex Co. v. Jacobson Prods. Co., Inc., 514 U.S. 159, 115 S. Ct. 1300, 131 L. Ed. 2d 248 (1995).

Toys "R" Us, Inc. v. Akkaoui, 1996 U.S. Dist. LEXIS 17090 (N.D. Cal. 1996).

University of Ga. Athletic Ass'n v. Laite, 756 F.2d 1535 (11th Cir. 1985).

University of Kansas v. Sinks, 565 F. Supp. 2d 1216 (D. Kan., 2008), *reh. denied*, 565 F. Supp. 2d 1216 (D. Kan., 2008).

USOC v. America's Team Properties, Inc., Cancellation Petition No. 92025167, Trademark Trial and Appeal Board (2003, September 30).

USOC v. San Francisco Arts & Athletics, Inc., 107 S. Ct. 2971 (1987).

World Wrestling Federation Entertainment, Inc. v. Big Dog Holdings, Inc. 280 F. Supp. 2d 413 (W.D. Pa., 2003).

Statutes

Anti-Cybersquatting Consumer Protection Act of 1999, 15 U.S.C. § 1125(d) (2003).

Copyright Act of 1976, 17 U.S.C. §§ 101–1332 (2003).

Digital Millennium Copyright Act, 17 U.S.C. 1201–1205 (2003).

Federal Trademark Dilution Act of 1995, 15 U.S.C. § 1125(c) (Supp. II 1996).

Sonny Bono Copyright Term Extension Act of 1998, 17 U.S.C. § 301–304 (2003).

Ted Stevens Olympic and Amateur Sports Act of 1998, 36 U.S.C. §§ 220501, 220506(a), and 220506(c)(3) (2000).

Trademark Act of 1946, 15 U.S.C. §§ 1051, 1114, 1127 et seq. (2003).

U.S. CONST. art. I, § 8, cl. 8.

Visual Artists Rights Act of 1990, 17 U.S.C. § 106A (2003).

Other Sources

Black's Law Dictionary. (2004). St. Paul, MN: West Publishing Co.

Dickson, J., Maxwell, K., & Kurtz, J. Tires r us: A case study in choosing a trade name or service mark. *The Journal of Legal Studies Education, 19*(1), 83–106.

Federal judge dismisses artist's claim against Alabama. (2005, November 18). *Sports Litigation Alert, 2*(19), 17.

Gluck, J. (2009, June 8). Sam Bass 'heartbroken' over Kyle Busch's guitar smash. Scenedaily.com. Retrieved June 18, 2009, from http://www.scenedaily.com/news/articles/nationwideseries/Artist_Bass_heartbroken_over_Kyle_Buschs_guitar_smash.html.

Grossman, M., & Feinsilver, A. (2001). A legal primer on domain names and trademarks. *Gigalaw.com.* Retrieved January 6, 2004, from www.gigalaw.com/articles/2001-all/grossman-2001-01-all.html.

In, S. (2002). Note: Death of a trademark: Genericide in the Digital Age. *The Review of Litigation, 21,* 159–189.

Lackman, E. M. (2003). Slowing down the speed of sound: A transatlantic race to head off digital copyright infringement. *Fordham Intellectual Property, Media, & Entertainment Law Journal, 13,* 1161–1208.

McCarthy, J. T. (2001). *McCarthy on Trademarks and Unfair Competition* (5th ed.). Deerfield, IL: Clark Boardman Callaghan.

Morgan Lewis pitches web address to Major League Baseball. (2000, September 6). Joint Press Release for Morgan, Lewis, Bockius and Major League Baseball.

Nimmer, M. B., & Nimmer, D. (2004). *Nimmer on Copyright,* Vol. 1, § 218(H)(3) and 203 (B).

Oswald, L. J. (1999). "Tarnishment" and "blurring" under the Federal Trademark Dilution Act of 1995. *American Business Law Journal, 36,* 255–300.

Richman, M. B., & Borden, V. W. (2003). Permitted but unauthorized use of trademarks. *The Legal Intelligencer, 229*(27), 5–9.

Salter, J. (2009, December 14). The North Face files suit over "South Butt" parody. *San Francisco Examiner.* Retrieved January 22, 2010, from http://www.sfexaminer.com/nation/the-north-face-files-lawsuit-claims-the-south-butt-parody-brand-is-trademark-infringement-79246772.html.

Schechter, F. I. (1927). The rational basis of trademark protection. *Harvard Law Review, 40,* 813–833.

United States Patent and Trademark Office. (2004). Trademark electronic application system. Retrieved March 6, 2006, from www.uspto.gov/teas/index.html.

Warren-Mikes, E. L. (1999). Note: December madness: The Seventh Circuit's creation of dual use in *Illinois High School Association v. GTE Vantage. Northwestern University Law Review, 93,* 1009–1052.

Washington Redskins win reinstatement of federal trademark registrations. (2003, November). *Entertainment Law Reporter, 25*(6). Available online at: Lexis-Nexis.com/universe.

Zamboni, Inc. (2006). Proper use of Zamboni trademarks. Retrieved February 1, 2006, from www.zamboni.com/copyright.html#trademark.

WEBSITE RESOURCES

www.copyright.gov ▪ The site for the U. S. Copyright Office provides resources for authors and for online copyright registration.

www.law.uconn.edu/homes/swilf/ip/statutes/vara.htm ▪ View the full text of the Visual Artists Rights Act at the University of Connecticut's law site. This act prevents others from falsely claiming authorship of a work or from distorting or misrepresenting a visual work.

www.uspto.gov ▪ The United States Patent and Trademark Office maintains a searchable database of registered trademarks and patents. This database should be used to search for similar marks when a new trademark is being developed.

www.ipmenu.com ▪ This website for Global Intellectual Property offers resources on patents, trademarks, design, domain names, and copyright.

Promotional and Operational Issues in Marketing

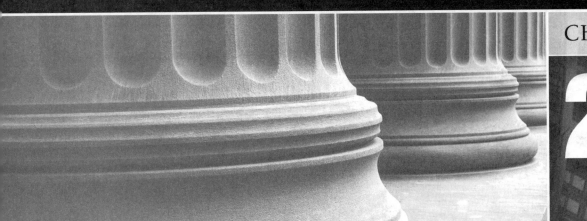

INTRODUCTION

I n the previous chapter, we discussed the legal issues associated with acquiring and protecting intellectual property (IP) rights. Intellectual property rights are the cornerstone for any sport organization to establish effective branding strategies and to begin implementing effective marketing strategies. This chapter focuses on how legal issues arise throughout the process of implementing marketing strategies. The chapter is divided into two sections relating to marketing implementation. The first section examines legal issues arising when sport organizations communicate about their products and services through advertising. It includes such topics as false advertising, deceptive trade practices, consumer protection, and Constitutional limitations on commercial speech. The next section examines legal issues arising when sport organizations interact with consumers, strategic partners, competitors, and the media, covering such topics as commercial sales transactions, licensing and sponsorship contracts, broadcasting agreements, publicity rights, ambush marketing, invasion of privacy, and defamation. Exhibit 20.1 outlines the managerial contexts, legal issues, and relevant laws and cases covered in this chapter.

EXHIBIT	20.1	Management contexts in which issues related to marketing promotion and operations may arise, with relevant laws and cases.

MANAGEMENT CONTEXT	MAJOR LEGAL ISSUES	RELEVANT LAW	ILLUSTRATIVE CASES
Advertising development and placement	False advertising and deceptive trade practices regulations	FTC Act State DTPA	
	Other regulations or limitations of commercial speech or advertising activities	First Amendment free speech	*Central Hudson, Bailey, Nike*
Celebrity endorsements	Scope of the right of publicity	Unfair competition law and Tort of Invasion of Privacy	*Haelan, Zacchini, C.B.C. v. M.L.B., Pirone*
	Liability of celebrity endorsers for false product claims	FTC Act, 16 CFR § 255.0	*FTC v. Garvey*
Competitors' advertising practices	Ambush marketing and misappropriation of goodwill	Common law misappropriation	*NHL v. Pepsi, NFL v. Delaware*
		Lanham Act—trademark infringement	*NCAA v. Coors*
Sales	Consumer contract rights	Uniform Commercial Code	
Developing partnerships and business relationships	Negotiating and drafting effective contracts	Contract and agency law	
Interacting with and through the media	Liability for disclosure of private information	FERPA; Tort of Invasion of Privacy	
	Defamation	Tort of Defamation	*Woy, Montefusco, Curtis Publishing*

COMMUNICATIONS WITH
CONSUMERS THROUGH ADVERTISING

S port marketers naturally want to communicate with their customers and clients about a sport organization's goods and services. This communication is usually accomplished through some method of advertising. The sport marketer confronts a number of state and federal regulations on advertising. False advertising and deceptive consumer practices are illegal under a variety of federal laws. In addition, all 50 states have adopted some form of protection for consumers and businesses from unfair, false, or deceptive advertising and consumer practices (Sheldon & Carter, 2004). Most of the regulations are designed to protect consumers from false and deceptive advertising.

Restraints on advertising and communications necessarily implicate the First Amendment guarantee of free speech because commercial speech enjoys limited constitutional protection from governmental restraint. (See Chapter 7 for information on the First Amendment protections relating to speech.) The modern commercial speech doctrine reflects an understandable desire to empower government to protect people from fraudulent or deceptive trade and consumer practices and to promote the general public welfare. Thus, we first explain the commercial speech doctrine, which permits governmental regulation and control over commercial speech activities such as advertising and business practices. Next, we discuss the application of several specific government regulations on commercial speech as they apply to the sport industry.

Commercial Speech Doctrine

To fully understand the interplay between government restraints on speech and the First Amendment, we must refresh ourselves on the First Amendment. The First Amendment to the U. S. Constitution describes the limitations imposed upon the government if and when it attempts to inhibit expressive activities such as prayer, speech, assembly, and the press. These constitutional limitations were initially presented in Chapter 7. In this chapter, we expand on the First Amendment protections specifically as they relate to what is known as commercial speech. The key question is whether speech by a commercial enterprise such as Nike or the National Football League is entitled to any protection under the free speech provisions of the First Amendment. The amount of protection, if any, will then determine whether the government can regulate that speech without violating the Constitution.

All speech is not protected under the First Amendment, and some speech receives more protection than other types of speech. For example, obscene speech receives no First Amendment protection, while political speech receives the highest level of protection. The Supreme Court has held that the First Amendment embodies the principle that free expression is both vital in its own right and essential to representative government. Political speech, even if erroneous or false, has been protected from government interference. The Supreme Court in *New York Times v. Sullivan* (1964) observed that "erroneous statement is inevitable in free debate, and it must be protected if the freedoms of expression are to have the 'breathing space' that they need to survive" (pp. 271–272). Thus, a government restraint on political speech will be subject to exacting scrutiny so as not to violate the First Amendment (*McIntyre v. Ohio Elections Commission,* 1995). Now that we know politcal speech receives the highest constitutional protection, let's examine what level of protection is afforded commercial speech.

Commercial speech has been defined as speech that does no more than propose a commercial transaction. Advertising is the most notable example of commercial speech; the Focus Cases in this section provide several more examples. Prior to 1975, it appeared clear that commercial advertising simply was not "speech" for the purposes of the First Amendment (Piety, 2005). However, in 1975, the Supreme Court in *Bigelow v. Virginia* suggested that it was erroneous to assume advertising was entitled to no First Amendment protection. And the Supreme Court affirmed in *Virginia State Board of Pharmacy v. Virginia Citizens Consumer Council* (1976) that speech does not lose its First Amendment protection "because money is spent to project it" (p. 761). The protection for commercial speech flows more from the consumer's right to hear about the information rather than the advertiser's right to speak (Piety, 2005).

Now that it is clear commercial speech is entitled to some protection under the First Amendment, the next step is to determine when the government may regulate or restrict commercial speech. As presented in Chapter 7, when the government attempts to regulate or restrict a constitutionally protected right, those regulations are subject to some level of scrutiny or review to determine if they are constitutionally permissible. As mentioned above, for example, restrictions on political speech are subject to strict or exacting scrutiny similar to that used for suspect classifications under the Equal Protection Clause. However, government restrictions on commercial speech must meet an intermediate level of constitutional scrutiny.

The intermediate level of scrutiny requires that the governmental purpose or objectives must be *sufficiently important* to warrant the intrusion on the First Amendment and that the proposed restrictions be *directly connected* to achieving those objectives. In other words, there must be a *direct connection* between the *important* goals or objectives of the regulation and the actual accomplishment of those goals or objectives. The Supreme Court also held in *Central Hudson Gas & Electric Co. v. Public Service Commission of New York* (1980) that the First Amendment only protects commercial speech that is truthful and not misleading. Thus, governmental restrictions on false, untrue, or deceptive advertising have been deemed constitutional restraints on commercial speech.

The Supreme Court developed a four-factor test in *Central Hudson* (1980) to determine whether a state's restrictions on commercial speech satisfy intermediate scrutiny (see Exhibit 20.2).

EXHIBIT	20.2	The four-factor test to determine whether a state's restrictions on commercial speech are constitutional (*Central Hudson,* 1980).

1. The commercial speech must concern a lawful activity and not be misleading.

2. The state must have a substantial interest in the restriction of the speech.

3. The regulation must directly advance the state's interest.

4. The regulation must be no more extensive than necessary to meet the state's interest.

The following Focus Case presents an example of how the *Central Hudson* factors, along with the intermediate level of scrutiny, are applied when a state imposes restraints on commercial speech.

Bailey v. Kentucky Racing Commission

496 F. Supp. 2d 795 (W.D. Ky. 2004)   **FOCUS CASE**

FACTS

The Kentucky Racing Commission (now known as the Kentucky Horse Racing Authority, KHRA) imposed rules prohibiting jockeys from wearing advertising on their clothing during a race. This rule first came under scrutiny soon after the 129th Kentucky Derby in 2003 when a group of jockeys (the Bailey plaintiffs) were denied permission to wear commercial endorsement patches during the 2003 Spring Meet at Keeneland Racetrack in Lexington, Kentucky. Thoroughbred horse racing is subject to tremendous state regulation and control in states with a horse racing industry. Kentucky, like other states with horse racing, has expressly designated horse racing as an important and vital industry to the state and has vested a horse racing commission with broad authority and responsibility to regulate, control, and maintain the industry. As the 130th Kentucky Derby approached, many jockeys desired to pursue sponsorship opportunities; thus the Bailey plaintiffs filed suit to enjoin enforcement of the advertising ban on commercial sponsorships during the 2004 Kentucky Derby.

HOLDING

The district court ruled in favor of the Bailey plaintiffs.

RATIONALE

It was undisputed that the Bailey plaintiffs' desire to wear corporate logos was expressing commercial speech (essentially an advertisement): thus the four-factor test established in *Central Hudson* (1980) must be used to determine whether the state's restrictions on commercial speech were unconstitutional. (See Exhibit 20.2.) It was undisputed that the Bailey plaintiffs' commercial speech was neither unlawful nor misleading and that the state has a substantial interest in regulating the sport of horse racing. However, the state needed to demonstrate how this *specific regulation was directly connected* to the accomplishment of its stated goal or objective (emphasis added).

The KHRA is authorized to promulgate administrative regulations prescribing conditions under which all horse racing is conducted and establishing requirements for jockeys and apprentice jockeys (810 KAR 1:1009). These regulations cover such areas as license qualifications, amateur status, weight allowances for apprentices, jockey fees, and the contested regulation—jockey attire. Section 14 of the Kentucky regulations states that "Advertising, promotional, or cartoon symbols or wording which in the opinion of the commission are not in keeping with the traditions of the turf shall be prohibited" (810 KAR 1:009, Section 14(3)).

Thus, on its face, the objective of the regulation is to ensure that jockey attire and appearance are in keeping with the "traditions of the turf." However, KHRA produced no evidence of what specific "traditions" would warrant restricting advertising or other symbols on jockeys' attire. It was arguable that traditions of the turf related to preserving the genteel, pristine appearance, and atmosphere at the racetracks. Permitting logos on jockeys' attire could create the commercialized appearance that is often associated with other sports but is not in keeping with the traditions of the turf. However, despite these obvious arguments, the KHRA instead argued that the state interest at stake was protecting the integrity of horse racing and that the restriction on sponsor logos and advertising would (1) ensure an unobstructed view of the jockey if misconduct is alleged and (2) foster confidence in the betting public by avoiding collusion among jockeys sponsored by the same advertiser. The court did not question that Kentucky's interest in avoiding collusion connected with horse racing was a "laudable objective." However, "to intrude on one's First Amendment rights . . . requires more justification than simply establishing a substantial state interest. Logically enough, *the regulation that limits speech must itself bear some direct and material relationship to that interest*" (p. 15). The regulation at issue and as applied appears to have nothing to do with assessing foul play or avoiding collusion. Instead, the express purpose of the regulation related entirely to a jockey's appearance as that appearance reflects on maintaining the traditions of the turf.

Notice that the federal district court did not question that the Commonwealth of Kentucky had an *important* interest in regulating the sport of horse racing, including the attire and manner of dress of the jockeys. However, the government must do more than just have an important objective for regulating speech, even commercial speech. There must be a "reasonable fit" between the regulation and the objective. If the regulation and the objective are not sufficiently related or connected, the regulation is likely to be found unconstitutional. The decision in the Kentucky Derby jockey case precipitated immediate response from several sectors of the horse racing industry. Shortly after the court's ruling, the KHRA issued a statement that in fairness to all jockeys, the KHRA would apply the ruling to all jockeys racing in Kentucky ("Press Release," 2004). Churchill Downs announced "House Rules" for jockey advertising and said it would allow jockeys competing in the 2004 Spring Meet and 130th running of the Kentucky Derby and Kentucky Oaks to wear advertisements and promotional logos on their race riding apparel; however they would be subject to several exceptions and conditions (Churchill Downs, 2004).

It was undisputed that the speech involved in the Kentucky Derby jockey case was commercial speech, but this is not always so clear. For example, if a business speaks about matters related to commerce or its business, must that be commercial speech simply because the speaker is a business? What if the matters being discussed are also questions of public policy, as in *Nike, Inc. v. Kasky* (2002), presented below. To determine whether particular speech is properly categorized as commercial or noncommercial speech requires consideration of three elements: the speaker, the intended audience, and the content of the message. See Exhibit 20.3.

In the following Focus Case, the California Supreme Court had to determine whether statements made by Nike as part of a public relations campaign would be considered commercial or noncommercial speech. The distinction is impor-

Elements used by courts to categorize speech as commercial (*Nike, Inc. v. Kasky,* 2002).	EXHIBIT	20.3

The speaker: Someone engaged in commerce. Generally involved in the production, distribution, or sale of goods or services, or acting on behalf of a person so engaged.

The intended audience: Actual or potential buyers or customers of the speaker's goods or services, or persons acting for actual or potential buyers or customers, or persons (such as reporters or reviewers) likely to repeat the message to or otherwise influence actual or potential buyers or customers.

The factual content of the message: Message is commercial in character. In the context of regulation of false or misleading advertising, this typically means that the speech consists of representations of fact about the business operations, products, or services of the company made for the purpose of promoting sales or other commercial transactions.

tant since the California deceptive trade practices act applies only to commercial speech. Thus, if Nike's statements were determined to be noncommercial speech, it would not be subject to the state law.

Nike, Inc. v. Kasky

27 Cal. 4th 939, 45 P.3d 24, 119 Cal. Rptr. 2d 296 (Cal. 2002)	**FOCUS CASE**

FACTS

Plaintiff Marc Kasky sued Nike on behalf of the general public of the State of California under Business and Professions Code §§ 17204 and 17535. Nike manufactures and sells athletic shoes and apparel. Most of Nike's products are manufactured by subcontractors in China, Vietnam, and Indonesia. Beginning at least in October 1996 with a report on the television news program *48 Hours,* and continuing at least through November and December of 1997 with the publication of articles in the *Financial Times,* the *New York Times,* the *San Francisco Chronicle,* the *Buffalo News,* the *Oregonian,* the *Kansas City Star,* and the *Sporting News,* various persons and organizations alleged that, in the factories where Nike products are made, workers were paid less than the applicable local minimum wage; required to work overtime; allowed and encouraged to work more overtime hours than applicable local law allowed; subjected to physical, verbal, and sexual abuse; and exposed to toxic chemicals, noise, heat, and dust without adequate safety equipment, in violation of applicable local occupational health and safety regulations.

In response to this adverse publicity, Nike made statements to the California consuming public. Kasky alleged that Nike's statements were false and misleading. Nike made these statements in press releases, in letters to newspapers, in a letter to university presidents and athletic directors, and in other documents distributed for public relations purposes. Nike also bought full-page advertisements in leading newspapers to publicize a report that GoodWorks International, LLC, had prepared under a contract with Nike.

HOLDING

The California Supreme Court concluded that Nike's allegedly false and misleading statements were properly characterized as commercial speech.

RATIONALE

The issue here is whether the defendant corporation's false statements are commercial or noncommercial speech as determined by the constitutional free speech analysis under the state and federal constitutions. The Supreme Court has stated that the category of commercial speech consists at its core of "speech proposing a commercial transaction." The high court also cautioned, as it had in past cases, that statements may properly be categorized as commercial "notwithstanding the fact that they contain discussions of important public issues" and that "advertising which 'links a product to a current public debate' is not thereby entitled to the constitutional protection afforded noncommercial speech." The Court further explained that "[a]dvertisers should not be permitted to immunize false or misleading product information from government regulation simply by including references to public issues." (See Exhibit 20.3.)

Here, the first element—a commercial speaker—is satisfied because the speakers, Nike and its officers and directors, are engaged in commerce. Specifically, they manufacture, import, distribute, and sell consumer goods in the form of athletic shoes and apparel.

The second element—an intended commercial audience—is also satisfied. Nike's letters to university presidents and directors of athletic departments were addressed directly to actual and potential purchasers of Nike's products because college and university athletic departments are major purchasers of athletic shoes and apparel.

The third element—representations of fact of a commercial nature—is also present. In describing its own labor policies and the practices and working conditions in factories where its products are made, Nike was making factual representations about its own business operations. In speaking to consumers about these working conditions and labor practices, Nike addressed matters within its own knowledge. Thus Nike was in a position to verify the truth of any factual assertions it made on these topics. To the extent that application of these laws may make Nike more cautious and cause it to make greater efforts to verify the truth of its statements, these laws will serve the purpose of commercial speech protection by "insuring that the stream of commercial information flow[s] cleanly as well as freely" (*Va. Pharmacy Bd. v. Va. Consumer Council, supra,* 425 U.S., p. 772 (96 S. Ct., p. 1831)).

Applying the reasoning of the California Supreme Court in *Nike v. Kasky,* could statements during an interview made by an organization's representative, such as Roger Goodell, commissioner of the NFL, be deemed commercial speech because he had commercial motives? Consider the number of sport administrators who have testified before Congress on the matter of steroid use in professional sports, clearly an issue of significant interest to the public. When they speak in that setting is their speech considered private speech relevant to a public debate? If their motive in speaking is in part to influence consumers' perception of their league or company, is the speech more correctly classified as commercial speech? All of these questions relate to the critical distinguishing characteristic between political or private speech and commercial speech—that is, the tolerance of false speech when made in a political or public debate and the intolerance for false speech when made in the commercial marketplace. A first step in understanding the various laws regulating advertising and business practices is knowing that they apply only to speech that is categorized as commercial speech. Any application of those laws to noncommercial speech would be challenged as unconstitutional.

Consumer Protection Laws

A **consumer** is any individual who purchases goods or services for personal or household consumption. Consumer protection laws arose as a response to the perceived inequities of the common law following America's change to a consumer society. The common law as it relates to consumers and consumer transactions was developed in times when merchants and customers engaged in face-to-face transactions and all parties were required to protect their own interests. This was known as the doctrine of **caveat emptor**—let the buyer beware. However, this doctrine left consumers without a remedy in consumer transactions by placing the burden on the buyer to inspect goods prior to purchase and to ensure they conformed to expectations. The consumer could rely only on himself or herself when entering into business transactions.

Under federal law, the Federal Trade Commission (FTC) Act is the basic consumer protection statute. It empowers the FTC to enforce prohibitions against "unfair or deceptive acts or practices in or affecting commerce," including prohibiting false or deceptive advertising (15 U.S.C. § 45(a)(1)). The FTC Act empowers the Federal Trade Commission to prevent trade practices that are unfair or deceptive and thereby harmful to consumers. The individual consumer may not bring a private action under the FTC Act; instead, alleged violations of the FTC Act are investigated by the FTC.

Recognizing that the FTC could not fully protect consumers, state legislatures began enacting their own consumer protection laws to protect the public. Today each of the 50 states has adopted consumer protection laws related to false or deceptive advertising. However, the specific scope of the consumer protection laws varies from state to state because each state may adopt various forms of model acts or create its own unique consumer protection laws. Sport marketers must take care to become informed about the specific consumer protection laws applicable in the states in which they work.

All states have also passed Deceptive Trade Practices Acts (DTPAs). DTPAs prohibit deceptive acts or practices in the conduct of trade or commerce, along with a laundry list of deceptive trade practices relating to unfair competition. They were enacted in response to the consumer empowerment movement of the 1960s and are patterned after the FTC Act. Most of these statutes provide for enforcement either by the state attorney general's office or an administrative agency in charge of consumer protection.

In general, the FTC Act regulates business practices that are either deceptive or unfair (15 U.S.C. § 45(a)(1)). According to the FTC Act, advertising (1) must be truthful and nondeceptive; (2) must have evidence to back up claims; and (3) cannot be unfair (Federal Trade Commission Regulations, 2001). Not every deceptive practice is unfair, and vice versa. Thus we focus first on deceptive practices, since those are more likely to involve advertising.

Deceptive business practices: False advertising

The FTC has issued a Deception Policy Statement defining a **deceptive advertisement** as one that contains a statement or omission that is likely to mislead a reasonable consumer and that is important to the consumer's decision to buy or use the product (Federal Trade Commission Regulations, 2001). Deception can result from innuendo, not just an outright false statement. In addition, deceptive advertising may cause consumers to make inferences that go beyond what is claimed in the ad (Burke, DeSarbo, Oliver, & Robertson, 1988; Gaeth & Heath, 1987).

Advertisements containing implied claims that are false may also meet the legal definition of deception (Sheldon & Carter, 2004, pp. 165–166). However, actions such as puffing, incomplete comparisons, and implied superiority claims can deceive the consumer within the limits of the law (Lord, Kim, & Putrevu, 1997).

The distinction between actual deception and sales puffing is not clear, but generally expressions of opinion not made as factual representations are considered **sales puffing**. For example, an advertising campaign used by the University of Louisville referring to the City of Louisville as the "Best College Sports Town in America" would be a clear example of puffing: exaggeration that is an expression of opinion, not actual product facts about the University of Louisville sports program or the city itself. Thus, a seller has some latitude in the use of sales puffing, but he may not misrepresent the benefits or virtues of his products or services. Thus, when a sport organization develops an advertising message containing specific factual claims about its products, those advertising claims must be truthful or have a reasonable basis. For example, assume Nike claims that in a recent *Consumer Reports* survey Nike's Shox "received CR's highest rating, 'excellent.'" If, in fact, the *Consumer Reports* survey rated the Nike shoe *among the highest rated shoes* and specifically found it to have *excellent cushioning capability,* Nike's factual claims may be considered untruthful and deceptive. If advertisements contain false or deceptive information, the FTC can conduct an investigation and impose fines and penalties against the advertiser.

The following hypothetical case illustrates how statements contained in advertising and public statements (as discussed earlier) may create a situation where a claim of false or deceptive advertising could be raised.

considering . . .   **DECEPTIVE ADVERTISING**

The following statement is made by a manager of a local health food store during an interview with a local newspaper: "Sport supplements do not pose any health risks for athletes." The newspaper is writing a story regarding sports supplements. The headline of the story reads: "Local Health Food Store Says Supplements Are Safe." The article is quite lengthy and ultimately concludes that many sports supplements are shipped in from foreign countries with little or no product testing. The manager of the store cuts out the first page of the article with the headline, makes a number of copies, and posts them throughout the store for customers to read while they shop. But the entire article, including the portion discussing the risks associated with sports supplements, is not included on the copied page.

Question

- Can either the manager's statements to the newspaper or his posting of the article be considered false or deceptive advertising?

Note how you would answer the question and then check your response using the Analysis & Discussion at the end of this chapter.

The restrictions imposed in the FTC Act are designed to protect consumers as a whole and assure that advertisers are truthful in their advertising to consumers. In addition to the remedies available under the FTC Act, competitors can sue under the Lanham Act. As we discussed in regard to trademark infringement, the Lanham Act permits individual and corporate consumers to enforce various protections provided for under the act. No federal agency is responsible for enforcement of the Lanham Act. The act permits an individual or company to sue another individual or company (its competitor) for false or misleading representations of facts, including **false advertising** (see Exhibit 20.4). It empowers companies and individuals with remedies that can be used to protect against deceptive business practices engaged in by competitors in the marketplace. The remedies provided in the Lanham Act for false advertising enable individuals and companies to protect their own interest in their intellectual property. The intended benefit is to avoid confusing consumers about the source or origin of products and services. The FTC Act and the Lanham Act work cooperatively to limit false advertising in the marketplace.

Specifically, the Lanham Act makes a defendant liable for false advertising where all of the following conditions are met:

1. the defendant made a misrepresentation in commercial advertising or promotion of goods, services, or commercial activities;
2. the misrepresentation actually deceived or tended to deceive its recipients;

Section 43(a) of the Lanham Act, pertaining to false advertising (15 U.S.C. § 1125(a)).   EXHIBIT   **20.4**

(1) Any person who, on or in connection with any goods or services, or any container for goods, uses in commerce any word, term, name, symbol, or device, or any combination thereof, or any false designation of origin, false or misleading description of fact, or false or misleading representation of fact, which—

(B) in commercial advertising or promotion, misrepresents the nature, characteristics, qualities, or geographic origin of his or her or another person's goods, services, or commercial activities, shall be liable in a civil action by any person who believes that he or she is or is likely to be damaged by such act.

3. the misrepresentation was likely to influence purchasing decisions;
4. the misrepresentation injured or was likely to injure the plaintiff; and
5. the misrepresentation was made in commerce.

Two recent cases provide good examples of how and when false advertising arise in sport.

First, Pepsi sued Coca-Cola, accusing Coke of false advertising and other unfair competition in connection with a two-week advertising campaign for Coke's Powerade ION4 sports drink (Berlik, 2009). In the advertising campaign, Powerade which is marketed as "the complete sports drink," was claimed to be superior to Pepsi's Gatorade due to Powerade's inclusion of trace amounts of two electrolytes, calcium and magnesium. According to the lawsuit, no evidence exists to suggest that the addition of these two minerals—especially in such tiny quantities—provides any nutritional or physiological benefits. Pepsi said Coke was misleading consumers when it displayed a photo of a Gatorade bottle cut in half alongside the slogan "Don't settle for an incomplete sports drink." As the trial moves forward, the key issues will be whether the statements in Coke's advertising were *actually* false and whether labeling Gatorade an "incomplete sports drink" tends to deceive consumers and/or influence purchasing decisions.

A second example involved the false advertising claims made in *Baden Sports, Inc. v. Kabushiki Kaisha Molten* (2008). A jury awarded Baden more than $8 million to compensate it for Molten's intentionally falsely advertising that its basketballs were "innovative technology that is proprietary to Molten." However, the court of appeals reversed the jury verdict, holding that since the claim of innovation was merely a claim that the technology was actually created or owned by Molten, rather than a claim relating to 'nature, characteristics, [or] qualities' of the basketballs themselves, the Lanham Act did not apply to such claims of authorship or invention" (*Baden Sports, Inc. v. Molten USA, Inc.*, 2009). In such cases, patent or copyright law was the appropriate remedy, not trademark law or false advertising.

These two cases demonstrate how closely advertising claims must be monitored, both from the perspective of the company making the claims and from the perspective of competitors. Even a two-week advertising campaign can have a tremendous impact on consumers. Seeking a legal remedy alone may not be an adequate response for marketers. Often companies will immediately counter what is believed to be a false or misleading advertisement with their own advertising campaign to correct the allegedly false claims. You may recall the ongoing ad wars between A.T.&T. and Verizon in which Verizon emphasizes its superior 3G coverage using the comparative maps (Paul, 2009). Even though A.T.&T. is pursuing legal action against Verizon, it also launched a full-scale advertising rebuttal.

Deceptive business practices: Unfair competition

The FTC's Policy Statement on Unfairness (1980) identifies three factors used to determine whether a business practice is unfair:

1. Whether the practice injures a consumer
2. Whether the practice violates public policy
3. Whether the practice is unethical or unscrupulous

With regard to the first factor, consumer injury, three additional criteria must be considered:

a. The injury is substantial (trivial or speculative harms are not sufficient).
b. The injury could not reasonably have been avoided.
c. The injury is not outweighed by any countervailing benefits to consumers or competition. (FTC, 1980)

The evaluation of unfairness can consider whether the practice offends public policy, is immoral, or is unethically oppressive or unscrupulous. Generally, the FTC expects the marketplace to be self-regulating, and it relies on consumer choice to govern the market. However, sellers may adopt business practices that interfere with or hinder consumer choice and free market decisions. For example, withholding or failing to provide critical price or performance data may leave buyers with insufficient information to make informed comparisons. Some sellers may engage in overt coercion, such as dismantling a treadmill or other sport equipment for "inspection" and then refusing to reassemble it unless a service contract is signed. Others may exercise undue influence over a highly susceptible class of purchases, such as promoting a weight loss product as a cure for obesity.

With regard to violations of public policy, the policy must be clear and well-established in sources such as statutes, judicial decisions, or the Constitution. For example, a cigarette manufacturer's distribution of cigarette samples at a NASCAR race in such a way that they could come into the hands of children would likely violate the public interest and public policies in place to prevent underage smoking (FTC, 1980). Regarding benefits outweighing the injury, the FTC recognizes that many sales practices involve a tradeoff between consumer and competitive interests. For example, a seller may omit technical data on a product in order to reduce the cost it must charge for the product (FTC, 1980).

Deceptive business practices: Athlete endorsements

Athletes frequently endorse products or services. These product endorsements can earn a professional athlete substantial sums of money, and indeed some professional athletes can earn more from endorsements than their player salaries. The FTC advertising regulations do apply to athlete endorsements. 16 C.F.R. § 255.0 *et seq.* address endorsements. For a celebrity endorsement not to be deceptive, it must meet the following criteria:

1. The endorsement must reflect the honest opinion, findings, beliefs, or experience of the celebrity.
2. The advertiser must substantiate the accuracy of the celebrity's claims.
3. Efficacy claims must be substantiated, if capable of substantiation, if such claims were made by the advertiser.
4. If the advertisement claims the celebrity uses the product or service, the celebrity must in fact be a bona fide user.
5. The advertiser can use the endorsement only so long as it has a good faith belief that the celebrity continues to hold the views expressed in the advertisement.

As the regulation states, an endorsement would be considered deceptive if the athlete does not in fact use or prefer the product or service, and the advertiser may not continue to use the endorsement if the athlete stops using the product or service. Despite these specific regulations on celebrity endorsements, it is an area where enforcement is difficult. For example, unless a professional athlete who is a celebrity endorser admitted that he or she no longer used a product or did not in fact ever use the product, it would be difficult to prove a violation.

The FTC has attempted to impose endorser liability upon a former professional athlete, Steve Garvey (a former Los Angeles Dodgers player), in *FTC v. Garvey* (2004). The FTC sued Garvey based upon statements that Garvey made during an infomercial and television interviews endorsing weight loss products, the Enforma System products Fat Trapper, Fat Trapper Plus, and Exercise in a Bottle. The court held that Garvey's statements that Enforma was "all natural," "safe," and "it works" were sufficiently substantiated by some scientific materials Enforma had provided to him. The court observed that to find Garvey liable would require a showing that he was recklessly indifferent to the truth of his statements. In addition, his representations about his and his wife's personal weight loss experiences did reflect his honest opinion or beliefs about the product. Finally, the court acknowledged that there is no settled standard for the level of inquiry to which a celebrity spokesperson should be held when he is hired to participate in an advertisement. Although the court did not find Garvey liable, this case reveals the potential for liability of celebrity endorsers who make false or unsubstantiated claims about a product or misrepresent actual use of the product.

INTERACTIONS WITH CONSUMERS, STRATEGIC PARTNERS, AND COMPETITORS

The previous section identified several instances when managers working in marketing may encounter legal issues as they communicate about their products and services. This section focuses on the legal issues that may be implicated in a manager's interactions with consumers, strategic partners, and competitors.

Interactions with Consumers

Contracts and sales

Interactions with customers in the sale of products and services raise several unique challenges for sport managers, especially since contract law is a matter of state law. (Contract law principles were presented in Chapter 4.) If your organization is in one state and you want to sell products in another state, you must know which state's law will apply to the transaction. The easiest way to handle this problem is to include what is known as a *choice of law clause* in contracts. A choice of law clause simply specifies that the parties agree that if a dispute arises regarding the agreement, the law of a specified state will be applied to resolve the dispute. Since contract law is a matter of state common law, before agreeing to be bound by the law of a particular state, a sport marketer or sport manager should become familiar with the specific consumer protection statute and contract law in that state.

Due in part to the economic downturn in the late 2000s, coupled with the rising ticket prices and increased pressure on teams to generate revenue, some professional and college sports teams experienced strained relationships with their season ticket holders. For example, the Washington Redskins and New England Patriots were sharply criticized for suing several season ticket holders who were unable to pay for their season tickets and defaulted on their multi-year ticket agreements (Grimaldi, 2009). The practice is criticized since it is not clear whether the teams have actually suffered any damage from the ticket holders' breach. As we studied earlier, a party to a contract has a general duty to mitigate his damages. In many cases when a season ticket holder fails to pay for and forfeits the tickets, the team should be able to resell the tickets. The monies received from the resell should reduce the amount of damages owed from the ticket holder. However, the Redskins and Patriots ticket agreements include liquidated damages provisions that arguably give them a right to payment for every year on the multi-year ticket agreements regardless of whether or when they resell the tickets. A liquidated damages provision in the Patriots multi-year personal seat license (PSL) agreement was upheld by a Massachusetts appellate court in *NPS, LLC v. Minihane* (2008). In *NPS*, the terms of the PSL provided that Minihane would pay $3,750 per seat, per season from 2002 to 2011 for a total commitment of $75,000. The PSL agreement included a liquidated damages clause that further provided that in the event of a default, Minihane's payments would be accelerated such that he would be required to pay the entire balance remaining on the 10-year agreement. The trial court held that the accelerated damages clause was unenforceable because the amount due was "grossly disproportionate to a reasonable estimate of actual damages made at the time of contract formation." NPS appealed to the Massachusetts Supreme Judicial Court. The appellate court utilized a two-pronged test to determine the legality of the disputed clause:

1. the actual damages flowing from a breach must have been difficult to ascertain at the time of contracting, and
2. the sum agreed upon in the liquidated damages clause must represent a "reasonable forecast of the damages expected to occur in the event of a breach."

The court agreed the terms were harsh, but not unreasonably and grossly disproportionate to the actual damages. Thus, in this case, Minihane not only was ordered to pay the $65,500 owed on the PSL agreement, but he also lost his luxury seats (Saltzman & Finucane, 2008). Despite these examples, however, most teams elect not to sue defaulting ticket holders.

Ticket holders have also sued teams for a variety of reasons. A New York Jets season ticket holder sued the Patriots and Bill Belichick for deceiving consumers under the New Jersey Consumer Fraud Act and the New Jersey Deceptive Business Practices Act, asserting that secret videotaping by the Patriots violated contractual expectations and rights of Jets ticket holders. Two ticket holders for the Indianapolis 500 sued the speedway for breach of contract due to how the race track handled several postponements due to rain. The suit alleged that the race was postponed for the second time on May 29 and rescheduled on May 30 "subject to clear race conditions." However, according to the complaint, rain was forecast for the 30th; thus, the race should have been rescheduled to a date when clear weather was forecast. Finally, season ticket holders sued the New York Giants and Jets claiming that the Jets and Giants PSL agreements are illegal restraints of trade in violation of federal antitrust laws and a violation of the New Jersey Consumer Fraud Act (Larson, 2009). The suit alleges that 45,000 season ticket holders are forced to purchase a PSL for a one-time payment of between $1,000 to $25,000 in order to renew or purchase season tickets in the new stadium (*Oshinsky v. New York Football Giants, Inc*, 2009).

Generally, a sport organization's relationship with its season ticket holders is a mutually agreeable, harmonious, and beneficial relationship. However, the above disputes remind us of the importance of understanding basic contract law as we draft and negotiate season ticket renewal agreements and PSL agreements, and the importance of familiarizing ourselves with a state's consumer protection laws as we promote and sell our products and services.

Commercial transactions such as sales are also governed by the Uniform Commercial Code (UCC). The UCC is a model state law proposed by the National Conference of Commissioners on Uniform State Laws (NCCUSL). (You may recall that the NCCUSL also drafted the Uniform Athlete Agent Act, discussed in Chapter 10.) Much like the Uniform Athlete Agent Act, the objective of the UCC was to standardize commercial law between the states so that businesses conducting business in multiple states would have more consistency and predictability in the legal impact of their business transactions. The UCC has multiple parts, referred to as articles. Article 2, which applies to the sale of goods, is the focus of this section.

The UCC provides for each stage of a contractual relationship, from formation to performance. It includes provisions governing implied and express warranties, risk of loss, statute of frauds, parol evidence (terms of a written contract cannot be contradicted by evidence of a prior or contemporaneous oral agreement), interpretation, "gap filling" terms that apply when parties fail to reach agreement, breach of contract, and remedies for breach of contract.

A **sale** is a contract by which title to goods is transferred from one party to another for a price. **Goods** are tangible moveable objects and do not include real estate or securities. Most items of tangible personal property would be considered goods. Thus, many transactions that a sport marketer, sport manager, recreation manager, coach, or athletic director may enter into would be covered by the UCC. For example, retail merchandise (T-shirts, caps, jackets), athlete clothing (practice clothes, shoes, uniforms), fitness and training equipment, and computer equipment are all tangible items that are goods under the UCC.

One advantage of the UCC, in addition to its consistency and uniformity, is that it eliminates some of the rigid common law contract rules. For example, as you may recall from Chapter 4, the essential elements of an offer include identification of the parties, the subject matter, price to be paid, and time and place for performance. An offer that does not contain the price may not form the basis of a valid contract. However, the UCC allows missing elements to be supplied, rather than finding that a contract does not exist. The UCC requires only three elements for a valid contract:

1. An indication that an agreement exists
2. That the reflection of the agreement is signed by the party against whom enforcement is sought
3. A statement of the quantity of the goods to be sold

The UCC will fill in any terms that were left out or not addressed by the parties, including price, time and place for performance, payment terms, and remedies.

Sweepstakes and contests

Each state regulates sweepstakes and contests, so it is vital that sport marketers understand the laws of each state in which they plan to conduct a sweepstakes or contest. These are popular promotional strategies for sport organizations, and particularly for corporate sponsors, who often include sporting events among their prize packages.

In conducting contests and giveaways an issue may arise as to whether the contest represents some form of illegal gambling. Courts generally distinguish between bona fide entry fees, and bets or wagers. Generally, entry fees do not constitute bets or wagers where they are paid unconditionally for the privilege of participating in a contest, and the prize is for a specified amount that is guaranteed to be won by one of the contestants (but not the entity offering the prize). When the entry fees and prizes are unconditional and guaranteed, the element of risk necessary to constitute betting or wagering is missing.

An online fantasy sports contest was challenged as illegal gambling under New Jersey law in 2006 in the case *Humphrey v. Viacom*. The district court dismissed the case and stated that Courts throughout the country have long recognized that it would be "patently absurd" to hold that "the combination of an entry fee and a prize equals gambling" (*State of Arizona v. Am Holiday Ass'n, Inc.*, 1986). The district court cautioned that to hold otherwise would result in countless contests engaged in every day being construed as unlawful gambling, including "golf tournaments, bridge tournaments, local and state rodeos or fair contests, . . . literary or essay competitions, . . . livestock, poultry and produce exhibitions, track meets, spelling bees, beauty contests and the like," and contest participants and sponsors could all be subject to criminal liability (*Humphrey*, pp. 19–20).

According to the district court, gambling represents an activity where parties voluntarily make a bet or wager. The act of doing so inherently involves a monetary risk: participants can lose the wager and receive no corresponding reward. When multiple parties bet, they may pool their collective monies, creating a purse to be awarded to the winning party. All participants have the opportunity to win or lose the purse. Conversely, with online fantasy sports leagues, the court interpreted the fee as part of a contractual agreement between the online provider and the participant—not a wager or bet. The participant pays the fee, and the provider in turn offers services, including conducting a virtual draft where participants select players for their respective teams, providing player and team statistical data, and determining weekly and total season winners. Neither side places a bet or assumes a monetary risk with online fantasy sports. Both parties know in advance the terms of the agreement, and both benefit mutually from the arrangement.

Keep in mind, however, that the cases discussed above were in the State of New Jersey and each state may regulate these types of promotional activities differently. The best practice for a direct promotional giveaway would be to permit consumers to obtain at least one entry into the contest without a purchase or entry fee and to obtain any additional entries through the purchase of products or services.

Interactions with Strategic Partners

In today's competitive marketplace, especially in the sport industry, strategic alliances are more important than ever. We see these strategic alliances in a variety of relationships in sport, such as corporate sponsorships, facility naming rights, co-branding, and cross-promotion. All of these alliances offer advantages to a company wanting to connect to a specific customer base, particularly the customer base of major sporting events and sport leagues and teams. These relationships open doors to new markets that would otherwise take months to develop and penetrate. However, developing these strategic relationships involves a number of legal issues requiring research and extensive planning. To be successful in relationships with strategic partners, a sport manager often needs a solid knowledge of contract law and contract negotiation. In addition to having a good grasp of contract law, the sport manager should take a number of steps and precautions as these strategic alliances are formed to avoid costly litigation later (Wyman, 2003). These include researching the potential partner, planning an exit strategy, and preserving intellectual property.

Research your potential partner

Know as much as possible about potential partners before approaching them. Study not just their products and business structure, but also their management, corporate culture, third-party relationships, intellectual property rights, and financial condition before deciding whether they are the right partners for you. To appreciate the importance of research and advance planning, consider the number of corporate naming partners whose failing financial conditions created serious challenges for their sport organization partners. In 1999, Wayne Huizenga reworked the naming rights contract between the Miami Dolphins home field, "Pro Player Stadium," and Fruit of the Loom, owner of the Pro Player trademark and clothing line (Ratner, 2001). The new contract allowed Huizenga to cancel the agreement but with two months' notice. Shortly after the contract revision, in February 2000, Fruit of the Loom filed for Chapter 11 bankruptcy and began liquidating Pro Player. After a bankruptcy filing, the naming rights agreement becomes an asset of the bankrupt estate, which can create legal problems for the sport organization and stadium owner partner. Perry Ellis International purchased the Pro Player trademark from the bankrupt estate of Fruit of the Loom but did not acquire the naming rights agreement. Thus, while Huizenga was shopping for a new naming rights partner, Perry Ellis was getting exposure for the Pro Player mark for free.

Similar scenarios occur when corporate partners' reputation becomes tainted or when partners are drawn into a public controversy. For example, after Enron was involved in massive consumer fraud, the Houston Astros found themselves in a challenging position as they attempted to distance themselves from Enron and remove Enron as a stadium naming rights owner. Similarly, a number of financial organizations and automotive companies were criticized for entering or continuing sport sponsorship and naming rights agreements after receiving government bailout funds in 2008. For example, consider the 2009 college football bowl games. Citigroup, Inc., presented the Rose Bowl, and Capital One Financial Corp and GMAC were named sponsors of bowl games. All of these financial organizations received funds from the Troubled Asset Relief Program (TARP). Bank of America received $15 billion from TARP and sponsored the Pioneer Las Vegas Bowl. Eagle Bancorp, Inc., received approximately $38.2 million dollars and sponsored the Eagle Bank Bowl, held in RFK Stadium in December 2009.

In addition to sponsoring bowl games, a number of financial institutions entered into naming rights agreements with sport stadiums. AIG and Citibank renewed or continued multi-million-dollar sponsorship agreements with, respectively, Manchester United ($125 million) and the New York Mets ($400 million) after receiving taxpayer support. These activities were heavily criticized in the media and by public reform groups as vanity advertising and irresponsible (Crittenden, 2009). Most sponsors and sport organizations defended partnerships as a good marketing investment and an integrated marketing practice that had been committed to well before the economic crisis. Fortunately, these activities did not result in litigation, but the controversy illustrates that when entering into a partnership agreement, it is important for a sport organization to assess a partner's financial stability and understand how a partner's financial activities can impact the sport organization.

Plan an exit strategy

Strategic alliances will not endure indefinitely. At some point, one of the partners will seek to end it. How one ends a strategic relationship can be more important than how one entered the relationship. Plan the exit strategy, and include it in all agreements. At a minimum, address issues of who will retain the rights to any joint intellectual property and how the rights and responsibilities for ongoing operations will be divided.

As indicated above, an economic crisis can affect sport partnerships. Sport organizations need to be aware that their corporate partners may seek to escape contractual commitments or forgo future sponsorships. In 2008, for example, General Motors began scaling back its sports sponsorships (Thomas, 2008), and at least two suits were filed against sponsors who tried to pull out of a sponsorship. The Chicago Cubs sued Under Armour for Under Armour's alleged breach of their five-year, $10.8 million sponsorship contract (Katz, 2009), and the PGA Tour sued Ginn Development after Ginn dropped its sponsorship of the Champion's Tour Ginn Championship and the LPGA's Ginn Open. Ginn still had three years remaining on its sponsorship contract (AP, 2009). These lawsuits illustrate the importance of addressing whether extreme financial distress will permit one party to terminate the sponsorship agreement and the need to plan for such an eventuality when agreements are drafted and executed.

Preserve intellectual property

Preserving intellectual property (IP) is a crucial legal issue (see Chapter 19). Whether your organization owns the IP, the partner owns it, or it is co-owned, these issues must be addressed. This is especially important if you or your partner does not own the IP rights to a brand or a technology that is critical to the partnership.

Interactions with Competitors

Naturally, in a competitive marketplace, your competitors may take actions that interfere with your property or contract rights, or business opportunities. Two fairly common examples of this in the sport industry relate to the use of a professional athlete's image or likeness without his consent and a marketing practice known as ambush marketing. Both of these examples are explored in detail in the next section.

Right of publicity

Publicity rights are either created by common law or by statute and are a matter of state law. In other words, there is no federal right of publicity (McCarthy, 2003). Currently, 30 states have some form of protection for the right of publicity. Eleven states have recognized this right based upon common law, and 19 have statutory protection for publicity rights.

In essence, a right of publicity is the right of a famous individual, such as a professional athlete or sport celebrity, to control the commercial value and use of his or her name, likeness, and image. This right is protected based upon principles related to invasion of privacy claims. The common law tort of invasion of privacy has recognized that misappropriation of a person's identity, image, name, or likeness interferes with an individual's personal right to privacy. The modern right of publicity claims have evolved beyond the original misappropriation and personal invasion of privacy notions to protect the commercial interest a person has in the exclusive use of her identity. This is particularly relevant in the sport industry since athletes, coaches, sports reporters, and many others are highly visible, and a significant part of their success is connected to their ability to market their image and name (Grady, 2004).

The right of publicity was recognized in 1953 in *Haelan Laboratories, Inc. v. Topps Chewing Gum, Inc.* Haelan claimed that a competing chewing gum company, Topps, had induced professional baseball players to breach their baseball card contracts with Haelan. Topps argued that any contract between Haelan and the baseball players was merely a release that protected Haelan from liability for violating the players' right of privacy. However, the court acknowledged the commercial value present in a famous person's persona. The court stated,

> For it is common knowledge that many prominent persons (especially actors and ball-players), far from having their feelings bruised through public exposure of their likenesses, would feel sorely deprived if they no longer received money for authorizing advertisements, popularizing their countenances, displayed in newspapers, magazines, busses, trains and subways. This right of publicity would usually yield them no money unless it could be made the subject of an exclusive grant which barred any other advertiser from using their pictures. (Haelan, 1954, p. 868)

Elements for a right of publicity claim. The following elements have been developed in the Restatement (Third) of Unfair Competition, § 46 for a right of publicity claim:

1. Use of a person's identity
2. Without consent
3. To gain a commercial advantage

Note that the harm must be a commercial loss. The original misappropriation claim did not contain the commercial element—the nonconsensual use of a person's name just had to be done for some advantage to the person making the unauthorized use, and the plaintiff could recover for monetary losses as well as emotional harm (Grady, 2004). The right of publicity claim, on the other hand, requires that the advantage gained must be a commercial advantage, and the plaintiff can recover only for commercial losses. **Commercial advantage** is defined narrowly; typically, it includes uses in advertising or the promotion or sale of a product or service.

First Amendment limitations on publicity rights. The right of publicity does not prevent or prohibit the use of an athlete or sport celebrity's name, image, or likeness in news reporting, commentary, or entertainment, or in advertising related to those uses. This limitation of the right of publicity is intended to maintain a balance between First Amendment protections for a free press and free speech, and the individual privacy interests involved. A First Amendment challenge was raised in 1977 in *Zacchini v. Scripps-Howard Broadcasting Co.* The U. S. Supreme Court acknowledged the right of publicity and held that the defendant violated the common law rights of Hugo Zacchini, known professionally as the "Human Cannonball," by secretly taping his performance and then broadcasting it on the evening news. The Court acknowledged that the right of publicity is not always trumped by the right of free speech. Explaining the competing rights, the Court observed that "the rationale for protecting the right of publicity is the straightforward one of preventing unjust enrichment by the theft of goodwill. No social purpose is served by having the defendant get free some aspect of the plaintiff that would have market value and for which he would normally pay" (*Zacchini,* 433 U.S., 1977, p. 576).

The Zacchini Court also distinguished claims for right of publicity or name appropriateness from claims for defamation like those adjudicated in *New York Times v. Sullivan* (1964), which is presented later in this chapter. Because property interests are involved in right of publicity cases but not involved in defamation cases, the Court refused to apply the *New York Times v. Sullivan* "actual malice" standard that speech was privileged unless it was "knowingly false or was published with reckless disregard for the truth."

Since *Haelan* and *Zacchini,* several right of publicity cases have been decided affecting athletes and sport celebrities and involving First Amendment issues. Right of publicity cases often focus on the threshold legal question of whether the use of a person's name and identity is "expressive," in which case it is fully protected under the First Amendment and will probably trump a right of publicity claim, or "commercial," in which case it is less protected and a right of publicity claim will likely prevail. The use of a person's identity in news, entertainment, and creative works for the purpose of communicating information or expressive ideas about that person is protected "expressive" speech. On the other hand, the use of a person's identity for purely commercial purposes, like advertising goods or services or placing the person's name or likeness on merchandise, is not expressive speech but is instead commercial speech.

Expressive vs. commercial speech tests. The courts have struggled with how to distinguish between expressive speech and commercial speech. Since publicity rights are a matter of state law, each state that protects publicity rights must adopt a test for distinguishing expressive speech and commercial speech. At least three different tests have been used by the courts.

Relatedness test. Some states follow the Restatement (Third) of Unfair Competition and use a "relatedness" test that protects the use of another person's name or identity in a work that is "related to" that person. Related uses include "the use of a person's name or likeness in news reporting, whether in newspapers, magazines, or broadcast news[;] . . . use in entertainment and other creative works, including both fiction and nonfiction[;] . . . use as part of an article published in a fan magazine or in a feature story broadcast on an entertainment program[;] . . . dissemination of an unauthorized print or broadcast biography; [and use] of another's identity in a novel, play, or motion picture . . ." However, "if the name or likeness is used solely to attract attention to a work that is *not related* to the identified person, the user may be subject to liability for a use of the other's identity in advertising. . . ."

Transformative test. California courts use a different approach, called the "transformative test," that was most recently invoked in *Winters v. D.C. Comics,* (Cal. 2003). In that case, Johnny and Edgar Winters, well-known musicians with albino complexions and long white hair, brought a right of publicity action against defendant D.C. Comics for its publication of a comic book featuring the characters "Johnny and Edgar Autumn," half-worm, half-human creatures with pale faces and long white hair. The California Supreme Court considered whether the action was barred by the First Amendment. The court adopted "a balancing test between the First Amendment and the right of publicity based on whether the work in question adds significant creative elements so as to be transformed into something more than a mere celebrity likeness or imitation" (*Winters,* 69 P.3d, p. 475; citing *Comedy III Productions, Inc. v. Gary Saderup, Inc.,* Cal., 2001). Concluding that the comic book characters Johnny and Edgar Autumn "are not just conventional depictions of plaintiffs but contain significant expressive content other than plaintiffs' mere likenesses," the court held that the characters were sufficiently transformed so as to entitle the comic book to full First Amendment protection.

In another case involving famous sports artist Rich Rush's creation and sale of lithographs featuring a collage of images of golfer Tiger Woods, the court again applied the "transformative use" test and concluded that Rush's artwork was more than a literal depiction of Woods and that the artist "added a significant creative component of his own to Woods' identity" (*ETW Corp. v. Jireh Publishing Co.,* 2003).

Predominant use test. In a well-publicized case, *Twist v. TCI Cablevision* (2003), the Missouri Supreme Court created its own balancing test—called a predominant use test. The Missouri Supreme Court stated that its test would better address cases where speech is both expressive and commercial: If a product is being sold that predominantly exploits the commercial value of an individual's identity, that product should be held to violate the right of publicity and not be protected by the First Amendment, even if there is some "expressive" content in it that might qualify as "speech" in other circumstances. If, on the other hand, the predominant purpose of the product is to make an expressive comment on or about a celebrity, the expressive values could be given greater weight.

The following focus case reviews the elements of a right of publicity claim and examines a common defense to such claims, First Amendment free speech.

C.B.C. Distribution and Marketing, Inc. v. Major League Baseball Advanced Media, L.P.

FOCUS CASE   505 F.3d 818 (8th Cir. 2007)

FACTS

C.B.C. Distribution and Marketing, Inc., (CBC) sells fantasy sports products via its Internet website, by email, by mail, and over the telephone. Its fantasy baseball products incorporate the names, along with performance and biographical data, of actual major league baseball players. Before the commencement of the major league baseball season each spring, participants form their fantasy baseball teams by "drafting" players from various major league baseball teams. Participants compete against other fantasy baseball "owners" who have also drafted their own teams. A participant's success, and his team's success, depends on the actual performance of the fantasy team's players on their respective actual teams during the course of the major league baseball season. Participants in CBC's fantasy baseball games pay fees to play and additional fees to trade players during the course of the season.

From 1995 through the end of 2004, the MLB Players Association licensed to CBC "the names, nicknames, likenesses, signatures, pictures, playing records, and/or biographical data of each player" to be used in association with CBC's fantasy baseball products. In 2005, however, the Players Association licensed to Advanced Media the exclusive right to use baseball players' names and performance information "for exploitation via all interactive media." Advanced Media began providing fantasy baseball games on its website, MLB.com, the official website of major league baseball. Advanced Media offered CBC, in exchange for a commission, a license to promote the MLB.com fantasy baseball games on CBC's website but did not offer CBC a license to continue to offer its own fantasy baseball products.

CBC sued to establish its right to use, without license, the names of and information about major league baseball players in connection with its fantasy baseball products. The district court held that CBC was not infringing any state law rights of publicity that belonged to major league baseball players.

HOLDING

CBC's First Amendment rights in offering its fantasy baseball products supersede the players' rights of publicity; therefore summary judgment is affirmed.

RATIONALE

The Right of Publicity Claim

An action based on the right of publicity is a state law claim. See *Zacchini v. Scripps-Howard Broad. Co.*, 433 U.S. 562 (1977). In Missouri, "the elements of a right of publicity action include: (1) That defendant used plaintiff's name as a symbol of his identity (2) without consent (3) and with the intent to obtain a commercial advantage." The parties all agree that CBC's continued use of the players' names and playing information after the expiration of the 2002 agreement was without consent. The district court concluded, however, that the evidence was insufficient to make out the other two elements of the right of publicity claim and addressed each of these in turn.

Symbol of Identity

With respect to the symbol of identity element, the Missouri Supreme Court observed that "the name used by the defendant must be understood by the audience as referring to the plaintiff." The state court further held that "[i]n resolving this issue, the fact-finder may consider evidence including 'the nature and extent of the identifying characteristics used by the defendant, the defendant's intent, the fame of the plaintiff, evidence of actual identification made by third persons, and surveys or other evidence indicating the perceptions of the audience.'" The court entertained no doubt that the players' names that CBC used are understood by it and its fantasy baseball subscribers to refer to actual major league baseball players. CBC itself admits that much. In responding to the appellants' argument that "this element is met by the mere confirmation that the name used, in fact, refers to the famous person asserting the violation," the court reasoned that "identity," rather than "mere use of a name," "is a critical element of the right of publicity." The district court did not mean that when a name alone is sufficient to establish identity that the defendant's use of that name satisfies the plaintiff's burden to show that a name was used as a symbol of identity.

Commercial Advantage

It is true that with respect to the "commercial advantage" element of a cause of action for violating publicity rights, CBC's use does not fit neatly into the more traditional categories of commercial advantage, namely, using individuals' names for advertising and merchandising purposes in a way that states or intimates that the individuals are endorsing a product. But a name can be used for commercial advantage when it is used "in connection with services rendered by the user." The plaintiff need not show that "prospective purchasers are likely to believe" that the plaintiff endorsed the product or service. The court determined that the players' identities were being used for commercial advantage and that the players therefore offered sufficient evidence to make out a cause of action for violation of their rights of publicity under Missouri law.

First Amendment Defense

CBC argued that the First Amendment nonetheless trumps the right of publicity action under Missouri law. The Supreme Court has affirmed that state law rights of publicity must be balanced against First Amendment considerations. The CBC court concluded that state law must give way to the Constitution. First, the information used in CBC's fantasy baseball games is all readily available in the public domain, and it would be a strange law that denied a person the First Amendment right to use information available to everyone.

While it is true that CBC's use of the information is meant to provide entertainment, "[s]peech that entertains, like speech that informs, is protected by the First Amendment because '[t]he line between the informing and the entertaining is too elusive for the protection of that basic right.'" The court also found no merit in the argument that CBC's use of players' names and information in its fantasy baseball games is not speech at all. On the contrary, "the pictures, graphic design, concept art, sounds, music, stories, and narrative present in video games" is speech entitled to First Amendment protection. Similarly, here CBC uses the "names, nicknames, likenesses, signatures, pictures, playing records, and/or biographical data of each player" in an interactive form in connection with its fantasy baseball products. This use is no less expressive than the use that was at issue in *Interactive Digital*.

It is important to note the Missouri Supreme Court did find the players could prove violations of their publicity rights, but the First Amendment permits the unauthorized use as constitutionally protected speech.

Survival of publicity rights on death. Another issue that relates to publicity rights is whether they survive the death of the athlete or sport celebrity. The law is divided on this and varies from state to state. Some states hold that rights of publicity cease at death, while around 12 states view the right of publicity as an economic interest that the heirs of an athlete or sport celebrity may protect. See the following Focus Case involving Babe Ruth's heirs and publicity rights under the law of New York.

Pirone v. MacMillan, Inc.

894 F.2d 579 (2d Cir. 1990)

FOCUS CASE

FACTS

Babe Ruth was one of the greatest baseball players of all time. A standout pitcher in his early years; his renown derives principally from his prowess as a hitter. His place in the pantheon of baseball legends is secure, and his name is among those "that have sparked the diamond and its environs and that have provided tinder for recaptured thrills, for reminiscence and comparisons, and for conversation and anticipation in-season and off-season" (*Flood v. Kuhn,* 1972). While he lived, Ruth was paid by manufacturers for the use of his picture or name in promoting the sale of various products. In 1987, MacMillan published *The 1988 MacMillan Baseball Engagement Calendar.* The calendar included three Babe Ruth photos. A picture of Ruth helping a small boy with his batting grip appears on its cover. Another shows Ruth saluting General John Pershing, and the third shows a baseball autographed by Ruth. Though Pirone, one of Ruth's heirs, claimed no particular ownership interest in these specific photographs, Pirone objected to the use of Ruth's likeness. Pirone filed suit, alleging infringement of the common law right of publicity. The district court dismissed the right of publicity claim for failure to state a claim on which relief might be granted.

HOLDING

The court of appeals affirmed the district court's dismissal.

RATIONALE

Pirone's claims were based on an asserted common law "right of publicity" under New York's statutory right to privacy. The privacy law forbids the use for advertising or trade purposes any portrait or picture without the consent of the subject. The right of privacy protection, however, is clearly limited to "any living person." (A right to privacy claim is personal to the individual and expires upon his death.) Pirone claimed the common law right of publicity, barring the unauthorized commercial use of a person's image or likeness, survived the death of Babe Ruth. The New York court said "no such non-statutory right has yet been recognized by the New York State courts." The court added, "Since the 'right of publicity' is encompassed under the Civil Rights Law as an aspect of the right of privacy, which . . . is exclusively statutory in this state, the plaintiff cannot claim an independent common-law right of publicity."

Ambush marketing

Ambush marketing has been defined as an intentional effort to weaken or "ambush" a competitor's official association with a sports organization, an association secured through payment of sponsorship fees (McKelvey, 1992, 1994). Another definition is a marketing practice with the "ability to reasonably confuse" the consumer regarding the ambushing company's status as an official sponsor (McAuley & Sutton, 1999). The first significant legal contribution to the evolution of ambush marketing was *NHL v. Pepsi-Cola Canada Ltd.* (1992) presented in the following Focus Case.

National Hockey League v. Pepsi-Cola Canada Ltd.

FOCUS CASE   70 B.C.L.R.2d 27 (BCSC 1992)

FACTS

Pepsi-Cola Canada (Pepsi) utilized numerous ambush marketing techniques to associate itself with the 1990 Stanley Cup hockey playoffs. Pepsi conducted a nationwide promotional campaign in Canada in which consumers were eligible for up to $10,000 if they matched certain information on bottle caps and specially marked cups with the outcome of the Stanley Cup playoffs. The Stanley Cup pits the winner of the NHL's Campbell Conference against the winner of the Wales Conference in a seven-game playoff series. The Pepsi campaign worked like this: Assume that the Edmonton Oilers won the Stanley Cup in the fifth game of the series in 1990, and a lucky consumer had acquired a Pepsi bottle cap reading "If Edmonton wins in 5 games you win $10,000." That consumer would be eligible to win the $10,000 prize once she submitted the contest entry form and winning game piece and had successfully completed a skills test included on the entry form. Several other prizes, such as free Pepsi products and merchandise and small cash awards, were also available.

Pepsi ran extensive television advertising during the television broadcasts of the NHL playoffs to promote its prize contest. The NHL sued Pepsi in an effort to protect the rights it had sold to Coca-Cola as the official sponsor of the NHL. Unfortunately, in 1989, when the NHL entered into its sponsorship agreement with Coca-Cola, television broadcast advertising rights were not among the rights included in the agreement. The broadcast advertising rights had been licensed to Molson Breweries, who in turn granted Pepsi the right to be the exclusive advertiser of soft drinks during the broadcast of all NHL postseason and playoff games.

HOLDING

The Canadian court rejected each of the NHL's claims and dismissed the action.

RATIONALE

The NHL alleged four theories of recovery: common law tort of passing off, statutory passing off, trademark infringement, and interference with economic relations and future business relations. The passing off claims were rejected since the NHL's consumer survey evidence was not adequate to demonstrate that Pepsi's promotional activities had created a false impression that the product or activity was authorized, approved, or endorsed by the NHL. Even if the survey evidence had been acceptable to the court, the court cited *NFL v. Delaware* (1977) in stating that Pepsi's disclaimers would have been sufficient to dispel any impressions of sponsorship or approval. The trademark infringement claims were easily dismissed since none of the NHL's actual registered marks were used by Pepsi. Finally, the court dismissed the interference with economic relations claims since NHL could not base its claim on the rights of another (i.e., Coca-Cola), and none of Coca-

Cola's rights under its sponsorship agreement with NHL had been interfered with. The court noted that Coca-Cola's sponsorship agreement did not include any advertising rights with respect to television broadcasts.

The court's opinion in *NHL v. Pepsi-Cola Canada* confirmed what many sport managers at the time suspected: that most common law and statutory remedies simply do not encompass common ambush marketing practices. Thus, many companies viewed the Canadian decision as an open invitation to engage in ambush marketing (McKelvey, 1992). As a result, sport organizations were forced to identify additional business and legal strategies to combat ambush marketing practices. One such strategy, a misappropriation claim, is explained below.

In turn, ambush marketers have developed a wide range of tactics. The most common and effective of these strategies are the following:

1. Purchasing advertising time during an event broadcast
2. Conducting sweepstakes or contests using event tickets as prizes
3. Creating premium offers thematically tied to the event
4. Using notable athletes affiliated with the sport or event to endorse the products or be featured in advertising (Lefton, 2003)
5. Hiring fans to hold up signs bearing logos during a televised event

Other strategies include flyover blimp advertising, stadium advertising, individual team sponsorship, and even forehead tattoos (Jensen, 1996; Liberman, 2003). Ambush marketing is effective. Studies show that fans do associate the ambushing company with the ambushed event (Moorman & Greenwell, 2005). Exhibit 20.5 provides a few examples of prominent ambushes.

Probably the most outright and unapologetic brand to embrace ambush marketing is Nike (Sauer, 2002). Examples of Nike ambush campaign "victims" include Converse in Los Angeles in 1984; Reebok in Atlanta in 1996; and adidas on just about every continent (Sauer, 2002). Nike's tactics at the 1996 Olympics seriously eroded the IOC's credibility and forced sport organizations into adopting more assertive and aggressive anti-ambushing strategies. However, in most ambush marketing situations, the marketers do not make any false claims about their products or services, and the athletes do in fact endorse the products or services. Thus, false and deceptive advertising laws are not very effective in combating ambush marketing. Similarly,

Competitive Advantage
STRATEGIES

Consumer Communications and Advertising Practices

- Managers must recognize that their communications with consumers about competitors may have legal consequences. Procedures should be in place to verify the accuracy of any statements or representations contained in advertising.

- A sport organization must have the consent of any person whose likeness is being used in an advertisement or promotion. For example, if a collegiate or professional sport team wants to feature a student-athlete or professional athlete in its marketing efforts, the athlete must have given consent or else a right of publicity claim could result.

- To combat ambush marketing, sport organizations and sponsors must build as many protections as possible into their sponsorship agreements and broadcasting agreements. Sport organizations may be requested to assume the responsibility to pursue legal recourse against ambush marketing companies. This could involve significant legal expense, so care should be exercised during contract negotiations.

- A sport organization must actively monitor the advertising practices of its competitors and notify competitors promptly if it believes an advertising practice is illegal or unethical.

EXHIBIT	20.5	Examples of prominent "ambush" marketing campaigns.

1984 Los Angeles Olympics: Kodak sponsors TV broadcasts of the games as well as the U. S. track team, despite Fuji's being the official sponsor. Fuji returns the favor during the Seoul 1988 Games when Kodak is the official sponsor.

1992 Barcelona Olympics: Nike sponsors press conferences with the U. S. basketball team despite Reebok's being the official sponsor.

1996 Atlanta Olympics: Nike's Atlanta ambush is still seen as the ambush of all ambushes. Saving the $50 million that an official Olympic sponsorship would have cost, Nike plasters the city with billboards, hands out "swoosh" banners to wave during the competitions, and erects an enormous "Nike center" overlooking the stadium.

2000 Sydney Olympics: Qantas Airlines' slogan "The Spirit of Australia" sounds strikingly similar to the Games slogan, "Share the Spirit." Qantas claims it's just a coincidence, while official sponsor Ansett Air helplessly protests.

2002 Winter Olympics in Salt Lake City: Anheuser-Busch pays more than $50 million to become an official Olympic sponsor. In accordance with its agreement, it has exclusive rights to use the word "Olympic" and the five-rings logo. Schirf Brewery, a local (and very small) company, rather ingeniously (and apparently legally) marks its delivery trucks with "Wasutch Beers. The Unofficial Beer. 2002 Winter Games." In accordance with copyright and trademark laws, Schirf has used neither the word "Olympics" nor the five-ring logo. (Sauer, 2002.)

2007 U. S. Open: Arizona Beverage Company hands out free samples of their sports drink to fans around the event facility. Andy Roddick was an endorser of the Arizona Beverage product; however, Gatorade is the official sports drink sponsor of the event (Kaplan, 2007).

Euro 2008: Heineken passes out large green hats to fans buying their beer prior to a Dutch soccer match ("Playing the Game," 2008).

companies that employ ambush marketing techniques rarely use the actual marks or logos of the event or their competitors; thus trademark and copyright laws are of little help (McKelvey & Grady, 2004).

A few sport organizations have sued ambush marketers under common law principles of unfair competition. This remedy allows recovery for the misappropriation of goodwill and reputation of a sport organization. The remedy for misappropriation is fairly simple. The sport organization need only show the following:

1. It is the owner of the event or right in question.
2. The ambusher has participated in unauthorized activity.
3. Its goodwill or reputation has been appropriated or damaged through the use of false representations in relation to products or services. (McKelvey, 1992)

Sport organizations have not had much success with misappropriation claims to date because of the difficulty of proving actual damage to goodwill or reputation. Also, for a misappropriation claim to succeed the objectional activity must include false representations. To counter this, many ambush marketers simply use a disclaimer indicating "truthfully" that their promotional activity is in no way endorsed or associated with the sport organization in question. For example, the

Delaware federal district court rejected the NFL's misappropriation of goodwill claims against the Delaware State Lottery for a lottery game based on NFL games. The ruling rested on the fact that the Delaware State Lottery used a disclaimer indicating the NFL had not endorsed the lottery game (*NFL v. Delaware*, 1977).

The *NFL v. Delaware* case has been most often cited for its holding permitting ambush marketers to avoid trademark infringement and unfair competition claims by using disclaimers in their advertising. The NFL presented survey evidence that between 19 percent and 21 percent of those surveyed were confused as to the NFL's sponsorship or endorsement of the state lottery game. The court agreed that this was sufficient evidence to demonstrate consumer confusion and stated that "one may not . . . advertise one's services in a manner which creates an impression in the mind of the relevant segment of the public that a connection exists between the services offered and the holder of the registered mark when no such connection exists" (*NFL v. Delaware*, 1977, p. 1380). However, the district court determined that an adequate remedy for this transgression was for the state lottery to include a clear and conspicuous statement that the game was not associated with or authorized by the NFL (p. 1381). The impact of the *NFL v. Delaware* decision has made it very difficult for sport organizations to challenge ambush marketing practices using unfair competition theories.

In the more recent case *NCAA v. Coors Brewing Company* (2002), the NCAA sued Coors Brewing Company to thwart the beer company's use of tickets to the NCAA Men's Basketball Championship Tournament in an advertising promotion. This was the first lawsuit to challenge the use of sports tickets in an unauthorized sweepstakes promotion as unfair competition (McKelvey, 2003). Because the case was settled before trial, we do not know how the court would have ruled on the NCAA misappropriation claims. However, Coors did cease its promotion.

INTERACTIONS WITH PUBLIC MEDIA AND BROADCAST PARTNERS

Media relations is an umbrella term that includes managers who may also be called sport information directors, publicity directors, or media relations directors. The functions of these managers are quite diverse, and media relations personnel may be asked to participate in negotiating broadcasting agreements or working with broadcasters once an agreement has been entered into. In addition, the duties of media relations personnel may include collecting and disseminating factual information about the organization through press kits, press releases, press conferences, media guides, stat sheets, fact sheets, public announcements, and websites. In the process of collecting and disseminating this information, media relations personnel must be aware of federal and state privacy laws and state defamation laws that could be invoked in the event of a false and negligent release of information. Below we explore the key elements of a broadcasting agreement, privacy issues, and the tort of defamation, with regard to media relations.

Broadcasting Agreements

Sport marketers and sport administrators are often involved in negotiations with the media for the sale of broadcast rights to sport events. When entering into an agreement that relates to the broadcasting of a sporting event, both the rights owner (sport organization) and the broadcaster must consider a number of issues as they negotiate.

Quantification of coverage

Quantify the exact broadcast coverage desired. For example, if the NFL is seeking to negotiate an agreement for broadcast rights for an entire season, the exact number of games to be broadcast must be established. Of course, the NFL has hundreds of potential games and team combinations and often negotiates with multiple broadcasters. In a more confined scenario, consider a Division I-A college athletic department seeking to negotiate for the broadcast of all home games. The team has exactly seven home games, and the exact dates of the games and the identities of the opponents have been determined. However, the broadcaster may want to approve the timing and scheduling of the events. For example, a game scheduled for Saturday afternoon at 3:00 may be perfect for the home team, but the broadcaster may have already scheduled that particular time slot. In this situation, the broadcaster will likely want to move the game to another time or even another day. This change will require the home team to negotiate with its opponent or to include in its game contracts provisions for moving the game day or time to accommodate broadcasting needs.

Mode of transmission

The broadcasting agreement should establish the mode of transmission, such as satellite or cable, and whether the broadcast will be free to the public or pay-per-view. The parties must also negotiate whether the event will be broadcast live and simultaneous with the event, tape delayed, or broadcast as highlights only. For example, pay-per-view event agreements for boxing matches frequently permit moving images (live or tape-delayed) to be broadcast only by a single provider. A secondary provider, including the media, would only be permitted to broadcast still photos of select moments during the fight. A broadcaster will want the highest priority for its broadcast coverage to maximize its usage, and often the broadcaster will seek designation as the exclusive broadcaster for an event. This exclusivity does not prevent the news media from using small amounts of footage for legitimate news reporting purposes (see Chapter 19 regarding copyright protection and the scope of the media's fair use of copyrighted materials).

Access to the event

Access to the event is also a concern for the broadcaster. The broadcasting agreement should specify details such as the number and positioning of cameras; availability and construction of scaffolding and rigging; positioning of commentary teams; and parking, power, and electrical requirements. As digital technology continues to expand, advanced technological capabilities should be addressed in the broadcasting agreement. The broadcaster will likely also want access to event personnel and participants for interviews.

Cancellation of the event

The parties to the broadcasting agreement will want adequate event cancellation insurance, and they must determine who is responsible for securing the insurance and, of course, who will pay for the insurance. Event cancellation insurance protects parties from financial losses they may suffer should an event be cancelled, losses such as missed revenue, promotional expenses, and production expenses.

Protection against ambush marketing

The sport organization may seek a commitment from the broadcaster to protect actively against ambush marketing. The sport organization should request that official sponsors be given a first option to purchase advertising time during the broadcast. The sponsors may even desire to negotiate with the broadcaster for exclusivity, to prevent competitors from purchasing advertising time during the broadcast and attempting to ambush the official sponsors.

These are only a few of the issues that are important in a broadcasting agreement and that sport marketers should consider when negotiating with the media.

Privacy Rights and Defamation

In the sport industry, invasion of privacy claims and defamation claims are raised in a variety of settings. These may include disclosure of personal information about a coach or athlete; statements made by an athletic director about reasons for terminating a coach; statements made by a coach about an assistant coach; statements made by a professional athlete about his agent; statements published by a newspaper about an athlete; and statements published on an Internet discussion board about an athlete, a coach, or an owner of a professional sport team.

Any of these examples could easily form the basis of an invasion of privacy or defamation action. First, we explore the concept of privacy and the tort of invasion of privacy; then we examine the law of defamation.

Privacy rights

Privacy is the expectation that confidential personal information disclosed in a private place will not be disclosed to third parties, when that disclosure would cause either embarrassment or emotional distress to a person of reasonable sensitivities. "Information" is a broad term that includes facts, images such as photographs, videotapes, audiotapes, and even disparaging opinions. Privacy rights exist both under the common law as expressed in the Restatement (Second) of Torts at §§ 652A–652I and also under a number of statutes that prohibit disclosure of certain kinds of information, such as the Family Educational Right to Privacy Act (FERPA), which protects the privacy of student records.

This section focuses on common law rights of privacy. The Restatement classifies four basic kinds of common law privacy rights. These are defined in Exhibit 20.6.

Only the second of these four rights is widely accepted in the United States. The distinction between the right of publicity as discussed previously and this second type of privacy right is that a personal right to privacy protects against "injury to personal feelings," whereas the right of publicity protects against unauthorized commercial exploitation of a person's name or face. As a practical matter, a sport celebrity would generally sue under the right of publicity, and an ordinary citizen would sue under right to privacy.

The first type of privacy right is the one most likely implicated by the release of private information about an individual, such as an athlete, coach, or athlete director. Unreasonable intrusion upon seclusion applies only to secret or surrepti-

EXHIBIT	20.6	Four types of common law privacy rights.

1. Protection from unreasonable intrusion upon the seclusion of another—for example, physical invasion of a person's home (e.g., unwanted entry, looking into windows with binoculars or a camera, tapping the telephone), searching a person's wallet or purse, repeated and persistent telephone calls, or obtaining financial data (e.g., bank balance) without a person's consent.

2. Protection from appropriation of a person's name or likeness. This is similar to the concept of the right of publicity discussed previously.

3. Protection from publication of private facts—for example, income tax data, information about sexual relations, personal letters, family quarrels, medical treatment, or photographs of a person in his home.

4. Protection from publication that places a person in a false light. This is similar to defamation. A successful defamation action requires that the information be false. In a privacy action, the information is generally true, but the information creates a false impression about the plaintiff.

tious invasions of privacy. An open and notorious invasion of privacy would be public, not private, and the victim could choose not to reveal private or confidential information. For example, the recording of telephone conversations is not wrong if both participants are notified before they speak that the conversation is, or may be, recorded. Further, if two college athletes make extravagant purchases of sportswear at a local mall, those purchases are made in a public place, and the sales clerk and other customers do not owe the athletes any duty of confidentiality. Therefore, under current law, there is no expectation of privacy. The store clerk could report the amount that the athletes spent and the items they purchased even if the disclosure may be harmful to the athletes (e.g., if the purchases were a violation of NCAA regulations regarding benefits to student-athletes).

Businesses have no right of privacy (*California Bankers Association v. Schultz*, 1974; *U.S. v. Morton Salt Co.*, 1950; Restatement [Second] of Torts, § 652I, comment *c*, 1977; Prosser, *Privacy*, 1960; Am. Jur. 2d *Constitutional Law* § 606, 1979). Privacy law is phrased only as an individual person's rights. However, businesses have rights analogous to the right of privacy. For example, corporate espionage might be prosecuted as an improper acquisition of a trade secret (Restatement [Third] of Unfair Competition § 43, 1995). Trade secrets, criminal proceedings, and patents are beyond the scope of this text, but we note that many of those statutory protections are also grounded in privacy law. Further, trademark law, discussed in Chapter 19, permits a business to own a product logo and to prevent others from using the same mark or logo.

Defamation

Defamation cases are common in the sport industry and are a significant concern for sport organizations in their interactions with media outlets, as well as for media outlets when reporting events. For example, Evel Knievel sued ESPN, Inc. based on a photo caption published on the website espn.com. The photo showed the aging daredevil motorcyclist with his wife and another woman with a caption that read, "Evel Knievel proves that you're never too old to be a pimp" (Anderson Publications, 2002b). The district court dismissed Knievel's suit, concluding that the photo was the tenth photo among a 17-photo slideshow and that the word "pimp" had meanings other than its literal meaning (*Knievel v. ESPN*, 2002). The district court noted that calling someone a pimp in the abstract was capable of defamatory meaning, but it lost such meaning in the context used here, and no reasonable person would believe that espn.com was actually accusing Evel Knievel of being a pimp or soliciting prostitution. The dismissal was affirmed on appeal (*Knievel v. ESPN*, 2005).

ESPN, Inc. was also sued by John Montefusco, a former major league baseball pitcher, for statements made by ESPN during a SportsCenter broadcast regarding Montefusco's pending criminal proceedings for sexual and physical violence toward his ex-wife (Soocher, 2002). Several times during the broadcast, Montefusco's case was compared to that of O.J. Simpson as yet another ex-athlete accused of domestic violence. The case was dismissed based on the district court's finding that the statements were not defamatory and that the news program was privileged to report such a comparison pursuant to New Jersey's fair reporting privilege. Montefusco appealed to the Third Circuit Court of Appeals, which affirmed the dismissal (*Montefusco v. ESPN, Inc.*, 2002). Thus, despite the cost and time involved in these types of actions, numerous defamation actions continue to be filed against sport broadcasting organizations.

In another case, a former athletic director and men's basketball coach at Green River Community College (GRCC) in the state of Washington sued GRCC for defamation surrounding his firing. McGraw was fired after an investigation by conference officials revealed that he had knowingly used an ineligible player during a game (Anderson Publications, 2002a). College officials stated to others that the ineligible player had played with McGraw's knowledge. McGraw presented substantial evidence at trial demonstrating that these statements were not true and that he had no knowledge of the player's ineligibility. The jury awarded McGraw $1 million on the defamation claim, and the award was upheld on appeal (*McGraw v. Green River Community College*, 2001).

In another case, Mike Price sued Time, Inc. for defamation based on a *Sports Illustrated* article reporting his alleged misbehavior (*Price v. Time, Inc.*, 2003). Price sued for $20 million, claiming he was defamed and slandered by the story, which detailed his alleged actions the night he visited a topless bar in Pensacola, Florida, in April 2003, shortly after being hired as the new head coach at Alabama. He acknowledged being heavily intoxicated but denied allegations of having sex at his hotel. Alabama fired Price a few days before the article was published. The parties ultimately settled for an undisclosed sum without any admission of wrongdoing on the part of Time (Caldwell, 2005).

Defamation claims are intended to protect a person from false statements that are damaging to his or her reputation, or that diminish the esteem, respect, goodwill, or confidence in which a person is held, or that cause adverse, derogatory, or unpleasant feelings or opinions against a person. Generally, a **defamatory act** is defined in the Restatement (Second) of Torts as follows:

1. A false statement
2. Published to a third party

Competitive Advantage
STRATEGIES

Consumer Interactions and Marketing Practices

- Document any strategic alliances with a memorandum of understanding. It can be used to define the parameters of the partnership and the basic interests of the partners. It does not have to bind the parties to a deal, but it should allow them time to explore the possibility without other parties intruding.

- Do not hesitate to involve lawyers in drafting agreements, participating in negotiations, and researching business practices and intellectual property ownership. Lawyers can force the parties to ask hard questions and raise negative scenarios without pitting the parties against one another.

- Communicating with the media is a critical part of media relations, but it is also imperative that any personnel dealing with the media verify and confirm any information provided and avoid disclosures about personnel, employment issues, or employment status of coaches.

- If a coach is being reassigned, is resigning, or is being fired, consider the following strategies. If possible, allow a resigning coach to make the official announcement, rather than the team or university. If the coach is terminated, the organization will have to issue the press release or announcement; however, the reasons for dismissal must be carefully worded to avoid damaging the coach's reputation.

- Media relations personnel working in college athletics should be aware of limitations on the type of information that can be disclosed about a student-athlete's academic performance and medical treatments or conditions.

3. Involving some degree of fault or negligence on the part of the publisher

4. Causing actual damage

The tort of defamation includes both **slander** (spoken) and **libel** (written). Libel is broader than slander in that any number of tangible communications would fall under the heading of written communication, such as written comments, photographs, cartoons, and publications. Each state may define defamation slightly differently, but typically a verbal or spoken comment is *per se* defamatory if it falls into one of the following categories:

1. Imputes that a person has engaged in criminal conduct

2. Imputes that a person has a loathsome disease

3. Imputes that a person has engaged in adultery or fornication

4. Imputes that a person has engaged in misconduct in public office

5. Imputes that a person is incompetent or unfair in that person's profession, business, or trade

If a statement falls into one of these categories, it is presumed as a matter of law that the reputation of the individual about whom the statement was made will be injured. A statement is defamatory *per se* if its harm is obvious and apparent on the face of it (*Green v. Rogers*, 2009). For example, false comments accusing a coach of sexual misconduct with an athlete or illegal recruiting practices could be construed as slanderous *per se* because these comments will always be considered damaging to the coach's reputation. In other words, a reasonable person could not interpret such statements as a positive reflection upon the coach.

Notice that the third element from the Restatement involves some degree of fault or negligence. This is the element most often at issue in defamation cases. The degree of fault required to extend liability varies depending upon whether the person allegedly defamed is a public figure. The Supreme Court held in *Curtis Publishing Co. v. Butts* (1967) that a **public figure** (in that case the athletic director of the University of Georgia, Wally Butts) was an individual who has, because of his or her activities, "commanded sufficient continuing public interest."

This designation as a public figure is very important. In order for a public figure to recover for defamation, she must prove that the defamatory statements were made with "actual malice." That is, the statements were made with knowledge that they were false or with reckless disregard for whether they were false or not. The courts have often classified professional athletes and coaches as public figures. Requiring professional athletes or other high-profile sport celebrities to prove actual malice is appropriate because they have voluntarily placed themselves in the public eye and, having done so, are exposed to greater public scrutiny. In addition, public figures have more ready access to the media and other public forums in which they can defend against public criticism. A private person does not have to prove actual malice; thus, a private person must only prove that a false and defamatory statement was published negligently (unreasonably) in order to recover damages. Truth is an absolute defense to all claims of defamation.

A public figure is one who either has gained notoriety from his achievements or seeks public attention through vigor and success. The U. S. Supreme Court reduced the "public-figure question to looking at the nature and extent of an individual's participation in the particular controversy giving rise to the defamation." That is, the Court looked at the following:

- The extent to which the individual's participation is voluntary
- The extent to which the individual has access to the media to counteract the false statements
- The prominence of the individual's role in the public controversy

The Court recognized a limited purpose public figure as "an individual [who] voluntarily injects himself or is drawn into a particular public controversy."

The following Focus Case explores the issue of the limited purpose public figure and how defamation law applies in that context.

Woy v. Turner

| 573 F. Supp. 35 (N.D. Ga. 1983) | **FOCUS CASE** |

FACTS

After Bob Horner's first season with the Atlanta Braves National League Baseball Club, Woy acted as Horner's agent in negotiations for a new contract with Bill Lucas, the general manager and representative of the Braves. Prior to the resolution of the heated contractual dispute, Mr. Lucas died. Subsequently, defendant Ted Turner, owner of the Braves, made statements to the press and on a telecast to the effect that Woy's tactics and accusations regarding the character of Mr. Lucas during the course of the negotiations had contributed to or caused his death. Plaintiff William "Bucky" Woy sued Ted Turner for libel and slander pursuant to O.C.G.A. § 51-5-1 et seq. (Ga. Code Ann. § 105-7). At trial, Turner moved for a declaration that plaintiff was a public figure at the time defendant made the alleged defamatory statements.

HOLDING

Bucky Woy was a public figure during the time of the contractual dispute between Bob Horner and the Atlanta Braves and at the time Ted Turner issued the statements to the news media concerning the death of Bill Lucas. Because of this, Woy would only be entitled to recover damages on his claim of libel and slander upon a showing that Turner's statements were made with "actual malice."

RATIONALE

The Supreme Court held in *The New York Times v. Sullivan* (1964) that a state cannot award damages to a "public official" for defamatory falsehoods unless the official proves "actual malice," which is defined as the issuance of a statement with knowledge of its falsity or with reckless disregard for whether the statement is true or false. Furthermore, in order to find that the defendant acted with reckless disregard of whether the statements were true or false, the plaintiff must prove that a false statement was made with a high degree of awareness of its probable falsity by the defendant. Otherwise there must be sufficient evidence to permit the conclusion that the defendant in fact entertained serious doubts as to the truth of his statement.

The New York Times standard formulated for defamatory falsehoods published about "public officials" was later extended to "public figures" in *Curtis Publishing Co. v. Butts* (1967), where the court defined a "public figure" as: "(a) One who commands a substantial amount of public interest by his position alone (special prominence), or (b) One who voluntarily thrusts himself into the 'vortex' of an important public controversy."

Turner argued that Bucky Woy was a public figure due to his special prominence and introduced evidence that Woy used the media (i.e., the press, television, and sports magazines) constantly to promote himself as a sports agent and to express his views on a wide variety of subjects. Evidence was also presented showing that Woy represented several celebrity clients and used the media in the representation of those clients. Woy also coauthored a book about himself entitled *Sign Em Up, Bucky*. In support of his argument that Woy was a "public figure" due to his special prominence, Turner cited several cases to demonstrate the type of activity that would typically generate the classification of one as a "public figure." See, e.g., *Chuy v. Philadelphia Eagles Football Club*, (1979) (professional football player was held to be a public figure as to his playing career); *Vandenburg v. Newsweek, Inc.*, (1975) (college track coach was a public figure for some issues); *Curtis Publishing Co. v. Butts* (football coach was a public figure due to his position and due to his easy access to media for purpose of broadcasting a response or counterargument). However, Woy elicited testimony from a sports journalist who had not heard of the plaintiff until the time of the contractual dispute that led to the incident complained of in this lawsuit. The court found that Woy was widely known in the "community" for his general fame or notoriety as a sports agent, well enough to qualify as a public figure based on *special prominence*.

Turner further contended that Woy was a public figure because Woy voluntarily thrust himself into the forefront of the public controversy at issue. The defendant introduced evidence that the plaintiff was in contact with the media numerous times regarding the contractual dispute, including several times at his own initiation. Woy argued that he was a private person thrown into the public controversy when he received media attention owing to his professional service to a client associated with the public controversy.

In making the determination as to whether Woy was a public figure because he voluntarily thrust himself into a public controversy, the court considered the three prong test:

1. Did the plaintiff voluntarily thrust himself into the vortex of this particular controversy?

2. What was the nature and extent of the plaintiff's participation in the particular controversy?

3. Did the plaintiff encourage the public's attention in an attempt to influence the outcome of a particular controversy?

The court found that during the period of the contractual dispute until the time when the defendant made the alleged defamatory statements, the plaintiff had voluntarily thrust himself into the contractual dispute and was a public figure at the time Ted Turner issued his statements to the news media. The evidence established that Woy was as much a major participant in the public controversy as Ted Turner and Bob Horner, and much of this was due to his own efforts.

CONCLUSION

This chapter covered legal issues that may arise as sport marketers and sport managers implement marketing strategies and interact with consumers, competitors, strategic partners, and the media. We examined legal issues that are relevant when sport organizations communicate about their products and services with consumers through advertising, including such topics as false advertising, deceptive trade practices, and constitutional limitations on commercial speech. We also examined legal issues relevant to a sport organization's interactions with consumers, the media, strategic partners, and competitors, including such topics as commercial sales transactions, sponsorship and broadcasting agreements, publicity rights, ambush marketing, and defamation.

discussion questions

1. What is the most common form of commercial speech?

2. What are the four criteria for determining whether a state's restriction on commercial speech is constitutional?

3. Which of the four criteria was not satisfied in the *Bailey v. Kentucky Racing Commission* case?

4. How are remedies under the Lanham Act for unfair business practices different from remedies under the FTC Act?

5. When is a business practice unfair?

6. What are five recommended strategies for developing strategic partners such as corporate partners?

7. What is an exit strategy in strategic partnerships?

8. How does a right of publicity claim differ from a claim for common law misappropriation?

9. Explain the relatedness, transformative, and predominant use tests related to free speech and publicity rights.

10. What is ambush marketing?

11. When is a verbal or spoken comment defamatory *per se*? Why are these types of statements defamatory *per se*?

12. According to *Woy v. Turner*, what are two ways a private person may become a public figure?

learning activities

Locate your state's attorney general's office website and search the links to the consumer protection division or consumer protection regulations. Does the website provide good and readily accessible information about consumer rights and regulations regarding deceptive trade practices? What special programs does your state operate to protect against consumer fraud or deceptive trade practices that may impact a sport organization in your area?

CASE STUDY

Consider the popular Hanes underwear advertisements featuring Michael Jordan. During the launch of new ComfortSoft waistband underwear, Hanes issued numerous press releases promoting its ad campaign. One press release contained the following statements made by Michael Jordan: "Hanes and I have been together for more than a decade spreading the word about comfort and style. Last year, we urged everyone in America to 'Go Tagless' with the Tagless undershirt. Now, we've done it again to men's underwear with the ComfortSoft Waistband. It truly is a beautiful thing."

1. Would this be considered a celebrity endorsement?
2. What FTC regulations define celebrity endorsements?
3. Assume that Michael Jordan does not actually wear Hanes underwear. Can the FTC bring an action against Hanes or Michael Jordan?

considering . . .   **ANALYSIS & DISCUSSION**

Deceptive Advertising (p. 616)

Since the Federal Drug Administration has determined that a number of sport supplements, particularly those containing the stimulant ephedra or metabolic steroids, have been connected to athlete deaths and illnesses, we may assume that the manager's statement to the reporter is at best deceptive and more likely false. However, if a false statement made by a sport manager as part of a public debate (e.g., on the public health risks created by the use of sport supplements) is treated as political speech, laws prohibiting false advertising, permitting private defamation actions, and regulating deceptive business practices would likely not provide any remedy for that false statement. However, if that same statement were instead treated as commercial speech, either because of the speaker's motive or the commercial context in which it was made, or simply because it was made by a corporate representative, laws relating to false advertising, deceptive trade practices, and defamation would likely prohibit the speech and provide a legal remedy for anyone injured by the speech, including the general public.

The manager's posting of the article throughout the store would likely be a deceptive advertisement. Since the manager has omitted an important part of the article (namely the risks of using sports supplements), it is likely that a reasonable consumer could be misled into thinking the article concurred with the manager's statements and verified them as truthful.

R E F E R E N C E S

Cases

Baden Sports, Inc. v. Kabushiki Kaisha Molten, 541 F. Supp. 2d 1151 (W.D. Wash. 2008).

Baden Sports Inc. v. Molten USA, Inc., 556 F.3d 1300 (Fed. Cir. 2009).

Bailey v. Kentucky Racing Comm'n, Civil Action No. 3:04CV-243-H (United States District Court, Western District of Kentucky, 2004).

Bigelow v. Virginia, 421 U.S. 809 (1975).

Board of Trustees, State Univ. of N. Y. v. Fox, 492 U.S. 469 (1989).

California Bankers Ass'n v. Schultz, 416 U.S. 21 (1974).

Cardtoons v. MLBPA, 335 F.3d 1161 (10th Cir. 2003).

C.B.C. Distribution and Marketing, Inc. v. Major League Baseball Advanced Media, L.P., 505 F.3d 818 (8th Cir. 2007).

Central Hudson Gas & Elec. Co. v. Public Serv. Comm'n of N.Y., 447 U.S. 557 (1980).

Chuy v. The Philadelphia Eagles Football Club, 595 F.2d 1265 (3rd Cir. 1979).

Curtis Publ'g Co. v. Butts, 388 U.S. 130 (1967).

ETW Corp. v. Jireh Publ'g Co., 332 F.3d 915 (6th Cir. 2003).

Flood v. Kuhn, 407 U.S. 258 (1972).

FTC v. Garvey, 383 F.3d 891 (9th Cir. 2004).

Green v. Rogers, 917 N.E.2d 450 (Ill. 2009).

Haelan Laboratories, Inc. v. Topps Chewing Gum, Inc., 202 F.2d 866 (2nd Cir. 1953).

Humphrey v. Viacom, Inc., 2007 U.S. Dist. LEXIS 44679 (D. N.J. 2007).

Knievel v. ESPN, 223 F. Supp. 2d 1173 (D. Montana 2002).

Knievel v. ESPN, 393 F.3d 1068 (9th Cir. 2005).

McGraw v. Green River Community College, 2001 Wash. App. LEXIS 2627 (Wash. App. 2001).

McIntyre v. Ohio Elections Comm'n., 514 U.S. 334, 115 S. Ct. 1511 (1995).

Montefusco v. ESPN, Inc., 2002 U.S. App. LEXIS 19740; 30 Media L. Rep. 2311 (3rd Cir. 2002).

NCAA v. Coors Brewing Co., Case No. 49D01-Z207-PL-001290, Marion County, Indiana (2002).

New York Times v. Sullivan, 376 U.S. 254 (1964).

NFL v. Delaware, 435 F. Supp. 1372 (D. Del. 1977).

NHL v. Pepsi-Cola Canada Ltd., 70 B.C.L.R. 2d 27 (BCSC 1992).

Nike, Inc. v. Kasky, 27 Cal. 4th 939, 45 P.3d 24, 119 Cal. Rptr. 2d 296 (2002).

NPS, LLC v. Minihane, 886 N.E.2d 670, 451 Mass. 417 (Mass. 2008).

Oshinsky v. New York Football Giants, Inc., Class Action Complaint, Civil Action No. 09-cv. 1186 (PGS), United States District Court, District of New Jersey (March 16, 2009).

Pirone v. Macmillan, Inc., 894 F.2d 579 (2d Cir. 1990).

Price v. Time, Inc., Jefferson County Circuit Court, State of Alabama. Complaint, Civil Action: CV 03 3855 (June 20, 2003).

Spalding Sports Worldwide, Inc. v. Wilson Sporting Goods, Co., 198 F. Supp. 2d 59 (D. Mass. 2002).

State of Arizona v. American Holiday Ass'n, Inc., 727 P.2d 807 (Ariz. 1986).

Twist v. TCI Cablevision, 110 S.W.3d 363 (Mo. 2003).

United States v. Morton Salt Co., 338 U.S. 632 (1950).

Virginia State Bd. of Pharmacy v. Virginia Citizens Consumer Council, 425 U.S. 748 (1976).

Winter v. DC Comics, 69 P.3d 473 (Cal. 2003).

Woy v. Turner, 573 F. Supp. 35 (N.D. Ga. 1983).

Zacchini v. Scripps-Howard Broadcasting Co., 433 U.S. 562 (1977).

Statutes

Family Educational Right to Privacy Act Regulations 34 C.F.R. § 99.31 (2005).

Federal Trade Commission Act, 15 U.S.C. § 45 *et seq.*

Federal Trade Commission Regulations, 16 C.F.R. § 255.0 *et seq.* (2001).

Kentucky Revised Statutes, § 230.210 to 230.260 (West 2004).

Kentucky Administrative Regulations, 810 KAR 1:009 (1975).

Lanham Act, 15 U.S.C. § 1125 *et seq.*

Restatement (Second) of Torts, § 652A-I (1977).

Restatement (Third) of Unfair Competition, § 43, 46 (1995).

Other Sources

American Jurisprudence, 2d. *Constitutional law* § 606 (1979).

Anderson Publications, Inc. (2002a, February). Highlight case. *Legal Issues in Collegiate Athletics,* 3(4), 3.

Anderson Publications, Inc. (2002b, August). Focus on: Pending litigation. *Legal Issues in Collegiate Athletics,* 3(10), 4.

Anderson Publications, Inc. (2002c, October). Court dismisses Evel Knievel's defamation suit against espn.com. *Computer and Online Industry Litigation Reporter,* 20(8), 5.

Associated Press. (2009, January 30). PGA Tour sues Ginn for breach of contract after it drops event. *PGA.com.* Retrieved March 15, 2010, from www.pga.com/2009/news/industry/01/30/ginn.ap/index.html.

Berlik, L. E. (2009, April 14). Trademark litigation between Coke and Pepsi enters another round. *Virginia Business Litigation Lawyer Blog.* Retrieved January 22, 2010, from http://www.virginiabusinesslitigationlawyer.com/2009/04/trademark-litigation-between-c.html.

Burke, R. R., DeSarbo, W. S., Oliver, R. L., & Robertson, T. S. (1988). Deception by implication: An experimental investigation. *Journal of Consumer Research, 14,* 483–494.

Caldwell, A. A. (2005, October 10). Mike Price, Time Inc. settle SI lawsuit. *SFGate.com.* Retrieved January 27, 2006, from http://sfgate.com.

Churchill Downs, Inc. (2004, April 29). Churchill Downs releases House Rules on jockey advertising. Retrieved January 27, 2006, from www.churchilldowns.com/bet_the_races/racing_news/04292004.html.

Crittenden, M. (2009, January 3). The bailout bowl: Big-game sponsors scored billions. *The Wall Street Journal,* p. A2. Retrieved March 15, 2010, from http://online.wsj.com/article/SB123094249710750433.html.

Federal Trade Commission. (1980). FTC policy statement on unfairness. Retrieved January 26, 2006, from www.ftc.gov/bcp/policystmt/ad-unfair.htm.

Federal Trade Commission. (2001). *Frequently asked questions: Answers for small business* (agency information booklet). Washington, DC: Federal Trade Commission.

Gaeth, G. J., & Heath, T. B. (1987). The cognitive processing of misleading advertising in young and old adults: Assessment and training. *Journal of Consumer Research, 14,* 43–54.

Grady, J. (2004). Right of publicity and trademark case: Implications for marketing professional athletes. *Sport Marketing Quarterly, 13,* 59–60.

Grimaldi, J.V. (2009, September 3). Washington Redskins react to fans' tough luck with tough love. *Washington Post,* p. A01.

Jensen, J. (1996). Flaunting the rings cheaply: Non-sponsors of Olympic games instead back teams. *Advertising Age,* 67(28), 4.

Kaplan, D. (2007, September 10). USTA blocks marketers looking to ambush Open. *Street & Smith's Sports Business Journal,* p. 6. Retrieved April 13, 2010, from www.sportsbusinessjournal.com/article/56282.

Katz, J. (2009, January 27). Economy's toll on sports sponsorships evident in Cubs-Under Armour dispute. Retrieved March 15, 2010, from www.findingdulcinea.com/news/sports/2009/jan/Economy-s-Toll-on-Sports-Sponsorships-Evident-in-Cubs-Under-Armour-Dispute-.html.

Larson, E. (2009, March 18). Giants, Jets sued by fan over arena seat 'licenses.' *Bloomberg.com.* Retrieved March 15, 2010, from www.bloomberg.com/apps/news?pid=20601079&refer=amsports&sid=aRg_rO52oBWg.

Lefton, T. (2003, November 3). Ambush tactics evil, effective. *Street & Smith's SportsBusiness Journal.* Retrieved January 27, 2006, from www.sportsbusinessjournal.com.

Liberman, N. (2003, April 28). Marathon ambush a real head-scratcher. *Street & Smith's SportsBusiness Journal.* Retrieved January 27, 2006, from www.sportsbusinessjournal.com.

Lord, K. R., Kim, C. K., & Putrevu, S. (1997). Communication strategies to counter deceptive advertising. *Review of Business, 18*(3), 24–29.

McAuley, A. C., & Sutton, W. A. (1999). In search of a new defender: The threat of ambush marketing in the global sport arena. *International Journal of Sports Marketing and Sponsorship, 1,* 64–86.

McCarthy, J.T. (2003). *Rights of publicity and privacy* (2nd ed.). Eagan, MN: West.

McKelvey, S. (1992). NHL v. Pepsi-Cola Canada, uh-huh! Legal parameters of sports ambush marketing. *The Entertainment and Sports Lawyer, 10*, 5–18.

McKelvey, S. (1994). Atlanta '96: Olympic countdown to ambush Armageddon? *Seton Hall Journal of Sport Law, 4*, 397–445.

McKelvey, S. (2003). Unauthorized use of event tickets in promotional campaign may create new legal strategies to combat ambush marketing: NCAA v. Coors. *Sport Marketing Quarterly, 12*(2), 117–118.

McKelvey, S., & Grady, J. (2004, Summer). An analysis of the ongoing global efforts to combat ambush marketing: Will corporate marketers "take" the Gold in Greece? *Journal of Legal Aspects of Sport, 14*(2), 191–220.

Moorman, A. M., & Greenwell, T. C. (2005). Consumer attitudes of deception and the legality of ambush marketing practices. *Journal of Legal Aspects of Sport, 15*(2), 183–211.

Paul, I. (2009, November 9). Verizon vs. AT&T: The ad wars shift. *PC World*. Retrieved January 22, 2010, from http://www.pcworld.com/article/181717/verizon_vs_atandt_the_ad_wars_shift.html.

Piety, T. R. (2005, Spring). Grounding Nike: Exposing Nike's quest for a constitutional right to lie. *Temple Law Review, 78*, 151–200.

Playing the game. (2008, July 5). *The Economist, 388*(8587), 77.

Press Release of the Kentucky Horse Racing Authority. (2004, April 30). Statement from William Street, Chairman, Kentucky Horse Racing Authority.

Prosser, W. (1960). Privacy. *California Law Review, 48*, 383–423.

Ratner, A. (2001, June 8). Stadium name game may get ugly: Divorce has been smooth in St. Louis, but bizarre in Miami: Millions of dollars at stake. *The Baltimore Sun*. Retrieved March 7, 2006, from www.savefenwaypark.com/newscass_detail.cfm?ID=127&SORTBY=ID%20DESC.

Saltzman, J., & Finucane, M. (2008, May 16). Patriots ticket buyer bound to contract. *Boston.com*. Retrieved March 15, 2010, from www.boston.com/news/local/articles/2008/05/16/court_patriots_ticket_buyer_bound_to_contract.

Sauer, A. (2002, May 27). Ambush marketing steals the show. Brandchannel.com. Retrieved January 26, 2006, from www.brandchannel.com.

Sheldon, J., & Carter, C. L. (2004). *Unfair and deceptive acts and practices* (6th ed.). Boston: National Consumer Law Center, Inc.

Soocher, S. (2002, October). Bit parts. *Entertainment Law & Finance, 18*(7), 10.

Thomas, K. (2008, November 16). As GM begs for a bailout, sports sponsorship takes a hit. *The New York Times*. Retrieved March 15, 2010, from www.nytimes.com/2008/11/16/business/worldbusiness/16iht-16sponsor.17856078.html

Wyman, A. M. V. (2003, May 19). Take pains to craft the right strategic alliances. Mass High Tech.com. Retrieved March 7, 2006, from www.masshightech.com/displayarticledetail.asp?art_id=62584&search=wyman+.

WEBSITE RESOURCES

www.law.cornell.edu/uniform/ucc.html ▪ This site provides the text of all provisions of the Uniform Commercial code as enacted in the various states.

http://dca.lacounty.gov/tsFalseAdvertising.htm ▪ This site provides a sample of consumer protection information like that generally available in most major cities and counties regarding consumer practices.

www.eff.org/about ▪ The Electronic Frontier Foundation is a nonprofit advocacy organization that tracks litigation on numerous issues involving digital rights, publicity rights, media rights, and consumer rights.

www.ftc.gov/bcp/guides/guides.shtm ▪ The Federal Trade Commission offers guides for advertising, including a deception policy statement that defines false advertising. Organizations that create promotional materials should be aware of laws against deceptive marketing practices.

www.state.id.us/ag/ ▪ Consumer protection laws are easily found on state government websites, like this one for Idaho. Usually they fall under the office of the attorney general.

www.nccusl.org/Update/ ▪ The National Conference of Commissioners on Uniform State Laws "provides states with non-partisan, well-conceived and well-drafted legislation that brings clarity and stability to critical areas of state statutory law." Its website offers a searchable listing of its acts, either by title or by state. The organization is responsible for sport-related laws such as the Uniform Athlete Agent Act and the Uniform Commercial Code.

Glossary

Acceptance An agreement to the terms of an offer as stated.

Act of God A defense to negligence. A person has no liability if an unforeseeable natural disaster resulted in injury to the plaintiff.

Actual authority In agency law, the principal conveys to the agent what his or her limits of authority may be.

Actual cash value The replacement value of property, minus depreciation.

Actual notice Having been informed directly of something or having seen it occur; implies that the landowner knows of a danger through inspection by employees; *also known as* actual knowledge.

Affirmative action Preferential treatment to members of protected classes where their qualifications are essentially the same as those of members of a nonprotected class.

Affirmative defense A defense used between private parties in civil litigation; it works to excuse a defendant's liability even if the plaintiff's claim is true, based on facts additional to those asserted by the plaintiff.

Agency The "fiduciary relation that results from the manifestation of consent by one person to another that the other shall act in his behalf and subject to his control and consent by the other so to act" (Restatement [Second] of Agency, §1(1)).

Agency contract An agreement in which a student-athlete or professional athlete authorizes a person to negotiate or solicit on behalf of the athlete a professional-sports-services contract or an endorsement contract.

Agency law Defines how and when agency relationships are created, what rights and responsibilities exist between a principal and an agent, and what legal effect will be given to the acts of an agent in his or her dealings with third parties.

Agency relationship A consensual relationship established for a lawful purpose by informal oral or formal written agreements; both parties (agent and principal) must have the legal capacity to enter into an agreement.

Agent In agency law, the person acting on behalf of another party (the principal).

All risk policy Insurance policy that seems to be all-encompassing, although some losses may not be covered because they are listed in the "exclusions" section of the policy.

Alternative dispute resolution Methods other than trial for resolving legal conflict; most common forms are arbitration and mediation.

Ambush marketing An intentional effort to weaken or "ambush" a competitor's official association with a sports organization that had acquired its rights through payment of sponsorship fees.

Apparent agency A relationship that is created by the conduct of the principal that leads a third party to believe another individual serves as her agent.

Apparent authority An instance when the principal has somehow conveyed to a third party that the agent has the authority to act, even though the agent does not have the actual authority.

Arbitrary mark Trademark comprising words, names, or symbols that are in common linguistic use but that neither suggest nor describe any quality or characteristic of the good or service.

Arbitration Submission of a dispute to a neutral decision maker for final and binding resolution.

Area of sport activity That portion of a room or space where the play or practice of a sport occurs.

Assault An intentional tort involving some type of menacing or threatening behavior.

Assumption of risk A defense that a participant in an activity knows of the inherent risks of an activity, or those risks that are obvious and necessary to the conduct of the activity; assumption of risk is frequently discussed as being either primary or secondary.

At will Regarding employment, the employer may fire the employee at any time, for any reason or for no reason; the employee also may quit at any time for any reason.

Athlete agent An individual who enters into an agency contract with a student-athlete or professional athlete or, directly or indirectly, recruits or solicits a student-athlete or professional athlete to enter into an agency contract.

Attractive nuisance doctrine A doctrine providing that there is an affirmative duty on landowners to use reasonable care to protect child trespassers who may be attracted to the property because of some manmade or artificial feature of the land that poses some serious danger to a child.

Back pay A remedy for discrimination under Title VII of the Civil Rights Act of 1964; compensation for earnings for work missed due to the adverse employment action.

Bad faith cyber-squatting Instances where Internet domain names that are similar to trademarks are registered with the purpose of reselling the name or diverting consumers from their desired website to the cyber-squatter's site.

Battery The unwanted touching or striking of one person by another, with the intention of bringing about a harmful or offensive contact.

Binding precedent The decisions of higher courts that establish the rule of law to be followed in similar cases in lower courts within the same jurisdiction.

Blurring The effect of a similar mark being used by a non-competitor in a way that, over time, will diminish the famous trademark's value by detracting from its exclusiveness.

Bona fide membership clubs Social clubs and country clubs that are truly exclusive with regard to their membership policy.

Bona fide occupational qualification (BFOQ) defense A defense to a discrimination claim in which the employer must show that the criteria used that resulted in an adverse employment action were genuine qualifications for the job.

Breach of contract An instance when one party fails to perform essential aspects of a contract.

Breach of duty The second element in a negligence case; a failure to meet the required standard of care.

Building ordinance insurance Insurance that covers the increased cost necessary to rebuild property to meet new building code standards that were not in effect when the building was originally constructed.

Burden of production The defendant's responsibility to produce evidence supporting the defense without any accompanying burden to prove that the defense is true.

Burden of proof The responsibility of proving the truth of a claim.

Business interruption insurance Insurance that compensates for lost income if you have to close your business due to a covered occurrence on your property.

Business invitee An individual who is on another person's premises with the assent of the landowner and who brings some economic benefit to the landowner.

Buy-out A provision that states that if the exact amount of damages to be suffered when a party breaches the contract cannot be ascertained at the time the contract is signed, the parties may agree to an amount of damages that reasonably approximates the damages that would be sustained. Another term for liquidated damages.

Canon of statutory construction Time-honored maxims that a court uses to guide and justify its interpretations of statutes.

Canons of interpretation In contract law, a few basic principles on how courts interpret contracts.

Capacity The principle that parties to a contract are legally competent to enter into a contractual relationship.

Capologist Industry-invented term for experts with labor and financial know-how who manage a team's salary cap.

Case brief A succinct one- or two-page summary of a case that allows one to read it quickly and compare it with other cases.

Case law *See* Common law.

Causation The third element in a negligence case; the act of causing something to happen that results in damage to the plaintiff.

Caveat emptor Let the buyer beware.

Certiorari A request for an appeal to be heard by a higher court.

Choice of law clause Clause that states that the lease agreement will be governed by the laws of a particular state.

Civil causes of action The legal grounds upon which to sue.

Civil courts The location where cases that involve controversies of a noncriminal nature are heard.

Collective bargaining agreement (CBA) The contract that results from collective bargaining negotiations in which employees through their union and employers through a management negotiating team negotiate over mandatory subjects of bargaining.

Collective mark Trademark that is used to indicate membership within an organization such as a labor union.

Collective work Content compiled from a number of contributions, created as separate and independent works, which are assembled into a collective whole for distribution and use; each separate contribution represents a distinct copyright from the work as a whole.

Commercial advantage Commercial use in advertising or the promotion and sale of a product or service.

Commercial speech Speech that does no more than propose a commercial transaction, such as an advertisement.

Common law The body of law created by courts when they render decisions interpreting existing laws as they apply to a particular case brought before them.

Community of interests Similarities in workers' jobs that will lead to common needs, desires, and goals being addressed through collective bargaining to make it more likely to create a labor settlement.

Comparative negligence A system that allows a plaintiff to recover some portion of the damages caused by defendant's negligence even if the plaintiff was also partially negligent and responsible for causing the injury.

Compensable injury A physical injury or illness that a worker must suffer in order to receive workers' compensation.

Compensatory damages Damages that an injured party can collect to compensate for the loss suffered.

Complaint A summary of allegations in a case.

Concerted action   Joint action between two or more parties.

Concurrent jurisdiction   The jurisdiction of two or more courts that are each authorized to deal with the same subject matter; state courts hear both state law and federal law claims.

Consent   The willingness that an act or invasion of an interest will take place.

Consideration   Something of value, such as money or personal services, given by one party to another in exchange for an act or promise.

Constitution   A foundational document that sets forth the basic operating principles of a government, including limits on governmental power.

Constructive discharge   A reassignment of an employee in which the employee has not actually been fired but the impact of the reassignment has been to essentially take away the responsibilities for which he or she was hired.

Constructive notice   Presumed knowledge of dangers that a reasonable prudent facility owner would be aware of; *also known as* constructive knowledge.

Consumer   Any individual who purchases goods or services for personal or household consumption.

Contract   A promise or set of promises, the breach of which the law gives a remedy, or the performance of which the law in some way recognizes a duty.

Contract damages   Damages designed to put a nonbreaching party in the position it would have held if the contract had been performed as promised.

Contributory negligence   A plaintiff who contributed in any way to the injury may not recover for any damages.

Counteroffer   An offer made in response to the initial offer.

Covenant not to compete   *See* Restrictive covenant.

Covenant of good faith and fair dealing   An expectation that both parties to a contract act fairly in their contractual dealings.

Criminal courts   The location where persons who are charged with a crime are prosecuted.

Cyber-squatter   Someone who registers a domain name for improper purposes such as extorting money from another person.

Damages   The final element in a negligence case; the loss caused by the defendant to the plaintiff or to his property.

Deceptive advertisement   An advertisement that contains a statement or an omission that is likely to mislead a reasonable consumer and that is important to the consumer's decision to buy or use a product.

Defamatory act   A false statement, that is published to a third party, involving some degree of fault or negligence and causing actual damage.

Denial of certiorari   A decision whereby either the U. S. Supreme Court or the highest state appellate court declines to hear a case and, having done so, allows the decision of the next lowest court to stand.

Depositions   Oral testimony obtained under oath from witnesses or the parties in a case.

Descriptive mark   Trademark that describes the intended purpose, function, or use of the good.

Design defect   A product defect that exists when the very design of the product is flawed so as to render each item of that product unsafe.

Disabling impairment   An impairment that is permanent or long-term and that is not likely to be overcome with rest or treatment.

Disclosed principal   A classification of a principal in which a third party is aware of the identity of the principal and the fact that the agent is acting on behalf of the principal.

Disparate impact   A theory of liability used in deciding Title VII cases in which an employer's neutral employment practice has had a discriminatory effect on a protected class.

Disparate treatment   A theory of liability used in deciding Title VII cases in which an employer has intentionally discriminated against a member of a protected class.

Disparity of bargaining power   A situation in which one party gains an unfair bargaining position because it has much more power to make the contract terms in its favor.

Distraction doctrine   A doctrine providing that, in some cases, even though a condition appears to be open and obvious, the plaintiff may somehow be distracted from appreciating the danger.

Diversity of citizenship jurisdiction   An instance where a state law case may be brought in federal court because the parties to a lawsuit are residents of different states; this allows an objective decision to be made about which state's law should be applied.

Dram shop acts   Statutes that provide for liability against those who commercially serve alcohol to minors or to persons who are visibly intoxicated when the inebriated individual subsequently injures third parties.

Due process   A constitutional provision that guarantees a person fair treatment in the process of a governmental decision to deprive them of life, liberty, or property.

Duties test   Part of a test for exemption from overtime pay in which the employee's duties must be primarily involved in the executive, administrative, or professional duties of the business.

Duty   The first element in a negligence case; the defendant must have some obligation, imposed by law, to protect the plaintiff from unreasonable risk.

Duty of fair representation A requirement that a union represent all employees in the bargaining unit fairly, even if the employees are not union members.

Eminent domain The power of the state to appropriate private property for its own use without the owner's consent.

Employment practices liability (EPL) insurance Insurance that covers injury to employees caused by wrongful employment practices such as sexual harassment, wrongful termination, defamation, invasion of privacy, breach of the employment contract, and discrimination based on race, religion, age, gender, disability, and so forth.

Enterprise coverage Coverage that applies to employees who work for certain businesses or organizations that have at least two employees and that do at least $500,000 a year in business.

Equal Protection Clause Found in the Fourteenth Amendment to the U. S. Constitution; it says that no state shall "deny to any person within its jurisdiction the equal protection of the laws."

Errors and omissions insurance Insurance that covers the negligent or accidental acts of those who have professional knowledge or training.

Essential facility doctrine A doctrine that states that refusing to share an essential facility that is economically unfeasible for a would-be competitor to duplicate (when that refusal would constitute a severe impediment to prospective market entrants) is an unreasonable restraint of trade.

Establishment Clause Found in the First Amendment to the Constitution; it protects us from the government establishing a preferred religion; interpreted to mean that the government must be neutral with respect to religious matters.

Exculpatory agreement Contract in which an individual or entity that is legally at fault tries to excuse itself from fault.

Exculpatory clause A contractual provision that relieves an individual or entity from any liability resulting from a negligent act.

Express agency An agency relationship based on a formal written or oral agreement made between two parties.

Express warranty A warranty that is explicitly made by a manufacturer or seller, either orally, in writing, or as a visual image; it makes an assertion of fact or a promise regarding the quality of the goods.

Fair use Using a copyrighted work in a reasonable and limited way without the author's permission; fair use is a defense to a copyright infringement claim.

False advertising A form of unfair and deceptive commerce.

Fanciful mark The most distinctive trademarks; coined words that have been invented for the sole purpose of functioning as a trademark.

Fiduciary A person who acts primarily for the benefit of another.

Fiduciary relationship A relationship that is founded on trust or confidence, when one person has entrusted his or her interests to the integrity and fidelity of another.

First use The first person to use a trademark in commerce has the superior rights to the mark, even if the mark has not been formally registered.

Fixation A requirement that work being copyrighted be put into a tangible form, such as by being written down or recorded.

Force majeure clause Contract clause that excuses or relieves a party from having to perform due to natural disasters or other "acts of God," war, or the failure of third parties.

Fraud Intentional misrepresentations that are intended to induce action by another party, thus resulting in harm.

Fraudulent concealment A person knowingly withholds or conceals information from the plaintiff concerning the plaintiff's medical condition.

Free Exercise Clause Found in the First Amendment to the Constitution; it protects our fundamental right to the free exercise of religious beliefs; interpreted to mean that the government may not target a particular religion for suppression.

Front pay A remedy for discrimination under Title VII of the Civil Rights Act of 1964; compensation for future earnings that would have been received absent the discrimination.

Functional mark A trademark that does not describe or distinguish the product or service but that is necessary for the product to exist.

General duty The requirement that an employer shall provide a place of employment that is free from hazards that cause or are likely to cause death or serious physical harm to employees.

Generic mark The common descriptive name of a product or service; considered part of the public domain.

Good cause A legally sufficient reason, such as unsatisfactory job performance or violation of workplace rules, that allows an employer to discipline or discharge an employee.

Good Samaritan statutes State statutes providing that persons who act to help others in distress may not be sued for ordinary negligence based on their efforts to assist.

Goods Tangible moveable objects, not including real estate or securities.

Goodwill The favor that the management of a business wins from the public.

Hazing Any activity by which a person recklessly endangers the health or safety of an individual, or causes a risk of bodily injury, for purposes of initiation into, admission into, or affiliation with an organization or team.

Hold harmless clause Contract clause in a lease stating that one party, usually the lessee, assumes the liability in the transaction in question. *See also* Idemnification clause.

Holding The final ruling on a specific issue being decided.

Horizontal price fixing A generally illegal arrangement among competitors to charge the same price for an item.

Horizontal restraints Agreements between competitors that restrain free trade; for example, the player draft system spreads talent across teams in a league by preventing teams from vying economically for the best players.

Hostile environment harassment A type of sexual harassment that occurs when an employee is subjected to repeated unwelcome behaviors that do not constitute sexual bribery but are sufficiently severe and pervasive that they create a work environment that interferes with the harassed employee's ability to perform his or her job.

Immunity The ability to escape legal responsibilities; precludes a suit from being brought against a party.

Impasse A stalemate in negotiations that often leads to an economic weapon being used by the union in the form of a strike or by management in the form of a lockout.

Implied agency An agency relationship that is implied by the conduct of the parties.

Implied warranty of fitness A warranty that accompanies a sale in which the seller has reason to know the particular purpose of a purchase and the buyer relies on the seller's expertise in providing a product that is appropriate for that purpose.

Implied warranty of merchantability A warranty that is an implied promise that the product is fit for its ordinary intended use and thus is merchantable.

Indemnification clause Contract clause that provides for reimbursement to a party for a loss incurred by that party. *See also* Hold harmless clause.

Independent contractor A person or business that provides goods or services to another entity under terms specified in a contract; an independent contractor is not an employee.

Individual coverage Coverage for an employee of an organization that does not qualify as an enterprise, but the employee regularly engages in activities involving interstate commerce or the production of goods for interstate commerce.

Individualized inquiry Requirement under the Americans with Disabilities Act that a fact-specific inquiry relative to the stated purpose of a rule and a person's individual disability and circumstances must be undertaken to determine whether a requested modification of the rule is reasonable.

Injunctive relief A remedy for discrimination under Title VII of the Civil Rights Act of 1964; orders the employer to cease unlawful practices or to engage in affirmative action.

Intent The planning and desire to perform an act.

Intentional tort A category of torts in which someone intentionally causes harm to person or property.

Interest arbitration A method of settling disputes over the terms of contracts in which a neutral third party arbitrator chosen by the parties renders a final and binding decision.

Intermediate scrutiny A test to determine whether the Equal Protection Clause has been violated; assumes that rarely, but occasionally, the government may have an important reason to rely on a rule that contains a quasi-suspect classification (e.g., gender).

Interrogatory Answers written under oath to a list of written questions.

Invitee An individual who has a specific invitation to enter another person's property or is a member of the public in a public place.

Joint work A collaboration between two or more authors, in which they are co-owners of the copyright of the work unless they have entered into an agreement to the contrary.

Jurisdiction The authority to hear a case.

Just cause Termination of a contract because the employee has engaged in behavior that violates the standards of job performance established by the employer.

Lease agreement Contract giving rise to the relationship of lessor and lessee; contract for the exclusive possession of lands or premises for a determinate period of time.

Legal error An erroneous interpretation of the law or application of legal procedure.

Legality To be enforceable, the subject matter of a contract must not violate state or federal law.

Lessee One who rents or leases property from another.

Lessor One who rents or leases property to another.

Liability insurance Insurance that covers bodily injury or property losses to a third party.

Libel Written or published defamation of character; broader definition than slander, because any number of tangible communications might fall under the heading of written communication.

License Agreement that creates a privilege to go on the premises of another for a certain purpose but does not operate to confer on the licensee any title or interest in such property.

Licensee An individual who is on the premises with the consent of the owner but who does not bring any economic benefit to the property owner.

Likelihood of confusion The evidentiary burden that a trademark owner must meet to prove infringement of a trademark; consumers would be likely to associate the goods or services of one party with those of the other party as a result of the use of the marks at issue by both parties.

Limited duty rule A rule used in baseball that provides a baseball facility has met its duty of care to spectators by providing seating that is protected from projectiles that leave the field of play.

Liquidated damages A provision that sets up a reasonable approximation of damages required to satisfy a loss resulting from breach of contract. In employment contracts it may also be known as a buy-out clause.

Major life activity Fundamental aspects of human living, such as walking, seeing, hearing, speaking, breathing, learning, and working.

Mandatory subjects Topics that management must bargain over or risk being charged with an unfair labor practice; these topics include hours, wages, and terms and conditions of employment.

Manufacturing defect A product defect that is the result of an error in the manufacturing and production process that flaws one or more of the manufactured items, even though the design itself is a safe one.

Mediation Submission of a dispute to an impartial decision maker who assists the parties in negotiating a settlement of their dispute.

Mens rea The requisite intent to commit a crime; literally, "guilty mind."

Mitigation of damages A principle that states that a non-breaching party must act reasonably to lessen the consequences of a breach.

Modified comparative negligence Generally a plaintiff may not recover damages if the proportion of his or her negligence exceeds the defendant's negligence.

Morals clause Just cause termination based on immorality, criminal behavior, or behavior that reflects poorly on the employer.

Named peril policy Insurance policy that covers only the specific risks set forth in the policy.

National Letter of Intent (NLI) An agreement between the institution and the prospective college student-athlete stating that the student will attend the institution for one year and will be provided with a financial aid award.

Negligence Conduct that falls below the standard established by law for the protection of others against unreasonable risk of harm.

Negligence per se There is conclusive proof that a defendant has breached the standard of care when an injury is caused by a failure to meet a statutory requirement that was established for safety reasons.

Negligent hiring The failure to properly screen employees, resulting in the hiring of someone who is not suitable for the position; the basic question is whether a manager acted reasonably in choosing a particular person to fill a position.

Negligent misrepresentation A false statement given negligently to another party and that the party reasonably relies upon, resulting in harm.

Negligent referral The failure of an employer to disclose complete and factual information about a former or current employee to another employer when the failure to do so may result in harm to a third party.

Negligent retention The retention of an employee after the employer became aware of the employee's unsuitability, thereby failing to act on that knowledge; the basic question is whether a manager acted reasonably in retaining an employee's services.

Negligent selection The employer has a duty to choose an independent contractor in a reasonable fashion; similar to negligent hiring.

Negligent supervision The failure to provide the necessary monitoring to ensure that employees perform their duties properly; the basic question is whether a manager acted reasonably in providing guidance and in overseeing an employee's actions.

Nonexempt employees Workers who receive an hourly salary and who are entitled to overtime pay after working more than 40 hours in a five-day work week.

Offer A conditional promise made to do or to refrain from doing something.

Open and obvious A condition that the invitee knows of or that a reasonably careful person would have discovered upon careful inspection.

Originality Requirement that a work be created by the author himself or herself and that it contain some minimal amount of creativity.

Partially disclosed principal A classification of a principal in which a third party is aware that the agent is acting on behalf of another but does not know the identity of the principal.

Penalty provision Provisions that do not bear a reasonable relationship to the damages to be sustained and that are simply punishing a party for breaching a contract. Courts will not enforce penalty provisions.

Per se violations Usually related to antitrust law, wrongdoings that are so obviously improper restraints on free trade that little other analysis is needed.

Permissive subjects Topics that management is not obligated to negotiate over and the union cannot bargain to impasse over.

Perquisites (perks) Benefits that an employee may receive beyond a base salary and fringe benefits; for a coach these may include use of an automobile, payment for housing, or payment from endorsement contracts.

Persuasive precedent Cases that a court may use but is not required to follow when deciding its cases.

Place of public accommodation A place that accommodates the paying public; the place must affect interstate commerce and be principally engaged in selling food for consumption on the premises or exist for the purpose of exhibition or entertainment.

Preponderance of the evidence The level of proof required to prevail in most civil cases; the winning party's evidence is more likely than not preponderant.

Preventive law A position that looks at *all* risks that could affect an institution's financial health; a broader view of risk management.

Prima facie case A situation where the plaintiff's evidence is sufficient to prevail unless controverted by a defendant's evidence; a plaintiff has made out her prima facie case.

Primary assumption of risk The plaintiff understands and voluntarily agrees to accept the inherent risks of an activity.

Principal In agency law, the person hiring or engaging the agent to act on behalf of the principal or to perform certain duties for the principal.

Prior similar incidents rule A rule used to determine whether a certain incident was foreseeable by looking at what has occurred previously at that location; a sufficiently similar incident might make it foreseeable that another occurrence of that kind could happen.

Private right of action Circumstance under which a court determines that a statute or provision that creates rights also supports a private plaintiff's remedy that can be achieved through a lawsuit, even though no such remedy is explicitly provided for in the statute.

Privity of contract A direct contractual relationship between user and provider.

Promissory estoppel A quasicontractual remedy in which a party may have some recourse despite the fact that all the elements of a contract may not exist, based on reliance on a promise made.

Property right Provision to the creator or owner of a copyright the exclusive economic and property interests to the work.

Protected classes Classes of people designated as protected by a law; in the case of Title VII of the Civil Rights Act of 1964, these include race, color, religion, sex, and national origin.

Proximate cause An act or failure to act, unbroken by any intervening act, that directly produces an event and without which the event would not have occurred.

Public figure An individual who has, because of his or her activities, commanded sufficient continuing public interest.

Public invitee An individual who is legally on public land.

Punitive damages Compensation in excess of actual damages that is awarded under certain circumstances, to punish the offender in the case of intentional torts.

Pure comparative negligence A plaintiff may recover damages even if the proportion of his or her negligence exceeds the defendant's negligence.

Qualified privilege Acting in good faith, the privilege for employers to disclose information concerning an employee's work performance to those inside the current employer's operation or to prospective employers.

Quid pro quo harassment A type of sexual harassment that occurs when an employer conditions a job-related benefit, such as a promotion or pay raise, on an employee's willingness to engage in sexual behavior; sexual bribery.

Ratification When no actual agency exists, but a principal accepts or ratifies an agent's unauthorized acts after the fact.

Ratification/condonation principle The acceptance or confirmation of a previous act done by another.

Rational basis review The easiest test to determine whether the Equal Protection Clause has been violated; the government must simply have a rational basis for adopting the challenged rule in order to accomplish a legitimate goal. It is used for all group classifications other than suspect (e.g., race) or quasi-suspect (e.g., gender) classifications.

Rationale The reasoning used by the court to justify its decision.

Reasonable accommodation A modification in the work or academic environment that enables a qualified person with a disability to apply for a job, perform the essential functions of a job, or have equitable access to an educational program.

Reasonable factors other than age A defense used when an employer has taken an adverse employment action that was motivated by an age-neutral factor.

Reasonable force Lawful force that is reasonably necessary to accomplish a particular end, such as preventing theft or compelling obedience from a child.

Reasonable person A reasonable person exercises judgment that meets societal expectations for prudence in decision making; an objective standard applied to judge behavior using a hypothetical individual; *also known as* reasonably prudent person.

Reasonably prudent person *See* Reasonable person.

Reasonably prudent plaintiff   A hypothetical individual who is used as a standard to determine what the plaintiff should have done in a particular circumstance to protect his or her own safety.

Reassignment clause   A clause that gives an employer the right to transfer an employee to a different employment position in an organization.

Reckless misconduct   An individual does an act or intentionally fails to do an act that it is his or her duty to do, knowing or having reason to know not only that the conduct creates an unreasonable risk of physical harm to another but also that such risk is substantially greater than that which is necessary to make the conduct negligent; *also known as* gross negligence or willful and wanton misconduct.

Recreational use statute   Provision of some level of immunity for landowners who open their property to recreational use by the public with no fees charged.

Regulations   Rules created to operationalize statutes by providing more specific guidance.

Replacement value   An amount sufficient to replace property or equipment, subject only to the maximum amount set forth in the insurance policy.

Rescission   The right of a party to undo a contract and return the parties to the positions they had prior to the contract.

Reserve clause   A clause that has been used in professional sports contracts that functions to give teams a perpetual right to keep their players unless traded or released.

Respondeat superior   *See* Vicarious liability.

Restitution   An equitable remedy that involves returning the goods and/or property that were transferred under a contract.

Restrictive covenant   A clause in an employment contract that protects the interests of the employer by restricting the ability of the employee to take a comparable position in another organization.

Retaliation   Action taken in return for an injury or offense. Often refers to action by an employer against employees' efforts to obtain justice.

Revocable license   A license that may be revoked, withdrawn, or cancelled.

Right of attribution   A right that prevents others from claiming authorship or attributing authorship falsely to an individual.

Right of integrity   A right that prevents others from distorting, mutilating, or misrepresenting an author's work.

Right of publicity   The right of a famous individual to control the commercial value and use of his or her name, likeness, and image.

Rights arbitration   A method of setting disputes over the interpretation or application of a contract in which a neutral third party arbitrator chosen by the parties renders a final and binding decision.

Rights to register   Rights that are created by both state and federal statutes and that provide certain benefits to the registrant.

Rights to use   Rights that are grounded in common law and that are created when a mark is used in commerce to identify a product or service.

Risk assessment   The process of determining the probability that particular risks will result in claims during a specific period, as well as determining the magnitude of the potential liability arising from such claims.

Risk evaluation   The process in which one assesses risks in conjunction with the mission of the organization and importance of certain activities to that organization.

Risk management   The function or process by which an organization identifies and manages the risks of liability that arise from its activities.

Rollover clause   A clause that provides that, at the end of each year of a contract's term, the contract's term is automatically renewed for another year unless one party notifies the other of the intention not to roll over.

Rule of reason analysis   The requirement that a court balance the procompetitive (economically) effects of a rule against its anticompetitive effects.

Salary basis test   Part of a test for exemption from overtime pay in which the employee must be paid a set and fixed salary that is not subject to variations because of quantity or quality of work.

Salary test   Part of a test for exemption from overtime pay in which the amount of salary must meet a minimum level.

Sale   A contract by which title to goods is transferred from one party to another for a price.

Sales puffing   Expressions of opinion that are not made as factual representations about a product or service.

Scope of employment   The range of reasonable and foreseeable activities of an employee that further the business of the employer.

Secondary assumption of risk   A plaintiff deliberately chooses to encounter a known risk and, in so doing, acts unreasonably.

Secondary meaning   Requirement that a trademark has become associated in the mind of the public with a particular source or origin; allows descriptive marks to obtain protection that they would otherwise not be entitled to receive.

Section 10(j) injunction   Refers to a section (10(j)) of the NLRA. It grants the NLRB discretionary authority to seek a court order to prohibit an unfair labor practice.

Self-defense Justified use of force when a person reasonably believes that it is necessary to defend himself or herself from attack.

Service mark A trademark that relates to a service rather than a good or product.

Shared responsibility statute A statute that states that participants in an activity assume the risks inherent in the activity; if the participant chooses to assume those risks, the activity provider does not owe a duty of care to the participant relative to those risks.

Slander Spoken defamation of a person.

Sovereign immunity A doctrine precluding the institution of a suit against the sovereign government without its consent; rooted in the inherent nature of power and the ability of those who hold power to shield themselves.

Specific hazard standard A benchmark that must be met by an employer; it requires that employers adopt specific practices, means, methods, or processes that are reasonably necessary and appropriate to protect workers on the job.

Specific performance A remedy provided by a court that orders the breaching party to perform the contract. May only be used when the subject of the contract is a unique good.

Standard of care The degree of care a reasonable prudent person would take to prevent an injury to another.

Stare decisis "Let the decision stand"; a refusal by a court to change a ruling on an issue that has already been decided.

State actor A term used in constitutional law to describe an entity that is acting with the sufficient authority of the government and therefore is subject to regulation under the Fifth and Fourteenth Amendments, which prohibit the federal and state governments, respectively, from violating the rights laid out elsewhere in the Constitution.

Statute of Frauds A requirement that certain types of contracts must be in writing.

Statute of limitations A defense that a cause of action has not been filed in a timely fashion.

Statutes Written laws created by legislatures, which are law-making bodies composed of elected representatives.

Strict scrutiny The strictest test applied to determine whether the Equal Protection Clause has been violated; based on the premise that there is almost never a good reason for a law to differentiate on the basis of an immutable characteristic such as race.

Student-athlete An individual who engages in, is eligible to engage in, or may be eligible in the future to engage in any intercollegiate sport.

Suggestive mark A mark that subtly connotes something about the service or product but that does not actually describe any specific quality or characteristic of the good or service.

Suspect classifications A classification that is likely to be based on illegal discrimination; includes race, ethnicity, national origin, and alienage.

Tarnishment The effect of a similar mark being used in such a way as to disparage or harm the reputation of a famous trademark; often used in connection with shoddy products or sexual, obscene, or socially unacceptable activities.

10(j) injunction A court order to stop an employer from committing an unfair labor practice.

Territorial rights Franchise relocation restrictions that prevent a competitor franchise from relocating into another team's market territory without league permission and adequate compensation for the potential loss of market share caused by the incursion.

Tort A civil wrong other than a breach of contract; usually refers to the causing of damage or injury to property, a person, a person's reputation, or harm to a person's commercial interests.

Trade dress Distinctive packaging, including distinctive shape and appearance of a product or service.

Trade name Any name used by a person to identify his or her business or vocation.

Trademark A word, name, symbol, or device that has been adopted and used by a manufacturer or merchant to identify goods and to distinguish them from those manufactured or sold by others.

Trademark dilution Damage to or weakening of famous trademarks, lessening their distinctiveness, even in the absence of any likelihood of confusion or competition.

Trademark infringement The unauthorized use of another person's or business's trademark.

Trainee status The status of a trainee, student, or intern who meets the eligibility criteria for exemption from the minimum wage and overtime pay requirements of the FLSA.

Trespasser An individual who is on the premises without permission.

Trial on the merits If a sufficient controversy remains after discovery is completed, then the issues will be fully argued and a final decision reached.

Undisclosed principal A classification of a principal in which a third party is not aware that the agent is acting on behalf of another party.

Undue hardship An accommodation that would impose an excessive cost or administrative burden on an organization; a court will not find an accommodation reasonable if it would impose an undue hardship or burden on the organization.

Unfair dominance A principle that states that a waiver will not be upheld if the party getting the benefit of the waiver has so much power in the transaction that it is not a fair deal.

Unfair labor practice   According to the National Labor Relations Act (NLRA), employers may not discriminate in regard to any term or condition of employment to encourage or discourage membership in any labor organization, nor interfere with employees in the exercise of their rights to associate with a labor union.

Unidentified principal   An agency relationship where a third party is aware that an agent is acting on behalf of another but does not know the identity of the principal.

Unrelated business income tax (UBIT)   A tax on income generated by a trade or business carried on by a tax-exempt organization that is not substantially related to the performance of its tax-exempt function.

Vicarious liability   A doctrine that holds an employing organization (employer) responsible for certain acts of its employees, not because of any wrongdoing by the employer, but because the law has deemed it appropriate for the employer to be held accountable for the actions of its employees.

Waiver   A type of contract in which one party gives up his or her right to sue the other party when that party has been negligent, thus altering the outcome that would transpire under the usual tort law principles.

Warranty   An assertion of fact or promise made by a manufacturer or seller that is relied upon as part of the consumer transaction.

Whistleblower statutes   Statutes that provide a system to protect, against discrimination and retaliation, those employees who report wrongful conduct by their employer to authorities.

White-collar exemption   Exemption from minimum wage and overtime pay received by worker employed in a bona fide executive, administrative, or professional capacity; the worker is usually salaried and receives a higher rate of pay than an hourly worker.

Willful and wanton misconduct   *See* Reckless misconduct.

Work for hire   A work prepared by an employee within the scope of his or her employment, or contracted work that has been specially ordered or commissioned.

Work week   A period of 168 hours in seven consecutive days (7 x 24 = 168); may begin on any given day and hour as determined by the employer.

Worst case scenario   In contract law, drafting contracts to envision the worst that could happen in order to protect the client's interests.

Writ of certiorari   An order issued by the U. S. Supreme Court or a state's highest appellate court that directs a lower court to send up the case record for review.

Wrongful termination   A termination when the employee has been fired contrary to the terms of the contract or in violation of the law.

Case Index

Index